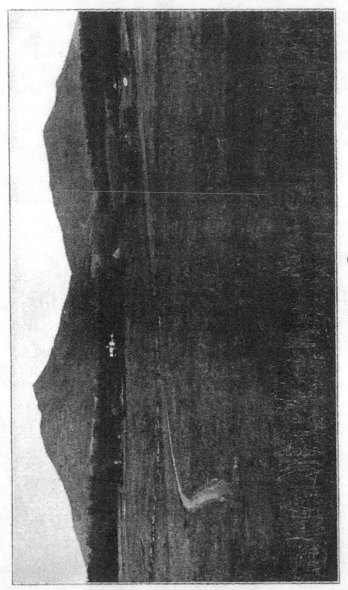

THE PEAKS OF OTTER
Bedford County, Virginia

"OUR KIN"

The Genealogies

OF SOME OF THE EARLY
FAMILIES WHO MADE
HISTORY *in the Founding
and Development of*
BEDFORD COUNTY
VIRGINIA

By
MARY DENHAM ACKERLY
and
LULA EASTMAN JETER PARKER

SouthernwHistorical Press, Inc.
Greenville, South Carolina

Please direct all correspondence and book orders to:
SOUTHERN HISTORICAL PRESS, Inc.
PO Box 1267
Greenville, SC   29602-1267

Originally printed: Lynchburg, VA 1930
Copyrighted by: Mary D. Ackerly and
Lulu E.J. Parker
ISBN #978-1-63914-147-06
Printed in the United States of America

DEDICATION

With sincere affection I dedicate

my part in this book

to my

MOTHER AND FATHER

MARY DENHAM ACKERLY

And my part I dedicate

to my

CHILDREN

with the hope that a

knowledge of their forbears may be

an incentive to right living and noble deeds

LULA EASTMAN JETER PARKER

PREFACE

"OUR KIN" is intended to be a brief, but by no means complete, family history. Every effort, consistent with our limited time and financial ability, has been made to make it a just and true record. All available sources of information have been followed and, as far as possible, exhausted. It may contain some inaccuracies. These are likely to occur in any work of this kind. Such as exist, however, are errors of the hand and not of the heart. It is presented as a labor of love, rather than profit, with the hope that the information contained will prove of interest and value to all who read, and perhaps, an inspiration to higher ambitions and nobler deeds by the present and future generations of "our kin." Yet if it serves only as a stimulus to others to make further investigations along the same line, our labor will not have been in vain, as much valuable information has already been lost to posterity by reason of the lack of similar endeavor in generations past.

Grateful acknowledgment is hereby made of the helpful assistance of Mr. D. W. Parker, Miss Georgie Tillman Snead, Dr. Elbert Berkley Talbot, Mrs. Stuart Buford, Dr. J. D. Eggleston, Mrs. Cornelia Burks Dillard, Mrs. H. W. Scott, Miss Bessie Penn, Miss Alice Page Callaway, Mr. C. D. DeMott, Miss Ruth Callaway Pannill, Mrs. Hugh Davis Poindexter, Mr. Ernest G. Robinson, Captain William White Ackerly, Miss Louise C. Jennings, and the late Rowland D. Buford of Virginia; Dr. Benjamin Sledd of North Carolina; Mr. M. R. Jeter, Mrs. E. M. Wilson, and Lt. Gov. T. B. Butler of South Carolina; Mr. John Randolph Bolling and Mrs. Edith Bolling Wilson of Washington, D. C.; Mrs. E. S. Porter of Kentucky; Mr. Bertrand Jeter of Illinois; Mrs. Donald C. Dickson and Dr. Jas. E. Gwatkin of Louisiana; Rev. F. S. Moseley of Alabama; Judge John H. Hatcher and Mr. George H. Alderson of West Virginia; Mrs. C. H. Heard of Texas; Mrs. Charles W. Byrd of New York; Miss Fannie Jeter of Tennessee; Mrs. Thomas R. Moseley of Mississippi; Rev. William E. Gwatkin, Mrs. Virginia Gwatkin Campbell, Mrs. L. M. Ottofy, and Mr. William Penn Amfahr of Missouri; Mrs. W. W. McPherson of Chicago; and all others who have in any way aided us in this undertaking.

"He who cares not whence he came, cares
not whither he goes."

MARY DENHAM ACKERLY,
LULA EASTMAN JETER PARKER.

February 21, 1930.

Contents

CONTENTS—*Continued*

PUBLISHER'S NOTE
REGARDING
THE ADDENDUM

The "Addendum", pages 821 through 837 (immediately following the index), has been prepared from information supplied by Miss Georgette Parker of Lynchburg, Virginia, daughter of co-author Mrs. Lula Eastman Jeter Parker.

Subsequent to the publication of "Our Kin" in 1930, and prior to her death in 1954, Mrs. Parker accumulated considerable information from various sources, regarding additions, deletions and corrections. This information is recorded in the "Addendum".

We are deeply grateful to Miss Georgette Parker for the contribution she has made to this reprint edition.

The Publisher

Illustrations

BEDFORD COUNTY, VIRGINIA

As is true of most of the counties in this section of Virginia, Bedford was once the home of the red man. Tomahawks and arrow heads picked up in various parts of the county bear testimony to his dominion; while human skeletons and implements of war have been exhumed in the vicinity of Montvale, and an old barrow still remains there on the south bank of Goose Creek. An Indian fort, in which Mary Ingles sought refuge after her captivity and eventful life among the savages, stood near this barrow; and from here two Indian trails led in directions of other settlements—one to the north between the Peaks of Otter, and the other to the west through Buford's Gap (now Villamont) in the Blue Ridge Mountains.

As immigration increased in Virginia and settlers pushed further and further west, it became necessary for their convenience to divide old counties and form new ones, so Bedford was taken from Lunenburg in 1754, as Lunenburg had been taken from Brunswick in 1746, and Brunswick from Prince George, Surry, and Isle of Wight in 1732. A small portion of Albemarle was also included in Bedford's territory. In November, 1753, by Act of the House of Burgesses, to take effect the 10th of May, 1754, the new county was formed, and named Bedford in honor of John Russell, fourth Duke of Bedford, and Secretary of State of Great Britian, 1721-1757.

New London, which had been the county seat of Lunenburg, was now in Bedford and was retained as the seat of the new county.

The first Court held for Bedford was on May 27, 1754, "at the house of Mathew Talbot, Gent.," at which the following Justices were sworn in: John Pane, William Callaway, John Smith, Zachary Isbell, Robert Page, Thomas Pullin, and Edward Manion. Benjamin Howard produced a commission to be Clerk of the Court and took oath of office.

John Harvey, Clement Reade, and James Cary, Gent., took oath of attorneys and were admitted to practice law in this Court.

Clement Reade was also sworn his Majesty's Attorney-General.

At the next Court, held at the same place on July 22nd, John Phelps, Richard Callaway, and Robert Ewing, Gent., were sworn in as Justices, and Joseph Ray as Sheriff, his securities being Obadiah Woodson, Turner Hunt Christian, Richard Burks, John Partree Burks, Edward Watts, Jr., James Walker, Thomas Walker, Benjamin Orrick, Joseph Mays, and John Goad.

The house of Mathew Talbot continued to be used as a court house until November, 1754, when it was ordered that the "Court be adjourned until tomorrow 10 o'clock at the Courthouse at William Callaway's," which was a rude structure erected for county purposes on land given to the county by William Callaway and his wife "on the road below his Mill Creek."

NOTES TAKEN FROM ORDER BOOKS, 1754 TO 1800:

November 25, 1754. Ordered that the Sheriff of this County collect from each of the Tithable Person 27 lb. Tobo. towards defraying the Levy for this County.

George White's ear mark, a swallow fork in the left ear and a half moon under it and a slit in the right ear, ordered to be recorded.

November 25, 1755. Richard Callaway, Zachary Isbell and Ben. Howard are appointed County Trustees to receive in fee simple one hundred acres of land from William Callaway, to be sold in lots as previously agreed upon, for the establishment of a town, this town to be "called by the name of New London."

June 23, 1761. Leave is granted the inhabitants of Bedford County to build a meeting house on Sherwood Walton's land on the wagon road from the Peaks of Otter to Warrick.

June 24, 1766. On the motion of Sundry Presbyterian Protestant Dissenters of the County the New meeting house lately erected near the Six Mile tree is set apart for the worship of God and established accordingly.

July 23, 1766. Ordered that a Courthouse be built in this County, to-wit, twenty four by thirty six feet, 12 feet pitch, two 12 feet square rooms with a brick chimney, a fire place in each room . . . the house to be underpinned with brick one foot and a half above the ground, the bench to be built in a quarter circle, with a bar and two sheriff's desks, a Clerk's table, etc. (This was Bedford's first court house and was used as such until 1782, when Campbell County was cut from Bedford with New London in its territory, making it necessary to establish a new county seat.)

April 23, 1782. William Callaway, Gent., is appointed to make a survey of the County for the purpose of ascertaining the centre thereof where to fix the Courthouse and other public buildings.

July 22, 1782. William Mead, William Leftwich, William Trigg, Henry Buford, James Buford, and Charles Gwatkin, Gent., are appointed to view a place on Bramblett's Road for the purpose of fixing the Courthouse and other public buildings and make report tomorrow at 10 o'clock.

July 23, 1782. The Gentlemen appointed yesterday to view a place on Bramblett's Road for the purpose of fixing the Courthouse and other public buildings reported as their opinion that the proper place is in a tract of one hundred acres of land on Bramblett's Road, this day given to the County by William Downey and Joseph Fuqua. Whereupon the Court is of the opinion and doth order and direct the Courthouse and other public buildings to be erected thereon accordingly, etc. James Buford, Gent., is appointed to contract for Courthouse, Prison, and Stocks. (Court was held in this building August 26, 1782.)

April 28, 1783. Liquor rates. (Fixed by the Court):

Diet	1	3
" cold		8
Lodging p. night with clean sheets		8
" without		6
Rum p. gallon	10	
Brandy p. "	10	
Whiskey "	8	
Small Beer	1	3
Cider p. Gallon	2	6
Stableage 24 hours		8
Fodder p.		2
Corn p. gallon		6
Pasteurage 24 hours		6

February 23, 1789. James Callaway recommended as Presiding Member in the County Court of Bedford for singular services rendered.

September 22, 1800. On motion of John Otey leave is granted to build a meeting house on the Courthouse lot beyond the Spring. (This house still stands, and has been used in recent years as the rectory for the Episcopal Church.)

In Deed Book W, page 116, it is recorded that in October, 1782, the General Assembly of Virginia passed an act vesting the title to "the said one hundred acres" in certain trustees for the benefit of the county, and thereby also "established a town by the name of Liberty." The surrender of Cornwallis at Yorktown just the year before probably inspired the name. In 1890 a real estate boom swept over this part of Virginia, and for advertising purposes the names of many of the old towns were changed. Liberty fell a victim to this fad and changed its name to Bedford City, and in a few years, despairing of its becoming a city as a result of the boom, dropped the word from its name, and has since been called Bedford.

In 1789 a new court house was built in Liberty—a brick building, which was much more imposing, convenient and comfortable than the first one. This stood until 1834, when it was torn down and a still more imposing and commodious building erected upon the same spot. And now—1930—this old lank mark, dear to the hearts of many of Bedford's citizens, has also had to go the way of its predecessors, and has been razed to the ground to give place to a still larger and handsomer structure, in order to meet the demands of this ever prosperous and progressive county.

Just before the county seat was moved from New London the celebrated "Johnny Hook Case" was tried, when Patrick Henry delivered his famous "Beef Speech," and Jemmy Steptoe, the Clerk of the Court, not being able to control himself, rushed from the court room and threw himself upon the ground, rolling in paroxysms of laughter. It seems that Hook, a wealthy Scotchman was accused of being unfriendly to the American cause, and, during the distress of the American Army, a Mr. Venable, an army commissary, had taken two of Hook's steers for the use of the troops, which act was not strictly legal, and Hook sued for damages. Mr. Henry appeared for the defendant, using his wonderful oratorical powers first to excite indignation against Hook, and then to ridicule him, until his audience roared with laughter. The verdict rendered was, "for the plaintiff, one penny damages." Mr. Henry's speech did not stop here, however, for the people had been aroused to such indignation by the audacity of such a suit that it is said only a precipitate flight and the speed of his horse saved Hook from being tarred and feathered.

Jemmy Steptoe, Clerk of Bedford County for fifty-four years, and great-great-grandfather of Lady Astor, M. P., lived at "Federal Hill," near New London. The old manor house, built more than a hundred years ago, still stands, and in a window pane in the hall, carved with a diamond in a boyish prank, no doubt, is the name of his son, James Callaway Steptoe, who succeeded him in office, and is as unmistakably his writing as his signatures upon the books of the Bedford County

"Poplar Forest"

Court. Jemmy Steptoe's wife was Frances Callaway, daughter of James, and grand-daughter of Col. William Callaway, whose ancestral home can be seen from the porch of "Federal Hill."

Near by is Thomas Jefferson's handsome old estate, "Poplar Forest," to which he often repaired for rest and freedom from the cares of state and the hospitality for which he was famous at "Monticello." Here he lived the life of a simple country gentleman, mingling with his neighbors on common ground, and lending himself sympathetically to the local point of view. They knew and loved him as "The Squire."

While riding over this estate of five thousand acres he was thrown from his horse and severely injured, from which he was confined to his bed for several months. During this period of lameness at "Poplar Forest" he wrote his "Notes on Virginia," practically without library or books of reference.

Tradition says that the beautiful Scotch broom which grows so prolifically in the eastern part of the county came from seed brought over in hay for Mr. Jefferson's horses.

"Poplar Forest," still in a perfect state of preservation, is owned by C. S. Hutter of Lynchburg, and used by him as a summer home.

Bedford County has been the birthplace of many great men in many walks of life; among them, Bishop Early of the Methodist Episcopal Church, South; Bishop Otey, of the Protestant Episcopal Church, founder of Sewanee University of Tennessee; Bishop Nicholas Cobbs, also of the Episcopal Church; Rev. John Holt Rice of the Presbyterian Church, founder of the Union Theological Seminary of Virginia; Rev. Jeremiah Bell Jeter, D. D., and Rev. William Eldridge Hatcher, D. D., of the Baptist Church; Judge Edward Calohill Burks, founder of the Virginia Law Register, and his illustrious son, Judge Martin Parks Burks of the Supreme Court of Virginia; Honorable John Goode, member of Secession Convention of Virginia; and others.

It is claimed by Virginians who have traveled all over the world that there is no mountain scenery more interesting nor more beautiful than that afforded by the spur of the Blue Ridge on the north side of Bedford County. Here the celebrated Peaks of Otter lift their rock crowned heads four thousand feet above the level of the sea and thirty-one hundred feet above the level of the surrounding country. Flat Top has the larger base and is said to be the taller, but the difference is not appreciable to the eye. Sharp Top is considered the greater curiosity because of its steep ascent and the magnificent view from its summit—as totally unobstructed as from an airplane—and is the one exclusively visited by vacationists and tourists, who come from all parts of the globe, thousands registering on top each season.

A stone from this peak was Virginia's contribution to the Washington monument in Washington, D. C. It bears the following inscription:

> "From the summit of Otter
> Virginia's loftiest Peak
> To crown the monument
> To Virginia's noblest son."

REVOLUTIONARY SOLDIERS OF BEDFORD COUNTY, VIRGINIA

BEDFORD COUNTY MILITIA
Taken from Order Book, 1774-1782

Adams, James—Captain.
Adams, James—2nd Lieut.
Alexander, Robert—Captain.
Anderson, Jacob—2nd Lieut.
Anthony, Joseph—2nd Lieut.
Arthur, Benjamin—Captain.

Baldwin, Jonas.
Beard, Adam.
Beard, David—Captain.
Beard, Samuel—Captain.
Biggs, John.
Boline, Barnabas.
Boyd, James.
Bryan, William—Ensign.
Bryant, William—Ensign.
Buford, Henry—Captain.
Buford, James—Captain.
Bullock, James—Captain.
Bullock, Josiah—Captain.
Burnley, Harry—Ensign.
Burnley, Henry—1st Lieut.
Burnley, Zachariah—Captain.
Burns, James—2nd Lieut.
Butler, Alexander—1st Lieut.
Butterworth, Benjamin—Lieut.

Callaway, Charles—Captain.

Callaway, Chesley Dudley—1st Lieut.
Callaway, James—County Lieut.
Callaway, James, Jr.—Captain.
Callaway, John—Major.
Callaway, Richard—Colonel.
Callaway, William—Lieut.-Colonel.
Campbell, John—Ensign.
Charter, Thomas—Captain.
Cheatwood, Jace—Ensign.
Cheatwood, Joel—Ensign.
Chiles, John—Captain.
Clark, Micajah—Ensign.
Clark, Robert—Captain.
Clayton, ————, Ensign.
Claytor, John—Captain.
Cobb, Charles—Captain.
Cobb, Edward—2nd Lieut.
Cobb, Jesse—Ensign.
Coggett, Charlton—Captain.

Davis, Henry—1st Lieut.
Davis, Joseph—2nd Lieut.
DeMoss, Thomas—1st Lieut.
Devine, ————.
Divers, John—1st Lieut.
Dooley, George—1st Lieut.

Early, Jacob—Captain.

Early, Jacobus—1st Lieut.
Early, Jeremiah—Colonel.
Early, Thomas.
Eidson, Henry—Ensign.
Ewing, William—1st Lieut.

Farley, Frances—Ensign.
Franklin, Edmund—Ensign.
Franklin, Owen—Ensign.
French, Daniel—Ensign.
Fuqua, Moses—2nd Lieut.

Garvin, Hugh.
Gilbert, Daniel—2nd Lieut.
Gilbert, John W.—Captain.
Gilbert, Preston—Lieut.
Gilbert, Samuel—1st Lieut.
Gilliam, Zachariah—2nd Lieut.
Glass, Charles.
Going, William.
Goggin, Stephen—1st Lieut.
Goodman, Ansel.
Goodman, ————.
Graham, James.
Green, James—2nd Lieut.
Greer, James—1st Lieut.
Griffith, Benjamin—Ensign.
Gwatkin, Charles—Captain.

Haile, Richard—Ensign.
Haynes, Parmenas—Captain.
Haythe, Thomas—1st Lieut.
Heath, William—Substitute for Francis
    Luck.
Helm, John—2nd Lieut.
Helm, Thomas.
Henderson, William, Gent.—Ensign.
Hudnall, William—1st Lieut.
Hunter, John—Ensign.
Hutts, Jacob.
Hurte, Moses—Ensign.

Innes, Harry—Ensign.
Irvine, Abraham—1st Lieut.
Irvine, Andrew—1st Lieut.
Irvine, John—2nd Lieut.
Irvine, Robert—1st Lieut.

James, William—1st Lieut.
Jeter, Henry—1st Lieut.
Johnson, Thomas—Ensign.
Johnson, Christopher.
Jones, Thomas—Ensign.
Jones, William—1st Lieut.
Jordan, William—Captain.

Kelley, Michael.
Kelly, ————.
King, Matthew—Substitute for James
    Mays.

Lahorn, Henry.
Leftwich, Uriah—Ensign.
Leister, William.
Logan, Benjamin—Captain.
Logwood, Thomas—Captain.
Lynch, Anselem—1st Lieut.
Lynch, Charles, Esq.—Colonel.

Martin, David—2nd Lieut.
Mead, William—Major.
McIlroy, Hugh—1st Lieut.
McNininy, William.
McReynolds, Thomas—Captain.
Miller, Simon, Jr.—Ensign.
Mitchell, Daniel—Ensign.
Moon, Jacob, Jr.—Ensign.
Moore, Jacob—2nd Lieut.
Moseley, Arthur—2nd Lieut.
Murray, Thomas—Lieut.

Nance, Thomas—Ensign.
Newell, Cornelius—2nd Lieut.
Noell, Cornelius—2nd Lieut.

Otey, John—Captain.

Parrin, ————.
Parrow, Daniel—Ensign.
Parsons, Daniel—Ensign.
Paramanas, ————, 1st Lieut.
Pate, Anthony—Captain.
Pate, Jesse.
Pate, Matthew—1st Lieut.
Pate, Jeremiah—Captain.
Pate, Thomas—Ensign.

Patrick, John F.—Ensign.
Patterson, Nathaniel—Lieut.
Piles, Henry.
Phelps, John—1st Lieut.
Poindexter, Joseph—Captain.
Prewitt, ————.
Price, Bowen—Captain.
Price, Brown—1st Lieut.

Quarles, John—Colonel.

Rames, Bailey.
Rentfree, Isaac—1st Lieut.
Rentfree, William—Captain.
Rentfro, John—Captain.
Rentfro, Mark—Ensign.
Richeson, Jonathan—Captain.
Robinson, Stephen.
Rose, Thomas.
Ruff, Benjamin.
Runnels, Jesse.
Russell, James—2nd Lieut.
Runyon, John.

Slaughter, John—Ensign.
Smith, James.
Smith, Henry.
Smith, Jonathan—2nd Lieut.
Snow, Henry.
Starkey, John—Ensign.
Steel, Alexander—1st Lieut.
Stith, Joseph—Ensign.
Suter, Charles.

Talbot, Haile—Captain.
Talbot, Williston.
Torbert, John—Captain.
Tate, Edmund—2nd Lieut.
Tate, Jesse—1st Lieut.
Tate, Nathaniel—Captain.
Taylor, Shelton—1st Lieut.
Terrill, Harry—Major.
Terrill, Peter—Captain.
Terry, John.
Terry, William—Captain.
Thornhill, William—Ensign.
Trigg, John—Captain.
Trigg, William—Lieut.-Colonel.
Turnbull, George—1st Lieut.

Vardiman, William—1st Lieut.

Walden, Richard—Ensign.
Ward, Peter.
Watkins, Charles—Captain.
Watkins, Robert—Captain.
Watts, Aaron.
Watts, Thomas—Captain.
Watts, William.
Webb, Isaac—Captain.
Wilkerson, John—Captain.
Wood, Peter—1st Lieut.
Woosten, Hinman.
Wooten, Himan—Ensign.
Wright, David—Captain.

BEDFORD COUNTY SOLDIERS

Taken from Eckenrode's List of Virginia Soldiers in the Revolution

Adams, Henry.
Adams, Robert.
Andrews, Thomas.
Arthur, John.
Arthur, William.

Bailey, Phillip.
Bailey, Savage.
Baker, Glover.
Baldwin, James.
Barton, Elisha.
Blankenship, David.

Blankenship, Abraham.
Blankenship, Henry.
Boley, Priestly.
Bond, Wright.
Brown, Henry.
Brown, Robert.
Brown, Sheldrake.
Brown, Thomas.
Bryant, Alexander.
Bryant, Andrew.
Buford, Henry.

Caldwell, William.
Callaway, Joseph.
Callaway, ———, Colonel.
Camfield, Aaron—Captain.
Campbell, Anthony.
Campbell, William.
Carter, John.
Cowender, William.
Childress, ———.
Church, Robert.
Citty, Jacob.
Clement, Adam.
Cobb, Robert.
Conner, ———.
Crews, Joseph.
Crouch, William.
Cummins, Alexander—Captain.
Cundiff, Isaac.

Davenport, William.
Daverson, James.
Davis, Samuel—1st Lieut.
Dixon, James.
Dixon, Thomas.
Dobins, Alexander.
Donoho, James.
Donoho, Robert.
Doss, Stephen.

Ewing, Samuel.

Ferris, John.
Fielding, Samuel.
Franklin, Samuel.
Fraser, William.
Frazer, Thomas.

Greer, Moses.
Gibbs, John.
Gillman, Archer.
Goff, Abraham.
Goff, Zachariah.
Goodman, ———.
Goswell, George.
Graham, Michael.
Groom, Jonathan.

Hackworth, Thomas.
Hackworth, William.

Hall, Isham.
Hall, Robert.
Hancock, Edward.
Hancock, Samuel.
Haney, Michael.
Haynes, John.
Hinson, ———.
Holly, ———.
Holly, John.
Hudson, William.
Huddel, John.
Himbrick, Joseph.

Jackson, William.
Jones, Charles.
Jones, Gray.
Jones, Stephen.

Kennedy, John.
Kerr, Thomas.
King, Herman.

Laine, Thomas.
Laine, Daniel.
Lambert, Charles.
Lambert, George—Captain.
Lee, William.
Leftwich, ———, Captain.|
Leftwich, John.
Leftwich, Thomas—Captain.
Leister, ———.
Littlepage, John.
Lockard, Philip.
Lowry, Henry.
Lowry, John.
Lumpkin, Thomas.
Lynch, Patrick.

McGrane, Thomas.
McGrady, Jacob.
McLaughlin, Thomas.
McReynolds, James.

March, John P.
Markham, John.
Markham, Thomas.
Marshall, Thomas.
Martin, Robert.

Meador, Benjamin.
Melson, Charles.
Merritt, ———, Major.
Middleton, John.
Milam, Benjamin.
Milam, William—1st Lieut.
Miller, Jacob.
Miner, Thresswelers.
Miner, William.
Mitchell, John.
Mitchell, Samuel.
Moon, ———, Captain.
Moore, Robert.
Moore, James.
Moseley, James.

Nelms, Charles.
Nowman, Nimrod.

Overstreet, Thomas.

Padgett, Frederick.
Powell, Aaron.
Pullen, Thomas.

Quarles, James.
Quarles, John—Captain.

Read, Robert.
Ready, ———.
Reid, Nathan—Captain.
Reynolds, Alexander.
Reynolds, Jesse.
Rice, Benjamin—1st Lieut.
Robertson, Benjamin.
Rogers, Ezekiel.
Ross, Job.
Ross, William.
Rouse, Peter (negro).

Saunders, David.
Scantling, Jeremiah.
Scruggs, Gross—Capt.

Sharp, John.
Shepherd, Jacob.
Simpkins, Garrett.
Slaughter, Reuben.
Smith, George.
Spearman, John.
Steel, John.
Stiff, James.
Stovall, John.
Swain, George.

Talbot, Charles M.
Tanner, Nathan.
Tate, Adams.
Thomasson, John.
Tracy, William.
Triggs, I. ———, Captain.

Valentine, Luke.
Vest, John.

Williams, Edward.
Williams, John.
Wilson, Samuel.
Winn, Joshua.
Witt, Jesse.
Wood, Francis.
Wood, Joseph.
Woodward, George.
Worley, Joshua.
Wright, John.
Wade, Jacob.
Walker, Charles.
Walker, William J.
Ward, Henry.
Watkins, John.
Watts, ———.
Watts, Aaron.
Watts, John—Captain.
White, Joseph.
Wigginton, John.

The following list of soldiers was picked up here and there in the records in the Congressional Library:

Oliver, William.
Gross, Isaac, Sr.
Hudnall, John.
Dokin, Jonathan.
Gill, John.

Arthur, John, Sr.
McCormahoy, John.
Buford, John.
Austin, Richard.

THE PIONEERS OF BEDFORD

By J. E. GWATKIN

In early days a hardy folk
  Pressed on beyond the near frontier,
Passed on to where the sky-line broke,
  And there, in narrow valleys drear,
    They made their homes in Bedford.
They bravely met the dangers great;
  They beat their backs to labors;
Nor quailed before the red-man's threat,
  With only mountain neighbors;
    In the sunny vales of Bedford.

They built their guardian circle fires
  Around their lonely camps by night:
Inspired by love that never tires,
  Took up their tasks at morning light;
    Those pioneers in Bedford.
The forests rang with axe and saw;
  Their cabin homes went up apace;
For soon their coming loved ones saw
  The homes of an all conquering race,
    Amidst the hills of Bedford.

Where crystal streams burst from the hills
  They cleared each one his fertile field,
And by these rapids built their mills
  To grind the golden grain they yield,
    In fair and fruitful Bedford.
With daily toil they fenced these farms,
  They built their barns and stables,
And soon amidst such scenic charms
  Appeared the roofs and gables
    Of these first homes in Bedford.

So now from all our common land,
  Where they have wandered far,
Descendants of this noble band
    Are proud to claim their natal star
      Shone brightly there in Bedford.
From every worthy walk of life,
  From North and South and West,
From country's calm and city's strife,
  They turn for peace and rest,
    In heart and soul to Bedford.

Hail native land of high blue hills!
  Hail valleys cool and quiet!
How at your name each exile thrills
  Amidst our rush and riot!
    Hail rare old name of Bedford!
Ye favored ones who now reside
  Within her blessed bound,
Know that in all this world beside
  No region can be found
    So sweet, so dear as Bedford.

New Orleans, November 3, 1929.

WHITE

When Virginia was still in her infancy, a minister, William White, came from Wiltshire, England, and settled in York County. All we know of him is that he died in Lancaster County in 1678, leaving a will which mentions his sons, John, William and Edward; daughter, Deborah; and daughter-in-law, Mary Alford or Afford. His brother, Rev. Jeremiah White, of London, was made one of the guardians of his children.

The names of the descendants of these Whites appear frequently in the records of York, Lancaster, King William, Spotsylvania, Orange, Culpeper, Albemarle, and other counties in that section of the state; but because of the almost universal custom, in those days, of using family names, it has been well-nigh impossible to separate the different branches of the family. That they are all one family is certain for the same reason—these names have clung to them, even down to the present day.

In "Extracts from King William County records," in the *Virginia Historical Magazine*, Vol. 25, page 174, we find that in 1705 Thos. Ellett deeded land to his son-in-law, John White and wife, Mary. In Spotsylvania County records we find them mentioned again in 1730.

The following items are taken from Crozier's "Records of Spotsylvania County":

Deed Book "B"—1729-1734 of Spotsylvania Co., April 4, 1730, deed of John White of St. John's Parish, King Wm. Co., Gent., to Thomas Crothers of St. George Par., Spotsylvania Co., Planter, witnesses, Richard Gregory, Joe Roberts and Thos. White. Mary, wife of John White, acknowledged her dower.

March 6, 1743. James White and Sarah, his wife, of Hanover Co., to Thos. White of Spots. Co. L 29 Curr. 300 a. (devised to sd James White by the will of his father, John White, dec'd., recorded in King Wm. Co.).

Jeremiah White and wife, Mary, of Spotsylvania County, mentioned in 1747.

Chilion White and Millicent White also mentioned.

Wm. White of Spotsylvania County, 1766.

It is believed by those who have searched these records and followed the history of the family that Jeremiah White, who died in Orange County in 1774 and Daniel White, who died in Culpeper County in 1790, were sons of John and Mary Ellett White, but we can only take up the lines with absolute certainty where the court records, now extant, begin.

Daniel White's will (recorded in Culpeper County, Virginia, Will Book "C," page 40), made November 23, 1788, and probated December 20, 1790, mentions sons, Henry White, John White; granddaughter, Polly White, daughter of John White; daughter, Tabitha Rogers; grandchildren, Reuben Harrison, John Harrison, Richard Harrison, James Harrison, Elizabeth Tinsley, Frances Lee, wife of Richard Lee, children of daughter, Frances. To his son, Henry, he leaves five negroes, Phyllis, Moll, Jack, Dick and Charles, but no land.

In Orange County, Daniel White's name appears in the list of tithables, in 1739, and in the records of the same county we find in Deed Book No. 15: "Henry White, James Madison, George Taylor and John Carter, Gent., 37 lbs.—154 acres, lot No. 9, Aug. 24, 1769."

In 1787, we find Henry White in Buckingham County; but whether he was the son of Daniel, mentioned above, it has been impossible to prove (though we have not a doubt but that he was), first, because his father left him no land, by which he might have been traced, and, second, because the records of Buckingham County were destroyed by fire many years ago—only a Tax Book, which happened to be out of the Courthouse at the time of the fire, is now in existence. This shows, however, that Henry White owned property in Buckingham County.

1787, List of land owners, Buckingham Co. Peter Guerrant Com., Dist. No. 1.

Henry White (weaver), 260 acres of land.

1793, Henry White, 1 tithe, 1 slave over 16, 1 under 16, and 4 horses.

Other Whites mentioned in the above Tax Book: Henry, Dabney, Hugh and William, 1804-1806.

Henry White came from Buckingham to Bedford County about 1800, evidently to spend his declining years with his son, Jacob, who had preceded him several years. His will, dated August 18, 1800, and probated September 27, 1802, in Bedford (Will Book "B," page 366), reads:

I, Henry White, of the County of Bedford, do make and constitute this to be my last Will and Testament in manner following:

My will and desire is, first—that all my lawful debts be paid, after which I leave the money now arising from the sale of my land to all my sons, to be equally divided among them. The money now arising from the property already sold in Buckingham County on the first and second days of November, 1799, also my money that I have lent out, with my personal estate that I brought up from Buckingham, to wit: Abraham, Rachel and Maryan, to be equally divided between all my Sons and Daughters including my Granddaughter, Judith David, equal with my own Daughters, that is to say that she shall have an equal part with each of them: if Judith David should depart this life before she becomes of age then her part to be equally divided amongst the rest of my children.

Item, I also leave my household furniture that I brought up with me from Buckingham to Bedford and a horse, bridle and saddle to my son Jacob White. I do hereby nominate and appoint my son Jacob White and my son William White my Executors of this my last Will and Testament by me made this thirtieth day of August, Eighteen Hundred.

his

HENRY x WHITE [SEAL].

mark

Signed, sealed and declared
in presence of

    CHAS. GWATKIN
    FELL LESEUR
    JULIUS HATCHER, SR.

At a court held for Bedford County the 27th day of September, 1802. This last Will and Testament of Henry White deceased was proved by oaths of Fell Leseur and Julius Hatcher witnesses thereto and ordered to be recorded. And on motion of Jacob White one of the Exors. named in said Will, who made oath thereto certificate is granted him for obtaining probate therefor in due form, giving security whereupon he together with Thomas Logwood his security entered into acknowledged their bond in the penalty of six thousand dollars conditioned for the said Exors. due and faithful administration of said decedents Estate and performance of his will: Liberty being reserved William White the other Exor. named in the said will to join in the probate thereof when he shall think fit.

Teste: J. STEPTOE, C. B. C.

Appraisement of the property of Henry White, made November 30, 1802.

One negro man named Abram.. 115.
One negro woman named Rachel.. 80.
One negro girl named Mary Ann... 20.
One negro child named Charity.. 15.
                                                                                                                       ———
                                                                                                                       230.

(Will Book "B," page 394.)

William White married Polly Price in Bedford County in 1799.

Thomas White married Jane Lusk in Bedford County in 1783. In 1785 he bought land on Otter River, and sold the same in 1788. Nothing more is known of him.

Daniel White married Margaret Caldwell in Bedford County in 1780.

Jeremiah White died in Bedford County in 1816.

His appraisement shows no property in this county.

These are all family names and they were no doubt closely related, but whether or not they were sons of Henry White it has been impossible to tell.

The following is the coat of arms used by the descendants of Henry White of Buckingham County:

Arms: gu (red) a chevron vain,
          between three lions rampant-or (gold).

Crest: Out of a ducal coronet or (gold),
           a dimi eagle, wings expanded sable (black).

Motto: Loyal unto death.

Jacob White, son of Henry White of Buckingham County, Virginia, came to Bedford soon after the Revolutionary War, and settled near James River, in the northeastern part of the county.

He bought, November 4, 1794, from Samuel Waddy 350 acres of land, adjoining Henry Hatcher, Thomas Hubbard, Edmund Winston and Charles Gwatkin. (Deed Book "J," page 164.)

His second purchase was from Francis Halley in 1805 "West side of No Business Mountain and on waters of James River. Beginning at Jeremiah Hatcher's line." (Deed Book "K," page 1196.)

A historical sketch of Jacob Samuel White, grandson of Jacob White, in Hardesty's Encyclopedia, page 434, says: "His parents were natives of this (Bedford) County and his grandfather, after serving with distinction and with rank of captain through the greater part of the Revolutionary War, was an early and prominent settler here. The county was almost a wilderness when he came here, and with his own hands he cleared and improved the beautiful place on Otter Creek, where the subject of this sketch resides."

(The place above spoken of, except for a period of a few years, remained in the White family until 1928, when Samuel J. White, son of Jacob Samuel White and great grandson of Jacob White, to whom it descended, sold it and moved his family to Roanoke, Virginia. In 1805, when Jacob White made his purchase of land from Francis Halley "on waters of James River," he moved his family there, where he lived until his death in 1832. Some of this property is owned today by his descendants; but not the manor house tract. This, known as "Charlemont Lodge," descended to his son, Col. William Allen White and the present owners of the part of it on which was located the home are Messrs. C. S. Nelson and M. N. Moorman, Jr., of Lynchburg, Virginia.)

Jacob White, born October 20, 1765, son of Henry White of Buckingham County; married (first) before coming to Bedford, Hannah Spiers. He became a wealthy landowner of Bedford County; and was prominent in all local affairs, holding positions of trust and responsibility. Served in the Revolutionary War with the rank of Captain and was a Justice of the Peace in Bedford County for a number of years.

His wife, Hannah (Spiers) White, died January 11, 1816, and is buried in the family burying ground at "Charlemont Lodge," Charlemont, Bedford County, Va. After her death he married (second), December 10, 1816, Nancy Oglesby, daughter of Richard Oglesby, of Bedford County. There were no children by his last marriage.

Jacob White died in 1832, and was buried by the side of his first wife. The inscription on his tombstone reads:

CAPTAIN JACOB WHITE
BORN
OCTOBER 20, 1765
DIED
JUNE 2ND, 1832
AGED 66 YEARS 7 MONTHS AND 12 DAYS

The children by his first marriage, all of whom married in Bedford County except one, Samuel D., who settled in Kentucky, were as follows:

(1) Sallie, born August 18, 1787; married, November 12, 1801, David Douglas. (See Douglas family.)

(2) John A.; married, April 4, 1808, Elizabeth Robinson, daughter of Benjamin Robinson, and settled in Warren County, Kentucky. Nothing more known of him.

(3) Nancy R., born 1789; married (first), August 15, 1805, Abraham Robinson; married (second), Jesse Spinner. Died 1831. (See Robinson and Spinner families.)

(4) Jacob Washington, born March 5, 1792; married, December 17, 1812, Matilda Buford. (See forward.)

(5) Rebecca H.; married, December 23, 1807, Charles Lewis Davis. (See Davis family.)

(6) Elizabeth; married, February 4, 1812, Henry Hatcher. (See Hatcher family.)

(7) William Allen; married (first), November 3, 1828, Caroline Poindexter; married (second), May 10, 1841, Lucy McDaniel Reese. (See forward.)

(8) Samuel D.; settled in Simpson County, Kentucky. Nothing more known of him.

(9) Polly; married, January 28, 1817, Julius W. Hatcher. (See Hatcher family.)

(10) Catherine; married, November 27, 1818, Thomas Hatcher. (See Hatcher family.)

(11) Henry Milton, born January 31, 1805; married, October 4, 1826, Mary Ann Gwatkin. (See forward.)

(12) Edna A.; married, October 19, 1824, Moses Penn. (See Penn family.)

(13) Editha S.; married, July 16, 1827, Gabriel S. Fisher. Nothing more known of her.

The will of Jacob White, recorded in Will Book "H," page 94 of the Bedford County records is as follows:

I, Jacob White, a citizen of the County of Bedford and State of Virginia do make constitute & ordain this as my last will and testament hereby revoking & annulling all former wills by me heretofore made.

I desire that all my just debts be speedily paid—I give to my wife Nancy White should she survive me all the land I own on the left hand side of the road leading from Meadow and Reed Creek to Sledd's Shop and the following Negroes to wit: Racheal and her children now born and any which may be born previous to my death, Elvira and her children now born and any which may be born previous to my death. I give this property to my wife during her natural life, and after her death to be divided amongst my children as hereinafter directed. I give to my said wife one feather bed and furniture, one horse to be chosen by her out of my stock of horses, six head of cattle to be allotted her of cows and young cattle, six head of sheep, twenty head of hogs, and a sufficient quantity of grain to support her for one year from my death. I desire that the residue of my estate be divided into twelve equal parts by sale or otherwise as may be deemed most expedient by those interested.

I give to my executors hereinafter named one twelfth part of my estate to be held by them as trustees during the life of my daughter Sally Douglas and they are to apply the profits arising from the said portion to the support and maintenance of my said daughter during her life, and at her death they are to convey the same to the children of my said daughter,—and I also give them for the same purpose to be by them held in like manner one-twelfth part of the property above given to my wife for life at the death of my said wife should she survive me, should she die before me, this devise is to take effect at my death.

I give to my son John A. White one-twelfth part of my estate, also one-twelfth part of the property given to my wife for life at the death of my said wife should she survive me, should I outlive her this devise is to take effect at my death.

I give to the children of Abraham Robertson (Robinson) by my daughter Nancy who has since intermarried with ———— Spinner one-twelfth part of my estate, also one-twelfth part of the property given to my wife for life should she survive me to take effect at her death, should I outlive her to take effect at my death.

I give to my son Jacob W. White one-twelfth part of my estate, also one-twelfth part of the property given to my wife for life to take effect at her death, should she survive me, should I outlive her to take effect at my death.

I give to the children of my daughter Rebecka Davis one-twelfth part of my estate, also one-twelfth part of the property given to my wife for life to take effect at her death should she survive me, should I outlive her to take effect at my death.

I give to the children of my daughter Elizabeth Hatcher one-twelfth part of my estate, also one-twelfth part of the property given to my wife for life to take effect at her death should she survive me, should I outlive her to take effect at my death.

I give to my son William A. White one-twelfth part of my estate, also one-twelfth part of the property given to my wife for life, to take effect at her death should she survive me, should I outlive her to take effect at my death.

I give to my son Samuel D. White one-twelfth part of my estate, also one-twelfth part of the property given to my wife for life to take effect at her death should she survive me, should I outlive her to take effect at my death.

I give to my daughter Polly Hatcher one-twelfth part of my estate, also one-twelfth part of the property given to my wife for life to take effect at her death should she survive me, should I outlive her to take effect at my death.

I give to my daughter Catharine Hatcher one-twelfth part of my estate, also one-twelfth part of the property given to my wife for life to take effect at her death should she survive me, should I outlive her to take effect at my death.

I give to my son Henry M. White one-twelfth part of my estate, also one-twelfth part of the property given to my wife for life to take effect at her death should she survive me, should I outlive her to take effect at my death.

I give to my daughter Edna A. Penn one-twelfth part of my estate, also one-twelfth part of the property given to my wife for life to take effect at her death, should she survive me, should I outlive her to take effect at my death.

My daughter Editha S. having married without my consent and contrary to my wishes, I desire she shall have no part of my estate.

I do hereby constitute and appoint my sons William A. White and Henry M. White Executors of this my last will and testament and desire that they shall not be required to give security, hereby revoking and annulling all former wills & testaments by me made. I do hereby make constitute publish & declare this as my last will & testament. In testimony whereof I have hereunto set my hand & seal this 9th day of October in the year 1827.

JACOB WHITE [SEAL].

Signed, sealed, published and declared as & for his last will & testament in presence of us

JEREMIAH HATCHER
ALBERT M. HATCHER
GEORGE LAMBERT
SAMUEL HOBSON

At a Court held for Bedford County the 25th day of June, 1832.

The within last will & testament of Jacob White deceased was produced in court proven by the oaths of Jeremiah Hatcher and Samuel Hobson two of the subscribing witnesses thereto and ordered to be recorded. And on the motion of William A. White and Henry M. White the executors in said will named who made oath thereto according to law, and severally entered into & acknowledged their bond in the penalty of Twelve Thousand Dollars each, conditioned according to law, without security, according to the provisions of the will, certificate is granted them for obtaining probat thereof in due form.

Teste,

Ro. C. MITCHELL, *C. B. C.*

A copy,
Teste:

V. W. NICHOLS,
*Clerk of the Circuit Court of
Bedford County, Virginia.*

Deed Book "H," page 94.

....

From the Bedford County records we have the following: September 21, 1832. Samuel D. White of Simpson County, Kentucky, gives Power of Attorney to John.A. White, of Warren County, Kentucky, "to demand and receive" his part of his father's estate.

....

November 19, 1832. Both John A. and Samuel D. White sold the land which they inherited from their father's estate to Micajah Davis, Jr., of Lynchburg, Va.

....

JACOB WASHINGTON WHITE

Jacob Washington White, born March 5, 1792, son of Captain Jacob and Hannah (Spiers) White, married, December 17, 1812, Matilda Buford, born February 11, 1793, daughter of William and Martha Hill (Logwood) Buford, of Bedford County, Va. Jacob W. White, died May 20, 1829, and his widow, Matilda (Buford) White, married, November 18, 1835, William Thaxton, born September 23, 1782; died May 5, 1839. She died March 10, 1876, at the home of her daughter, Mrs. Mary Starr (White) Nimmo, with whom she had spent her last years, having outlived her second husband also.

CHILDREN:

(1) Celine Catherine Spiers, born October 18, 1813.
(2) William Allen Buford, born May 15, 1815.
(3) Adeline Martha, born March 30, 1817.

(4) John Henry, born February 6, 1819; died June 30, 1828.

(5) Virginia Ann, born July 28, 1820.

(6) Parmelia Elizabeth, born June 2, 1822.

(7) Mary Starr, born July 27, 1824.

(8) Hillary Alexander, born May 11, 1826; died November, 1849.

(9) Sarah Frances, born January 18, 1829.

....

Celine Catherine Spiers White, born October 18, 1813; daughter of Jacob Washington and Matilda (Buford) White, married Fountaine M. Hawkins.

CHILDREN:

(1) Matilda; married Henry Cobb.

(2) Francis Lewis; married Francis Edward Hopkins, son of Jesse Turner and Mildred (Hewett) Hopkins, of Bedford County.

CHILDREN:

(a) Jesse M., born November 26, 1857; married, December 15, 1880, Elizabeth M. Hatcher, born October 1, 1861, daughter of Henry Milton and Maria (Hawkins) Hatcher. (See Hatcher family.)

CHILDREN:

(aa) Samuel M., born August 23, 1881; married Elizabeth Lindsay. Their children are:
(aaa) Jacob M., born March 29, 1919.
(bbb) Jesse R., born June 1, 1921.
(ccc) William, born February 22, 1925.

(bb) Fannie M., born July 1, 1884.

(cc) Jesse Claude, born October 5, 1891; married, June 30, 1915, Minnie Sale Ballard, born October 1, 1891, daughter of James W. and Margaret (McGhee) Ballard. Their children are:
(aaa) Margaret E., born October 18, 1917.
(bbb) James C., born October 23, 1919.
(ccc) Dorothy J., born October 23, 1922.
(ddd) Frank K., born October 31, 1927.
(eee) William, born December 1, 1928.

   (b) George C.; married Annie Newsom, daughter of Major
       David M. and Susan (Williamson) Newsom. They live
       in California.

   (c) Lillian M.; married George Stiff. One son living—
       F. P. Stiff.

   (d) Fannie Davis; married ———— Rudwisheold.

   (e) Edward, twin of Davis; married Witcher Wright.

   (f) Elizabeth; married C. N. Horsley.

(3) Harvey; died unmarried.

(4) Martha; married Pleasant Meador.

(5) John; married Mary Jane Hurt.

(6) Edward; married Lottie Hopkins.

(7) Bettie; married Henry Huddleston.

(8) Spottswood Brown, born May 20, 1852; married, October 18,
    1876, Lelia Newsom, born May 29, 1855, died December, 1924,
    daughter of Major David M. and Susan (Williamson) New-
    som.

CHILDREN:

   (a) William Edward, born July 10, 1877; died August 9,
       1877.

   (b) Hillary Houston, born July 22, 1879; went to Kansas
       in early life and there married Maud Karney. They and
       all their children live in Kansas.

CHILDREN:

       (aa) Kenneth C.
       (bb) Dayton Spottswood.
       (cc) Lelia Katherine.
       (dd) Hillary Houston, Jr.
       (ee) Glenn.
       (ff) Robert Lee.
       (gg) Bertha.
       (hh) Tuila.

   (c) Sallie Eugenia, born August 7, 1880; unmarried.

   (d) Edna Rieley, born July 9, 1882; married, March 24,
       1907, W. Abbott Saunders.

CHILDREN:

(aa) Virginia.
(bb) Lelia Edwin.
(cc) Hillary Abbott.
(dd) James Hayden.
(ee) Nelly Rieley.
(ff) Mary and Martha, twins.
(gg) Joseph Spottswood.

(e) Susie Irene, born January 29, 1884; married, August 19, 1918, Charles S. Spradlin.

CHILDREN:

(aa) Charles S., Jr.
(bb) Ruth Spottswood.

(f) Annie Gertrude, born December 31, 1885; died August 11, 1887.

(g) Ora Jopling, born July 21, 1891; married, March 25, 1920, Claud Griffin, of North Carolina.

CHILDREN:

(aa) Ralph Hawkins.
(bb) Sydney Bivens.

....

THE MISSOURI WHITES

William Allen Buford White, born May 15, 1815, eldest son of Jacob Washington and Matilda (Buford) White married in Kanawha, West Virginia, January 16, 1840, Sarah Leftwich. He later went to Missouri, settling in Cass County, where he died in 1904. Sarah (Leftwich) White died before her husband.

CHILDREN:

(1) Jacob William, born December 22, 1841; married, June 12, 1873, Mrs. Selina Garland Bradford. She died August 29, 1904.

CHILDREN:

(a) Ann Selina, born January 23, 1875.
(b) Sarah Pottenger, born November 7, 1876.

(c) Florence Allene, born February 14, 1879.

(d) William Allen Buford, II, born March 13, 1881.

(e) D. V., born February 19, 1884.

(2) Mary Adeline, born May 27, 1843; died 1845.

(3) Matilda Jane, born August 16, 1845; married, May 28, 1873, Tinsley W. Jeter; died March 15, 1919. (See Jeter family.)

(4) John Alexander, born May 5, 1848; married (first), June 27, 1873, Lydia Dodson. He married (second), September 16, 1893, Mary Burns. John Alexander White died in Cass County, Mo., March 20, 1904.

CHILDREN:

Child by first marriage:
(a) Maude.
Children by second marriage:
(b) James Corbett, born September 14, 1894.

(c) Matilda Frances, born November 26, 1896.

(d) Sarah Elizabeth, born August 7, 1898; married, November 20, 1919, Edward Luster.

(5) James Hillary, born July 18, 1850; married, November 6, 1879, Missouri Reed Hudson. She died March 20, 1911.

CHILDREN:

(a) Samuel Buford, born July 2, 1885; died December 22, 1905.

(b) Malinda Jane, born September 26, 1886; died June 23, 1913.

(c) James D., born October 2, 1890; married Blanche Reynolds.

CHILDREN:

(aa) Martha Reed, born August 20, 1920.

(bb) Jane Dee, born March 27, 1922.

(d) William Allen, born November 9, 1891; married, April 1, 1922, Evelyn Reyburn.

(e) Infant; died 1894.

(f) Clark Hudson, born September 16, 1896; married, May 27, 1922, Effie DeYoung.

CHILD:

(aa) James Truman, born March 28, 1923.

(6) Milton Starr, born November 12, 1852; unmarried.

(7) Infant; died January 19, 1855.

(8) Ann Celine, born July 16, 1896; married, October 30, 1879, James Lee Dyer.

CHILDREN:

(a) William Henderson, born September 30, 1880.

(b) Edna May, born May 4, 1882.

(c) Infant; died January 23, 1884.

(d) Eva Virginia, born June 26, 1885.

(e) Zoula Frances, born November 3, 1887; married, April 9, 1911, William Snodgrass.

CHILD:

(aa) Ruby White, born September 25, 1913.

(f) Infant; died June 27, 1889.

(g) Grace Leonidas, born September 2, 1893; married, July 4, 1918, Allen Hargie.

(h) Eugene Vest, born November 2, 1895.

(i) Roy Bryan, born February 10, 1898.

Adeline Martha White, born March 30, 1817, daughter of Jacob Washington and Matilda (Buford) White, married, September 26, 1833, Alexander A. N. Plunkett and went to Texas, where she died in 1835, soon after the birth of her only child, William, whose descendants now live in and around Ft. Worth, Texas.

Virginia Ann White, born July 28, 1820, daughter of Jacob Washington and Matilda (Buford) White, married, December 30, 1836, Fielden H. Jeter; died April 9, 1877. (See Jeter family.)

Parmelia Elizabeth White, born June 2, 1822, daughter of Jacob Washington and Matilda (Buford) White, married in 1840, James Clark Thaxton, who died in 1848. For many years she was an invalid and a great sufferer from rheumatism. Her hands and feet were so drawn that she could neither walk nor use her hands. She died at her home at Thaxton, Va., September 12, 1890.

CHILDREN:

(1) William White, born November 8, 1842, in Montgomery County, Virginia; married in April, 1867, Frances Elizabeth Newsom, daughter of William and Sophia (Hancock) Newsom, of Bedford County. William White Thaxton was a merchant in Lynchburg, Va., for many years before his death, which occurred in that city, November 6, 1896. His widow, Frances (Newsom) Thaxton, lives in Farmville, Va., with her daughter, Mrs. Elizabeth (Thaxton) Gilbert.

CHILDREN:

(a) Walter; married, in 1893, Mary Elizabeth Hopkins and lived only a few years. No children.

(b) William Clark; married, in 1901, Florence Lowden; went to Albuquerque, N. M., in 1907, and is now State Senator from his district.

CHILD:

(aa) Frances, born 1906.

(c) Mary Jimmie; married in 1895, Walter Gish, born 1870; died 1906.

CHILDREN:

(aa) William Griffin; married Gertrude Howl.

(bb) Ethel May; married Randolph Asley Wilmoth.

(d) George Rufus; married in 1896, Cora Lee Craddock.

CHILDREN:

(aa) William White.

(bb) George Rufus, Jr.

(cc) Louise Virginia.

(e) Jacob Elmore; married Addie Virginia Craft.

CHILDREN:

(aa) Jacob Elmore, Jr.

(bb) Doris.

(f) Elizabeth Ann; married, in 1911, Aubrey Powertan Gilbert. She was educated at Randolph-Macon Woman's College and was a most successful teacher and school supervisor before her marriage. She lives in Farmville, Va., where her husband is agent for the Norfolk and Western Railway.

(g) John F.; married, September 23, 1908, Lelia Ella Johnson. He studied medicine at the Medical College of Virginia (1906-1908) and at the University of Kentucky (1908-1910). He is now a popular and successful physician at Tye River, Nelson County, Virginia.

CHILDREN:

(aa) Virginia, born in Louisville, Ky., July 13, 1909; died in Nelson County, Va., December 23, 1922.
(bb) John F., Jr., born November 15, 1911.
(cc) Elizabeth Ann, born November 5, 1913.

(h) Hillary White; married in 1910, Willie Jordan Laughon. He died of influenza in the epidemic of 1918.

(2) Mary Frances, born 1843; married Rufus Brugh, of Botetourt County, Virginia.

CHILDREN:

(a) Ora Elizabeth; married Ira Lee Graybill and died in Roanoke, Va., in 1924.

CHILDREN:

(aa) Louise.
(bb) Elsie.
(cc) Ralph.

(b) Walter Jacob; married Claudine Linkenhoker.

CHILDREN:

(aa) William.
(bb) Virginia.

(3) Jacob Nathaniel, born 1845; died 1884.
(4) Matilda James, born 1848; married, in 1870, George T. Rieley (born 1848; died 1882).

CHILDREN:

(a) Ollie C.; married Florence Sheffield.

CHILDREN:

(aa) Matilda White.
(bb) Edith Eugenia.
(cc) James Whitcomb.

(b) Cordelia Edith; married Edward A. Gilbert; lives in Tallahassee, Florida. No children.

(c) Maud; unmarried; lives in Roanoke, Va.

(d) Anna White; married Russell McMillan.

....

Mary Starr White, born July 27, 1824, daughter of Jacob Washington and Matilda (Buford) White; married, November 7, 1854, Josiah H. Nimmo, born October 29, 1819. Josiah H. Nimmo was the son of Robert Nimmo, born June 2, 1773; died February 12, 1851, and Lydia Holland, born December 5, 1781; died December 14, 1839. He was a local preacher of the Methodist Episcopal Church, South, and a most excellent man. He died at his home near Chamblissburg, Bedford County, Va., November 20, 1890.

After the marriage of her son and the death of her husband, Mary Starr (White) Nimmo lived alone, except for the faithful attendance of "Patsey," the daughter of one of the old family slaves, whom she raised and taught to be a very fine cook.

"Aunt Starr," as she was called throughout the family, was noted far and wide for her lavish hospitality, her kindness of heart, and her keen sense of humor. Her home was the neighborhood center for old and young—even the girls, living near her, would take their visiting beaux on Sunday afternoons to see "Aunt Starr," and to enjoy her delicious cake and wine. She was seriously offended if a stranger came to visit in the neighborhood and did not "break bread" with her. There was no such thing as refusing when she pressed you to eat more at her table, and upon one occasion, when she was entertaining a party of young people at dinner, after they had eaten to their own satisfaction of ham, fried chicken, the best pickles ever made, all the vegetables of the season, ice cream and old-fashioned pound cake, "Aunt Starr" said, "Now, Mary, honey, have a clean plate and some more snaps."

While she was a devout Methodist, she was much beloved by all denominations, and her home was ever the home of the preacher, no matter what his faith. Many a circuit rider of the old days has found shelter beneath her roof and has left her house with buggy laden with products of her garden, her pantry, and her orchard.

She died November 28, 1905, at the ripe old age of eighty-one years, and was buried by the side of her husband in the family burying ground, just back of her garden.

(1) John William, born July 10, 1856; married, December 20, 1882, Lucy James Stewart, born June 1, 1861, the daughter of Samuel Givens Stewart (born in Botetourt County, March 9, 1823; died in Bedford County, October 8, 1886) and Mary Jane Arrington (born in Franklin County, November 6, 1830; died February 22, 1880) who were married May 6, 1847.

CHILDREN:

(a) Edmund H., born October 11, 1883; unmarried.

(b) Mary Elizabeth, born August 10, 1885; married, January 14, 1914, Samuel Walton Huddleston, born April 2, 1881, son of John H. Huddleston (born April 4, 1849; died December 30, 1907) and Ann Missouri Field (born June 4, 1849; died 1929), who were married, June 9, 1880. Ann Missouri (Field) Huddleston is the daughter of William Millen Field (great-grandson of Capt. Thomas Buford, who commanded a company at the Battle of Point Pleasant, and was killed in that battle) and Louisa W. Adams.

CHILDREN:

(aa) William Walton, born November 9, 1914.

(bb) Stewart Edwin, born December 19, 1915.

(c) Frank Stewart, born July 10, 1888; died April 14, 1919, in the Naval Hospital at Chelsea, Mass., while in service during the World War.

(d) Robert Parrish, born May 6, 1891; accidently shot himself while out hunting, and died immediately—May 1, 1901.

(e) Matilda Starr, born July 11, 1893; unmarried.

(f) Louis Embree, born September 13, 1896; unmarried.

(2) Robert Alexander, born January 7, 1859; died January 12, 1889.

Sarah Frances White, born January 18, 1829, daughter of Jacob Washington and Matilda (Buford) White, married, July 14, 1847, Septimus Ligon Williams, born January 20, 1819, the son of Samuel Williams (born 1781, and Betsey Wingo, born 1784). He moved his family to Missouri in 1867 and lived there until his death in 1882. Sarah (White) Williams died in Newburg, Mo., January 1, 1912. Of their twelve children, eleven were born in Virginia—the youngest one in Missouri; now living in St. Louis.

CHILDREN:

(1) Matilda Elizabeth, born May 6, 1848; married, November 14, 1867, Winfield T. Jones. He has been dead many years and she lives in St. Louis, Missouri.

CHILDREN:

(a) Walter Ligon Jones, born September 8, 1868; married Jennie Foulks in Arkansas. They have several small children and live near Newburg, Missouri.

(b) Annie Gray Jones, born January 12, 1871; married Ivy Hawkins. Lives in Newburg, Mo. Had one daughter, Lenna, who died in childhood.

(c) Robert Leonidas Jones, born February 21, 1874; married Jessie Rogers. Now live in St. Louis and have five children as follows:

    (aa) Marie.

    (bb) Ernest.

    (cc) Robbie.

    (dd) Lydia; married Albert Buck and have a baby daughter, Anita Lee.

    (ee) Walter.

(d) Emmett Albert Jones, born June 26, 1876; married Kate Sitz and lives in California. Had one daughter, Helen, who died in childhood.

(e) Thomas Monroe Jones, born October 28, 1879. Unmarried and living with his mother in St. Louis.

(f) Charles Castilla Jones, born March 5, 1881. Unmarried and living with his mother in St. Louis.

(2) Hillary Albert, born June 22, 1850; married Jane (Jennie) Wingo; is a prosperous merchant in Forth Worth, Texas. Had one son, Wingo, who died in 1912 at the age of 26. He had just completed his education as a doctor, and contracted scarlet fever while an interne in a hospital.

(3) Leonidas Rosser, born October 25, 1851; married Emma Wilhite. He died in St. Louis in 1914. They had four children, two of whom died in childhood. Of the remaining two, Connor, is married to Dollie Dickson, in Alabama, and has two little girls. Steve is unmarried and lives in Birmingham, Alabama.

(4) Missouri ("Zoula"), born October 16, 1853; married Stephen Douglas Barlow, who died several years ago. His widow now lives in Springfield, Ill., with her only daughter, Margaret, who is married to Dr. Frederick P. Cowdin, and has one daughter, Lucy Frances Cowdin.

(5) Edward Emmett, born December 6, 1855. Unmarried. Employed at the Missouri Baptist Sanatarium in St. Louis.

(6) Virginia Celine, born January 28, 1858; married William W. Logan, of Meridian, Miss., where they lived until his death several years ago. No children, and Mrs. Logan now lives in St. Louis.

(7) Charles Henry, born March 10, 1859; married Mary Zachritz. He died January 8, 1897. There are two daughters, Minnie and Gertrude, both of whom are now married and live in Oklahoma.

(8) Davis Connor, born April 20, 1861; married Lillie Gardner. He died in 1923. There were three children, Richard, William and Frances, all of whom are married and living in Fort Worth, Texas. Frances married William Milner and they have one child.

(9) William White, born July 5, 1863; died August 31, 1899. Unmarried.

(10) Septimus B., born October 16, 1865; married Dora Hansard. He died October 24, 1891. One child that died in infancy.

(11) Samuel Jacob, born June 16, 1867; married Blanche Buntyn. No children. Living in Alabama.

(12) James Buford, born March 26, 1871, in Missouri; married Maggie Vernon. Living in St. Louis, Mo.

CHILDREN:

(a) Margaret.
(b) Buford.
(c) Dorothy.
(d) Virginia.

COL. WILLIAM ALLEN WHITE

Colonel William Allen White, born 1800, son of Captain Jacob and Hannah (Spiers) White; married (first), November 3, 1828, Caroline Poindexter, born 1809, only daughter of Captain Samuel and Ann Poindexter (Slaughter) Poindexter, of Bedford County, Va.

On her father's side she was a granddaughter of Joseph and Elizabeth James (Kennerly) Poindexter, who came to Bedford County from Louisa County, later moving to Campbell County, where he died June 29, 1826. Joseph, being a son of John and Christian Poindexter and a descendant of George Poingdestre, the emigrant, who first settled in Virginia, was a Captain of the Militia from Bedford County in the Revolutionary War (McAllister's *Virginia Militia*, Section 254). Her mother, who was Ann Poindexter Slaughter, was a daughter of Reuben and Bettie (Poindexter) Slaughter. Reuben Slaughter, born 1733 in Culpeper County, Virginia, Captain of Militia in Revolutionary Army from Bedford County, Va. (Eckenrode's *Revolutionary Soldiers*—Index 8-405), was the third son of Colonel Francis Slaughter, born 1701; died 1766, and Ann (Lightfoot) Slaughter, born September 22, 1708; died 1748; married, June 3, 1729. Colonel Francis Slaughter was a large land holder in Culpeper and Orange Counties and the eldest son of Robert and Frances Anne (Jónes) Slaughter, who were married in 1700. Robert Slaughter was born about 1680, had large holdings in Spotsylvania County and was a prosperous planter of Essex County, where he lived and died. He was the eldest son of Francis and Margaret (Hudson) Slaughter, a planter of Richmond County. Francis, born about 1653, was a son of Captain Francis, who married in 1652, Elizabeth Underwood, and a grandson of John Slaughter, the emigrant, who settled in Virginia prior to 1620.

Ann (Lightfoot) Slaughter, born 1708; died 1748, was a daughter of Major Goodrich and Mary (Chew) Lightfoot, of Spotsylvania County, Va., and the granddaughter of Colonel John Lightfoot, the emigrant, who married Ann Goodrich. Colonel John Lightfoot was the son of John Lightfoot, of Gray's Inn, London, and Elizabeth Phillips, his wife, and the grandson of the Rev. Richard Lightfoot, of Stoke Bruene, Northamptonshire, England, born 1562, died 1625, who married Jane Jones. Ann Goodrich, the wife of Col. John Lightfoot, was the daughter of Lieut. Gen. Thomas Goodrich who was in command of the troops in Northern Virginia during Bacon's Rebellion, he being the son of John Goodrich, the emigrant, and grandson of Richard Goodrich and Muriel, his wife, of Goodrich Castle, Hertfordshire, Wales. (See Poindexter and Slaughter families.)

Colonel William Allen White was a prosperous planter of Bedford County, owning vast tracts of land and many slaves. He was a kind and lenient master to his slaves, giving them always a half-holiday on Saturday, for their own pleasures and amusements. The plantation, he inherited from his father, was a village in itself. On it were located the manor house, slave quarters, store, mill, shop, etc. He was a man of fine mind, pleasing personality, well educated, public spirited, honorable, and highly esteemed. He was a Christian gentleman of the highest type, a friend to the poor, an affectionate father, and a man of great influence in his county, holding positions of trust and responsibility. In 1832, he was commissioned Captain of 91st Virginia Militia, and in 1835, was commissioned Colonel of the same company. An old roll book once belonging to him, is now the prized possession of Dr. Benjamin F. Sledd, Professor of English at Wake Forest College, a great grand-nephew of Colonel White, and the son of William E. Sledd, for whom on the death of his father, James Sledd, Colonel White was made guardian in 1840.

His wife, Caroline (Poindexter) White, died in 1839. She is said to have been a very gracious and beautiful woman—a lovely Christian character. She bore her husband two sons, who, grown to manhood, were a credit to the influence and early teachings of their lovely young mother.

On May 10, 1841, he married, for his second wife, Lucy McDaniel Reese, daughter of Joseph T. and Elizabeth (Tinsley) Reese. She was very young when married to Colonel White—scarcely more than a girl. She was noted for her marvelous beauty and gracious personality. After the death of Colonel White, she married (second), October 23, 1848, Edmund Logwood, by whom she had two children. The daughter, Lizzie, a woman of rare beauty and attractiveness, married General James G. Field, Attorney-General of Virginia; and the son, William, died when about sixteen years of age. (See Logwood family.)

Colonel William Allen White, died in 1844—just in the prime of life. He was laid to rest in the family burying ground at "Charlemont Lodge" by the side of his parents. He was survived by his young widow, an infant daughter and his two sons.

The boys were, financially, well provided for; but were brought up without the loving care and influence of home and parents. However, the memories cherished, and so often spoken of in later years, of the days spent in the home of their aunt, Sallie (White) Douglas, was a loving tribute of their appreciation of her love and motherly kindness to two orphan boys.

CHILDREN BY FIRST MARRIAGE:

(1) Jacob Samuel, born July 27, 1829; married, August 11, 1847, Catherine Spiers White, daughter of Captain Henry Milton and Mary Ann (Gwatkin) White. (See forward.)

(2) John Milton, born July 31, 1831; married December 9, 1852, Mary Virginia White, daughter of Captain Henry Milton and Mary Ann (Gwatkin) White. (See forward.)

CHILD BY SECOND MARRIAGE:

(3) Sallie Spiers, born January 5, 1843; married, September 18, 1860, William Holcombe Bolling, son of Dr. Archibald and Ann E. (Wigginton) Bolling, of Bedford County. She died November 21, 1925. (See Bolling family for descendants.)

JACOB SAMUEL WHITE

Jacob Samuel White, born in Bedford County, Virginia, July 27, 1829, was the eldest son of Col. William Allen White and his first

Richard Emmett White

Jacob Samuel White

wife, Caroline Poindexter, she being the daughter of Samuel and Ann Poindexter (Slaughter) Poindexter, of Bedford County. (See Poindexter and Slaughter families.) He married, on August 11, 1847, his first cousin, Catherine Spiers White, born March 9, 1829, the second daughter of Captain Henry Milton and Mary Ann (Gwatkin) White. Her maternal grandparents being Charles, Jr., and Catherine (Clayton) Gwatkin and her great grandparents Col. Charles and Mary (Callaway) Gwatkin. (See Gwatkin-Clayton-Callaway families.)

Jacob Samuel White was educated in private schools and at "The Valley Union Seminary," now Hollins College. When a youth of less than twelve years of age, he unfortunately suffered the loss of his left arm in a threshing machine accident. Left orphans at an early age in life, and he, being of rather a frail delicate constitution, his brother, John Milton, would always look out for his interests as he would his own. When the two brothers finally came into their share of their father's estate, they purchased from John P. Chilton a part of the estate that had originally belonged to their grandfather, Jacob White. A historical sketch of Jacob Samuel White in Hardesty's *Encyclopedia*, page 434, says: "His parents were natives of the county, and his grandfather after having served with distinction and with rank of captain through the greater part of the Revolutionary War, was an early and prominent settler here. The county was almost a wilderness when he came here, and with his own hands he cleared and improved the beautiful place on Otter Creek where the subject of this sketch resides." During the period of Mr. Chilton's ownership, he built and operated there a mill. In the division of the estate between the two brothers, it was agreed that Jacob Samuel should have the part upon which was located the mill and the manor house, known as "Otter View." His brother took the remaining half—later known as "The Locusts." This property remained in the same family for more than seventy-five years, being sold in 1928 by the last owner, his son, Samuel Jacob White, when he removed to Roanoke. The adjoining estate, "The Locusts," owned by John Milton White, still remains in the White family. Jacob Samuel White was a man of genial disposition and an engaging personality. He took an active interest in public affairs and served Charlemont District as Supervisor for a number of years. Their home, noted for its gracious hospitality, was always the center of a host of merrymaking among the young people.

Catherine Spiers White, "Kitty," as she was affectionately called, was a lovely woman of sweet and amiable disposition. She and her husband were faithful Methodists. Jacob Samuel White, died April 29, 1885, and was buried in the family burying ground at "Otter View." His wife died on September 1, 1902, and was laid to rest by the side of her husband.

CHILDREN:

(1) Mary Allen, born July 28, 1848; married, January 21, 1874, John C. Hatcher, son of Uriah and Susan (Witt) Hatcher. She died August 5, 1914. Their only child died in infancy.

(2) Richard M., born May 14, 1850; married, January 29, 1873, Lucy Frances Major, born December 27, 1851, daughter of Harwood M. and Cleopatra A. McD. (Tinsley) Major and a granddaughter of John Major, born in Prince Edward County and Lucretia (Tinsley) Major, born in Bedford County. Her maternal grandparents, being William and Betsy (Burks) Tinsley. Richard M. White, early in life, engaged in the mercantile business, and had a promising and successful future before him. He died March 13, 1878. His wife later married a Mr. Smith, and had by this marriage, one son, Duncan C. Smith, of St. Louis, Missouri.

CHILDREN:

(a) Sammie McDaniel, born 1874; died November 20, 1883.

(b) Richard Emmett, born March 10, 1876; married, October 26, 1898, Magnolia Pendleton Wright, daughter of William H. and Emma (Pettigrew) Wright of Bedford County.

He is a member of the Rotary Club of Bedford, a steward in the Main Street M. E. Church, South, and teacher of the R. E. White Bible Class of that church. He was cashier of the Citizens National Bank of Bedford from its organization in 1914 until 1921, when he was elected vice-president. In August, 1922, he was again promoted and made president of the bank. The *Bedford Democrat* of that date had this to say of him:

"He is a Bedford boy, born and reared on Bedford soil, and comes from a long list of noble ancestors, upon whose shoulders has rested in part, for generations past, the development and best interests of their native land. His boyhood was spent on the farm and he has risen from the ranks, having climbed the ladder, rung by rung, by virtue of conscientious and efficient service. . . . To his business friends he is courteous, accommodating, honest, always looking to the best interest of those whom he serves; to his personal friends he is kind, sympathetic, loyal; to all he is a high-toned Christian gentleman."

CHILDREN:

(aa) Marion Louise; educated at Randolph-Macon Institute and Hollins College; married, October 24, 1928, Wilbur Eugene Bakke, son of John Edward Bakke of Detroit Lakes, Minn. They live in Oklahoma. One child: Wilbur Eugene, Jr., born September 10, 1929.

(bb) Magnolia Pendleton; died in childhood.

(cc) Isabel; now a junior in the Bedford High School.

(3) Samuel Jacob, born February 12, 1852; married, March 31, 1885, Sophia Emma Hardy, daughter of Joseph S. and Jane (Nichols) Hardy of Bedford County.

CHILDREN:

(a) Harry Hardy, born March 14, 1886; married, November 5, 1913, Cleopatra Elizabeth Major, daughter of Robert Henry Major, born in Bedford County, March 1, 1849, and his wife, Georgia A. McDaniel Burks, born September 15, 1850, daughter of John Dabney and Dolly (Cheatwood) Burks. (See Burks family.)

(b) Mary Will ("Billy"), born October 8, 1890; married, October 16, 1912, William Staples Engleby, son of Thomas Joseph and Estelle (Staples) Engleby, of Roanoke, Virginia. He graduated in Law at Washington and Lee University in 1911, and is now practicing his profession in Roanoke where they reside.

CHILDREN:

(aa) Emma Jane, born October 1, 1920.

(bb) William Staples, Jr., born August 9, 1924.

(c) Jacob Henry, born September 8, 1892; married Nelle Charlton, daughter of Dr. Charlton of Williamson, West Virginia. He is an official of the N. & W. R. R. and located at Williamson where they live. Have one child: (aa) Ann Marie White.

(d) Frederick Leonidas, born September 8, 1897; unmarried. He was educated at Washington and Lee University. Living in Roanoke, Va.

(4) William Allen, born January 25, 1854; unmarried. For many years he was a popular and successful merchant in Bedford City—now retired from business.

(5) Walter Blount, born February 14, 1856; married, January 28, 1880, Ida Clemintine Jennings, born January 21, 1862, daughter of Samuel S. Jennings, who enlisted in Jordan's Artillery Company August 12, 1861, and was transferred to Company "E," 34th Virginia Infantry, with which he served till wounded near Petersburg in May, 1864, dying at Richmond, June 20, 1864. Her mother was before marriage a Miss Wheat. Walter Blount White died at the home of his daughter, Mrs. Eugene C. Eggleston in Richmond, Va., on February 20, 1925. He was a man of fine character and ability. He served as Commissioner of the Revenue for James River District a number of years. His wife died November 13, 1909. Both he and his wife were members of Mt. Herman Baptist Church.

CHILDREN:

(a) Annie Davis, born April 21, 1882; married, January 31, 1905, J. Griffin Hardy, son of Joseph Hardy, of Bedford County, Virginia.

CHILDREN:

(aa) Marguerite, born February 27, 1906.

(bb) Joseph Allen, born October 18, 1907.

(cc) Sara Clemintine, born March 2, 1909.

(dd) Mary Elizabeth, born July 16, 1910.

(ee) James Griffin, born May 25, 1912; died September 9, 1912.

(ff) Walter Glenwood, born August 21, 1913.

(gg) Ralph Hall (twin), born September 5, 1914.

(hh) Ray Davis (twin), born September 5, 1914.

(ii) J. Griffin, Jr., born October 21, 1917.

(jj) Jane Watts, born July 23, 1919.

(kk) Rachel White, born March 7, 1923.

(b) Samuel Jennings, born October 11, 1885; married, August 12, 1909, Virginia Whealton. He died January 4, 1917. One child: (aa) Samuel Jennings White, Jr., born May 19, 1910. Now living in Roanoke, Va., with his mother, who after the death of her husband, married J. H. Morris of that city.

(c) Katherine Leo, born June 12, 1887; married, September 6, 1910, Dr. Eugene Conway Eggleston, born July 6, 1887, at Chula, Virginia. There are no children by this union.

Dr. Eugene C. Eggleston was educated in Richmond Public School, McGuire's University School and Medical College of Virginia. Doctor of Medicine, practicing in Richmond, Va.; volunteered in medical corps in 1917 and turned down physically. He is a member of the Medical Society of Virginia, Richmond Academy of Medicine and Manchester Medical Society—Scottish Rite Mason, 32nd Degree, Past Master Dixie Lodge No. 202 A. F. & A. M. Also a member of order of Woodmen of the World, Modern Woodmen of America, and Junior Order, United American Mechanics. He was the son of Dr. Joseph William Eggleston, born Servia, Indiana, August 12, 1844, and his wife Lucy Jefferson Eggleston, born 1844, a daughter of John Garland Jefferson (direct descendant of Peter Jefferson, brother of Thomas Jefferson, President of U. S. A.) and his wife Otelia Jefferson Booker who was born in Chesterfield County. His father, Dr. Joseph W. Eggleston, served four years in the Confederate Army — Sergeant of Artillery. Past Grand-Master of Masons of Virginia;

author of Tuckahoe; Masonic Life of Washington, &c. He was a descendant of Richard Eggleston, one of three brothers, who settled in Jamestown, early in the history of Virginia.

(d) James Allen, born February 14, 1889; drowned in Tug River, West Virginia, July 22, 1907.

(e) Roberta ("Bert") Madge, born August 13, 1891; married, November 25, 1919, James G. Clark. Living in Coral Gables, Florida.

CHILDREN:

(aa) Peggy Ann, born November 9, 1923.
(bb) Marjorie Leigh, born June 23, 1925.

(f) Louise Ida, born October 10, 1893; married, December 14, 1916, Dr. Harlow Richard Connell, born July 7, 1892, at Prescott, Ontario, Canada, son of William Samuel and Mary Connell of Prescott, Ontario, Canada.

Dr. Connell was educated at Queen's University, Kingston, Ontario, Canada, and the Medical College of Virginia at Richmond. Internship in Lewis-Gale Hospital, Roanoke, Va., and New York Post Graduate Hospital. Served two years overseas with the 315th Field Artillery, 80th Division A. E. F. as Battalion surgeon. Served on Artois Sector, St. Mehiel and Argonne Fronts. Wounded November 4, 1918, at Bantherville, France. Arrived home May 23, 1919; and discharged August 9, 1919, with rank of Major. Still in regular army on inactive list with rank of colonel. Dr. Connell is now practicing physician at Elkhorn, W. Va. His wife was a graduate nurse of Lewis-Gale Hospital, Roanoke, Va. One child: (aa) Harlow Richard, Jr., born April 23, 1923.

(g) Walter Stephen, born November 16, 1895; died September 15, 1896.

(h) Ralph Gordon, born April 18, 1902; unmarried. Living in Richmond, Va.

(6) Sarah Roberta, born September 6, 1857; married, December 20, 1882, Frank C. Breazeal, son of Edward Munford and Lydia

Alice Breazeal. She was a woman of engaging personality and greatly loved by all who knew her for her many lovable qualities. She died May 15, 1892. (Her husband later married her brother's widow, Mary Walter (Barnett) White.)

CHILDREN:

(a) Katie Alice; married, July 5, 1909, Acree S. Jones, son of Moseley and Ann Jones. They are living in Los Vegos, Nevada.

CHILDREN:

(aa) Roberta Carroll, born October 2, 1914.

(bb) Virginia Lee, born January 11, 1919.

(b) Sammie May; married, October 17, 1922, William C. Ballard, son of James Winston and Margaret (McGhee) Ballard. Living in Bedford, Va. They have one child:

(aa) Sara Margaret, born May 18, 1924.

(c) Iba Lee; married, April 14, 1917, Herbert Diuguid Wills, son of Willis Tyler and Mamie Wills. They live at Shawsville, Va.

CHILDREN:

(aa) Mary Katherine, born August 7, 1918.

(bb) Herbert Diuguid, Jr., born March 21, 1921.

(7) Leonidas Rosser, born March 11, 1859; married, November 11, 1884, Mary Walter Barnett, daughter of David and Fannie (Schenk) Barnett. He died November 21, 1891, and on November 11, 1895, his widow married Frank C. Breazeal. No children by this second marriage.

CHILD BY FIRST MARRIAGE:

(a) Mamie Leo White; married, December 2, 1905, Henry Austin Wilson. They live in Bedford, Va. Have one child:

(aa) Mary Rebecca Wilson, a senior at Randolph-Macon College, Lynchburg, Va.

(8) Holcombe Davis, born July 28, 1860; married, December 12, 1882, Mary Jennings, daughter of Zachariah Edward and Lucy Amanda Jennings, of Bedford County. For a number of years

Holcombe Davis White owned and operated the farm inherited from his father. He was a man well beloved by all who knew him and very popular in his community. After the two older girls were grown the family removed to Roanoke; and he died there on November 9, 1924. He was a Methodist.

CHILDREN:

(a) Elizabeth Walter, born September 25, 1883; married, June 27, 1911, Russell J. Watson, son of Hubert F. and Willie A. Watson. For some years Russell J. Watson has held the position of Clerk of Court, Roanoke, Va.

CHILDREN:

(aa) Elizabeth White, born February 25, 1912; now a student at Mary Baldwin College, Staunton, Va.

(bb) Russell Jordan, born March 26, 1918; died July 29, 1919.

(cc) Jeanne Stuart (adopted daughter), born February 14, 1922.

(b) Estelle Louise, born September 27, 1885; married, April 24, 1918, John T. Taylor, son of James T. and Lula Taylor. John T. Taylor was educated at Virginia Military Institute.

CHILDREN:

(aa) Kitty White, born June 13, 1921.

(bb) Jack Louis, born May 1, 1925.

(c) Clemmie Spiers, born October 14, 1890; married, December 18, 1917, Horace Edmunds Mayhew, son of James A. and Edith E. Mayhew. He received his education at Washington and Lee University. Living in Roanoke, Va. Clemmie Spiers (White) Mayhew died on July 2, 1928.

CHILDREN:

(aa) Janice Allen, born September 21, 1922.

(bb) Horace White, born October 18, 1918; died October 21, 1918.

MARY VIRGINIA WHITE
wife of John Milton White

JOHN MILTON WHITE

(d) Carlton Davis, born July 17, 1900; married, July 10, 1928, Etta Melville Bondurant, daughter of Mr. and Mrs. John Lee Bondurant. Now living in Roanoke, Virginia.

(e) May Catharine, born October 20, 1903; a teacher in the public schools of Roanoke, Va.; unmarried.

JOHN MILTON WHITE

John Milton White, born July 31, 1831, was the second son of Colonel William Allen White and his first wife, Caroline Poindexter, she being the daughter of Samuel and Anne Poindexter (Slaughter) Poindexter, of Bedford County, Virginia. (See Poindexter and Slaughter families.) He married, December 9, 1852, his first cousin, Mary Virginia White, born December 20, 1836, a daughter of Captain Henry Milton and Mary Ann (Gwatkin) White, her maternal grandparents being Charles Gwatkin, Jr., and Catherine Clayton (daughter of John Willis and Mary Clayton), and her great grandparents, Col. Charles and Mary (Callaway) Gwatkin. (See Gwatkin-Clayton-Callaway families.)

John Milton White was educated in private schools and at "Hollins College," at that time known as "The Valley Union Seminary," which was a co-educational institution. Often have we heard him tell of their "going away to school"—how he and his brother rode horseback, while the negro slave, who accompanied them as body-guard, rode another horse, carrying their luggage,—the "little leather trunk." He served the four years of the Civil War; was Lieutenant in Company "E" 34th Virginia Infantry, C. S. A., participating in all the engagements of that command: Seven Pines, Williamsburg, "The Crater," Hatcher's Run, etc.; helped in the construction of the defenses of Richmond and Petersburg, and helped to defend the same in the memorable battles fought there. He was taken prisoner at Hatcher's Run (beyond Petersburg) on March 31, 1865; imprisoned at Johnson's Island, Lake Erie, from which he was released June 17, 1865. He was wounded only once during the four years service and that was in the Battle of Seven Pines. Returning from the army, he set his musket in the corner and bade his children never to touch it. His home-coming marked much rejoicing both among the white and colored—"Bles'

Gawd! heah's Mars Milton!" Many of these old slaves, through love
for their master and mistress, refused to leave them and remained on
the old plantation.

The years following the surrender were lean years in old Virginia;
and many were the families who had to part with their treasures and
heirlooms to buy the actual necessities of life. The old musket and
the watch carried through four years of hardship and suffering were
among the articles parted with by him; and his wife willingly sacrificed
her jewels to help keep things together. And here we must pay tribute
to the brave little wife and mother—scarcely more than a girl herself,
who during those four long, anxious years, with the help of the true
and faithful slaves, ran the plantation, and kept the hearth fires burning
against the "dawn of peace" and the homecoming of her soldier
husband. Four years of exposure during the war brought on rheumatism, from which he suffered for a number of years. However,
this did not daunt his spirit; and he engaged largely in farming,—
tobacco raising principally,—and grazing. He took an active interest
in public affairs, especially schools, being Clerk of the School Board
for Charlemont District for more than sixteen years; and was also
magistrate for a number of years. He was an ardent Democrat. Both
he and his wife were faithful Methodists. However, their home was
always open to ministers, regardless of their faith, and there were
many of other denominations entertained there for days at a time.

John Milton White was a man of medium height with black hair,
and dark blue eyes which usually beamed with kindliness, but which
could become exceedingly stern when he was greatly displeased. He
loved all children; but even in old age displayed a special foundness
for little girls with black hair. He was possessed of a fine mind, high
ideals and unbounded energy. He was a faithful husband and father,
a kind and generous friend and neighbor, a useful Christian gentleman,
beloved and honored by all who knew him. The poor and needy of his
community, both white and colored, came to him for aid, knowing they
would always receive it. His home, "The Locusts," was noted, far
and wide, for its typical old Virginia hospitality.

His wife, Mary Virginia White, died January 25, 1916. She was
a noble character, sweet and gentle,—a good wife, a devoted mother,
a sincere Christian, a true friend; simple in her tastes and manners and
faithful to every trust and duty. Her sweet, loving, and gracious

personality will always remain as a hallowed memory to bless those of her grandchildren who remember her. She possessed that remarkable quality of seeing only the good in everyone—a rare virtue!

John Milton White died January 1, 1920, and was laid to rest by the side of his wife in the family burying ground at "The Locusts."

"Fading away like the stars of the morning,
    Losing their light in the glorious sun—
Thus would we pass from the earth and its toiling,
    Only remembered by what we have done.

Only the truth that in life we have spoken
    Only the seed that on earth we have sown;
These shall pass onward when we are forgotten,
    Fruits of the harvest and what we have done."

CHILDREN:

(1) John Allen, born March 25, 1854; died January 20, 1869.

(2) Edward Henry, born October 18, 1855; married, May 12, 1880, Laura Porter Turpin, born April 13, 1855, a daughter of Captain John and Mary M. (Lambert) Turpin, of Bedford County, Va. (See Turpin family.) He was educated in private schools; but early in life, due to conditions following the Civil War, had to go to work on the farm, which occupation he has followed very successfully for many years. He owns "The Cedars," one of the ancestral homes still remaining in the family, and being a part of the Poindexter estate inherited by his father from his uncle, Anderson Poindexter. Soon after Edward Henry's marriage, he moved there to help manage the estate, and has made this his home ever since.

CHILDREN:

(a) William Ashby, born July 27, 1883; unmarried. Holds a responsible position with Armour and Company.

(b) John Lewis, born April 14, 1890; married, June 11, 1920, Vixella Rucker, daughter of Waller J. and Russell (McDaniel) Rucker, of Forest, Va. Living at Grand Rapids, Michigan, where he is successfully engaged in business.

CHILDREN:

(aa) Lewis Marian, born August 22, 1921.

(bb) Philip Ashby, born June 4, 1923.

(cc) Barbara Jean, born August 23, 1925.

(dd) Polly Pendleton, born August 26, 1928, Lynchburg, Va.

(c) Edward Lawrence, born April 10, 1893; married, November 29, 1928, Genevieve Daniels, daughter of G. C. Daniels, of Cedar Rapids, Iowa. Edward Lawrence White was a soldier in the World War, having enlisted September 22, 1917, at Bedford, Va.; served the entire period with the 80th Division, Company F, 318th Infantry. Appointed Corporal, January, 1918. Battles, engagements, skirmishes, expeditions, A. E. F., May 22, 1918, to May 27, 1919. Artor's Sector, July 23, August 18, 1918. St. Mihiel offensive (Corps Reserve) September 12, September 16, 1918. Meuse Argonne, September 26, October 12, 1918; November 1, November 7, 1918. Discharged at Camp Lee, Va., June 4, 1919. He and his wife make their home at Cedar Rapids, Iowa, where he holds a responsible position.

(3) Charles Alonza, born February 16, 1857; died July 17, 1858.

(4) Ceril Davis, born November 9, 1858; married (first), December 9, 1885, his cousin, Julia Gertrude Spinner, daughter of Dr. Jesse Frank and Martha (Snead) Spinner, of Bedford County, Va. (See Spinner and Snead families.) She died on April 3, 1910; and he married (second), May 26, 1922, Mrs. Dollie M. (Pierson) Taylor (widow), born March 26, 1856; died April 6, 1923. He married (third), August 18, 1925, Rena (Wilson) Martin (widow), born February 15, 1876, daughter of J. M. and Matris (Padgett) Wilson. Early in life Ceril D. White went to Texas; but a short stay there convinced him Virginia was his home. He returned to Bedford; and shortly after his arrival developed typhoid fever. From the effects of this disease, he suffered the loss of his left leg. A great portion of his life has been spent in the mercantile business. In 1911, he was elected Commissioner of the Revenue for James River District, a position he held for sixteen years, performing

his duties with promptness and efficiency. Declining re-election to this office in 1927, he retired from public life to spend his remaining days at his home at Charlemont, Va.

CHILDREN:

(a) Roy Spinner, born October 18, 1886. He served in the World War, having enlisted with the Canadians, and was killed in service.

(b) Guy Judson, born January 31, 1888; married, November 29, 1922, his first cousin, Mattie Weda Turpin, born March 19, 1897, daughter of Thomas Mosby and Annie (Spinner) Turpin, of Bedford. (See Spinner and Turpin families.) They live in Bedford; no children.

(c) William Sherman (twin), born November 11, 1890; unmarried; living at Clifton Forge, Va.; where he holds a responsible position with the C. & O. R. R.

(d) Nannie Snead (twin), born November 11, 1890; married Harold J. Smith; living in Philadelphia. She was a trained nurse.

(e) John Milton, II, born May 13, 1893. Saw service in the World War. Enlisted in New York. Received his training at Greenville, S. C., and went overseas with the 27th Division—was gassed. Now living in Detroit, Mich., and unmarried.

(f) Jesse Neale, born July 7, 1896; married, November 2, 1922, Pheobe Veronica McCarthy, born May 6, 1905, daughter of Frank Charles and Sarah McCarthy, of Newport, R. I. Served with the U. S. Marines from 1917 until 1921. Received training and enlisted in Mare Island, California, in 1917. Foreign service Guam. Now living in Brooklyn, New York, where he is successfully engaged in business.

CHILDREN:

(aa) Jessie Lee, born April 2, 1924.

(bb) John Raymond, born November 29, 1926.

(g) Gladys Gertrude, born May 9, 1899; married, June 29, 1920, Lon James Milam, born January 5, 1882, son of William and Mary (Grant) Milam. She was a teacher.

CHILDREN:

(aa) James Winston, born March 27, 1921.

(bb) Claude White, born July 21, 1923.

(cc) Shirley William, born May 4, 1927.

(dd) Marshall Garnett, born May 20, 1929.

(h) Frances Marshall, born January 28, 1903; married, August 12, 1926, William Lee Robbins, born March 1, 1898, son of John Wiley Robbins, born April 8, 1866, and Elizabeth H. (Hinesley) Robbins, born May 10, 1869, of Brownsville, Tenn. No children.

(5) Mary Conna Blount, born May 12, 1862; married, February 21, 1883, John Paul Ackerly, born August 3, 1850; died August 4, 1927, a son of William and Lucy Douglas (Turpin) Ackerly, of Rockbridge County, Va. (See Ackerly and Turpin families.) She was educated in private schools; noted for her great beauty of face and charm of manner.

CHILDREN:

(a) Mary Denham, born May 29, 1885.

(b) William White, born June 15, 1890.

(c) Lucy Pauline, born November 8, 1892.

(d) Kate Thelma, born October 17, 1895; died February 7, 1897.

(e) John Paul, Jr., born December 28, 1899.

(f) Eugene Glasgow, born July 11, 1903.

(g) Frank Douglas, born May 13, 1911; died June 30, 1911.

(6) Luther Wilmer, born September 30, 1866; married Belle M. Scott, of Tennessee. He died January 13, 1924, at Waverly, Va. There was one child, a boy, by this marriage.

(7) Robert Atherton, born March 27, 1868; died March 27, 1868.

(8) Waddell Allen, born March 7, 1869; married, February 25, 1902, Anna Shepherd Dameron, born March 19, 1873, a daughter of Charles Dibrell and Mildred Jane (Joyner) Dameron, of Amherst County. (Charles Dibrell Dameron, born March 9, 1834, soldier in C. S. A., was a son of Charles Dameron (born 1780) and Mary E. MacGann (whom he married in 1820) daughter of Joseph P. MacGann, who came from Scotland and

John Milton White and Family

settled in Amherst County, Va. The Damerons came from England and first settled in Northumberland County, Va. Charles Dameron, born 1780, son of Dunmore and Lucy (Thomas) Dameron of Albemarle County, Va., served in the War of 1812. Mildred Jane Joyner, born 1845, was the youngest child of Peter Garland Joyner, born 1799 (son of Peter and Mildred (Dillard) Joyner) who married in 1841, his first cousin, Oney Dillard Tyler, born in Amherst County, in 1800. Oney Dillard Tyler was the daughter of John and Elizabeth (Dillard) Tyler and the widow of Col. Richard Huckstep of the British Army. Peter Joyner and John Tyler were soldiers in the Revolutionary War. John Tyler was the son of Charles Tyler, one of three brothers who came from England. Mildred Dillard and Elizabeth Dillard were daughters of William Dillard, son of James Dillard who rode as sheriff under George III of England, and by whom he was granted a 10,000-acre tract of land along the James River in Amherst County.) Waddell Allen White received his education in the public schools of Bedford and New London Academy. Early in life he began teaching; but for a number of years past, has been successfully engaged in farming. Now owns a part of the Poindexter property inherited by his father from his uncle, Anderson Poindexter, also his father's old homestead, "The Locusts." He is an earnest worker in Nazareth Methodist Church, the church of his parents.

CHILDREN:

(a) Katherine Dameron, born January 18, 1903; a successful teacher in the public schools of Va.

(b) William Davis, born September 10, 1904, unmarried—living in Chicago where he is taking an Electrical course.

(c) Dibrell Tyler, born October 7, 1905; unmarried—living in Bedford, where he is engaged in the mercantile business.

(d) Dorothy Eugenia, born May 3, 1907; Senior at State Teacher's College, Farmville, Virginia.

(e) Rebecca Joyner, born March 5, 1909; in training at Maryland University Hospital, Baltimore, Md.

(f) Mary Ann Elizabeth, born May 13, 1912, a Senior in the Bedford High School.

(9) Clifton Egbert, born November 30, 1870; died April 29, 1916. He was educated in the public schools of Bedford and at New London Academy. Except for the years he spent on the farm, most of his life was spent in the mercantile business. He was of a quiet, gentle disposition and loved by all. Was never married.

(10) Kate, born July 19, 1872; died January 25, 1904. Was educated at New London Academy and the Jeter School for girls in Bedford City. She was a popular teacher in the schools of Bedford County, and her untimely death was a great sorrow to the family and to her many friends. Hers was a bright and lively disposition, and she was a favorite with the old and young.

(11) John Otis, born May 29, 1874; married, October 26, 1909, Naomi Wiley, born July 25, 1888, daughter of William and Lucy Wiley, of Campbell County. For many years he remained with his parents and managed the farm for his father. In 1919 he removed to Roanoke where he now resides and is engaged in business there.

CHILDREN:

(a) Lucille Virginia, born July 31, 1910; a student at Virginia Intermont College, Bristol, Virginia.

(b) Nellie Marion, born January 26, 1912; died January 16, 1919—a sweet and lovely child.

(c) John Earl, born July 17, 1919.

(12) Eugene Graham, born March 30, 1876; married, April 8, 1908, Bertie Rachel McMann, of West Virginia, born March 31, 1886, daughter of John Anderson and Martha Elizabeth (Davis) McMann (who was the daughter of Thomas and Nancy (Macbe) Davis, of Virginia). Eugene White received his education in the public schools of Bedford County and New London Academy. For several years he was engaged in teaching; but is now living in Bluefield, Virginia, where he holds an important position with the Chicago House Furnishing

Company. He is a member of the Elks Lodge, and is held in high esteem by his fellow citizens.

CHILDREN:

(a) Hugh Edward, born January 26, 1909; married, January 1, 1929, Rachel Barkley, of Princeton, West Virginia.
(b) Mary Elizabeth, born September 30, 1917.
(c) Eugene Graham, Jr., born January 19, 1927.

(13) Frank Anderson, born November 3, 1879; died July 9, 1910. Educated at New London Academy and after arriving at the age of maturity, left home to engage in the mercantile business. However, most of his life was spent traveling for Armour and Company. He was a member of the Odd Fellows Lodge, the Elks and U. C. T. Was very popular, and of an engaging personality. Never married.

(The following is a copy of a letter written by John Milton White from the trenches at Petersburg, Va., in 1865, to his wife. My mother was the "precious little daughter" spoken of here.—M. D. A.):

My Own Dear,   Petersburg Defences, Jany 12th, 1865:

I will now endeavor to respond to yours of the 3rd & 6th which were received on the 9th. I was relieved of a great deal of uneasiness & apprehension of mind on ascertaining through them that our precious little Daughter had recovered from the severe cold she had taken, which you seemed to manifest considerable alarm in regard to, in your letter of the 1st. Ever since the death of our Dear Alonzo, whenever any of the children are afflicted or suffering from a deep cold and I am apprised of the fact; feel restless & uneasy & fear that it may result in something serious. How grateful we ought to feel for the many manifestations of the Lord's goodness to us, I am never forgetful of his beneficence to us & when reflection brings to memory his tokens of love for us, My Soul yearns to humble itself before his Majesty in thankfulness & praise, that we are still permitted to make supplication before his rich throne of grace and reverence his holy & exalted name. Mary, I regret that I am not the Christian that I ought to be, I feel sometimes that I am too vile & sinful to dare to call upon the Lord for Mercy that he would in his indignation spurn me from his presence and withhold forever his blessings. But the more I doubt my prospect for eternal joy & happiness in that celestial abode where dwelleth our bright & happy little Boy and our Dear Parents, many years ago we trust gone to glory; the more I agonize in prayer and manfully strive against the powers of the wicked one; and oh I certainly do derive a comfort, joy and a peace of mind that the world cannot give. Merciful God defend us from our Enemies and that wicked Adversary the Devil and may we fight manfully the battles of the living God. I will now turn my attention to the consideration of two highly interesting and important letters above alluded to. Since I wrote last we have had to contend with the most terrific rain, fallen since we have been in the trenches; & mud, it makes me feel muddy to think of the immense quantity we have had to deal with. Tuesday Morn when we awoke our bed was fully 3 inches deep in water; the floor of our tent in a few minutes afterwards was not less than 6 inches deep in mud & water. It rained incessantly the day out & every body in the trenches was flooded with mud & water. I went over to Town yesterday and examined into my box more carefully, found the meats & chickens you sent, a bag of flour with some lard in it. If ever a fellow enjoyed anything he ate, I did those cakes, pies & apples. I resalted my meats and brought to camp one of the B. bones, sausage & the chickens. I am very close & stingy with my cakes, apples & chestnuts, intend to enjoy the most of them myself. What things you sent will last me two months. You inquired if I was messing to myself. I took in Woolfolk with me after Hatcher left and I procured for us a tent. As soon as the Capt left—Lowry gave his tent to some of the men, they having no shelter whatever & he & Tom by my consent moved into my tent & since that we four have been cooking & eating together. Lowry & Tom both received a very nice box each from Home since Christmas and we four fared alike off of the contents. Woolfolk is not a married man & is a very nice & good fellow,—he will go home in a few days on furlough & will bring a good box with him. C. Lowry got a box from Bettie yesterday by express the charges on it were $23.50 and I would not have paid that much hardly for all that was in it. I had to lend him the money to pay for it. Two F. shirts a Counterpane some cakes & pies were all that it contained. The present I had reference to was a pr. of Yarn Gloves, and the Donor was a member of our *Co.-Hayden.* You need not longer consider that you are indebted to me for a Christmas treat I think you have rewarded me very liberally indeed for all claim upon you, but you are to reserve for me a Christmas *kiss* will you not. I will try and get Johny & Ned a *sachel* like yours; it will be of much help to them when going to school. I am still in arrest, Goode has preferred no charges against me yet. I presume he intends for me to have a good long rest spell & then release me. I will be greatly obliged to him for the favor. I will write again soon, closing for the present. My love to all the boys, you & Sissy accept of many kisses & much love from your loving & dear one.

MILTON.

Write when you can to your own dear Milton.

CAPTAIN HENRY MILTON WHITE

Captain Henry Milton White, born January 31, 1805, son of Captain Jacob and Hannah (Spiers) White; married, October 4, 1826, Mary Ann Gwatkin, born April 13, 1810, daughter of Charles Gwatkin, Jr., and Catherine Clayton, who was the daughter of John Willis and Mary Clayton. (See Clayton family.) Mary Ann Gwatkin was the granddaughter of Charles Gwatkin, Sr. (died 1806), a Captain in the Revolutionary War (McAllister's *Virginia Militia*—Section 254; Chalkley's *Abstracts of Augusta County, Virginia,* Vol. 2, page 486), who married, November 6, 1767, Mary Callaway (died 1829), a daughter of Richard and Frances (Walton) Callaway. (See Gwatkin and Callaway families.)

Henry Milton White was a planter and owned many slaves and large tracts of land near the present St. Thomas Church. The home is now owned by the heirs of Richard Burks. He was a commissioned Captain in the Virginia Militia. His wife died February 4, 1846. He never married again. The loss of his only son in the Civil War was a great blow to him. Soon after the close of the war, his daughters all married except one, he decided to give up housekeeping and make his home with his two daughters, Mary and Catherine—the wives of his two nephews, John Milton and Jacob Samuel White, respectively. He died October 12, 1867, at the home of his daughter Catherine, and was buried in the family plot on the estate, originally owned by his father, Jacob White, when he first came to Bedford County, and where he was born. He was a man highly honored and beloved by all who knew him—one of the outstanding men of his day in that county.

CHILDREN:

(1) Nancy ("Ann") Logwood, born July 22, 1827; married, December 21, 1850, Nathaniel W. Thomson, born December 7, 1829, son of Jesse L. and Rhoda Morris (Wharton) Thomson, of Bedford County. She died July 17, 1851; and she and her infant son were buried together. She was a very beautiful woman and her untimely death was lamented by her many friends. (See Thomson family.)

(2) Catherine Spiers, born March 9, 1829; married, August 11, 1847, her first cousin, Jacob Samuel White, son of Col. William Allen and Caroline (Poindexter) White. She died September 1, 1902. (See Jacob Samuel White family.)

(3) Eliza Frances, born September 5, 1830; married, August 8, 1850, Dr. William Henry Jennings, physician and surgeon, born in Bedford County, December 15, 1824, a son of James Chapel Jennings, born in Chesterfield County, Va., and Elizabeth L. (Wheat) Jennings, born in Bedford County. Eliza Frances (White) Jennings, lovingly known as "Aunt Fan," died October 1, 1882. For many years she was an invalid and bore her many sufferings and afflictions with Christian fortitude.

CHILDREN:

(a) James Henry, born August 27, 1854; never married; deceased.

(b) Charles William, born January 29, 1859; married, November 12, 1884, Nannie Deans Horsley, born October 4, 1864, daughter of Nicholas Cabell and Nannie Cooper (Deans) Horsley, and a granddaughter of John Horsley (son of William, Jr.), and Mary Mildred Cabell (second wife). John Horsley died at Mt. Retreat in Nelson County, September 6, 1890. Mary Mildred Cabell was born at "Soldiers Joy," January 15, 1802, and died March 3, 1880, at Mountain Retreat. Charles William Jennings was a man of genial disposition, honored and respected by all who knew him. He was a prosperous farmer, and owned his father's old home near the Peaks of Otter. Here he died April 28, 1913.

CHILDREN:

(aa) William Elbert, born April 23, 1886; married, December 10, 1913, Essie Dodson. Educated at Randolph-Macon Academy, Bedford, Va.; V. P. I., Blacksburg, Va.; Graduated in Medicine from Medical College of Virginia, 1909; served as an interne at Memorial Hospital, Richmond, Va. Head Doctor at Catawba for five years; since 1917, practicing at Danville, Va. He is a Mason and a member of Chi Phi Fraternity. No children.

(bb) Marie Frances, born July 2, 1892; married, December 28, 1922, Robert Edward Rowe. She was educated at Jeter Seminary, Bedford, Va., and University of Virginia. Taught for several years in public schools of Greensboro, N. C., where she is now living. One child:

(aaa) Dorothy Rowe, born August 29, 1925.

(cc) Charles Horsley, born April 2, 1896; married, November 20, 1917, Lucile Frances Boone. Educated at Randolph-Macon Academy, Bedford, Va., and the Chatham Training School. He is a prosperous farmer of Bedford County, living near Thaxton.

CHILDREN:

(aaa) Charles William, born June 28, 1923.
(bbb) Wallace, born March 27, 1925.

(dd) Edward Davis, born December 9, 1900. Unmarried; educated at Bedford High School, and Davidson College, N. C., with degree of B. S. Now in bank in St. Louis, Mo.

(ee) Louise Cooper, born May 31, 1902. Unmarried. Educated at Queens College, Charlotte, N. C.;

M. A. degree from Columbia University; now
working on Ph. D. from Cornell University. At
present teaching Psychology at Virginia Intermont College, Bristol, Va.

(ff) Catherine Cabell, born November 20, 1904;
married, June 17, 1924, Joseph Clarence Holmes.
She was educated at Bedford High School and
University of Virginia. Living in Roanoke, Va.

CHILDREN:

(aaa) Joseph Charles Holmes, born March
27, 1925.

(bbb) Anne Cabell Holmes, born April 3,
1929.

(gg) Nicholas Watkins, born October 27, 1907. Now
a student at the University of Virginia studying
law.

(c) Olivia White, born July 7, 1860; died September 30,
1862.

(d) Raphael Semmes, born November 12, 1864; never married—deceased.

(e) Othello Booth, born March 18, 1867; married and has a
family.

(f) Robert Sidney, born October 1, 1870; went West.

(g) Helen Maude, born May 29, 1875—deceased.

(4) William Davis, born January 3, 1832. For a number of years
was editor of the *Bedford Sentinel*. Joined the Confederate
cause and saw service in a western state where he was killed in
battle. Was never married.

(5) Charles Henry, born July 21, 1835; died February 15, 1841.

(6) Mary Virginia, born December 20, 1836; married, December 9,
1852, her first cousin, John Milton White, son of Col. William
Allen and Caroline (Poindexter) White. She died January 25,
1916. (See John Milton White family.)

(7) Sarah Lucy, born November 28, 1840; married, February 17,
1870, Paul Bedford Vaughan, born in Halifax County, October
13, 1847; died in Bedford County, August 29, 1901. He was a
son of Paulus Bedford Vaughan and Mary Jane Tuck who

were married in Halifax County, June 22, 1841. The Vaughans are mentioned in the History of Halifax County as being among the earliest and most prominent citizens of that county. Sarah Lucy (White) Vaughan died April 20, 1921.

CHILDREN :

(a) William Lee, born January 17, 1871; married, November 23, 1898, Perine Carl Toms, born December 22, 1881, daughter of James Adam and Berta Edith (Cottrell) Toms.

CHILDREN :

(aa) Walter Eugene, born November 22, 1899.
(bb) Lucy Edith, born August 8, 1901; married, July 22, 1923, Leslie Ray Arrington, born December 22, 1897, son of John Howard and Mary Amanda (Forbes) Arrington. They have the following,

CHILDREN :

(aaa) Julius Edward, born April 28, 1924.
(bbb) William Ray, born July 28, 1928.
(cc) Nellie Belle, born October 25, 1903.
(dd) George Paul, born March 14, 1906.
(ee) Rachel Aurelia, born June 7, 1908.
(ff) William Carl, born October 6, 1910.
(gg) Eddie Wilson, born February 16, 1913.
(hh) Gussie Jane, born January 10, 1916.
(b) Mary Emma, born August 6, 1872; married, in 1900, Frank Eddie Wood, son of Fleming Lee and Mildred (Coleman) Wood.

CHILDREN :

(aa) Alvin Vaughan, born May 9, 1902; married Mary Willie Watson and they have one child, Mary Christine.
(bb) Elizabeth Blanche, born July 3, 1904.
(cc) Frank Lee, born May 18, 1906.
(dd) Lucy Pauline, born July 20, 1908.

(ee) Claradeen Otis, born February 28, 1910.

(ff) Katie Mae, born February 20, 1913.

(gg) Margaret Orender, born June 30, 1916.

(c) Veola Price, born April 5, 1874; married Leah Wade Allen.

CHILDREN:

(aa) Edwin Allen.

(bb) Lurie.

(cc) Mae Kathrine; married Louis H. Bennett and they have one child, Rachel Mae.

(dd) Voda Virginia; married Herman Harrison and have one child, Thomas Estes, born August 6, 1928.

(ee) Agnes Price.

(ff) Dorcas Wade.

(gg) Hansford Willard.

(d) Maria Blanche, born December 20, 1875; married, 1902, William H. Agee.

CHILDREN:

(aa) Harry Morgan, born November 12, 1904.

(bb) Mary Jimmie, born March 15, 1906.

(cc) Sarah Josephine, born May 25, 1908.

(dd) Eddie Miller (twin), born August 11, 1910.

(ee) Willie Frances (twin), born August 11, 1910.

(ff) Robert Hugh, born December 18, 1915.

(e) Paulus Powell, born March 18, 1878; married, June 30, 1909, Rhoda Florence Wilkerson. They have no children.

(f) Aurelia White, born June 20, 1882; married Wood Meador.

CHILDREN:

(aa) Tazewell Bedford.

(bb) Margie Mae.

(cc) Lucy White.

(dd) Willie Frances.

Marriages of the White family from 1780 to 1915, inclusive, taken from the records of Bedford County, Virginia. The Northside Whites came from Buckingham County, Virginia, and are indicated thus *. The Southside Whites came from Pittsylvania County, Virginia:

Daniel White and Margaret Caldwell, daughter George Caldwell, 27 July 1780.

Wm. Vaughan White and Mary Holligan, 18 September 1782.

James White and Lucy Terry, daughter Thos. Terry, 6 March 1783.

Thomas White and Jane Lusk, 23 March 1783.

James Callaway and Lucy White, daughter Stephen White, 13 July 1783.

Obadiah White and Pheola Arthur, 24 April 1785.

Henry Harris and Sarah White, daughter Sarah White, 25 October 1786.

Robert Roland and Tabby White, 12 August 1790.

Wm. White (Southside) and Charlotte Cundiff, daughter Elisha Cundiff, 18 May 1792.

John Dallice and Sally White, 19 February 1795.

*Wm. White and Polly P. Price, 5 April 1799.

Lewis Morgan and Frankey White, 21 January 1800.

George White and Anne Dowdy, daughter Ezekiel Dowdy, 11 November 1800.

John Burnett and Elizabeth White, daughter Joseph White, 26 October 1801.

*David Douglas and Sally White, 12 November 1801.

Aquilla Moulden and Doshia White, 18 February 1802.

John Witt and Jane White, daughter Joseph White, 17 June 1803.

Israel Wildman and Sarah White, daughter Lucy White of Pittsylvania County, 23 February 1804.

Vintsent C. Sterrmen and Nancy White 22 September 1804.

John Safoy and Mary White, 10 January 1805.

*Abraham Robinson and Nancy R. White, daughter Jacob White, 28 October 1805. (John White, security.)

Jeremiah White and Lucinda Buford, daughter Wm. Buford, 31 March 1806. (Edmund Logwood, security.)

*Lewis Davis and Rebecca H. White, daughter Jacob White, 14 December 1807. (John White, security.)

*John White and Elizabeth Robinson, daughter Benjamin Robinson, 4 April 1808. (John Robinson, security.)

George White and Sarah Freeman, daughter James Freeman, 27 February 1809.

Thos. T. White and Eleanor G. Latham, daughter Henry and Mary B. Latham, 13 June 1810.

Jeremiah Overstreet and Lucy White, daughter of Lucy White of Pittsylvania County, 16 October 1810. (Israel Wildman, security.)

Littleberry White and Mary Stone, 21 October 1811. (Geo. Stone, security.)

Pleasant White and Polly Hunt, 18 January 1812. (Jno. Dallis, security.)

*Henry Hatcher and Elizabeth White, daughter Jacob White, 4 February 1812.

Jacob White (Southside) and Rachel Allen, daughter Wm. Allen, 10 December 1812.

*Jacob W. White and Matilda Buford, daughter Wm. Buford, 18 December 1812. (Henry Hatcher, security.) Thos. Logwood, guardian.

John White and Polly Harris, daughter Sam'l. Harris (Southside), 7 November 1813.

Joshua Crouch and Polly White, daughter Jacob White, 26 August 1816.

Stephen White and Panky Overstreet, 12 November 1816.

*Jacob White (son of Henry) and Nancy Oglesby (Northside), 10 December 1816. (J. W. Noell, security.) Second marriage.

*Julius W. Hatcher and Polly White, daughter Jacob White, 28 January 1817. (Wm. A. White, security.)

Jasper Clayton and Lucinda H. White, 17 September 1817. (Lewis Wright, security.)

*Thomas Hatcher and Catharine White, daughter Jacob White, 27 November 1818. (Wm. A. White, security.)

Wm. White and Mary Ogden, daughter Henry Ogden, 22 January 1821. (Merritt M. White, security.)

Wm. Lowry, Jr., and Mary White, daughter Jarvis White, Sr., 1 February 1821.

Benjamin Hughes and Polly White, 24 August 1821.

Howson S. White and Catherine E. Moore, 22 October 1821. (Jno. N. Anderson, security.)

Wm. Naly and Polly White, 1822.

*Moses Penn and Edney A. White, daughter Jacob White, 19 October 1824. (Henry M. White, security.)

Joseph White and Penelope Taylor (Thos. Alsop Taylor), 14 March 1826.

*Henry M. White and Mary A. Gwatkin, daughter Charles Gwatkin, deceased, 2 October 1826. Jacob White, guardian. (Wm. A. White, security.)

Crawford E. White and Elizabeth W. Martin, daughter George Martin, 23 January 1827. (Abner Martin, security.)

*Gabriel S. Fisher and Editha S. White, daughter Jacob White, 16 July 1827. (Absalone Hunter, security.)

*Wm. Allen White and Caroline Poindexter, daughter Captain Sam'l Poindexter, 3 November 1828. (Sam Poindexter, security.)

Julius H. Hatcher and Frances B. White, 24 February 1829. (Crawford E. White, security.)

John White and Julian Fuqua, daughter A. Fuqua, 10 February 1830.

*Alexander A. N. Plunkett and Adaline White, daughter Mrs. Matilda Buford White, 26 September 1833. (Dan'l. P. Jones, security.)

*Wm. Thaxton and Matilda White (widow of Jacob W. White, daughter of Wm. Buford, 18 November 1835.

James Wood and Matilda Jane White, 12 December 1837.

Simeon A. White and Martha A. Turpin, 27 June 1839. (Philip Turpin, security.)

*Wm. Allen White and Lucy McD. Reese, daughter Joseph T. Reese, 10 May 1841. (Cyrus Robinson, security.) Second marriage.

Alexander H. Logwood and Theodosia A. White (widow), daughter Charles B. Reynolds, 11 November 1841.

Perciville C. White and Frances Overstreet, daughter Thos. Overstreet, 27 July 1846.

George White and Susan Lauwhorn, daughter Joshua Lauwhorn, 21 December 1846.

*Jacob Samuel White and Catherine S. White, daughter Henry M. White, 26 July 1847. (Wm. D. Hatcher, security.)

James W. Stuart and Martha Ann White, 29 September 1847. (Philip Turpin, security.)

George W. Mimmick and Catherine White, daughter Stephen White, 19 April 1849. (Jeremiah C. White, security.)

*Wm. H. Jennings and Eliza J. White, daughter Henry Milton White, 29 July 1850. (Jacob S. White, security.)

*Nathaniel W. Thomson and Ann L. White, daughter Henry Milton White, 24 December 1850. (Jacob S. White, security.)

*Jno. Milton White and Mary V. White, daughter Henry Milton White, 29 November 1852.

Joshua Lawhorn and Mary E. White, 13 December 1852.

Alexander White and Sophia Jane Johnson, 12 December 1853.

James M. White and Mary R. Gray, daughter John and Mary Gray, 1 November 1854.

Wm. G. White (from Campbell County) and Pocahontas R. Bolling, 1 February 1853.

*Josiah H. Nimmo and Mary Starr White, daughter Jacob W. and Matilda White, 7 November 1854.

Wm. H. McGhee and Lucy J. White, daughter James W. and Theodosia White, 8 May 1857.

Thomas T. White and Sarah E. Bondurant, daughter Jasper and Matilda Bondurant, 8 October 1857.

Wm. H. White and Lucy D. Wheat, daughter Hazarel and Eliza Wheat, 13 April 1858.

*Wm. Holcombe Bolling and Sally S. White, daughter Wm. A. White and Lucy McD. White, 18 September 1860.

John M. White and Flora B. Lowry, daughter Nelson and Sarah Lowry, 26 January 1864.

Thomas S. White and Lizzie F. DeWitt, daughter Elisha and Susan DeWitt, 8 June 1867.

Richard D. McClintock and Lucy D. White (widow), daughter Hazarel and Eliza Wheat, 12 September 1867.

Peter J. Hill and Pocahontas R. White (widow), daughter Archibald and Catharine Bolling, 10 October 1867.

James M. Lacy and Ann M. White, daughter Geo. and Susan White, 31 October 1867.

Charles Turner and Viny White, 28 December 1868.

Coley Sanderson and Sarah White, daughter C. E. W. and Parmelia White, 13 May 1869.

George Walden and Ellen White, daughter Littleberry and ——— White, 17 October 1869.

Richard C. Noell and Lucie T. White, daughter Jeremiah and Elvira White, 16 January 1872.

Jas. W. White and Emma D. Wilson, daughter John N. and Ann Wilson, 19 December 1872.

*Richard M. White and Lucie F. Major, daughter Harwood and Cleopatra Major, 15 January 1873.

Issac W. White and Sarah N. Witt, daughter John E. and Alice Witt, 22 January 1873.

Frebnigkugson Wills and Valeria White, daughter Samuel G. and Catharine J. White, 13 March 1873.

Henry White and Margaret Bates, daughter Wm. and Malinda Bates, 29 January 1873.

Anson Updike, Jr., and Isabella White, daughter George and Susan White, 10 December 1873.

Thos. W. White and Sallie A. Wooldridge, daughter Peter H. and Margaret Wooldridge, 14 January 1874.

*Julius C. Hatcher and Mary A. White, daughter Jacob S. and Catherine S. White, 21 January 1874. (E. H. Pritchett.)

Samuel J. White and Missouria J. Dobyns, daughter Griffin A. and Eliza. F. Dobyns, 28 June 1874.

R. M. White and Virginia Dunning, daughter Joseph and Eliza Dunning, 31 July 1874.

John F. Moore and Fannie A. White, daughter James and Martha A. White, 5 November 1874.

Fletcher White and Victoria Field, daughter John N. and Elizabeth Field, 24 December 1874.

John W. Coleman and Mary E. White, daughter Jeremiah C. and Elvira White, 21 April 1875.

Davis Buford White and Anna A. Newsome, daughter John W. and ——— Newsome, 9 February 1876.

R. A. Whorley and Phedora C. White, daughter J. C. and Elvira W. White, 19 September 1877.

Ansolem Hogan and Mary R. White, daughter Alex. and Sophia J. White, 20 December 1877.

Ranson White and Sallie F. White, daughter Jas. M. and Rebecca White, 20 October 1878.

Joseph G. Thompson and Nannie D. White, daughter Wm. H. and Lucy D. White, 10 September 1879.

Hubert F. Watson and Willie A. White, daughter Wm. H. and Lucy D. White, 10 September 1879.

*Walter B. White and Ida C. Jennings, daughter Stephen F. and A. E. Jennings, 28 January 1880.

*Edward H. White and Laura P. Turpin, daughter John and Mary Turpin, 12 May 1880.

Jas. M. White and Lavina E. Lawhorn, daughter Joshua and Elizabeth Lawhorn, 21 December 1881.

James Burnett and Cora Ella White, daughter Samuel G. and Catharine J. White, 21 October 1882.

John M. White and Sallie G. Crank, daughter Wm. J. and Legus M. Crank, 13 December 1882.

*Holcombe D. White and Mary C. Jennings, daughter Zachariah E. and Lucy A. Jennings, 12 December 1882.

*Frank C. Breazel and Roberta S. White, daughter Jacob S. and C. A. White, 20 December 1822.

Geo. W. Myers and Cora E. White, daughter Jerry C. and Elvira W. White, 28 January 1883.

*John P. Ackerly and Connie B. White, daughter John M. and Mary V. White, 21 February 1883.

Samuel H. White and Kitty H. Hensley, daughter Jos. E. and Lucy Hensley, 2 September 1883.

Robert Taylor (Logwood) and Rosa E. White, daughter John W. and Mary A. White, 14 December 1883.

*Leonidas Roper White and Mary Walter Barnett, daughter David and Fannie Barnett, 11 November 1884.

*J. Sam White, Jr. and Sophia E. Hardy, daughter Joseph S. and Jane S. Hardy, 31 March 1885.

Samuel White and Leana S. Dobyns, daughter Griffin A. and Eliza Dobyns, 12 August 1885.

*Ceril D. White and Julia G. Spinner, daughter Jesse F. and Martha Spinner, 9 December 1885.

Junior E. Lacy and Mattie White, daughter Geo. and Susan White, 22 December 1885.

John W. Wheat and Etta S. White, daughter Jeremiah C. and Elvira W. White, 27 February 1889.

Wm. S. Tankersley and Lilly E. White, daughter John W. and M. A. White, 19 February 1890.

Albert Howard Moore and Mary Julia White, daughter Jno. W. and Mary A. White, 11 September 1890.

Sibnah Y. White and Mary Lucas Callahan, daughter James and Sarah E. Callahan, 11 November 1890.

Jas. A. White and Sallie B. Feagans, daughter Martin E. and Mary Feagans, 17 December 1890.

Wm. H. Burnett and Vellaire F. White, daughter Samuel J. and Virginia White, 14 October 1891.

David W. Stevens and Ada F. White, daughter Samuel J. and M. J. White, 9 December 1891.

Davis R. White and Rosa O. Feagans, daughter Martin E. and Mary Feagans, 23 December 1891.

Houston S. White and Mary C. Wilson, daughter James E. and Elizabeth Wilson, 28 November 1896.

John W. Ogler and Alina J. White, daughter E. W. and Eliza C. White, 18 December 1896.

Charles E. White and Cora A. Blanks, daughter Obadiah and Amanda Blanks, 16 January 1895.

Ollie B. White and Mary J. Burnett daughter Joseph and Josephine F. Burnett, 12 June 1895.

Charles D. White and Carrie Knight, daughter Osson P. and Emma Knight, 9 October 1895.

*Frank C. Breazeal and Mary Walter White (widow), daughter David and Fannie Barnett, 11 November 1895.

George W. Austin and Mary M. White, daughter Richard and Jane White, 9 September 1897.

John A. Smith and Jennie B. White, daughter Alexander and Sophia J. White, 11 October 1897.

Eugene G. Wood and Ella M. White, daughter Thomas S. and Elizabeth White, 22 December 1897.

*Richard E. White and Magnolia Wright, daughter Wm. H. and Emma N. Wright, 26 October 1898.

Francis E. Watson and Mary J. White, daughter Thomas H. and Lizzie F. White, 2 November 1898.

Jas. W. White and Sallie D. Wilkes, daughter Corbin and Nettie M. Wilkes, 21 December 1898.

Robt. A. Beard and Berta White, daughter Scott and Lizzie White, 1 November 1899.

Jas. N. White and Lizzie B. Ballard, daughter Jacob B. and Ellen F. Ballard, 20 December 1899.

*Waddell A. White and Anna S. Dameron, daughter Chas. D. and Mildred Dameron, 25 February 1902.

Harvey C. Barton and Julia Ella White, daughter Montgomery P. and Sallie G. White, 3 April 1902.

Bruce White and Louisa Gaddy, daughter Wm. and Nannie C. Gaddy, 19 July 1903.

Robt. Julian Key and Ottie May White, daughter Edward and Eliza C. White, 16 December 1903.

David White and Alcora L. Nichols, daughter H. Walter and Jennie D. Nichols, 4 April 1904.

Ira F. White and Estelle Spencer Key, daughter E. W. and Elizabeth Frances Key, 27 April 1904.

John Claude Draper and Texie Newsom White, daughter Davis B. and Emma O. White, 27 December 1904.

Jas. Raleigh Watson and Susan Elizabeth White, daughter Thos. S. and Elizabeth White, 1 February 1905.

*J. Griffin Hardy and Annie Davis White, daughter Walter B. and Ida O. White, 31 January 1905.

Rufus M. Leftwich and Mary Leanna White, daughter Frank O. and Dora Elizabeth White, 8 March 1905.

*Henry Austin Wilson and Mannie S. White, daughter Leonidas R. and Mary W. White, 20 December 1905.

W. L. White (Hanover County) and Kate Henson (Amherst), daughter Marshall and Margaret Henson, 19 June 1906.

Clarence Henry White and Mary Ethel Perrow, daughter Henry J. and Mattie C. Perrow, 16 January 1907.

Judson E. Overstreet and Eleanor H. White, daughter Jas. H. and Jennie E. White, 31 July 1907.

Roy C. Beard and Pearle K. White, daughter P. Scott and Elizabeth White, 9 October 1907.

Daniel Edward Davis and Bessie A. White, daughter Frank O. and Bettie E. White, 22 June 1910.

Oscar B. White and Myrtle G. Freeman, daughter Scott and Lou Freeman, 16 August 1910.

*Eugene Conway Eggleston and Katharine Lee White, daughter Walter B. and Ida C. White, 6 September 1910.

John White and Maggie Hogan, daughter G. Whitsell and Ida Hogan, 14 December 1910.

Andrew Bruce White and Lola Mabel Canada, daughter Lewis H. and Bettie L. Canada, 27 December 1911.

Henry D. White and Elizabeth Florence Wooldridge, daughter Robert C. and Cora Lee Wooldridge, 10 January 1912.

*Wm. Staples Engleby and Mary Will White, daughter Samuel J. and Emma White, 16 October 1912.

Theodore H. Campbell and Eva White, daughter Jno. M. and Sallie G. White, 17 December 1913.

James White and Carrie Leftwich, daughter ———— and Eliza Leftwich, 29 September 1915.

DOUGLAS

The Virginia Douglases are descended from the Scottish family of Douglas—described by historians as the most powerful and widely celebrated family that Scotland ever produced. There are many legends of the origin of this family, but the first recorded is William of Douglas, the name being derived from the wild pastoral dale he possessed on the small river Douglas in Lanarkshire-Gael, "duf-glas" or "du'glas," meaning dark grey, from the color of its waters. William of Douglas appears as a witness to charters by the King and the Bishop of Glasgow between 1175 and 1213. He was either the brother, or the brother-in-law, of Sr. Freskin of Murray and had six sons, of whom Archibald, or Erkenbald, was his heir, and Brice rose to be Bishop of Moray. Archibald is a witness to charters between 1190 and 1232, and was knighted. Sir William of Douglas, apparently the son of Sir Archibald, figures in records from 1240 to 1273, and was the father of another Sir William, distinguished in family traditions as William the Hardy, who had three sons, viz: (1) The Good Sir James, (2) Hugh, and (3) Archibald. The Douglases had, since the time of William the Hardy, held the title of Lords of Douglas; but in 1357, Sir William, who had fought at Poitiers, was made Earl of Douglas, and by marriage became Earl of Mar. He died in 1384. The family rose into power under King Robert Bruce of whom "the good Lord James of Douglas" was the most distinguished adherent, but suffered a partial eclipse when the ninth Earl, James, rebelled against King James II. The Earls of Angus, however, partly restored the ancestral glory of the house, which has always continued to be one of the most important in Scotland.

The Good Sir James of Douglas is known as the greatest Captain of Bruce in the long war of independence. "The Black Douglas," as he was called, was victor in fifty-seven fights, his name being a terror to the border country. When his sovereign Robert Bruce lay dying, he told his knights of a longing he had always felt to make a pilgrimage to the Holy Land, and begged Sir James, as his most trusted and best beloved knight, to carry his embalmed heart to Jerusalem and bury it under holy soil. Sir James gave his promise upon his knighthood. Bruce died 7 June 1329. Receiving the heart carefully embalmed and laid within a silver case, Sir James with a long train of Scotland's most gallant knights, set forth on his long pilgrimage to Palestine. While on his way to Jerusalem (though Hume the historian of the family, says it was on his return from Jerusalem), he was killed fighting against the Moors in Spain, and the silver casket containing the heart of Bruce was brought back with the body of Douglas and buried in the Monastery of Melrose.

Remembering his gallant death, the Douglases have ever since that time worn a bloody heart bearing a crown upon it. The origin of the original arms of the family, which were simply "three silver stars on a blue field" is not known. Following are the armorial bearings of the family most generally seen and used.

> "Arms.—Argent, a man's heart
> gules ensigned with an
> imperial crown proper;
> on a chief azure three
> stars of the first."

(Reference: *Patronymica Britannica,* Lower; *Scottish Clans and Their Tartans,* Johnston.)

It is by no means unusual to find in our early records the name spelled with an additional "s" as Douglass; but now, generally speaking, the family use the original spelling—Douglas.

....

In 1690, a Charles Douglas patented land in Henrico County, in Varina Parish—again 1692 in Charles City County, Bristol Parish. As early as 1700, we find them patenting land in the counties of King William and King and Queen.

From the early land grants in Virginia we have the following patents:

(B. 9, p. 559) 1703.

George Douglas, pat. 180 A. lying between the lands of Wm. Morris and Wm. Rawlins, King William County.

(B. 9, p. 600) 16 April 1704.

Robert Douglas pat. 150 A. on branch of Pampatike Creek in St. John's Parish in King and Queen County.

(B. 10, L. Gr.) 1710.

Wm. Douglas pat. 275 A. land in King William County on the Mattapony Creek.

(B. 13, p. 401) 27 September 1727.

George Douglas and Wm. Dutton pat. 400 A. in King William County on Chandle's Branch.

(B. 19, p. 1031) 6 July 1741.

John Douglas pat. 430 A. land in Goochland County.

(B. 24, p. 1031) 20 September 1745.

John Douglas pat. 129 A. land on west branch of Bear Garden Cr. of the Fluvanna River.

(B. 31, page 733.)

John Douglas pat. 400 A. in Albemarle County on both sides of Rockfish Cr. at Wm. Matlocks—adj. Robert Waltons—adj. Abraham Childs—175 A. being formerly granted to John Douglas, 20 Aug. 1708. 225 A. more having been granted 10 September 1755.
(Deed Book IV, p. 218, Goochland County Records.)

13 Aug. 1743, James Bleving of Goochland sold to Robert Douglas of same county 295 A. on Little Muddy Creek, south side of James River, adj. Ashford Hughes.
From Albemarle County Records (D. B. II, p. 131), 12 June 1759.

Charles Lewis, Sr., of Goochland County to George Douglas of Albemarle Co. 400 acres land in the Rich Cove—pat. 6 July 1741.

Wit.—JAMES DOUGLAS.	WM. MAXWELL.
MICHAEL SMITH.	JOHN ADKINS.

In 1752, John Douglas owned land on the Northside of Fluvanna River, adj. Daniel Scott and George Nicholas.
Amherst County Records (Deed B. "C," p. 412) October 15, 1772.

George Douglas (Sen.), and wife Mary of Albemarle County, and son, James Douglas of Amherst deed land to George Blain of Amherst.

In 1792, George Douglas and wife—Mary of Amherst Co. sold land on Hoop Creek—a branch of Hickory.

Following marriage records from Amherst County, Virginia:

George Douglas married Mary Tucker, daughter of Drury, April 13, 1769. (James Douglas, a witness.)

John Douglas, married December 25, 1803, Nancy Rucker, daughter of Wm. Rucker (John, John, Peter Rucker).

David Douglas married Polly Ham, December 25, 1805. (Robert Douglas on the bond.)

Robert Douglas married Susanna Ham, September 30, 1806. (David Douglas on the bond.)

Wm. Douglas married Susanna Davis, daughter of Charles Davis, November 13, 1809.

Bedford County Records:

Surveyed to Robert Douglas, December 12, 1764, situated in Bedford County, 330 acres of land.

November 30, 1784.

Survey to David Douglas 22 Acres of land by virtue of Land office warrant granted to Wm. Logwood for 500 acres, October 16, 1781.

....

There came to Virginia October 6, 1750, one, William Douglas, Minister, who was born August 3, 1708, in ye shire of Galloway, Parish of Pennington, Scotland, son of William and Grishield (McKeand) Douglas; married, November 27, 1735, Nicholas Hunter, born September 1715 in Nithsdale County, Glencavin Parish, Scotland. He died December 31, 1781. Had charge of St. James Northern Parish in Goochland County, Virginia for twenty-seven years; Maniken Town (King William Parish) for nineteen years, and ministered to a charge in Buckingham County for four years. He had only one child, a daughter, Margaret or "Peggy" Douglas, who married (first) Nicholas Merriwether; (second) Chiles Tyrril.

Rev. Wm. Douglas, had a brother, John (died 1761); married Martha Heron and had five children, viz:—(1) William, (2) James, (3) George, (4) Peggie, (5) Samuel.

George Douglas, son of John, died at age of fifty, leaving six children, viz:—(1) Elizabeth (died at age of fourteen years), (2) George, (3) William, (4) Margaret, (5) Harriet, (6) Elizabeth Mary.

It has been thought by some who have searched the records that George, who lived in Albemarle, may have been the son of John Douglas; and by others that he was from King William or King and Queen. Since it has not been proven, as yet, satisfactorily, either way, we will take up the line where the records are intact—beginning with George Douglas, Sr., and wife, Mary, of Albemarle County, Virginia, whose son George, Jr., married April 13, 1769, Mary Tucker, daughter of Drury Tucker and his wife, Susanna Douglas, whom he married in Goochland, about 1740.

(Drury Tucker and wife, Susanna Douglas had a number of children, among them being the two who married as follows:

(1) Martha Tucker; married George Rucker.

(2) Mary Tucker married, 1769, George Douglas, Jr., son of George, Sr., their son, John, married in 1803, Nancy Rucker (Wm.,[4] John,[3] John[2], Peter[1]), who was a niece of George Rucker as well as niece of his wife, Martha Tucker. No doubt George Douglas, Sr., of Albemarle was a brother also to Susanna who married Drury Tucker. The Tucker family came from Prince George County, Virginia. I am indebted to Mrs. Sudie Rucker Wood (Mrs. Wm. P.), of Richmond, Virginia, who is a descendant of Drury and Susanna (Douglas) Tucker, for records of early land grants, records of Albemarle, King William, Goochland and King and Queen Counties, as well as the Rucker-Tucker notes: M. D. A.)

Among other children of George, Sr., and Mary Douglas of Albemarle County, was a son, James, who lived in Amherst and was, probably, the same who died in Rockbridge County, Virginia, in 1810. David Douglas, who died in Bedford County in 1791 (leaving children), is thought, also, to be a son of George, Sr., and Mary Douglas of Albemarle County.

James Douglas, who died in 1810 in Rockbridge County, Virginia, left a will (Will Book 3, page 360) in which he mentions wife, Elizabeth, and the following children, viz: Sons, William, John, James, Jr., George, and Robert. Daughters, Agnes (Douglas) Dixon and Elizabeth Douglas.

We have from Eckenrode's List of Colonial Soldiers in Virginia, page 35, the following: James Douglas, Thomas Douglas, William Douglas, George Douglas.

George Douglas, whose will we find probated in Bedford County, November 24, 1812, son of George Douglas, Senior, and his wife, Mary, of Albemarle County, married, April 13, 1769, Mary Tucker, daughter of Drury and Susanna (Douglas) Tucker, of Amherst County. We find him listed in Hardesty's *Enclycopedia*, page 410, as a soldier in the Revolutionary War from that county, also on page 35 of Eckenrode's *List of Colonial Soldiers of Virginia*.

Under date of 1792, Amherst County records we find that George Douglas and wife, Mary, sold land on Hoop Creek, a branch of Hickory Creek. He evidently moved to Bedford County soon after this. Early in 1797, his daughter, Lucinda, married John Willis Clayton in Bedford County. George Douglas died in 1812, and left surviving, besides his widow, the following children:

(1) Lucinda Douglas married, March 21, 1797, John Willis Clayton, Jr., son of John Willis and Mary Clayton. She married (second) November 15, 1832, Jesse Spinner. (See Clayton, Turpin, and Spinner families.)

(2) David Douglas, born February 26, 1776; married, November 12, 1801, Sallie White, daughter of Captain Jacob and Hannah (Spiers) White, of Bedford County. (See forward.)

(3) Susannah Douglas married, January 8, 1800, Henry Lane, Jr., son of Henry Lane, Sr. A daughter by this marriage, Sarah Lane, married Vincent Turpin, son of Thomas and Rachel (Cheatwood) Turpin, of Bedford County. (See Turpin family.)

(4) John Douglas married, December 25, 1803, Nancy Rucker, daughter of William Rucker. In addition to other children by this marriage, there were the following:

> (a) Catherine Willis Douglas; married, November 3, 1825, Jonathan W. Eads. Among other descendants of this marriage are the children of the late J. E. Moose, of Rockbridge County.

> (b) Alfred Douglas; married (first), December 12, 1833, Agnes Paxton, of Arnold's Valley. One child, a daughter by this union. He married (second), Mary Jones (widow), of Bedford County. One child, a son. No children by his third wife, who was Lucy Spriggs, of Lancaster County, Virginia.

> (c) Murphy Douglas; married, February 22, 1849, Catherine Louisa Luster, of Rockbridge County. Several children by this marriage living in Botetourt County, Virginia.

(5) Murphy Douglas.

(6) Polly Douglas married, March 1, 1805, John Ballard.

(7) Sally Douglas married, January 4, 1806, John Coward.

(8) William Douglas married, November 13, 1809, Susanna Davis, daughter of Charles Davis and Rosanna (Ellis) Davis, of Amherst County, Virginia. (See Davis family.)

In Will Book "D," page 68 of the Bedford County records, we find the will of George Douglas as follows:

IN THE NAME OF GOD, AMEN: I, George Douglass of Bedford County in perfect health and of sound memory do make this my Last Will & Testament. Imprimis, I lend to my beloved wife during her life or Widowhood the Lands I own in the County of Bedford with all the rest of my Estate real & personal except such part as is hereafter given & particularly devised. Item, I give & bequeath to my Daughter Lucinda Claton one negro woman Nancy. I give & bequeath to my son David Douglass one negro man named Ratter, & one Bay Horse to make him equal with the others. Item, I give & bequeath to my Daughter Susannah Lane one negro man named Lesor, then received back from Henry Lane forty Pound in order to make her equal with the rest of my children. Item, I give & bequeath to my son John Douglass one negro woman named Betsy. Item, I give and bequeath to son Murphey Douglass one negro man named Jessey. Item, I give and bequeath to my Daughter Polly Ballard one negro woman named Ellen. I give and bequeath to my Daughter Sally Coward one negro woman named Edy & one horse to make her equal with the others of my children. Item, My son William Douglass I have not given *narrow* negro, but it is my Will & desire that he should be made equal with the rest of my children in a negro, then they received t*hern*. Item, my Will & desire is that at the decease or marriage of my wife, all the Estate lent to her & not otherwise devised above shall be equally divided among my eight children to-wit, Luc*indy,* David, Susannah, John, Murphy, Polly, Sally, William to them & their children forever & I do hereby constitute and appoint my Wife Mary Douglass, my son Murphy Douglass, & Waddy Cobbs to execute this my Last Will & Testament.

his

GEORGE x DOUGLASS [SEAL].

mark

Signed, Sealed & Published this first day of April, One thousand eight Hundred & twelve.

Teste, JOSEPH R. CARTER, THOS. WRIGHT
JOHN WRIGHT.

SALLIE WHITE
wife of David Douglas

At a Court held for Bedford County at the Courthouse the 24th day of November, 1812. This last will and testament of George Douglass dec'd was exhibited in Court and on examination of the witnesses thereto subscribed on oath the same was admitted to record.

Teste:

J. STEPTOE, *C. B. C.*

A copy,

Teste:

V. W. NICHOLS,

Clerk Circuit Court of Bedford County, Va.

Will Book "D," page 68.

....

David Douglas, born February 26, 1776, son of George, Jr., and Mary (Tucker) Douglas, of Amherst and Bedford Counties, married November 12, 1801, Sallie White, born August 18, 1787, eldest daughter of Captain Jacob and Hannah (Spiers) White, of Bedford County. She was married at the age of fourteen years and was the mother of fifteen children, twelve of whom lived to be grown. Three of her grandchildren were also reared in her home. She died July 31, 1878, having lived to be almost ninety-one years of age. She was a most remarkable woman, noted for her kindness of heart, sympathetic nature, and her lavish hospitality. She inherited from her father much land which is still in the possession of some of her descendants.

[Sallie (White) Douglas was an aunt of my maternal grandparents and her husband, David Douglas, a brother of my paternal great, great grandmother, Lucinda (Douglas) Clayton, wife of John Willis Clayton, Jr.—M. D. A.]

David Douglas served in the War of 1812, for which service his widow drew a pension before she died.

CHILDREN:

(1) James, born October 31, 1803.

(2) Nancy, born November 19, 1804; married James Sledd. (See Sledd family.)

(3) George W., born November 22, 1806.

(4) Elizabeth, born March 13, 1808; married, September 24, 1827, Alexander H. Logwood and had children: Mary, Nannie, and James.

(5) William B., born January 27, 1810.

(6) Louisa Jane, born October 20, 1811; married Milton Hatcher.

(7) Edward H., born May 14, 1813.

(8) Mary Ann R. L., born October 21, 1816.

(9) Martha Ann, born April 5, 1819; married David Witt. (See forward.)

(10) Lamira, born March 1, 1821.

(11) Sarah, born January 31, 1823; married her cousin, Robert Douglas.

(12) Editha S., born February 7, 1826; married Benjamin Hobson, of Bedford County and had children: Richard, Sallie, and Edward.

(13) Robert Henry W., born March 1, 1828; married Elizabeth Ann Major. (See forward.)

(14) Edna America, born August 11, 1830; never married. Was a mother to her youngest sister's children, who, after the death of their mother, were reared in their grandmother's home.

(15) Catherine H., born August 20, 1833; married Spottswood A. Major. (See forward.)

....

Martha Ann Douglas, born April 5, 1819, ninth child of David and Sallie (White) Douglas; married David Witt, born July 15, 1811, son of Dennet and ———— (Oglesby) Witt, of Bedford County, Virginia. David Witt resided in Poplar Hills, Rockbridge County, Virginia, where he devoted his life to farming. He died July 3, 1899, and his wife died May 5, 1903.

CHILDREN:

(1) William Edward Witt, born March 3, 1840; married Laura L. Brice, of Baltimore, Maryland. He was a dentist. Lived in Newport News, Virginia, where he died September 12, 1908.

CHILDREN:

(a) William Edward, Jr.

(b) David Henry.

(c) Laura.

(d) Emmett.

(e) Glasgow.

(2) David Henry Witt, born April 1, 1842. Lived in California and while home on a visit was drowned August 20, 1888, crossing a swollen stream at Cedar Grove, Rockbridge County, Virginia. Never married.

(3) Robert Richard Witt, born July 17, 1851; married, April 20, 1876, Margaret Newman Williams, born March 8, 1857, daughter of George Rader Williams (son of Hazael and Nancy (Rader) Williams) and Margaret Elizabeth Eubank (daughter of John and Catherine (Rose) Eubank), of Amherst County, Virginia. Robert R. Witt was educated in the Lexington Schools and Richmond College. While his earlier activities were devoted to farming, his life was largely spent in public service—holding, first, the office of deputy sheriff, then sheriff of Rockbridge County, and, for a number of years prior to his death, was clerk of the circuit court, then deputy county clerk for Rockbridge County, Virginia. He held the confidence and esteem of his fellow citizens and performed his duties with promptness and efficiency. He was a member of the Baptist Church and belonged to the Masonic order. He died December 27, 1923.

CHILDREN:

(a) George William, born February 2, 1877; married Ellen Yates. One child:
    (aa) George William Witt, Jr.

(b) David Edward, born September 22, 1879; married Belle Almond, daughter of Charles and Eliza (Rucker) Almond, of Lynchburg, Virginia. Two children:
    (aa) Nancy Almond Witt.
    (bb) Margaret Williams Witt.

(c) Margaret Thomas, born December 25, 1881; married George Amna Rucker. Two children:
    (aa) Margaret Eubank Rucker.
    (bb) Robert Parks Rucker.

(d) Robert Eubank, born March 28, 1884; unmarried.

(e) Hugh McCluer, born March 12, 1887; married (first) Grace Verdier; (second) Aline Parker.

(f) Robert Richard, Jr., born August 27, 1889; married Harriet Means. Two children:

(aa) Ellison Means Witt.

(bb) Sallie Prescott Witt.

(g) Infant, born July, 1893; died in infancy.

(h) Dora Winborne, born September 8, 1895; unmarried.

(4) Sarah White Witt, born August, 1846; died of diphtheria at age of two years.

(5) Bettie Barker Witt, born April 25, 1854; married, October 31, 1876, Robert Shafer McCluer, born June 28, 1856, son of John William and Bettie (Shafer) McCluer, of Rockbridge County, Virginia. Living in Roanoke, Virginia.

CHILDREN:

(a) William Henry McCluer, born October 28, 1878; married, November 29, 1900, Maude Parsons, daughter of Colonel Chester and Nellie (Loomis) Parsons, of Natural Bridge, Virginia. Living in Roanoke, Virginia.

CHILDREN:

(aa) Chester Parsons McCluer, born December 28, 1903.

(bb) Nellie Loomis McCluer, born June 29, 1907.

(cc) Elizabeth Douglas McCluer, born July 8, 1909.

(dd) Robert Shafer McCluer, II, born October 13, 1912.

(ee) Collette McCluer, born June 8, 1915.

(b) Elizabeth Douglas McCluer, born November 25, 1887; died August 11, 1889.

(c) David Childs McCluer, born September 29, 1891; married, June 7, 1920, Mrs. Julia Tucker (widow). One child:

(aa) John William McCluer, born August 14, 1921.

(6) Lamira Oglesby Witt, born March 23, 1857; married Emmett Wilson, of Rockbridge County. Living in California. Two children:

(a) Charles Wilson.

(b) Douglas Wilson (deceased).

(7) Charles Margrave Witt, born 1859; married ————. Died in California, December 1, 1916. Left issue.

Robert Henry W. Douglas, born March 1, 1828, thirteenth child of David and Sallie (White) Douglas; married, October 30, 1855, Elizabeth Ann ("Betty") Major, born August 4, 1837, daughter of Harwood Major, born in Bedford County, Va., September 20, 1807, and Cleopatra A. McD. (Tinsley) Major, born in Bedford County, January 19, 1815, and they were married December 7, 1831. (The parents of Harwood Major were John Major, born in Prince Edward County; died 1844, and Lucretia (Tinsley) Major, born in Bedford County; died in 1839.) Cleopatra A. McD. (Tinsley) Major, his wife, was a daughter of William and Betsy (Burks) Tinsley. Her father was born in Bedford County and her mother in Amherst County. Harwood Major was a magistrate for more than forty years.

Robert Henry W. Douglas served in Company A, Twenty-Eighth Virginia Infantry, C. S. A. Enlisted September 1, 1864; wounded at Hatcher's Run, March 31, 1865. He was public spirited and active in all affairs concerning the interests and welfare of the community. Was one of the substantial men of Bedford County where he owned and cultivated an estate. He died in 1915.

CHILDREN:

(1) Lemira Susan, born January 7, 1857; married, February 28, 1883, William Sherman Burks, born September 24, 1856, son of John Dabney and Dollie Waller (Cheatwood) Burks. (See Burks family for descendants.)

(2) John Letcher born April 4, 1859; married, December 21, 1892, Georgie W. Penn, born November 9, 1864, daughter of James Jacob and America ("Mitt") (Turpin) Penn. (See Penn and Turpin families.)

CHILDREN:

(a) Emmett Penn, born November 15, 1893; unmarried.

(b) Elizabeth, born March 28, 1895; married, October 12, 1918, William Elston Hedges of West Virginia.

CHILDREN:

(aa) Margaret Hedges, born January 22, 1919.

(bb) Elizabeth Hedges, born October 21, 1923.

(c) John Letcher, Jr., born July 26, 1897; married, August 12, 1920, Vesta Peale Turpin, born December 21, 1899, daughter of Edward J. and Mary (Rieley) Turpin, of Montvale. Va.

CHILDREN:

(aa) Edna Penn, born June 3, 1921.

(bb) Thomas Turpin, born January 3, 1923.

(cc) Joseph Rieley, born November 12, 1926.

(d) Robert James, born November 24, 1898; married, May 20, 1922, Annie Elizabeth Penn, born March 8, 1896; died April 26, 1926, daughter of Robert Reid and Jennie (Chapman) Penn, of Callaway, Franklin County, Va. Child:

(aa) Robert James Douglas, Jr., born April 3, 1926.

(e) George William, born March 19, 1900; married, February 12, 1923, Maude Underwood, born April 8, 1897, of Chase City, Va. Living at Asheville, N. C. No children.

(f) Mary Jackson, born September 15, 1902; married, February 28, 1923, Lester Pleasant Bailey, son of Andrew and Nannie (Lawson) Bailey, of Lynchburg, Va. One child:

(aa) Lester Pleasant Bailey, Jr., born September 11, 1924.

(g) Lily Katherine, born August 4, 1904; unmarried.

(h) Sallie Enid, born December 22, 1907; married, October 12, 1923, Robert A. Scott, son of D. H. and Connie (Gatewood) Scott, of Bedford County. They have one child:

(aa) Patsy Penn Scott, born May 12, 1928.

(i) Rebecca Virginia, born August 11, 1910.

(3) Willie Catherine, born September 27, 1861; married, November 20, 1886, Martin Cabell Parks, born June 15, 1856, son of Samuel Goode Parks and Amanda Theresa Burks (daughter of Samuel C. and Pamela M. (Hunter) Burks), of Rockbridge County. (Martin and Nancy Parks his grandparents were originally from Amherst County.) Willie C. (Douglas) Parks died May 17, 1928.

CHILDREN:

(a) Clarence Letcher Parks, born September 5, 1888; married, October 16, 1913, Bertha Lee Middleton, of Greenfield. Ohio.

CHILDREN:

(aa) Wayne Middleton, born November 9, 1914.

(bb) Helen Clare, born July 5, 1917.

(cc) Martin Cabell, born March 21, 1921.

(b) Samuel Robert Parks, born March 2, 1890; married, February 3, 1926, Mary Lucille Overstreet, of Bedford County. They have one child:

(aa) Samuel Robert, Jr., born October 15, 1927.

(c) Katherine Welch Parks, born February 24, 1893; married, December 12, 1917, Wilton Baxter Long, son of Lafayette and Julia Gertrude May Long, of Nelson and Bedford counties.

CHILDREN:

(aa) Carol Parks Long, born September 11, 1918.

(bb) Wilton Baxter Long, Jr., born February 11, 1920; died September 30, 1921.

(cc) Infant girl (not named), born November 10, 1922.

(dd) Edna Earle Long, born July 24, 1924.

(ee) Infant boy (not named), born January 29, 1927.

(4) Cleopatra McDaniel, born December 27, 1863; married, June 7, 1887, Frank Oscar Parks, born January 9, 1859; died March 16, 1925, son of Tranval B. and Laura (Fulton) Parks.

CHILDREN:

(a) Oscar Douglas Parks, born May 24, 1888; died November 23, 1893.

(b) Robert Clayton Parks, born March 10, 1890; unmarried.

(c) Laura Elizabeth Parks, born September 21, 1893; married, February 10, 1917, Samuel Burks.

(d) Jessie Louise Parks, born August 9, 1897; married, November 28, 1927, Edward Davis.

(e) Frank Oscar Parks, Jr., born July 19, 1901; unmarried.

(5) Jesse Spinner, born December 26, 1873; married (first), December 22, 1903, Lottie L. Turpin. (See Turpin family.) He married (second), November 23, 1915, Mrs. Eva S. (Booker) Yoder, daughter of T. J. and Annie E. (Moore) Booker.

CHILDREN BY FIRST MARRIAGE:

(a) Jack F. Douglas.

(b) J. Linwood Douglas.

CHILDREN BY SECOND MARRIAGE:

(c) William C. Douglas.

(d) Henry M. Douglas.

(6) Sallie White, born November 3, 1878; married, December 18, 1902, Edward Richard Burks, born November 7, 1874, son of George Wellington and Harriett Eliza (Hopkins) Burks. (See Burks family for descendants.)

Catherine H. Douglas, born August 20, 1833, youngest child of David and Sallie (White) Douglas; married in 1852, Spottswood Alexander Major, born in Bedford County, September 20, 1832, eldest son of Harwood and Cleopatra A. McD. (Tinsley) Major, who was the daughter of William and Betsy (Burks) Tinsley. Harwood Major was the son of John Major, born in Prince Edward County, died in 1844, and Lucretia (Tinsley) Major, born in Bedford County, died in 1839.

He owned and cultivated a fine farm in Bedford County and gave his time during the winter months to teaching. Catherine H. (Douglas) Major died July 28, 1863. Her husband married, for his second wife, December 19, 1866, Cleopatra A. Harrison, daughter of James S. and Nancy (Thomas) Harrison, of Bedford County. Three children, by the first wife, were reared in the home of their grandmother, Sallie (White) Douglas—Spottswood A. Major died June 15, 1919.

The children of Spottswood A. Major and his first wife Catherine H. Douglas are:

(1) Walter Pendleton Major, born November 19, 1854; died June 12, 1927. Never married.

(2) Edna Douglas Major, born October 7, 1856; married, February 3, 1885, William Beverley Watts, born 1851; died 1927, eldest son of Ludwell and Nancy Sallings (Davis) Watts. Maternally, he was the grandson of Charles Lewis Davis and his second wife, Nancy Morris, of Amherst County. On his father's side he was the grandson of Curtis and Nancy (Brown) Watts, and

great grandson of Caleb Watts, of Amherst County, who was a son of Thomas and Elizabeth Watts. Mrs. Edna D. (Major) Watts is living at Big Island, Va.

CHILDREN:

(a) Hubert Ashby Watts, born November 1, 1885; married, October 23, 1911, Rob May Miller. They have one child:
   (aa) Hubert Ashby, Jr., born January 1916. Living in Lynchburg, Va.
(b) Walter Douglas Watts, born October 7, 1887; unmarried. Living with his mother at Big Island.
(c) Katherine Sallins Watts, born November 11, 1889; married, July 8, 1922, Henry Judson Noell. (See Turpin family.) She is a graduate of Hollins College. They have one child:
   (aa) William Judson Noell, born March 2, 1924.

(3) William Edward Major, born October 5, 1858; married Mrs. Lizzie (Wright) Turpin, daughter of George W., and Fanny L. (Turpin) Wright. (See Philip Turpin family.)

CHILD:

(a) Mamie Kathleen Major; married Ashby Perrow, of Bedford County.

CHILDREN:

(aa) Jack Perrow.
(bb) Shirley Perrow.
(cc) Louise Perrow.

(4) Harwood A. Major; died in childhood.

———

Some of the early marriages of the Douglass family from the records of Bedford County, Virginia:

Elizabeth Douglass and Joshua Halley, March 12, 1792, with William Halley as surety.

William Douglass and Kitty Gissag Slaughter, January 26, 1795, with Reuben Slaughter as surety.

Lucinda Douglass and John Willis Clayton, March 21, 1797. Surety, Thomas L. Clayton.

Susannah Douglass and Henry Lane, Jr., January 8, 1800, with George Douglass as surety. Consent of Henry Lane, Sr., father of Henry, Jr.

David Douglass and Sally White, November 12, 1801, with Jacob White as surety.

Nancy Douglass and John Halley, December 28, 1801.

Robert Douglass and Pamelia Noell, October 13, 1803, with Wm. Chasteen as surety. Consent of Thomas Noell, father of Pamelia.

Elizabeth Douglass and Francis Halley, November 9, 1803.

Polly Douglass and John Ballard, March 1, 1805. No consent with bond.

Sally Douglass and John Cowhard, January 4, 1806. Consent of father, George Douglass.

Murphy Douglass and Nancy A. Hubbard, March 14, 1814, with Richard Wright as surety. Consent of Stephen Hubbard.

John Douglass and Catharine Centz (Autz, Antz), December 4, 1822, with Isaac St. Clair a surety.

Elizabeth Douglass and Alexander H. Logwood, September 24, 1827. She was a daughter of David Douglass. James Sledd, security.

Edwin H. Douglass and Mary J. Ogden, May 2, 1834, with Wm. H. White as surety. Consent of Henry M. Ogden, father of Mary.

Alfred Douglass and Frances S. Jones, January 4, 1837, with James D. Watts as surety.

Early marriages of the Douglas family from the records of Botetourt County, Va.:

John Douglass and Ann Morris, daughter of Richard Morris, 1788.

Wayman Sinclair and Elizabeth Douglass, daughter of Benjamin Douglass, January 2, 1801.

George Anderson and Polly Douglass, September 27, 1805.

John Jamison and Elizabeth Douglass, March 5, 1807.

Hugh Douglass and Mary Myers, January 21, 1818.

John Douglass and Mary Douglass, October 24, 1839.

William Douglass and Catherine Fuluster, June 14, 1841.

Early marriages of the Douglas family from the records of Halifax County, Va.:

Martin Miller and Rebecca Douglass, January 31, 1788.

Adam Windows and Mary Douglass, December 6, 1788.

James Douglass and Judith Wall, August 24, 1789.

Robert Juniel and Salley Douglass, December 16, 1789.

Andrew Douglass and Susannah Willis, November 18, 1790.

Thomas Douglass and Betsey Davenport, December 1, 1790.

William Douglass and Betsey Holt, January 20, 1791.

William Douglass and Anney Crenshaw, April 14, 1791.

George Douglass and Elizabeth McFarland, October 12, 1791.

Drury Mays and Nancy Douglass, January 25, 1793.

John Douglass and M. Browner, May 10, 1793.

Lewis Crenshaw and Sary Douglass, July 24, 1794.

Nathaniel Douglass and Polly Douglass, April 30, 1796.

John Hart and Polly Douglass, January 5, 1798.

John Douglass and Hannah Douglass, December 18, 1798.

Arthur Fowler and Sally Douglass, July 31, 1800.

John Douglass and Frances Green, November 19, 1818.

James Gregory and Caly Douglass, November 26, 1823.

Hamilton Dougliss and Polly Gill, December 27, 1827.

Early marriages of the Douglas family from the records of Rockbridge County, Va.:

William Douglass and Agnes McCluer, December 29, 1803.

James Dickson and Nancy Douglas, January 19, 1804.

John Jamison and Elizabeth Douglass, March 5, 1807.

William Viers and Ivia Ann Douglass, November 5, 1818.

James Douglass and Eliza Hamilton, April 15, 1819.

Jacob Matthews and Patsy Douglass, August 19, 1819.

Jacob Saunders and Malinda Douglass, June 22, 1820.

Samuel McCorkle and Jane M. Douglass, December 29, 1824.

John Eades and Catherine W. Douglass, November 3, 1825.

Alfred Douglas and Agnes A. C. Paxton, December 12, 1833.

James S. Richeson and Nancy M. Douglass, September 22, 1842

William A. Richeson and Mary Douglass, November 2, 1843.

John R. Maben and Sarah Douglass, July 15, 1847.

Murphy Douglass and Catherine Louisa Luster, February 22, 1849

Julius H. Noell and Frances Ann Douglass, daughter of Wm. Douglass, deceased May 13, 1851.

Marshall B. Pynce and Margaret S. Douglass, daughter of Wm. Douglass, deceased September 12, 1853.

Robert H. Douglass and Bettie A. Major, daughter of Howard (Harwood) Major, October 31, 1855.

James G. Davidson and Agnes I. Douglass, daughter of Alfred Douglass, May 28, 1856.

SLEDD

The ancestors of the Sledd family were English, coming from Sledton, a lovely little village near York—nearby there is a beautiful lake still called Sledd's Mere. Sweet's *Oldest English Texts* (page 179) says, "The Sledds were Kings of the East Saxons for several generations. The family were ardent Cromwellians and had to give up everything and come to America about 1662."

Owing to the destruction of the Colonial Records by the Federals, we take up the family here with James Sledd, a soldier of the Revolution and living in Albemarle County. His son, John, came to Bedford County in 1792. He erected the old brick house now owned by Jesse Douglas, and in 1827, moved to Benton, Marshall County, Kentucky, where he died in 1834. He was married three times, and in the words of old Ed, "de ole Boss married a Miss Burford from Amherst."

His son, James Sledd, born August 20, 1800; married, in 1824, Nancy Douglas, born November 19, 1804, eldest daughter of David and Sallie (White) Douglas. (See White and Douglas families.) James Sledd died August 22, 1840, leaving a son, William Edward Sledd, for whom his great uncle, Col. William Allen White, was made guardian. Nancy (Douglas) Sledd died July 26, 1872.

William E. Sledd, Sr., born January 8, 1826; married September 2, 1847, Arabella Hobson, born August 23, 1829, daughter of Richard and Louisa (West) Hobson. A biographical sketch of him in Hardestry's *Encyclopedia,* page 430, says, "The grandfather of Mr. Sledd was one of the pioneers of Bedford County, and amassed a large property, all of which is still owned by the subject of this sketch. He adds a custom milling business to the conduct of his fine estate, and is one of the substantial men of the county." William E. Sledd, Sr., died November 6, 1888; and his wife died March 31, 1889.

CHILDREN:

(1) Ann Hobson, born July 28, 1848; married in 1873, Charles L. Campbell. She died in 1913.

(2) James Richard, born November 10, 1849; married, January 22, 1873, his first cousin, Mattie Lee Penn, daughter of Paul Silas and Mary Charlotte (Hobson) Penn. (See Penn family.) He lived in Pike County, Missouri, where he died in 1910. His

widow, a number of years after his death, married Joseph G.
Gilchrist and now living at Chillicothe, Missouri.

CHILDREN:

- (a) Charles Oscar Sledd, born October 27, 1873; died September 30, 1924; married, ————; no children.
- (b) William Paul Sledd, born October 5, 1875; died January 16, 1925; married, ————; no children.
- (c) Frances Lillian Sledd, born March 29, 1883; died
  October 17, 1903; married, ————; no children.

(3) Eliza Susan, born May 14, 1851; married, January 17, 1872,
William R. Cornelius, born in Bedford County, November 26,
1846, son of William and Anna (Hobson) Cornelius, both of
whom died when he was an infant one year old. She is still
living.

CHILDREN:

- (a) Ottie M. Cornelius, born May 25, 1873; married Jesse
  S. Burks, son of Hiram C. and Charlotte (Sale) Burks.
  (See Burks family.)
- (b) Anna S. Cornelius, born January 10, 1875.
- (c) Selma Cornelius, born May 12, 1876.
- (d) Eliza Cornelius, born April 19, 1879.
- (e) Samuel H. Cornelius, born August 27, 1883; married
  Lucy Ogden, daughter of William M. and Willie (Turpin) Ogden, of Bedford County. (See Captain John
  Turpin family.)

(4) William Robert, born June 24, 1853; died August 11, 1855.

(5) (Dr.) Samuel David, born July 31, 1855; married in 1884, Belle
Mason. Lived at Fort Wayne, Indiana where he died in 1924.
Left one daughter, Mabel.

(6) Ida Nelson, born November 28, 1857; married in 1875, Charles
M. Garnett. Living in Farmville, Virginia.

(7) Charlotte Louisa, born January 31, 1860; married in 1879, John
Wilson. She died in Lynchburg, Virginia, in 1922.

(8) William Edward, Jr., born March 28, 1862; never married. Died
September, 1927.

(9) Benjamin, born August 27, 1864; married, June 11, 1889, Neda
Purefoy, daughter of Frederick M. and Temperance (Jones)

DR. BENJAMIN SLEDD

Purefoy, of Wake Forest, North Carolina. She died July 30, 1928. Benjamin Sledd, entered Washington and Lee University at Lexington, Virginia, as a student, in 1881, from which he graduated, with the degree of M. A., in 1886; Litt. D., 1905.

A sketch of his work, while a student at Washington and Lee University, is found in the Alumni Record of that institution and is as follows:

"Honorary Scholarship, 1882; Latin Scholarship, 1883; F. O. French Scholarship, 1884; Early English Text Society Prize, 1885; Santini Prize Medal, 1886; Robinson Prize Medal, 1886."

He was a student at John Hopkins University, 1886-87; but took no degree on account of failing eye sight. Became Professor of English in Wake Forest College, North Carolina, September, 1888. Professor of English, University of Virginia (summer term) since 1916. Member Phi Beta Kappa, Virginia (Mother) Chapter, Williamsburg, 1913. Traveling Fellow of Albert Kahn Foundation, 1914-15.

The following sketch of his literary work is taken from "Who's Who in America, 1928":

"Author: (Poems) From Cliff and Scaur, 1897; The Watchers of the Hearth, 1901; When Freedom Came, 1910; At Lexington, a Memorial Poem, 1913; A Virginian in Surrey, 1914; To England; Afterthought, 1919; The Dead Grammarian, 1924; The Modernist and The Megatherium, 1927.

Editor: La Princesses de Clèves, 1892."

CHILDREN:

(a) Arthur Purefoy Sledd, born 1895; married, 1922, Elsie Brantley. Now head of the science department of Judson College in Alabama. One son:

    (aa) Hassel Brantley Sledd, born May 9, 1926.

(b) Gladys Hobson Sledd, born 1899; unmarried.

(c) Elva Douglas Sledd, born 1903; unmarried.

ROBINSON

Christopher Robinson, of Cleasby, in Yorkshire, England, who settled at "Hewick," near Urbanna, in Middlesex County, about the year 1666, is said to be the ancestor of the distinguished family Robinson in Virginia. He was the brother (or nephew) (*Virginia Magazine,* Vol. 3, p. 169) of the Right Reverend John Robinson (born 1650; died 1722), a distinguished prelate and statesman, who was Bishop of London as well as ambassador to Sweden.

Christopher Robinson was born in 1645; married, first, Agatha Bertram, secondly, Katherine, daughter (or widow) of Theophilus Hone, and widow of Robert Beverley, of Virginia. (*Virginia Magazine,* Vol. 3, p. 169.)

....

Abraham Robinson, born in 1783, son of Benjamin and Mar. (North) Robinson; married, August 15, 1805, Nancy R. White, born in 1789, second daughter of Captain Jacob and Hannah (Spiers) White, of Bedford County, Virginia. Abraham Robinson died November 26, 1821. His father, Benjamin Robinson, served with honor in the War for Independence. (Record of Benjamin Robinson No. 1780832 War Department, Washington, D. C.—Adj. Gen. Office.)

After the death of her husband, Nancy R. (White) Robinson married Jesse Spinner, a wealthy citizen of Bedford County, and who also was, a widower (his first wife having been Celia (or Sillah) Cheatwood, daughter of William Cheatwood, of Powhatan County). She died May 8, 1831, in the forty-second year of her age. (See Spinner and Snead families for descendants.)

CHILDREN:

(1) William W., born September 12, 1807.

(2) Lucinda S., born October 8, 1809; married, October 2, 1826, Robert R. Logwood.

(3) Eldred (Eldridge) Herbert, born October 9, 1811. (See forward.)

(4) Jacob H., born October 10, 1814; married Miss Julia Jones. They had no children of their own but adopted Corrie Jones, the daughter of Rev. Wesley Jones, the brother of Julia Jones Robinson. Corrie Jones Robinson died in 1928, at the home of

her half-brother in Richmond, Virginia. Jacob H. Robinson was for a number of years, City Collector of Lynchburg, Virginia.

(5) Rebecca N., born August 4, 1817; died February 6, 1827.

....

Eldred (Eldridge) Herbert Robinson, third child of Abraham and Nancy R. (White) Robinson, of Bedford County, Virginia, was born October 9, 1811; married, in 1833, Elizabeth Ann Cornelia Moorman, born 1815, died 1848. He died in 1845, leaving the following worthy sons and daughters.

CHILDREN:

(1) John William White Robinson, born in Bedford County, August 6, 1837; married, November 21, 1867, Miss Elizabeth ("Bettie") Graham, of Wythe County, Virginia, born September 1, 1845; died June 15, 1921. He died July 16, 1906, at his home in Wythe County. He was a man of the finest type—one of the outstanding men of his day in that section of the state.

CHILDREN:

(a) David Graham, born September 24, 1868; died November 28, 1928; married, April 19, 1892, Julia Rebecca Gill, of Baltimore, Md., who died March 22, 1897. He afterwards married Sarah Price, of Prince Edward County, Va. No children by this marriage.

CHILDREN BY FIRST MARRIAGE:

(aa) Agnes.
(bb) Julia; married Auther Koch, of Minersville, Pa.
(cc) Rufus; deceased.

(b) Malcom G., born September 7, 1870; died June 25, 1925; married (first) Maggie Stuart Raper, of Wythe County, Va., who died August 3, 1896. No children by this marriage. He married (second) Maggie Taylor Crockett.

CHILDREN:

(aa) Virginia Lewis; married Lewellen Harvey, of Richmond, Va.
(bb) Elizabeth; married William Bond, of Richmond, Va.

      (cc) Margaret.

      (dd) Malcolm G.

(c) Harry G., born July 19, 1872; died September 15, 1918; married, June 18, 1907, Emily Brown Miller, of Wytheville, Va.   CHILDREN:

      (aa) Frances.

      (bb) Bettie.

      (cc) Harriet.

(d) Ernest G., born October 16, 1874; married, March 30, 1911, Laura Keene Gleaves, of Wytheville, Va. He is a prominent business man at Max Meadows, Va. No children by this union.

(e) John W., Jr., born December 13, 1876; married, December 24, 1891, Nannie Councilman, of Wythe County, Va.

CHILD:

      (aa) Miriam; married T. E. Simmerman, of Wythe County, Va.

(f) Julia G., born February 15, 1879; married, October 12, 1905, Dr. Paul Kernan, of Norton, Va.

CHILDREN:

      (aa) John Robinson.

      (bb) Elizabeth Krema.

(g) Mary Belle, born March 5, 1881; married, April 10, 1906, Campbell C. Hyatte, of Jonesville, Va.

CHILDREN:

      (aa) Campbell C., Jr.

      (bb) Bettie.

      (cc) Ann.

      (dd) John R.

      (ee) Mary Belle.

(h) Elizabeth G., born September 11, 1883; married, April 30, 1907, John Ingles, of Radford, Va.

CHILDREN:

      (aa) Bettie.

      (bb) Angeline.

      (cc) John.

(2) James Madison Abraham, born 1835, died 1892; married in 1859, Elizabeth Mary Morgan, born 1839, died in 1923, daughter of Samuel and Elizabeth Ann (Bernard) Morgan.

CHILDREN:

(a) William Henry; married Elinor Montgomery. He died in 1902.

CHILD:

(aa) Elizabeth Lewis; married Allen Kessenger. They have three children, a girl and two boys.

(b) Mary Bernard; married, February 18, 1885, Charles Ellis Finch, born December 16, 1853, in Wilmington, N. C., a son of Gilbert Lafayette Mortier Finch, a prominent Baptist minister (born September 15, 1824, in Louisberg, N. C.; died October 30, 1863), and Sarah Ellis (born April 25, 1829, in Wilmington, N. C.; died March 5, 1890). Charles Ellis Finch died in Norfolk, Virginia, August 20, 1928.

CHILDREN:

(aa) Charles Ellis Finch, Jr., born January 30, 1886, in Bristol, Va., a graduate of Virginia Polytechnic Institute. Unmarried. Defective eyesight and hearing since childhood—now sightless.

(bb) James Lafayette Finch, born January 1, 1887; died in Norfolk, Va., April 25, 1892.

(cc) Henry Bridges Finch, born January 30, 1889; married, November 22, 1916, Marie Mahone.

They have one child:

(aaa) Marie Mahone Finch.

(c) Charles Wharton; died in infancy.

(d) Edgar Morgan; married Mary Esther Edwards. She died in 1916 and he died in 1928.

CHILD:

(aa) Esther Morgan; married Wallace Towe. They have one child:

(aaa) Frances Elizabeth.

(e) Claude Raymond; married Elizabeth Landreth.

CHILDREN:

    (aa) Samuel Landreth.

    (bb) James Madison.

    (cc) Elizabeth.

  (f) John Ellis (twin); married Almeda King. No children.

  (g) Eldred Herbert (twin); married Mary Allen Pierce.

CHILDREN:

    (aa) Evelyn Herbert.

    (bb) Samuel Allen.

    (cc) James Madison.

    (dd) Eldred Herbert, Jr.

  (h) Samuel Allen; died in 1909.

  (i) Emma Lewis; married Hampden Warwick Scott, son of Dr. Samuel Burke and Sallie Donald (Patteson) Scott. Living near Lynchburg, Va. No children.

(3) Clay; unmarried.

(4) Emma Cornelia; married W. A. B. Hill.

CHILDREN:

  (a) Samuel Roger; married Willie Chapman Mitchell.

CHILDREN:

    (aa) Roger Chapman.

    (bb) Mary Bell; married Burdett Holmes.

  (b) Willie Wilburn; married Joseph Tuley Wright. Living in Woodville, Mississippi.

CHILDREN:

    (aa) Mary Belinda; died infant.

    (bb) Joseph Tuley, Jr.; married Elsie Lambert. Have two children: Joseph Tuley, 4th, and Shirley.

    (cc) Virginia Marguerite; married Van Dyke Brooke. He died 1929. No children.

    (dd) Laurence; in school George Washington University, Washington, D. C.

    (ee) Roger; in school in Memphis, Tenn.

  (c) Jacob Robinson; married Dollie Kinter, Falls Creek, Pa.

CHILD:

(aa) Emma Rebecca.

(d) Effie Hope; unmarried. Lives in Scotland.

(5) Eldridge Herbert, Jr.; married (first) Margurite Hall, (second) Elva Quesenberry; all deceased.

CHILDREN BY FIRST MARRIAGE:

(a) Mary.

(b) Herbert, deceased.

(c) John, deceased.

(d) Hugh.

(e) Roland.

(f) Margurite.

(g) Ann.

CHILD BY SECOND MARRIAGE:

(h) Heiter.

....

Some records found in a Bible that once belonged to Abraham and Nancy R. (White) Robinson, now in the possession of Mr. Ernest G. Robinson, of Max Meadows, Va. Part of the pages containing the records are torn off; but the following are an exact copy of the remaining half all in good condition and well written. (M. D. A.)

MARRIAGES:

Abraham Robinson and Nancy White, his wife were married August the 15 in the year of our Lord 1805 in the 22 and sixteenth years of their ages.

BIRTHS:

William W. Robinson, son of Abraham and Nancy, his wife, was born September the 12, 1807.

Lucinda S. Robinson was born October the 8, in the year 1809.

Eldred H. Robinson was born October the 9, in the year 1811.

Jacob H. Robinson was born October the 10, in the year 1814.

Rebeckah N. Robinson was born August the 4, in the year 1817.

(Page torn here; but enough seen to know this was not the last entry on the page.)

DEATHS:

Abraham Robinson died November the 26th, 1821, in the thirty-seventh year of his age.

Rebecah H. Robinson died February 6th, 1827, in the tenth year of her age.

Nancy Spinner died May the 8th, 1831, in the forty-second year of her age.

....

The following are marriages of the children of Benjamin Robinson and Mar. (North) Robinson from Bedford County records:

Abraham Robinson and Nancy R. White, daughter of Jacob White. 28 October 1805. (John White, security.)

John White and Elizabeth Robinson, daughter of Benjamin Robinson. 4 April 1808. (John Robinson, security.)

Jesse Jeter and Susan Robinson, daughter of Benjamin Robinson. 17 December 1821.

John S. Poindexter married Nancy Robinson, daughter of Benjamin N. Robinson. (See Poindexter family.)

MARTIN PARKS BURKS, SR.

SPINNER-BURKS

Jesse Spinner came from Goochland County to Bedford where he became a wealthy land owner. He was a man of fine mind, honorable and highly esteemed. He married (first) Celia (or Sillah) Cheatwood, daughter of William Cheatwood, of Powhatan County. After the death of his first wife, he married (second) Nancy R. (White) Robinson, daughter of Captain Jacob and Hannah (Spiers) White, and the widow of Abraham Robinson. (See White and Robinson families.) She died May 8, 1831; and on November 15, 1832, he married his third wife, Lucinda (Douglas) Clayton, widow of John Willis Clayton, Jr., and a daughter of George and Mary Douglas. (See Douglas and Clayton families.)

CHILD BY FIRST MARRIAGE:

(1) Louisa Claiborne. (See forward.)

CHILDREN BY SECOND MARRIAGE:

(2) Anne, born October 21, 1828; never married.
(3) Jesse Frank, born September 27, 1829. (See forward.)
(4) Martha Davis, born May 3, 1831; married Captain George Tillman Snead, son of Moses and Martha (Yates) Snead. (See Snead family for descendants.)

....

Louisa Claiborne Spinner, daughter of Jesse Spinner and his first wife Celia (or Sillah) Cheatwood, married (first) William Gooch, of Goochland County and (second), January 18, 1820, Martin Parks Burks, of Bedford County, a son of Samuel Burks and Margaret Parks, of Amherst County, who were married December 21, 1789.

The Virginia Law Register (September, 1897) records the following:

"Martin Parks Burks, Sr., was a man of the highest character, of excellent sense, and one time the senior in commission of the justices of the old Bedford County Court, a tribunal before which the best lawyers of Virginia delighted to practice, and whose judgments were rarely reversed.

His wife was a type of the Virginia matron and housewife of her day. She had a family of nine sons. In addition to these she had the care of a large number of slaves, and reared seven others in her family. Yet with the cares incident to the management of this large family, she performed her duties with such ease and grace that no one under her control ever felt that he was controlled at all."

CHILDREN BY SECOND MARRIAGE:

(1) Edward Callohill, born May 20, 1821; died July 4, 1897; married, October 15, 1845, Mildred Elizabeth Buford (born November 19, 1822; died January 4, 1873), daughter of Captain Paschal Buford and Frances Ann Otey. (See Buford family.)

The Virginia Law Register (September, 1897) records the following:

"Judge Edward Callohill Burks first attended 'The Old Field Schools' of Virginia, in some of these, classics were taught, and he commenced the study of them when only ten or eleven years old. He afterwards studied for several sessions at New London Academy, in the fall of 1838 he matriculated at Washington College (now Washington and Lee University), Lexington, Va., and was graduated from there in 1841, having been chosen to deliver the Cincinnati Oration, the highest honor of his class at the time of his graduation. In the fall of 1841, he went to the University and entered the law class under Prof. Henry St. George Tucker. Here he graduated in one session, taking the degree of Bachelor of Laws in the summer of 1842. He practiced law in Liberty, Bedford County, Va. He was too frail to enter the army (1861-1865), but from a sense of duty consented to go to the Legislature. He was elected Judge of the Court of Appeals in 1876, and was one of the Codifiers of the law of the State."

In 1891 Judge Burks was elected president of the Virginia Bar Association, and in 1895 he founded, and became editor of *The Virginia Law Journal.*

He died in Bedford City (formerly Liberty), July 4, 1897, at the home of his daughter, Mrs. Frances C. Kasey, with whom he had lived since the death of his wife, many years before.

Children of Edward Callohill and Mildred Elizabeth (Buford) Burks were:

      (a) Frances Claiborne, born November 5, 1847; died January 22, 1916; married, April 14, 1870, John Singleton

Kasey (born February 17, 1842; died March 23, 1898), son of Alexander and Marcella (Cundiff) Kasey. (See Cundiff family.)

Frances C. Burks Kasey was never physically strong, and during her last years was practically a shut-in. Her memory was remarkably good, and one of her pleasures was to gather her children and their friends about her on winter evenings before a big open fire, and, while she busily plied her knitting needles, tell them tales of her young life, of the Civil War, and of the doings about town "before their day."

One story that they never tired of hearing was of Hunter's Raid during the Civil War. This was Bedford's only real war experience and it was also recounted, for many, many years, in sick rooms for the pleasure of convalescent patients by "Aunt Ellen Terry," a typical "black mammy" and a good nurse, who was a slave of Judge G. A. Wingfield "in time o' the War" and lived across the road from "Woodford," the home of Judge Burks.

HUNTER'S RAID

On their way from the Valley of Virginia to Lynchburg, Hunter and his men crossed the mountains between the Peaks of Otter and marched through Liberty, setting fire to the depot, tobacco factories, and saw mills as they went. They were met in Lynchburg by General Jubal A. Early and turned back.

When the people of Liberty heard that the enemy was returning, they feared the town would be shelled, and many of the women and children on the south side of the town fled for protection to "Woodford," the home of Judge Burks, which was on the hill just south of the town.

The raiders marched in that direction and drew up in line of battle on Burks' Hill. The Confederate forces were on Piedmont Hill, just east of the town. The women and children who had gone to "Woodford" for protection, were driven from the house and out in front of the enemy, between the two firing lines, and made to lift their skirts, so that the Confederate soldiers could see their white petticoats and know that they were women, and thus put an end to the firing.

After the women left the house, the raiders entered it and searched the smokehouse, closets, cellar, pantry, etc., and finding some men's underwear in the bureau drawers, they tied knots in the legs of the slips, filled them with flour, meal, and sugar, and, placing them in front of them on their horses, rode away. The things they could not carry with them, they piled in the middle of the cellar floor and poured molasses and kerosene oil over them.

Judge Burks was a member of the Legislature at this time, and when he heard that Hunter was coming this way, he left home, knowing that he would be captured by the enemy if he remained, so his wife and small children were unprotected, except by the slaves. Realizing that with Yankees all about her, she could not spend the night at home, she took her children and started to a nearby farm house. On the way she was overcome by fatigue and excitement and sat down on a rail of a fence to rest, with her little boys on either side of her, and in a moment a minie ball, fired by the enemy, whizzed within a foot of her head.

Reaching the home of the neighbor she asked to be allowed to spend the night, but was refused admission and made her little family as comfortable as possible on the front porch.

The next morning, when she returned to her home, she found everything in confusion—the Yankees were gone, but they had left desolation in their wake.

> "Who bade us go with smiling tears?
> Who scorned the renegade,
> Who, silencing their trembling fears,
> Watched, cheered, wept, and prayed?
> Who nursed our wounds with tender care,
> And then, when all was lost,
> Who lifted us from our despair
> And counted not the cost?
> THE WOMEN OF THE SOUTH."

Children of John Singleton Kasey and Frances C. (Burks) Kasey:

    (aa) Kate Singleton Kasey, born May 29, 1871; married, December 31, 1890, John Scruggs Burks, son of Samuel Jackson and Aurelia (McClure) Burks.

CHILDREN:

    (aaa) Buford Singleton Burks, born August 29, 1892; married, September 5, 1925,

Susan Doswell Epes. He is now a popular dentist of Crewe, Va.

Dr. Burks enlisted in the World War, May 27, 1918. Was appointed Corporal, June 15, 1918, and Sergeant July 13, 1918. Sailed for France July 17, 1918—arriving in France July 27, 1918, and was stationed at Le Mans, France, where he was attached to the 323rd Machine Gun Battalion. Sent to school for two months, after which he did interpreting work the rest of the time of the war. Honorably discharged the 15th of April, 1919.

(bbb) John Sale Burks, born May 18, 1895; married in Bonham, Texas, November 5, 1925, Nina White. They live in Bonham, Texas. He was a World War soldier.

(bb) Margaret Burks Kasey, born January 23, 1874; married, November 25, 1896, Dr. James Elliott Walmsley, who at that time was a teacher at Randolph-Macon Academy, Bedford, Va.

The following article is taken from "Who's Who in America, 1928":

"James Elliott Walmsley, born June 24, 1873, son of Rev. Columbus Steele and Harriet See (Stalnaker) Walmsley; A. B., Randolph-Macon College, 1893, A. M., 1894; Ph. D., Illinois Wesleyan University, 1909. Instructor Randolph-Macon Academy, 1894-96; professor history and political science, Kentucky Wesleyan College, 1896-1903; Millsaps College, Jackson, Miss., 1903-12; professor history, Winthrop College, S. C., 1912-25; professor history and political science, State Teachers College, Farmville, Va., since 1925. Member History Association of South Carolina; Virginia History Teachers Association (president, Kappa Alpha, Pi Gamma Mu, Pi Kappa Delta) (governor South Carolina province); Associate Editor, Social Science; contributor to Dictionary of American Biography. Author, European

History (800-1911), 1911; The Making of South Carolina, 1921; The Shadow of the Mighty Peaks, 1922; also brochures and historial articles."

CHILDREN:

(aaa) Margaret, born December 9, 1894; married Joseph Louis Bellus. They live in New York and have two children— Margaret and Dorothy.

(bbb) Frances, born April 13, 1907.

(cc) Bettie Buford, born May 4, 1877; died May 7, 1917; married George Winston Schenk, January 14, 1909.

CHILDREN:

(aaa) Mary Buford, born January 26, 1910.

(bbb) George Winston, Jr., born April 2, 1912.

(ccc) Bessie Singleton, born August 4, 1913.

(ddd) John Beryl, born September 13, 1916.

(dd) Louise Claiborne, born May 29, 1884; died December 17, 1914; married, February 24, 1911, William Vincent Jordan, son of Henry Vincent and Mary (Buford) Jordan.

CHILDREN:

(aaa) Frances Elizabeth.

(bbb) Louise Claiborne.

(b) Edward Callohill, Jr., born May 30, 1849; died August 20, 1877; married, March 5, 1875, Josephine Porterfield Bell, daughter of Orville P. and Nannie (Gladding) Bell. (See Bell family.)

CHILDREN:

(aa) Orville Gladding; died in youth.

(bb) Edward Callohill, III, born in October 1877; married, October 25, 1904, Virginia McClaren Mosby, daughter of William H. and Lucy (Boothe) Mosby.

JUDGE MARTIN PARKS BURKS

JUDGE EDWARD CALLOHILL BURKS

CHILDREN:

(aaa) Josephine Bell; married, October 25, 1928, Benjamin Vincent Pearman.
(bbb) Virginia Mosby.
(ccc) Elizabeth Gladding.
(ddd) Nancy Stuart.

(c) Martin Parks, born January 23, 1851; died April 30, 1928. He was educated at "Sunnyside," a boys' school near his home at Liberty, Va., taught by Rev. Alexander Eubank; at Washington and Lee University; and at the University of Virginia, where he completed the two years law course in one year. He began the practice of his profession in his home town—Liberty—in 1872. In 1899 he accepted a position as a member of the law faculty of Washington and Lee University, and in 1903 was made dean of that faculty. In 1917 he was appointed, by Governor Stuart, to the bench of the Supreme Court, and was later elected by the General Assembly for a full term of twelve years.

Judge Burks held the degree of LL.D. from Roanoke College and from Washington and Lee University. He was one of the revisors of the Code of Laws of Virginia in 1919.

He married December 31, 1874, Roberta Gamble Bell, daughter of Orville P. and Nannie (Gladding) Bell. (See Bell family.)

CHILDREN:

(aa) Elizabeth Gladding; died in childhood.
(bb) Martin Parks, Jr.; married, February 4, 1909, Laura Mangum Ogesby.

CHILDREN:

(aaa) Martin Parks, III.
(bbb) Albert Ogesby.
(ccc) Laura Mangum.
(ddd) Edward Callohill, IV.

(d) Paschal Buford; died unmarried.

(e) Elizabeth Blackburn (Nora); married, June 15, 1887, Alexander Spotswood Payne.

CHILD:

(aa) Nora Burks; married William Ragland Hill, and had one son:

(aaa) Russell Spotswood.

(f) Margaret; died unmarried.

(g) Rowland; married Eliza F. Lloyd.

CHILD:

(aa) Eliza Fontaine.

(2) Jesse Spinner, born March 20, 1823. Attended Washington College, one year and graduated from Virginia Military Institute, in 1844. Helped to organize the 42nd Virginia Regiment of which he was Colonel; was honorably discharged after the battle of Kernstown, in which he was injured. He served in the Virginia Legislature, 1853-54, and again in 1874-75-76-77. He was married three times. Married (first), December 3, 1845, in St. Charles County, Mo., Elizabeth Royal Otey, daughter of William L. and Mary Gwatkin (Logwood) Otey. (Three sons by this marriage.) Married (second), February 17, 1855, Charlotte F. Thomson, daughter of Jesse L. and Rhoda Morris (Wharton) Thomson. (See Thomson family.) Seven children by this union. In 1883 he married for his third wife, Mrs. Mary J. (Tinsley) Claggett, of Powhatan County, Va. No children by this marriage. He died at his home "Rockhaven," Bedford County, June 15, 1885, and is buried at St. Thomas's Episcopal Church near his home.

CHILDREN BY FIRST MARRIAGE:

(a) Thomas Otey, born October 26, 1846; died June 26, 1847.

(b) William Parks, born July 29, 1848. Now living at "Rockhaven," the old home of his father. He married (first) Elizabeth C. Gray, of Maryland and had one son. He married (second), December 4, 1901, Edmonia Arrington, daughter of J. W. Arrington, of Bedford. No children by this marriage.

CHILD BY FIRST MARRIAGE:

(aa) Harry Gray, who married Elizabeth Watts, daughter of John H. and Rebecca (Hurt) Watts.

> CHILDREN:
>
> (aaa) Harry Gray, Jr.; educated at University of Virginia and Boston "Tech."
> (bbb) William Watts; married Anna Haile.
> (ccc) Rebecca; A. B. of Randolph-Macon Woman's College.
> (ddd) Philip Parks, B. L. of University of Virginia; now practicing law with Landon Lowry in Bedford, Va.
> (eee) George Beverly; now a student at Hampden-Sidney College.

(c) Alonza Otey, born March 9, 1850; married Mattie Burks. Both now deceased. Had five sons and one daughter.

CHILDREN BY SECOND MARRIAGE:

(d) Ida Temple; married Hunt Tardy. Both died in St. Louis, Mo.

(e) Edward Lewis; died unmarried.

(f) Mary Campbell; unmarried; lives in St. Louis, Mo.

(g) Sallie Thomson; married Otto Eisenhart; lives in St. Louis, Mo.

> CHILDREN:
>
> (aa) Lucille Eisenhart.
> (bb) Edward Eisenhart.

(h) Kate Davis; married George Logan; lives in Salem, Va.

> CHILDREN:
>
> (aa) Jesse Burks Logan.
> (bb) Charlotte Wharton Logan.
> (cc) Katharine Tardy Logan.

(i) Minnie B.; unmarried; lives in St. Louis, Mo.

(j) Charlotte F.; died young.

(3) John Dabney, born April 2, 1826; died in 1912 at his home near Charlemont, Bedford County, Va. He was educated by private tutors. He married, December 12, 1849, Dolly Waller Cheatwood, daughter of Hiram and Harriett (McDaniel) Cheatwood, of Amherst and Bedford counties. He was for many years Justice of the Peace, and a member of the Board of Supervisors. He served in Company C, 28th Virginia Infantry, C. S. A.

CHILDREN:

(a) Georgiana McDaniel; married Robert H. Major. Deceased.

(b) Robert L.; married Mrs. Nannie (Hurt) Chamin, daughter of William O. and Sarah Hurt. Deceased.

(c) William Sherman, born September 24, 1856; married, February 28, 1883, Lemira Susan Douglas, born January 7, 1857, eldest daughter of Robert Henry W., and Elizabeth Ann (Major) Douglas, of Bedford County, Virginia. (See Douglas family.)

CHILDREN:

(aa) Nina McDaniel Burks, born February 26, 1884; married, March 3, 1917, Horsley Barnes Camden, born August 14, 1893, son of Horsley Barnes and Willie T. Camden, of Bedford County.

CHILDREN:

(aaa) Sherman Burks Camden, born May 2, 1918.

(bbb) Heyden Barnes Camden, born June 1, 1920.

(ccc) Dorothy Leigh Camden, born October 15, 1924.

(bb) Nannie Acree Burks, born August 2, 1886; died August 1, 1888.

(cc) Infant (not named), born August 19, 1888.

(dd) Annie Cheatwood Burks, born September 26, 1889; died September 4, 1890.

(ee) William Sherman Burks, Jr., born January 6, 1894; died October 21, 1918, in France from wounds received in battle during the World War.

(d) Hiram Parks; married May P. Wright, daughter of Wm. H. Wright, of Bedford County.

(e) Louisa Spinner; unmarried.

(f) Harriet Cheatwood; unmarried.

(4) Martin Parks, Jr., born July 15, 1828; died December 18, 1839. (Thrown from a horse.)

(5) Samuel, born October 1, 1830; died January 18, 1833. (Died from burns.)

(6) Wm. Lynchfield,. born November 30, 1832; died February 19, 1876. He married, April 23, 1860, Maria Louisa Sale, daughter of Dr. Richard Sale, of Bedford. He enlisted April 3, 1863, in Company C, 28th Virginia Infantry, C. S. A., and served till the close of the war.

CHILDREN:

(a) Martha, born December 5, 1865; married, April 12, 1887, Marshall U. Griggs, born March 29, 1863, son of Samuel and Eva Kefauver Griggs, of Roanoke County, Va. She died February 9, 1913, and on April 29, 1914, Mr. Griggs married for his second wife, Miss Bettie M. Collins, daughter of William J. and Amanda Price (Rice) Collins, of Bedford County. He died April 1, 1917. There were no children by the second marriage.

CHILDREN BY FIRST MARRIAGE:

(aa) Samuel, born July 17, 1888; died June 12, 1890.

(bb) Lynchfield Burks, born October 3, 1889; died May 9, 1890.

(cc) Clarence Marshall, born October 25, 1890; married, June 9, 1915, Hallie Meade. She died June 26, 1922. Left issue.

(dd) Douglas Merriwether, born May 22, 1892; married, November 27, 1917, Douglas Smith Crafford. She died August 15, 1928, leaving an infant son, Douglas, Jr.

(ee) John Franklin, born April 12, 1894; married, December 14, 1914, Ruth Meade. They have several children.

(ff) William Claude, born October 25, 1896; married, September 23, 1927, Wilda Kunkle.

(gg) Louis Wharton, born March 18, 1901. Studying for the ministry.

(hh) Richard Sale, born August 8, 1902.

(b) Richard Albert; married Annie D. Griggs, daughter of Samuel and Eva Kefauver Griggs, of Roanoke County. He is deceased. Left issue.

(c) William Lynchfield, Jr.; married Willie Watson, daughter of Barney C. Watson. He is deceased. Left issue.

(d) John Franklin; married (first) Miss Fisher, of Alexandria, Va. A minister of the Episcopal Church.

(7) Hiram Claiborne, born July 15, 1836; married, March 25, 1857, Charlotte Sale, daughter of Nelson and Anna A. (Wharton) Sale, of Bedford. He was educated at the Virginia Military Institute and served in Company G, 2nd Virginia Cavalry, C. S. A. Promoted to first lieutenant; made prisoner at Westminister, Md., and sent to Fort Delaware, thence to Johnson's Island, thence to Point Lookout and again to Fort Delaware. Discharged June, 1865.

CHILDREN:

(a) Annie M.; married ———— Dean, of Kansas; deceased.

(b) Lucy C.; married ————.

(c) Sallie S.; married Wm. De Witt.

(d) Jesse S.; married Ottie M. Cornelius, daughter of Wm. R. and Eliza S. Cornelius. (See Douglas-Sledd families.)

(e) Channing L.; married ———— James, of Chicago.

(f) Nelson; unmarried.

(g) Fannie S.; married Gordon Seay, of Roanoke; deceased.

(h) Virginia W.; married Gordon Seay, of Roanoke.

(8) Albert Sherman, born March 17, 1838; died April 11, 1913. He attended New London Academy, also Prof. Winston's School near Lynchburg, Va., known as the Westwood Academy. He finished under Gen. Pendleton, who at that time conducted a

school at Lexington, Va. He enlisted in Company C, 28th Virginia Infantry, C. S. A., May 15, 1861. This Company became Capt. C. M. Bowyer's Company, about August 20, 1861, and later became J. R. Johnson's Company, Virginia Light Artillery. The latter being disbanded October 4, 1862. He was then transferred to Captain Pegram's Company, Light Artillery. Discharged November 12, 1862, sending a substitute. He married (first), June 2, 1869, Virginia Catherine Rucker, daughter of James Monroe and Marinda (McDaniel) Rucker, of Bedford, Va. Married (second) in April, 1884, Mary Emma McDaniel, daughter of Judge John R. McDaniel, of Campbell County, Va.

CHILDREN BY FIRST MARRIAGE:

(a) Cornelia Waller; married, July 14, 1903, Willis Howard Dillard, of Nelson County. No children. Living in Lynchburg, Va.

(b) John Lodowick; married, February 21, 1906, Evelyn Marshall, daughter of Dr. E. L. Marshall, of Bedford County. Living in Bluefield, W. Va. Two children:
 (aa) Dorothy Virginia.
 (bb) Lionel Lodowick.

(c) Margaret Elizabeth; married, October 3, 1901, Sloan Lewis Stroud, of South Carolina. Living in Lynchburg, Va. One child, Virginia Burks Stroud; married, September 12, 1928, Dr. J. W. Nuttycombe, of Charlottesville, Va. Now Prof. University of Tenn, Knoxville, Tenn.

(d) Charles Albert; married, January 6, 1913, Grace Young, daughter of Dr. Benj. F. Young, of Knoxville, Tenn. Children:
 (aa) Cornelia.
 (bb) Elizabeth (Betty).
 (cc) Charles Cheatwood.

(e) Leighton Cheatwood; never married. Died at Lexington, Ky., May 14, 1928.

(f) Ernest Rucker; married, May 13, 1911, Mary M. ("Doll") May, daughter of Sam'l. May, of Tazewell, Va. Living in Bluefield, W. Va. Children:

(aa) Ernest Rucker, Jr.
(bb) Leighton Jackson.

CHILDREN BY SECOND MARRIAGE:

(g) Wellington Sherman, Charleston, W. Va.
(h) Herbert McDaniel, Princeton, W. Va.
(i) Temple Pendleton, Mullens, W. Va.

(9) George Wellington, born April 4, 1840; died September 5, 1912.
Educated at New London and Westwood Academies and fin-
ished under Gen. Pendleton at Lexington, Virginia. He served
first in Company C, 28th Virginia Infantry, C. S. A., and later
21st Virginia Cavalry. Was under Gen. McCausland at the
Battle of Lynchburg. Married, November 20, 1867, Harriet
("Hallie") Eliza Hopkins, daughter of Edward and Lucy
(Cheatwood) Hopkins, of Amherst County, Virginia.

CHILDREN:

(a) Harriet Louise; died young.
(b) Lucy Elizabeth; married, October 10, 1886, Granville
Beauregard Parks.

CHILDREN:

(aa) Harry Ashby Parks; married, May 7, 1919,
Katie Vernon Wildman, of Bedford County.
Have three children:
(aaa) Louise Elizabeth.
(bbb) James Beauregard.
(ccc) Nancy Lee.
(bb) William Wellington Parks; married, October 17,
1918, Jettie Pearl Carter. Have two children:
(aaa) Dorothy Jean.
(bbb) Ruth Elizabeth.
(cc) Lucy Lee Parks; married, February 16, 1918,
Ferdinand Clayton Ford, of Lynchburg, Va.
Have two children:
(aaa) William Clayton Ford.
(bbb) Allan Parks Ford.

(c) Sue Lelia; deceased.
(d) Edward Richard, born November 7, 1874; married,

December 18, 1902, Sallie White Douglas, born November 3, 1878, daughter of Robert Henry W., and Elizabeth Ann (Major) Douglas, of Bedford County, Va. (See Douglas family.)

CHILDREN:

(aa) Robert Wellington Burks, born October 3, 1903.
(bb) Douglas Harriett Burks, born June 14, 1905; married, October 29, 1923, Waller S. Perrow, born February 17, 1900, son of Waller S. and Willie (Walker) Perrow. They have one child:
　(aaa) Betty Burks Perrow, born September 5, 1925.
(cc) Dan Randolph Burks, born March 15, 1912.
(dd) Louise Cheatwood Burks, born September 7, 1914.
(ee) Claude McDaniel Burks, born May 8, 1916.
(e) Frank Wellington; married, September 15, 1909, Sallie Wheat, of Bedford County.

CHILDREN:

(aa) Hallie Burks.
(bb) Frances Burks.
(cc) Reed Smith Burks.
(dd) Mary Burks.
(ee) Doris Burks.
(f) Mary Waller; never married; deceased.
(g) Roberta Leighton; married, March 12, 1905, Thomas Marvin Turpin, son of Thomas M. ("Tom Phil") and Caroline W. (Penn) Turpin. (See Penn and Turpin families.)
(h) Paschal Buford; married Kate Bullard, of North Carolina. Living at Roseboro, North Carolina.

CHILDREN:

(aa) Margaret Carroll Burks.
(bb) Paschal Buford Burks, Jr.
(cc) Annie Dean Burks.
(dd) Edward Burks.

(i) Martin Parks; served in the World War; died the year following the Armistice.

(j) Annie Dean; deceased.

Dr. Jesse Frank Spinner, born September 27, 1829, only son of Jesse Spinner and his second wife, Nancy R. (White) Robinson; married, November 17, 1852, Martha Judson Snead, born September 15, 1833, daughter of Moses and Martha (Yates) Snead. (See Snead family.) Dr. Spinner practiced his profession in Bedford County, where he was eminently successful and highly esteemed for his many sterling qualities.

CHILDREN:

(1) Annie Marshall; married, February 28, 1882, Thomas Mosby Turpin (called "Tom Henry"), son of Spotswood Henry and Lucetta (Lambert) Turpin, of Bedford County. (See Turpin family for descendants.)

(2) Sophie; unmarried.

(3) Dr. William; married (first) Miss Genevieve Adams; (second) Miss Nannie Lackes. For a number of years, he practiced medicine at Montvale, Bedford County. Now deceased. There were no children by either marriage.

(4) Julia Gertrude; married her cousin, Ceril Davis White, son of John Milton and Mary Virginia White. (See White family for descendants.)

(5) Frank Lee, born May 25, 1863; married, November 29, 1893, Ida Boxley, born August 9, 1875, daughter of E. D. and Mary C. Boxley.

CHILDREN:

(a) Marion; married C. H. Thurber and have one son:
    (aa) Jack Thurber.

(b) Reeves Boxley.

(c) William Sherman; married Mary Frances Handly.

CHILDREN:

(aa) Frank Lee Spinner, II.

(bb) Virginia Ellener.

(6) Loula; married James Daniel Brown, of Bedford. There were several children by this union.

Marriages in Bedford County, Virginia, in family surnamed Burks:
John Burks and Mary Stevens, 1 May 1786. Phillips Owens, security on marriage license bond.

Moses Blackwell and Nancy Burks, 18 January 1799, by Rev. James Turner. Joseph Holt, security.

Nathaniel D. Burks and Elizabeth John, 25 January 1810, by Revd. George Rucker. Robert Tinsley, security.

Robert Burks and Sally City, 29 April 1818, by Revd. James Scott. Jacob City, security.

Martin P. Burks and Louisa C. Gooch (widow), daughter Jesse Spinner, 15 January 1820. Charles M. Christian, security.

Charles L. Burks and Levinia P. Cheatwood, 21 November 1821, by Revd. Enoch W. Terry. Martin P. Burks, security.

Henry Burks and Sally Smith, 19 August 1822. Wm. Tinsley, security.

David Burks and Elizabeth Wilkerson, 7 November 1822, by Revd. Enoch W. Terry.

John P. Burks and Judith Tinsley, 25 November 1826. Absalom Tinsley, security.

Samuel Burks and Sarah Ann Millner, daughter Wm. Millner, 16 October 1829.

Edward C. Burks and Mildred E. Buford, daughter Paschal and Frances A. Buford, 15 October 1845. John W. Holt, Jr., security.

George M. Burks and Martha A. Burton, daughter James L. Burton, 15 August 1849. John W. Burton, security.

John D. Burks and Dolly W. Cheatwood, daughter Hiram Cheatwood, 7 December 1849. John W. Sherman, security.

William R. Scott and Louisa V. Burks, 15 January 1851, by Revd. Nelson Sale (daughter of Charles L. and Levinia P. (Cheatwood) Burks).

Jesse S. Burks and Elizabeth Royall Otey, daughter William L. and Mary Gwatkin Otey (Mr. Burks' first marriage in Missouri).

Jesse S. Burks and Charlotte F. Thomson, daughter Jesse L. and Rhoda M. Thomson, 1 February 1855, by Revd. Nelson Sale (Mr. Burks' second marriage).

Jesse S. Burks and Molly J. Claggett (widow), daughter Peter and Jane R. Tinsley (Mr. Burks' third marriage).

Hiram C. Burks and Charlotte A. Sale, daughter Nelson and Ann A. Sale, 25 March 1857, by Revd. Richard Wilmer.

William L. Burks and Mariah L. Sale, daughter Richard A. Sale, 23 April 1860, by Revd. John A. Wharton.

John S. Kasey and Fannie C. Burks, daughter Edward C. and Mildred E. Burks, 14 April 1869, by Revd. John A. Wharton.

Albert S. Burks and Virginia C. Rucker, daughter James M. and Marinda Rucker, 2 June 1869, by Revd. R. N. Sledd.

Robert H. Major and Georgie McD. Burks, daughter John D. and Dolly W. Burks, 8 November 1871, by Revd. Alexander S. Berkeley.

Edward C. Burks, Jr., and Josephine P. Bell, daughter Orville P. and Nannie P. Bell, 5 March 1874, by Revd. Henderson Suter.

Martin P. Burks and Roberta G. Bell, daughter Orville P. and Nannie P. Bell, 31 December 1874, by Revd. Henderson Suter.

Alonzo H. Tardy and Ida T. Burks, daughter Jesse S. and Charlotte S. Burks, 27 November 1878.

Robert W. Withers and Josephine P. Burks (widow), daughter Orville P. and Nannie P. Bell, 25 May 1882, by Revd. John K. Mason.

Alonzo O. Burks and Mattie L. Burks, daughter Charles L. and Mattie M. Burks, 17 May 1882, by Revd. John A. Wharton.

Richard A. Burks and Annie D. Grigg, daughter Samuel and Eva Grigg, 15 November 1882, by Revd. John A. Wharton.

William S. Burks and Lemma S. Douglass, daughter Robert H. and Elizabeth Douglass, 28 February 1883, by Revd. A. Judson Reamy.

Marshall U. Griggs and Martha W. Burks, daughter Wm. L. and Maria L. Burks, 12 April 1887, by Revd. ————.

Alexander Spottswood Payne and Nora Elizabeth Blackburn Burks, daughter Edward C. and Mildred E. Burks, 15 June 1887, by Revd. Robert W. Forsythe.

John S. Burks and Katie Singleton Kasey, daughter John S. and Frances C. Kasey, 31 December 1890, by Revd. Thomas W. Jones.

William M. DeWitt and Sallie S. Burks, daughter Hiram C. and Charlotte A. Burks, 7 September 1892, by Revd. Thomas W. Jones.

Jessee S. Burks (son of H. C. B.) and Ottawa M. Cornelius, daughter Wm. R. and Eliza Cornelius, 6 November 1895, by Rev. Thomas W. Jones.

Edward M. Burks and Emma C. Coleman, daughter George W. and Mildred F. Coleman, 5 February 1896, by Revd. S. J. Liggan.

Robert L. Burks and Nannie Chamin (widow), daughter Wm. O. and Sarah Hurt, 9 January 1896, by Revd. Charles M. Chumbley.

Harry G. Burks and Mary Elizabeth Watts, daughter John H. and Rebecca Watts, 28 December 1897, by Revd. Joseph W. Schackford.

William P. Burks and Edmonia Arrington, daughter J. W. and J. F. Arrington, 4 December 1901, by Revd. J. McD. Reynolds (second marriage).

Edward R. Burks and Sallie W. Douglass, daughter Robert H. and Bettie Douglass, 18 December 1902, by Revd. J. P. McCabe, Jr.

William L. Burks (son of Wm. L. and Mariah Burks) and Willie Watson, daughter Barney C. and M. C. Watson, 24 December 1903, by Revd. R. B. Scott.

Hiram P. Burks and May P. Wright, daughter Wm. H. and Emma Wright, 26 July 1904, by Revd. B. R. B. Scott.

Edward Calohill Burks, Jr., of first Jr., and Virginia McLaren Mosby, daughter Wm. H. and Lucy B. Mosby, 25 October 1904, by Revd. Dallas Tucker.

Thomas M. Turpin, Jr., and Bertha L. Burks, daughter Wellington and Harriett Burks, 12 March 1905, by Revd. Dallas Tucker.

John Lodowick Burks and Evelyn Louise Marshall, daughter Edward L. and Dorothy C. Marshall, 21 February 1906, by Revd. Dallas Tucker.

Frank W. Burks and Sallie Ethel Wheat, daughter Joseph F. and Eliza H. Wheat, 15 September 1909, by Revd. W. W. Royall.

Robert J. Burks and Clara Graves, daughter Peyton and Ossie M. Graves, 16 April 1910, by Revd. J. P. Luck.

Irvine W. Parr and Maria E. Burks, daughter Richard A. and Annie G. Burks, 29 May 1911, by Revd. J. F. Burks.

Andrew Jackson Burks and Annie Cornelia Neas, daughter W. C. and Mary W. Neas, 25 May 1915, by Revd. P. F. Arthur.

Harry Douglass Burks and Carrie Nichols, daughter William and Cynthia Ann Nichols, 13 August 1916, by Revd. Geo. E. Booker.

Samuel Dennis Burks and Laura Elizabeth Parks, daughter Frank and Pate Parks, 8 January 1917.

SNEAD

Sneyde, Snede, Snead or Sneed. Sneyds of Keel in the County of Stafford—a family whose lineage is as ancient as the valor of her sons is famous. Arms—argent, a scythe, the blade-in-chief, the sned, or handle, in bend sinister, sable; on the fesse point; a fleur-de-lis of the second.

> Crest: A lion passant,
> guardant sa.

> Motto: Nec opprimere nec opprimi
> (Neither to oppress, nor to be oppressed.)

Captain George Tillman Snead, born December 12, 1824, son of Moses and Martha (Yates) Snead and grandson of Jesse Snead near Richmond; married, March 12, 1851, Martha Davis Spinner, born May 3, 1831, second daughter of Jesse Spinner and his second wife, Nancy R. (White) Robinson. Nancy R. White was the second daughter of Captain Jacob and Hannah (Spiers) White and the widow of Abraham Robinson. (See White, Robinson, and Spinner families.)

For many years Captain George Tillman Snead lived in Bedford County. He later moved to Lynchburg, Va., where he died, October 10, 1892, and his wife the following year, May 20, 1893. Both were buried in Spring Hill Cemetery in that city. They were faithful members of the Big Island Baptist Church.

CHILDREN:

(1) Dr. Edward Franklin; married Mollie L. Couch; lived in Lynchburg, Va. He was a dentist by profession. Deceased.

CHILDREN:

   (a) Edward (deceased); married May Reaves, lived in Athens, Ga.

   (b) William C.; married ————.

   (c) Maude; married Charles A. Scott; living in Lynchburg, Va.

   (d) Lawrence; deceased.

(2) Nannie Marshall; married Otho W. Wheat, of Bedford County, Va.

CHILDREN:

(a) Harry (deceased); married Marie —————.
(b) Ward; deceased.
(c) Floy; married Frank Huddleston.
(d) Curtis; married Daisy Booth; living in Richmond, Va.
(e) Hugh; married Eunice Logwood; living in Bedford County, Va.
(f) Bessie; married Aubrey H. Camden, son of Horsely Barnes and Willie T. Camden, of Bedford County, Va. Live at Chatham, Va., where Major Camden is head of the Chatham Training School.

(3) Louisa Burks; married A. J. Trevy, of Bedford County. This was Mr. Trevy's first marriage. After the death of his wife, he married (second) Maizie Turpin, daughter of Thomas Nelson and Elizabeth (Harrison) Turpin, of Bedford County, Va. (See Turpin family for descendants of this marriage.)

CHILDREN:

(a) Lucille; married Thomas Nelson Turpin, Jr., son of Thomas Nelson and Elizabeth (Harrison) Turpin, of Bedford County, Va. (See Turpin family.) There was one son by this marriage:
(aa) Ray.
(b) Mary Lawrence; married Frank Faucett, of Amherst, Va.
(c) Maxwell; married Belle Jordan, daughter of Henry Jordan, of Bedford City, Va. (See Jordan family.)

(4) Dr. Charles Haddon Spurgeon; married Dollie Couch. He died several years ago in Lynchburg, Va., where he made his home. He was a prosperous druggist of that city.

CHILDREN:

(a) Charles Dabney; married Anna Lithicum, of Richmond, Va. Living in Montgomery, Alabama.
(b) Louise; married Frank K. McVeigh, of Lynchburg, Va., where they live.
(c) Etherton; deceased.
(d) Dr. George C.; married Grace Neff, of Wythe County, Va. Now practicing medicine at Moss, Va.

(e) William Haddon; married (first) Kittie Hancock; (second) Phyllis Robey. Living in Lynchburg, Va.

(5) Willie Eubank; married Mark Fletcher, of Upperville, Virginia, where they live.

CHILDREN:

(a) Snead; married Rose Beitzel Allen, of Washington, D. C.

(b) Martha; married her first cousin, Frank Spencer Snead, son of Henry C. and Nannie B. (Spencer) Snead, of Lynchburg, Va. They live at Covington, Va.

(c) Freda; unmarried.

(d) Kathleen; deceased.

(6) Georgie Tillman; unmarried; living in Lynchburg, Virginia. Authoress and teacher; has written several prose volumes and a book of poems. Her books have been accorded very high praise throughout the country. There is a peculiar charm to her style, and her writings are of the highest ideals and purity of thought.

(7) Roberta Lee, born March 9, 1863, in Smyth County, Virginia; married, November 1, 1882 at Big Island, Va., John Bunyan Cox, born July 13, 1853, a son of Dr. Robert Humber and Sarah Ann Cox, of Amherst County, Va. Roberta Lee (Snead) Cox, died at Big Island, Va., June 16, 1903.

CHILDREN:

(a) Elsie Edgeworth; married (first), May 1, 1904, Claude Hyte Ridings, son of W. H. and Frances Ridings, of Buena Vista, Virginia. Died August 11, 1909 at Buena Vista, Va. Married (second), October 9, 1915, Vernon Thaddeus Strickler, son of Reuben T. and Martha Ann Strickler, of Luray, Virginia. Living in Buena Vista, Va.

CHILDREN BY FIRST MARRIAGE:

(aa) Garvice Hyte, born July 9, 1905; married, August 7, 1928, at Buena Vista, Va., Emma Graham Dold, daughter of Dr. Charles Graham Dold and Linda (Manly) Dold. Living at Elizabeth, New Jersey.

(bb) Dorothy Snead, born December 2, 1906. Educated at State Teachers College, Harrisonburg. Now teaching in city school of Buena Vista, Va.

CHILD BY SECOND MARRIAGE:

(cc) Vernon Thaddeus Strickler, Jr., born June 13, 1917, at Buena Vista, Va.

(b) Robert Humber; married, September 22, 1909, at San Marcos, Texas, Trammell Jeannette Beall, daughter of Dr. Edward Foster and Flora (Eames) Beall. Living in Lynchburg, Va.

CHILDREN:

(aa) Flora Eames ("Texas"), born September 21, 1911 (twin).
(bb) Roberta Snead ("Virginia"), born September 21, 1911 (twin).
(cc) Robert Humber, Jr., born December 25, 1912.
(dd) Edward Beall, born July 15, 1915.
(ee) Elsie Claire, born January 6, 1917.
(ff) James Trammell, born August 25, 1921.

(c) John Bunyan, Jr.; married, August 25, 1921, at Brownsville, Tenn., Virginia Bond, daughter of William J. Thomas and Virginia Bond. Living in Lynchburg, Va.

CHILDREN:

(aa) John Bunyan Cox, III, born June 26, 1922.
(bb) Virginia Bond, born January 30, 1925.
(cc) Mamie Bond, born March 13, 1926.

(d) Lawrence Snead; married, June 20, 1922, May Allen Page at Lynchburg, a daughter of Ambrose and Della May (O'Shell) Page. May Page Cox died September 18, 1923; and her husband resides at Tupelo, Miss.

(e) Charles Franklin; married at Lynchburg, Va., September 4, 1928, Ruth Marion MacGregor, daughter of George and Ida (Peterson) MacGregor. Living in Charlottesville, Va.

(f) Ruth; married, November 14, 1914, at Big Island, Va., James Fitzhugh Lee Mattox, son of Alexander Ransom and Lelia Dudley Mattox. Live at Big Island, Va., where Mr. Mattox holds the position of cashier in the Bank of Big Island.

CHILDREN:

(aa) Addison Lee, born October 19, 1915.
(bb) Roberta Snead, born July 5, 1917.
(cc) Margaret Lawrence, born October 9, 1919.
(dd) Fitzhugh Lee, Jr., born December 28, 1922.
(ee) Ruth, born June 17, 1925.
(ff) James Alexander, born September 1, 1927.

(8) Henry Clarence; married Nannie B. Spencer, daughter of Dr. Spencer, of Lynchburg, Va. He devoted the greater portion of his life to Y. M. C. A. work. Died in Lynchburg, Va., where he had lived for many years.

CHILDREN:

(a) Lucille; married Walter C. Cousins. Living in Lynchburg, Va.
(b) Marguerite; married Frank Dillon, of Lynchburg. Living in Winchester, Ky.
(c) Bessie; married Frank Lowe. Living in Greenville, N. C.
(d) Frank Spencer; married his first cousin, Martha Fletcher, daughter of Mark and Willie E. (Snead) Fletcher, Upperville, Va. Living at Covington, Va.
(e) Terry S.; married Dorothy Urquhart. Living in Montgomery, Alabama.
(f) Dorothy; unmarried. Living in Lynchburg, Va.
(g) Carol; unmarried. Living in Lynchburg, Va.

(9) Jesse Spinner; married (first) ————. Married (second) Mrs. Zoe Brown, of Atlanta, Georgia, where they reside.

(10) Sophie; deceased in infancy.

DAVIS

Nathaniel Davis, the emigrant ancestor of the family, married Elizabeth Hughes. Their son, Robert Davis, married ———— and had, among other children, a son, Nathaniel Davis, who married Elizabeth Atkins, of Amherst County, Virginia.

CHILDREN:

(1) Charles; married Rosanna Ellis. (See forward.)
(2) Robert.
(3) Isham.
(4) James; married Sarah Dudley Ragland. (See forward.)
(5) Nathaniel, Jr.
(6) Elizabeth.
(7) Sarah.
(8) Theodosha.
(9) Matilda; married John Bagby, December 19, 1792.
(10) Nancy.

Charles Davis, eldest son of Nathaniel and Elizabeth (Atkins) Davis, of Amherst County, married June 30, 1782, Rosanna Ellis, born November 30, 1755, the youngest daughter of Charles and Susanna (Harding) Ellis, of "Red Hill," Amherst County. The Ellis family, tradition says, is of Welsh extraction and traced to John Ellis, emigrant from Wales, who settled on Peter's Creek, a branch of Tuckahoe Creek in Henrico County; he was born about the year 1661 and emigrated in 1683. Rosanna (Ellis) Davis is buried in the family burying ground at "Red Hill." In Hardesty's *Encyclopedia,* we find on page 409 among the listed Revolutionary soldiers from Amherst County, the names of both Charles Davis and Nathaniel Davis.

CHILDREN:

(1) Charles Lewis, born February 4, 1784. (See forward.)
(2) Elizabeth; married George Morris, of Amherst, Va.
(3) Susanna; married, November 13, 1809, William Douglas, of Bedford, Va. (See Douglas family.)

(4) Sarah; married Thomas Montgomery, a lawyer by profession. Emigrated to Kentucky. One son, Dr. Thomas Montgomery.

....

Charles Lewis Davis, born February 4, 1784, eldest son of Charles and Rosanna (Ellis) Davis; married (first), December 23, 1807, Rebecca H. White, daughter of Captain Jacob and Hannah (Spiers) White, of Bedford County, Va. (See White family.) After the death of his first wife, who died in 1815, he married (second), September 16, 1816, Nancy Morris, daughter of Thomas and Elizabeth (Sallings) Morris, of Amherst County, Va. Charles Lewis Davis died September 18, 1849, and his wife October 4, 1862.

CHILDREN BY FIRST MARRIAGE:

(1) Rosanna, born January 13, 1809.
(2) Dabney W., born April 22, 1810.
(3) Overton L., born October 20, 1811.
(4) Eliza Ann, born April 5, 1813; married Col. George Alderson, of West Virginia, son of Joseph and Polly Alderson. She was his second wife and the mother of fourteen (14) of his twenty-eight (28) children. His first wife, whom he married, July 8, 1813, was Jennet C. McCleary.

Colonel George Alderson was, for many years before the Civil War, toll collector for the James River and Kanawha Turnpike, now the Midland Trail. He would go on horseback from Western Virginia to Richmond to take the taxes he had collected for the state; and it was on one of these trips, he met Eliza Ann Davis, his second wife. He kept a stage stand at Lookout, Fayette County, and in 1844, Henry Clay was a guest at the Inn. Col. Alderson said to Clay, "What shall we name our baby boy?" Clay replied, "Name him for the two greatest men in the United States—yourself and myself." Hence the name, George and Henry Clay, together, was given the baby boy, and he carried it to manhood, but finally dropped writing Clay. Col. Alderson represented that part of Virginia in the Legislature and made several trips to the Capitol at Richmond. "Alderson" town in Greenbrier County was named for the family; and the first Baptist Church, west of the Alleghany Mountains was built by the Alderson forefathers at Alderson.

ELIZA ANN DAVIS
wife of Col. George Alderson

Col. George Alderson died January 22, 1881; his wife in September, 1882. The names and births of the children of Col. Alderson and his second wife, Eliza Ann Davis, are as follows:

(a) Jennet Creigh, born July 30, 1838; married (first) Mason McClung, of Greenbrier County, West Virginia; (second) James Sivain; two children survive:
   (aa) Irene (McClung) Hatch.
   (bb) Lyda (McClung) King.
(b) Eliza Ann, born July 8, 1840.
(c) Georgia Ann, born May 9, 1841; married Samuel McClung, of Nicholas County, W. Va.

CHILDREN:

   (aa) Henry McClung.
   (bb) Mary (McClung) —————.
   (cc) Sara Martha (McClung) Tyree.
(d) Infant son (not named), born April 4, 1842.
(e) Rebecca White, born March 29, 1843; married William Swope, of Monroe County, W. Va.

CHILDREN:

   (aa) John Swope (deceased).
   (bb) George Swope.
   (cc) Anna Swope.
   (dd) Mary Swope.
   (ee) Walter Swope (now a minister).
   (ff) Opie Swope (physician in Kansas).
   (gg) Bernard Swope.
   (hh) Eugene Swope.
   (ii) Marcella Swope; married W. S. Wray.
(f) George Henry Clay, born October 28, 1844. (See forward.)
(g) Josephine Davis, born March 26, 1846; married James Norton.

CHILDREN:

   (aa) Lou Norton; married L. J. Walker.
   (bb) Chloe Norton; married T. C. Cavendish.
   (cc) William Norton (deceased).
   (dd) Parks Norton (deceased).

(ee) Hugh Norton (deceased).

(ff) Lewis Norton, of Evanston, Ill.

(gg) Otis Norton.

(hh) Calvin Norton.

(ii) Carey Norton.

(jj) Bessie Norton; married Thomas Mahood.

(h) Infant son (not named), born June 24, 1847.

(i) Alice Ellis, born July 15, 1848; married (first) Eugene Norton; married (second) W. S. Richardson, of Virginia.

CHILDREN BY FIRST MARRIAGE:

(aa) Camilla Norton.

(bb) Eugenia Norton; married Dr. Lyle Austin.

(cc) Mary Norton; married J. S. Wilson, of Richmond, Va.

(dd) Annette Norton (deceased).

CHILDREN BY SECOND MARRIAGE:

(ee) George Richardson (deceased).

(ff) Willie Richardson; married W. S. Woodward.

(gg) Frances Richardson; married Joseph Alderson.

(j) Frances Lewis, born March 26, 1850; married Samuel Moore.

CHILDREN:

(aa) Della Moore; married R. H. Carter.

(bb) Eugene Moore.

(cc) Hattie Moore (deceased).

(dd) Margaret Moore; married ———— Anderson.

(k) Infant son (not named), born June 23, 1851.

(l) Infant son (not named), born July 24, 1852.

(m) Overton Davis, born November 18, 1853; married Ollie Neal.

CHILDREN:

(aa) Lee.

(bb) Blanche.

(cc) Cleo.

(n) Lewis Newman, born July 21, 1855; married Cassie Bryant; died November, 1928.

CHILDREN:

(aa) Hattie; married C. T. Lloyd.
(bb) Clara.
(cc) Coleman.
(dd) Nellie; married John Evans (deceased).
(ee) Grace; married David Dunbar.
(ff) Willa; married H. Herold.

(5) Jane Amanda, born December 14, 1814.

CHILDREN BY SECOND MARRIAGE OF CHARLES LEWIS DAVIS TO
NANCY MORRIS:

(6) Samuel, born June 12, 1817.
(7) Henrietta M., born June 20, 1818; married George Morris, II, son of Maurice Morris and grandson of Thomas and Elizabeth (Sallings) Morris.
(8) Thomas M., born January 11, 1820.
(9) George, born April 20, 1821.
(10) Charles D., born January 29, 1822.
(11) Nancy Sallings, born July 4, 1824; married Ludwell Watts, son of Curtis and Nancy (Brown) Watts and grandson of Caleb Watts, of Amherst County, Va. [These were the parents of Mrs. Lucy Dudley (Watts) Noell, of Lynchburg, Va., to whom I wish to express my appreciation and give due credit for the early data on the Davis family herewith submitted.—M. D. A.]

CHILDREN:

(a) William Beverley Watts, born 1851; died 1927; married Edna Douglas Major. (See Douglas family.)
(b) Charles Lewis Watts, born ———; died 1925; married Mary Poindexter.

CHILDREN:

(aa) Lewis Poindexter.
(bb) Richard.
(cc) Mary Ellen.

(c) Susan Frances Watts, born ———; died 1926; married William Sandidge. No children.
(d) Callie Watts; married James Huntley.

CHILDREN:

(aa) Howe M. Huntley.

(bb) Louise Huntley.

(cc) Joseph L. Huntley.

(e) Nannie Watts (deceased); never married.

(f) Lucy Dudley Watts; married James T. Noell, Jr.

CHILDREN:

(aa) James Burroughs Noell.

(bb) Hortense Noell.

(cc) Shirley Watts Noell.

(dd) William Cedric Noell.

(g) Overton Ludwell, born ————; died 1928; married Harriet Miller.

CHILDREN:

(aa) Nancy.

(bb) William Miller.

(12) William Ludwell, born June 22, 1826; married, Sarah Turpin, daughter of Roland and Margaret (Logwood) Turpin, of Bedford County, Va. (See Turpin family.)

(13) Susan Frances, born December 11, 1828; married John Childress.

(14) Caroline L., born April 2, 1832; never married.

(15) Henry M., born June 15, 1835.

....

George Henry Clay Alderson, born October 28, 1844, son of Colonel George and Eliza Ann (Davis) Alderson; married (first), November 21, 1871, Mary C. Jones, daughter of Levi and Letha (Peters) Jones, of Fayetteville, West Virginia. He married (second), January 5, 1889, Sabina Huffman, daughter of William and Sarah (Stickler) Huffman, of Nicholas County, West Virginia. On July 24, 1921, he married for his third wife, Mrs. Bettie (Brock) Ward, daughter of Samuel and ———— (Gross) Brock, of Summersville, West Virginia.

George Henry C. Alderson, now 85 years of age, is living at Enon, W. Va., in the home he built fifty years ago. He served three years in Company A, 14th Virginia Cavalry (Greenbrier Cavalry),

C. S. A., having volunteered November, 1862, at Salem, Va.; served with gallantry and distinction through the war, in the same company, participating in all the engagements of that command—Martinsburg, Winchester, Opeckan, Droup Mountain in Greenbrier County, Lynchburg, Gettysburg, Richmond, Petersburg and others. Was paroled at Appomattox, April 9, 1865; and when he brought the news of Lee's surrender to Lewisburg, was placed in the guard house, by Major Sweeney, as a deserter, for two hours, until the other soldiers reached the town.

He has been a merchant until his recent retirement from business, having lived eighteen years in Summersville, W. Va. He is the oldest Past Master of the Summersville Lodge No. 76, A. F. and A. M., also the oldest member of this Masonic Order. Has been a lifelong member of the Baptist Church, and is a Democrat.

CHILDREN BY FIRST MARRIAGE:

(1) Ida May, born December 2, 1872; married A. C. Masters. She died June 17, 1907.

CHILDREN:

 (a) William Alderson Masters, born July 31, 1900; died June 21, 1928.
 (b) Clifford Masters, born August 29, 1902; unmarried. Lives in Baltimore, Md.
 (c) Julian Jones Masters, born 1904; unmarried. Cashier of the bank at Lewisburg, W. Va. Educated at University of Maryland, Johns Hopkins, and Harvard.
 (d) Lester Masters, born 1906; unmarried. Lives in St. Petersburg, Fla.

(2) Otis Hambra, born January 30, 1874; unmarried. Has lived in Spokane, Wash., for many years; now living in Montana.

(3) Evalena, born March 5, 1875; married September 11, 1912, Frederick A. Hummel. He died April 13, 1923, at Mt. Hope, W. Va., where his widow is now living, and a teacher in the schools of that place. There were no children.

(4) Cecil Warren, born November 8, 1876; married July 1921, Maude Mearns. Living in Charleston, West Virginia. Have one child:
 (a) Cecil Warren, Jr., born April 28, 1923.

(5) Alice Eloise, born November 7, 1879; married, April 8, 1903, Isaac Henry Fry, a descendant of Colonel Joshua Fry of Revolutionary fame. (Col. Joshua Fry was at one time Lieut. George Washington's commanding officer.) Living at Princeton, West Virginia.

CHILDREN:

(a) Irene Imogene Fry, born February 5, 1904. Educated at Marshall College, Huntington, and "The Sorbonne," Paris, France.

(b) Alderson Francis Fry (twin), born March 26, 1906. Educated at Marshall College; now teaching in High School.

(c) Alfreda Frances Fry (twin), born March 26, 1906. Educated at Concord Normal; now teaching.

(d) Phil Henry Fry, born July 16, 1907. In Aviation School—in Panama Canal Zone.

(e) Hale Fry, born June 17, 1909. Senior in High School.

(f) Donald Klein Fry, born September 5, 1910. In College

(g) Lena Eloise Fry, born July 26, 1913. In High School.

(h) George Warren Fry, born October 10, 1915. In High School.

(i) Cecil Wilmot Fry, born March 10, 1920.

Four of these six (6) boys have won many letters in athletics, the eldest being barred by losing a foot when thirteen years old.

(6) Zela Irene, born February 22, 1883; married, June 12, 1901, Arch Wesley Grant. Live in Memphis, Tenn., where he conducts a jewelry business. No children.

(7) Herbert C., born September 2, 1887; married, November 30, 1916, Emma V. Smith, of Oakland, California. He died, December 6, 1928, at his home in Spokane, Washington. He was prominent in Masonic Circles, Elks Lodge, Rotary Club, Chamber of Commerce, and was a very successful business man.

CHILDREN:

(a) Virginia, born 1918.
(b) Winona Lee, born 1921.

CHILD BY SECOND MARRIAGE OF GEORGE HENRY C. ALDERSON TO
SABINA HUFFMAN

(8) Roy C., born December 21, 1895; married, May 2, 1916, Hattie Hutchinson. Live at Summersville, W. Va.

CHILDREN:

(a) Nancy Marion, born May 8, 1918.

(b) Bettie Jo, born December 18, 1919.

(c) Peggy Anita, born May 15, 1921.

(d) Dorothy Lee, born May 20, 1923.

(e) John Henry, born April 22, 1925.

James Davis, the fourth son of Nathaniel and Elizabeth (Atkins) Davis, of Amherst County; married, October 13, 1800, Sarah Dudley Ragland, daughter of John and Nancy (Dudley) Ragland. Nancy Dudley was the daughter of John Dudley, of Virginia.

CHILDREN:

(1) John Dudley, born September 22, 1801, in Amherst County, Va.; married (first), December 7, 1837, Margaret Newman Eubank, born at "The Wilderness," Amherst County, June 9, 1818, a daughter of Thomas Newman and Jane Shelton (Ellis) Eubank, of Amherst County. She died June 23, 1841, and was buried in the family burying ground at "The Wilderness." In April 1843, he married (second) Lucy McDaniel Tinsley, born 1825, daughter of Nelson and Ann (Burks) Tinsley. Col. John Dudley Davis died 1871 and his wife died in March, 1910.

CHILDREN BY SECOND MARRIAGE:

(a) Bettie; married (first) Mr. Pleasants, (second) Mr. Woods.

(b) Sallie; married Harry Williams.

(c) Dolly; married Silas Ogden.

(d) Anna; married Mr. ———— Williams.

(e) Pinkie; married Marshall Barrett.

(f) John Dudley, Jr.; married Jennie Perrow.

CHILDREN:

(aa) Elizabeth Hubbard; married George Lewis, son of Henry and Emma (Dameron) Lewis.

(bb) John Dudley, III; married Miss Woods, daughter of James and Belle Waugh Woods.

(cc) Robert Guy.

(dd) Willie Clayton.

(g) Jimmie; married Rosa Parr.

(2) Nancy Beverly; married Elliott Wortham.

(3) Louis Jane; married Dr. Micajah Pendleton.

[I am indebted to Dr. E. Pendleton Tompkins of Lexington, Virginia, a great grandson of James Davis and Sarah Dudley (Ragland) Davis, of Amherst County, Virginia, for the following notes on the Davis, Dudley, and Ragland families.
—M. D. A.]

DAVIS FAMILY

The progenitor of the Davises of Amherst County was Robert Davis, who was originally from Wales, but married, probably, in Hanover County, a Miss Hughes, and moved from there to the County of Amherst about the year 1720, and entered a large tract of land in the triangle formed by the James and Pedlar Rivers and a line drawn from Waugh's Ferry to Pedlar Farm, also, a large tract of land on Chestnut Mountain in Bedford County. He had seven children, viz.: (1) Nathaniel, (2) Isham, (3) Robert, (4) John, (5) Abby, and two daughters whose names I have been unable to ascertain. His wife having died he married the second time, Anna Atkins, of Amherst County, about the year 1750. Soon thereafter, he had some difficulty with Nicholas Davis [Note: I think this should be Nicholas Davies— M. D. A.], of Bedford County in regard to the Chestnut Mountain land, and (to use the expression of Uncle Nat Davis from whom this information is obtained) he damned Nick Davis and the Governor of the Colony, and was compelled to fly the country, and moved with his wife and the two sons of his second marriage, Lewis and Landon, to the neighborhood of Raleigh, North Carolina, where another son, Hugh, was born. He afterwards moved to Florida and settled on an Island in the St. John's river, where both he and his wife died some years afterward, leaving four sons, Lewis and Landon born in Amherst County,

Virginia, Hugh born in North Carolina, and Absalom born in Florida. The sons subsequently moved to the territory of Mississippi and settled on the Homochitto River below Natchez.

Nathaniel Davis, eldest son of Robert Davis, married, in Amherst in 1752, Elizabeth Atkins, a sister of his stepmother. He lived at the place known as the "Old Orchard," subsequently owned by Chas. I. Ellis, and during the Revolutionary War was engaged in the manufacture of fire arms. He had eleven children, viz.: (1) Elizabeth, who married John Burks, of Arnold's Valley; (2) Charles, who married (first) Rosa Ellis and (second) Susanna Ragland, born October 18, 1765; (3) Nancy, who married John Francis Penny Lewis, of Kentucky; (4) Robert, who was killed by the Indians on the Mississippi River; (5) Sally, who married Stephen Terry, of Arnold's Valley; (6) Theodosia, who married Jarrett Gilliam; (7) Isham, who moved to Kentucky, married and died about 1840; (8) James, who married Sally Dudley Ragland, of Louisa County; (9) Matilda, who married John Bagly and moved to Kentucky; (10) Nathaniel, Jr., who married Polly H. Tate of Bedford and died 1866; (11) Oliver, who died in infancy. Nathaniel Davis, senior, and his son Robert were both killed in the Homochitto County.

James Davis, born May 4, 1770, son of Nathaniel and Elizabeth (Atkins) Davis, of Amherst County, Virginia, married, October 13, 1800, Sallie Dudley Ragland born April 4, 1764, daughter of John and Nancy (Dudley) Ragland, of Louisa County, Virginia. They had three children, viz: John Dudley Davis, born 22nd of September, 1801; Nancy Beverly Davis, born 27th of March, 1803; and Louisa Jane Davis, born 29th of December, 1806. Sallie Dudley (Ragland) Davis died at her residence in Amherst County in December, 1852, in the 90th year of her age.

(1) John Dudley Davis, married, December 27, 1837, Margaret N. Eubank, who died without issue on the 23rd of June, 1841. He married the second time, at the same house and by the same minister, Lucy McDaniel Tinsley, on the 10th of April, 1844. He died April, 1872, leaving seven children, viz.: (1) Louisa Ann, (2) Sally James, (3) Betty Nelson, (4) John Dudley, Jr., (5) Dolly, (6) James, and (7) Pinkey or Roberta.

(2) Nancy Beverly Davis, married, in the year 1823, Elliott Wortham and died June 16, 1841, leaving seven children, viz.: (1) Sally Jane, (2) James Davis, (3) Louisa Jane, (4) Charles Elliott, (5) Samuel Ragland, (6) Fanny Dudley, and (7) Richard Beverly, who married (second wife), Judith Emma Tompkins.

(3) Louisa Jane Davis, born December 29, 1806; married, September 20, 1822, Dr. Micajah Pendleton, died in Buchanan, Virginia, September 23, 1840, leaving five children, viz.: (1) Edmund Pendleton, born September 29, 1823, a lawyer by profession; married Cornelia Morgan; children: (a) Willie, died young; (b) Elizabeth Carter; married Dr. Walter Coles; (c) Ephraim Morgan; married Laura Tucker, daughter of John Randolph Tucker. (2) Ann Garland Pendleton, born September 15, 1826; married Lewis Brugh, of Fincastle, Virginia; had five daughters. (3) James Dudley Pendleton, born November 3, 1829, a physician by profession and for twenty-five years clerk of the Virginia Senate; married Clara Rock—one daughter, Willie (married Speece). (4) Susan Frances Pendleton, born March 5, 1832—never married. (5) Sarah Dudley Ragland Pendleton, born March 18, 1834; married first, George W. Johnson, no issue; married second, on June 5, 1867, John Fulton Tompkins, born May 15, 1830, died October 3, 1899; children: (a) Edmund Pendleton Tompkins; married, June 6, 1905, Sarah Casterline Souther—two children, viz: Pendleton Souther Tompkins and Souther Fulton Tompkins. (b) Sallie Louisa Tompkins; married, March 31, 1908, William Morton McNutt—no issue. (c) George Johnson Tompkins; married Elizabeth Dillard—five children. (d) Bertie Lee Tompkins, unmarried.

RAGLAND FAMILY

The "Raglan" or "Ragland" family of Wales are descended from Evan Herbert who was a blood relation of William the Conqueror, and came over with that monarch from Normandy.

The family of Herbert intermarried with the family of Beauforts, who were lineal descendants of John of Gaunt and Catherine Swineford, and came into possession, through the Beauforts of "Raglan Castle" in Wales, thence were called Raglans and subsequently Raglands.

John Ragland, the first of the name who came to America, married his kinswoman, Anne Beaufort, and came to Virginia about the year 1720, and settled upon Mechamps Creek, near the mouth of the Chickahominy River. He obtained grants for some fifteen thousand acres of land in the counties of Hanover and Louisa, and imported slaves directly from Africa. His country seat was known as "Ripping Hall," and remained in the Ragland family till 1823, when it was destroyed by fire. He had nine children, viz.: (1) John, who married, in 1759, Nancy Dudley, of Hanover; (2) William, who married a Miss Lipscomb; (3) Samuel; (4) James, who married Catherine Davis; (5) Evan, who married ———— and settled in Halifax County; (6) Pettus, who married Elizabeth, daughter of John Davis, of Hanover County; (7) Martha, who married Thomas Tinsley; (8) Frances, who married Jeremiah Pate; (9) ————, who married a Mr. Bowe.

DUDLEY FAMILY

John Dudley, of Hanover County, Virginia, who married, about 1725, Ursula Beverly, daughter of Robert Beverly, Jr., and his wife Ursula Byrd (daughter of Col. Wm. Byrd), is thought to have been the only son of Ambrose Dudley, who emigrated from England to this country early in the eighteenth century and settled on James River, not far from Jamestown, at a place known as Hall's Landing, where he died about the year 1750, leaving three children, viz.: (1) John, (2) Mary, and (3) ————, a daughter, name unknown. John, married as above stated, Ursula Beverly, and the issue of this marriage was six children, viz.: (1) William, (2) Nancy (who married, in 1759, John Ragland, of Louisa County, Va.), (3) Mary, (4) Jane, (5) Ursula, and (6) ————, a daughter, name unknown.

"The Cabells and Their Kin," page 43:

"I can not vouch for it but will give it as I find it in the Floyd tradition. Opechancanough, the celebrated chief of the Powhatans, * * * left a lovely young daughter, the child of his old age, the Princess Nicketti,—'she who sweeps the dew from the flowers.' Some years after this graceful Indian maiden had reached the years of mature womanhood, a member (the name is not given) of one of the old cavalier families of Virginia fell in love with her and she with him, and the result was a clandestine marriage, and a half-breed Indian girl, who married about the year 1680, a Welshman (others say a native of Devonshire, England), named Nathaniel Davis, an Indian trader, and according to some accounts a Quaker; and from this alliance many notable people in the East and in the West have descended. Their daughter, Mary Davis, born about 1685, married Samuel Burks, of Hanover (the ancestor of the Burks family of Virginia), and their daughter, Elizabeth Burks, married Captain William Cabell, the ancestor of the Cabells.

"Martha Davis, another daughter, married Abraham Venable, the ancestor of the Venables.

"Robert Davis, senior, a son (the ancestor of the 'black Davises' of Kentucky and from whom Jefferson Davis descended), had a daughter, Abadiah (or Abigail) Davis, who married William Floyd, the ancestor of the Floyds of Virginia and of the West.

"A daughter or granddaughter of the Quaker married General Evan Shelby, of Maryland, the ancestor of the Shelbys of the West.

"Samuel and Philip Davis, of the Blue Mountains, were sons, and there may have been other sons and daughters.

"William Floyd left the eastern shore of Virginia, went up the country as far as the present Amherst County, which was then a very wild region, where he met with this family of Davises, who had traded with the Indians and gotten much property this way. (The Quakers were much given to friendly trading with the Indians.)

"William Floyd and his wife's brother, Robert Davis, junior, with their families emigrated to Kentucky with the first settlers, and finally located in the Bear-grass region near Louisville, where the kinsmen (Floyds and Davises) had a fort, called Floyds' Station.

*　　*　　*　　*　　*　　*　　*

"The Princess Nicketti's name has not been popular among her traditional descendants (it may be because the marriage was clandestine). The first Governor John Floyd named one of his daughters for her. I know no other namesake, but if tradition is true, no more lovely woman ever 'swept the dew from the flowers'."

Judge John H. Hatcher

Hatcher.

HATCHER

There are two accounts given of the derivation of the name Hatcher, both of which are likely correct. In Norman French the word "hache" meant a light battle axe. The name was applied to one who wielded such a weapon. After the Norman invasion of England, the word was anglicised into the present form. In ancient England, a gate was frequently built across the highway in forest districts to prevent the escape of deer. This gate was called a "hatch." The suffix "er" means "at" or "near." Hence "Hatcher" was the name given one who resided at or near such a gate.

In a report to Robert Hatcher of Georgia an English genealogist stated that the Hatchers "recorded their pedigree at the visitation of Lincoln in 1634, when they had their arms, a chevron between six escallops, confirmed and allowed to them." In Fairbanks' *Book of Crests* is the following: "Hatcher Lincs, an arm embowed, vested az, charged with three bars holding in the hand ppr a branch of olives vert." "Hatcher Lincs" evidently refers to the Hatchers of Lincolnshire. Not being versed in heraldic terms, I cannot translate Fairbanks. A family coat of arms is not to be lightly dismissed, however. It may serve a purpose. For example see "Lorna Doone."

The first Hatcher who came to Virginia was undoubtedly an Englishman and was named William. The genealogists refer to him as "William the Immigrant." He was born about 1614, and secured a patent for land in Henrico County in 1636, where he lived until his death about 1680. There were four other Hatchers who came to Virginia shortly after the arrival of William, but as they did not locate in Henrico County and the records disclose no connection between them and William, I have made no effort to trace them.

Dr. Wm. E. Hatcher is credited with the statement that William "The Immigrant" came from the Hatchers of Careby Manor, Lincolnshire, England, where an inscription on a tombstone dated 1564, records that they were "of the ancient family of Hatchers, for many generations the Lords of this Manor." In this I dare say the Doctor was correct. Personally, though, I have never been able to connect our first Virginia ancestor with any branch of the English family. His name does not occur in the Lincolnshire pedigree recorded in 1634. It does not appear on any of the emigrant lists kept by the various shipping companies of England. In a sketch of our family appearing in the Woodson book, it is stated that there is a family tradition that "the immigrant came over with Sir Harry Vane." I could find no mention of William Hatcher in the Vane Books. But what's the use of a tradition if it has to be bolstered up with proof?

There was a Wm. Hatcher of Careby, a member of Parliament, who was indicted for treason in 1643, because he had taken up arms against the King. There was also a Sir Thomas Hatcher who was a colonel in Cromwell's army and who was indicted for treason in 1643. "The Immigrant" could have been the son of either one of these "Round-heads." If so, the Vane tradition would be strengthened, as Vane also served under Cromwell. This might account for the absence of William's name from the shipping lists, as he may have fled the country under an assumed name. It could also account for the little respect he showed the officials of the Virginia Colony, who were, loyal to the King. In 1654 he was forced to apologize in the House of Burgesses for having stated that its mouthpiece, meaning its Speaker Col. Ed. Hill, "was a devil." In 1676 at the time of Bacon's Rebellion he was fined 10,000 pounds of tobacco "and caske" for "uttering divers mutinous words tending to the disquiet of this, his majesty's country." The Court order provides that as he was an "aged man," he might instead pay 8,000 pounds of dressed pork for the support of his Majesty's Soldiers. The immigrant had a notoriously high temper. If any of his descendants have that weakness, it may be some comfort to them to learn that they come by it honestly, as it can be charged directly to him. He was appointed a viewer of tobacco by Act of the Assembly of 1639. This was a position of importance at that time, as tobacco was the medium of exchange. He was a member of the Virginia House of Burgesses from Henrico County in 1644-5-6, 1649, 1652 and 1658-9. He patented in all 1,500 acres of land, and was evidently a leader in his county. I have not been able to find the name of his wife or that of any daughter. His sons were Edward, Henry, Benjamin, John, and William. The last named died unmarried. John went to North Carolina early in life and so passed out of the Henrico records. Benjamin married Elizabeth Greenhaugh, accumulated some property, and was generally called "Mr." which in that day meant he was a person of some importance. His descendants are scattered from Henrico to the far West, and have seemingly prospered.

Edward, born about 1635, was a swearing, fighting, horse-racing swash buckler, who was the sporting member of the family. In 1694 he was indicted for raising a band to fight the Indians. As a similar act by Nat'l Bacon, but on a larger scale, is now championed by all Virginians, we need not condemn Uncle Edward for that. He married Mary ———— and had quite a number of children to whom he was very generous. He must have been honest, whatever other faults he had, as the records contain a deed from Edward Hatcher to Nat'l Bacon's son, upon arrival at his majority, for a tract of land which the elder Bacon had paid Edward for many years before. Edward owned several fine plantations, and, out-living his brothers, died in 1711.

In an article written by the eminent Virginia genealogist, Mr. Wm. G. Stanard, on page 401 of Volume 17 of the *Virginia Historical Magazine* is the following:

"Jane, daughter of Edward Hatcher, married ———— Branch of Henrico, afterwards married Abell Gower. The will of Mrs. Jane Gower was proved in Henrico, October, 1699. Through a child of her first marriage, Mrs. Jane Gower was an ancestress of Thomas Jefferson." Now Mr. Wm. Torrence, another Virginia genealogist equally eminent, demonstrates to his own satisfaction that the Henrico records do not prove that Jane, referred to by Mr. Stanard, was the daughter of Edward Hatcher. He correctly states that the records do not affirmatively show that Edward had a daughter named Jane. I read Mr. Stanard's article first and marked the biggest branch on our family tree "Thomas Jefferson." I would lop off that branch with great reluctance. While Mr. Torrence's argument appeals to me judicially, I prefer to indulge my fancy as an individual. The will of Jane Gower gives some household articles to one whom she designates as "Sister Hatcher." Now who "Sister Hatcher" was, the records do not disclose. Mrs. Gower was of the age to have been the daughter of Edward. She was the ancestress of Thomas Jefferson, and she had a sister by the name of Hatcher. I side with Stanard!

The other son, Henry, married Anne Lound. He was beloved of the gods more than his brother Edward and died young (about 1677), leaving to survive him several children, the oldest of whom was another Henry. This Henry (2) married Dorothy Batte. The records show him sowing some wild oats early in life, after which he evidently settled down. He was a successful planter and frequently served his county as juror and grandjuror. He died in 1743. One of the witnesses to his will was Edmund Logwood. Henry (2) had a son Henry (3) who married Margaret ————, became independently wealthy, and died in 1762 in Chesterfield County (cut off from Henrico in 1749). He left several daughters (Frances married Joseph Jackson and Lucy married Joseph Terry), and three sons, Henry (4), Jeremiah, and Julius.

Henry (4) was given a plantation by his father in 1756. In 1780 a deed from this Henry refers to his wife as Edith "late widow and relict of Godfrey Hill." Then on March 4, 1783, is recorded a marriage settlement between him and Ann Hampton of Chesterfield. Sometime thereafter he moved to Bedford County. His will recorded in 1799 mentions his wife Ann. One of his sons, another Henry (5), served under Washington at Brandywine and Germantown. Henry (5) married Nancy Hoskins in Chesterfield County and moved to Kentucky, where some of his descendants have acquired wealth and honorable position.

Jeremiah married Edith Logwood in Chesterfield County in 1773, was in Cumberland County in 1775, was in Powhatan County in 1777 and 1780, and shortly thereafter moved to Bedford County where he lived until his death, in 1804. In 1780 he sold the plantation in Chesterfield County which was willed him by his father to the Rev. Eleazer Clay for five thousand pounds in money. Some plantation that! His wife, Edith, was a daughter of the same Edmund Logwood who witnessed the will of Jeremiah's grandfather, Henry (2), in 1743. Two of her brothers, Thomas and Edmund, moved to Bedford County before the Revolutionary War. These two and another brother, Archibald, were soldiers in that war, Thomas serving as a captain.

In addition to Henry (5) the following members of the Hatcher family were soldiers in the Revolutionary War: William, Seth, Samuel, Obadiah, Josiah, John (Major), John (Lt.), Gideon, Fredrick, Daniel, Benjamin and Thomas (Capt.). We may take pride in this list showing that our family did not blanch before the storm of war. Our ancestor Jeremiah was a minister of the gospel and a man of peace. That he also was not afraid of the long arm of Britain is shown by the fact that he openly took the oath of allegiance to the State of Virginia, in Powhatan County on October 16, 1777.

By the year 1800 the descendants of "The Immigrant" were scattered from Henrico County to Kentucky. Of these colonial Hatchers, the same Mr. Torrence writes: "In the beginnings in Henrico the Hatchers and" (here he names other families) "were very well to do people." After explaining how the wealth of Henrico County became concentrated in just a few families, he continues: "Nearly all of these older families continued to maintain good social position and remained comfortably off, but they were overshadowed by the large activities of some of their neighbors. The Hatchers * * * moved up James River to new lands, and at a later day we find them holding offices of responsibility and profit in the counties of Goochland, Cumberland and Powhatan." *William and Mary College Quarterly,* Volume 24, pages 266-7.

In the history of Bristol Parrish (by Slaughter), page 121, Hatcher is included in the list of "representative names" in that section during the colonial period.

Following the Revolution, the Hatchers seem to have taken very seriously the biblical injunction to be fruitful and multiply. Ten to twelve children in the family became the rule rather than the exception. Consequently our forefathers were unable to accumulate or distribute much property to the individual child. Eleven children are mentioned in the will of the Rev. Jeremiah. They were: Hardaway, Jeanne (or Jane who married Pleasant Jeter and was the mother of Rev. Jeremiah Bell Jeter), Jeremiah, Jr., Harvey, Edmond, Peggy (Margaret), Archer, William, Julius (married Polly White), Thomas (married (first) Catharine White and (second) Elizabeth M. Baughan), and Henry (married (first) Elizabeth White and (second) Mary Latham, and was the father of Rev. Wm. E. Hatcher).

The Rev. Jeremiah was pastor of the Tomahawk Church in Chesterfield County and upon his removal to Bedford County he became the pastor of a church on the North Fork of Otter, called "Hatcher's Meeting House." In a sketch of him in Virginia Baptist Ministers, it is stated that the Otter Church "was built up principally under his ministry, and enjoyed his indefatigable labors without fee or reward until the time of his death * * *. He was greatly beloved by the people of his charge; and by all that knew him, whether saint or sinner, he was recognized as a devout man of God." (Page 338.)

His fame as a preacher is overshadowed by that of his more renowned grandsons, Dr. Wm. E. Hatcher and Dr. Jeremiah Bell Jeter. If families, like nations, have their rise and fall, then likely the Hatcher family reached its zenith in the generation which produced these two remarkable men, who were the most prominent preachers in the southern Baptist Church for half a century. That generation produced another grandson of the Rev. Jeremiah, who was perhaps as talented but not quite so famous as his cousins—the Hon. Robert Hatcher who served in Congress from Missouri for some twenty odd years. (My grandfather Caleb Hatcher told me that this Robert Hatcher was the smartest man he ever knew.) Another grandson, Dr. Harvey Hatcher (brother of Wm. E.) was quite prominent in the Baptist Church in Georgia.

Jeremiah, Jr., in 1803, married Elizabeth Jeter, the daughter of Lieutenant Henry Jeter and his "beautiful Betsy Bell" and died in 1816. His wife survived him until about 1861-2. His children were: Nancy Elliot (married J. W. Hawkins), Wm. Logwood (married Nancy Hurt), Jane Jeter (married John Williamson), James Harvey, Jeremiah Gibson (married Angeline Wainwright), Archibald Presley (married Mary Buford), Wilson Cary (who died in childhood) and Caleb Henry, whom the records show was born shortly after the death of his father.

Caleb Henry married Florentine Hurt in 1836. She was a daughter of Henry Hurt and Rhoda Wright (a daughter of John Wright, a Rev. Soldier of Bedford County). One of their children was my father, Wilson Cary, born in 1846. He joined Company B, 10th Virginia Batallion of the Confederate Army when he was seventeen years old and served continuously until severely wounded and captured in the fighting around Richmond. He married Anne Bulman of King and Queen County in 1874, who still survives him. He engaged in the merchandise business in Bland County and died in 1892. It will surely be permitted me to write of him, that he was a high type of Christian gentleman and was known for his business integrity and honor.

The other children of Caleb Henry were: William (who was a Lieutenant in the Confederate Army and married Mary Grey Jones), Sallie (married Tom Sublett), Mildred (married Charles Bradley), James (married Willie D. Anderson), Lee (married Willie Davis), and Davis (married Jennie Tate).

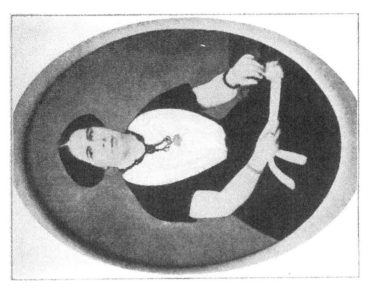

DEMARIS HATCHER PERKINS FORD
grand-daughter of Rev. Jeremiah Hatcher

REV. JEREMIAH HATCHER

In addition to the Logwoods, Jeters, Hurts and Wrights, I proudly record relationship through maternal lines with the Stratton and Turner families of Bedford County. As I have lived all my life away from Bedford County, I am not informed as to the Hatchers outside of my direct line—so this sketch is necessarily incomplete in that respect. My grandfather once said to me of the Hatchers of his generation, "The men have been honest and the women virtuous." What better heritage could one desire!

I have been requested to include my own family in this sketch. I was born in 1875, and in 1900 married Leona Lyle Bowman, of the brilliant North Carolina family of Bowmans. We made our home at Beckley, West Virginia, where I practiced law, and three children came to us. Our first born, Lois, married F. M. Simpson of Huntingdon, Pennsylvania, and has a son, Cary Hatcher. She is an expert musician, but her music is no sweeter than Lois. To our second daughter was given her mother's name and in special measure her mother's beauty and intellect. She married H. L. Bennett, an attorney of Charleston, West Virginia. Our third child, John H., Jr., married Violet Walker of Mabscott, West Virginia, and has a son, John Walker. Our boy follows my footsteps and is studying law. He is to me all I could ask of a son. My wife passed away this year. Whatever of happiness and of success has come to me, I owe to her. She lead me even unto "marble halls," and now her smile lights for me the dark portal of death. JOHN H. HATCHER.

Charleston, West Virginia.

November 1, 1929.

John H. Hatcher was elected to the bench of the Supreme Court of Appeals of West Virginia in 1924, and, in 1928, was re-elected for the full term of twelve years. Since the death of his wife, Judge Hatcher has established his home permanently in Charleston, W. Va.

Henry Hatcher (3), born prior to 1712, married Margaret ————, and died in 1762. They had three sons, Jeremiah, Henry, and Julius; and three daughters, Lucy, Frances, and Mary.

Jeremiah Hatcher, son of Henry (3) and Margaret Hatcher, was born in Henrico County, Va., subsequent to 1741. He married Edith

Logwood, July 2, 1773, in Chesterfield County, and died in Bedford County, July, 1804. (See Logwood family.)

CHILDREN:

(1) Hardaway; married Elizabeth Snelson. (See forward.)
(2) Jane; married Pleasant Jeter. (See Jeter family.)
(3) Jeremiah; married Betsy Jeter. (See forward.)
(4) Henry; married (first) Elizabeth White; (second) Mary Latham. (See forward.)
(5) Edmund.
(6) Margaret (Peggy); married Jonathan Rucker.
(7) Archibald.
(8) William; married (first) Lucy Rucker; (second) Cathron Payne.
(9) Julius, Jr.; married Polly White, daughter of Jacob and Hannah (Spiers) White.
(10) Thomas; married Catherine White. (See forward.)
(11) Harvey.

REVOLUTIONARY RECORD OF (REV.) JEREMIAH HATCHER, SR.

(Found in Order Book No. 1, pages 11 and 14, of the records of the County Court of Powhatan County, Va., for October term and year 1777.)

"At a court held for Powhatan County at the house of Littlebury Mosby, Gentleman, on Thursday, October 16th, A. D. 1777. Present in Court: John Netherland, John Mayo, William Smith, Vincent Markham, and Edward Logwood, Gentlemen, Justices.

"Edward Maxey and Jeremiah Hatcher, both Baptist preachers, took the oath of fidelity to the State and agreeable to an Act of Assembly in that case made and provided are exempted from Military duty.

(Signed) JOHN NETHERLAND.

Testo: TH. MILLER, *Clerk*."

Hardaway Hatcher, son of Rev. Jeremiah and Edith (Logwood) Hatcher; married, in Bedford County, Va., February 11, 1801, Elizabeth Snelson (perhaps Nelson), and died in 1822.

CHILDREN:

(1) Nelson.
(2) Polly; married William Witt.
(3) Sally.
(4) Frances; died in 1840.
(5) Caroline M., born March 13, 1812; died July 19, 1895; married George Johnson. (See Johnson family.)

....

Jeremiah Hatcher, Jr., son of Rev. Jeremiah and Edith (Logwood) Hatcher; married, September 26, 1803, Betsy Jeter, daughter of Henry and Elizabeth (Bell) Jeter. (See Jeter family.)

CHILDREN:

(1) Nancy Elliott; married George Hawkins.

CHILDREN:

(a) Jeremiah W.; died unmarried.
(b) Thomas B.; married Bettie M. Hatcher, daughter of John Calvin, Sr., and Rebecca (Hatcher) Hatcher.
(c) James D.; married Fannie Cox of Campbell County.
(d) Jane; married Jesse Goodwin.
(e) Susan; married William L. Bowman.
(f) Catherine; married Robert E. Hatcher, son of Thomas and Catherine (White) Hatcher.
(g) Virginia; married Edward Womack. Lived and died in Texas.
(h) Maria; married Henry Milton Hatcher, son of Thomas and Catherine (White) Hatcher.

(2) William Logwood; was a local Baptist preacher, and lived near Salem, Va. It was through his efforts that the Fort Lewis Church of Roanoke County, Va., was built. He was pastor of this church for many years. He married Nancy Hurt.

CHILDREN:

(a) Cary; married Mary Zircle.
(b) John; married Nannie ————.
(c) Jeremiah; married Jennie Jeter.
(d) Robert E.; married Rebecca Dyerle.

    (e) Susan; married Jones Ligon.
    (f) Emmett; married Clara Benson, of Maryland.
    (g) Laura; married C. W. Chapman.
    (h) Charles; married Susan Thomas.

(3) Jane; married ——— Williamson.
(4) James Harvey; died unmarried.
(5) Jeremiah Gibson, born in 1807; died January 28, 1889. (See forward.)
(6) William Cary; died unmarried.
(8) Caleb Henry. (Previously given.)

Jeremiah Gibson Hatcher, son of Jeremiah, Jr., and Betsy (Jeter) Hatcher; married (first), March 27, 1838, Angeline Wainwright (born 1814; died November, 1867); (second) Mrs. Martha A. Hurt, by whom he had no children.

CHILDREN BY FIRST MARRIAGE:

(1) Mary E.; married James W. Halley and went to Missouri.

CHILDREN:
    (a) Hubert H.; married Bulah Fox.

CHILD:
      (aa) Lucile.
    (b) J. Page; now deceased; married W. H. McCall.

CHILDREN:
      (aa) Ray McCall; now deceased.
      (bb) Wheeler McCall.
      (cc) Grady McCall.
      (dd) Halley McCall.
      (ee) Harvey McCall.
    (c) J. Sydney; married Mabel Ewing.

CHILDREN:
      (aa) James Ewing; now deceased.
      (bb) Ray Sydney.
      (cc) Laura May.

(d) May P.; married George McCall; both now deceased.

(e) Lena V.; married J. W. Dickey.

CHILD:

(aa) Halley K.

(f) Ada J.; married M. R. Guthrie.

CHILDREN:

(aa) Genevieve.

(bb) Harold; now deceased.

(cc) Eugene.

(dd) Margaret.

(ee) Dwight.

(ff) Ewell.

(gg) Ethel.

(g) Emma C.; married J. I. White.

CHILDREN:

(aa) Mary Frances.

(bb) Halley.

(h) Boyce; now deceased.

(i) G. C.; married Jessie Vaughan.

CHILDREN:

(aa) Martha.

(bb) Thomas.

(j) Loutie M.

(k) C. D.; married Peggy Rush.

CHILD:

(aa) Jack.

(l) C. J.—twin of C. D.; married Offie Lane.

CHILDREN:

(aa) Frances Mary.

(bb) C. J., Jr.

(2) Charles W.; soldier in the Civil War—member of Company A, Fitzhugh Lee's Brigade, Stuart's Division, 2nd Virginia Cavalry. He married, May 20, 1863, Amanda Lunsford, and died July 23, 1923.

CHILDREN:

(a) Sallie Wilson; married Alfred L. Woolfork of Louisa County, Va.

CHILD:

(aa) Charles.

(b) Charles Judson; married Edmonia C. Watkins.

(c) Clarke Chesterfield; married Emma Day; lives at Montvale, Va.

(d) Acree; died in childhood.

(e) Fannie; died in childhood.

(f) Mary Angeline; married James R. Maupin, her cousin.

(g) William H.; married (first) Mamie Bush; (second) Sally Larus; (third) Kate Brown. No children.

(h) Bessie Mildred; married J. Harry Rusher; lives at Thaxton, Va.

CHILDREN:

(aa) Margaret.

(bb) Sallie.

(3) Rebecca Jane, born September 21, 1843; died July 8, 1904; married, September 8, 1872, William Clarke Tate, born July 22, 1848; died October 10, 1901.

CHILDREN:

(a) Mary Willie Armistead, born July 28, 1873; died July 2, 1902; married, July 14, 1896, Harry S. Fraine, of Canada. Their home was in Lynchburg, Va., where she died. He has married a second time and still lives there.

CHILDREN:

(aa) Harold S., Jr., born June 6, 1897; married, May 3, 1927, Rose Ferry, of Springfield, Mass.

(bb) Edith May, born February 2, 1899; married, June, 1929, Robert Martin, of New York; now living in New York City.

(cc) James; died in infancy.

(b) Charles Judson; married Mrs. Evie (Jennings) Carter, June 15, 1903; lives in California.

(c) John Winfree Clarke, born July 18, 1878; died September 23, 1913. Unmarried.

(d) James Henry, born December 28, 1880; married, Mary Lucy McGhee, daughter of Rice and Lucy (Walker) McGhee; lives in Florida. (See Walker family.)

CHILDREN:

(aa) Virginia, born November 16, 1908; died in childhood.

(bb) Henryetta McGhee, born February 8, 1912.

(e) Louise Rebecca, born February 18, 1885; married Emmet J. Atkinson, son of Joseph and Theresa (Schenk) Atkinson, and grandson of Captain Paul Atkinson, B. S. N., and Jenny (Bassett) Atkinson, of Liverpool, England.

CHILDREN:

(aa) Louise.

(bb) Josephina.

(4) Sarah W.; born in 1871; married William Carey Maupin (died November, 1912).

CHILDREN:

(a) Robert Washington, born June 26, 1873; married Florence Smith.

CHILDREN:

(aa) Dorothy.

(bb) Robert W., Jr.

(b) Addison, born September 17, 1874; married Beulah G. Pritchard.

CHILDREN:

(aa) William Carey.

(bb) Lillian Gertrude.

(cc) James.

(c) William Hart, born January 26, 1876; died 1911.

(d) John Warwick Daniel, born 1877; married Louise Blake.

CHILD:

(aa) Lloyd.

(e) Socrates, born 1878; unmarried; killed in Spanish-American War in 1899.

(f) Jeremiah Gibson; born in 1879; married Margaret Mackay, of Paris, Texas.

(g) James Rawlings; born in 1882; married Angeline Hatcher, daughter of Charles W. and Amanda (Lunsford) Hatcher.

CHILDREN:

(aa) James Rawlings, Jr.
(bb) Angeline.
(cc) Elizabeth.

(h) Rex Corbin, born in 1884; married Margaret Lewis Maupin.

(5) William Gibson; married Mary Susan Key; lived and died in Missouri.

CHILDREN:

(a) Jennie Judson; married ———— Sowers.
(b) William Luther; married Myra ————.
(c) Charles Curry; married Lena Barton.

(6) Emma Wainwright, born October 9, 1847; died June 13, 1919; married Dr. Charles Auville Board, of Bedford, Va. (See Board family.)

CHILDREN:

(a) Charles Auville, Jr.; died in infancy.
(b) Florence Hatcher; married James Edmond Luttrell.
(c) Howard Eager; killed in World War.

(7) Lena W.; died September 9, 1927; married James Edward Tate, who died October 21, 1915.

CHILD:

(a) Minnie Lena; lives in Washington, D. C.

(8) Armistead Cary, born January 16, 1851; died June 13, 1922; married, June 15, 1898, Ida Burroughs, daughter of Joseph Nicholas and Sarah (Morgan) Burroughs. (See Robertson family.)

CHILDREN:

(a) Ada Burroughs, born January 26, 1900.
(b) Angeline Wainwright, born February 12, 1902.
(c) Sallie Anthony—twin of Angeline Wainwright, born February 12, 1902.

William Ralph Clements, M. D.

William Robin Clements

(9) Luther, (10) Judson, (11) Jimmie, all died in infancy.
(12) Lizzie Otey; married Henry Scott. No children.

....

Henry Hatcher, son of Rev. Jeremiah and Edith (Logwood) Hatcher; married (first), February 4, 1812, Elizabeth White, daughter of Jacob and Hannah (Spiers) White of Bedford County, Va. (See White family.)

CHILDREN:

(1) Alexander; died unmarried.
(2) Henry; died unmarried.
(3) Allen D.; married Emily Reese; had one son who died in youth.
(4) Demaris; married (first) John Perkins; (second) ———— Ford.

CHILD BY FIRST MARRIAGE:

(a) Bettie Alexander, born 1848; died June 4, 1905, at Brooklyn, N. Y.; married, November 20, 1871, William Robin Clements, who was born in Petersburg, Va., July 18, 1846. He enlisted in the Confederate Army at the age of sixteen; was elected Lieutenant of a company from Petersburg, and was at that time the youngest officer in the Confederate service; later, was promoted to Captain; surrendered with Lee at Appomattox, after having served with fidelity throughout the war.

William Robin Clements was a journalist by profession, and at one time a member of the editorial staff of the *Petersburg Courier*. During the last year of his life he was associated with the editorial conduct of the *Progress*. He died in Petersburg, Va., October 17, 1872.

CHILD:

(aa) William Ralph, born in Petersburg, Va., September 10, 1872; until thirteen years of age, under instruction of a governess; later, a private tutor, in preparation for college; M. D. degree, Medical College of Virginia, 1894. Member Phi Kappa Sigma Fraternity; elected a grand officer at Baltimore, 1898; Sons of the American Revolution; Kiwanis Club of Woodbury, N. J.

Master Mason, Florence Lodge No. 87, Woodbury, N. J.; Ancient Accepted Scottish Rite, Excelsior Consistory; 32nd Degree, Camden, N. J.; Tall Cedars of Lebanon, Glassboro Forest No. 1, Woodbury, N. J.; Veiled Prophets, Philadelphia, Pa.; Mystic Shrine, Crescent Temple, Trenton, N. J.

Dr. Clements is Surgeon; Haematologist; Chemical Pathologist; Toxocologist; now in charge of Repauno Hospital, Gibbstown, N. J., under control of E. I. du Pont de Nemours and Company, of Wilmington, Delaware.

He was appointed by President of United States Director of Draft Board of Gloucester Section of New Jersey, during the World War.

He married, August 26, 1913, Mrs. Bertha (Schnell) White, daughter of August and Louisa (Maier) Schnell, born in Worms, Rhein Hessen, Germany. They have no children.

(5) Rebecca Spiers; married John Calvin Hatcher, Sr.

(6) Margaret, born October 11, 1823; died June 15, 1908; married, January 25, 1848, Dr. Alexander Spotswood Thomson. (See Thomson family.)

Henry Hatcher married (second) Mary A. Latham, daughter of Henry and Mary (Ball) Latham.

CHILDREN:

(7) Harvey, born 1832; married Polly Hatcher; died 1904.

CHILDREN:

(a) Harvey.
(b) Halley.
(c) Frances.

(8) William Eldridge, born July 25, 1834; died 1912. From "Who's Who in America" we take the following:

"Hatcher, William E., clergyman, born in Bedford County, Va., July 25, 1834; son of Henry and Mary Latham Hatcher; A. B. of Richmond College in 1856; D. D., Richmond; LL. D., Denison; L. H. D., Colgate; married Oranie Virginia Snead in

EDITH HATCHER
wife of O. M. Harcum

REV. WILLIAM ELDRIDGE HATCHER, D. D.

1864. President Board of Trustees of Richmond College, 1893-1908; Woman's College, Richmond, 1892-1893; and now Fork Union Academy; President Baptist Education Board of Virginia, 1875-1901; President Baptist Orphanage of Virginia since 1891. Editor *Religious Herald, Baltimore Baptist* and *Baptist Argus*. He was author of the following: 'Life of Rev. J. B. Jeter, D. D.,' 1889; 'The Pastor and the Sunday School,' 1902; 'John Jasper,' 1908; 'Along the Trail of the Friendly Years,' 1910."

He collaborated with his wife, Oranie Virginia Snead Hatcher, in Life and Works of Dr. A. B. Brown, who was her teacher. Mrs. Hatcher wrote "Snead of Fluvanna" also. She was the daughter of George and Oranie (Pollard) Snead of Fluvanna County, Va.

CHILDREN:

(a) Eldridge Burwell, born at Fork Union, Va., October 16, 1865.

"Who's Who of America" says, "M. A. of Richmond College, studied at Johns Hopkins, Th. M., Southern Baptist Theological Seminary, Louisville, Kentucky. Married Annie G. Denson of Norfolk, Va. Children: William Eldridge and Anna Cranville. Pastor First Baptist Church, Norfolk, ten years; Editor, *Baptist World* and of *Western Recorder*. Head of Department of Christianity. Author, 'Dorothy Page,' 'Young Professor,' 'Woodrow Carlyle,' 'L i f e of William E. Hatcher'."

(b) Virginia Mabel, born at Baltimore, Md. Active in religious work in Richmond. Died 1900.

(c) Orie Latham, born in Petersburg, Va.

"Who's Who of America" says, "A. B., Vassar College, 1888; Ph. D., Chicago University. Joined faculty Bryn Mawr College. Head of Department Comparative Literature, same college. Founder and president of Southern Women's Educational Alliance. Clubs, Virginia Writers, (founder) Women's University Club, Washington, Chairman Committee on Patriotic Education of Daughters of American Revolution. Author of

'John Fletcher,' 'A Study in Dramatic Methods' (1904), 'Shakespeare Plays and Pageants' (1915), Editor, *Occupations for Women* (1927). Home Office, Gresham Court, Richmond, Virginia."

(d) Kate Jeter, born in Petersburg, Va.; married Charles Leonard DeMott of Lynchburg, Va. Ex-Chairman, committee on Patriotic Education, Daughters American Revolution.

CHILDREN:

(aa) Virginia Bagby; married Edwin Cox, of Richmond, Va.

(bb) Katherine; married Jacqulen Payne, of Columbia, Va.

CHILD:

(aaa) Katherine DeMott.

(e) Elizabeth Herndon White, born in Richmond, Va.; married Harry Winn Sadler, of Richmond. She was engaged in educational work for several years; wrote "The Bloom of Monticello."

(f) Edith Logwood, born in Richmond, Va.; married Octavius Marvin Harcum. Graduate, Woman's College, Richmond, Va.; Studied piano with Theodor Leschetizky in Vienna and I. Philipp in Paris. Founder and Head of the Harcum School in Bryn Mawr, Pennsylvania. Concert Pianist. Composer. Mentioned in "Who's Who in America," "Musical Blue Book" and "Women of America."

....

Thomas Hatcher, son of Rev. Jeremiah and Edith (Logwood) Hatcher; married (first), November 27, 1818, Catherine White, daughter of Jacob and Hannah (Spiers) White, of Bedford County, Va. (See White family.)

CHILDREN:

(1) Jacob White; married Bettie A. Turpin. (See Turpin family.)

SONS:

(a) William Richard. (See forward.)

(b) Overton L.

(c) Charles Henry. (See forward.)

(2) Alexander Monroe; married Amanda Falls.

(3) Thomas A.; married Mary Etta Meador.

(4) Robert E.; married Catherine Hawkins. (See forward.)

(5) Edward M.; married Theodosia C. N. Baughan.

(6) Henry Milton; married Maria Hawkins, daughter of George and Nancy (Hatcher) Hawkins.

CHILD:

(a) Elizabeth, who married Jesse M. Hopkins. (See White family.)

Thomas Hatcher married (second) Elizabeth Baughan.

CHILDREN:

(1) John E.; married Mamie Lupton, of Winchester, Va.

CHILDREN:

(a) Minnie; married John Putt.

(b) Lillie; married ———— Tankersley.

(c) Elizabeth; married Joseph Felton; lives in Richmond, Va.

(d) Frank; married; lives in Roanoke.

(e) Oscar; unmarried.

(f) Grace; married John Bower; lives in Bedford and has one son:

(aa) Jack.

(2) Whitfield; died unmarried.

(3) Scott; died unmarried.

(4) Theodosia; died unmarried.

(5) Margaret; never married; died December 25, 1929, aged 81 years.

(6) Ellen; died unmarried.

———————

William Richard Hatcher, son of Jacob White and Bettie A. (Turpin) Hatcher, was born in Bedford County, Va., July 23, 1845; married, May 27, 1869, Elizabeth Harrison Watson, daughter of James Fleming and Cynthia (Wilkerson) Watson. She was born in Botetourt County, Va., November 2, 1847.

CHILDREN:

(1) Myrtle White, born March 5, 1870; married, October 12, 1892, William Baily McNair.

(2) Oscar Burford, born August 4, 1871; married, April 3, 1899, Virginia E. Barger.

(3) Minnie Sarah, born May 10, 1875; married, July 9, 1896, James Brosius Waskey.

(4) William Lewis, born December 17, 1877; married, May 4, 1904, Bessie Rebecca Cash; died November 5, 1921.

(5) Otis Watson, born April 23, 1880; died August 15, 1881.

(6) Mabel Elizabeth, born July 28, 1882; unmarried.

(7) Lawrence Turpin, born March 27, 1884; died April 5, 1884.

All of the above children were born in Botetourt County, Va.

William Richard Hatcher saw service in the Confederate Army, having enlisted in December, 1863, at the age of eighteen years, in Company "G," Bedford County, Va. He joined his company in South Carolina, spent a few months there and then came to Petersburg, Va., where he remained most of the time until he was captured in 1865.

He was a member of the 34th Virginia Regiment, Wise's Brigade, Johnston's Division. Captain, William V. Jordan; Colonel, Goode; Major, Bagby.

He was in the Battle of The Crater; received a slight wound on the head; was captured near Hatcher's Run, March 29, 1865; taken to Point Lookout, Maryland, Prison, from which he was discharged, June 22, 1865. He was in service nineteen months, never asked for a furlough, and never missed a roll call nor a meal.

......

Charles Henry Hatcher, son of Jacob White and Bettie A. (Turpin) Hatcher, was born July 4, 1848, and died October 3, 1924. He married, December 3, 1872, Cynthia Agnes DeWitt, born January 13, 1853; daughter of William DeWitt.

CHILDREN:

(1) William H.; married Maude Wright, daughter of Ashby Wright. Two children: Ruby and Edward.

(2) Nannie Sue; married Andrew J. Key, son of Y. P. Key. Five children: Roy, Ruby, Woodrow, Burford, and Lucy West.

(3) Lemuel S.; married Ola Key, daughter of Benjamin F. Key. One child: Helen Gray.

(4) Maude Seay; married J. Frank Key, son of Benjamin F. Key. Five children: Willie Scott, Louise, Frank Edward, Russell, and Arline.

(5) Clayborne Otis; married Minnie Watts Logwood, daughter of Robert R. Logwood. Children: Maurice Reid, Cathryn Lloyd, Claude Johnson, and Mary Virginia.

(6) Samuel H.; married Sallie Elizabeth Vaughn, daughter of William Vaughn. Children: Lillian, Luella, Elizabeth, Maurice, Evelyn, and Doris.

(7) Bessie Lou; married Kent Arrington, son of William Arrington. One child: William Earl.

(8) Frank S.; married Lottie Coffee, daughter of George Purnell Coffee. Children: Francis Purnell and Charles Robert.

(9) Harry J.; married Marian Watson, daughter of Elmo Watson.

(10) Lottie Shackford; died November 16, 1906.

Robert E. Hatcher, son of Thomas and Catherine (White) Hatcher; married Catherine Hawkins, daughter of George and Nancy (Hatcher) Hawkins.

CHILDREN:

(1) Emmett D.; married (first) Margaret Smith, and had one son:
(a) Walter.
He married (second) Catherine Hawkins, and had one daughter:
(b) Catherine.

(2) Elmo Allen; married Mrs. Jane (Upshur) Vest.

CHILDREN:

(a) Katherine; married Harry Butler and lives in Premier, West Virginia.

CHILDREN:

Jane, Harry, Jr., Katherine, James, and Virginia.

(b) Virginia Wilcox; married Granville Curtis Sexton. Lives in Welch, W. Va. No children.

(c) Elmo Allen, II; married Ennis Bower. Lives in West Virginia.

CHILDREN:

Althea, Elmo Allen, III, and John D.

....

Julius Hatcher, son of Henry (3) and Margaret Hatcher, was born in Henrico County, Va., about 1735. He married Nancy ———.

CHILDREN:

(1) Julius F., born 1775; died January 2, 1867; married, September 2, 1799, Celia Fuqua, of Bedford County, Va.

CHILDREN:

(a) Granville L.; married Calistia Hatcher.
(b) Ann; married, March 11, 1819, Caleb Noell, son of Cornelius Noell, lieutenant of Bedford County Militia in Revolutionary War. (See McAllister's Data.)
    They had four sons and six daughters—among them Julius Hatcher Noell, who was born November 9, 1828, and died in Kansas in 1924. Caleb Noell died in West Virginia at the home of his daughter, Catherine. C. W. Noell, son of Julius Hatcher Noell, lives in Syracuse, Kansas, where he is Registrar of Deeds of Hamilton County, Kan.
(c) Thomas F.; married Caroline Noell.
(d) Julius Harmon; married, February 24, 1829, Frances B. White, daughter of James B. White; died 1864.

CHILDREN:

(aa) Mary C.; married Hannibal Hatcher, November 27, 1855.
(bb) Lucy; married Robert H. Jeter. (See Jeter family.)
(cc) Marinda; married William L. Turpin. (See Turpin family.)
(dd) Laura; married James W. Hatcher, son of John Calvin and Rebecca (Hatcher) Hatcher.
(ee) Florella; married Benjamin Noell, November 21, 1867.
(e) Judith; married Lafayette Noell.
(f) Angeline; married David Jones, Jr.

 (g) Julia Ann; married ——— Crank.

 (h) John Calvin; married Rebecca Spiers Hatcher; died 1868. (See forward.)

(2) Jesse; married Milly Edens, November 8, 1808.

(3) Betsy; married Joshua Taylor, January 18, 1801.

(4) Uriah; married (first) Elizabeth Jones, December 4, 1811.

CHILDREN:

 (a) Pleasant P., born November 11, 1812.

 (b) Susannah, born October 17, 1814.

 (c) Cincinnatus, born September 25, 1816.

He married (second) Nancy Noell. No children. His (third) wife was Susan Witt, and their children were:

 (a) Kittie, born February 17, 1822; married Alexander Noell.

 (b) Calistia, born September 29, 1823; married her first cousin, Granville L. Hatcher.

 (c) Hannibal, born October 21, 1825; married his cousin, Mary C. Hatcher, daughter of Julius H. and Frances (White) Hatcher.

 (d) Julius Caesar (Jack), born 1827; married Molly White, daughter of Jacob S. and Catherine (White) White. (See White family.)

 (e) Celine, born July 30, 1829.

 (f) Hillary, born November 8, 1832; married Gillie Jones.

 (g) Luvenia, born January 4, 1835; married John Sanderson.

 (h) Abner Uriah, born April 2, 1837; killed in Richmond, Va.

 (i) Kany; killed in Battle of Seven Pines.

(5) Sophia; married Henry Hatcher, son of Henry (4), March 8, 1806.

(6) Polly; married Thomas W. Taylor, June 18, 1808.

(7) Hillary; married Margaret Hensley, October 14, 1816.

(8) Lucy; married, perhaps, William Hatcher in 1815.

John Calvin Hatcher, son of Julius F. and Celia (Fuqua) Hatcher, married Rebecca Spiers Hatcher, daughter of Henry and Elizabeth (White) Hatcher. (See White family.)

CHILDREN:

(1) James Wellington, born September, 1838; married, November 25, 1866, Laura Frances Hatcher; died May, 1895.

CHILDREN:

(a) Julius Eldridge, born August 25, 1867; married Hattie Monger.

CHILD:

(aa) Julius Eldridge, Jr.; died May, 1925.

(b) Jimmie Calvin, born May 3, 1870; married Archibald Alexander Jones, June 16, 1897.

(c) Lillian Frances, born April 8, 1873; married, March 25, 1895, Robert Hugh Luck, son of George P. and Nancy (Buford) Luck.

CHILDREN:

(aa) James Wellington; married Gladys Arrington.

CHILDREN:

Zelma Gladys, James Paul, Josephine, Geraldine, Bettie Ann, and Robert Hugh.

(bb) Edward W.; married Virginia Hall.
(cc) Effie Golden; married Gardner Wright Bond.

CHILD:

(aaa) Gardner Wright, Jr. (See Bond family.)

(dd) Julian Aubrey; married Grace Snead.

CHILDREN:

Eloise, Dorothy, and Sallie Lillian.

(ee) Archibald A.
(ff) George Simeon.
(gg) Helen Frances.

(d) Fonza Ernest, born March 8, 1876; married Bessie Capps.

CHILDREN:

Frances Gwendolin, who married Joseph Baker; Fonza Bertram; and Ralph Stewart.

(e) Laura Gilmer, born March 21, 1878; married Robert Beryl Schenk, Jr.

CHILDREN:

Earl Nelson, William Eldridge, George Philip, and Robert Calvin.

(2) Bettie M.; married Thomas B. Hawkins.

CHILDREN:

(a) Novell O.; married Mary Turpin; died May, 1927. No children.

(b) Steptoe C.; married Kate Winfrey.

CHILDREN:

Thomas B., Pauline, Elizabeth, Alice, and John.

(c) Alfred L.; married Lola Browning.

CHILDREN:

Bettie M., and Alfred L., Jr.

(d) Jennie; married R. E. Doyle.

CHILDREN:

R. E., Jr., and Clarence.

(e) Celia; married Emmett D. Hatcher.

CHILD:

Catherine.

(f) Ruth; married ———— Minnick.

(3) Henry B.; died unmarried in 1862, while in the Civil War.

(4) John Calvin, Jr.; married, February 16, 1871, Ann Stitira Cobbs, daughter of James Valentine and Sarah (Jeter) Cobbs. (See Jeter family.)

CHILDREN:

(a) Connie Gwatkin; married William Hopkins.

CHILDREN:

Ralph, Kenneth, Calvin, and Coral, who married Louise Wright and has one child: Marguerite.

(b) Courtney Valentine; married, January 19, 1929, Frances Cofer.

(5) Martin Luther, born November 6, 1848; married, December 3, 1876, Mary Ella Read (born December 10, 1852; died September 22, 1928), daughter of Edward T. and Eliza (Garner) Read.

CHILDREN:

(a) Zelda, born November 8, 1877.

(b) Mabel Claire, born November 25, 1879; married (first), November 29, 1899, A. R. Ferrill (died February 17, 1901); (second) Philip H. Johnson, January 7, 1906.

CHILDREN:

(aa) Frank Everett, born April 17, 1907; killed in automobile accident, September 12, 1929.

(bb) Mabel Claire, born September 2, 1908.

(cc) Philip H., Jr., born February 11, 1910.

(dd) Leonard, born October 8, 1914.

(c) Ella Pearl, born July 6, 1886; married John Winston Overton, September 24, 1907.

CHILDREN:

(aa) John Winston, Jr., born October 3, 1908.

(bb) Samuel Hatcher, born March 18, 1916.

(d) Lelia Belle, born September 13, 1888; died July 11, 1908.

(e) Edward Calvin, born December 18, 1890; married, February 15, 1912, Edna Louis Clingenpeel.

CHILDREN:

(aa) Martin Teaford, born February 21, 1913.

(bb) Edward Calvin, Jr., born March 31, 1916.

(6) Julius Watson; married Cora Obenchain; died, leaving one son:

(a) Julian Guy, who lives in Memphis, Tenn.

(7) Edward Perkins, born July 9, 1854; died February 8, 1902; married, March 29, 1883, Fannie R. Cobbs, daughter of James Valentine and Sarah (Jeter) Cobbs. (See Jeter family.)

CHILDREN:

(a) Sammie; married Joseph Garnett, of Farmville, Va. No children.

(b) Watson Calvin; married, August 8, 1923, Viola Spillsbee Bush, daughter of William Griffin and Mary R. (Woolfork) Bush.

CHILDREN:

Calvin Perkins and Barbara Ann.

(c) Harry Cobbs; married Marie Lewis.

(d) Harvey Spinner; unmarried.

(8) Celia D.; married Rev. Samuel M. Richardson. One daughter:

(a) Ruth, who married Paul Wood and died soon after.

(9) Birdella Eldridge; married Nathaniel Thurman Wright. Died at birth of only son:

(a) Bernard.

BOARD

John Board, the immigrant, was born in England. He settled in Bedford County, Virginia, where he died in 1787. His wife was Jemima ————.

CHILDREN:

(1) Stephen; married Judy ————.
(2) Absalom; married Martha ————.
(3) James; married Mary Ferguson. (See forward.)
(4) William.
(5) Mary; married Jesse Hix.
(6) John; married Jane Harwood. (See forward.)

....

James Board, son of John the immigrant and Jemima Board, lived in Bedford County, Va., moved to Franklin County, and then to Breckinridge County, Ky., where he died.

He was a private in the Colonial Army under Colonel Byrd, 1761-62 (Bedford records). He married Mary Ferguson, daughter of Alexander and Mary Ferguson of Bedford and Franklin counties. Alexander Ferguson was a patriot, for he proved in court, April 22, 1782, that he furnished John Ward, Commissary, 650 lbs. of beef and 325 lbs. of beef.

CHILDREN OF JAMES AND MARY (FERGUSON) BOARD:

(1) Henry.
(2) Christopher.
(3) Robert.
(4) Jefferson.
(5) William.
(6) Elijah.
(7) Micajah.
(8) Nehemiah.
(9) Richard; died 1873.
(10) Joel.
(11) Polly; married Nehemiah Dowell.
(12) Nancy; married Nathaniel Shrewsbury, son of Samuel and Elizabeth Dabney (D'Aubigne) Shrewsbury. He was Ensign 1st Battalion, 10th Reg't., 1799; in 1800, was Lieutenant and Captain of Militia of Bedford County. They removed to Breckinridge County, Ky. Among their children was Nancy, who married Burwell Horsley. (See forward.)
(13) Elizabeth.
(14) Jemima; married ———— Dowell.

....

John Board, son of John the immigrant, and Jemima Board, was born January 3, 1754; died 1821; married Jane Harwood (died 1874), daughter of Francis and Margaret Harwood of Charlotte County, Va.

He proved in court (Bedford), April 22, 1782, that he furnished Com. John Ward with 13 diets, 5 pecks Corn, 43 bundles of Fodder. He was also employed by John Ward, Commissioner, ten days in collecting Public Beeves. (Virginia State Archives.)

He was Captain of Militia of Bedford County in War of 1812, and was thus the head of the Processioners—August 26, 1825.

CHILDREN :

(1) Polly; married William Horsley. (See forward.)
(2) Nancy, born September 22, 1778; married Jehu Meador.
(3) Jemima, born December 25, 1780; married Thomas Squires.
(4) Esther, born September, 1783; married William Dent.
(5) Francis, born February 13, 1786; married Maria Preston. (See forward.)
(6) John, born August 27, 1787; married Elizabeth McCabe. Among their sixteen children was Francis Harwood Board, born February 10, 1832, who was killed in battle near Winchester, Va., July 20, 1864. His son, Dr. John Board resides at Altavista, Va., and his daughter, Mrs. Lillie (Board) Dennis, widow of Dr. T. C. Dennis, resides at Bedford, Va.

Polly Board, daughter of John and Jane (Harwood) Board, married William Horsley. They were living in Bedford County in 1800, in Franklin County in 1810, and he died in Breckinridge County, Ky., before 1817. Among their children was—

Burwell Horsley, born December 5, 1800; died in Bentonville, Arkansas, in 1870; married, March 25, 1824, Nancy Shrewsbury. Their youngest son—

Louis Langley Horsley married Florentine Gunn, and their daughter—

Clara Horsley married William Tollerton, and lives at 10502 S. Seeley Avenue, Chicago, Ill.

Francis, son of John and Jane (Harwood) Board, married Maria Preston.

CHILDREN :

Green B; Jemima; John; Joseph; Jane; Francis; Thomas, married Elizabeth Wright; Charles Auville (see forward); James Garland (see forward); Samuel; Henry; and Septimus Maxton.

Charles Auville Board, son of Frank and Maria (Preston) Board, was born in Bedford County, November 14, 1832, and died February 26, 1910. He was educated at the University of Virginia, taking courses in both medicine and dentistry. After practicing medicine for some years in Bedford County he entered the Confederate Army and was assistant surgeon in the hospital service for three years, being attached to the 1st Division.

He was active in church work—superintendent of the Sunday School and deacon of the Baptist church of Bedford, and, for many years, moderator of the Baptist Strawberry Association.

He was, also, much interested in civic affairs; was twice mayor of the town of Bedford, and clerk of the Municipal School Board for a great many years.

Dr. Charles Auville Board married (first) October 11, 1855, Lizzie Adelaide Gish (born March 21, 1835; died May 18, 1870), daughter of William and Sarah E. (Bush) Gish.

CHILDREN:

(1) Olive May; married Rev. John Howard Eager, October 6, 1880; went to Rome, Italy, in the service of the Southern Baptist Convention, living there ten years and in Florence, Italy, six years. They returned to the United States in 1896 and have since lived in Louisville, Ky., Baltimore, Md., and are now living in New York City.

Their children, now all married, are as follows:

(a) John Howard, Jr., born in Rome, Italy, 1881.

(b) Alice Rivier, born in Rome, Italy, 1883.

(c) George Taylor, born in Rome, Italy, 1885.

(d) Elizabeth Gish, born in Bedford, Va., 1888.

(e) Auville, born in Rome, Italy, 1889.

(f) Harriet Ide, born in Florence, Italy, 1891.

(g) Paul Roman, born in Baltimore, Md., 1896.

(h) Olive May, born in Louisville, Ky., 1899.

(2) Alice Maria; married, April 14, 1896, Benjamin Franklin Reese of Kansas City, Mo. (See Reese family.)

CHILD:

(a) Mary Eager, born February 15, 1897; married, June 18, 1921, in Kansas City, Mo., Dr. Herbert L. Mantz, who was born June 28, 1896, in West Plains, Mo.

CHILDREN:

(aa) Ben Reese, born April 7, 1922.

(bb) Alice Virginia (twin), born August 14, 1926.

(cc) Mary Elizabeth (twin), born August 14, 1926.

(3) James McHenry, born in Nicholas County, West Virginia; died in Texas, December, 1920.

(4) Sallie Elizabeth; married in Florence, Italy, March 22, 1892, by Rev. John H. Eager, James Shannon Miller of Pulaski, Virginia, who was educated at the University of Virginia and has been Professor of Mathematics in Emory and Henry College, Va., since 1893, with the exception of three years, when he held a similar position in Hampden-Sydney College, Va.

CHILDREN:

(a) William Berkeley, born February 16, 1894; died in infancy.

(b) James Shannon, Jr., born October 5, 1898; married at Niagara, in 1920, Isabel Painter Holladay of Charlottesville, Va.; now teaching in the Electrical Engineering Department of the University of Virginia.

DR. CHARLES AUVILLE BOARD

CHILDREN:

(aa) Isabel Holladay, born May 24, 1922.

(bb) Sarah Elizabeth, born September 12, 1928.

(c) Juliet Eager, born September 23, 1906.

(5) Mary Dawkins; unmarried; now living in New York City.

(6) Lizzie Gish; died in childhood.

Dr. C. A. Board's (second) wife was Emma Wainwright Hatcher, whom he married, October 19, 1886. (See Hatcher family.)

CHILDREN:

(7) Charles Auville, Jr., born February 4, 1889, died in infancy.

(8) Florence Hatcher, born September 22, 1891; married, April 1, 1929, James Edmond Luttrell; lives in Craig, Colorado.

(9) Howard Eager, born March 29, 1893; died in France, July 21, 1918, from wounds received in action at a point five miles east of Chateau Thierry, death coming almost at the beginning of the great offensive which finally ended the World War. His body was laid to rest in the beautiful Aisne-Marne Cemetery—Grave 26, Row 7, Block A, at Belleau Wood, France.

That he met his death while bravely performing his duties as an American soldier is amply substantiated by the following communications from the commander of the Sixth Brigade, General Hunt, with whom he served.

HEADQUARTERS SIXTH BRIGADE
13 July 1919

Mrs. Emma W. Board,
330 N. Bridge Street,
Bedford, Va.

My dear Madam:

I am sending you a service ribbon with three bronze stars and one silver star for your son, Private Howard E. Board, Headquarters Detachment Sixth Brigade.

The three bronze stars are for the battles and the occupation of the one defensive sector in which he participated. The silver star is for the citation, copy of which I enclose.

BATTLES:

Aisne Defensive, June 1st to June 5th, 1918.

Champagne-Marne Defensive, July 15th to 18th, 1918.

Aisne-Marne Offensive, July 18th to 21st, 1918.

DEFENSIVE SECTOR:

Chateau Thierry Sector, June 6th to July 14th, 1918.

Your son was wounded at St. Eugene, France, five miles directly east of Chateau Thierry, on the afternoon of July 21st, 1918, and died at 7:45 P. M. the same day.

He was highly esteemed by all the officers and men with whom he served, and you have my sincere sympathy in his loss.

Very truly yours,

O. E. Hunt,

Brigadier General, U. S. A.

HEADQUARTERS SIXTH BRIGADE

13 July 1919

GENERAL ORDERS:

No. 3.

I, The Commanding General Sixth Brigade, cite the following named officers and enlisted men for distinguished service rendered in action:

Private Howard E. Board, Headquarters Det.

"For extraordinary ability and heroism in the Aisne-Marne Offensive near Crezancy, France, the 21st of July 1919, for repeatedly carrying messages under severe shell and machine gun fire, distinguishing himself by his ever willingness to perform any duty called upon.

By command of Brigadier General Hunt,

W. S. Maxwell,
Major Infantry,
Brigade Adjutant.

UNITED STATES ARMY

U. S. A.—A. E. F.

In Memory of

Private Howard E. Board, Headqrs. Det. 6th Infantry Bde.

who died July 21st, 1918

He bravely laid down his life for the cause of his country. His name will ever remain fresh in the hearts of his friends and comrades. The record of his honorable service will be preserved in the archives of the American Expeditionary Forces.

John J. Pershing,
Commander-in-Chief.

As a testimony of the high esteem in which he was held by his comrades, the Bedford County Post of the American Legion was named in his honor.

....

James Garland Board, son of Frank and Maria (Preston) Board, was born January 8, 1834; married, April 21, 1858, Anna M. Bond, daughter of Pleasant and Elizabeth (Jeter) Bond. (See Bond family.)

CHILDREN:

Lulie B., Edgar C., James P., Walter G., Emma C., Daisy A., Florence J., Lizzie M., Pearl O., Frank W., and Nina May.

James G. Board was one of six brothers who were soldiers in the Confederate Army. He was Captain of Company "E", 28th Virginia Infantry, for three years, and lost a leg at Boonesboro, Md., September 14, 1862, while in service.

THOMSON

Jesse L. Thomson, born in Amelia County, Virginia, married Rhoda Morris Wharton. He died May 4, 1842, and she died in September, 1864, both in Bedford County, Va.

CHILDREN:

(1) Alexander Spotswood, born July, 1827; attended Emory and Henry College; later graduated in medicine, which profession he practiced in Bedford County. Married, January 25, 1848, Margaret R. Hatcher, born October 11, 1823; daughter of Henry and Elizabeth (White) Hatcher. (See White and Hatcher families.) Dr. Alexander Spotswood Thomson died September 15, 1907, and his wife died June 15, 1908.

CHILDREN:

(a) Sallie W., born December 21, 1849; died November 11, 1852.

(b) Demaris Ann ("Malie"), born October 4, 1851; married, April 11, 1876, Callohill Minnis Gibbs, born March 18, 1840, son of John Dent and Lucy Jane (Moorman) Gibbs, of Bedford County. Callohill Minnis Gibbs enlisted May 28, 1861, in Company G, 2nd Virginia Cavalry, and served with honor until the close of the war. Both he and his wife are deceased.

CHILDREN:

(aa) Mabel Hope, born February 24, 1877 (deceased).

(bb) Maurice Thomson, born February 7, 1879; married ————; has several children. Practicing medicine at Huddleston, Va.

(cc) Alexander Dent, born January 25, 1881 (deceased).

(c) Emily Morris, born March 21, 1854 (deceased).

(d) Lelia, born December 2, 1856; died June 9, 1858.

(e) Mary Louis, born January 16, 1859; unmarried. Living in Chicago.

(f) Olivia Alexander, born January 30, 1861; unmarried. Living in Chicago.

(g) Spotswood Edward, born January 30, 1864; married, December 5, 1888, Jessie Frances, daughter of James Jacob and America (Turpin) Penn. (See Penn family.)

CHILDREN:

(aa) Lewis Edward; died at his home, "Shady Acres," in Macon, Georgia, on October 9, 1929; unmarried.

(bb) Harry Penn; married Stella Marie McClellan. Living in Waxahachie, Texas.

CHILD:

(aaa) Emily Frances.

(cc) James Ralph; married Blanche Isaac. Living in Dallas, Texas.

CHILD:

(aaa) James Ralph, Jr.

(dd) William Alexander; married Monroe Tate. Living in Hattiesburg, Mississippi.

CHILD:

(aaa) William Alexander, Jr.

(ee) Helen Temple; married Marcellus Leslie Slaughter, of Lynchburg, Va.

CHILDREN:

(aaa) Margaret Helen.
(bbb) Shirley Penn.

(ff) Lillian Olivia; married William McDuffy Woodson. Living in Lynchburg, Va.

(gg) Marian Jessie, of Macon, Ga.

(hh) Edith Hatcher; married, February 22, 1929, Staley Butler Johnson, of Lynchburg, Va.

(ii) Louise Evelyn, of Macon, Ga.

(jj) Polly Penn, of Macon, Ga.

(kk) Virginia Spotswood, of Macon, Ga.

(h) Henry, born December 21, 1868; married, May 18, 1892, Lula May Lupton, born March 10, 1876, daughter of

NANCY ("ANN") LOGWOOD WHITE
wife of Nathaniel W. Thomson

Cornelius and Jennie Watts (Shelton) Lupton, of Bedford County, Va.

CHILDREN:

(aa) Herbert Bruce, born September 10, 1898; married, February 5, 1921, Elizabeth Kabler, daughter of Dr. Kabler, of New London. Living in Chicago.

CHILDREN:

(aaa) Herbert Bruce, Jr., born November 5, 1921.
(bbb) Emmy Lou, born August 4, 1923.
(ccc) Betty Kabler, born April 13, 1925.

(bb) Alexander Spotswood, born May 15, 1900. Educated at New London Academy. Living in Topeka, Kansas.

(cc) Virginia Elizabeth, born January 26, 1902. Graduate of William and Mary College.

(dd) Margaret Louis, born April 24, 1903; graduate of William and Mary College; married, April 6, 1926, Arthur Copeland, of Charles City, Va., now living in Madison, Wisconsin.

(ee) Cornelius Lupton, born December 1, 1906. Educated at New London Academy and Virginia Polytechnic Institute. Living in Rock Island, Illinois.

(ff) Frances Olivia, born February 11, 1908. Graduate of William and Mary College, 1928.

(gg) Christine Henry, born December 27, 1911. Senior at William and Mary College.

(2) Nathaniel W., born December 7, 1829; married, December 21, 1850, Ann Logwood White, born July 22, 1827, a daughter of Captain Henry Milton and Mary Ann (Gwatkin) White. (See White family.) She was noted for her beauty and was a sweet and lovely character. Her untimely death brought much sadness to those who loved her. She died July 17, 1851, and with her infant son, was buried in the family plot. On December 5, 1865, he married Sarah Virginia Wharton, born May 13, 1835,

a daughter of John A. and Isabella (Brown) Wharton, of Bedford County, Va. Nathaniel W. Thomson served in the Confederate Army, enlisting first, in Company C, 28th Virginia Infantry, which was afterwards changed to Bowyer's Battery and known as the Bedford Light Artillery. He participated with honor in all the engagements of his company until the battle of Sharpsburg, Maryland. In this battle he was so severely wounded that his recovery was considered a miracle. He lived at "Locust Hill," Bedford County, and died December 10, 1918.

CHILD BY FIRST MARRIAGE:

(a) Infant son; born dead—unnamed.

CHILD BY SECOND MARRIAGE:

(b) Isabella M., born October 31, 1869; married, November 1, 1901, William Steptoe Foster, born September 23, 1857, son of Henry J. and Elizabeth (Steptoe) Foster, of Bedford, Virginia.

CHILDREN:

(aa) Virginia Thomson, with the National Geographic Magazine Co., Washington, D. C.

(bb) William Steptoe, Jr.

(3) Sarah; married Dr. John Temple.

(4) Catherine; married John Sanderson.

(5) Isabella; married William Allen Hayden, of Missouri, where they lived.

(6) Sophia Davis; married ———— Gregg, of Missouri.

(7) Charlotte F., born March, 5, 1836; married, February 17, 1855, Col. Jesse S. Burks, son of Martin P. and Louisa C. (Spinner) Burks, of Bedford County, Va. She was his second wife. (See Burks family.)

(8) Jesse Lewis; married Anna Trask.

PENN

In his Patronymica Britannica, Mr. Lower says the family of William Penn, the founder of Pennsylvania, derived their name, at an early period, from the parish of Penn, in the County of Buckingham, England.

The earliest record of the Penns in Virginia is 1621-1635—long before William Penn, the Quaker, was born, though, we are told, they were his ancestors. These early Penns first settled in Maryland—many of their descendants, after the Revolutionary War, moving west to Ohio and Kentucky.

William Penn, the founder of Pennsylvania, was born in London, October 14, 1644. He was the son of William Penn, who was an Admiral and served in the navy of Parliament, and his wife, Margaret Jasper, the daughter of a Dutch merchant. He entered Christ Church College, Oxford in 1660—matriculating as a "gentleman Commoner, and the son of a knight." He became a Quaker, and, though, his father died in 1670, leaving him a wealthy man, he continued to be a very ardent Quaker. He married in 1672, Gulielma Springett, who died in February, 1694, leaving three children (two boys and one girl), viz.: (1) Springett, (2) William, III, and (3) Letitia.

In 1675, he first became connected with America, and, on June 24, 1680, asked the Crown of England for a grant of land in America, described as a "tract of land in America, north of Maryland, bounded on the east by Delaware, on the west limited as Maryland (i. e., by New Jersey) northward as far as plantable."

In 1696, he married for his second wife, Hannah Callowhill and she bore him three sons: (1) John, (2) Thomas, and (3) Richard. From 1699 to December, 1701, Penn was in Pennsylvania. He was noted for his friendly trading with the Indians. William Penn died May 30, 1718, and was buried at Jourdan's meeting-house Chalfont St. Giles in Buckinghamshire, England.

....

The following is the Penn coat of arms as given by Burke:

Arms. Ar. on a fesse sa. three plates.
Crest. A demi lion ramp ar. gorged
with a collar sa. charged with
three plates.
Motto. Dum clarum rectum teneam.

In Drysdale Parish, Caroline County, Virginia, between 1730-1746, we find John, George, Joseph and Moses Penn, purchasing land.

1761-1763—Deeds made by Joseph Penn of Spottsylvania County, Virginia, mentions wife, Elizabeth; children, John, Philip, Moses, Thomas, Catherine (wife of Larkin Gatewood), Mary, and Frances. (This Joseph was deceased in 1773.)

1764—Gabriel Penn of Amherst County, Virginia, deeds to John Penn of Spottsylvania County, Virginia. Witness, John Penn, Jr., Thomas Penn.

1771—Will of John Penn, Spottsylvania County, Virginia, mentions wife, Mary; children, John, Thomas, George, William, Mildred, Sally and Frances.

From the First Census of the United States, taken in 1783, we find in Amherst County, Virginia, the following Penns listed as "Heads of Families": Gabriel, George, John, Moses, Philip, Sr., Philip, Jr., Rawley, and Thomas.

The foregoing are all family names having been handed down, for generations, from father to son; and since then, found in many counties of Virginia, in Ohio, Kentucky and other western states. There were many Moses Penns in Virginia.

....

John Penn, third Signer of the Declaration of Independence on behalf of the province of North Carolina, born in Caroline County, Virginia, May 17, 1741, was the son and only child of Moses Penn. His mother was Catherine Taylor, born December 30, 1719; died November 4, 1774, and married, July 4, 1739, Moses Penn, who died November 4, 1759. Catherine Taylor was the daughter of John Taylor (born November 18, 1696; died March 22, 1780, son of James and Mary Taylor) and Catherine Pendleton (born December 8, 1699; died July 26, 1774, daughter of Philip and Isabella Pendleton), who were married, February 14, 1716. (*William and Mary Quarterly*, Vol. 12, p. 129.) John Penn married in July, 1763, Susan Lyme and had three children—only one surviving infancy—a daughter, Lucy M., who married in 1781, Col. John Taylor, of Caroline County, Virginia, said to be the son of James and Ann (Pollard) Taylor. In 1774, John Penn took up his residence in North Carolina. His death occurred in September, 1788.

In Hardesty's *Encyclopedia*, we have the following Penns listed as Revolutionary Soldiers from Amherst County, Virginia: Gabriel, Philip, Sr., Rolly, Captain George, Philip, Jr., and Thomas. William, also, was a Revolutionary soldier from Amherst and died 1777. (See forward; will of William Penn.)

....

George Penn, of Caroline County, Virginia, brother of Moses Penn who married Catherine Taylor and were the parents of John Penn, the third Signer of the Declaration of Independence, married Ann ———. Prior to 1750, this George and Ann (———) Penn moved from Caroline County to Amherst—then Albemarle County, Virginia, and were the progenitors of the Penns we find in Amherst at the beginning of the Revolutionary War. We have already seen that Gabriel Penn, of Amherst County deeded in 1764, land in Spottsylvania County, Virginia.

CHILDREN OF GEORGE AND ANN (———) PENN

(1) Frances, born January 9, 1735; married (first), Ambrose Lee, who died in 1764, leaving her with three children, viz.: (1) Frank (Francis) Lee, (2) Richard Lee, and (3) Nancy Lee. She married (second), Drury Tucker, of Prince George County, Virginia, and died in 1812. She was Drury Tucker's second wife, his first wife being Susanna Douglas.

(2) George, born December 12, 1737. (See forward—will of George Penn.)

(3) Philip, born January 27, 1739. Had several daughters.

(4) Gabriel, born July 17, 1741. (See forward.)

(5) Abraham, born December 27, 1743; married, 1768, Ruth Stovall, daughter of James and Mary (Cooper) Stovall, of Amherst County, Virginia. Colonel of Henry County Militia. A man of prominence and influence in that section of the state. Died 1801. There were twelve children, viz.: (1) George Penn; married Miss Gordon and afterwards moved to New Orleans. (2) Lucinda Penn; married Samuel Staples, for many years Clerk of Patrick County, Va. (3) Gabriel Penn; married Jinsy Clark, of Patrick County. (4) Horatio Penn; married Nancy Parr, and moved to Missouri. (5) Polly Penn; married Charles Foster, of Patrick County. (6) Greenesville Penn; married (first) Miss Leath, of Manchester, Va.; (second) Mar-

tha Reed, of Bedford County, Va.   (7) Thomas Penn; married (first) Frances Leath, of Manchester, Va.; (second) Mary Christian Kennerly, of Amherst County, Va.   (8) Abram Penn; married Sally Kreitz (or Critz); moved to Tennessee. (9) James Penn; married (first) Miss Leath, of Manchester, Va.; (second) Mary Shelton, daughter of William and Pattie (Dillard) Shelton.   (10) Luvenia Penn, died young.   (11) Edmund Penn; married Pollie Ferris, of Patrick County and moved to Kentucky. (12) Philip Penn; married Louise Briscoe, of Bedford County, Va.   (The Penn Family of Virginia—Clemens.)

(6) William, born April 7, 1745. Never married. Lieutenant in Continental Army. (See forward—will of Wm. Penn.)

(7) Moses, Jr., born January 13, 1748—never married. (See forward —will of Moses Penn, Jr.)

The following is a copy of the will of George Penn, eldest son of George and Ann (————) Penn, filed February 5, 1790, Will Book No. 3, page 267, Amherst County, Virginia, gives names of his ten children. No mention being made of wife—evidently deceased.

IN THE NAME OF GOD, AMEN. I, GEORGE PENN, of Amherst County, being weak of body but of sound mind and memory, do make and ordain this my last will and testament in manner and form following (to-wit).

Item. I give unto my daughter, Frankey Burton, two negroes, Peter and Jude, and one feather bed which she has now in possession to her and her heirs forever.

Item. I give unto my daughter, Molly Harrison, two negroes, Simon and Virgin, and one feather bed which she has in possession, to her & her heirs forever.

Item. I give unto my daughter, Nancy Savage, two negroes, Candis & Davy, and one feather bed the feather and negro Candis she has now in possession the other at my decease to her and her heirs forever.

Item. I give to my daughter, Lucy Penn, two negroes, Moses and Rachel, and one feather bed and furniture to her and her heirs forever.

Item. I give unto my daughter, Sally Penn, two negroes, Charlotte and Betty, and one feather bed and furniture to her and her heirs forever.

Item. I give unto my son, William Penn, two negroes, Henry & Rose, and one feather bed and furniture, the feather bed and furniture and negro Henry he has at present in possession to him and his heirs forever.

Item. I give to my son, George Penn, two negroes, Diner and Sam, with one feather bed and furniture, the negro Diner and feather bed has already in possession to him and his heirs forever.

Item. I give unto my son, Wilson Penn, two negroes, Benn & Lucy, and one feather bed & furniture to him and his heirs forever.

Item. I give unto my son, Thomas Penn, two negroes, Sampson & Delf, and one feather bed & furniture to him and his heirs forever.

Item. I give unto my son, Moses Penn, two negroes, Adam & Hanner, & one feather bed and furniture to him and to his heirs forever.

Item. It is my will and desire that whatever negroes I may die possessed of not already bequeathed be equally divided between my ten children, to-wit, William Penn, George Penn, Thomas Penn, Wilson Penn, Moses Penn, Molly Harrison, Frances Burton, Nancy Savage, Lucy Penn, & Sally Penn, to them and their heirs forever.

Item. It is my will and desire that what right and title I may have to any lands in the State of Kentucky be hereby vested in my five sons equally, William Penn, George, Wilson Penn, Thomas Penn, and Moses Penn, to them and their heirs forever.

Item. I give to my son, Moses Penn, my riding horse and saddle to him and his heirs forever.

Item. I give to my daughty, Lucy Penn, the next choice beast out of my estate and saddle to be furnished by Executors to her and her heirs forever.

Item. I give unto my daughter, Sally Penn, the next choice beast out of my estate and saddle to be furnished out of my estate to her and her heirs forever.

Item. It is my will and desire that my Executor hereafter named do dispose of all my personal estate not already bequeathed which I may die possessed of not allready or heretofore bequeathed on twelve months tender for the best price that can be had and the money arising from such sale to be applied to the discharging all my just debts after which the balance of money arising from such sale to be equally divided between my five sons, William Penn, George Penn, Wilson Penn, Thomas Penn and Moses Penn, to them and their heirs forever.

Item. It is my will and desire that the land whereon I now live with the appurtenances be sold by my executors on twelve months credit and the money arising from such sale to be equally divided between my five sons, William Penn, George Penn, Wilson Penn, Thomas Penn, and Moses Penn, to them and their heirs forever after paying all of my just debts.

Item. Lastly I do appoint my sons William Penn, George Penn, Wilson Penn, and Thomas Penn, and my friend, David S. Garland, executors to this my last will and testament hereby revoking and disannulling all former wills and legacys. In Witness Whereof, I have hereunto set my hand and seal this 5th day of February, 1790.

GEORGE PENN [SEAL].

Teste
    MATHEW WATSON
    JAMES M. BROWN
    JAMES BALLINGER.

At a Court held for Amherst County the 15th day of February, 1790.

This will was produced in Court and proven by the oaths of James M. Brown, Matthew Watson, and James Ballenger, witnesses thereto, sworn to by William Penn, George Penn, Thomas Penn, and David S. Garland, four of the executors therein named and ordered to be recorded, and certificate for obtaining a probate thereof in due form was granted the said Executors they having given bond with Thomas Powell and Micajah Pendleton their securities in the penalty of five thousand pounds current money conditioned as the law directs.

Teste

W. S. CRAWFORD, *Clk*.

Will Book No. 3, page 267,
    Amherst County, Va.

....

From the Amherst County marriage bonds we have the following— no doubt, both were the sons of George Penn as mentioned in above will:

1796, September 12—Wilson Penn and Frances Taliaferro.
1797—Thomas Penn and Beth. Stevens.

The Will of Moses Penn, Junior (born January 13, 1748; died 1774, youngest child of George and Ann (———) Penn) recorded in Will Book No. 1, page 268, of the Amherst County records is as follows:

In the Name of God Amen. I, MOSES PENN, of the County of Amherst being weake and low of body but of perfect sences and sound of memory, do make and ordain this my last will and testament in manner and forme as followith. Item first it is my will and desire that all my just debts should be paid. Item. I give unto my brother Philip Penn my negroe fellow named Jacob, to him and his heirs forever. Item, I give unto my niece and Godchild Parmelia Penn daughter of my brother Gabriel my negroe woman named Tamar with her future increase, to her and her heirs forever. Item. I give unto my nephew and Godson, George Penn (son of my brother George), my negroe fellow named Gabe which said negroe I have lent to my brother William Penn to attend him on his journey in some of the Southern Provinces, and in case the said negroe should die in the possession of my said brother William I charge him my said brother William seventy-five pounds to be paid to my said God son George Penn in lew of the said negroe, to him and his heirs forever. Item. I give unto my brother William Penn the sum of fifty pounds to be collected and paid him out of the debts due me, part of which is already in his own hands. Item. I give unto my nephew Frank Lee my riding horse saddle & bridle and one-half of my wearing apparel. Item. I give unto my nephew Richard Lee halfe of my wearing apparel. Item. I give unto my God son Ben Phillips son of William Phillips ten pounds out of the debts due me in any remain after my just debts are paid. For the care and diligence of John Conner in wateing on me in my sickness I desire he may be amply recompenced out of my estate for the same at the discretion of my executors. Item. All the remainder of my whole estate if any such remaining I give unto my niece Nancy Lee to be applied towards her maintenance and education & lastly do appoint as Executors to this my last will and testament my beloved brothers George Penn and Gabriel Penn. In witness whereof I have hereunto set my hand and seal this third day of August An. dom. one thousand seven hundred and seventy-foure.   MOSES PENN, JUN. [L. S.]

Sealed & acknowledged in presence of
    EDMD. WILCOX, JOHN LAMONT
    DAVID SHEPHERD.

At a Court held for Amherst County the third day of October, 1774. This last will and testament of Moses Penn, Jr., deceased, was presented in Court by George and Gabriel Penn, Executors, therein named, who made oath thereto according to law, and the same being also proved by the oaths of Edmund Wilcox, John Lamont & David Shepherd, subscribing witnesses thereto, is ordered to be recorded.

Teste:

BEN. POLLARD, D. Clk.

Will Book No. 1, p. 268,
Amherst County, Va.

The will of William Penn (born April 7, 1745; died 1777, Lieutenant in Cont. Army) recorded in Will Book No. 1, page 355, of the Amherst County records is as follows:

I, WILLIAM PENN, of the County of Amherst and Colony of Virginia, being perfectly sound in mind, and well in health, but fully sensible of the uncertainty of human life, have thought proper (as I intend going into the Armies of the United Colonies of America) do dispose of the estate money or effects I may die possessed of in manner following,—but first as I have a firm reliance on the wisdom and goodness of God, when it shall please him to take me out of this transitory life, I cheerfully resign my soul into his hands who knows best how to dispose of it, who gave it and who alone can take it away. My will and desire is that whatever estate real and personal I may die possessed of may be sold and converted into money by my Executors hereafter mentioned, and out of the money arising therefrom all of my just debts may be paid with all convenient speed, and the balance of any remaining, I give and bequeath in manner following, To my brother George Penn I give and bequeath one fourth part to him and his heirs. To my brother Phillip Penn I give and bequeath one fourth part to him and his heirs forever. To my brother Gabriel Penn I give and bequeath one fourth part to him and his heirs forever. To my brother Abraham Penn I give and bequeath one-fourth part to him and his heirs. And I do hereby constitute and appoint the aforesaid George Penn and Gabriel Penn (my brothers) to be Executors of this my last will and testament, whom I require and enjoin to dispose of the same according to the true intent and meaning of this will notwithstanding any forms of ceremonies of law that may be wanting. In witness whereof I have hereunto set my hand in the presence of three subscribing witnesses this thirteenth day of August in the year of our Lord one thousand seven hundred and seventy-six.

Signed by the testator   WILLIAM PENN [L. S.]
William Penn and declared
to be his last and only
Will & Testament, in
presence of us,

 EDMD. WILCOX
 DAVID SHEPHERD
 THOMAS LANDRUM.

At a Court held for Amherst County the Seventh day of July, 1777. This last Will and Testament of William Penn, deceased, was presented in Court by George Penn and Gabriel Penn, the Executors therein named, and proved by the oaths of David Shepherd and Thomas Landrum, two subscribing witnesses, and ordered to be recorded, and on the motion of the said Executors who made oath according to law, certificate is granted them for obtaining probate thereof in due form, giving security, whereupon they with Edmund Wilcox their security is to give bond in the Clerk's Office in the penalty of Two Hundred pounds with the condition required by law.

Test:

Will Book No. 1, p. 355,   EDMD. WILCOX, *Clk.*
 Amherst County, Va.   Exd by WM. LOVING, *D. Clk.*

Gabriel Penn, born July 17, 1741, fourth child of George and Ann (———) Penn; married, September 20, 1761, Sarah Callaway, daughter of Col. Richard and Frances (Walton) Callaway, of Bedford County, Virginia. (See Callaway family.) In 1764, Gabriel Penn was Sergeant 1st Virginia Regiment under Col. Wm. Byrd; a Colonel of Amherst County Militia; served till surrender of Yorktown. Member of Revolutionary Convention. Died in 1798.

CHILDREN OF GABRIEL AND SARAH (CALLAWAY) PENN

(1) Elizabeth (Betsey); married (first), James Callaway; (second) Wm. Long.

(2) James R.; married Mary Major. (See forward.)
(3) Sophia; married Wm. S. Crawford.
(4) Permelia; married Thomas Haskins.
(5) Matilda; married 1792, Abner Nash.
(6) Fannie; married William White.
(7) Nancy; married (first), Alex. Brydie; (second) John McCredie.
(8) Edmund.
(9) Sally; married Thomas Crowe.
(10) Catherine; married John W. Holder, her first cousin. (See Col. Richard Callaway family.)

The Will of Gabriel Penn, recorded in Will Book No. 3, page 506, of the Amherst County records is as follows:

I, GABRIEL PENN, of Amherst County and State of Virginia, being of sound mind and recollection, do make and ordain this to be my last will and testament in writing.

Imprimis. I give to my son James Penn to him his heirs and assigns forever my right and interest in and to one fourth part of a Military Land Warrant, or the lands surveyed and secured under it, which was granted to the executors of my deceased brother, William Penn, I also give to him his heirs and assigns forever all the property which he has already received from me and which he has had in possession.

Item. I give to my daughter Betsey Calloway two debts due to me from the estate of David Shepherd, deceased, viz., one of one hundred and six pounds eight shillings with the interest thereon, it being the amount of a bond which I paid to Carter Braxton, bearing date the 16th of February, 1775, given in consideration of lands purchased by said Shepherd from said Braxton. The other bond of Ezekiel Gilbert amounting to forty-one pounds thirteen shillings and four pence specie which bond I lent to the said David Shepherd in his life to discount in the payment of land purchased from said Gilbert.

Item. I give to each of my daughters, Sophia Crawford, Permelia Haskins, Matilda Nash and Fannie White all the property which they respectively have received from me and have had in possession since their respective marriages, to them their heirs and assigns forever.

Item. I give to my daughter Nancy Penn (besides the negroes to which I have made her deed of gift) on her marriage or arrival at the age of twenty-one years the following property, viz.: two cows and calves a riding horse and saddle, a feather bed and furniture, and such pewter as have been usually given to my other daughters on their respective marriages.

Item. I give to my son Edmund Penn to him his heirs and assigns forever, and to take in possession after the decease of my beloved wife eight hundred and seventy acres of land being part of the tract on which I now live, and which has lately been laid off by a survey made the 8th day of January, 1794, by James Higginbotham, Surveyor of Amherst County, and besides the six negroes, which I have already given him by deed of gift. I give to him his heirs and assigns forever upon his marriage or arrival to the age of twenty-one years one-sixth part of my stock of horses, cattle, sheep and hogs, a good feather bed and furniture and book case and such other of my household furniture as my wife in her discretion may think proper to allot to him.

Item. I give unto each of my daughters, Sally Penn & Catherine Penn respectively (besides the four negroes which I have given to each of them by deed of gift) a good feather bed and furniture, a riding horse and saddle, two cows and calves and such pewter as has been usually given to my other daughters on their respective marriages or becoming of age, to each of them their heirs and assigns forever.

Item. I lend unto my beloved wife Sarah Penn during her natural life the tract of land on which I now live containing eight hundred and twenty acres and being the land which in a preceding clause of this my will I have given to my son Edmund after the decease of my said wife. Also I lend her for life all the remainder of my slaves, stock, household and kitchen furniture and plantation utensils for the purpose of her comfortable maintenance and support and the bringing up and educating my younger children and the management and direction of the estate which I have thus lent to my wife I entrust to the prudence and management of my executors hereinafter mentioned.

Item. It is my will and desire and do direct that all the remainder of my real estate (not hereinbefore given) including the ballance of the tract on which I now live and which I have given to my son Edmund Penn, and containing three hundred and fifty seven acres laid off and surveyed by James Higginbotham, the 7th day of January, 1794, also Higginbotham's Mill Creek tract containing three hundred and sixty five acres, one other tract on Freelands Creek near Buffaloe

River containing one hundred and forty-six acres as also what lands
I may be entitled to in Kentucky shall be sold by my executors or the
survivor or survivors of them whenever they may think it most convenient and necessary, and the money arising therefrom to be considered as personal estate and to be applied as hereinafter directed.

Item. It is my further will and desire that after the decease of
my beloved wife all the slaves with their natural increase, stock of all
kinds, household and kitchen furniture, and plantation utensils which
I have lent to her as hereinbefore mentioned, excepting such as may be
necessary and convenient for my executors to sell for the payment of
my lawful debts as also all the money which may arise from the sale of
my lands my share in the James River Company which my executors
may at any time sell when necessary and also all the remainder of my
property of every kind whatsoever not before herein mentioned, may
be equally divided among all my children, viz.: Betsey Calloway,
James Penn, Sophia Crawford, Permelia Haskins, Matilda Nash, Fannie White, Nancy Penn, Edmund Penn, Sally Penn & Catharine Penn
to each of them their heirs and assigns forever.

Item. I appoint my son James Penn guardian to my son Edmund
Penn, Thomas Haskins guardian to my daughter Sally Penn and
James Calloway guardian to my daughter Catharine Penn, who are
hereby authorized and required to suffer to remain in the bulk of my
estate for their comfortable support and the conveniency of my beloved
wife until they become of age or marry, if their or either of their
conveniences should require it to remain there so long the property
which I have heretofore given the said wards,—for which at any
future day they are not to be called to account.

Lastly. I appoint my son James Penn and my two sons-in-law
Wm. S. Crawford and James Calloway executors of this my last will
and testament, hereby revoking all former wills. Given under my hand
and seal this 21st day of November Anno Domini 1794.

GABL. PENN [SEAL].

Signed, sealed and acknowledged
in the presence of

> GEORGE DILLARD
> REUBIN CRAWFORD
> JAS. BALLINGER
> WIATT SMITH
> GEO. PENN
> JAS. M. BROWN.

At a Court held for Amherst County the 16th day of July, 1798.

This will was proved by the oath of James M. Browne a witness thereto, and George Penn, Senr., another subscribing witness to the said will being dead, William Penn and George Penn being sworn deposed that they are well acquainted with the handwriting of the said George Penn, decd., and verily believe that his name subscribed as a witness to the said will is in the proper handwriting of the said George Penn, and the said will is ordered to be recorded: Whereupon William S. Crawford, one of the executors in the said will named, refused to take on himself the burthen of the execution thereof and on the motion of James Penn, another executor in said will mentioned, certificate is granted him for obtaining a probat thereof in due form he having made oath and given bond with Philip Gooch, Joseph Burrus, George Penn, William Penn, Thomas Penn and William S. Crawford, his securities in the penalty of seven thousand pounds current money conditioned as the law directs.

Teste,

W. S. Crawford, Clerk.

Will Book No. 3, p. 506,
    Amherst County, Va.

....

James R. Penn, eldest son of Gabriel and Sarah (Callaway) Penn, of Amherst County, Virginia; married, December 5, 1791, Mary Major. From the language of his father's will, written November 21, 1794, probated in Amherst Court, July 16, 1798, Will Book No. 3, p. 506, he, James, was at this time, living in Amherst County. His father, having inherited from his brother an interest in some Kentucky lands; at some date, probably, about 1818, James R. Penn moved to Kentucky, settled in Taylor County, where he lived and died. He is buried near a little town called Spurlington. Names of all his children are not known. However, by those who have searched the records, it is believed that Harwood M., born 1794; died 1880; William and James (the youngest brother and only eight (8) years old when the family moved to Kentucky to live) are sons of this same James R. Penn, who moved to Kentucky around 1818. These three brothers, after marriage, settled in Missouri and there reared families. Among other children of James R. and Mary (Major) Penn, were Moses Penn, of Bedford

County, Virginia, born 1796; died 1878 (see forward), and Thomas Major Penn, of Taylor County, Kentucky, born June 11, 1798; married Lou Ann Spurling, of Kentucky.

Children of Thomas Major Penn and Lou Ann (Spurling) Penn, of Taylor County, Kentucky:

(1) Martha Ann Penn; married James Newton. There were six children—one, James Newton, Jr., very old but still living in Indianapolis, Ind.

(2) Edmund Penn; married Frances Mann, of Mannsville, Ky. He was a captain in the Union Army in the Civil War. A daughter, Mrs. G. W. Peterson lives in Campbellsville, Ky.

(3) Mary Ann Penn; married Moses Mann.

(4) Anna Liza Penn; married Josiah Mann.

(5) Sarah Elizabeth Penn; married Joshua Mann. (These Manns were from Virginia and all brothers and sisters.)

CHILDREN:

(a) Florence Mann; married Wm. Waller, of St. Petersburg, Florida. Two children.

(b) Myrtle Mann; married John Thompson, of Florence, Alabama. No children.

(c) Sanford Mann; married Miss Beard. Two children—Hatcher, Ky.

(d) Redford Mann; married Mary Lee Tucker—one child. Lives in Stockton, California.

(e) Benjamin F. Mann; married Lulu A. Frazee, of Arcadia, Indiana.

CHILDREN:

(aa) Sarah Elizabeth Mann, married Earl Barker, of Arcadia, Ind. Their daughter Imogene Barker, married W. E. Pullen. Living in Charleston, West Virginia. They have one child:

(aaa) John Thomas Granville Pullen, age four years.

(bb) Cecil Mann, married Frank Graham.

(cc) Virgil F. Mann; married Mabel Bibe. Living in Indianapolis, Ind.

(dd) Marjorie Mann; married W. F. Mann. Living in Indianapolis, Ind.

(6) Sanford Penn; married Elizabeth Harding.

(7) John Penn; married Laura Anne Roley.

....

Moses Penn, of Bedford County, Virginia, born March 6, 1796, a son of James and Mary (Major) Penn, of Amherst County, Va., later of Kentucky; married, October 19, 1824, Edna A. White, daughter of Captain Jacob and Hannah (Spiers) White, of Bedford County, Va. (See White family.) Moses Penn served with honor in the War of 1812. He was a man of kindly disposition, interested in the activities of the community, and noted for his generous hospitality. Being a farmer, by occupation, he owned and cultivated the fine farm his wife inherited from the Jacob White estate, adding to the conduct of this estate a custom milling business. Much of this property is still in the possession of their descendants. His wife, Edna A. (White) Penn, died in 1844; he never married again. He died in 1878, at the age of 82 years.

CHILDREN:

(1) Paul Silas, born December 17, 1829; married (first), on September 15, 1853, Mary Charlotte Hobson, of Bedford County, Virginia, born October 10, 1834; died October 18, 1865, and buried at Prairieville, Pike County, Missouri, where they were at that time living. She was the daughter of Richard and Louisa (West) Hobson. After the death of his wife, he returned to Virginia and settled on part of the estate his mother had inherited from her father, Captain Jacob White, and engaged in farming. He married (second), October 8, 1868, Hannah Rachel Turpin, born July 19, 1842, a daughter of Roland Green and Elizabeth (Wilson) (Reid) Turpin. (See Turpin family.) Paul S. Penn served in the Civil War from Missouri where he was living at that time. He died July 20, 1884; and his wife died October 17, 1928, leaving a worthy family of children.

CHILDREN BY FIRST MARRIAGE:

(a) Mattie Lee, born August 9, 1854; married (first), January 22, 1873, James Richard Sledd, born November 10, 1849, a son of William E., born January 8, 1826, and Arabella (Hobson) Sledd, born August 23, 1829, a daughter of Richard and Louisa (West) Hobson. They lived in Pike County, Mo. (See Sledd family.) A number of years after the death of her first husband, she married Joseph G. Gilchrist and is now living in Chillicothe, Mo. No children by the second marriage.

CHILDREN BY FIRST MARRIAGE:

(aa) Charles Oscar, born October 27, 1873; died September 30, 1924; married; no children; lived in Missouri.

(bb) William Paul, born October 5, 1875; died January 16, 1925; married; no children; lived in Missouri.

(cc) Frances Lillian, born March 29, 1883; died October 17, 1903; married; no children; lived in Missouri.

(b) Edna Frances, born December 20, 1857; married, September 1, 1886, Robert Henry Parks, born July 13, 1864, a son of Samuel G. and Teresa Amanda (Burks) Parks, of Rockbridge County and grandson of Martin and Nancy Goode Parks originally, of Amherst County, Va.

CHILDREN:

(aa) Charles Samuel, born August 5, 1887; married Marion Amelia England and they have the following children:

(aaa) John England, born March 18, 1916.

(bbb) Paul Gordon, born May 15, 1920.

(ccc) Robert Henry, born September 7, 1924.

(ddd) David Reid, born November 23, 1925.

(bb) Mattie, born December 1, 1889; married, January 3, 1910, Thomas Nelson Turpin, Jr. (See Turpin family.)

(cc) Dora Arlene, born October 16, 1891; married, December 12, 1913, Clarence John Baker, born March 31, 1889, son of Charles W., and Elizabeth (Walker) Baker. They have two children as follows:

WILL PENN AMFAHR

(aaa) Charles Parks, born September 7, 1915.

(bbb) Edna Clare, born July 9, 1918.

(dd) Robert Henry, Jr., born June 14, 1893; married Mary Smith and they have one child:

(aaa) Robert Henry, III, born July 20, 1922.

(ee) Martin Goode, born July 15, 1896; died October 3, 1918.

(ff) Reid Eliza, born November 20, 1897; married, December 5, 1923, Lambert Marshall Turpin. (See Turpin family.)

(gg) James Amfahr, born December 18, 1899.

(hh) Francis Burks, born March 23, 1903.

(c) Willie C., born February 29, 1855; died January, 1916. Married in the West where he lived and died. No children.

(d) Susan, born Prairieville, Pike County, Missouri, January 1, 1860; married, September 25, 1885, William Christopher Amfahr, born February 21, 1848; died February 20, 1915. He was a native of Germany; and their residence was Louisiana, Missouri, where he is buried and his widow now makes her home. Wm. C. Amfahr was Supt. Construction C. B. & Q. R. R.

CHILDREN:

(aa) James Dreyfus, born November 30, 1886, Louisiana, Mo. Educated in the Public Schools of Louisiana; now living in Slater, Mo., where he holds position of Conductor of the C. & A. R R.

(bb) William Penn, born August 31, 1888, in Louisiana, Mo., where he received his education. He married, September 2, 1913, Sallie Aletha Daniel, born December 15, 1891, died April 4, 1919, a daughter of Charles Gillum and Fannie (Mc-Pike) Daniel, of Vandalia, Missouri. William P. Amfahr volunteered for service in the World War, April 8, 1917, and served as 2nd Lieutenant, Infantry. Discharged December 4, 1918;

now holds his Reserve Commission. A successful young merchant, of Vandalia, Mo. His
children are:

> (aaa) Marjorie Louise, born January 19,
> 1915; in school at Wheaton, Illinois.
> (bbb) Frances Sue, born March 13, 1916;
> in school at Wheaton, Illinois.

(cc) Florence Minnie, born November 17, 1891,
Louisiana, Mo. Received her education at the
Central Missouri State Normal, Warrensburg,
Mo., and State Teacher's College, Macomb, Ill.
Now teaching in the Public Schools of Quincy,
Illinois.

(dd) Annie Gertrude, born December 2, 1893; living
in Louisiana, Missouri.

(ee) Lena, born October 25, 1895; married, August
6, 1922, Walter W. Schanbacher, of Hannibal,
Missouri, where they live.

(e) Paul Silas, Jr., born July, 1861; married Ora Alger,
of Denver, Colorado, where they now live. No children
by this union.

CHILDREN BY SECOND MARRIAGE:

(f) Eliza, born November 19, 1873; died September 2,
1898; unmarried.

(g) Ben Hobson, born January 18, 1877; died March 29,
1895; unmarried.

(h) Roland Reid, born January 5, 1875; married, June 10,
1908, Goldie May McLaughlin, a daughter of Smelser
and Emma (Harper) McLaughlin, of Hollins, Virginia.
For many years R. Reid Penn was a guard at the Virginia State Penitentiary, and in 1920 was made
Superintendent of the State Farm, which position he
has held since with credit and honor.

CHILDREN:

(aa) Emma Louise, born April 3, 1909.
(bb) Helen Turpin, born September 30, 1912.
(cc) Dorothy May, born December 17, 1915.

(dd) Frances Elizabeth, born August 2, 1919.

(i) Henry Clay, born March 20, 1879; married, April 7, 1928, Cornelia Frances Weaver, daughter of John L. and Lula (Kipps) Weaver, of Richmond, Virginia. They reside in Richmond, Va.

(j) Bessie Hannah, born July 19, 1881, living at the old home place in Bedford County with her brother John.

(k) John Thomas, born March 12, 1884; unmarried. He and his only sister, Bessie, are still living at their old home. They tenderly cared for their mother the many years of her declining health and invalidism.

(2) James Jacob, born May 22, 1834; married December 7, 1859, America ("Mitt") Turpin, born July 22, 1838; died October 4, 1884, a daughter of Thomas and Mary Polina (Clayton) Turpin. (See Turpin family.) James Jacob Penn, was of a jolly, good-natured disposition. In appearance, he was like the "Whites," his mother's family. He, and his first cousin, John Milton White, were often taken for each other. The genial, hospitable nature of the parents and their pretty daughters made of their home the gathering place for great crowds of young people. He, too, inherited a part of his grandfather White's many acres of land; some of his descendants still live at the old home place. He died June 9, 1909, and was buried in the Penn burying ground. [He was a first cousin of my maternal grandparents and his wife, a sister of my paternal grandmother, Lucy Douglas (Turpin) Ackerly.— M. D. A.]

CHILDREN :

(a) Mary Cora, born October 24, 1860; died July 25, 1861.

(b) Lilly Bell, born July 24, 1862; died April 15, 1883; unmarried.

(c) Georgie W., born November 9, 1864; married, December 21, 1892, John Letcher Douglas, born April 4, 1859, a son of Robert Henry and Betty (Major) Douglas, of Bedford County. (See Douglas family.)

(d) James Walter, born March 2, 1867; married, November 28, 1888, Sallie Lula Turpin, born June 19, 1866, a daughter of William L. and Marinda J. (Hatcher)

Turpin, and a grand-daughter of Captain John and Mary M. (Lambert) Turpin, of Bedford County, Va. (See Turpin family.) James Walter Penn and his wife reside at the old home of his wife's grandfather, Captain John Turpin, where he is successfully engaged in farming. He is a substantial citizen of the community, taking part in public affairs. Has been a Justice of the Peace for a number of years.

CHILDREN:

(aa) William Julius, born December 11, 1889; married, December 16, 1913, Hester Honea, a daughter of John A. Honea. Have two children:

    (aaa) Florence Virginia, born August 4, 1915.

    (bbb) William J., Jr., born July 2, 1924.

(bb) John Earle, born August 9, 1892, served in World War, September 22, 1917-July 29, 1918. Killed in action July 29, 1918.

(cc) Maurice James, born October 8, 1896; married, March 26, 1918, Lizzie Bell Noell, daughter of Cary and Belle (Logwood) Noell. Have one child:

    (aaa) Gerald Luck, born November 10, 1920.

(dd) Eva Mae, born February 26, 1900; married, June 8, 1919, Robert M. Madron, son of John E. and Ollie (Reese) Madron. Have three children:

    (aaa) Juanita Penn, born October 12, 1920.

    (bbb) Earl Essex, born October 1, 1922.

    (ccc) James Shirley, born July 2, 1924.

(ee) Walter Lloyd, born April 7, 1902; graduated Virginia Polytechnic Institute, June, 1926. Unmarried.

(e) Jessie Frances, born January 27, 1870; married, December 5, 1888, Spotswood Edward Thomson, born January 30, 1864, son of Alexander S. and Margaret R. (Hatcher) Thomson, and a grandson of Henry and

JOHN EARLE PENN

Elizabeth (White) Hatcher, of Bedford County. (See Hatcher and White families.) Spotswood Edward Thomson died February 18, 1922. His widow lives with her children in Macon, Ga. (See Thomson family for descendants.)

(f) Emmett Clifford, born May 29, 1873; married, December 26, 1900, Mary Forbis, born December 18, 1881, a daughter of William R. Forbis (born April 23, 1847), and Mary N. (McCulloch) Forbis (born October 7, 1859), who were married November 19, 1878 — no children. Living in Princeton, West Virginia.

(g) Sallie Lula, born August 12, 1876; married, September 19, 1897, George Thomas Smith Davis, born July 21, 1868, a son of Lysander and Julia Ann (Graves) Davis, of Bedford County, Va. Sallie Lula Davis died October 3, 1904.

CHILD:

(aa) Betty Elise, born January 20, 1901. Unmarried. A successful teacher.

Mr. Davis later married, Enid Day, a daughter of Charles Edwin and Emma Jane (Furcron) Day, of Richmond, Va. They make their home in Clifton Forge, Virginia, where Mr. Davis holds an important position with the C. & O. R. R.

(h) Maude Lee, born August 11, 1878; married, October 11, 1900, Thomas Joseph Bannister, born April 28, 1876, a son of Thomas J. and Rosa (Lee) Bannister, of Richmond, Va. Now living in Richmond, Va.

CHILDREN:

(aa) Thomas, born October 10, 1901; died January 6, 1902.

(bb) James (twin), born March 27, 1904; died August 28, 1904.

(cc) Thomas, II (twin), born March 27, 1904; unmarried.

(dd) Lula Elizabeth, born June 10, 1905.

(ee) Louise Rosalie, born August 14, 1911.

(ff) Virginia Lee, born January 30, 1917.

    (i) Daisy Blanche, born November 1, 1880; married, November 19, 1902, Channing Sale, a son of John Wharton Sale, born December 14, 1827, in Amherst County; died April 30, 1913, Bedford County; married, June 9, 1854, Anne Rebecca Campbell, born in Bedford County, April 22, 1832; died January 19, 1903, in Bedford County. Channing Sale and his wife are now living at Hopewell, Va., no children by this marriage, but he has three children by a former marriage.

    (j) Willie Edward, born April 1, 1883; died June 17, 1883.

    (k-l) Twins; one born dead and the other one lived twenty-four hours.

(3) Fannie; died at age of eighteen years; unmarried.

(4) William H.; private in Captain Irvine's Company G, 2nd Virginia Cavalry. Died at age of 21 years.

(5) Sarah D., born September 2, 1840; married (first) Paul A. Turpin, a son of Thomas Turpin, Jr., and Mary Polina (Clayton) Turpin, of Bedford County, Va. He enlisted April 20, 1861, Company "F", 58th Virginia Infantry. Was second lieutenant; wounded at Fredericksburg, Va., December 23, 1862. (See Turpin family.) Married (second), December 18, 1878, Benjamin Wilkes, Jr., born May 13, 1844, a native, of Campbell County, Va., and a son of Benjamin and Matilda (Duffell) Wilkes.

CHILDREN BY FIRST MARRIAGE:

    (a) Edward J. Turpin, married Mary Riley.

    (b) Anna Turpin, married Henry Wilkes.

    (c) Charlie Turpin, never married.

    (d) Richard Turpin, died young.

CHILD BY SECOND MARRIAGE:

    (e) Leora Walker Wilkes, born July 30, 1880.

(6) Caroline W., married (first), February 27, 1861, James A. Logwood; married (second), December 8, 1874, Thomas M. ("Tom Phil") Turpin, a son of Philip and Elvira (Clayton) Turpin. (See Turpin and Logwood families.)

CHILD BY FIRST MARRIAGE:

(a) Samuel R. Logwood, born February 27, 1862; married Lenna Elvira Turpin. (See Turpin family.)

CHILDREN BY SECOND MARRIAGE:

(b) Russell A.
(c) Edna Sale.
(d) Thomas Marvin. (See Turpin family.)

(7) Lucy McD., born September 8, 1842; married, December 22, 1862, James M. Turpin, born October 6, 1832, a son of Philip and Elvira (Clayton) Turpin. Were the parents of nine children. (See Turpin family.)

(8) Edna Ann, born August 3, 1844; married, November 19, 1867, Benjamin Wilkes, Jr., born May 13, 1844, a native of Campbell County, Virginia, and a son of Benjamin and Matilda (Duffell) Wilkes, Sr. His father was born in Montgomery County, Virginia, and his mother in Frederick County. Both his father's and mother's families were Virginians for several generations. Benjamin Wilkes, Jr., entered the Confederate States Army as third lieutenant of Company "A," 28th Virginia Infantry and after about six months service in this capacity was promoted quartermaster in which service he continued till close of war. He was a wealthy land owner and after the war continued the farming of his estate. Edna Ann (Penn) Wilkes died June 20, 1877.

CHILDREN:

(a) Moses Penn, born July 29, 1869; married Roena Prior. (Have three (3) daughters.)
(b) Caroline D., born June 6, 1870; married James Goodrich. (One son and one daughter.)
(c) Vergia O., born August 5, 1871; married Russell A. Turpin. (Four sons.) (See Turpin family.)
(d) Nora Osman, born July 23, 1873; married Henry Helbig. (One daughter and two sons.)
(e) James Duffell, born August 16, 1876; married Mrs. Malcom Cox. (Three sons.)

BEAUFORT, BEAUFORD, BUFORD

Richard Beauford, the first of the name in Virginia, "was examined by a minister of the Church of England, as to loyalty to the King took the prescribed oath of allegiance, etc., age eighteen," and emigrated on the ship, "Elizabeth," August 1, 1835, from Gravesend, England. (Hotten.)

The following FISH STORY concerning that voyage of the good ship, "Elizabeth," has been handed down in the Buford family, from generation to generation, since that day:

It is said that the ship, on her way over, struck a snag and sprung a leak which threatened to sink her, and that all on board were forced to take turns at baling out the water. Suddenly the water ceased to pour in, but it was not until they reached shore that they knew the suction had caught a big fish, and the pressure was so great that it was held fast against the side of the ship, thus stopping the leakage and allowing the ship to land safely.

Richard Beauford settled in Lancaster County, Va., about 1656. Where he lived from the time he arrived in Virginia up to that time is not known, but in the Lancaster records, under date of April 15, 1656, "John Vause assigned Richard Beauford three hundred acres of land, lying on the south side of the Rappahannock River." He married the daughter of John Vause. This was no doubt the reason for this assignment.

In the Register of Christchurch, Middlesex County (formerly Lancaster County), 1653-1812, the sixth entry is that of the marriage of John Blueford (Beauford) and Elizabeth Parrott, on April 11, 1662. John was the son of Richard, the immigrant, and ————— Vause.

John Beauford died April 18, 1722.

Children of John and Elizabeth (Parrott) Beauford: Thomas, born 1663; Ambrose, born 1665; Susannah, born 1667; Elizabeth, born 1669.

Elizabeth (Parrott) Beauford, born 1645, was the eldest child of Richard and Margaret Parrott, who came from England by way of Barbadoes, as early as 1649, and settled in Lancaster County, Va. The Christchurch Register gives the following memorandum: "Richard, sone of Richard Perrott, Sr., was borne the 24th of February, 1650, being the first man child that was begott and borne on Rappahannock River of English parents."

Richard Parrott, Sr., was a vestryman of Christchurch; a Commissioner of Lancaster County in 1656; elected High Sheriff June 5, 1657; and Senior Justice of Middlesex County Court from 1673 until his death, November 11, 1686.

Margaret, wife of Richard Parrott, Sr., died January 30, 1687.

Thomas, son of John and Elizabeth (Parrott) Beauford, married Mary ————. Children: Thomas, Jr., born 1682; Henry, born 1684; Mary, born 1688. Thomas Beauford died December 9, 1716, and his wife, Mary, died December 29, 1720.

Thomas Beauford, Jr., son of Thomas and Mary Beauford, married Elizabeth ————. Children: Agatha, born August 13, 1705; John, born 1707; Elizabeth, born 1709; Sarah, born 1712; Mary, born 1716; and Ann, born 1718. Thomas Beauford, Jr., died in 1761, and his wife died later.

John, son of Thomas and Elizabeth Beauford, born in Middlesex County, Va., in 1707; married in 1735, Judith Phillippe, daughter of Count Claude Phillippe, minister de Richebourg, who came over with the first band of Huguenots that settled in Manakin Towne, Va., and was one of their first two ministers. (See Phillippe family.)

John and Judith (Phillippe) Beauford settled in Bromfield Parish, Culpeper County, Va., on a tract of land situated on the Rapid Ann and Beautiful Run, the deed to which bears date of August 9, 1735. He continued to increase his acreage until he became one of the largest land owners of the county.

His homestead was acquired from William Phillips, perhaps his brother-in-law, of Orange, St. Marks Parish, on the 26th day of June, 1739. The deed—in part—reads: "From the day after date of these presents and during the term of one hole year from thence. Next to be completed and ended, yealding and paying therefore yearly the Rent of one peper corn at the feast of St. Michael, the archangle, if the same be lawfully demanded." The residence built upon this estate was the first two-story house erected in this part of the country, and people came from far and near to see it.

CHILDREN OF JOHN AND JUDITH (PHILLIPPE) BEAUFORD:

(1) John Thomas, born 1736. (See forward.)
(2) Anne, born 1738.
(3) James, born 1740. (See forward.)
(4) Elizabeth, born 1742.

(5) William, born 1745. (See forward.)

(6) Abraham, born July 31, 1749.

(7) Henry, born September 19, 1751. (See forward.)

(8) Mary, born 1753.

(9) Frances, born 1754.

(10) Simeon, born 1756.

John Beauford died in 1787, and, as his will does not mention his wife, it is presumed that she preceded him to the grave.

Thomas, James, William, and Henry Buford, sons of John and Judith (Phillippe) Beauford, came to Bedford County about the time of the formation of this county, acquired large boundaries of land, married and became influential citizens.

Thomas Buford was an officer in the Colonial Army and served under Braddock, Washington, and Byrd. For these services he was allowed six hundred and sixty-six acres of land on the Ohio River.

He married Ann Watts in 1756 and lived near what is now Mont-vale on the Holstein Plantation (now owned by Samuel W. Huddleston, his great-great-great-grandson), not far from the old Block House, which was erected by the Whites for protection against the Indians. This block house was built of logs, closely fitted together, with numerous gun holes on all sides, and was no doubt a popular resort in those troublous times. There was a settlement of Cherokee Indians in this vicinity, as shown by a barrow, which has been unmolested to this present day, and numerous tomahawks of stone and arrow heads which have been picked up about it. In going back and forth to visit other members of this tribe, whose headquarters were on the head waters of the Tennessee River, these Indians crossed the Blue Ridge at what was later known as Buford's Gap, now Villamont.

In 1774, when trouble with the Indians on the western frontier necessitated sending an army to drive them back, Thomas Buford raised a volunteer company in Bedford County, and, joining General Andrew Lewis beyond the Blue Ridge, marched with him on to Point Pleasant, and was killed in that famous battle on October 10, 1774.

The members of CAPTAIN THOMAS BUFORD'S VOLUN-TEER COMPANY were:

Thomas Buford, Captain	Nicholas Meade
Thomas Dooley, Lieutenant	William Kennedy
Jonathan Cundiff, Ensign	Thomas Fliping
	Sergeants

Abraham Sharp

Absalom McClanahan

William Bryant

William McColister

James Scarbara

John McClanahan

James McBryde

John Carter

William Overstreet

Robert Hill

Samuel Davis

Zachariah Kennot

Augustine Hackworth

William Cook

Uriah Squires

Thomas Hall

William Hamrick

Nathaniel Cooper

John Cook

Mr. Waugh

John McGlahlen·

John Campbell

William Campbell

Adam Lin

Thomas Stephens

William Keer

Gerrott Kelley

James Ard

William Deal

John Bozel

John Welch

Robert Boyd

Thomas Hamrick

James Boyd

James Dale

Robert Ewing

Francis Seed

William Hackworth

John Roberts

Joseph White

Joseph Bunch

Jacob Dooley

Thomas Owen

John Read

John Wood

(Crozier's *Virginia Colonial Militia*.)

Seven years after the Battle of Point Pleasant General Andrew Lewis, while returning from Williamsburg to his home in Botetourt County, was taken ill en route and stopped at the old home of his comrade, Captain Buford, where he died September 25, 1781. He was buried temporarily near the Buford home and a thorn bush marked the spot for more than a century. There are members of the Buford family still living who remember the thorn bush and know the exact location of General Lewis' grave. His remains were afterwards removed to his home and re-interred near what is now Salem, Virginia.

CHILDREN OF THOMAS AND ANN (WATTS) BUFORD WERE:

(1) John; married Rhoda Shrewsbury in Bedford County in 1786.

CHILDREN:

(a) Elizabeth; married James Field.
(b) Nancy; married John Haynes and lived in Missouri.
(c) Frances; married ——— Cleveland; lived in Kentucky.
(d) Mildred; married George Foutz.
(e) Rhoda; married Lawson Lawhorn.
(f) Julia; married Berry Settles; lived in Tennessee.
(g) Thomas; died in infancy.
(h) John.
(i) Samuel.
(j) William.
(k) Thomas (2); probably died unmarried.

A pension was allowed John Buford for fifteen months and eighteen days for active service in the Revolutionary War. He had also served three years under his father in the French and Indian War.

(2) William; married Ann Pate and moved to Breckenbridge County, Ky., and from there to Missouri.

(3) Nancy; married Martin Wales or Weele and moved to Kentucky.

James Buford, son of John and Judith (Phillippe) Beauford of Culpeper County, Va., and one of the four brothers who settled in Bedford when that county was first formed, became a prominent citizen and large land owner in his adopted county. He was one of the pioneers who laid out the town of Liberty for the new county seat; was presiding Justice for many years; a member of the House of Burgesses in 1778; and in 1782 was appointed by the Court to let the contract for the erection of the Court House, Prison, and Stock. He was one of the trustees of Liberty in 1786.

In the Revolutionary Archives of the Virginia State Militia, under date of March 22, 1777, Captain James Buford was allowed pay, rations, etc., for his company to the 15th. inst., 997 pounds, 1 shilling, 9 pence.

James Buford was executor of the estate of his brother, Capt. Thomas Buford, and guardian of his children.

He married in Bedford County, Va., July 14, 1761, Elizabeth Bramblett, daughter of William Bramblett, one of the oldest settlers of Bedford County, and a Sergeant in the Colonial Army (Hening's Statutes). In 1792 he moved his family to Kentucky and died in Scott County after 1798.

MATILDA BUFORD
wife of (first) Jacob W. White
(second) William Thaxton

CHILDREN:

(1) Elizabeth, born 1762; married William Scruggs.

(2) John, born 1764; married in Lincoln County, Ky., Frances Turpin Banton; died in Kentucky after 1833.

(3) William, born 1866; married, October 11, 1783, Martha Hill Logwood, daughter of Capt. Thomas Logwood, of Bedford County (see Logwood family); and was killed by the Indians near Crab Orchard, Ky., in 1794, while looking for a place to settle.

CHILDREN:

(a) Lucinda; married Jeremiah White, March 31, 1806.

(b) Pamela; married Alexander Gibbs in 1802; settled in Madison County, Ky.

(c) Hillary; went West and was never heard of again.

(d) Parthena; married Levi Wheat, December 15, 1810.

(e) Matilda, born February 11, 1793; died March 10, 1876; married (first), December 18, 1812, Jacob W. White (see White family); (second) William Thaxton.

After the death of William Buford his widow, Martha Hill (Logwood) Buford, married Stephen Hubbard of Bedford County and had five children. (See Logwood family.)

(4) James, Jr., was left in Virginia when his father moved to Kentucky in 1792.

(5) Simeon K.; went to Kentucky and married (first) Mary Barr, of Lancaster County; (second) Mrs. Ann Mary (Fisher) Gaines.

(6) Abraham, born in Bedford County, Va., April 13, 1772; went to Bourbon County, Ky.; married Mary Moody, and later moved to Missouri, settling near New London.

(7) Ambrose; married Nancy Kirtley, daughter of Francis and Elizabeth Kirtley, of Orange County, Va.; went to Kentucky in 1827.

(8) Henry; went to Mt. Vernon, Ky., in 1800; married Elizabeth Terrill, of Crab Orchard, Ky.

(9) Judith; married, March 1, 1787, Thomas Scruggs.

(10) Frances, born 1779; married her cousin, Thomas Buford, son of Capt. William and Mary (Welsh) Buford; lived and died in Kentucky.

William Buford, son of John and Judith (Phillippe) Buford, married Mary Welsh, thought to have been the daughter of Nicholas Welsh of Bedford County, Va. He enlisted in the Revolutionary Army, December 17, 1776, to serve three years, and was "Honorably discharged December 2, 1779." He was afterwards made Captain.

CHILDREN OF WILLIAM AND MARY (WELSH) BUFORD:

(1) Judith; married (first) Thomas Scruggs; (second) ———— Noell.
(2) Thomas, born 1776; married, December 21, 1797, Frances Buford (born 1779) daughter of James and Elizabeth (Bramblett) Buford.
(3) Polly; married Elijah Kirtley.
(4) Elizabeth, born 1781; married Capt. Abner Baker, October, 1796, in Lincoln County, Ky.
(5) Frances; married ———— Young.
(6) Amelia; married ———— Tilford.
(7) William; married Rebecca Day.

William Buford moved his family to Lincoln County, Ky., about 1788, and in 1805 he moved again to Rockcastle County, where he was still living in 1814. In 1798 he wrote the following letter to his brother Henry, who was the only one of the four brothers, who came to Bedford County, that lived and died on his original estate.

"Kentucky, May 15th, 1798.

Dear Brother,

"We Recd. yours dated 25th of month last by Mr. Sasteen, which informs us of your health, & you also mention that you have Recd. No Letters from us for some time which must be owing to Miscarriages as I am fond of writing you at all opportunity. I have made enquiry for those letters you wrote to Brother Js. Mr. John Meux Informed me that such Letters came to his hand and that he sent them forward to Brother James. I also wrote to Bro. James upon that subject But have Recd. no answer. His son Simeon Left my house the Day before I Recd. your Letter on his way to yr. Country, as I was not at home did not know his Business to your Country—the suit Talbot vs. myself and Brother James is now before the Court of Appeals, the Judgment of which will be Reversed or set at nought tomorrow, it will then come back to Lincoln & I suppose will be Leavelled against me with all force and ambition on the part of Talbot. Brother Abraham was at my house a few days ago & says our friends are all well on the other side of Kentucky. I have never seen Cousin Prudence since she came to this Country, But I expect Jonathan and her over in a few days. Your son Tommy and his wife and her Relations is well, and Tommy is house keeping on a very fine tract of first Rate Land of 106 acres, adjoining his father-in-law which the old man has given him. But it is so heavy timbered that he wont get much cleared this Crop, Tommy tells me he is in want of money. I think he is very Industrous and very Saving, his wife also. I shall see that he wants for nothing I have in my power. Money is amazing scarce in this Country and dont know how we shall get along without it should become more plenty.

"We are all in a Tolerable state of health at present & hope by the blessing of God that you are all in a state of health and prosperity.

"We have no news to Write you. Our Country is full of a confused noise of a war with the Republick of France, which I suppose is no news to you. I expect yr. son Tommy would be glad to have known of this opportunity of writing to you, But Mr. John Roberson who is the bearer of this Letter cant wait.

We are with every sentiment of esteem,
Your affectionate Brother and Sister,

W. M. Buford."

Henry Buford, born in Culpeper County, Va., September 19, 1751, son of John and Judith (Phillippe) Beauford and youngest of the four brothers who settled in Bedford County, was a captain in the Revolutionary War from 1776 to 1778; was presiding magistrate of Bedford County; High Sheriff from 1790 to 1795; and owned a large estate which he called "Locust Level." This place is near what is now Montvale (formerly Bufordsville) and has been owned and occupied by descendants of Henry Buford down to the present time.

Captain Henry Buford married, March 22, 1771, Mildred Blackburn.

CHILDREN:

(1) Elizabeth, born August 8, 1773; married, April 1, 1790, John Hopkins Otey, of Bedford County. (See Otey family.)

(2) Thomas, born March 11, 1776; married Elizabeth Pierce, of Lincoln County, Ky. Lived in Kentucky.

(3) Abraham, born December 13, 1778; married (first) Sophia Lumpkin, December 22, 1796; (second) Nancy Eidson, August 25, 1817.

(4) Henry, Jr., born February 17, 1781; married, August 22, 1799, Jane Sherman.

(5) Prudence, born July 23, 1783; married, November 6, 1797, Jonathan Blackburn, her first cousin. Lived in Kentucky.

(6) Paschal, born February 14, 1791; married, October 31, 1820, Frances Ann Otey, daughter of Major Isaac and Elizabeth (Matthews) Otey, of Bedford County. (See Otey family.) He, being the youngest son, inherited "Locust Level" and lived and died there. He built the brick residence which is now standing.

CHILDREN:

(a) James Hervey, born July 6, 1821, a twin, Neeta, died in infancy; married, October 8, 1857, Lucy E. Hanson.

(b) Mildred Elizabeth, born November 19, 1822; married, October 15, 1845, Edward Callohil Burks. (See Burks family.)

(c) John Quincy Adams, born July 29, 1824; married, February 12, 1857, Jane Smith Terry.

(d) Mary Charlotte; died in infancy.

(e) Rowland Dabney, born September 20, 1827; died February 3, 1921; was Clerk of the Circuit Court of Bedford County twenty-seven consecutive years; Clerk of the County Court six years; vestryman, lay reader, and superintendent of the Sunday School of St. John's Episcopal Church for many years. He was intensely interested in the history of his county, and possessing a remarkably retentive memory for dates and details, he was rarely appealed to in vain for any information concerning the happenings in the county. He spent a great deal of time, during his later years, studying the records in the Clerk's Office, and made lists of marriage bonds of many of the old families of the county. Many of those appearing in this book are his work, and were presented to the authors by him.

He married (first), March 4, 1856, Josephine Victoria Wilson. They had one child, Nancy Lightfoot, who died in infancy, and his wife died soon after. He married (second), December 5, 1866, Sarah Augusta Bell, daughter of Alfred A. and Mary Isabel (Lowry) Bell. (See Bell and Lowry families.)

CHILD:

(aa) Isabel, born December 5, 1867; died September 28, 1927; taught many years in the Bedford High School, where she was ever loved and respected by her pupils for her ability as a teacher, her rare common sense, and her interest at all times in their welfare.

(f) Ann Jane, born April 22, 1830; married, November 16, 1858, William Hampton Hall.

(g) Julius Blackburn, born November 22, 1832; married, April 11, 1871, Letitia Terry Campbell.

(h) Margaret Letitia, born February 17, 1835; married, December 27, 1883, Capt. Thomas N. Cobbs.

(i) Isaac Henry, born September 25, 1838; married, August 31, 1859, Sarah McGavock Kent, of Pulaski County, Va.

(7) Julia Ann, born April 17, 1793; married, August 25, 1811, David Kyle, of Botetourt County, Va.

(8) Mary Malinda (Polly), born July 14, 1795; married, September 7, 1814, Jacob Kent, of Wythe County, Va.

Mildred (Blackburn) Buford died April 19, 1802, and Captain Buford married (second) Mrs. Jane Kent Quirk, October 17, 1805. He died December 31, 1814.

(Material for this sketch of the Buford family has been gathered from many sources, but most of it, perhaps, from the Buford Genealogy, by Mrs. Mildred Buford Minter.)

PHILLIPPE

The history of the religious persecution of the Huguenots in France, from the Massacre of St. Bartholomew in 1572 to the infamous outrages which preceded and followed the Revocation of the Edict of Nantes in 1685 is too well known to be repeated here. Refuge in Great Britain was sought by the Huguenots early in the sixteenth century and they continued to emigrate to that country, going in great numbers immediately after the Revocation of the Edict of Nantes.

Many of these refugees soon turned their eyes toward America, which at that time was offering many inducements to colonists, and sought a home in Virginia, settling along the Potomac, Rappahannock and James rivers.

In the year 1700 more than five hundred Huguenot emigrants were landed in Virginia by four successive debarkations. Three ministers—Claude Phillipe de Richbourg, Benjamin de Joux and Louis Latane—and two physicians—Castaing [Chastain (?)] and La Sosee—were among the number.

These emigrants appear to have settled at different points in Virginia, but more than two hundred of them established their homes upon land which was given to them on the south side of the James River, twenty miles above Richmond (now in Powhatan County), and which had been occupied by the Manakin tribe of Indians. This settlement took the name of these Indians and was henceforth called Manakin Towne.

Two of the ministers who came with these Huguenots—Claude Phillipe de Richbourg and Benjamin de Joux—settled in Manakin Towne, while Louis Latane became the minister of South Farnham Parish in Essex County, and continued in office until his death in 1732.

Claude Phillipe de Richbourg and his wife head the list of passengers in the first ship which left Gravesend, England, in the spring of 1700. He was a relative of Isaac Porcher de Richbourg, the ancestor of a prominent Huguenot family in South Carolina, both being descended from the Counts of Richbourg, of St. Sévère. Owing to disputes in his parish, which were referred to the Council of Virginia, September 2, 1707, Mr. Phillipe, with numerous followers, left Virginia soon after this date and settled in the Carolinas.

(The above is taken from the "Huguenot Emigration to Virginia," by R. A. Brock.)

In Baird's Huguenot Emigration, Vol. II, page 105, it is stated that Claude Phillippe de Richebourg left Virginia for South Carolina where he became minister of the French settlement at Santee, dying in 1719.

We have not been able to learn just where he died, nor have we been able to secure a copy of his will, though there are references to it in the records of the Huguenot Society of the Founders of Manakin.

Huguenot settlers of Manakin Town, Virginia, from whom some of our kin and other residents of Bedford County, Virginia, are descended:

Agee	Goin	Prouitt
Apperson	Grahame	Parratt
Bondurant	Gardner	Pemberton
Brooks	Howard	Perry
Brian	Hamton	Richebourg
Barnett	Jordan	Robinson
Bernard	Joanes	Richard
Beaufort (Buford)	Kempe	Robin
Brousse (Bruce)	LeSeur	Rogers
Barbie (Barber)	Lacy	Roussel (Russell)
Booker	LeFevre	Smithe
Cosby	LeGrande	Sublett
Crouch	Louys (Lewis)	Scot
Clarke	LeRoy	Shorte
Cabiness	Lansdon	Tammas (Thomas)
Chastain	Martin	Teler (Taylor)
Cocke	Monford	Temple
David	Michel (Mitchell)	Trent
DuPuy	Maupin	Woolridg
Daniel	Ormund	Watkins
DuVal	Oliver	Witt
Duncan	Porter	Woodson
Forde	Perault (Perrow)	Wever
Flournoy	Powell	Williamson
Forqueran	Patterson	Younge

LOGWOOD

Edmund Logwood and his wife, Jane (Eke) Logwood, came from England and settled in Chesterfield County, Virginia, where he died in 1775. His will, made January 13, 1773, and recorded in Chesterfield County (Will Book No. 2, page 295), mentions children: Thomas, Edmund, William, Archibald, Mary Lockett, Elizabeth Chasteen, Edith Hatcher, Sarah, and Milly. His wife is not mentioned, so she evidently died before her husband.

His children married as follows:

(1) Thomas; married (first) Ann Aiken; (second) Mrs. Martha Minnis. (See forward.)
(2) Edmund; married Mary Dandridge of Powhatan County and settled in Bedford County before the Revolutionary War.
(3) William; married Jane Walker of Chesterfield County.
(4) Archibald; married Nancy Friend of Chesterfield County.
(5) Mary; married Edmund Lockett of Chesterfield County.
(6) Elizabeth; married ———— Chastain, a Huguenot of Manakin Town, Virginia.
(7) Edith; married Rev. Jeremiah Hatcher. (See Hatcher family.)
(8) Sarah.
(9) Mildred; married William Woolridge of Chesterfield County.

Thomas Logwood, born in 1740; died September 10, 1821, son of Edmund and Jane (Eke) Logwood, of Chesterfield County, Va., came to Bedford County before the Revolutionary War and took up a large boundary of land on the north side of the county, which included the "Locust Hill" farm (now (1930) owned by Elmo Wright), the old "Davis Place," the farm of Col. Jesse Burks, called "Wyoming," and others—in all, about 5,000 acres. He also went to Kentucky with Daniel Boone and took up land there—two tracts in Harrison County, one of 2,000 acres, and the other of 14,000 acres. He did not remain in Kentucky but a short while.

Thomas Logwood was a Major in the Continental Army and, later, a Captain in the Bedford County Militia. He fought in the battle of Guilford Court House and was wounded three times.

He was High Sheriff of Bedford County, an office which, at that time was not filled by popular election, but by commission from the

Governor upon recommendation of the Bench of Magistrates—a self-perpetuating body, who presided at the County Court. He was a member of the General Assembly in 1798. He had considerable reputation as a surveyor, and is said to have laid out the road from Big Island to Liberty (now Bedford). He was a member of the Presbyterian Church, and a man of commanding presence, genial and popular in his manners, and had great influence in his community.

Thomas Logwood married (first) Ann Aiken in Chesterfield County, and brought her with him to Bedford, where their seven children were born. She died, and he married again at the age of seventy-five, his (second) wife being Mrs. Martha Minnis, widow of Calohill Minnis of Bedford County. They had no children.

He died September 10, 1821, and is buried by the side of his first wife at "Locust Hill." His will, made August 6, 1821, and proved September 24, 1821, mentions: "wife, Martha; son, Burwell; grandchildren, Sally Ann, Margaret, Martha, Eliza, Jane, and Valentine Logwood, children of son, Burwell; grandsons, Thomas P., Alexander, John, Robert, and Edmund, sons of son Burwell; grand-daughter, Nancy Douglass, formerly Nancy Hubbard; grandsons, Thomas Hubbard, Jr., Edmund, William and Margaret Hubbard (children of Stephen Hubbard); grand-daughter, Lucinda Clayton; daughter, Sallie Wharton; daughter, Nancy Scruggs; and heirs of Thomas G. Logwood." Jacob W. White was his executor.

CHILDREN OF THOMAS AND ANN (AIKEN) LOGWOOD:

(1) Burwell; married Prudence Peyton of Albemarle County, Va.; died in 1863, when more than ninety years of age.

CHILDREN:

(a) Sally Ann; married Benjamin Johnson.
(b) Margaret R.; married Roland G. Turpin. (See Turpin family.)
(c) Martha; married James M. Johnson.
(d) Eliza; died unmarried.
(e) Jane; married ———— Murrill.
(f) Valentine.
(g) Thomas Peyton.
(h) Alexander H.; married (first) Elizabeth Douglass. (See Douglas family.)

CHILDREN:

(aa) Nannie; married R. Gilbert.
(bb) Kitty.
(cc) May; married Jack Bondurant.
(dd) Eliza; married A. W. Clayton.
(ee) James A.; married (first) Sarah J. Jennings; (second) Caroline W. Penn. (See Penn family.) Child by second marriage:

    (aaa) Samuel R.; married Lenna Elvira Turpin. (See Turpin family.)

Alexander H. married (second) Mrs. Theodocia A. (Reynolds) White, widow of James White. (She had one child by her first marriage: Lucy, who married William H. McGhee, and had children: Margaret, married J. W. Ballard; Bettie, married George Saunders; James W., married Florence Steele; Lucy Logwood, married George D. Wingfield; Benjamin, married Frances Walthall; Willie, married Emmett Thomas; and Walter Bain (Bob), married Genella McGhee.)

CHILDREN:

(ff) John C., married (first) Sallie McClintock; (second) Annie Akers; (third) Fannie Logwood.
(gg) Margaret; married Holcombe Wilkins.
(hh) Charles; married Mary Overstreet.
(ii) Elizabeth; married A. Overstreet.
(jj) Thomas; married Elvira Minnick (?).
(i) John.
(j) Robert; married (first) Lucinda Robinson (see Robinson family); (second) Lydia Wheat; (third) Elizabeth Johnson.
(k) Edmund.
(2) Thomas G.; married Kitty Gwatkin. (See Gwatkin family.)

CHILDREN:

(a) Polly; married Wm. L. Otey.
(b) Edmund; married Mrs. Lucy McDaniel (Reese) White,

widow of Col. William Allen White. (See White family.)

    (c) Thomas.

    (d) Nancy.

(3) Martha Hill; married (first) William Buford. (See Buford family.)

CHILDREN:

    (a) Hillary.

    (b) Parthenia; married ———— Wheat.

    (c) Lucinda; married (first) Jeremiah White; (second) Jasper Clayton.

    (d) Matilda; married (first) Jacob W. White (see White family); (second) William Thaxton.

    (e) Parmelia; married Alexander Gibbs.

Martha Hill (Logwood) Buford married (second) Stephen Hubbard.

CHILDREN:

    (a) Nancy; married Murphy Douglass.

    (b) Thomas, Jr.

    (c) William.

    (d) Margaret; married Benjamin Williamson.

    (e) Edmund.

(4) Nancy; married Gross Scruggs.

CHILDREN:

    (a) William.

    (b) Gross.

    (c) Edmund.

    (d) Ann.

    (e) Polly.

    (f) Martha.

(5) Mildred.

(6) Edmund; married Euphan Tate.

CHILDREN:

    (a) Nancy A.; married William Callaway.

    (b) Peggy.

    (c) Adalaline.

(7) Sally Lilbourne, born December 16, 1779; died February 16 1864; married John Wharton. (See Wharton family.)

Marriages in the Logwood family in Bedford County to about 1870:

Gross Scruggs and Nancy Logwood, 31 May 1792, by Rev. Jeremiah Hatcher.

Burwell Logwood and Prucy Peyton, 19 July 1794. (Gross Scruggs, security.)

John Wharton and Sally Logwood, daughter of Thomas Logwood—June 1, 1797. Rev. Jeremiah Hatcher. Hardaway Hatcher, security.

Thomas G. Logwood and Catherine (Kitty) Gwatkin, daughter of Col. Charles Gwatkin, February 16, 1802. Rev. Jere. Hatcher, Jno. Wharton, security.

Edmond Logwood and Fanny Tate, 22 February 1807. John Tate, security.

Thomas Logwood and Martha Mennis, 1 January 1816. Revd. James Hatcher.

Wm. L. Otey and Mary G. Logwood, daughter of Catherine Logwood, 17 April 1820. James Campbell, security.

Robert R. Logwood and Lucinda S. Robinson, daughter of Abraham Robinson, 2 October 1826. Wm. A. White, security.

Alexander H. Logwood and Elizabeth Douglass, daughter of David Douglass, 24 September 1827. James Sledd, security.

Wm. Callaway and Ann Logwood, daughter Euphan Logwood, 2 September 1828. Jno. S. Leftwich, security. Rev. Nicholas H. Cobbs.

Roland Turpin and Margaret Logwood, 31 March 1831. Rev. Jas. Leftwich.

Benjamin Johnson and Sarah Ann Logwood, daughter Burwell Logwood, 16 September 1836. George Jones, security.

James M. Johnson and Martha D. Logwood, daughter Burwell Logwood, 16 September 1836. George Jones, security.

Alexander H. Logwood and Theodosia A. White, daughter Charles B. Reynolds, 11 November 1841. Rev. Wm. Harris. Edwin Reynolds, security.

Edmund Logwood and Lucy McDaniel White (widow of Wm. Allen White), daughter of Joseph T. Reese, 23 October 1848. J. R. Hatcher, security.

Robert R. Logwood and Edith B. Wheat, daughter of Z. Wheat, 2 July 1841. Jack O. Wheat, security.

Robert R. Logwood and Mary E. Johnson, daughter of L. H. Johnson, 17 April 1851. Alex. H. Logwood, security.

John P. Bondurant and Mary Logwood, 28 January 1852. Revd. Joseph Spriggs.

James A. Logwood and Sarah J. Jennings, daughter of James C. Jennings, 4 February 1857. Rev. Jas. R. Waggener.

Benjamin R. Gilbert and Nannie A. Logwood, daughter of Alexander H. Logwood, January 1858. Revd. Wm. C. Blount.

James A. Logwood and Caroline W. Penn, 27 February 1861. Rev. Leml. S. Reed.

Charles E. Logwood and Mollie V. Overstreet, daughter of Henry A. Overstreet, 27 April 1864. Rev. Wm. Harris.

John Logwood and Sallie W. McClintock, daughter of Lee McClintock, 19 December 1865. Rev. Lyman B. Wharton.

WHARTON

John Wharton, son of the immigrant, married Rhoda Morris of Hanover County, Virginia, and died "the Wednesday before March 3, 1816," in Nashville, Tennessee, at the home of their son, Jesse, with whom they were spending their old age. She died after 1825.

John Wharton, son of John and Rhoda (Morris) Wharton, was born February 2, 1771; died February 7, 1845; married, June 1, 1797, Sally Lilbourne Logwood. They lived at "Locust Hill," the home of her father, Major Thomas Logwood, from whom they inherited it.

CHILDREN:

(1) Rhoda Morris, born July 1, 1798; died September 8, 1864; married Jesse Thomson. (See Thomson family.)

(2) Ann Aiken, born February 5, 1880; married Nelson Sale.

(3) Sophia Hill, born August 10, 1801; died January 25, 1849; married Richard Davis.

(4) John Austin, born March 22, 1803; died June 20, 1888. (See forward.)

(5) Dabney Miller, born December 27, 1804; married (first) Ann Ophelia Pierce; (second) Virginia Hungerford.

(6) Martha, born March 18, 1807; died April 21, 1861; married Richard Sale.

(7) Catherine Amanda, born April 20, 1809; died October 27, 1857; married Lee McClintock.

(8) Thomas Jefferson, born January 24, 1811; died December, 1856.

(9) Edmund, born December 17, 1812; died May 17, 1837.

(10) Sally Temple, born December 25, 1814; died March 17, 1847.

(11) Maria Louisa, born June 4, 1817.

(12) William Adolphus, born May 23, 1819; died October 10, 1846.

(13) Charlotte Eliza, born August 20, 1821; died August 19, 1861; married Rev. Jeremiah Bell Jeter. (See Jeter family.)

(14) Mary Johnson, born January 13, 1827; died June 27, 1848.

....

John Austin Wharton, son of John and Sally (Logwood) Wharton, married, in 1830, Isabella Brown, born December 4, 1810, in Berkshire County, Massachusetts, died December 31, 1895, in Bedford

County, Virginia. John A. Wharton was lawyer, judge, and clergyman of the Protestant Episcopal Church. He lived in Liberty, in the residence now (1930) occupied by Mrs. Ellen Davis Gregory.

CHILDREN:

(1) Lyman Brown; clergyman of Protestant Episcopal Church; Professor at William and Mary College, Williamsburg, Va.; married Paulina S. Taylor.
(2) Frances Isabelle; died in childhood.
(3) Sarah Virginia; married Nathaniel W. Thomson of Bedford County. (See Thomson family.)

CHILD:

(a) Isabelle; married William Steptoe Foster.

CHILDREN:

(aa) Virginia Thomson.
(bb) William Steptoe, Jr.

(4) Mary Jane; died unmarried.
(5) Frances Isabelle, born February 8, 1844; died September 30, 1898; married, December 26, 1869, John T. Meade.

CHILDREN:

(a) John Wharton; married Helen Brown.
(b) Frances; married George Eugene Moore.

CHILDREN:

(aa) George Eugene, Jr., born October 4, 1897; married, August 16, 1921, Ruth P. Dickey.
(bb) Frances Wharton, born August 13, 1899; married, October 19, 1921, Edgar Anderson, who was born February 7, 1899.

CHILDREN:

(aaa) Frances, born March 15, 1923.
(bbb) George Eugene, born February 8, 1926.

(c) Florence.
(d) Mary.
(e) Joseph.

(6) John Edmund; married Mattie McClintock.

(7) Charlotte Eliza; died unmarried.

(8) Alice; died unmarried.

(9) Charles William, born June 1, 1852; died February 16, 1913; married, December 10, 1879, Estelle Steptoe, daughter of LaFayette and Maria (Watson) Steptoe.

CHILDREN :

(a) Charles William, Jr., married Merrie Louise Bibb. Lives in Bedford, Va. (See Bond family.)

(b) Marie Louise; married George W. Slicer, son of Captain Joseph S. and Eliza (Williams) Slicer, of Bufordsville (now Montvale), Va. They live in Huntington, W. Va.

CHILDREN :

(aa) Charles Wharton.

(bb) George W., Jr.

(Data for the sketches of both Logwood and Wharton families were furnished by Charles W. Wharton, of Bedford, from a family tree made by his uncle, Dr. Lyman B. Wharton, of William and Mary College.)

MEADE

The following early history of the Meade family is taken from the *William and Mary Quarterly,* Vol. X, page 191:

Most of the Meads of Loudon, Bedford, and other counties of Virginia are descended from one Richard Mead of Mursley, Buckinghamshire, by his wife, Joane, through his second son, Rev. Matthew Meade, of Stepney, who was born in 1629, at Leighton Buzzard, Bedfordshire, and died Oct. 16, 1699.

Rev. Matthew Meade was a prominent clergyman of the Church of England, and was a man of very liberal views. He was ejected from his charge for non-conformity, in 1662. He seems to have been implicated in the Rye House Conspiracy, and was for some time imprisoned; but was set free by the king.

Rev. Matthew Meade (Mead) married and had issue fifteen children, among them being Nathaniel Mead, Richard Mead and William Mead. William Mead married and had issue, among them being John, William, Robert, Samuel, Pleasant, Sarah, and others, who came to America about ——, and settled in Bucks Co., Pa.

John Mead married Mary ————, and, so far as known, had two sons, Robert Mead, and William Mead born Oct. 10, 1727. Nothing is known of him, however, as he died in Bedford Co., Va., in 1754, and letters of administration were granted on his estate in that county in the year 1754. These letters were granted to his son, William Mead. He was buried in the burial ground of the Mead family, near New London, Bedford Co., Va.

William Mead, brother of John Mead, married in Bucks Co., Pa., Ellen Worrell, daughter of Thomas and Ellen Worrell. He was a resident of Bucks Co., Pa., in 1744, as in that year Andrew Ellett conveyed to Wm. Meade 220 acres of land in Lower Wakefield Township, Bucks Co., Pa., on the Delaware. He sold it in 1747, to Hezekiah Anderson, and left the township and went to Fairfax Co. (that part of it which is now Loudon Co., Va.), and afterwards to Bedford Co., Va. He remained in Bedford Co. for seven years, and returned to Loudon Co., where he died and was buried at the Friends burial ground, near Leesburg. His will is of record in Loudon Co., Va., at Leesburg, it having been probated Jan. 17, 1780. He left issue, the descendants of whom are numerous in Loudon and other counties of Virginia and elsewhere.

....

From the *Virginia Gazette,* by Dixon and Hunter, October 21, 1775:

Whereas the alarming situation of the country at this time is such that Gentlemen of property and distinction have thought it necessary to move their families for safety: In tender consideration whereof, I do hereby declare that I think the indispensable duty of every frontier county to be aiding and assisting all those who are exposed to imminent danger; I, therefore, as a private individual, being blessed with a considerable quantity of land, do freely offer, for the relief of such distressed families, 10,000 acres of land in the counties of Bedford and Pittsylvania, which will settle fifty families, on paying only the quitrents of such land until times shall be changed.

WILLIAM MEAD.

New London, Bedford County, Va.

....

Of the children of William and Ellen (Worrell) Mead, William, Jr., married Mary Shreve, daughter of Benjamin and Ann (Berry) Shreve.

CHILDREN:

(1) William, III, born April 18, 1786; died in Bedford County, Virginia, July 20, 1854; married Mary Crenshaw of Bedford County.
(2) Ellen, born 1787; died 1788.
(3) Ellen (second child by same name); married Robert C. Moffet, of Loudon County, Virginia.
(4) Elizabeth; died unmarried.
(5) Ann; married Eli Schooley.
(6) Thomas; married Mary Ann Worsley, of Bedford County, Virginia.
(7) Mary; married Thomas Saunders.
(8) Joseph, born June 29, 1799; died August 13, 1870; married Jane Worsley.

CHILDREN:

(a) William Worsley; married Cornelia F. Mead.

(b) Mary Elizabeth; married Benjamin S. White.

(c) Frances Ann; married Nelson Head.

(d) John Thomas, born September 1, 1843; died September 16, 1912; married Frances I. Wharton. (See Wharton family.)

CHILDREN:

(aa) John Wharton.

(bb) Frances Worsley; married James E. Moore.

(cc) Florence.

(dd) Mary E.

(ee) Joseph; married Ada Lockard.

(9) Hannah; died unmarried.

(10) Martha; married Frederick Carper.

OTEY

From the register of St. Peter's Parish, New Kent County, Va., are taken the following data which are believed to be the earliest records of the Otey family:

"John, son of John Otey, born July 19, 1713.
Mary, daughter of John Otey, born July 17, 1715.
William Otey, son of John Otey, born March 18, 1719.
Martha, daughter of John Otey, born July 23, 1717.

William, son of John Otey, deceased September 20, 1724.
Martha, daughter of John Otey, deceased October 3, 1721.

Betty, daughter of Isaac and Frances Otey, born May 13, 1737.
Sarah, negro girl belonging to Miss Elizabeth Otey, born June 5, 1738.
Mary, daughter of Isaac and Frances Otey, born August 24, 1738."

On the fly leaf of his Bible, Dr. John A. Otey (born January 13, 1818; died December 26, 1892) of Liberty, Va., wrote this interesting bit of family history, which was told to him by his father, Col. Armistead Otey, an officer in the Virginia line of troops in the War of 1812:

"John Otey—from whom all of the Oteys in upper Virginia, Tennessee and Alabama descended—came to the County of Bedford, Virginia, about the time of the Revolutionary War. He left one brother in the County of New Kent, and all the persons of that name, that their descendants have been able to find, descended from these two brothers.

"John Otey served in the Revolutionary War and held the office of captain. Upon one occasion, when the British soldiers had sailed up the River Pamunkey in a vessel, for the purpose of robbing the citizens of their cattle, John Otey assembled his company of riflemen and stationed them along the bank of the river, fifty paces apart, and as the vessel was returning he hailed it and commanded it to come to shore; the British aboard were unused to the rifle, and musket (which they supposed the little band were armed with) shot so inaccurately, that they supposed themselves out of danger, and began to taunt Otey's men and defy them. John Otey ordered his men to commence firing. The second shot brought down a man, the third did likewise. The commander gave orders to land, which was done, and the entire crew made prisoners. Otey then gave orders that they were not to give any sign to their comrades, under pain of being shot down; and when night came on he marched them in single file very near the British line of encampment, which he passed, and landed them safely in the American camp. He then returned to the vessel which he found to contain some valuable silver plate, some of which remains in the Otey family at the present time. John Otey's descendants were too proud to claim a pension for his services, and consequently the country was never taxed by him or his descendants to pay for the service which he rendered. John Otey was a man of very large stature and commanding appearance, of great moral firmness, and with all an humble Christian. His children were all, except Armistead, the youngest son, men of powerful physical strength and activity, and of great bravery. They all occupied high positions in society and had the confidence of the people among whom they lived."

John Otey qualified as captain in Bedford County, March 23, 1778. He died in 1817, and his will is recorded in Bedford. He and his wife are buried in the old Otey Cemetery in the town of Bedford (formerly Liberty) and the inscription on their tombstone reads:

IN MEMORY OF

JOHN OTEY AND HIS WIFE MARY HOPKINS

ALSO THEIR CHILDREN

JOHN OTEY	WALTER OTEY
FRAZIER OTEY	ARMISTEAD OTEY
JAMES OTEY	FRANCES OTEY
ISAAC OTEY	

Mary Hopkins, wife of Captain John Otey, was the daughter of John Hopkins, and grand-daughter of Dr. Arthur Hopkins and his wife Elizabeth Pettus.

Elizabeth Pettus was the daughter of Col. Thomas Pettus, and grand-daughter of Sir John Pettus, who was a knight, and one of the founders of the Colony of Virginia.

See Smith's *History of Virginia,* Vol. II, page 52; and Burk's *History of Virginia,* page 345.

John Hopkins Otey; married Elizabeth Buford. (See Buford family.)

Isaac, born October 18, 1765; died October 18, 1839. (See forward.)

Frazier Otey, married (first) Mildred Leftwich; (second) Mrs. Mary (Lane) Latham. (See forward.)

Walter.

Frances, born October 5, 1772; died October 10, 1825; married William Leftwich.

James, born May 4, 1774; died unmarried.

Armstead, born March 1, 1777; died November 23, 1866; married (first) Sally Gill (born September 12, 1788; died August 12, 1891; (second) Nancy Lumpkin.

Isaac Otey, son of John and Mary (Hopkins) Otey, married, February 5, 1789, Elizabeth Matthews (born February 22, 1767; died March 4, 1855).

The following family record was taken from a folio Bible which belonged to Isaac Otey, and was given by his widow to their son, the Rt. Rev. James Hervey Otey, first Bishop of Tennessee:

"February 5, 1789—Isaac Otey and Betsy Matthews married at 6 P. M. by Rev. Wm. Graham.

(1) Sarah M. Otey, born 17 Dec. 1789; died 1 June, 1832.
(2) William Otey, born 13 Feb. 1791; died 13 Feb.
(3) John M. Otey, born 2 Dec. 1792; died 3 Feb. 1859.
(4) Mary J. A. Otey, born 18 July 1794.
(5) Isaac N. Otey, born 23 May 1796.
(6) Frances Ann Otey, born 17 March 1798.
(7) James H. Otey, born 27 Jan'y 1800.
(8) Armistead Otey, born 11 Nov. 1801.
(9) Mildred L. Otey, born 23 April 1804.
(10) Walter L. Otey, born 9 July 1806.
(11) Littleton W. T. Otey, born 30 Aug. 1808.
(12) Robert Taylor Otey, born 23 Aug. 1811."

The following marriages of some of the above children of Isaac and Elizabeth (Matthews) Otey have been furnished by Mrs. Frances Otey (Buford) Buford:

John Matthews Otey married, December 10, 1817, Lucy Wilhelmina Norvell.

James Hervey Otey (Bishop) married, October 13, 1821, Eliza Pannill, of Petersburg, Va.

Armistead Otey married (first), September 9, 1847, Mrs. Susan J. (Terry) Russell; (second) April 8, 1858, Martha Ann Nolley.

Mary J. A. Otey married Col. Edward Gwatkin. (See Gwatkin family.)

Sarah M. Otey married William Cook.

Frances Ann Otey married Capt. Paschal G. Buford. (See Buford family.)

Mildred L. Otey married her cousin, John Hopkins Otey.

....

Frazier Otey, II, son of Frazier Otey, I, and his second wife, Mary Lane, was born in Liberty, Va., December 27, 1818, and died in Knoxville, Tenn., September 11, 1908. He married, September 23, 1841, Syrena K. Newlee, of Christiansburg, Va., and moved in covered wagons to Cumberland Gap, Tenn., in 1851. In 1865 he was ordained to the ministry of the Baptist Church, and preached chiefly among the mountain people of East Tennessee.

CHILDREN:

(1) William R., born November 4, 1842; died September, 1909; married, November 15, 1866, Frances Cadle, of Cumberland Gap, Tenn.

CHILDREN:

(a) Charles A.; married Nannie E. Holman, of Ft. Smith, Ark.

(b) Mary Olive; died December 27, 1879.

(c) Rufus P.

(d) Sarah S.; married Robert G. Pettigrew.

(e) Lucy P.; married Nuton A. Kobric.

(f) Annie M.; married William K. Kinkade.

(g) John W. C.

(h) Lydia Grace.

(2) James T., born April 16, 1845; died October 1, 1926; married, April 10, 1890, Nancy Sharp, of Powells Valley, Tenn.

CHILDREN:

(a) Minnie E.; married Jacob D. Templin.
(b) Ella Vestie; married H. Frank Price.
(c) Charles F.; married Alice ————.
(d) Mary; married Thomas Tiller.
(e) Mellie V.; married Marshall S. Cottrell.
(f) Irene; married J. Carl Baldwin.

(3) John M., born February 2, 1847; married, June 2, 1874, Margaret Hale, of Mossy Creek, Tenn., and, like his father, became a Baptist preacher.

CHILDREN:

(a) Syrena; married William A. Hudson.
(b) William S.; married (first) Margaret Carpenter; (second) Elizabeth Bates.
(c) Annie Ruth; married Joseph T. McKinney.
(d) Robert N.; married Maud Mitchell.
(e) Eula K., twin to Robert N.; married G. Otis Butler.
(f) Buford T.

(4) Robert N., born December 31, 1849; died April 9, 1852.

(5) Charles H., born August 20, 1852; died April 9, 1926; married, December 23, 1885, Mary Sharp, of Cumberland Gap, Tenn.

CHILDREN:

(a) Newman Frazier.
(b) Neil Sharp.

(6) Mary V., born August 1, 1854; married, October 27, 1878, T. C. Bates, of Knoxville, Tenn.

CHILDREN:

(a) Elizabeth.
(b) Grace; married John Weaver, of Spokane, Wash.
(c) Ellen; married Robert Lovejoy.
(d) Albert.

(7) Mellie H., born July 7, 1857; died January 24, 1925; married (first), September 25, 1879, Richard E. Hale, of Mossy Creek, Tenn.

CHILDREN:

(a) Effie; married Robert L. Crawford.
(b) Nettie; married Eugene Trent.

Mellie H. married (second) J. T. Bryan, of Jefferson County, Tenn.

CHILDREN:

(a) Fannie Lee; died unmarried April, 1921.

(b) Robert Otey; married Achsa Freeman.

(8) Frances B., born November 14, 1861; married, October 13, 1885, Dr. Reuben Neil Kesterson, of Richmond, Ky. She is a member of the Daughters of the American Revolution and of the United Daughters of the Confederacy; is prominent in club and social circles, and a zealous worker in the Baptist Church.

Reuben Neil Kesterson, born in Claiborne County, Tenn., July 12, 1858, is the son of Reuben and Adeline (Henderson) Kesterson. She was a daughter of Jeremiah and Betsy (Mills) Henderson, and granddaughter of Thomas Henderson, who was a second cousin to George Washington.

Reuben Neil Kesterson was educated at Mosey Creek College, now Carson and Newman College, of Jefferson City. He studied dentistry at the University of Tennessee and graduated in 1881, receiving the degree of D. D. S. He began the practice of his profession in Richmond, Ky., and after four years went to Knoxville, Tenn., and continued his professional work until 1908.

Dr. Kesterson is a public spirited citizen, and wields a great influence for good, both in Knoxville and the surrounding country. He is a man of culture and high intellectual attainments, and is particularly interested in music and art.

CHILDREN:

(a) Robert Neil, born November 4, 1887; died August 8, 1890.

(b) Thomas Otey, born in Knoxville, Tenn., January 11, 1890; married, April 18, 1922, Barbara Davis, daughter of W. P. Davis, of Louisville, Ky.

CHILD:

(aa) Thomas Huntingdon Davis, born January 31, 1925.

POINDEXTER

"The first of the Poindexter family in Virginia was George Poindexter who, in the seventeenth century, settled at Middle Plantation, now Williamsburg. He was a merchant, part owner of ships, and a planter. The entire destruction of the records of New Kent and James City counties and the almost entire destruction of those of Hanover, have prevented the preparation of a connected genealogy of the family. Members of the family, prior to the Revolution, had settled in half a dozen different counties in Virginia and the names are now represented by descendants throughout the country.

The family, the original form of whose name is Poingdestre, is an ancient gentle line in the Island of Jersey. Fortunately, the pedigree preserved there includes the name of George Poingdestre or Poindexter and states that he settled in Virginia. This pedigree is contained in a work entitled 'An Armorial of Jersey,' Being an Account, Heraldic and Antiquarian of its Chief Native Families.

The account is as follows:

POINGDESTRE

Arms (used by present families in Jersey) Per fesse argent and or; in chief a dexter hand, clenched, ppr., cuffed of the second; in base a mullet of the first. Crest: An esquires' helmet ppr.

Two mottoes are used by different branches of the family, one: Nemo me impune lacessit, and the other; Dextra fidei pignus.

In the Armorial, the chart pedigrees are introduced by the following account:

As early as 1250 Geoffrey and Raoul Poingdestre are mentioned as land owners on the Island of Jersey, Great Britian, in certain documents preserved in the archives at S. Lo, in Normandy, France.

In 1424, John Poingdestre was bailly of the Island; in 1452, his son, another John, filled the same office; and in 1467, the grandson of the first named, a third son John, occupied this post. In 1485, John Poingdestre was Lieutenant-Bailly, as was his descendant, still named John, in 1669. This family has for several generations, possessed the fief of Grainville, in the parish of S. Saviour.

George Poingdestre, seigneur of the fief es Poingdestre, Island of Jersey, died in 1544. He married Girette, niece of Sir Thomas Ahier.

Children: John; Thomas, constable of S. Saviour, married Catherine, daughter of Thomas Lampriere, widow of Richard Langois and Clement Messervy.

(I) John Poingdestre, son of George and Girette Poingdestre, and seigneur of the fief es Poingdestre, died in 1583. His children were: Edward; John, who married Perrotine, daughter of Peter Laell.

(II) Edward Poingdestre, son of John Poingdestre, Seigneur of the fief es Poingdestre; married (first) Margaret, daughter of Clement Messervy, in 1562; and (second) Pauline, daughter of Guyon Ahier.

(III) Thomas Poingdestre, son of Edward Poingdestre, seigneur of the fief es Poingdestre, born in 1581; married Elizabeth, daughter of ———— Effard. Children: Philip, born in 1620, married Sarah Pinel; Jacob; George, who settled in Virginia, N. A.; Rachel.

(IV) George Poingdestre, son of Thomas and Elizabeth Poingdestre immigrated to America and settled in Virginia.

John Poindexter, a descendant of the emigrant, George Poingdestre, settled in Louisa County, Virginia, at the time of its formation, in or near, what was known as Gold Mine Creek, a small stream emptying into the North Anna River about eight miles northwest of Louisa Courthouse. He owned large landed estates, and at that time, was one of the most prominent men in the county, both in church and county matters. Was one of the first justices of Louisa County, December 13, 1742; also, one of the first vestrymen of Fredericksville Parish.

He died in 1753, and his will, dated January 10, 1753, probated in Louisa County, May 22, 1753, mentions Legatees: wife, Christian; sons, Thomas, John, William, Richard and Joseph; daughters, Anne, Sarah, and Frances Anderson. The widow, Christian Poindexter, qualified as executrix. (*Virginia Historical Magazine,* Vol. XIX, pages 439-440.)

Will of Christian Poindexter, dated June 25, 1778, proved in Louisa County, June 14, 1779. Legatees:

Item 1.   To my son William, one negro woman.

Item 2.   To my grandson William, Jr., one negro boy.

Item 3.   The balance of my estate to which I hold a fee simple, I wish divided among my children. Frances Anderson, being dead, her part to be given to her children. Richard's part to be divided between his children—Christian and Febey. The other children of hers named are John, William, Ann Slaughter, Joseph and Sarah Triton. She gives another part of her estate to her daughter, Frances Anderson's heirs, her son Richard's two daughters, and to her (the testator's) children: Thomas, John, William, Ann Slaughter, Joseph, and Sally Triton (Irion). (*Virginia Historical Magazine,* Vol. XX, page 107.)

Witnesses: John Slaughter, Sally Biggar, Elizabeth Poindexter, William White, Anne G. Poindexter.

Bond of executors of above will to Thomas Poindexter, Justice of the Peace, Louisa County."

(For proof of line of descent see *Virginia Historical Magazine,* Vol. XIX, pages 215-218.)

In the "Ellis Family of Virginia," is found a sketch of the *Shelton* family and there we note, that Sarah Shelton, the ancestress of the family married first, Richard C. Gissage; a merchant from London; one of her children, by this marriage, Christian, married a Poindexter. From dates, residence, etc., we feel reasonably sure it is our John Poindexter, son of the emigrant, George, that she married and whose will was probated in 1779 in Louisa County, Virginia.

Joseph Poindexter, thought to be the son of John and Christian Poindexter, of Louisa, was born June, 1736, and lived in Bedford County, later moving to Campbell County, where he died June 29, 1826, and his and his wife's tombs bear the following epitaphs:

"Capt. Joseph Poindexter
of the Revolution
died
June 29, 1826
aged 90 years."

"Elizabeth J., wife of
Capt. Joseph Poindexter
died
February 5, 1828
aged 82 years."

Joseph Poindexter was a Captain of the Militia from Bedford County (see McAllister's *Virginia Militia,* Section 254; and records in Virginia State Library), in the American Army in the Revolutionary War.

Joseph Poindexter married, February 10, 1763, Elizabeth James, daughter of James Kennerly. She was born February 28, 1747.

CHILDREN:

(1) Samuel; married (first) Anne Poindexter, daughter of Reuben Slaughter; (second) Sarah Garth, of Albemarle County; (third) Martha, daughter of Major Isaac Otey. (See forward.)

(2) James; married Mary, daughter of Waddy and Mary (Lewis) Thompson, of Albemarle County; has descendants living in California.

(3) Joseph; married Mrs. Harrison.

(4) William; married Judith, daughter of Waddy and Mary (Lewis) Thompson, of Albemarle. (Judith's mother, Mary Lewis, was a daughter of Robert Lewis. She married twice; her first husband being Samuel Cobbs; second, Waddy Thompson. (Page 213, Valume II, Chalkley's Abstracts of Augusta County)).

(5) Reuben.

(6) Thomas Kennerly; married Mrs. Mary (Rall) Kennerly; removed to South Carolina; left issue.

(7) John; married Judith Chilton. (See Chilton family.)

(8) Louis D.; married Ann Smith, lived in Campbell County and buried at the old homestead. (See forward.)

(9) Ann; married John Shelton, of Amherst County, Va.

(10) Elizabeth; married Raleigh Chilton.

(11) Richard; married ———— Ford; removed to the West.

Following is the will of Joseph Poindexter, found in Will Book No. 5, page 317, of the Campbell County records:

In the name of God Amen. I Joseph Poindexter Sr. of Campbell County Virginia in my proper *sences* and memory do make and publish the following as my last will and testament in the matter and form following toWit. I desire that my executors hereafter named to pay all my just and lawful debts out of my personal estate. I then give to my beloved wife Elizabeth J. Poindexter during her life or widowhood the tract of land where on I now live together with the following slaves toWit, Martin Patt, Sarah Cate, David Moses, Isbel Patrick, Lucina Billy Rose, Eliza Fountain, Louisa Milly and Violet with their future increase together with the whole of my hold and kitchen furniture with all my stock of every discription also my plantation tools including my waggon and horses together with the crop on hand and that that may be growing at the time of my Death and after the death or marriage of my said wife to be disposed of as hereafter directed.

I give and devise to my son Thomas Poindexter after the death or marriage of my wife the tract of land I now live on (Except seven and a fourth acres on Little Whipping Creek including a mill site which I do devise to my son Lewis for certain perposes, upon conditions that he the said Thomas pay to my son Lewis Poindexter nine hundred dollars lawful money of Virginia to him and his heirs forever. Item I give to my son William Poindexter one negro named Fanny with her increase during his and his wifes life and after their decease to be equally divided among his lawful representatives. Item I give to my grand daughter Franky Harrison Poindexter one negro girl named Rose with her future increase one feather bed & furniture one horse and saddle worth one hundred dollars to be possessed by her upon becoming of lawful age or marriage upon the condition that she die without issue leaving then & in that case to revert and go into the residue of my Estate. Item after the death or marriage of my said wife it is my will that all my Estate of every discription except what has heretofore been named and devised, be sold to the best advantage and the money arising therefrom be divided after the following manner; Item I give to my sons, James, Samuel, Joseph, William & Richard and Lewis Poindexter Five dollars each and no more as I have provided for them heretofore. Item I give to my daughter Ann Shelton Five hundred dollars. Item I give to the surviving children of my son James Poindexter lawfully begotten Five hundred dollars to be divided in equal and just proportions between them. Item I give to my son John Poindexter Eight Hundred Dollars. Item I give to the surviving children of my son William Poindexter five hundred dollars to be divided in *equeal* and just proportions between them. Item I give to the three sons of my son Joseph Poindexter toWit William Joseph & James and also to his daughter Franky one thousand dollars to be divided in *equeal* and just proportions between them. Item I give to the surviving children of my son Richard Poindexter lawfully begotten four hundred dollars to be divided in *equeal* and just proportions between them. Item I give to the surviving children of my deceased son Reubin Poindexter Five hundred dollars to be divided in *equeal* and just proportions between them. Item I give to my daughter Elizabeth Chilton one hundred dollars, now in case my Estate should sell for more or less then the amount of the specified legacies it is my will that the money be divided by the same proportions. It is my will & desire that after the death of wife that my two old and faithful servants Martin and Pate be let to live with such of my children as they may *chuse* and to be supported out of my estate during their lives. It is further my will that my Grand Daughter Fanny Harrison Poindexter do live with my said wife and be maintained as heretofore out of my Estate during my said wifes lifetime having disposed of my estate aforesaid I do hereby appoint my wife executrix and my sons Lewis Poindexter & John Poindexter and John Shelton Jr. executors of this my last will and Testament hereby revoking all other wills heretofore by me made. In witness whereof I have set my hand and *afixed* my seal this 12th day of July 1823.

JOSEPH POINDEXTER [SEAL].

Signed sealed and acknowledged in the presence of Jos. Scott, Francis Callaway, Richard Thornton, Philip Gibbs, Ro. Smith.

Memorandum; Since executing my last will and testament I have thought proper to annex a codicil to the same revoking that part wherein I have devised to my son Thomas Poindexter the Tract of land whereon I now live upon the condition that he should pay to my son Lewis D. Poindexter the sum of nine hundred dollars; And I do hereby devise the said tract of land with appertenances to same belonging after the death of wife to my said son Lewis D. Poindexter to him and his heirs and assignes forever upon condition he shall pay to my said son Thomas Poindexter the sum of sixteen hundred and sixty six dollars and sixty seven cents after the following manner ToWit three hundred and thirty three dollars thirty three and one third cents in twelve months after he becomes *compleatly* possessed of the premises and that sum annually *untill* the whole sixteen hundred & sixty six dollars & sixty seven cents is paid; In Witness whereof I have set my hand & seal this 11th day of July 1825.

JOSEPH POINDEXTER [SEAL].

Signed sealed and acknowledged in the presence of Jos. Scott, John D. Smith, Robert Smith.

At a Court held for Campbell County July 10th 1826. The foregoing last will and testament of Joseph Poindexter dec'd with the codicil annexed was produced in Court proved by the oaths of Joseph Scott and Robert Smith two of the subscribing Witnesses thereto and ordered to be recorded and on the motion of Lewis D. Poindexter one of the executors in said will named who qualified according to law certificate is granted him for obtaining probate thereof on his giving security whereupon he together with William Whitlow, Robert Smith, and Thomas A. Cobbs his securities entered into and acknowledged their bond in the penalty of fifteen hundred dollars conditioned as the law directs for said executors due & faithful administration of said decedents estate & performance of his will and at a Court held for the said County August 14, 1826, on the motion of John Poindexter another executor in said will named who qualified according to law leave is given him to join in the probat thereof on his giving security whereupon he together with Waddy Poindexter, Raleigh Chilton and Joseph Epperson his securities entered into and acknowledged their bond in the penalty of Ten Thousand dollars conditioned as the law directs for said executors due & faithful administration of said decedents estate & performance of his will.

Teste.

JOHN ALEXANDER, C. C. C.

A Copy;

Teste:

C. W. WOODSON, Clerk.

Will Book No. 5, page 317.

Samuel Poindexter, eldest son of Joseph and Elizabeth James (Kennerly) Poindexter, was born December 29, 1767, lived in Bedford County, where he owned large landed estates and was a prosperous planter of that section. He was a man of much influence and respected by all who knew him. Much of his land is still in the possession of his descendants. He married three times; (first), June 11, 1790, Ann Poindexter Slaughter, a daughter of Reuben and Betty (Poindexter) Slaughter. Reuben Slaughter was a son of Colonel Francis and Ann (Lightfoot) Slaughter, who was a large land holder in Culpeper and Orange counties, Virginia. (See Slaughter family.) There were five children by this marriage. After the death of his first wife, he married (second) Sarah Garth, of Albemarle County; and, by this union, there were three children. There were no children by his (third) marriage to Martha Otey, daughter of James Otey, of Kentucky. He died in 1841. (Family tradition says this Samuel reared his kinsman, George Poindexter, Governor of Mississippi, in his home.)

CHILDREN BY FIRST MARRIAGE:

(1) Dabney, born November 17, 1791; married Mary Eliza Watts. (See forward.)

(2) James; married Susan Shelton.

(3) John S., born January 26, 1796; married Nancy Robinson. (See forward.)

(4) Anderson; married, October 21, 1829, Denotia Furlony. There was one child, a daughter, who died. Anderson Poindexter inherited, the lovely old colonial home (now known as "The Cedars") from his father; and this estate, he willed to his nephew, John Milton White, father of Edward Henry White, the present owner.

(5) Caroline; married Col. William Allen White, son of Captain Jacob and Hannah (Spiers) White. (See forward.)

CHILDREN BY SECOND MARRIAGE:

(6) Garland; married Julia Bingham.

(7) Willis G.; married, October, 1836, Emily P. Slaughter, daughter of Joseph Slaughter. (See forward.)

(8) Samuel T.; married, September 4, 1845, Ann Maria Tucker. (See forward.)

WILL OF SAMUEL POINDEXTER OF BEDFORD COUNTY, VIRGINIA:

IN THE NAME OF GOD, AMEN, I Samuel Poindexter of the County of Bedford and State of Virginia, being weak and infirm in body but of sound and disposing mind and memory, do make and adopt this my last will and testament in the manner and form following, Viz.:

Item 1st, It is my will and desire that my funeral expenses and just debts be first paid. Item 2nd, It is my will and desire that —— wife Martha G. Poindexter receive at my death one third part of my real and personal estate, and her third part of my real estate to be located out of the lands hereafter mentioned and given to my four sons, Samuel, Willis, Garland & Anderson Poindexter, during her natural life. Item 3rd, I give and devise to my son Dabney Poindexter the whole of the tract of land on which he now lives and nothing more of my estate. Item 4th, I give and devise to my son John Poindexter that portion of my land on which he now lives, commencing at Sycamore Creek at the mouth of my ditch joining the lands of John C. Noell and running a South East course to the corner of the late Capt. C. Stewarts land and so running with said land South course to John Goodes line, so running with said lines to Thos. Wilson's lands, thence with said Wilson's lines to Sycamore Creek, and with the creek up to the beginning. Item 5th, I give and devise to my four sons Samuel, Willis, Garland & Anderson Poindexter all that portion or tract of land on which I at present reside, being the same which I purchased of Benj. Moore, equally, except that portion before reserved and given to my son John Poindexter, this being the lands out of which I design my wife's legal portion during her life. At her death I also give and devise her portion to my four sons named in this the above or 5th item, equally. Item 6th, It is my will and desire and I do hereby direct that one thousand dollars shall be raised out of my estate and to be retained in the hands of my executors hereinafter named and to act as trustees for the following purpose, viz.; the said thousand dollars to be put out on interest and the interest arising from the same to be applied by my executors who are hereby appointed as trustees, to the support of my son James Poindexter in the way and manner the trustees in the case may think best, during his natural life, and at his death the said thousand dollars to be equally divided between my sons Samuel, Willis, Garland and Anderson Poindexter. Item 7th, I give and bequeath to my grand children Samuel Jacob White and John Milton White one-eighth part of my personal and perishable estate equally, the said eighth part to be retained in the hands of my executors until they become of legal age respectively, my executors not to pay interest or hire during their minority. In the event of the death of either of my grandchildren above named before arriving at lawful age, then the legacy as above bequeathed to him to revert back to my sons John, Samuel, Willis, Garland & Anderson Poindexter equally, also in the event of the death of both of my grandchildren above named before arriving at lawful age, then the whole of the legacy bequeathed them to revert back equally to my five sons last named in this the 7th item. Item 8th, The interest on the one thousand dollars named in item 6th is all I intend or wish my son James Poindexter to receive, either real, personal or otherwise of my estate. Item 9th, I do hereby constitute and appoint my sons Samuel Poindexter, Willis Poindexter and Garland Poindexter as executors to this my last will and testament and as trustees for the purpose of seeing the foregoing sixth item faithfully executed.

Signed, sealed and acknowledged in the presence of,
this 5th day Sept. 1839.

SAMUEL POINDEXTER [SEAL].

NELSON A. THOMSON,
ALLISON JETER.

At a Court held for Bedford County the 27th day of September, 1841. This last will and testament of Samuel Poindexter deceased was produced in Court proved by the oath of Nelson A. Thomson and Allison Jeter, subscribing witnesses thereto and ordered to be recorded. And on the motion of Willis Poindexter, one of the executors in said will named, who made oath, and gave bond and security in the penalty of $40,000 conditioned according to law, certificate was granted him for obtaining a probat on said will in due form, and liberty was reserved to the other executors in said will named to join in the probat whenever they may think fit.

Teste,

Ro. C. MITCHELL, *C. B. C.*

A Copy,

Teste:

V. W. NICHOLS,
Clerk of the Circuit Court of
Bedford County, Virginia.

Will Book "K," page 394.

....

Wm. Dabney, eldest son of Samuel and Ann Poindexter (Slaughter) Poindexter, was born November 17, 1791; died September 27, 1848; married, September 6, 1819, Mary Eliza Watts, born March 15, 1801, a daughter of James Watts.

CHILDREN:

(1) Davis Durette, born September 11, 1820; married, November 15, 1849; Ann Elizabeth (born December 15, 1832, died October 11, 1900), a daughter of John and Nancy (Robinson) Poindexter. He died June 3, 1903. Served the Confederacy the four years of the Civil War.

CHILDREN:

(a) John Davis, born August 28, 1851; married, November 3, 1875, Amanda Freeman, born February 2, 1851, a daughter of Garland and Lucy (Burford) Freeman.

CHILDREN:

(aa) Eldridge Watts, born August 21, 1876; married, September 26, 1912, Lena B. Smith.

(bb) Annie May, born May 25, 1878; married, June 14, 1905, Albert Hopwood.

(cc) Warner J., born April 12, 1880; unmarried.

(dd) Sarah Douglas, born April 4, 1882; married, November 20, 1908, Dr. Robert E. Fortune.

(ee) Nannie Kathrine, born May 22, 1883; married, November, 1907, Herbert Davis.

(ff) Walker Garland, born January 9, 1885; married Helen Thomson.

(gg) Dr. Frank Wilmore, born December 22, 1887; married, January 15, 1918, Florence Page Jones; lives in Newport News, Virginia.

(hh) Fannie Burford, born April 5, 1889; unmarried.

(ii) William Overton Poindexter, born February 26, 1893; married, May 29, 1919, June Leola Shaner, born August 11, 1894, daughter of William Jackson and Agnes (Root) Shaner, of Lexington, Virginia. Wm. Overton Poindexter was educated at Washington and Lee University, Lexington, Va., and Virginia Medical College, Richmond, Virginia. Now practicing physician in Newport News, Virginia.

CHILDREN:

(aaa) William Overton, Jr., born October 30, 1921.

(bbb) John Eldridge, born April 10, 1923.

(b) Anne Eliza, born June 24, 1853, died September 13, 1854.

(c) Frances Susan, born April 7, 1856; married, November 18, 1874, Hugh Davis Poindexter, born 1849; died August 27, 1929; a son of Richard Watts and Mary (Durette) Poindexter.

CHILDREN:

(aa) Richard Davis, born August 28, 1875; married, September 25, 1907, Lelia Nelson Mitchell, born January 11, 1878.

(bb) Cornelia Elizabeth, born September 17, 1877; married, June 14, 1906, Ezra Thomas Carter. She died May 26, 1908.

(d) Emma Cornelia, born August 10, 1859; married, December 21, 1881, Gideon David Wildman. She died June 27, 1916.

(e) Joseph Samuel, born January 3, 1866; married a Miss Howard. He died October 25, 1893.

(f) Eldridge Lindon, born January 17, 1869, died July 14, 1870.

(2) Sarah W., born February 5, 1822; married, October 4, 1843, William Gills.

(3) Richard Watts, born October 8, 1823; married (first) in January, 1849, Mary Elizabeth Durette; (second) November 22, 1865, Mary Ellen Lee, a daughter of John Calhoun and Catherine Newell Lee, of Shenandoah County. He was one of five brothers who served the Confederacy as member of its Virginia troops. He enlisted in 1862; Company G, 11th Virginia Infantry; captured at Five Forks, 1865; held at Point Lookout.

CHILDREN BY FIRST MARRIAGE:

(a) Hugh Davis, born December, 1849; married Frances Susan, a daughter of Davis Durette and Ann Elizabeth Poindexter; two children were born to them, viz.:

Richard Davis and Cornelia Elizabeth. He died August 27, 1929.

(b) Elizabeth Mildred, born October 18, 1851; married Edward Gills.

(c) Frances Stark, born in 1853; died in infancy.

(d) Eliza Durette, born March, 1855; died December 11, 1883; unmarried.

CHILDREN BY SECOND MARRIAGE:

(e) Cora Lee, born October 18, 1866; married Richard Haden Penn.

(f) Lula Bell, born January 9, 1869; married Glenmore Torck Broune, of Georgia.

(g) Mary Richard, born July 27, 1870; married Charles Lewis Watts.

(h) Richard Newell, born April 8, 1872; married Daisy Byrd Long, of Alabama.

(i) John Samuel, born February 8, 1874; married Eller Sharp, of Tennessee.

(j) Dabney Thomas, born February 16, 1876.

(4) Caroline E., born October 6, 1825; married, March 8, 1844, Asa Gills.

(5) James W., born November 3, 1827; married, January 5, 1858, Sophia Nicholls. He served in the Civil War as a member of its Virginia troops. Moved to Texas. Had seven daughters and two sons.

(6) Samuel Thomas, born August 30, 1829; married, October 31, 1876, Benjamina James Hughes, daughter of Benjamin James and Sarah Matilda (Johnson) Hughes. Paternally she is a descendant of the Randolph and Woodson families of Virginia. Samuel Thomas Poindexter inherited a vast tract of land from his father and was a prosperous planter until the War Between the States. Soon after the beginning of active hostilities, he joined Company F. Second Regiment of Virginia Cavalry and served with this company throughout the duration of the war. After the war he entered the mercantile business in Lynchburg, establishing both a retail and wholesale grocery business from which he prospered greatly. He died in July, 1904, greatly

respected and loved by all who knew him. One son, Walker Watts Poindexter, survives and he is now living in the West.

(To his mother, Benjamina James (Hughes) Poindexter, and the *Virginia Historical Magazine,* I am indebted for much of the material used in the Poindexter genealogy. The early line as given to her family by "Aunt Benjie" as she was affectionately called, and published in *Virginia Magazine,* was turned over to me, to which I have added other complete lines and all extra data I could find pertaining to this line as well as some court records. M. D. A.)

(7) Paulina Ann, born May 3, 1832; married, October 4, 1849, Joseph Hardy.

(8) Frances Susan, born May 17, 1835; married Joseph Rucker.

(9) Mary Eliza, born June 3, 1838; married Charles Hardy.

(10) William Dabney, Jr., born December 20, 1843; died July 29, 1915; married, December 3, 1879, Mary Elizabeth Jeter, a daughter of Jesse R. and Susan M. (Poindexter) Jeter and grand-daughter of Samuel B. and Susan (Jeter) Poindexter and great-grand-daughter of John S. and Nancy (Robinson) Poindexter. (See John S. Poindexter family.) Served the four years of the Civil War.

John S. Poindexter, third son of Samuel and Ann Poindexter (Slaughter) Poindexter, born January 26, 1796, died April 14, 1874; married Nancy Robinson, born May 10, 1791, died September 8, 1879, a daughter of Benjamin N. Robinson.

CHILDREN:

(1) Samuel B., born May 12, 1830, died August 8, 1868; married Susan (Jeter) Poindexter, born December 8, 1837; died September, 1920.

(2) Ann Elizabeth, born December 15, 1832; married Davis Durette Poindexter.

(3) Susan M., born June 10, 1835; died August 12, 1909; married, December 4, 1851, Jesse R. Jeter, Jr., born February 25, 1830; died April 20, 1921. (See Jeter family.)

CHILDREN:

(a) Emma Ann, born September 23, 1852; died August 14, 1921; married Osson P. Knight.

(b) Samuel Cary, born February 12, 1855; unmarried.

(c) John Slaughter, born March 16, 1857; married Emma Wilson. Live in Iowa.

(d) Jesse Elliott, born June 27, 1859; died December 15, 1859.

(e) Mary Elizabeth, born July 9, 1861; married, December 3, 1879, William Dabney Poindexter, Jr., born December 20, 1843; died July 29, 1915, a son of Wm. Dabney, Sr., and Mary Eliza (Watts) Poindexter. William Dabney Poindexter, Jr., volunteered at the beginning of the Civil War, at the age of seventeen years. Was in the Home Guards from Lynchburg, Virginia, Company "G," 11th Virginia Regiment, Infantry, Terry's Brigade, Picket's division, Longstreet's Corps. Served the four years of the war; came home once during that period. Was wounded at Seven Pines.

CHILDREN:

(aa) Eula Willie, born September 13, 1881; married, April 20, 1906, George H. Feagans. Live at Holcomb Rock, Virginia.

CHILDREN:

(aaa) Mary Lucille, born May 12, 1907.
(bbb) Edward Jewett, born April 13, 1910.
(ccc) Margaret Eloise, born January 24, 1913.
(ddd) Cecil Leslie, born January 26, 1918.
(eee) Helen McRay, born June 27, 1921.

(bb) Ollie May, born November 14, 1884; married, May 22, 1923, Walter L. Martin. Live in Akron, Ohio.

(cc) Grover Talmadge, born February 3, 1888; married, July 27, 1915, Bessie O. Seay. Live at Coleman Falls. Va.

CHILDREN:

(aaa) William David, born August 30, 1916.
(bbb) Cora Lee, born July 4, 1918.
(ccc) Robert Talmadge, born September 23, 1920.
(ddd) Albert Merriweather, born December 15, 1922.

(f) Jessie Cornelia, born May 18, 1864; married Sterling E. Knight.
(g) Rosa Bell, born December 31, 1866; married A. Willis Milliner.
(h) James Perry, born May 28, 1871; married Annie Adams.

(4) Mary W., born March 23, 1837; died February 7, 1862.

....

Caroline Poindexter, only daughter of Samuel and Ann Poindexter (Slaughter) Poindexter; married, November 3, 1828, Col. William Allen White, a son of Captain Jacob and Hannah (Spiers) White, of Bedford County. (See White family.) She died in 1839; and in May, 1841, he married Lucy McDaniel Reese, daughter of Joseph T. and Elizabeth (Tinsley) Reese. William Allen White died in 1844.

CHILDREN BY FIRST MARRIAGE:

(1) Jacob Samuel, born July 27, 1829; married, August 11, 1847, Catherine Spiers White, daughter of Henry Milton and Mary Ann (Gwatkin) White. He died April 29, 1885. (See White family.)

(2) John Milton, born July 31, 1831; married, December 9, 1852, Mary Virginia White, daughter of Henry Milton and Mary Ann (Gwatkin) White. He died January 1, 1920. See White family.)

CHILD BY SECOND MARRIAGE:

(3) Sallie Spiers, born January 5, 1843; married, September 18, 1860, William Holcombe Bolling, son of Dr. Archibald and Ann E. (Wigginton) Bolling, of Bedford County. She died November 21, 1925, Washington, D. C. (See Bolling family.)

Willis G. Poindexter, son (by the second marriage) of Samuel and Sarah (Garth) Poindexter, and a grandson of Joseph and Elizabeth James (Kennerly) Poindexter; married, October, 1836, Emily P. Slaughter, daughter of Joseph and ————— (Sutton) Slaughter.

CHILDREN:

(1) Joseph; married ————; lives in Missouri.
(2) Edward P.; married twice; lived in Texas (deceased).
(3) Samuel; married Miss Hardy, of Bedford County; now lives in Texas. Had one daughter, Ella, who married and now lives near Roanoke, Virginia.
(4) Mary Harris, born August 12, 1840; married, May 8, 1860, Edwin R. Talbot, a son of Elbert A., and Maria S. (Everett) Talbot, of Campbell County. (See Talbot family.)
(5) Sallie Garth; married ————— McVeigh (deceased).
(6) Rosa, never married.
(7) Hugh, died infant.
(8) Caroline, died infant.

Samuel T. Poindexter, youngest child by the second marriage, of Samuel and Sarah (Garth) Poindexter and grandson of Joseph and Elizabeth James (Kennerly) Poindexter; married, September 4, 1845, Ann Maria Tucker.

CHILDREN:

(1) Sarah Ann, born February 21, 1848.
(2) Mary Elizabeth, born October 28, 1851; married, July 9, 1874, John H. Isbell, of Appomattox County, Virginia.

CHILDREN:

(a) Aubrey Tucker; married Emma Conway, of Paris, Texas.

CHILD:

(aa) Elizabeth Conway Isbell.

(b) Cleora; married Fauntleroy Lambert, of Staunton, Va.

(3) Rosa Ellen, born June 27, 1854.
(4) Virginia Tucker, born September 5, 1855; married, 1881, James Woodson Jones.

CHILDREN :

(a) Edna Earle Jones.

(b) Reginald Fairfax Jones.

(c) John Dillard Jones.

(5) William Samuel, born July 27, 1858; married (first), October 7, 1884, Alma Imogene Phelps, born in 1855, died September 29, 1894. Married (second), November 19, 1895, Lucy C. Barksdale. He died October 15, 1897.

CHILDREN BY FIRST MARRIAGE:

(a) William Samuel, Jr., born November 17, 1885.

(b) Jefferson Ward, born September 7, 1887.

(c) Ernest Lee, born May 2, 1889.

(d) Carl Tucker, born June 7, 1890.

(e) Frank, born October 9, 1891.

(f) Alma Terrell, born July 28, 1893.

(g) Frederick Augustus, born September 17, 1894.

CHILD BY SECOND MARRIAGE:

(h) Barksdale, born October 6, 1896.

(6) Orianna Beauregard, born July 16, 1861.

(7) Robert Lee, born July 25, 1865; married Effie Woolwine, of Pearisburg, Virginia. Now living in Bluefield, Va.

CHILDREN :

(a) William Donwreath.

(b) Robert Lee, Jr.

Louis D., son of Captain Joseph and Elizabeth James (Kennerly) Poindexter, of Bedford County, later, of Campbell County; married Ann Smith and lived in Campbell County and are buried at the old Poindexter homestead there.

CHILDREN :

(1) Thomas F.; married Harriet Billups Jennings daughter of John L. Jennings, of Halifax County.

CHILDREN:

(a) Mittie A.; married Mitchell Bass, of Appomattox County.
(b) Bettie J.; married Dr. W. R. Holland, of Halifax County.
(c) Robert L.; deceased; never married.
(d) Hattie; married Walter R. Bass.
(e) John T.; deceased; never married.
(f) J. B.; married Mattie E. Walthall of Campbell County.
(g) W. J.; married Ida Scott, of Halifax County.
(h) Lelia; deceased; never married.
(i) Rosa B.; married William Chilton, of Spottsylvania County.
(j) Samuel F.; married Bessie M. Taylor, of Lynchburg, Virginia, where they now live. Have three sons: (aa) Samuel F., Jr.; (bb) Arthur Louis; (cc) John Taylor.

(2) James; married Mary Ann Hamlett. Five children by this marriage.
(3) Jack; never married.
(4) Sallie; married William Payne and had a number of children.
(5) Jane; married Dr. William Jennings, of Halifax County (a half-brother of Harriet Billups Jennings), and had eight children.
(6) Mary; never married.

Thomas Poindexter, son of John and Christian Poindexter, resided in Louisa County. Justice of that county, 1766, &c. Married Lucy Jones, probably a sister of Gabriel Jones, "the Valley Lawyer."

CHILDREN:

(1) John, the eldest son, was Clerk of the County Court, of Louisa from 1790 to 1820 and was a prominent minister of the Baptist Church (known as Elder John Poindexter). He was married three times. His first wife was a Miss Green by whom he had only one child, William G. Poindexter, who left descendants. John Poindexter's second wife was a Miss Johnson by whom he had the following children, viz.: Nicholas, John, Thomas, Andrew, Waller, Lucy Jones (who died unmarried), and Mary who married Garrett M. Quarles. The descendants of this

marriage resided in Kentucky and Tennessee. Nicholas removed to Kentucky and there died. Among the sons he left was George Gilmer Poindexter. Thomas, whose wife was a Miss Schooler, died in Virginia, leaving children, two sons and a daughter. Waller married a Miss Talley, of Goochland County and went to Kentucky also, where he died, leaving children. John Poindexter's third wife was Margaret Maer, of North Carolina, by whom he had one daughter, Frances E. who married ———— Thompson.

(2) Gabriel, born 1758, died August 1881, in Clarke County, Indiana; married in Virginia, Mary Swift.

(3) Thomas, born 1760, died in Louisa County.

(4) Robert, went to Kentucky.

(5) James, died 1843 in Louisa County.

(6) Richard Jones, Baptist Minister, went to North Carolina.

(7) George, born 1770; died 1858. Attorney-General of Mississippi; Governor of that State, 1819-21; United States Senator, 1831-35.

(8) Elizabeth Jones; married Christopher and removed to Franklin County, Kentucky.

(9) Lucy Jones.

(10) Molly; married ———— Cosby; left children.

———————

Thomas Poindexter, son of John Poindexter, of Louisa County, died in Franklin County, Kentucky, where his will was probated December 12, 1796, a copy of which was also recorded in Louisa County, mentions sons as follows: James, Robert, Richard, George, Gabriel, Thomas; and daughters, Elizabeth Jones Commack, Lucy and my daughter Molly Cosby's heirs — viz.: Stith Cosby, Nicholas, Francis, Betsy and Garland. (*Virginia Magazine.*)

———————

In the "List of Revolutionary Soldiers," published by the Virginia State Library in 1912, the following Poindexters appear: Gabriel Poindexter, Jacob Poindexter, John Poindexter, Jonathan Poindexter, Joseph Poindexter (Captain, Bedford County Militia), Levil (Lovel) Poindexter, and Richard G. Poindexter.

Among the early records of Bedford County we find the following marriage bonds:

Samuel Poindexter and Ann Poindexter Slaughter, daughter of Reuben Slaughter, 11 June 1790.

Dabney Poindexter and Eliza M. Watts, daughter of James Watts, 6 September 1819.

John Poindexter and Nancy North, daughter of David North, 4 September 1820.

Samuel Poindexter and Martha Otey, daughter of Isaac Otey, 3 June 1822.

Anderson Poindexter and Denotia Furlony, 21 October 1829.

John S. Poindexter and Nancy Robinson, daughter of Benjamin N. Robinson, 5 August 1830.

Willis Poindexter and Emily P. Slaughter, daughter of Joseph Slaughter, 10 October 1836.

Richard W. Poindexter and Mary W. Durette, 5 February 1849. Jas. D. Watts (security).

Davis D. Poindexter and Ann E. Poindexter, daughter of John S. Poindexter, 10 November 1849.

....

From the records of Campbell County we take the following marriage bonds:

August 13, 1806, Reubin Poindexter to Sally McIvor by Obadiah Page.

January 28, 1812, Joseph Poindexter, Junr., to N. Rice by Edmund Johns.

December 7, 1831, John H. Hubbard to Elizabeth Ann Poindexter by Dade Fisher.

March 17, 1833, Jno. Murrell to Caroline Poindexter by H. Brown.

....

In "The Douglas Register" are the following marriages of the family, performed by the Rev. Wm. Douglas in Louisa County prior to 1800:

Poindexter, Jo: & Eliz: Thornton, both in Louisa, 1781, Dec. 26—p. 21.

Poindexter, Jo; & Frances Arnet, both of Louisa, 1785, July 14— p. 24.

Poindexter, Thos: & Eliz: Pledge, both of this parish 1760, Feby. 13—p. 5.

Poindexter, Will & Polly McGehee, both in Louisa, 1791—p. 27.

Poindexter, Eliz: in Louisa & Cha; Slaughter in Culpeper 1780, Feb: 3—p. 19.

Poindexter, Christian & Macon Biggar in Louisa, Jul. 22, 1779—p. 19.

Poindexter, Molly & Garland Cosbie both of Louisa, Jun: 27, 1782—p. 22.

Poindexter, Ann Gizage, & Rob: Cobb in Louisa, Nov: 19, 1783—p. 23.

CHILTON

Richard Chilton, the first of the name of whom we have authentic record, came from Culpeper County to Campbell County, Virginia, in December of 1798, and bought many acres of land, owning practically all of what is now West Lynchburg, Virginia. His old homestead, "Catalpa Grove," is still owned by his descendants. The old family cemetery is at "Catalpa Grove," and many members of the Chilton and Moorman families rest there. The Richard Chilton family Bible is owned by Mrs. John Key Walker, of Bedford, Virginia, and, from it the following records are taken:

"Richard Chilton and Judith, his wife, were married, June 6, 1761.

CHILDREN:

(1) William, born 1763.
(2) Stephen, born January 1, 1766.
(3) Elenor, born November 20, 1767.
(4) Elizabeth, born September 11, 1769.
(5) Richard, born August 6, 1771. (See forward.)
(6) John, born April 6, 1773.
(7) Harrison, born March 5, 1775. (See forward.)
(8) Raleigh, born December 18, 1776.
(9) Judith, born June 6, 1779. (Married a Poindexter; see Poindexter family.)
(10) Thadeus, born January 31, 1784.
(11) Joseph, born May 16, 1789.

Judith Chilton, wife of Richard Chilton, Sr., died in 1830.

Richard Chilton, Sr., died 1820, his will is recorded in Campbell County, Virginia. (Will Book No. 4, page 375.)

He mentions in this will his wife, Judith, and the following children: William, Stephen, Richard, Harrison, Elizabeth Allen, Eleanor Kabler, Judith Poindexter, Raleigh, and Joseph. He appoints Richard Chilton, Frederick Kabler, Raleigh Chilton, and John Poindexter, as his executors.

Richard Chilton, Jr., son of Richard, Sr., and Judith Chilton, was born August 6, 1771; died March 16, 1847; married (first), March 10, 1808, in Loudon County, Virginia, Dewannah Sydnor Bennett (born January 8, 1790; died September, 1814).

CHILD:

(a) Anne Sydnor, born January 9, 1809.

Richard Chilton, Jr., married (second) Eleanor Hough, in 1818. No children.

The will of Richard Chilton, Jr., is recorded in Campbell County, Virginia. Will Book No. 10, page 36.

Anne Sydnor Chilton, daughter of Richard, Jr., and Dewannah (Bennett) Chilton, born January 9, 1809; died March 20, 1886; married, October 29, 1829, Charles Hancock Moorman, born October 29, 1803; died April 9, 1881; son of Achilles and Frances Herndon Moorman.

CHILDREN :

(1) Dewannah Frances, born August 5, 1830; died December 25, 1899; married, May 2, 1849, Dr. Booker Flournoy Smith, born August 5, 1823; died August 23, 1891; son of Dr. Robert and Jane (Smith) Smith.

CHILDREN :

(a) Ella, born June 6, 1850; died January, 1852.
(b) Charles Robert, born September 25, 1851; married, April 15, 1885, Bessie Steele. No children.
(c) Jane Sydnor, born April 9, 1853; married, August 20, 1874, Captain Norment Doniphan Hawkins, born July 26, 1849. (See Hawkins family.)
(d) Etta Hutter, born January 15, 1855; died December 9, 1927.
(e) Ida Norman, born July 26, 1856; died October 2, 1860.
(f) Roy Booker, born April 1, 1856; died November, 1925; married, January 19, 1890, Florence Hatcher.

CHILDREN :

(aa) Roy Booker, Jr.
(bb) Mary Hatcher.
(cc) William Minor.

(2) Marietta L., born February 3, 1833; died May 2, 1881; married Col. William H. Hutter. No children.
(3) Marcellus Newton, born March 13, 1835; died May 29, 1904; married, January 20, 1863, Ellen Grace Moorman, born October 2, 1838; died October 5, 1923. Marcellus N. Moorman was a major and served with bravery throughout the Civil War. He was on Stonewall Jackson's staff, and was riding by Jackson's side when the general was shot at Chancellorsville, Virginia. He and his wife were faithful workers in Memorial Methodist Church in Lynchburg, Virginia.

CHILDREN :

(a) Two girls died in infancy.
(b) Marcellus Newton, Jr., now living in Lynchburg, Virginia.
(c) Pelham (deceased).
(d) Leftwich (deceased).

(4) Edmond Harrison, born February 9, 1838; died December 21, 1912; married, February 22, 1866, Lucy Jane Hamlet. He served through the Civil War.

CHILDREN :

(a) Trula Hicks.
(b) Mamie.
(c) Le Roy.

(5) Catharine Saunders, born November 12, 1840; died July 22, 1817; married, March 30, 1865, William W. Hurt.

CHILDREN:

(a) Tompkins.
(b) Charles Moorman.
(c) William W., Jr.
(d) Roscoe.
(e) Senora; married Frank Shorter.

CHILDREN:

(aa) Chilton.
(bb) Frank, Jr.
(cc) Senora.

(6) Charles Richard, born August 23, 1848; died October 4, 1922; married, May 17, 1876, Ella C. Jones.

CHILDREN:

(a) Annie May.
(b) Charles Hancock.
(c) Jessie Kathrine; married C. A. Ryburn.
(d) Richard.
(e) Clarence.
(f) Basil.

Harrison Chilton, born March 5, 1775; died unmarried, March 20, 1846. He was the son of Richard, Sr., and Judith Chilton. In July, 1831, Harrison Chilton was elected a trustee of New London Academy, New London, Virginia. His interest in its success was so great that, when he died, he left his entire estate to be converted into money and used as an endowment for this school, thus preventing a financial failure and saving the institution for the education of the youth of that section.

SLAUGHTER

Arms: Argent, a saltire azure.
Crest: Out of a ducal coronet, or, an
eagle's head between wings
addorsed, azure, beaked or.
Motto: Invictae Fidelitatis Praemium.

"The above described arms are found on a seal to a bond bearing date of 1685, signed by William Slaughter, High Sheriff of Essex County, Virginia. They correspond with the arms of the Slaughters, of Gloucester and Worcester in England, as given by Burke in his 'Landed Gentry'."

The Slaughters were among the earlier settlers in Virginia. There were two of the name, John and William, in Virginia prior to 1620. William was killed in the great Indian Massacre of March 22, 1622.

John Slaughter had numerous grants of land, between the years 1620 and 1635. He had three sons:

(1) Francis, the eldest son of John, was born about 1630 and died 1656 in Essex County. He was Captain of Militia, Justice for Rappahannock, a planter and merchant. Married, 1652, Elizabeth Underwood, daughter of Colonel William Underwood, and his wife Margaret. Elizabeth (Underwood) Slaughter married secondly, Colonel John Catlett, Presiding Justice for Rappahannock, who was killed by the Indians in 1671, while defending a frontier fort. In 1672-3, Elizabeth Underwood married her third husband, the Rev. Amory Butler. She died in 1673. By the first marriage to Captain Francis Slaughter there was born in 1653, one son, Francis Slaughter.

(2) William who was High Sheriff, of Essex County in 1685. He married Phoebe, daughter of Colonel Toby Smith, of Rappahannock, and widow of William Hodgkins, who died in 1673. She married as her third husband, William Peachey and died in 1710, her will having been proved in Essex County on April 10th of that year. William Slaughter left no issue.

(3) Richard, had grants of land in 1652, 1655, 1679, 1689, &c. No record of his marriage or having left issue. For the above line

of descent, see *Virginia Magazine*, Vol. 21, pages 306-307, Slaughter Genealogy as compiled by the late John S. Carpenter, of Louisville, Kentucky.

....

Francis Slaughter, only son of Captain Francis and Elizabeth (Underwood) Slaughter, was born in Essex County, Virginia, 1653. He was a planter in Richmond County where he died in 1718. He married in 1679, Margaret Hudson.

CHILDREN:

(1) Robert, born 1680. (See forward.)
(2) William.
(3) Martha; married John Taylor.
(4) Mary.
(5) Elizabeth.

....

Robert Slaughter, born 1680, eldest son of Francis and Margaret (Hudson) Slaughter and grandson of Captain Francis and Elizabeth (Underwood) Slaughter, was a prosperous planter of Essex County, where he lived and died. He had extensive grants of land in Spotsylvania County (1719 and 1723), part of which he transferred to his sons during his lifetime, and the remainder bequeathed to them by his will, which was dated February 5, 1725, and proved in Essex County, August 16, 1726. Robert Slaughter, married in 1700, Frances Ann Jones, daughter of Lieut. Col. Cadwallader and Katherine Jones, of Stafford County, he the son of Richard and Frances Ann (Townsend) Jones, of Devonshire, England. (*Virginia Magazine*, Vol. 21, page 309; Mackenzie's *Colonial Families of the United States.*)

CHILDREN:

(1) Francis, born 1701. (See forward.)
(2) Robert, born in Essex County; died in Culpeper in 1768; was commissioned Captain of Militia, September 2, 1729, later Colonel of Militia. He was Vestryman of St. Mark's Parish, 1731; Church Warden; member of the House of Burgesses, 1742; Presiding Justice for Orange County, 1745. He married in 1723, Mary Smith, daughter of Augustine Smith, of Essex

County, Virginia. Had issue. (See *Virginia Magazine*, Vol. 21, page 427.)

(3) Thomas, settled in Caroline County, Virginia; married Sarah Thornton, daughter of Francis and sister of Reuben Thornton. He was Colonel of Militia. He had issue.

....

Colonel Francis Slaughter, eldest son of Robert and Frances Anne (Jones) Slaughter was born in Essex County, 1701. After his father's death he removed to Culpeper where he died in 1766. He was a large landholder in Culpeper and Orange Counties, Virginia; was commissioned Captain of Militia on February 2, 1730; later Colonel of Militia, Justice, Vestryman, Church Warden and held numerous other civil offices. (*Virginia Magazine*, Vol. 21, page 309.) He married, June 3, 1729, Ann Lightfoot, born September 22, 1708; died 1748, a daughter of Major Goodrich and Mary (Chew) Lightfoot, of Spotsylvania County, Virginia. Major Goodrich Lightfoot was the son of Colonel John Lightfoot, the emigrant, who married Ann Goodrich. Col. John Lightfoot, member of the Virginia Council from 1692 until his death, May 28, 1707, Commander-in-Chief of King and Queen County, was the son of John Lightfoot, of Gray's Inn, London, and Elizabeth Phillips, his wife, and the grandson of Rev. Richard Lightfoot, of Stoke Bruene, Northamptonshire, England, born 1562, died 1625, who married Jane Jones. Ann Goodrich, the wife of Col. John Lightfoot, was the daughter of Lieut. Gen. Thomas Goodrich who was in command of the troops in Northern Virginia during Bacon's Rebellion, he being the son of John Goodrich, the emigrant, and grandson of Sir Richard Goodrich and Muriel, his wife, of Goodrich Castle, Hertfordshire, Wales. (Mackenzie's *Colonial Families of the United States.*)

CHILDREN:

(1) Francis, born 1730; was Colonel of Militia and served as an officer in the Revolutionary Army; married Sarah, daughter of Robert Coleman, of Culpeper. He and many of his family received extensive grants of land in Kentucky, in consideration of their military services. He died in Elizabethtown, Kentucky, in 1805. Had issue. (*Virginia Magazine*, Vol. 21, page 428.)

(2) John, born 1732; was Colonel of Militia and in the Revolutionary Army, he and his three sons, Lieutenants Robert, John, and

William Slaughter, having all been in the army at the same time. He married (first) Mildred Coleman, a sister of his brother Francis' wife. She was born in 1736 and died May 1, 1758. He married (second), on December 22, 1758, Elizabeth Suggett. Had issue. (*Virginia Magazine,* Vol. 21, page 429.)

(3) Reuben, born 1733. (See forward.)

(4) Cadwallader, born 1735; married (first) Miss Margaret Ransdell, of Fauquier County, Virginia; (second), December 26, 1790, Lucy, daughter of Francis Slaughter, of Jefferson County, Kentucky. He died in 1798. Had issue. (*Virginia Magazine,* Vol. 21, page 429.)

(5) Frances, born 1737; married Captain William Ball, Vestryman of St. Mark's Parish. He was the son of Samuel and Anna Catherine (Tayloe) Ball, and a cousin of Mary Ball, the mother of Washington. (*Virginia Magazine,* Vol. 21, page 309.)

(6) A daughter who married Edward Thomas. Their only son Edward Thomas removed to Kentucky and married Susannah Beall, daughter of Walter Beall of that state. (*Virginia Magazine,* Vol. 21, page 310.)

....

Captain Reuben Slaughter, born in Culpeper County, Virginia, in 1733; died in Bedford County, Virginia, about 1803. He was the third son of Col. Francis and Anne (Lightfoot) Slaughter, of Culpeper. His father having been born in Essex County about 1701, and his mother in Spotsylvania in September, 1708. Reuben Slaughter was Captain of Militia in Revolutionary Army from Bedford County, Virginia. (Eckenrodes' *Revolutionary Soldiers,* Index, 8-405; *Colonial Families of the United States,* by Mackenzie, Volume V, page 461; *Virginia Historical Mazagine,* XX.-219.) He was a large landholder in Bedford County; the family having been prominently identified with the interests of this section of Virginia since its settlement. He married about 1760, Betty Poindexter, of Louisa County, born 1739; died before 1800, a daughter of John and Christian Poindexter. (See Poindexter family.)

CHILDREN:

(1) Joseph; married Miss Poindexter.

(2) William; married Miss Thompson.

(3) Robert; married Miss Pendleton.

(4) Goodrich Lightfoot, born January 24, 1770, in Culpeper, Virginia; married Hannah Van Bibber, May 16, 1797, of Kanawha County, Virginia, she was a descendant of Isaac Jacobs Van Bibber, the emigrant, who founded the city of Germantown, Pennsylvania, 1684. Goodrich Lightfoot Slaughter died July 3, 1833, and his wife June 28, 1858. (Mackenzie's *Colonial Families of the United States*).

CHILDREN:

(a) Maria, born 1798; married Samuel Reed.

(b) Rhoda, born 1800; married Isaac Reed.

(c) Betsey, born 1802; married ———— Loring.

(d) Catherine Gizzage, born 1804; married, January 28, 1824, Levi Welch, of Kanawha County, Virginia, son of George and Hannah (White) Welch.

(e) Fanny Dawson, born 1806; married Charles Reynolds.

(f) Francis, born 1808; died young.

(g) Caroline Donnaly, born 1810; married James Cogar.

(h) John, born 1812.

(i) Chloe, born 1814; married James Norton.

(j) Miriam Van Bibber, born 1816; married Fred Walker.

(k) Edward, born 1818.

(5) Anne Poindexter, born about 1774; married, June 11, 1790, Samuel Poindexter, son of Joseph and Elizabeth James (Kennerly) Poindexter. She died before 1810. (See Poindexter family.)

CHILDREN:

(a) Dabney, born November 17, 1791; married Mary Eliza Watts.

(b) James; married Susan Shelton.

(c) John S., born January 26, 1796; married Nancy Robinson, daughter of Benjamin N. Robinson.

(d) Anderson; married, October 21, 1829, Denotia Furlony.

(e) Caroline, born about 1809; died 1839; married, November 3, 1828, Colonel William Allen White, son of Captain Jacob and Hannah (Spiers) White, of Bedford County, Virginia. (See White family.)

(6) Kitty Gissage; married, January 26, 1795, William Douglas.

TALBOT

From Charles Talbot, of Maryland, descends the family of that name which settled in Virginia.

Matthew Talbot, born September 26, 1699, son of Charles, moved to the state and married in 1722, Mary Williston, who died in 1736; had sons, Charles (see forward), Matthew, Jr., James and John. Matthew, Sr., married, second, in 1737, Jane Clayton, and children of this marriage were Isham and Martha. Members of the Talbot family were living in Lunenburg at the time of its division to form Bedford, and Matthew and Charles were appointed to define the boundary between the two counties. In May, 1754, the first Court held in Bedford County was in the home of Matthew Talbot. He offered to donate a site on his land for the court house; but it was not considered sufficiently central. In 1755, Matthew was made colonel and James lieutenant of Bedford militia; in 1757 Matthew was appointed sheriff of the county, and Matthew, Jr., was commissioned captain of militia in 1758. That year Colonel Matthew Talbot died and his estate was divided among his widow, Mrs. Jane Talbot, five sons and daughter, Martha Arthur. Charles was bequeathed the great family Bible.

Charles Talbot, son of Matthew and Mary (Williston) Talbot, born February 6, 1723; married, 1747, Drusilla Guinn, daughter of David Guinn, of Lunenburg County. He was appointed captain of militia in 1757; commissioner of the peace from 1773 to 1779 when he died. His will provided for his wife during her widowhood; gave land to sons, Williston (see forward), Charles Moile, David Guinn, Providence, George, and Ezekiel; and daughters, Mary Thurston and Christianna Talbot. He gave the family Bible to his son Williston.

Williston Talbot, born August 1, 1750, son of Charles and Drusilla (Guinn) Talbot, qualified as first lieutenant of militia in 1778, and in 1780 a commissary of provisions for collecting Revolutionary supplies. For many years he rode as high sheriff of Campbell County, Virginia. He was twice married, (first) December, 1769, to Elizabeth Cocke, born April 29, 1749, daughter of George and Agnes Cocke. He married (second), December 16, 1806, Nancy Keese, born November 27, 1780. He died in 1827.

CHILDREN BY FIRST MARRIAGE:

(1) Charles, born January 2, 1771.
(2) Salley, born August 10, 1772.
(3) Pleasant, born September 14, 1774.
(4) Levisa, born January 21, 1777.
(5) John, born April 21, 1779. (See forward.)
(6) Hillery, born September 24, 1781.
(7) Williston, Jr., born October 24, 1790; married in 1820, Ann Arnold.

(8) Betsey, born February 26, 1786.

(9) Edmond, born October 24, 1790.

(10) Allen, born August 7, 1793.

CHILDREN BY SECOND MARRIAGE:

(11) Elbert Adolphus, born January 9, 1808. (See forward.)

(12) Gale, born September 27, 1809.

(13) Mildred Ann, born April 18, 1813.

(14) Pollina Mettert, born August 10, 1815.

(15) Adeline Williston, born November 25, 1817.

(16) Melville Henry, born May 4, 1821.

John Talbot, fifth child of Williston and Elizabeth (Cocke) Talbot, born April 21, 1779; married Nancy Irby, daughter of John and Mary Irby.

CHILDREN:

(1) Nancy; died young.

(2) Mary; died young.

(3) Harrison; died young.

(4) Eliza; married Dickerson; left no children.

(5) Wilmoth Ann. (See forward.)

(6) John Allen.

(7) Panthea Agnes; married Elijah Harris Folkes.

Wilmoth Ann Talbot, daughter of John and Nancy (Irby) Talbot; married George Scott, born March 10, 1803, son of Pleasant and Nancy Ann (Witt) Scott.

CHILDREN:

(1) John Pleasant, born September 5, 1847.

(2) George Wheeler, born March 12, 1849.

John Pleasant Scott, son of George and Wilmoth Ann (Talbot) Scott, born September 5, 1847; married (first), Sarah Georgie Garrett, born April 24, 1848. John Pleasant Scott married (second), May 11, 1887, Virginia Hervey Wren, born October 5, 1860, daughter of Charles Carter and Virginia (Garrett) Wren.

CHILDREN BY FIRST MARRIAGE:

(1) Morton, born July 10, 1873; married (first), October 4, 1906, Norma Wilkes; (second) Lula Moore. No children by second marriage.

CHILDREN:

(a) Robert Wilkes, born July 21, 1908.

(b) Lois, born September 28, 1911.

(2) Ashby, born May 25, 1875; married, November 27, 1901, Martha Elizabeth Cooper, daughter of John A. and Ella (Jeter) Cooper, born May 21, 1874. (See Jeter family.)

CHILD:

(a) Wallace, born April 24, 1906.
(3) Vida E., born July 14, 1880; married, October 4, 1904, Herman W. Smith, born November 22, 1872, son of James E. and Nannie (James) Smith.

CHILD:

(a) George, born August 14, 1908.

CHILDREN BY SECOND MARRIAGE:

(4) Mertie M., born July 12, 1888; married, October 20, 1911, Claude Harrison, born January 3, 1888, son of Milton Thomas and Mary (Stump) Harrison.

CHILD:

(a) Claude, Jr., born February 19, 1913.
(5) Robert Pleasant, born March 5, 1893; married, July 16, 1924, Ella Mae Peay, born November 6, 1898, daughter of Walter Scott and Lena (Walker) Peay.
(6) Mary Rubye, born April 19, 1898.

Elbert Adolphus Talbot, born January 9, 1808, son of Williston and Nancy (Keesee) Talbot, married Mariah Everette, born November 11, 1807, a daughter of Thomas Y. Everette, who served in the War of 1812. Elbert Adolphus Talbot died in Bedford County, Virginia, February 13, 1864; and his wife, February 10, 1879. Had issue.

....

Edwin R. Talbot, born in Bedford County, October 5, 1833, a son of Elbert Adolphus Talbot, born in Campbell County and his wife, Mariah (Everette) Talbot, born in Bedford County; married, May 8, 1860, Mary Harris Poindexter, born August 12, 1840, daughter of Willis G. and Emily P. (Slaughter) Poindexter, of Bedford County. (See Poindexter family.) Both the Slaughter and the Poindexter families have been prominently identified with that section of Virginia since its settlement. Several of the name having served in the Revolutionary War. Edwin R. Talbot served as a non-commissioned officer through all the years of the War Between the States in Company G, 2nd Virginia Cavalry. A brother of his, Leslie C. Talbot was a lieutenant in Jordan's Artillery, and was captured and held prisoner twelve months, being released at the close of the war. Edwin R. Talbot, died July 26, 1909, in Bedford County and his wife passed away February 14, 1917, at the home of her youngest son, Dr. Elbert Berkley Talbot, in Richmond, Va.

CHILDREN:

(1) Emmett L., born February 18, 1861; educated at Bellvue under Professor Abbett; married Miss Lucy Andrews. He died in 1898. The widow married (second) Charles Lukin. Living in Roanoke, Virginia.

CHILDREN:

(a) Emmett L., Jr.

(b) Emily Susan.

(2) Edwin R., Jr., born October 15, 1864; educated at Bellvue and New London Academy; married a Miss Jennings, of Missouri and lives in Watonga, Oklahoma.

CHILDREN:

(a) Edna (deceased).

(b) Pauline; married ———— Arnette.

(c) Sue Betty.

(d) Harry Lee.

(e) Vivian.

(3) Minnie Garth, born October 23, 1867; married James W. Gannaway, of Tennessee; now living in New York City. Member of the Daughters of American Revolution.

CHILDREN:

(a) Eunice; married Robert Burney, of Alabama, a son of Judge Burney. Now living in Texas. Have one son.

(b) Mary Rix; married Robert Brunswick. They live in New York.

(4) Florence Williston, born November 17, 1869; now of St. Mary's School, Raleigh, North Carolina; never married; and in the words of her brother, "was the dearest daughter and sister—cared for us and for our dear mother in her declining years, when we were away."

(5) Robert Slaughter, born September 12, 1877; educated at New London Academy under Professor Warrick Daniel Read; was afterwards graduated in medicine at the Medical College of Virginia and post-graduate work at Columbia University, New York. Married Miss Gertrude Newland, of New York. Practiced his profession first at Petersburg under Dr. Wm. F. Drewry and later in Lynchburg, Virginia, where his health broke down. He died in Richmond, Virginia, December 10, 1914. Dr. Robert Slaughter Talbot was a member of the Medical Society of Virginia, Petersburg Country Club and the Piedmont Club of Lynchburg.

CHILD:

(a) Robert Slaughter, Jr.

(6) Elbert Berkley, born June 8, 1881; educated at New London Academy, graduated in medicine at Medical College of Virginia; elected a member of the adjunct faculty of that college, was resident physician at the Memorial Hospital of Richmond, Virginia, now doing general practice and some abdominal surgery in that city. Member of the University Club; the "Phi Chi" Medical fraternity. Dr. Elbert Berkley Talbot married Miss Madeline Wallace Loraine. They have no children living.

GWATKIN

The following as copied by R. D. Buford, Clerk County Court, Bedford City, Va., from an old book in possession of Mr. Lucien Freeman, the title, Family Devotion, &c., 10th Edition Williamsburg. Printed by William Parks, 1740, was published in William and Mary College Quarterly *Historical Magazine*, January, 1897, Volume V, pages 210-211.

SONS AND DAUGHTERS OF EDWARD AND MARY GWATKIN, HIS WIFE:

Charles Gwatkin was born the third day of April, in the year of our Lord 1741.

John Gwatkin was born the twentieth day of January, in the year of our Lord 1742-3.

Mary Gwatkin was born the thirty-first of May, in the year of our Lord 1745.

James Gwatkin was born the ninth day of April, in the year of our Lord 1747.

Margrait Gwatkin was born the fifth of April, in the year of our Lord 1749.

Prudence Gwatkin was born the fifth of April, in the year of our Lord 1749.

Colonel Charles Gwatkin, born in Scotland, April 3, 1741; first of the name, in Bedford County, Virginia, is said to be the eldest son of Edward and Mary Gwatkin, who were natives of Scotland and emigrated to America. Colonel Gwatkin, during his lifetime, filled several important civil offices as well as military offices in the County of Bedford; and was for a number of years, or until his death, a justice of the peace. He served as Captain of Virginia Militia in the Revolutionary Army. (McAllisters' *Virginia Militia*, Section 254; Chalkley's *Abstracts of Augusta County, Virginia*, Vol. 2, page 486.)

From the order book of the County Court of Bedford County, Virginia:

Col. Charles Gwatkin served in capacity of civil officer during Revolutionary War. Was a Justice of Peace in 1777. Lieut. Colonel of Militia in 1787. Sheriff in 1788. Colonel of Militia in 1791. Coroner in 1792. Colonel of Regulars in 1793.

Owning more than 3,000 acres of land, he built his home and settled near Charlemont, Bedford County, Virginia. According to family tradition, the old Colonel had been an officer in the English army and had been granted a large amount of land in that section, built his home there (Charlemont, Virginia) which descended from generation to generation in the family.

However this may be, he did have a grant from the King of England, owning a large estate in the section of Charlemont, Virginia, where he settled and built his home. Here he was married on November 6, 1767, to Miss Mary Callaway (born 1752), daughter of Colonel Richard Callaway (born June, 1722), and his wife Frances (Walton) Callaway, of Bedford County, Virginia. (See Callaway family.) Colonel Charles Gwatkin died in 1806 and his wife in 1829.

CHILDREN :

(1) Margaret ("Peggy") Gwatkin; married Waddy Cobbs, May 11, 1788, by Rev. Charles Clay.

(2) Frances ("Fanny") Gwatkin; married Simon M. Noell, November 19, 1801, by Rev. Jeremiah Hatcher.

(3) Catherine ("Kitty") Gwatkin; married Thomas G. Logwood, Jr., February 16, 1802, by Rev. Jeremiah Hatcher.

(4) James Gwatkin; married (first) Mary Thorp, November 6, 1802; (second) Parmelia Otey, daughter of John Hopkins and Elizabeth (Buford) Otey. (See forward.)

(5) Lucinda Gwatkin; married James Campbell, February 10, 1808, by Rev. Jos. Purnell. Descendants living in St. Louis. (See forward.)

(6) Charles Gwatkin, Jr., born September 24, 1781; married about 1808, Catherine Clayton, a daughter of John Willis and Mary Clayton. (See forward.)

(7) Mary C. ("Polly") Gwatkin; married Micajah Davis, Jr., October 6, 1810. (See Davis family.)

(8) Elizabeth Gwatkin; married Jeffrey Cobbs, September 13, 1811.

(9) Nancy H. Gwatkin; married Charles L. Mitchell, February 3, 1812, and settled in Kentucky.

(10) Edward Gwatkin; married Mary A. J. Otey, March 22, 1813, a

daughter of Major Isaac and Elizabeth (Matthews) Otey. (See forward.)

Captain Charles Gwatkin's Division, which mentions his children is recorded in Will Book "D," page 31, Bedford County, Virginia, records and reads as follows:

Division of Charles Gwatkin dec'd lands in the County of Bedford, amongst his heirs after deducting the widow's dower, which includes the mansion house tract, and a small part cut off of the squirrel mountain tract making 386 as pr. platt No. W, Viz.:

1st. Lucinda Gwatkin place called Taylors 71 acres as pr. platt No. 1.

2. Waddy Cobbs who married Peggy Gwatkin, place called Millers, 58 acres as pr. platt No. 2.

3rd. Thomas Logwood, Jr., who married Kitty Gwatkin part of the place called Wilson's 115 acres as pr. platt No. 3.

4. Simon Noel who married Fanny Gwatkin part of the place Wilkersons 122 acres as pr. plat No. 4.

5. James Gwatkin, place called Strattons, 86 acres as pr. platt No. 5.

6. Edward Gwatkin, place called Milams 84 acres as pr. platt No. 6.

7. Polly Gwatkin place called squirrel mountain 171 acres as pr. plat No. 7, also 8 acres and 16 po. as pr. 2nd plat No. 7, as well as 224 acres on the west side of Nobusiness mountain as pr. *pattant* granted Charles Gwatkin dec'd the 18th February, 1805.

8. Nancy Gwatkin land on Nobusiness mountain as pr. 3 pattants granted to Charles Gwatkin dec'd, viz.: One for 590 acres, one for 96 acres, both dated the 26th March, 1805, & one other for 470 acres dated 18th February, 1805.

9. Charles Gwatkin, Jackson mountain tract ——— and 63 acres to be added as pr. plat No. 9. This Lot to pay Lott No. 10—10. 0. 0. viz., to Elizabeth Gwatkin.

10. Elizabeth Gwatkin place called Godfreys ——— and to receive from Lot No. 9,-10, viz., from Charles Gwatkin.

The foregoing is an extract from the allotment and division of the real and personal estate of Charles Gwatkin, deceased, which was returned to Court and ordered to be recorded, June 26, 1809, and is of record in the Clerk's Office of Bedford County, in Will Book "D," page 31.

Teste: V. W. NICHOLAS,

Clerk of the Circuit Court of
Bedford County, Virginia.

....

James Gwatkin, son of Colonel Charles Gwatkin, Sr., and Mary (Callaway) Gwatkin, married (first), about November 6, 1802, Mary Thorp, probably, a grand-daughter of Captain Francis Thorp, of Campbell County, who married Elizabeth Callaway, a daughter of Col. William Callaway. He married (second) Parmelia, daughter of John Hopkins and Elizabeth (Buford) Otey, by whom he had the following

CHILDREN:

(1) Charles Anderson; married, October 7, 1845, Mary Isabella Blackford.

CHILDREN:

    (a) Thomas Blackford.

    (b) Charles Otey; married Nettie Kline.

    (c) Mary Sternberger; married Charles P. Stokes. They lived in Richmond.

    (d) Caroline Elizabeth; married Fielding Lewis Marshall, of Washington, D. C.

    (e) Royal.

    (f) Nannie McClellan; married Frederick Lewis Curtler, of Worchester, England.

    (g) William Graham; married Carlotta Smith, of Richmond, Va.

    (h) James; married Bolling Weisiger, of New York.

(2) Catherine; married Calvin Thompson, of Independence, Missouri.

(3) James; died young.

....

Charles Gwatkin, Jr., born September 24, 1781, son of Colonel Charles Gwatkin, Sr., and Mary (Callaway) Gwatkin, married about 1808, Catherine Clayton, a daughter of John Willis and Mary Clayton and grand-daughter of John and Elizabeth (Willis) Clayton, of Charlotte County, Va. (See Clayton family.)

By this marriage there were two children—early left orphans, Mary Ann Gwatkin and Charles B. Gwatkin. Captain Jacob White was made guardian of the children; and his son, Henry Milton White, married, October 4, 1826, Mary Ann Gwatkin, who was born April 13, 1810, and died February 4, 1846. (See Henry Milton White family.)

Copied from the Family Bible belonging to Henry Milton White:

Henry Milton White was born the 31st Jan. 1805. (Son of Jacob White: Gr. son of Henry White.)

Mary Ann Gwatkin was born 13th April 1810, and was married 4th day of October 1826 to Henry Milton White. Died February 4th 1846.

BIRTHS:

Nancy Logwood White, Born 22nd July 1827.
Catherine Spiers White, Born 9th March 1829.
Eliza Frances White, Born 5th Sept. 1830.
William Davis White, Born 3rd Jany. 1832.
Charles Henry White, Born 21st July 1835.
Mary Virginia White, Born 20th Dec. 1836.
Sarah Lucy White, Born 21st Nov. 1840.

Charles B. Gwatkin was born 6th March 1814. (Only brother of Mary Ann Gwatkin.)

Charlotte Ann Tinsley was born 12th Sept. 1819.

Charles B. Gwatkin and Charlotte A. Tinsley were married the 22nd September 1836.

BIRTHS:

Catherine Mildred Gwatkin, Born 8th July 1837.
Mary Ann Gwatkin, Born 12th March 1839.
Charles Henry Gwatkin, Born 4th April 1841.
Charlotte Virginia Gwatkin, Born 2nd Jan. 1843.
Fanny Callaway Gwatkin, Born 15th Oct. 1845.
Sarah Tinsley Theodosha Gwatkin, Born 23rd Oct. 1847.

(There were two younger children by this union whose births are not recorded in the Bible. Names are as follows:)

Edmund Logwood Gwatkin (date of birth not known), died in infancy in Lynchburg, Va.

Roberta Davis Gwatkin (date of birth not known), married John Richard Thomas, of Waverly, Missouri.

....

For the descendants of Henry Milton and Mary Ann (Gwatkin) White, see White family.

....

The descendants of Charles B. and Charlotte Ann (Tinsley) Gwatkin became widely scattered—many of them going West and settling there. While communication between the older members of the family was kept up, the younger ones have drifted apart. After years of trying to get in communication with some member of the present generation, only recently was any success had in locating this branch of the family whose record is given as follows:

Charles B. Gwatkin, son of Charles, Jr., and Catherine (Clayton) Gwatkin, born in Bedford County, Virginia, March 6, 1814; married, September 22, 1836, Charlotte Ann Tinsley, born September 12, 1819.

CHILDREN:

(1) Catherine Mildred, born July 8, 1837. (See forward.)
(2) Mary Ann, born March 12, 1839; married Thomas Howard. For a number of years, they lived in Bedford County, Va.; but on account of his wife's health, Mr. Howard moved his family to Missouri; and there in a few years she died leaving her husband and two sons, viz.: (a) Oscar Howard (now deceased), and (b) Charles Howard.
(3) Charles Henry, born April 4, 1841. (See forward.)
(4) Charlotte Virginia, born January 2, 1843; died unmarried.
(5) Fanny Callaway, born October 15, 1845, died in childhood.
(6) Sarah Tinsley Theodosia, born October 23, 1847; married, September, 1871, Samuel Walker Campbell, eldest son of Granville Kelley and Eliza Jane (Walker) Campbell, of Missouri.
(7) Edmund Logwood, died in infancy, in Lynchburg, Virginia.
(8) Roberta Davis; married John Richard Thomas, of Waverly, Missouri.

CHILDREN:

(a) Annie E.; married Cecil R. Wilson—living in Liberty, Missouri. Two children viz.: (aa) Richard T.; (bb) John O.

(b) Thelma Theresa; married Thomas Fiske Marbut. No children.

....

Catherine Mildred Gwatkin, born July 8, 1837, eldest child of Charles B. and Charlotte Ann (Tinsley) Gwatkin, of Bedford County, Virginia; married (first) Benjamin Steward; (second) April 17, 1866, George Washington Wyatt, born in Halifax County, Virginia, August 2, 1819. George W. Wyatt enlisted April, 1861, at Lynchburg, Virginia, in Company C, Virginia Heavy Artillery, C. S. A. After the seven days fight around Richmond, was made Commissary Sergeant of 34th Virginia Infantry, C. S. A., and paroled at Appomattox at close of the war. He was a member of the Jno. N. Edwards Camp of Confederate Veterans at Higginsville, Missouri, until his death, which occurred at Higginsville, September 29, 1905. His wife died December 11, 1889.

Child by first marriage of Catherine Mildred Gwatkin and Benjamin Steward:

(1) Frances ("Fanny") Steward; married Henry C. Baker. Died in the East about 1890, leaving two children.

Children by second marriage of Catherine Mildred Gwatkin and George W. Wyatt:

(2) Virginia Gwatkin Wyatt, born at Lynchburg, Virginia, September 18, 1868; married at Higginsville, Missouri, October 20, 1886, Hiram Farris Campbell, born in Lafayette County, Missouri, December 14, 1860, son of Granville Kelley Campbell and Louisa Jane (Walker) Campbell.

CHILDREN:

(a) Farris Campbell, born at Higginsville, Missouri, August 14, 1887. Graduated at the University of Missouri, 1908. Married at Kansas City, Missouri, August 14, 1909, Lily Bell Neal, daughter of George A. and Lily (Bell) Neal. Living in New York City.

CHILD:

(aa) Farris Campbell, Jr., born in New York City, November 22, 1917.
(b) Lyman L. Campbell, born at Higginsville, Missouri, January 8, 1890. Attended the University of Missouri, 1909-1911. Enlisted in the World War at Ogdon, Utah, May, 1917—was in Medical Corps, 12th Division, and served until Armistice. He married at St. Joseph, Missouri, May 7, 1923, Emily Catherine Holmes, daughter of Samuel Howard Holmes and Emma (Simms) Holmes. Living at Higginsville, Missouri.

CHILDREN:

(aa) Shirley Ann, born December 30, 1924.
(bb) Lyman L., Jr., born August 5, 1926.
(c) Carlyle Campbell, born at Higginsville, Missouri, May 28, 1894. Graduated from William Jewell College, Liberty, Missouri, 1916. Attended Harvard Law School one year. Enlisted in the World War, May, 1917, while at Harvard. Was paymaster in Naval Reserves, served until August, 1918. He married at Jacksonville, Florida, June 10, 1925, Helen Tunnell Scott, daughter of Mr. and Mrs. Roy Scott, of St. Petersburg, Florida, formerly of Chattanooga, Tenn. No children. Living at St. Petersburg, Florida.
(d) Catherine Louise Campbell, born at Higginsville, Missouri, August 2, 1897. Graduated from Stephens College, Columbia, Missouri, 1917. Married, October 17, 1917, Rev. Raymond Clifton Lippard, born March 11, 1888, at Woodleaf, North Carolina. Served as Chaplain in the World War from July, 1918, to December, 1918. Living at Excelsior Springs, Missouri.

CHILD:

(aa) Virginia Louise Lippard, born August 31, 1918, at Higginsville, Missouri.
(3) and (4) Twins—died in infancy.
(5) Eugene Wyatt, died in infancy.
(6) George McGrew Wyatt, born February 27, 1879.

Charles Henry Gwatkin, son of Charles B. and Charlotte Ann (Tinsley) Gwatkin, born April 4, 1841, in Bedford County, Va.; married Fredonia E. Chewning, born February 24, 1848, daughter of James T. and Catherine (Fuqua) Chewning, of Bedford County, Virginia. Charles Henry Gwatkin lived, for a number of years, in Bedford County, Va., then went West, later returning to Virginia to have his two sons educated at the University of Virginia. He died in Colorado, April 30, 1912. His wife, now nearing her 82nd year, is living with her son, Rev. Wm. Emmett Gwatkin, at Louisiana, Missouri.

CHILDREN:

(1) James Edward, born in Bedford County, Virginia, March 19, 1866. Educated at University of Virginia, B. A. degree. Southern Baptist Theological Seminary, Louisville, Kentucky, Th. M. and Th. D. degrees. Married, September 15, 1896, Rebecca S. Willis, of Locust Dale, Madison County, Virginia, daughter of Larkin Willis and Lelia A. (Turpin) Willis, who was a daughter of Miles and Rebecca M. (Garthwright) Turpin, of Richmond, Virginia. No children. Has been Baptist preacher in Virginia, Oklahoma, and Colorado—now, for last twelve years, professor of Biblical Introduction, and associate professor of New Testament Exposition in the Baptist Bible Institute at New Orleans, Louisiana. Poet and editor, having been for some five years associate editor of *The Baptist Argus,* of Louisville, Ky., writer of Sunday School lesson notes for a number of years, also a contributor to the *Baptist Teacher,* published by the S. S. Board of Nashville, Tenn.

(2) William Emmett, born in Bedford, County, Virginia, August 7, 1867. Educated at University of Virginia, B. A. degree. Southern Baptist Theological Seminary, Louisville, Kentucky. Th. M. degree. Married Anna E. Weakley, daughter of Judge Leonard A. Weakley and Victorine (Hammett) Weakley, of Shelbyville, Kentucky. Has been a Baptist preacher and pastor in Virginia, Kentucky, Oklahoma, Louisiana, and Missouri. Now pastor of the First Baptist Church at Louisiana, Missouri.

CHILDREN:

(a) William Emmett Gwatkin, Jr., born December 25, 1900. Educated at William Jewell College, B. A. degree Uni-

Rev. James Edward Gwatkin

versity of Indiana, M. A. degree Princeton, New Jersey, Ph. D. degree in process. Has taught at William Jewell College, University of Indiana, Princeton University, McMaster University, Toronto, Canada—now professor of Latin in the University of Missouri, Columbia, Mo. He married Le May Ryan.

CHILD:

(aa) William Emmett Gwatkin, III.

(b) Elizabeth Hammett Gwatkin, born May 20, 1903. Educated Junior College, Kansas City, and University of Indiana, B. A. degree Vanderbilt University, M. A. degree. Married Roy Ervin Baber, Ph. D. Now living in New York City, where Dr. Baber has chair Sociology in New York University.

CHILD:

(aa) Virginia Ellen Baber, four months old.

(c) Virginia Chewning Gwatkin, born January 15, 1905; died May 7, 1907.

....

Edward Gwatkin, son of Colonel Charles Gwatkin, Sr., and Mary (Callaway) Gwatkin, of Bedford County, Va.; married, March 22, 1813, Mary A. J. Otey, born 1794, a daughter of Major Isaac Otey, born 1765; died 1835 at Sandusky, and his wife, Elizabeth (Matthews) Otey, of Rockbridge County, born 1767; died 1855. Mary A. J. Otey was a sister of Frances Ann Otey, born 1798; died 1822; married Captain Paschal Buford, born 1791; died 1875, and were the parents of the late Rowland D. Buford, of Bedford, Virginia. (See Burks and Otey families.)

CHILDREN:

(1) James; died unmarried.

(2) Eliza Ann; married Edward Hunter, of Lynchburg, Virginia. (See forward.)

(3) Catherine; married William A. Hardy.

(4) Frances (twin); married John Otey.

(5) Mary Caroline (twin); married Charles Fant.

(6) Lucy Wilhelmina; married Edmund W. Horsley, of Bedford County, Va.

CHILDREN:

(a) Lucy Wilhelmina Horsley; died 1908; unmarried.
(b) Edmonia Winston Horsley; married Picton L. Saunders. His widow is living in Bedford, Virginia.
(c) Fannie Otey Horsley; married Judge John Callaway Brown. Judge Brown is deceased and his widow lives in Bedford. (See Callaway family for descendants.)

(7) Samuel; private in Civil War—enlisted with Colonel Price. Died at Ft. Delaware, the northern prison—unmarried.

(8) Edward; died unmarried.

....

Eliza Ann Gwatkin, daughter of Edward and Mary A. J. (Otey) Gwatkin, of Bedford County, Virginia, and a grand-daughter of Col. Charles and Mary (Callaway) Gwatkin; married (first) Edward Hunter, of Lynchburg, Virginia. After the death of her first husband she married (second) Steptoe Johnson.

CHILDREN OF ELIZA ANN GWATKIN AND HER FIRST HUSBAND, EDWARD HUNTER

(1) Molly Hunter, born 1832; died 1905; married George Deatherage.

CHILDREN:

(a) Blanche Deatherage, born 1872; unmarried. Living in Los Angeles, California.
(b) Hunter Deatherage, born 1874; married Lulu ————.

CHILDREN:

(aa) Blanche.
(bb) William.
(cc) Hunter.

(c) William Deatherage, born 1879. Died in World War.
(d) Kate Deatherage, born 1881; married Don P. Hall.

CHILD:

(aa) George Hall, born 1909.

(e) Robert Deatherage, born ————. (All living in Los Angeles, California.)

(2) Addie Hunter, born 1834; married Samuel Gaddis.

CHILD:

(a) Grace Gaddis, born 1869; unmarried and living in St. Louis, Mo.

(3) Edward Hunter, killed at Corinth, Mississippi, in war of 1861-65.

(4) Martha Hunter, born 1835, Lynchburg, Virginia; died 1871; married in 1860, Darius Heald, who died in 1904. She was his second wife, his first wife having been Caroline Virginia Campbell, a daughter of James and Lucinda (Gwatkin) Campbell. (See forward.)

CHILDREN OF DARIUS HEALD AND HIS SECOND WIFE MARTHA (HUNTER) HEALD

(a) Eliza (Lillian) Heald, born April 2, 1862; married in 1895, Joshua Richmond.

CHILDREN:

(aa) Nina Richmond, born 1896; married, 1920, John Barron.

CHILDREN:

(aaa) Lillian A. Barron, born 1922.
(bbb) John Barron, born 1927.

(bb) Edmonia Richmond; married in 1928, George Hay. (All live in St. Louis, Missouri.)

(b) Edmonia Heald, born 1864; married, 1889, Thomas McCluer.

CHILDREN:

(aa) Darius Heald McCluer, born 1892; served as Aviation Lieutenant in World War, Ft. Worth, Texas; married, 1920, Virginia Meyer. He died in 1925.

CHILD:

(aaa) Mary Elizabeth McCluer, born 1922.

(bb) Elizabeth E. McCluer, born 1894; married, 1920, Thomas Lee and living in Orlando, Florida.

CHILD:

(aaa) Elizabeth Lee, born 1924.

(cc) Hunter McCluer, born 1896; served in Marines in World War; married, 1921, Mary Sale.

CHILD:

(aaa) Hunter, Jr., born 1926.

(c) Rebecca Heald, born 1867; married, 1890, Arthur McCluer.

CHILDREN:

(aa) Virgil McCluer, born 1896; served Officer Corps Marine Aviation World War, Boston and Miami; married Gladys McCormick.

CHILDREN:

(aaa) Virgil, Jr., born 1922.
(bbb) Margaret Wells, born 1924.

(bb) Hugh McCluer, born 1898. Unmarried.

(d) Martha Hunter Heald, born 1869; married, 1897, Wright Johnson.

CHILDREN:

(aa) Charles Montgomery Johnson, born June 4, 1898. Served in World War—volunteer in U. S. Navy; married 1921, Helene Mason.

CHILDREN:

(aaa) Charles Montgomery Johnson, III, born 1922.
(bbb) Annette Mason Johnson, born 1924.

(bb) Carlisle Johnson, born July 11, 1899; unmarried. Served in World War—volunteer in U. S. Navy. Architect in New York City.

(e) Frances Otey Heald, born November 5, 1871; married, December 5, 1894, Dr. L. M. Ottofy, born March 11, 1865. Reside in St. Louis, Missouri.

The following is an excerpt taken from the *D. A. R. History of Missouri*, published in 1929 by the State Society D. A. R.:

Frances Otey Heald Ottofy (Mrs. L. M.), daughter of Darius Heald and Martha Hunter Heald, was born in St. Charles County, Mo., in the historic homestead, where her father was born in 1821.

Her grandparents, Major Nathan Heald, Commander of Ft. Dearborn (now Chicago) at the time of the massacre, and wife, Rebecca Wells Heald, Heroine of 1812 War, came to St. Charles County, Mo., and purchased the old Zumwalt Fort

FRANCES OTEY HEALD
wife of Dr. L. M. Offofy

and a Spanish Grant of 360 acres for their Homestead, in 1817—this Homestead was owned by the family for 100 years, a Granite Shaft was placed there to honor Major Heald and wife in 1929.

Her paternal ancestors were from New England and her maternal ones from Virginia; four revolutionary ancestors being colonels from Virginia and Kentucky, Col. John Otey, Col. Richard Callaway, Col. Samuel Wells, and Col. Charles Gwatkin. Stephen Hopkins, signer of the Declaration of Independence, John Hunter, and William Mathews were also Virginia Revolutionary ancestors. From New England, Col. Thomas Heald and Stephen Adams, the latter a descendant of Henry Adams the Ancestor of the Presidents.

Colonial ancestors, Lt. Thomas Adams and Lt. John Heald who came to Massachusetts about 1632.

She is a member of the Westminister Presbyterian Church; and in 1909 organized the Friday Literary Club. She has served on Historic and State Committees for the Federated Clubs, and as President of the Missouri Society Daughters of 1812 from 1919 to 1923 after serving for many years on the state board.

Mrs. L. M. Ottofy's first patriotic work for the Daughters of the Revolution was in 1897 during the Spanish-American War when she assisted in raising funds for the comforts of the soldiers.

In 1909 she was appointed organizing Regent of the Cornelia Greene Chapter and on June 17th officiated in organizing the chapter.

For seven years she served as State Parliamentarian for the D. A. R. and in 1917 was State Chairman of Real Daughters.

She is at present the Vice-Regent of Cornelia Greene Chapter and is serving on the State Finance Committee for Arrow Rock Tavern, is also Honorary State President and State Parliamentarian of the U. S. Daughters of 1812, National Society.

CHILDREN OF DR. L. M. AND FRANCES OTEY (HEALD) OTTOFY:

(aa) Martha A. Ottofy, born March 7, 1895.

(bb) Ladis Heald Ottofy, born June 11, 1897. Lieutenant in Aviation Corps, U. S. A., as a pilot in World War. Also, Aerial Observer. Holds commission in the Officer's Reserve of the Air Corps.

(cc) Justine Ottofy, born January 31, 1903; married, August 10, 1929, Elwood Rulon, who served in World War, Field Artillery, and was with a Missouri Unit over seas.

(dd) Frances Heald Ottofy, born June 11, 1904.

(ee) George Heald Ottofy, born November 13, 1907.

CHILDREN OF ELIZA ANN (GWATKIN) HUNTER AND HER SECOND
HUSBAND, STEPTOE JOHNSON

(5) Kate Johnson, born 1852; died October, 1912; married James L. Carlisle. At one time Postmaster of St. Louis, Missouri.

CHILD:

(a) Mary Kathryn Carlisle; married, in 1910, Douglas H. Jones.

CHILDREN:

(aa) Kathryn Jones, born May 15, 1912.
(bb) Douglas Jones, born June 25, 1914.
(cc) Stewart Jones, born January 2, 1919.
(dd) Shirley May Jones, born December 1, 1920. (All living in St. Louis, Missouri.)

(6) George Johnson, born 1854; married ————, Lizzie Bowman.

CHILDREN:

(a) Charles Sydney Johnson, born ————; served in Engineer Corps, U. S. A., World War, over seas; married Hallie Tate.

CHILDREN:

(aa) Hugh Johnson, born 1912.
(bb) Charles Sydney Johnson, Jr., born 1915.
(cc) Mary Shore Johnson, born 1925.

(b) George Johnson, Jr., born 1890. Served in Infantry, U. S. A., World War; married, 1925, Caroline McCluer.

CHILD:

(aa) Carol Johnson, born 1927.

(7) Charles F. Johnson, born 1856; died 1907; married Susan Miller.

CHILDREN:

(a) Kate Johnson; married in 1911, A. R. Ross.

CHILDREN:

(aa) Wm. J. Ross, born 1915.
(bb) Jane Ross, born 1917.
(cc) Charles Ross (twin), born 1921.
(dd) Reed Ross (twin), born 1921.

(b) Gussie Johnson; married Dr. Charles Emonts.

CHILDREN:

(aa) Charles Emonts, Jr., born 1914.

(bb) Robert Emonts, born 1915.

....

Lucinda Gwatkin, daughter of Colonel Charles Gwatkin, Sr., and Mary (Callaway) Gwatkin married, February 10, 1808, James Campbell. She died in 1853.

CHILDREN:

(1) Caroline Virginia Campbell, a daughter by this marriage, born 1824; married, November 5, 1846, Darius Heald, born January 27, 1822, died November 24, 1904. She was his first wife. His second wife was Martha Hunter, daughter of Edward and Eliza Ann (Gwatkin) Hunter. (See Edward Gwatkin family.)

CHILDREN:

(a) Dr. Nathan McCausland Heald, born 1849; died 1876; married Anna Ward. No children.

(b) John Campbell Heald, born February 20, 1851; died November 27, 1923, in California; married, in 1880, Carrie Pitman.

CHILDREN:

(aa) Virginia Heald; married, January 11, 1904, John L. McDowall.

CHILDREN:

(aaa) John Heald McDowall, born May 29, 1908.

(bbb) Jean McDowall, born May 1, 1912. (All reside in St. Louis, Missouri.)

(bb) Camilla Heald, born 1891. Living in California —unmarried.

(2) Lucinda Campbell, daughter of James and Lucinda (Gwatkin) Campbell; married, in 1854, James Sanford.

CHILDREN:

(a) Lelia Sanford, born 1855; married Dr. N. D. Barradall.

CHILD:

(aa) Lelia Barradall, born 1882; married, 1917, Dr. R. E. Gaston. No children.

(b) Elizabeth Sanford, born 1856; married, 1877, Joseph W. North.

CHILDREN:

(aa) Lucy North, born 1879; married Dr. W. R. North. No children.

(bb) Susan North, born 1881; married A. S. Miles. No children.

(cc) Maud North, born 1882; married Dr. J. H. Williams. No children.

(dd) Garrietta North, born 1888; unmarried. (All live in St. Louis County, Missouri.)

(c) Lucy Sanford, born 1860; married, November 2, 1882, J. M. Bixler.

CHILD:

(aa) Florence Bixler, born January 29, 1884; married, January 11, 1905, Robert Richardson.

CHILDREN:

(aaa) Preston Bixler, born February, 1907.

(bbb) Lucy Bixler (twin), born October, 1908.

(ccc) Robert Bixler (twin), born October, 1908.

(d) John McD. Sanford, born 1861; married, September 10, 1907, Lillian Mathews.

CHILD:

(aa) Mary Campbell Sanford, born October 10, 1909.

....

Marriages in the Gwatkin family from the Bedford County records:

Chas. Gwatkin (Batchelor) and Mary Callway (Spinster), daughter of Richard Callaway. 6 Nov. 1767. Security, Charles Gwatkin, Richard Callaway.

Jas. Gwatkin and Polly Thorp whose guardian was Nathan Reid. 6 Nov. 1802.

Edward Gwatkin and Polly Otey. 22 March 1813.

Charles B. Gwatkin and Charlotte A. Tinsley whose guardian was Wm. McDaniel, 16 September 1836. Security, Charles B. Gwatkin, Joshua Tinsley.

DAVIS (No. 2)

"The name 'Davis' is originally Welsh. It commenced with the introduction of Christianity into Wales. Missionaries went with the Roman Legions into Britian and began early to preach to the natives.

In Wales the bards of national poets, constituted a special class. They enjoyed hereditary privileges and were greatly esteemed by princes and people. Like the minstrels of Ireland and Scotland, the Welsh bards sang or recited with the accompaniment of the harp, the history and tradition of their country and the exploits in war of their chiefs and leaders.

When the scriptures were preached to the Welsh minstrels, they were especially attracted to the story of David, the Royal Bard of Israel. When they were baptized into Christianity they were required to take along with their barbarous patronymics a Christian or saint's name, and the Welsh bards frequently adopted that of King David spelled in their language 'Dyfedd' in earlier periods and 'Dafydd' in the thirteenth century. The letter 'F' in Welsh has the sound of 'V' in English.

Thus Davis became a popular name with the bards and was adopted as a family patronymic by numbers of them. In the course of time it appeared in the popular form Davy or Davie, from which were derived Davies, Davis, meaning sons of posterity of David, etc. The common English forms are Davidson, Davieson, and Davison, just as John and Johnson and Jones are derived from the name of the Beloved Apostle. It is worth noting that among the seven Champions of Christendom, Saint David was the special patron of Wales." *The Davis Family, 1698 to 1898.*

Extract by T. E. Davis, New Orleans, August 4, 1898, who was a son of Micajah Davis the Third.

Our family descended from John Davis of Shropshire, on the border of Wales. John, who flourished about the end of the seventeenth century was a considerable land-holder. The estate under the law of primogeniture being inheritable only by the oldest of the children, the younger were more or less dependent upon their own resources. In this case four of the younger sons, as not a few landless young lords and gentlemen had done before them in Raleigh's time, tried their fortunes in the British Colonies of the New World. These four Davis brothers in the order of their ages were: SAMUEL, WILLIAM, MICAJAH, and EVANS.

They all emigrated to America, landing in Virginia and settling in Louisa County in the Green Spring neighborhood. The rich lands nearer the mountains attracted their attention, they removed to Bedford County and engaged in farming, but subsequently William and Micajah went to what is now Lynchburg, but was then Lynch's Ferry, on James River. There they entered into mercantile operations, married and left numerous and prominent descendants.

....

The following compilation on this Davis family is taken, in part, from a paper compiled in 1898 by Mr. T. E. Davis, of New Orleans, La., son of Micajah Davis, the Third, and from the original notes of Dr. Alexander Brown, Virginia historian. The said note book of Dr. Brown's, now in the possession of Miss Kent Gregory, of Lynchburg, Virginia, was kindly loaned the compiler for which she makes grateful acknowledgment.

....

Dr. Brown gives the brothers as: (1) Samuel, (2) William, Sr., (3) Micajah, Sr., (4) ———, sons of John Davis and Susanna Smithson.

Samuel Davis, the eldest of the four brothers who emigrated to America, born 1740; married, August 15, 1769, Annis Lipscomb, daughter of a well to do Welsh farmer. He located in Louisa County, Virginia, near Green Springs, later moved to Bedford County, Virginia, where he died in 1779. His wife survived him, living to be 97 years old, and in the latter part of her life resided in Lynchburg with her eldest son, William.

CHILDREN:

(1) William Davis, second of this name in America, born July 3, 1770; married Zalinda Lynch, daughter of John Lynch, the founder of Lynchburg, Virginia.

CHILDREN:

(a) Samuel, died unmarried.
(b) John, died unmarried.
(c) Sarah Lynch, died unmarried.
(d) Mary Annis, born February 26, 1806; married Robinson Stabler, of Alexander, Virginia.

....

(2) John Davis, born September 24, 1774; married, July 7, 1805, Hannah (Anthony) Johnson (widow), a daughter of Christopher Anthony, of Campbell County, Virginia. He emigrated in 1815 to Cincinnati, Ohio and died August 13, 1830.

CHILDREN:

(a) Ann Maria Davis, born February 24, 1806; married, August 23, 1832, Archilles Pugh, of Cincinnati, born March 10, 1805, died October 31, 1876, son of Thomas and Esther Yatchell Pugh. She died February 14, 1877.

CHILDREN:

(aa) Esther Pugh, born August 31, 1834.
(bb) John Davis Pugh, born March 14, 1838; married, June 26, 1877, Laura Fay.
(cc) Mary Taylor Pugh, born September 26, 1840; married, November 29, 1865, John Wildman.
(dd) Achilles Henry Pugh, born November 24, 1846; married, June 14, 1875, Mary Lavinia Darr, born June 14, 1854.

CHILDREN:

(aaa) Achilles H., Jr., born March 13, 1876.
(bbb) Theresa Josephine, born October 21, 1879.

(ccc) Marie Louise, born October 23, 1883.

(ddd) Anna Charlotte, born May 18, 1885.

(b) Mary Jordan Davis, born October 10, 1808; married, January 1, 1830, Caleb Taylor, of Cincinnati, Ohio. She died May 9, 1875.

CHILDREN:

(aa) Hannah Taylor, born September 2, 1831; married, May 22, 1851, Murray Shipley and died November 19, 1891.

(bb) Wm. Henry Taylor, born December 25, 1836; married (first), December, 1861, Charlotte French, (second) in 1878, Mary Haines, (third) Helen Collard.

(cc) Elizabeth Lippincott Taylor; married George Dean.

(dd) Anna Maria Taylor; married Evan Lewis Johnson.

(c) Samuel Davis, born August 12, 1809; married, July 2, 1837, Rebecca Wallace, of Rushville, Indiana, and died July 2, 1887.

CHILDREN:

(aa) John Wallace Davis, of St. Louis.

(bb) Charles Henry Davis, of St. Louis.

(cc) Ellenor Davis; married Mr. Braithait, of England; living there.

(d) Sarah Annis Davis, born March 8, 1811; married Hugh Hall Smith, of Indianapolis and died November, 1888.

CHILDREN:

(aa) Colonna Smith.

(bb) Anna Mary Smith.

(e) Charlotte Davis, born February 21, 1813; died September, 1888.

(f) William Davis, born March 23, 1815; died 1837.

(g) John Davis, born April 15, 1818; died October, 1832.

(h) Charles Davis, born July 1820; died 1836.

(i) Hannah Davis, born October 21, 1823; married, 1842, Henry Stagg, of St. Louis, Missouri.

CHILDREN:

(aa) Charles Henry Stagg.

(bb) Virginia Isabella Stagg; married Moses Forbes, of St. Louis.

(cc) William Stagg, of Springfield, Illinois.

(dd) Charlotte Stagg.

(3) Thomas Davis, born February 18, 1777; married (first), 1798, Rachel Dixon, born 1770, daughter of George and Elizabeth Dixon, of Bedford County, Virginia. She died May 23, 1833 and in 1836, he married (second), Lucy Crenshaw, daughter of Colonel Richard Crenshaw, a prominent citizen of Bedford County. She bore him no children. Thomas Davis died in 1848 and his second wife died in 1855.

CHILDREN BY FIRST MARRIAGE:

(a) Samuel Lipscomb Davis, born 1800; died unmarried in 1828.
(b) George Dixon Davis; married Mary Ann Wills and died in 1879.

CHILDREN:

(aa) John Wills Davis, killed in battle in the Confederate Army in the War Between the States.
(bb) Thomas Dixon Davis.
(cc) Virginia Davis; married P. A. Krise, of Lynchburg, Virginia.
(dd) Alice Davis.
(ee) Micajah Davis.
(ff) Creed Wills Davis.

(c) John Thomas Davis, married Margaret Preston.

CHILDREN:

(aa) Mary Elizabeth Davis; married Camillus Christian, of Lynchburg, Virginia.
(bb) Margaret Preston Davis.
(cc) Thomas Bowker Davis, killed as Captain of his company in the Second Virginia Cavalry—C. S. A.

(d) Annis Elizabeth Davis; married Pleasant Preston.

CHILDREN:

(aa) Samuel Davis Preston; married Texana Saunders, of Albemarle County, Va.
(bb) Thomas Stephen Preston.
(cc) Pleasant Preston.
(dd) Elizabeth Preston.
(ee) Zalinda Preston.
(ff) John B. Preston.
(gg) Dr. George M. Preston, of Lynchburg, Virginia.

(e) Micajah Davis, third of the name, born November 5, 1813; married (first), November, 1833, Ellen Elizabeth Phillips, born November 11, 1816, daughter of Dr. Samuel Phillips and his wife, Ann Mitchell. Her father was from Maryland and her mother a daughter of Samuel Mitchell, of Botetourt, who had served in the war of the Revolution in the famous cavalry of Gen. Henry Lee known as "Light Horse Harry." Mrs. Ellen (Phillips) Davis died March 30, 1870, and in 1884, Micajah Davis, married (second), Miss Sarah W. Sheldon (Selden). Judge Micajah Davis died July 3, 1898, at the home of his daughter, Mrs. E. S. Gregory, in Bedford City, Virginia.

CHILDREN:

(aa) Thomas Edward Davis, born 1835; married, 1874, Mary Evelyn Moore, of Houston, Texas.

(bb) Mary Annis Davis, born 1837; married, 1856, William Wallace Berry, of Alexandria, Virginia, and died in 1883, leaving one daughter and four sons.

(cc) Samuel Phillips Davis, born 1838; married, 1857, Laura Virginia West, of Belleville, Illinois. He died in 1872.

(dd) Ann Rachel Davis, born 1841; married, 1862, Dr. Marcellus P. Christian, surgeon in U. S. Navy, and subsequently with the Confederate States Navy. She died in 1876, leaving one daughter only.

(ee) John Micajah Davis, born 1843; married, 1866, Virginia Finney Phillips, of Memphis, Tennessee, and died in 1875.

(ff) Ellen Buford Davis; married in 1869, Rev. Edward S. Gregory, of Lynchburg, Virginia, a brilliant and distinguished clergyman. They had one son, Edward.

(gg) George Wadsworth Davis; married 1878, Clara Hoffman. They had three sons and three daughters.

(f) Zalinda Lynch Davis; married Frazier Otey Stratton. One son, Frazier Otey, Jr.

---

(4) Micajah Davis, Jr., son of Samuel and Annis (Lipscomb) Davis, was born May 24, 1779; married, October 6, 1810, Mary C. Gwatkin (called "Polly"), daughter of Col. Charles Gwatkin, Sr., and Mary (Callaway) Gwatkin. (See Gwatkin and Callaway families.)

CHILDREN:

(a) William Davis; married Mary Alexander. He was a prominent physician, emigrated to Tallahassee, Fla., where his daughter, Mary, was married to Hon. William D. Bloxham, twice the Governor of the state.

(b) Charles Edward Davis.

(c) Samuel Gwatkin Davis.

(d) John Gwatkin Davis.

(e) Mary Annis Davis.

(f) Margaret Davis.

William Davis, Sr., the second of the four brothers, who emigrated to America, son of John Davis and Susanna Smithson; married Mary Gosney, daughter of Henry Gosney and Mary (born 1726) Shelton and a grand-daughter of Ralph and Mary (Pollard) Shelton, of King William County, Virginia.

CHILDREN:

(1) John Davis, born November 21, 1778; died December 11, 1863; married Ann Jennings.

(a) William Minor Davis, born in the town of Lynchburg, Virginia, January 22, 1813; married, May 27, 1841, Nannie Hunter Eubank, born February 10, 1820.

CHILDREN:

(aa) Thomas Newman Davis, born in the County of Amherst, Virginia, May 27, 1842; married Blanche Thompson and was for many years city collector of Lynchburg, Virginia, the same office later held by his son H. Minor Davis.

(bb) Jane Eubank Davis, born in the County of Amherst, Virginia, September 7, 1845.

(cc) Mary Gosney Davis, born in the County of Amherst, Virginia, July 19, 1847.

(2) Henry Davis; married, July 10, 1800, Sarah Anthony, born March 1784; died 1824.

CHILDREN:

(a) Lucy Davis; married Wm. Tudor Yancey.

(b) Mary Lou Davis, born July 26, 1804; married Hobson Johns. No issue.

(c) Samuel Davis, died unmarried.

(d) Sarah Ann Davis, born January 9, 1811; married (first) Wm. Smith, (second) Rev. Franklin G. Smith, a daughter by her first husband. Sallie Ward Smith married Dr. Gustine, of New Orleans.

(e) Robert Jordan Davis, born August 13, 1813; married Anne Carrington Cabell, of Amherst County, Virginia. He for a long time, represented Lynchburg in the State General Assembly.

CHILDREN:

(aa) Robert (died infant). (bb) Mary, (cc) Sallie, (dd) Paul, (ee) Nannie, (ff) Lucy, and (gg) William.

(f) Alexander Christopher Davis, born December 12, 1817.

(g) Charles Henry Davis.

(3) Susan Davis.

(4) Elizabeth Davis.

(5) Benjamin Davis; married Catherine Gilbert.

(6) Isaac Davis.

(7) Mary Davis; married Cornelius Pierce.

(8) Nancy Davis; married Peter Dudley.

(9) Louisa Davis.

(10) Deborah Davis.

Evan Davis, the youngest brother who emigrated from England, remained only a short time in Virginia. He emigrated to Georgia, and settled near Savannah. He resided there until the close of the Revolutionary War, in which he took an active part, serving in the Georgia Cavalry under Count Pulaski. Evan's son, Samuel, born in Georgia removed to Kentucky. He married there and became the father of Jefferson Davis, born in Christian County, Kentucky, in 1808; died 1889. This grandson of Evan Davis became a most illustrious citizen of Mississippi, filling many positions of trust and finally that of President and official head of the Confederate States of America.

....

It is stated that Micajah Davis, Sr., the third brother who emigrated from England, located in Bedford County. Among the notes from which this record has been compiled no further reference is made of him.

CALLAWAY

Arms: Norman. Fesse between three daggers.
The shield is black. The Fesse, a band
of color or metal that crosses the shield
horizontally and is one of the nine honorable
Ordinaries, Daggers or Conveys. The Daggers
are gold.

Crest: Helmet.

Motto: St. Callay Ora Pro Me.

The above is a description of the coat of arms used by the Callaway family—descendants of the emigrant. Following is an excerpt taken from Mrs. J. A. P. Hills' book, "History of Henry County and Fifty of its Oldest Families":

During 1500 John Call(a)way placed a window in the church at St. Neots and canonized the Monk, hence, "St. Callaway, Ora Pro Me." This window was still existing, January, 1915. William Callaway, a brother of John Callaway, married at St. Kew, 1577. In Patronymica Britannica (names of Britian) it is stated that Calway and Callaway are of one origin. In a "Historical Sketch of St. Neots" there is much information regarding the family taken from the Library of the British Museum there is evidence of both education and literary attainments. One, Henry Callaway, 11th child of a Somersetshire parent, born in January 17, 1817, was a teacher, a chemist, M. D., D. D., Bishop Kaffraria. Died March 26, 1890. Buried, Ottery Church, Devonshire. An entry at St. Kew, Cornwall, gives three brothers: Daniel Callaway, 1620; Richard, 1621; William (Guliel) Callaway, 1624.

The Callway family is one of the old families of Virginia and has become closely identified with the history of several other states of the union. They have taken prominent parts in the erection, and in shaping the organic laws of states of Virginia, Kentucky, and others. The founder of the Callaway family in Virginia is variously given as Joseph, William, and Francis—sometimes with the prefix "Sir," of England. Miss Ruth Early in *Campbell Chronicles* says that Lyman C. Draper in his "Life of Boone" gives a biographical sketch of Colonel Richard Callaway, in which he states that Joseph, the grandfather of

Richard, emigrated from England to Virginia, and that Richard's father (Joseph, Jr.) settled in Caroline County, Va., had seven sons and two daughters—that while Richard was still a youth, the father, mother and a brother having died of fever within a short period, the family remained at the old homestead for several years, then sold out, and settled about 1740, in Brunswick County (that part which afterwards became Bedford) locating on Big Otter River at the Eastern base of the Peaks of Otter. (The Callaways were the first men who had land cleared and raised corn on Big Otter River.) In 1754, when the war broke out, the country had become considerably populated and the people collected in forts which Washington occasionally visited. Three of the Callaway brothers held the commission of Captain: Thomas at Hickey's Fort, William at Pig River Fort, and Richard at Blackwater Fort. The frontiers were constantly alarmed, marauding parties pursued, and sometimes overtaken and punished. For services rendered in these engagements, two of the brothers, Richard and William, were promoted to rank of Bedford Militia Colonels. This account as given by Lyman C. Draper is accepted by members of the Callaway family.

From a list of soldiers in Revolutionary Army from Bedford County, Virginia, are found the following, bearing the name of Callaway.

> Callaway, Richard—Colonel.
>   "   Charles—Captain.
>   "   William—Lieutenant Colonel.
>   "   James, Junior—Captain.
>   "   John—Major.
>   "   James—Co. Lieutenant.
>   "   Chesley Dudley—First Lieutenant.
>   (Removed from county 1779.)

The family record in an old Callaway Bible belonging to Mr. James Franklin, Jr., of Lynchburg, Va., gives the two (2) sisters, Elizabeth and Ann, and five (5) brothers as follows:

———— Thomas, born 1712, appointed in March, 1738, constable in the upper precincts of James River Mountains. In 1747, removed from Orange to Lunenburg, which became Halifax in 1752. Vestryman and Church warden, 1752, of Antrian Parish,

Halifax County, Virginia; gentleman justice; commissioned captain of militia from that county, in the French and Indian Wars prior to 1755; emigrated, probably, to North Carolina.

———— William, born 1714. (See forward.)

———— Francis, born 1716; prominent in civil and military affairs. Was also commissioned sheriff of Bedford County; removed to North Carolina, then to Wilkes County, Georgia and had many descendants there.

———— James was a planter in Spotsylvania County, Virginia. Among other children of his, was a son, Flanders Callaway, who married Jemima Boone, daughter of Daniel Boone. (See Boone family.)

———— Richard, born 1722. (See forward.)

The names of the other two brothers are given as follows:

———— Joseph Callaway (Third), who died of a fever in early life.

———— John Callaway, lived and died in Bedford County, Virginia. (See Draper MSS., 15 C C 84.)

Colonel William Callaway, second son, (or grandson) of the founder, born 1714, was a prominent man in Virginia. He was colonel in the French and Indian Wars, 1755-61; presided at the first court held in Bedford County. In 1754, he gave one hundred acres of land for a town, courthouse, and prison, to be called New London, the County of Bedford, but recently (1753) taken from the County of Lunenburg had no courthouse. The following record of gift is copied from Bedford County records, Deed Book "A," page 113:

"This Indenture made this twenty-eighth of March one Thousand and seven Hundred and fifty-seven Between William Callaway, of the County of Bedford of the one Part and Richard Callaway, Zachary Isbell and Benjamin Howard Gents, Trustees for the said County of Bedford of the other part: Witnesseth: That Whereas the said William Callaway at a Court held for the said County the twenty-sixth day of August one Thousand seven hundred and fifty-four did agree to give the said County one Hundred Acres of Land at the Forks of the Roads near his house to erect a Courthouse and Prison for use of said County and to make a deed in fee simple to the Court for fifty acres, Part thereof at any time when Required, and to convey the other fifty Acres when he should obtain a Patent for the same:

"And Whereas at a Court continued and held for the said County of Bedford the twenty-fifth day of November one Thousand seven Hundred and fifty-five the said Richard Callaway, Zachary Isbell and Benjamin Howard by Order of the said Court were appointed Trustees for the said County, for the said William Callaway to make a Deed to in fee simple for the said land in trust, to be by them laid off into Lots and sold for the use of the said County upon such terms as shall be Prescribed by the said Court for each Lot or Parcel of Land, and to make conveyances for the same in fee simple. And the said Benjamin Howard was appointed Treasurer to Collect and Receive the money arising by the sale of the said Lotts. Now, this Indenture, Witnesseth that the said William Callaway for and in consideration of the sum of Five Shillings to him in hand, paid by the said Richard Callaway, Zachary Isbell and Benjamin Howard. The receipt whereof he doth hereby acknowledge, Hath Given, granted Bargained and Sold and by the Present Do Give, Grant, Bargain and Sell unto said Richard Callaway, Zachary Isbell and Ben. Howard, Trustees, as aforesaid, their Heirs and Assigns, forever, one certain Tract or Parcel of Land, Lying and being in the County of Bedford whereon the Courthouse of the County now stands, containing fifty acres, to the same more or less, Bounded as followeth, Viz.:

"Beginning at Pointers, Thence south seventy-three degrees East, Forty-five poles to Pointers on the Patent Line, Thence along the said Line North Thirty-three Poles to Pointers on the Patent Line, Thence along the said Line North Thirty-three Degrees East, One Hundred and thirty-eight and a half poles to Pointers, Thence of N. 73, W. 81 1-2 Poles to pointers, S. 17, W. 133 Poles to the first Station. Together with all the privileges and appertenances thereto Belonging, or in any wise appertaining to Have and to Hold the said Land and premises with all of the appertenances to them, the said Richard Callaway, Zachary Isbell and Benjamin Howard in trust to and for the use and Benefit of the said County and for no other use or Purpose whatsoever, and the said William Callaway for himself and his Heirs and assigns will Warrent and Forever Defend by these Presents the said Land and Premises against the claims or demands of any Person or Persons Whatsoever. In Witness whereof he, the said William Callaway hath hereunto set his hand and seal the day and year above written.

WILLIAM CALLAWAY (L. S.)."

INDENTURE RECORDED

At a court continued and held for Bedford County, March 29, 1757:

"This Indenture was acknowledged by William Callaway thereto and ordered to be recorded, Elizabeth, the wife of the said William Callaway, personally appeared in Court, and being first privily Examined, as the Law directs, Voluntarily Relinquished her Right of Dower in the Land Conveyed by said Indenture which is also ordered to be recorded.

"Teste, Ben Howard, C. B. C."

In 1767 in Deed Book C, page 97, in the County of Bedford we find recorded a deed to the other fifty acres. Trustees, William Mead, Richard Callaway and Richard Stith, Gents.

"Teste, Ben Howard, C. B. C."

At a court held for Bedford County, February 24, 1778:

"This court does recommend to his Excellency the Governor, Charles Lynch, Esq., for a Colonel, Jeremiah Early for a Lieu. Colonel; William Callaway for a Lieu.

Colonel; And William Trigg and William Leftwich, Esqrs. for Majors, as proper persons to act as Militia officers in this County."

At a court held for Bedford County, March 23, 1778:

"Jeremiah Early, Colonel; William Callaway, Lieu. Colonel and William Trigg and William Leftwich, Majors, produced commissions from his Excellency the Governor and qualified according to Law.

A copy—

"Teste: S. M. Bolling, Clerk of Bedford Court."

In 1755 fee book speaks of him as Major in French and Indian Wars.

In 1758 fee book speaks of him as Colonel in same war.

In 1758, November 28, fee book speaks of him as appointed County Lieutenant by the English government.

In deed book E, 1773, is recognized as colonel.

In deed book 74 and county court order book is recognized as colonel.

William Callaway, who made the gift of 100 acres of land lived near New London where he owned 900 acres of land and lot No. 1 in New London.

Dinwiddie's Official Records, Vol. 2, page 109, says that William Callaway had a patent from the English government of 15,000 acres of land in the counties of Lunenburg, Halifax and Bedford.

William Callaway was in the House of Burgesses of Virginia thirteen sessions, being the first Burgess from Bedford County. He died in 1778. On January 8, 1735, he married (first) Elizabeth Tilley, and (second), about 1752, Elizabeth Crawford. The children of Colonel William Callaway are as follows, five, being by his first wife and four by the second:

(1) James, born December 21, 1736. (See forward.)

(2) Major John, born June 10, 1738; married (first) Tabitha Tate, daughter of Henry and Sarah Tate; and (second) Agatha Ward, daughter of John Ward. He served in the Revolutionary War, distinguishing himself for gallantry at Guilford Courthouse. He lived in Campbell County where he died in 1821. (His will written January 28, 1821; probated March 12, 1821, Will Book 4, page 298, of Campbell County records; mentions Matilda, Dosha, and Sally Callaway, daughters of my son William Callaway, deceased, also grandson, George W. Callaway.) He had children: (a) James; (b) Elizabeth by his first wife; and by his second wife one child: (c) William.

(3) William, Jr., born 1748. (See forward.)

(4) Elizabeth, born June 18, 1743; married Captain Francis Thorp, of Campbell County. Their children were: (a) Betsey; married ———— Gwatkin (probably, James, son of Col. Charles Gwatkin); (b) Sophia; married James Reid; (c) Kitty (twin); married Captain Peter Grayson, of the United States Army; (d) Theodosia (twin of Kitty); married ———— Harris.

(5) Mary, born January 8, 1746; married Jacob Anderson, of Campbell County, son of George Anderson. Their children were as follows: (a) William; married Sally Early, daughter of Colonel Jeremiah Early; (b) Elizabeth; married Rev. Charles Price, of Bedford County; (c) Sarah; married David Jones; (d) John; married his first cousin, Sarah Callaway, daughter of Charles Callaway; (e) Millie, died young; (f) Dosha; married Abner Early.

(6) Charles, born June 18, 1754; lived in Campbell County; served in the Revolutionary War; commissioned first lieutenant, later captain. Was a man of wealth and prominence. He died June 3, 1827, and was buried in Pittsylvania County, Virginia. In 1768, he married Mrs. Judith (Early) Pate, daughter of Colonel Jeremiah Early (who served in the Revolutionary War) and his wife, Sarah (Anderson) Early. Their children were: (a) Joel, born 1769; (b) Achilles, born 1771; (c) William, born 1773; (d) Sarah, born 1775; married John Anderson; (e) James, born 1777; (f) Polly, born 1779; (g) Charles, born 1781; (h) Judith, born 1783; (i) John, born 1785; (j) Frances, born 1787; (k) Henry, born 1792.

(7) Joseph, born December 10, 1756; died 1838, in Campbell County, Virginia. Was a Revolutionary soldier. (Authority—9th Annual Report of Library Board, 1911-1912: Rev. Soldiers of Va.—Joseph Callaway, (lt.) Campbell County, Doc. F.) The will of Joseph Callaway, written March 15, 1833; probated December 10, 1838, Will Book 8, page 238, of Campbell County records; mentions daughters, Fanny Monroe (wife of John Monroe), Betsy Hudson, Polly Epperson, Susan Epperson, Nancy Gilchrist; son, Francis Callaway, and grandchildren, Joseph C. Epperson, Susan Wood and Patsy Scott (daughters of Fanny Monroe). A second will written January 26, 1837,

probated February 11, 1839, Will Book 8, page 257, of Campbell County, Virginia, revokes all former wills.

(8) Milly, born June 5, 1759, said to have married her first cousin, George Callaway, son of Col. Richard Callaway. The will of George Callaway, of Bedford County, Va., filed January 25, 1773; mentions wife, Milly, and daughter, Betty Callaway.

(9) Cathlena ("Cana"), born December 8, 1761; married William Bourne Price.

Colonel James Callaway, born December 21, 1736, eldest son of Colonel William and Elizabeth (Tilley) Callaway, was married three times and had twenty-two children. He married (first), November 24, 1756, Sarah Tate, born 1735, died 1773; (second) in 1777, Elizabeth Early, born 1759, died 1796, daughter of Col. Jerry Early; (third) in 1799, Mrs. Mary (Langhorne) Turpin. There were no children by this last marriage. He was a man of wealth and influence—a leading citizen of Bedford County, where he lived and died. He served in the French and Indian Wars; was a member of Bedford County patriotic committee of 1774; held by commission the successive militia offices; built the first iron furnace south of the James River; member of the House of Burgesses from Bedford County, 1766-1769; treasurer for New London Academy. Colonel James Callaway died November 1, 1809.

CHILDREN BY HIS FIRST WIFE, SARAH TATE:

(1) Elizabeth, born 1757, died 1791; married, 1775, Harry Innes, the first lawyer admitted to the bar of Campbell County, Va., later moving to Kentucky where he acquired office as Judge of Court —served in the Revolution as an ensign of Bedford Militia, born 1752. He was a son of Rev. Robert Innes, who emigrated from Scotland to Virginia before the middle of the eighteenth century and his wife, Catherine Richards, a native of the colony. They left issue.

(2) Polly, born 1759, died 1831; married, August 4, 1781, Dr. Daniel Brown; removed to New York.

(3) Frances, born 1760, died December, 1807; married, 1781, James Steptoe, born at "Hominy Hall," Westmoreland County, Va., July 16, 1750, died at "Federal Hill," near New London, Bed-

ford County, February, 1826. He was Clerk of Bedford County Court for fifty-four years — a personal friend of Thomas Jefferson, by whom he was appointed. He left nine sons and daughters. Of this union there are many descendants of great prominence; among them being Lady Nancy Astor, M. P., and Mrs. John H. Lewis, prominent throughout the State of Virginia as leader in the League of Women Voters and other civic movements.

(4) Lucy, born 1761; died 1839. Never married.

(5) Sarah, born 1763; died 1770.

(6) John, born 1764; died 1764.

(7) Nancy, born 1765; died 1775.

(8) William, born 1766; died 1770.

(9) James, Jr., born 1768; married Betsy Greer. (See forward.)

(10) Henry Tate, born 1769; married Martha Guerrant. (See forward.)

(11) Robert, born 1771; died 1794. Never married.

(12) Sarah, born 1773; died 1773.

CHILDREN BY HIS SECOND WIFE, ELIZABETH EARLY:

(13) Jeremiah, born 1778; died 1812. Never married.

(14) William, born 1779; married, 1807, Nannie Crump, daughter of Richard Crump, of Powhatan County, Va. He was a legislator from Franklin County, where he lived and died in 1855—left issue.

(15) John, born 1781; married (first) in 1811, Mary Hairston; (second) in 1821; America Hairston—both of Campbell County and cousins. He died 1865. (See forward.)

(16) Sally, born 1783; died 1788.

(17) (Dr.) George, born 1785; married, April 11, 1811, Mary Elizabeth Cabell, daughter of Col. William Cabell, of Union Hill, Nelson County and was the grandfather of Alexander Brown, Virginia historian. He died in 1822 and left issue.

(18) Abner Early, born 1787; married, January 23, 1809, Ann Eliza Lewis, daughter of Francis Lewis, of Powhatan County, Virginia. Said to have gone to Georgia—Missouri. Died 1834— left issue.

(19) (Rev.) Thomas, born 1789; married, June 20, 1811, Lucinda Anderson, daughter of William Anderson; moved to Missouri. Died 1877—left issue.

(20) Catherine, born 1792; married William Langhorne, moved to Botetourt County, has many descendants. Died 1871.

(21) Infant, born 1794; died infancy.

(22) Infant, born 1796; died infancy.

The will of James Callaway, recorded in Will Book "C," page 214, of the Bedford County records is as follows:

IN THE NAME OF GOD AMEN. I James Callaway the elder of Bedford County tho weak in body am of sound mind for the purpose of disposing of my worldly estate do make and declare this my last will & Testament in manner and form following. Imprimis, I desire and direct in the first place all my just Debts to be paid, and for that purpose shall hereafter make provision in the hands of my Executors. I will and bequeath unto my dearly beloved wife Mary Callaway my mansion house Tract of Land containing six hundred and forty acres be the same more or less with all the household and kitchen furniture the provisions and groceries that may be on hand at the time of my death her riding carriage and all the Horses and other stock attached to the plantation with the Mill on Lick-run and a small meadow on the same Creek already made and the following Negroe Slaves, Philis & her children, Caesar, Judy, Isaac, Sall Squire, Aaron, & Frederick, Kate & her children Dick, Tom, Bill, Winney, Ned & Darby, Robin, Frank, Dill, Patience, Anna, Amey & Joe, during her natural life. I do also give and relinquish unto her my beloved wife all the slaves I am in possession of or have right to by our intermarriage inclored those bequeath her by Mr. Trotter in absolute title and do declare that the provision now made is in lieu and full of her dower in my Estate real and personal I give & devise unto my son James Callaway his Heirs and assigns forever my Tract of Land on Chestnut Creek in the County of Franklin consisting of all the adjoining Lands, together with a small piece of Land called Rocky mount with the Tavern and all other improvements thereon except what has been reserved for the County on which the Courthouse stands. Item, I give and devise unto my son Henry T. Callaway all my Lands on Black-water in the said County of Franklin called Renfores embracing several adjoining Tracts and also a Tract of Land of three hundred & ten acres on pine

Run in the County of Montgomery to him and to his Heirs forever. Item, I give and bequeath unto my son William Callaway & to his Heirs forever the upper end of my Tract of Land in the said County of Franklin on both sides of Black-water called Doggets, & supposed to be a morty of the whole Tract. To be divided by a line comencing at the River in the Caroline road & running thence with the road southwardly to a sharp corner of the same, & from sd. sharp corner a straight line to the West end of the grassy Hill until it shall intersect the order line, On the North side of the River the dividing line shall commence at the mouth of a small branch a few steps below the ford & running the point of the hill to the top, leaving the siding ground of the branch on the North until it strikes the said order line not far from the big road. Also a small Survey on the upper lines purchased of Greer & one equal half of the undisposed of Land in the said order called Meads.

Item, I give and devise unto my son Abner Callaway all the residue of my said Lands on both sides of Black-Water called Doggets and the order Lands below the lines dividing his brother Williams with its appurtenances to him and to Heirs forever. Item, I give and devise unto my son John Callaway his Heirs and assigns forever all my Lands on Pig river in the said County of Franklin contiguous & adjoining the Land granted to William Callaway and purchased of Bartons, Manifies, Chitwoods, Duvalls & Eubanks with the reservation after to be made. Item, I give and devise unto my son George Callaway and his Heirs forever all my Estate in the Lands & Mills near Lynchburg held in copartnership with James Steptoe Esquire with all my Lotts and other Estate in the Towns of Madison & Lynchburg. Item, I give and devise unto my son Thomas Callaway and His Heirs forever all my Lands called my Staunton Lands, except what has already been disposed of & shall hereinafter be given to his sister Brown. Item, I give and devise unto my Executors hereinafter named, and whom for the following purpose I constitute Trustees and to the survivors and last survivor of them my Lands on Otter River and the new Mills thereunto attached with its appurtenances and so much of my other lands as shall not herein be specially devised and to be designated by them as will with the foregoing Lands and Mills with their appurtenances be equal in value in their estimation to the Land now devised to some one of my sons: to be held by them in Trust and for the use and sustenance of my son Jeremiah Callaway. With the priviledge to them or the last survivor of them from time to time if in their opinion the issues and profits shall be insufficient to give to him, or sell such part of the Estate as they may think proper for his additional support, or the payment of such of his Debts as they shall deem proper to discharge during his my sons natural life, and after his death the whole estate shall go and descend unto his Heirs. Item, I give and devise unto my daughter Polly Brown two Hundred Acres of my Staunton Lands, which I have for some time designed for her including her clearing last winter to be laid off compactly by my brother Charles for her, to her & to her Heirs forever. Item, I give & devise unto my Daughter Lucy Callaway & her heirs forever the Tracts of Lands called the Glebe Adam's old place & Holts all adjoining, with the remainder of the meadow on Lick run after the termation of my wifes life Estate & a negroe girl named Lydia & her two children Peter and Matilda & the sum of five hundred pounds to be paid to her by my Executors as shall be hereafter directed, and until that shall be done and compleated the interest shall be regularly discharged annually. Item, I give & bequeath unto my daughter Catharine Callaway the mansion House tract of Land with the Mill on Lick run and all the personal Estate except the Slaves that I have given unto my wife after the termation of her estate thereto unto my said daughter & her heirs forever. I also also give her one negro girl named Peggy & the sum of one thousand pounds to be paid to her by my Executors as hereinafter to be directed and until this is fully done and compleated they are to pay her annually the Interest thereon. Whereas I became the purchaser of part of the Estate in the County of Cumberland, formerly the property of Joseph Calland called the Long Ordinary under a Sale made by a decree of Chancery Court in favor of David Ross, and did promise that the Title should be made to sd. Land unto Mrs. Elizabeth Langhorn and requested the same to be done accordingly. Now to fulfil the promise and request aforesaid I do give & devise the said Lands to Mrs. Elizabeth Langhorn & to her Heirs & request & desire that the Title may be made to her accordingly. All the rest & remainder of my Estate both real and personal of every sort, kind, & description together with all mines, minerals, & metals on the Lands of John Callaway herein devised to him, I give and devise unto my Executors herein after named for the purpose of paying all my debts and legacys; that is to say, to pay & satisfy my daughter Lucys legacy as soon as in their opinion the circumstances of the Estate will justify. And the Legacy to my daughter Catharine at her intermarriage or arrival at the age of twentyone years. And to enable my Executors to do justice to the world and to my family they have full power and are hereby authorized the said Estate devised to them to sell dispose of, rent, hire out, keep together, work improve, manage & conduct in any & in such manner & ways as to them shall seem meet and prudent, and alterations in the same to make from time to time as to them shall seem proper. And after all the Debts and legacies are fully paid and satisfied the reservations of the mines, minerals, & metals in my son John Callaways Lands shall cease & the same shall belong with the Land to him & to his Heirs and all the rest & residue of the Estate shall be divided as my Executors shall approve either in share or by sale amongst my children James Callaway, Henry T. Callaway, William Callaway, John Callaway, George Callaway, Abner Callaway, Thomas Callaway, the Trustees of my son Jeremiah Callaway for the purposes of the trust thereto prescribed, my daughters Polly Brown, Lucy Callaway, Catharine Callaway, and the children or their descendants of my Decd. daughters Elizabeth Innes & Frances Steptoe so that the children of my two Deceased daughters shall each have a share and as my object & intention is & I do hereby declare the same to be to make all my children equal in point of property as the nature of the Estate will admit of. It is my will & desire that in the distribution of this residuary estate by my Executors it shall be so done that the estate either real or personal or both heretofore and now specifically given to my children or any of them shall be brought into estimate & each charged with what they may have received, & this residum to be so divided as to make each equal to the other:—I will & desire that if any of my Lands which I may have sold shall remain not conveyed to the purchasers that my Executors do make the necessary conveyances.

I appoint my Wife Mary Callaway, my son Henry T. Callaway & James Steptoe Esqr. guardians to my daughter Catharine Callaway until her full age.

Lastly I nominate and hereby appoint my sons Henry T. Callaway, John Callaway, George Callaway, my brother William Callaway, & my friends James Steptoe Esquire & Christopher Clark attorney at

Law Executors to this my last Will & Testament (contained in two sheets of paper) revoking all others declare this to be my last. Given under my hand and seal this 2nd day of May 1809.

CHARLES CALLAWAY, ACHILLES   JAMES CALLAWAY [SEAL].
CALLAWAY, WILLIAM GIBBS,
          his   his
LEONARD x HUTTS, ROBERT x OWEN.
          mark   mark

Whereas I did on the 2nd day of this instant duly make & publish my last Will & Testament, & in the distribution of my residuary estate I directed it to be so made that each of my children should receive an equal portion of my property, & for that purpose direct that each of my children should be charged not only with what I had previously given them but also with the provision made by the said Will. Now therefore to remove all uncertainty & to carry my intention into effect do make and declare this as a Codicil to my said last will & Testament & in aid and addition to the said residuary clause do now declare for the direction & government of my Executors that the following sums attached to the respective name of each of my children shall stand for & be estimate or true value of all the estate they have received or may specifically receive under the will, and for which they are bound to account in order to produce the equality contemplated by the Will to wit, My son James Callaways estate the sum of £4672. Henry T. Callaways estate the sum of £4520. John Callaways estate the sum of £3780. William Callaways estate the sum of £4654. Abner Callaways estate the sum of £4100. George Callaways estate the sum of £3000. Thomas Callaways estate the sum of £4000. The proportion for my son Jeremiah Callaways the sum of £2000. My daughter Elizabeth Innes the sum of £2400. My daughter Frances Steptoe the sum of £3700. Lucy Callaways the sum of £3000 three thousand. Polly Brown's the sum of £3618. Catharine Callaways the sum of £2300 two thousand three hundred. These sums are to be considered by my Executors as the standard value of the respective estates and no further estimate is to be made. Witness my hand & seal this 3rd day of May 1809.   JAMES CALLAWAY [SEAL].

Witness, CHARLES CALLAWAY,
ACHILLES CALLAWAY, JOHN CALLAWAY.

At a Court held for Bedford County at the Courthouse the 27th day of November 1809.

This last Will & Testament of James Callaway Senr. Decd. was proved by the oaths of Achilles Callaway, William Gibbs, Leonard Hutts, & Robert Owen witnesses thereto, & the Codicil endorsed on the said Will was also proved by the oaths of Charles Callaway, Achilles Callaway, & John Callaway witnesses to the same & ordered to be recorded: And on the motion of Christopher Clark, William Callaway, George Callaway & John Callaway four of the Ex'ors therein named who made oath thereto & together with John Watts, William Irvine, Jeremiah Callaway, John Callaway Senr., Charles Callaway, David Saunders, Jabiz Leftwich, Thomas Logwood, William Leftwich Junr. & Thomas Lumpkin their securities entered into & acknowledged their bond in the penalty of Two hundred thousand dollars conditioned as the Law directs, certificate is granted them for obtaining a probat of said Will in due form. Liberty being reserved the other executors named in said Will to join in the probat when they shall think fit. And afterwards at a Court continued & held for said County James Steptoe Senr another ex'or of the said James Callaway Senr. Decd. came into Court & made oath and gave bond with the secy, aforesd. conditioned according to law probat is granted him also on the said decedents Will.

Teste,

J. Steptoe, *C. B. C.*

A Copy—Teste:

V. W. Nichols,
*Clerk of the Circuit Court of
Bedford County, Virginia.*

Will Book "C," page 214.

....

James Callaway, Jr., born January 23, 1768, near New London, Bedford County, Virginia, son of Colonel James Callaway and his first wife, Sarah (Tate) Callaway; married Betsy Greer, a daughter of Captain Moses Greer and Anne Bailey, of Franklin County, Virginia. James Callaway, II, was educated at William and Mary College and, like his father and grandfather, was a large landowner and had many slaves. He was captain in the Bedford County Militia during the Revolutionary War. (*Campbell Chronicles*, page 272, and McAlisters' *Virginia Militia in the Revolution*, from Bedford County, Sec. 254, page 185.) He was Clerk of Franklin County from 1791 until 1813, and died in August 1851.

CHILDREN:

(1) Emily; married Jack Taylor, of Franklin County, left issue.
(2) Nancy; married Theo Webb, of Franklin County, left issue.
(3) Miranda; married James Leftwich, of Bedford County, left issue.
(4) Serena; married Wm. Leftwich, of Bedford County, left issue.
(5) Louisa; married ———— Turnball.
(6) Catherine; married Dr. Reese, of Franklin County, no issue.
(7) Langhorne Chiswell ("Lang"), never married.
(8) Walter C. ("Watt"); married Judith Hale, of Franklin County, left issue.
(9) Thomas Callaway, born February 14, 1824. (See forward.)

Henry Tate Callaway, the 10th child of Col. James Callaway and Sarah (Tate) Callaway and a brother of James Callaway, Jr., was born April 24, 1769, in Bedford County, Virginia. He was educated at William and Mary College and had a large estate in Franklin on Blackwater River and owned many slaves. He married Elizabeth Guerrant, a daughter of Col. Peter Guerrant, of Buckingham County, who came to Franklin in 1805 and settled on the headwaters of Blackwater River. The hamlet of Callaway, Virginia, derived its name from these two brothers and their descendants. He died in Franklin County in 1852.

CHILDREN:

(1) Lucy Frances, born January 11, 1820; died January 11, 1844; married Corbin Reynolds, of Glen Wilton, no issue.
(2) Amanda, born 1822; married Tazwell Taliferro, left issue.
(3) Susan Evelyn, born November 16, 1824; married 1845, Thomas Callaway Callaway, a first cousin. (See forward.)
(4) Malinda, born February 10, 1827; died February 14, 1851; married Peter Price, of Franklin, left issue.
(5) Mary, born 1829; married Edwin Tate, of Bedford County, Virginia.
(6) Peter Henry, born June 3, 1832; died August 24, 1859; married (first) Betty Guerrant; (second) Elizabeth McGuffin.

Thomas Callaway Callaway

(7) James Steptoe, born April 5, 1835; died May 16, 1874; married (first) Martha Reynolds; (second) Mary Saunders.

Thomas Callaway Callaway, third son of James Callaway, Jr., and Betsy (Greer) Callaway, born February 14, 1824, in Franklin County, Virginia, was educated at New London Academy, in Bedford, and Emory and Henry College (Emory, Va.). He enlisted in the Confederate Army in 1861, in Troop K, 24th Regiment, Virginia Cavalry, C. S. A., commanded by Captains T. G. Barham and William B. Smith. He served in the capacity of a Lieutenant and was discharged from this service in 1865. He married in June, 1845, his first cousin, Susan Evelyn Callaway, born November 16, 1824, daughter of Henry Tate Callaway. Her father gave her when she was married a grant of land on Blackwater, consisting of 6,000 acres together with thirty negroes. Thomas Callaway Callaway died on Blackwater River, October 10, 1902, leaving issue of three daughters and four sons.

CHILDREN:

(1) Lavinia Langhorne, born June 4, 1848, never married.
(2) George Edward, born February 12, 1850; died July 31, 1922—never married.
(3) James Henry, born May 5, 1852; died July 31, 1909—never married.
(4) Elizabeth Mary, born April 21, 1855; died June 18, 1864.
(5) John Peter, born April 26, 1858, on Blackwater in Franklin County, Va., was educated at Roanoke College (Salem, Va.), and Virginia Polytechnic Institute (Blacksburg, Va.). He married, June 28, 1890, Bettie Adline Renick, born October 27, 1860, daughter of Captain Calvin B. Renick, of Callaway, Virginia, and Greenbrier, West Virginia. He is now living (1929) on land in Franklin that was an inheritance from his grandfather, Henry Tate Callaway.

CHILDREN:

(a) Annie Lee Callaway, born May 29, 1891; married, October 5, 1924, Minor Franklin Johnson, son of Moses M. Johnson, of Albemarle County, Virginia.

CHILDREN:

(aa) Virginia Langhorne Johnson, born February 24, 1927.

(bb) Minor Franklin Johnson, Jr., born April 11, 1928.

(b) Susan Emerson Callaway, born January 13, 1893; married, in 1927, Lester T. Hutson, son of Wm. E. Hutson, of Maryland and Roanoke, Virginia. No issue.

(c) Flanders Brown Callaway, born October 16, 1895; married, October 3, 1922, Minnie E. Engleby, born March 29, 1897, a daughter of Thomas Joseph and Estelle (Staples) Engleby, of Roanoke, Virginia.

Flanders Brown Callaway enlisted in the World War on September 7, 1917, with the 1st Company, 2nd Air Service Mechanical Regiment. He served in the capacity of Sergeant, was with the American expeditionary forces eighteen months—discharged on June 23, 1919.

CHILDREN:

(aa) Flanders Brown Callaway, Jr., born October 23, 1923.

(bb) Russell Engleby Callaway, born February 15, 1927.

(d) Grace Callaway, born 1897; died in infancy.

(e) Helen Hunter Callaway, born February 16, 1899; died October 27, 1920—never married.

(f) Alice Page Callaway, born May 14, 1901. Educated at State Normal Schools at East Radford and Harrisonburg, Virginia, for a teacher, which profession she followed for four consecutive years; now in business at Roanoke, Virginia, where she lives. Member of United Daughters of the Confederacy and Daughters of the American Revolution.

(g) Mary Hale Callaway, born May 11, 1903; married in 1924, Marcus K. Dupree, son of John K. Dupree, of Botetourt County, Virginia. No issue.

(h) Hulda Penn Callaway, born April 24, 1906. Living at home (Callaway, Virginia).

(i) John Peter Callaway, Jr., born March 11, 1909; died January 13, 1913.

(j) George Edward Callaway ("Bill"), born September 28, 1913; studying preparatory for the medical profession.

(6) Charles Reynolds, born November 5, 1865; married in 1906, Florence Becker—one issue. He died June 24, 1907.

(7) Mary Lee, born August 20, 1868; married in 1905, Henry Hoy— no issue. She died September 27, 1918.

John Callaway, born 1781, near New London, Bedford County, Virginia, son of Col. James Callaway and his second wife, Elizabeth Early, born 1759; died 1796; daughter of Colonel Jerry Early; married (first) in 1811, Mary (Polly) Hairston, born 1793, of Campbell County, Virginia. He married (second) in 1821, America Hairston, born 1801, daughter of Colonel George Hairston and Bethenia Perkins (Letcher) Hairston, of Campbell County, Virginia, and a first cousin of his first wife. John Callaway died in 1865, leaving the following issue.

CHILDREN BY FIRST MARRIAGE:

(1) Samuel Hairston, born 1810; died 1846.

(2) Elizabeth Mary, born 1812; married Evan Davis.

CHILDREN:

(a) Elizabeth Davis.

(b) Ruth Davis; married ———— Haden.

(c) John Henry Davis; married Mary Pannill.

(d) Katherine Davis; married (first) ———— McCorkle, one daughter, (aa) May McCorkle; married (second) ———— McLarry, one son, (bb) John McLarry.

(3) James, born 1814; died 1829.

(4) Polly Hairston, born 1816.

CHILDREN BY SECOND MARRIAGE:

(5) George Hairston, born 1822; died 1894.

(6) Bethenia Ruth, born 1825. (See forward.)

Bethenia Ruth Callaway, born 1825, daughter of John Callaway and his second wife, America Hairston, married in 1841, George Pannill, born 1815, son of Morton and Mary Johns Pannill. He died in 1866 and she died in 1906.

CHILDREN:

(1) George Pannill; died in infancy.
(2) John Morton Pannill. (Was a V. M. I. Cadet.)
(3) William Hairston Pannill—Fell at Ream's Station, Confederate Army—Company K, 10th Virginia Cavalry, C. S. A.
(4) America Hairston Pannill; married William Arthur Campbell, of Scotch descent.

CHILDREN:

(a) Mary Bethenia Campbell; married Charles J. Stanley.

CHILDREN:

(aa) Roy Stanley.
(bb) Gertrude Stanley; married Philip Pannill, of Orange County, Virginia.

CHILD:

(aaa) Alice Bethenia Pannill, born 1919.
(cc) America Ruth Stanley; died in infancy.
(b) William Pannill Campbell; married Erie Brodie.

CHILDREN:

(aa) Edwin Ruthven Campbell.
(bb) William Arthur Campbell.
(cc) Frances Pannill Campbell.
(dd) Norman Taliaferro Campbell.
(ee) Raymond B. Campbell.
(ff) Evelyn Fairfax Campbell.
(gg) Charles Lamb Campbell.
(hh) James Stuart Campbell.
(ii) Ruth America Bethenia Campbell.
(c) Ruth Janet Campbell; married N. T. Shumate. Living in Charlottesville, Virginia.

CHILDREN:

(aa) Joseph Norman Shumate.
(bb) Ruth Shumate.
(cc) Louise Shumate.

(dd) William Wellford Shumate.

(ee) Mary Bettie Shumate.

(5) Mary Pannill; married John Henry Davis, son of Evan Davis and Elizabeth Mary (Callaway) Davis.

CHILDREN:

(a) George Evan Davis; married Amelia May Galloway, daughter of Dr. Galloway, of Philadelphia.

CHILDREN:

(aa) Amelia May Davis.

(bb) George Evan Davis, Jr.

(cc) Edith Davis.

(b) John Henry Davis, Jr.; married Hilda Forsberg, daughter of Colonel August Forsberg of the Confederate Army.

CHILDREN:

(aa) John Henry Davis, III.

(bb) August Forsberg Davis.

(c) Elizabeth Ruth Davis; married John Spottswood Taylor. Living at Stuart, Patrick County, Virginia.

CHILDREN:

(aa) Frances Pannill Taylor.

(bb) John Davis Taylor.

(cc) William Clay Taylor.

(dd) Katherine Langhorne Taylor.

(ee) James Spottswood Taylor.

(d) Edmond Pannill Davis; married Emily Rangeley.

(e) Ernest Davis.

(6) Edmond John Pannill, born 1853; married, 1885, Mary Eliza Reamey, born 1861, daughter of Dr. Peter Randolph Reamey and Sallie Jane (Waller) Reamey. Lived in Martinsville, Virginia, where he died in 1904.

CHILDREN:

(a) Sallie Reamey Pannill; married in 1917, John Redd Smith, attorney-at-law.

CHILDREN:

    (aa) Patsy Pannill Smith.
    (bb) John Redd Smith, Jr.
    (cc) Eliza Reamey Smith.

  (b) Ruth Callaway Pannill; an Instructor of Nurses at the Rockingham Memorial Hospital, at Harrisonburg, Virginia. Her home is in Martinsville, Virginia.

  (c) Bethenia Letcher Pannill.

  (d) Mariah Waller Pannill; married in 1921, William Brumfield Read.

  (e) Katherine Langhorne Pannill.

  (f) George Edmond Pannill, born 1896. Killed in action Chatteau-Thierry Soisson drive July 18, 1918. Company K, 9th Infantry, 2nd Division. They sleep in France.

  (g) Jeb Stuart Pannill, born 1897. Died August 4, 1918, as a result of wounds received in same battle in which his brother was killed. Company K, 9th Infantry, 2nd Division. Both were volunteers.

  (h) Mary Eliza Pannill.

  (i) America Hairston Pannill.

(7) Bethenia Ruth Pannill; married Martin T. Penn.

CHILDREN:

  (a) George Jackson Penn; married in 1922, Susie Lee.

  (b) Robert Edmond Penn, born 1880; died 1901.

(8) Harden Manson Pannill.

(9) Loulie Elizabeth Pannill.

(10) Sarah Ann Catharine Pannill, born 1863; married in 1898, Dr. Wm. T. Woodley, of Charlotte, North Carolina. He died in 1927.

———

William Callaway, Jr., born 1748, third son of Col. William Callaway and his first wife, Elizabeth Tilley, was prominent in the affairs of Bedford County, Va., where he lived and died. He was commissioned a Lieutenant Colonel, qualified and took the oaths in Revolutionary War (Court Order Book for March 23, 1778); vestryman; appointed surveyor of Bedford County and was commissioned a

Justice for Bedford Court and County, which office he held by re-appointment until his death, September 22, 1821. He married, 1772, Anne Booker Smith, born March, 1751; died November 2, 1834. (See Tombstones in Parrish burial ground between New London and the Academy.)

CHILDREN:

(1) Elizabeth, born May 18, 1773; married Samuel Read.
(2) Palinah, born October 26, 1774; died August 12, 1799.
(3) Matilda, born March 10, 1776; died October 6, 1805; married James Leftwich.
(4) John Smith, born December 8, 1777; died May 8, 1779.
(5) Permelia, born March 22, 1779; died January 15, 1803.
(6) William, III, born November 17, 1780; married Elizabeth Calland, of Pittsylvania County, Virginia, a very distinguished family. Her father was Col. Calland, supposed of Revolutionary fame. William Callaway, III, died November 27, 1813.

CHILDREN:

(a) William B.
(b) John, born about 1802; died 1863; married Lucinda Saunders, daughter of Col. David Saunders.

CHILDREN:

(aa) Robert W.; married Margaret Patton.
(bb) Elizabeth Calland, born about 1829; died 1861; married Dr. Granville L. Brown, born September 10, 1813; died 1876.

CHILD:

(aaa) John Callaway Brown, born April 7, 1859. (See forward.)
(cc) Lucinda ("Linda"), born about 1835; died about 1860; married James M. Harris, Esq.
(dd) Emma S.; married Richard Callaway.
(ee) Rosa Ella; married A. M. Doyle.

John Callaway Brown, born April 7, 1859, son of Dr. Granville L. Brown (born 1813) and Elizabeth (Calland) Callaway (born about

1829); married Fannie Otey Horsley, daughter of Edmund W. Horsley, who was born in Nelson County, Virginia, but lived the greater part of his life in Bedford County. (See Gwatkin family.)

CHILDREN:

(a) Granville Brown; died at the age of eighteen months.
(b) John Callaway Brown, Jr., born October 6, 1892; educated in the public schools of Bedford; Randolph-Macon Academy, 1908-1911; Hampden-Sydney College, 1911-1913; Washington and Lee University, 1913-1915; member Pi Kappa Alpha Fraternity; degree B. L., 1915.

Secretary-Treasurer Bedford County Fair Association since 1917; Member House of Delegates, 1918-1919; Chairman Municipal School Board, 1919-1924; Attorney for Town of Bedford, 1923-1926; Secretary-Treasurer of Bedford Chamber of Commerce since 1925; Mayor of Bedford since June, 1926.

President Kiwanis Club, 1927.

Trustee, Deacon, and Assistant Superintendent of Sunday School of Liberty Presbyterian Church.

Married, June 17, 1924, Margaret McKay McCutchen, daughter of Ernest E. McCutchen, of Augusta County and Rosalie McKay, of Warren County, Virginia.

CHILD:

(aa) John Callaway Brown, III, born June 2, 1928.

The foregoing will is of James Callaway, of Mercer County and State of Virginia, now West Virginia. This James Callaway is, probably, James, son of Charles and grandson of Col. William Callaway by his second wife, Elizabeth Crawford. The farm willed his son, Vinson, is, at present, owned by his great grandson, Robert H. Callaway, of Bluefield, West Virginia, son of James Preston Callaway. The aforementioned farm is located in the lower end of Monroe County and adjoins the Giles County, Virginia line.

The said Vinson Callaway was married three times: (first) to Miss Thompson; (second) ———; (third) Polly Pack—no children by this marriage. Among other children he had was James Preston Callaway, who married Elizabeth Harless. They had among other children, the above mentioned Robert H. Callaway, of Bluefield, West Virginia, and Henry Clay Callaway (Mayor of Bluefield, Virginia), who married Pearl Murray, of Botetourt County, Virginia, and have several sons.

WILL OF JAMES CALLAWAY

I, James Callaway, of Mercer County and State of Virginia do hereby make my last will and testament in manner and form following that is to say:

1st—I desire that all the perishable part of my estate be immediately sold after my decease, except such as I shall hereinafter name, and out of the money arising therefrom all my just debts and funeral expenses be paid also all the moneys coming to me by bonds, notes, deeds of trust or accounts be collected as they may become due and the moneys arising therefrom be applied to the payment of my just debts and the residue of any remain be disposed of by my executors hereinafter named in the manner hereinafter prescribed by me.

2ndly—I desire that the two hundred acres of land in the County of Monroe on the head waters of Dropping Lick along the foot of Peters Mountain adjoining the lands of John Miller & others be sold as my Exrs. may think best and the moneys applied as above mentioned.

3rdly—I give to my wife Margaret Callaway all the household and kitchen furniture, beds, bureaus, cupboards and all their containings but out of the above named property she is to give her daughter Lynn Olliver $52.00 worth of bedding and other things as she give Juley Crottey. (See my Day Book, page 31) also I give her one young mare called Pats, three cows as she may choose, ten head of sheep, one brood sow for her to keep during her natural life providing the debts can be paid out of the above named funds and should they fail rather than to take from her the above named property, I desire that the sawmill with about 700 acres should be rented out and the rents go to the payments of my debts and should the above funds and rents not pay as fast as the law may require I desire that the above named lands, say the tract & mill I bought of Joseph Summers and about 200 acres which I have sold to said Summers may be sold in three annual installments or as it may fetch the most and suit the payments of the debts best and I now will proceed to make a statement of what I have given to my heirs and what I now give and to whom I yet give to and what it is, to-wit:

1st.   I have given to my son Vinson Callaway in time past about one half of the old tract of land in Monroe County, Virginia, on Rich Creek or its waters joining the lands of John Fleshmons heirs and the lands of Jacob Pecks heirs and a deed is made to the same as also to about 15 acres which I sold him.   Also I have given him 1 mare, 3 cows, one bed and furniture and sundry other articles too tedious to mention which I find is as much as I am able to give and do what is right by other heirs.

2nd.   I have given to my son Granville Callaway in time past one young mare, 2 cows some sheep, one bed and furniture, one cupboard, one loom, one rifle gun sold to Carper, one saddle and sundry other things too tedious to mention and all old debts which I paid off in Monroe for him also all the land which he now lives on which was deeded to him sometime past by me and my wife which I find is as much as I find myself able to give and do what is right with my other heirs.

3rd.   I give to my three children hereinafter named all the tracts of lands which I now live on say 280 acres formerly belonging to Claud and Labon and all the big survey lands which I bought of Alex Mahood, Agent for McCullix & Co., up to the lines once run off to Sarah Jane Callaway, who was born Dec. 23rd, 1842, also Charles Wm. Callaway, who was born Nov. the 28th, 1844, also the James Mathew Callaway, who was born March 27th, 1847, who are all heirs and children of James Callaway and Margaret, his wife, subject to their Mothers dower her life also she is to have full control of the plantation until Sarah Jane may arrive at the age of 21 years then if found necessary it may be divided by the legal authorities and after my wifes dec'd, I give her thirds to the above named three children Sarah Jane, Charles Wm. Callaway and James Mathew Callaway, which I have given unto and their heirs forever.

5thly and lastly, I do hereby constitute and appoint my friends Alexander Mahood, R. B. McNutt and margaret Callaway, my wife, executors of this my last will and testament hereby revoking all other former wills or testaments by me heretofore made in witness whereunto I have set my hand and affixed my seal this 30th day of December 1853.

And it is further understood that I desire that Lynn Olliver still remain to live with her mother so long as she is willing to be governed by her mother and to have what her mother may think right out of what is made amongst them after the necessary expenses is paid off.

JAMES CALLAWAY [SEAL].

Signed, sealed, published and
delivered as and for the last
will and testament of the above
named James Callaway in presence
of us

ALEXANDER MAHOOD,
EDWIN GRANT,
JAMES (x) ROWLAND.
   (his mark)

Teste: R. B. McNUTT.

VIRGINIA: At a Court of quarterly sessions held for the County of Mercer at the Court House thereof on Wednesday the 13th day of June, 1855.

A proper writings purporting to be the last will and testament of James Callaway deceased, was presented in court proven by the oaths of James Rowland, Alexander Mahood and Robert B. McNutt, subscribing witnesses thereto and ordered to be recorded and on the motion of Margaret Callaway the Executrix and Robert B. McNutt, Executor in said will named, who made oath and together with Madison Karnes and William H. French, their securities entered into and acknowledged a bond in the penalty of $5,000 conditioned as the law directs leave is given them for obtaining probate of said will in due form.

A Copy Teste:

WM. T. HEPTINSTALL, *D. C.*

....

Colonel Richard Callaway, sixth son (or grandson) of the founder, was born in 1722; in Caroline County, Virginia. During the period, 1747-54, he patented lands in Brunswick and Lunenburg Counties and in Bedford County during 1762-70. An officer in the colonial army from the county in 1758, and appointed in 1761, one of the trustees of

New London. Sergeant, lieutenant and major of forces active in the French and Indian Wars. His first wife, whom he married in 1745, was Frances, daughter of Robert and Frances Walton. It has been said she was a daughter of George Walton, a landowner of Bedford County, Virginia. The Draper MSS. states she was a sister of Sherwood Walton, who, according to the register of St. Peters' Parish, New Kent (later Hanover) County, Va., was a son of Robert and Frances Walton. Frances (Walton) Callaway died in 1766, and the next year, 1767, Richard Callaway married Mrs. Elizabeth (Jones) Hoy, widow of John Hoy, of Buckingham County, Virginia. He was the father of fifteen (15) children, twelve by his first wife and three by his second wife.

Richard Callaway made several visits with Daniel Boone to Kentucky and moved his family there in 1775—about September 26th. In the affairs of the infant settlement, he became an efficient actor, his services being numerous and valuable. He assisted in the founding of Boonesborough, was one of the first burgesses to the general assembly of Virginia—justice of the peace and colonel of the county—member of the first legislature, which met at Boonesborough to organize the government of Transylvania—this legislature held its sittings under the shade of a large elm tree, near the walls of the fort—appointed on the commission for opening a road over Cumberland Mountain to Kentucky in 1779; and was placed in charge of the first ferry at Boonesborough. Callaway County, Kentucky, was named for him.

When his two daughters and Jemima Boone were captured by the Indians, July 14, 1776, he led a company which pursued the savages. There is a pretty little romance in connection with this incident, made mention of by Fenimore Cooper in "The Last of the Mohicans."

The following is quoted from Collins' *History of Kentucky*, Vol. II, rather than family tradition.

A KENTUCKY ROMANCE OF 1776

"Late in the afternoon of Sunday, July 14, 1776, Elizabeth Callaway and her sister Fanny, daughters of Col. Richard Callaway, and Jemima Boone, daughter of Col. Daniel Boone—the first named 16 and grown, the others 14 years old—were captured by Indians, while playing in a canoe in the Kentucky river, a short distance below the fort at Boonesborough. Though they screamed with fright, Elizabeth Callaway fought with her paddle, gashing an Indian's head to the bone. They were dragged from the canoe and hurried off, they knew not whither or to what fate. Colonels Boone and Callaway were absent at the time; but soon returned, and at the head of two parties, one on foot, the other on horseback, began the pursuit. With Boone on foot, were Samuel Henderson, Captain John Holder, and Flanders Callaway (the lovers of the three girls, in the order named, and who afterwards married them), Major Wm. B. Smith, Col. John Floyd, Bartlett Searcy, and Catlett Jones—who pressed forward in the direction the Indians had gone, but five miles before dark overtook them. By light, the next morning, and all day Monday, they pushed on rapidly, some 30 miles further, fearful the girls would grow weary of travelling and be put to death by the savages. The pursuers took fresh courage from every new sign of life in the carefully concealed, but as carefully followed trail—for Elizabeth broke twigs off bushes, and when her life was threatened, by upraised tomahawk, for this, tore small pieces of her dress and dropped along the way. She also impressed the print of her shoes, where the ground would allow it— having refused to exchange her shoes and put on moccasins, which the younger girls in their alarm, submitted to. The Indians compelled them to walk apart, as they did, in the thick cane, and to wade up or down the little branches of water, so as to hide their trail and deceive as to their number.

"On Tuesday morning, the whites renewed the chase; and after going about five miles, saw a gentle smoke curling in the air, over where the Indians had kindled a fire to cook some buffalo veal for breakfast. Says Col. Floyd, in a letter written the next Sunday:

*" 'Our study had been how to get the prisoners, without giving the Indians time to murder them after they discovered us. We saw each other nearly at the same time. Four of us fired and all of us rushed on them—by which they were prevented from carrying anything away except one shot gun without any ammunition. Col. Boone and myself had each a pretty fair shot, as they began to move off. I am well convinced I shot one thru the body. The one he shot dropped his gun; mine had none. The place was covered with thick cane; and being so much elated on recovering the poor little heart-broken girls, we were prevented from making any further search. We sent the Indians off almost naked; some without their moccasins, and none of them with so much as a knife or tomahawk. (Only one of them ever reached home: the others died from wounds or famine.) After the girls came to themselves sufficiently to speak, they told us there were five Indians—four Shawanese and one Cherokee; they spoke good English, and said they should go to the Shawanese towns. The war-club we got was like those I have seen of that nation; and several words of their language, which the girls retained, were known to be Shawanese.'

"Another circumstance attending the recapture is preserved. Elizabeth Callaway was dark complexioned, made more so by the fatigue and exposure. She was sitting by the root of a tree, with a red bandanna handkerchief around her, and with the heads of her sister and Jemima Boone reclining in her lap. One of the men mistaking her for one of the Indians, raised the butt of his gun, and was about bringing it down with all his muscular power upon her defenceless head—when his

---

*Letter to Col. Wm. Preston, July 21, 1776, also, letter of Dr. Matthew L. Dixon, son-in-law of said Elizabeth Callaway, afterwards Mrs. Sam'l Henderson, July, 1835. Also, depositions of Peter Scholl, nephew-in-law of Daniel Boone, April, 1818, and other depositions.

arm was arrested by one who recognized her. No harm was done; but the narrow escape from a most horrible death at the hands of a friend, produced a melancholy sensation never forgotten by the actors."

Like so many other daring spirits of the time, Col. Callaway was killed by the Indians. On March 8, 1780, while he and several companions were engaged about a mile above the settlement in the construction of his ferry boat, they were fired upon by a party of Shawnee Indians. Callaway was killed and scalped. His body was recovered two days later and buried within the old fort or stockade.

In 1777, Col. Charles Gwatkin, son-in-law of Col. Richard Callaway, raised a company of volunteers in the Revolution and was chosen captain. These men he took from Virginia through the Cumberland Gap and the Wilderness road into Kentucky, to defend the white settlers against the Indians carrying the British flag. George Rogers Clark met this company en route west and he reported them short of provisions. However, they reached their destination without undue hardship. Among the men in this company was Joseph Jackson, of Bedford County, a lifelong friend of Richard Callaway. This Jackson was captured by Indians at the Blue Licks in February, 1778, and was taken a prisoner to an Indian village in Ohio, where he remained for some years. While there he saw the Indians returning from an expedition. Among the scalps they waved in the air he recognized that of Richard Callaway, which he knew by the length and peculiar gray of the hair.

Colonel Callaway left a widow and children of both marriages, descendants of whom are in Virginia, Kentucky, Missouri, Alabama, Tennessee, Mississippi, and California.

CHILDREN OF COL. RICHARD CALLAWAY:

(1) Sarah, born May 7, 1746; married, September, 1761, Gabriel Penn, of Amherst County, Virginia, son of George and Ann (————) Penn. (See Penn family.)

(2) George, born January 12, 1748; married his first cousin Milly, daughter of Col. William Callaway. His will filed for probate January 25, 1773, in Bedford County Court, mentions wife, Milly and daughter, Betty Callaway.

(3) Lathaneath, born September 4, 1750. No record—evidently died in childhood.

(4) Mary, born in Bedford County, Virginia, 1752; died 1829; married, November 6, 1767, Col. Charles Gwatkin, born in Scotland, April 3, 1741; died in 1806. (See Gwatkin family.)

(5) Nancy, born 1754; died unmarried.

(6) Milly, born 1756. No record.

(7) Isham, born 1758. No record.

(8) Elizabeth ("Betsy"), born August 14, 1760; married, August 7, 1776, Samuel Henderson, younger brother of Col. Richard Henderson. (This was the first marriage in Kentucky and was performed in the fort at Boonesborough by Daniel Boone, a justice of the peace. Their first child, Fanny Henderson, was born in the fort, May 29, 1777—the first white child of parents married in Kentucky and the fifth white child born in the state.) She died October 14, 1815, near Winchester, Tennessee. There were ten (10) children.

(9) Caleb, born 1762. Executor of his father's will in Kentucky, in 1784.

(10) Frances, born June 16, 1763; first married Capt. John Holder. Her second husband was Col. John McGuire. She was the mother of nine children.

(11) Lydia, born October 14, 1764; married (first) Capt. Christophei Irvine; (second) General Richard Hickman, of Kentucky. Left issue.

(12) Theodosia, born August 8, 1766; married William Callaway, of Virginia.

(13) Keziah, born August 8, 1768; married Judge James French, of Kentucky. (See forward.)

(14) Richard, Jr., born June 14, 1771; married, in 1790, Margaret Wells. Died in Tennessee. Left issue.

(15) Col. John, born in Bedford County, Virginia, August 25, 1775; died in Henry County, Kentucky, July 31, 1825; married, May 12, 1796, Martha R. Booker. Left issue.

Hon. Richard French, for several years a judge in Kentucky, and one time member of Congress, was a grandson of Col. Richard Callaway.

Flanders Callaway, John Callaway, and Chesley Callaway were in the Revolutionary War at same place—Pioneer Soldiers, 1778 to 1781 of Kentucky, Collins' *History of Kentucky*. The above were nephews of Col. Richard Callaway and sons of James, and Sarah Callaway. (Spraker, *The Boone Family,* 516.)

The following is the will of Col. Richard Callaway, dated December 21, 1772, and found by Mr. Willard R. Jillson, recorded in Court of Appeals, Frankfort, Kentucky (Deed Book J, 9, 11). This was published for the first time in Vol. V. (October, 1927) of the *Missouri Historical Society Collections* in a sketch of "The Callaway Family," by Sarah Mercer Carpenter. This will was written when Col. Callaway was still a resident of Bedford County, Virginia. One of the witnesses and executors named, Charles Gwatkin, being his son-in-law.

WILL OF RICHARD CALLAWAY

In the name of God Amen, I Richard Callaway being low and weak but in perfect senses and memory and of Lawful mind of the morality of Life I do make this my last Will and Testament and first I give my soul to Almighty God who first Gave it to me and my body to the Earth to be Decently buried in a Christian like manner according to the discretion of my executors and as to my worldly goods I give and dispose of as follows. After all my just debts and funeral expenses are paid the remainder of my estate I dispose of as follows.

Imprimis I give and bequeath to my beloved Wife Elizabeth Callaway three negores named Jane, Doll and Sall to dispose of as she sees cause at her death. I also give her one feather bed and furniture such as would be suitable for her. Also one Roane mare saddle and bridle these only I give during her life or widowhood.

Item I give and bequeath to my daughter Sarah Penn one Crown and no more. I also give and bequeath to my son George Callaway one Crown and no more. I also give to my daughter Molly Gwatkin one Crown and no more. My desire is that when my son Caleb Callaway comes of age that this tract of Land whereon I now live may be equally divided between him and my son Richard Callaway—Caleb Callaway having the part whereon my mill stands and quarter at present, my son Richard Callaway to have the other part when he comes of age.

My desire is that my executors may collect and pay all my just debts and I further desire they may sell as much of my stock as they think proper only leaving enough for my wife and children that stays with her to subsist on. I further desire they sell all my Lands only the above mentioned Land that I am possessed with. I further desire that all my negores may be kept together and my executors will endeavour to raise as much cash as will purchase this Land here joining me of Dowsons (Dawsons) and give my children such education as they think will suit them and when they come of age all to be equally divided amongst them.

Lastly I appoint Simon Miller, John Callaway and Charles Gwatkin executors of this my last Will and Testament. In witness whereof I have set my hand and seal this 21st day of December in the Year of Our Lord 1772.

(Signed) RICHARD CALLAWAY.

Teste CHAS. GWATKIN,
      THOMAS BROWN,
         his
      JAMES x TAYLOR.
       mark

At a Supreme Court held for the District of Kentucky the 1st of March, 1784. This copy of the last Will and Testament of Richard Callaway deceased was produced in Court and ordered to be Recorded and on the motion of Caleb Callaway to be admitted to administration with the will annexed of said Deceased. Satisfactory proof was made to the Court that the Executors therein named had renounced their right of administration and Elizabeth Callaway, widow of said deceased having resigned her right of administration to the said Caleb Callaway. Thereupon administration is granted him he having executed and acknowledged Bond as the law directs.

Test JOHN MAY, *Clk.*

Some early marriages of the Callaway family found among the records of Bedford County, Virginia:

James Callaway and Sarah Tate, 24 November 1756.
John Callaway and Tabitha Tate, 6 March 1758.
Sarah Callaway and Gabriel Penn, 14th September 1761. (Daughter of Col. Richard Callaway.)
Elizabeth Callaway and Francis Thorp, 26 December 1762.
Mary Callaway and Charles Gwatkin, 6 November 1767. (Daughter of Col. Richard Callaway.)

Charles Callaway and Judith E. Pate, 14 December 1768.

Zachariah Callaway and Susanna Miller, daughter of Simon and Ann Miller, 12 December 1774.

Cana Callaway and Broune Price, 1774.

Elizabeth Callaway and Harry Innes, 1775.

Dudley Callaway and Polly Trent, daughter of Henry Trent, 12 December 1778.

Frances Callaway and James Steptoe, 1781.

Mary Callaway and Daniel Brown, 1781.

Mary Callaway and Jacob Anderson, 1781.

James Callaway and Susannah White, daughter of Stephen White, 12 February 1784.

Chesley Callaway and Christiana Galloway, daughter of John Galloway, 4 February 1785.

Elizabeth Callaway and John Patrick, 6 November 1787.

Some early marriages of the Callaway family among the records of Campbell County, Virginia:

James Callaway and Elizabeth Early, 22 September 1777.

Joel Callaway and Lucy Ashton, 1793.

Sarah Callaway and John Anderson, 1793.

James Callaway and Ellen Lewis, 1793.

Charles Callaway and Eliza Green, 1793.

Judith Callaway and William Shands, 1793.

Frances Callaway and John Monroe, November 1797. (Daughter of Joseph Callaway.)

Polly Callaway and Littleberry Epperson, 23 December 1807. (Daughter of Joseph Callaway.)

Nancy Callaway and Charles Gilchrist, 2 February 1808. (Daughter of Joseph Callaway.)

Margaret Callaway and Edmund Pate, 4 April 1820.

Susan Callaway and Joseph Epperson, 12 April 1824. (Daughter of Joseph Callaway.)

Sarah A. Callaway and John Hewit, 26 October 1826.

Doshia Callaway and William Butler, 13 December 1831.

Robert F. Callaway and Elizabeth Ann Whitton, 18 May 1836.

The following data on the Callaway family were kindly furnished by Mrs. A. E. Hart, of Los Angeles, California. She is a great-great-grand-daughter, of Col. Richard and Frances (Walton) Callaway.

There has been difference of opinion as to the name of the father of the seven Callaway brothers, some of whom were quite well known in Virginia history during the period from 1750 to 1800. One genealogist intimates they were sons of Francis Callaway. Others give William as their father, while in one instance they are named as sons of "Sir" William Callaway. After much study I have accepted the statement to be found in the Draper MSS, that they were sons of Joseph Callaway, Jr., and grandsons of Joseph Callaway, Sr., the immigrant from England to Virginia in the seventeenth century.

The year of birth of Richard Callaway, one of these seven brothers, has been variously given as 1717, 1720, 1722 and 1724, with an "about" cautiously placed in front of each year named. The old Anderson family Bible gives 1712 as the year of birth of his eldest brother, Thomas, but we may regard that date, placed in the Bible by a descendant of William (brother of Thomas and Richard) as less authentic than the date in 1700 given by a descendant of Thomas as marking the year of his birth. This same descendant, Elijah Callaway, placed about 1717 for the birth of Richard Callaway. There is no doubt as to the date of death of Richard. That is definitely fixed in history. He was killed by Indians at Boonesborough, Ky., March 8, 1780.

Born in Caroline County, Va., Richard Callaway lived on a farm there in boyhood. He was still quite young when his parents and his brother, Joseph, died of a fever within six weeks of one another. (See Draper MSS.) The family continued thereafter at the home farm until all the children were grown and some of them married, when, in order to have more land for their use, they sold out and moved to the then, undeveloped regions of Bedford County, Va. It is said that the brothers planted the first crop of corn ever raised in that county, and later Richard was to plant one of the very first crops of corn ever raised in Kentucky.

The family of which Richard Callaway was a member comprised of nine children (see Draper MSS.) namely:

(1) Thomas Callaway, born October 12, 1700 (Draper MSS., 5DD20), and died at his farm, Walnut Grove, Ashe County, N. C., in February, 1800, aged almost 100 years. He was a captain in the French and Indian Wars, and volunteered in the Revolutionary War, but on account of his age was honorably discharged without field service.

(2) Joseph Callaway (Third), who died of a fever in early life.

(3) William Callaway, probably the most successful of all the brothers. In 1754 was appointed the first county lieutenant in Bedford County, Va.; was a justice of the first court of that county, serving until 1775. Was a captain in French and Indian Wars (see Dinwiddie Papers, Vol. 2, page 109). Was a member of the House of Burgesses of Virginia most of the time from 1754 to 1765. In 1761, he made a free gift of 100 acres to Bedford County, to be settled into a town called New London. He died in 1777.

(4) Francis Callaway, commissioned sheriff of Bedford County, Va., by King George the Third, and was serving in that office at the opening of the Revolutionary War.

(5) John Callaway, lived and died in Bedford County, Va. (See Draper MSS., 15CC84.)

(6) Nancy Callaway. No record.

(7) Sarah Callaway. No record.

(8) Richard Callaway, born in Caroline County, Va., "about" 1717, and killed by Indians at Boonesborough, Ky., March 8, 1780. Married twice. Twelve children by first wife, Frances Walton, and three children by second wife, Mrs. Elizabeth (Jones) Hoy. Had more than eighty grandchildren.

(9) James Callaway, died intestate in Bedford County, Va., in 1773. (See Will Book A, 191-197, Bedford County.) In September, 1773, an account of his estate was filed with the court by the administrator, and in this inventory the name of the widow, Sarah Callaway, was mentioned. His children included:

(a) Flanders (1754-1828), married Jemima Boone.

(b) James, Jr. (1756-1835), captured by Indians and British during Revolutionary War.

(c) Micajah (1758-1849), also captured during the Revolutionary War. Applied for pension in 1832, giving his age as about 74 years.

(d) Chesley (1759-1846), a pensioner of the Revolutionary War (see Draper Notes of 1868, 23S142).

(e) Edmund (1764-1818), an officer in the War of 1812, also said to have served, as a mere boy, in the Revolutionary War, and to have been at the siege of Boonesborough, Ky.

....

Richard Callaway, a captain in the French and Indian Wars, and a colonel of militia in the Revolutionary War, was twice married. First, in 1745, to Frances Walton, sister of Sherwood Walton (a prominent surveyor and landowner) and daughter of Robert and Frances Walton. The Draper MSS. states she was a sister of Sherwood Walton, who, according to the register of St. Peter's Parish, New Kent (later Hanover) County, Va., was a son of Robert and Frances Walton. Frances Walton Callaway died in 1766, shortly after the birth of her youngest child. The next year, 1767, Richard Callaway married Mrs. Elizabeth (Jones) Hoy, widow of John Hoy, of Buckingham County, Va.

The following data concerning the children of Richard Callaway comes in part from my own studies; in part from the "Richard Callaway" Family Bible, now in possession of a descendant of his youngest son, Col. John Callaway; and in part from the researches of a capable Callaway genealogist and descendant, Mr. James H. French, of Winchester, Ky.

(1) Sarah, born May 7, 1746; married Capt. Gabriel Penn (born in Virginia, July 17, 1741); will recorded in Virginia, July 16, 1798. He mentions ten children in this will (which was dated November 21, 1794)—James, Elizabeth (Betsy), Sophia, Pamelia, Matilda, Fannie, Nancy, Edmund, Sarah, and Catherine.

(2) George, born January 12, 1748; will filed for probate in Bedford County, Va., January 25, 1773, mentions wife, Milly, and daughter, "Betty." This daughter appears later in Kentucky records as Elizabeth (Eliza), wife of John Patrick.

(3) Lathaneath, born September 4, 1750. No record. Is not mentioned in his father's will. Evidently died in infancy or childhood.

(4) Mary, born in Bedford County, Va., 1752, died there 1829. Married, November 6, 1767, Col. Charles Gwatkin, born in Scotland, April 3, 1741. In 1777 he led a company of men to Boonesborough, Ky., for service against the Indians. He was made their captain.

During the latter part of the Revolutionary War, Charles Gwatkin was colonel of militia of Bedford County. He died 1806. His widow survived him for twenty-three years. They were the parents of seven daughters and three sons:

(a) Margaret; married Waddy Cobbs, May 11, 1788.
(b) Frances; married Simeon M. Noell, November 19, 1801.
(c) Catherine; married Thomas G. Logwood, Jr., February 16, 1802.
(d) James; married (first) Mary Thorpe, November 6, 1802; and (second) Parmelia Otey.
(e) Lucinda; married James Campbell, February 10, 1808.
(f) Mary C.; married Micajah Davis, Jr., October 6, 1810.
(g) Elizabeth; married Jeffrey Cobbs, September 13, 1811.
(h) Nancy H.; married Charles L. Mitchell, February 13, 1812.
(i) Edward; married Mary A. J. Otey, March 22, 1813.
(j) Charles, Jr.; married Catharine Clayton.

(5) Nancy, born 1754; died unmarried, in Virginia, after September, 1806.

(6) Milly, born 1756. No record. Must have died in early life.

(7) Isham, born 1758. No record. Must have died in infancy or early life, as he is not mentioned in the will of his father, dated December, 1772.

(8) Elizabeth, born August 14, 1760; married Samuel Henderson. She died October 14, 1815, near Winchester, Tenn. Ten children.

(9) Caleb, born 1762. Records show that he and his wife were living in Bedford County, Va., in 1790, although some years prior to that he had been in Kentucky, as executor of his father's will. A letter written by him indicates that he was living in Logan County, Ky., in 1811. I have never been able to secure any information as to his descendants, indeed I do not know if he has descendants.

(10) Frances, born June 16, 1763, died in the early summer of 1803. There was no family Bible and her grave is unmarked. She married (first) Capt. John Holder, who died in the winter of 1797-98. Her second husband was Col. John McGuire, who survived her. She was the mother of nine children, namely:

(a) Theodosia, born 1782; married Capt. Samuel Richardson Combs, a soldier in the War of 1812, and a brother of Gen. Leslie Combs.
(b) Sophia, born 1784, died 1806 unmarried.

(c) John W. Holder, born latter part of 1785 or early in 1786; married his first cousin, Catherine Penn, and settled on a plantation in Franklin County, Tenn., where he died 1842.

(d) Caleb Holder, born 1788; married, but died childless in Georgia.

(e) Richard Callaway Holder, born 1790; married Harriet Dunbar Holder, widow of his brother, Caleb. He was a captain in the War of 1812, as was also his brother Caleb. His only son, William Dunbar Holder, was a member of Congress, C. S. A., and afterward for many years was a state officer in Mississippi.

(f) Lydia, born 1792; married Thomas G. Jones, and they had three children, one of whom, Caleb Holder Jones, a lawyer by profession, died November 4, 1847, at Pueblo, Mexico, while serving in the Mexican War. One of his sons, Edgar, became a leading banker in Nashville, Tenn.

(g) Frances W., born 1795; married Edward McGuire, a son of her step-father, and a soldier in the War of 1812. Edward McGuire died at Cape Girardeau, Mo., and his widow died at Aberdeen, Miss., when advanced in years.

(h) Catherine born in April, 1797, was less than a year old when her father died, and was nine when her mother passed away, December 12, 1812; she married Richard Gott Williams at Richmond Ky. (See forward.)

(i) Elizabeth McGuire was the only child of the second marriage of Frances Callaway Holder. After her mother's death, Elizabeth, then an infant, was taken to Tennessee by her father, Col. John McQuire, and settled in Franklin County. Both Capt. Holder and Col. McGuire were well known Indian fighters and both were with George Rogers Clark at Vincennes.

(11) Lydia, born October 14, 1764; married (first) Capt. Christopher Irvine, and (second) Gen. Richard Hickman, Lieutenant-Governor of Kentucky and in the War of 1812 its acting governor during the absence of Governor Shelby at the front. Eight children.

(12) Theodosia, born August 8, 1766; married William Callaway, of Virginia, whom she survived. Four children.

(13) Keziah, born August 8, 1768; married Judge James French, on Friday, June 27, 1783, at 3 o'clock, at Boonesborough, Ky. Eight children. Keziah was the eldest child of the second marriage of Richard Callaway, and was exactly two years younger than her half-sister, Theodosia.

(14) Richard, Jr., born June 14, 1771; married Margaret Wells in 1790. Died in Franklin County, Tenn., in the winter of 1849-50. Eleven children. From 1800 to 1804 he served from Madison County in the lower house of the Kentucky Legislature. In the War of 1812 he was captain and commanded a company of mounted riflemen at the battle of the Thames.

(15) Col. John, youngest of the fifteen children of Richard Callaway, was born in Bedford County, Va., August 25, 1775, and died in Henry County, Ky., July 31, 1825. Married Martha R. Booker, May 12, 1796. Ten children.

Many of his descendants still live in Henry County, honored and influential. In childhood he was captured by Indians, August 10, 1782, and exchanged about three years later. He was one of the most famous colonels at the Battle of the Thames, October 5, 1813, where his command of the 8th Regiment in the Volunteer Detachment from the militia of Kentucky made his name illustrious.

....

Catherine Holder, born April, 1797, daughter of Captain John Holder and Frances (Callaway) Holder and grand-daughter of Richard and Frances (Walton) Callaway; married, at the age of fifteen years, Richard Gott Williams, a descendant of David Williams, immigrant to Maryland, 1663; also a descendant of Richard Gott, who left London for Maryland in April of 1650, his father, Thomas Gott, having preceded him from England in 1642 as a member of the Richard Bennett expedition to Virginia.

There were thirteen children in the family of Richard Gott Williams (1786-1876) and his wife, Catherine (Holder) Williams (1797-1884), namely:

(1) John Holder, M. D., born 1813, died 1853 of yellow fever, contracted when caring for patients during an epidemic of that dread disease. He had served with distinction in the Mississippi state senate. Left two daughters.

(2) Frances Holder, born October 1, 1815; and married, November 15, 1834, to Charles K. Venable Martin, M. D., of Nashville, Tenn., who died young. A daughter of Mrs. Martin, Mary Catherine Casey, wife of an educator in New York City (compiler of the index of *Hening's Statutes*, etc.), was a charter member of the Daughters of the Revolution, and an early member of the Daughters of the American Revolution, being for almost twenty years registrar-general in the former.

(3) Eliza, Mrs. Matlock, 1817-1833, died childless.

(4) Jesse Caleb, born August 22, 1819, died December 5, 1917, survived by three of his seven children, namely: Judge O. W. Williams of Fort Stockton, Texas; Miss Susan Williams, of Alpine, Texas; and Mrs. A. E. Hart, of Los Angeles (compiler of the Hart Family History, also the Richard Callaway Family History, the History of Cabrillo Chapter, D. A. R., etc.).

(5) Sophia, Mrs. William Wilson, born 1823; married, 1838, and was the mother of twelve children.

(6) Rachel Amelia, 1823-24.

(7) Mary Catherine, born 1825; married M. Williamson Boulware and had one son, Richard William Boulware.

(8) Jacob John, born December, 1828, and died August 26, 1900. Had five daughters and one son.

(9) Oscar Waldo Williams, 1831-1850. Died in California unmarried.

(10) Susan Maria Virginia, Mrs. James Wilson, born March 1, 1833, and died in Monett, Mo., August 3, 1906. Survived by two sons.

(11) William H., born March 18, 1835, and died at Aztec, N. M., 1927, being the last of the thirteen children to pass from earth. One son and three daughters.

(12) David Napoleon, born April 27, 1838, and died April 4, 1910. Survived by four sons and one daughter.

(13) Harriet Louise, born 1841, twice married. No children.

The following data were submitted by J. H. French, of Winchester, Kentucky, a descendant of Judge James French and Keziah Callaway, daughter of Col. Richard and Elizabeth (Jones) Callaway.

Keziah Callaway, born 1769; married, June 27, 1783, in the Fort at Boonesborough, James French, born November 5, 1756, Prince William County, Virginia, son of William and Winifred French who were born in North Ireland. William French was the son of James French who emigrated from Ireland to America and was a planter in Stafford County, Virginia. James French attended William and Mary College where he qualified as a surveyor and later joined the Continental Army. Was at Valley Forge and served until the Revolution was over.

On April 10, 1781, he was appointed deputy surveyor of Mongolia County, Va. (now W. Va.) under John Madison, later went to Kentucky and December 10, 1782, was appointed deputy surveyor of Fayette County. Locating later at Boonesborough was appointed on March 24, 1783, surveyor of Madison County by Gov. Isaac Shelby, Kentucky's first governor. In 1802 he moved to Montgomery County, Ky., and was appointed Associate Circuit Judge. He held other offices and was for thirty years Clerk of the North District Baptist Association.

CHILDREN:

(1) William, captain in War of 1812.

(2) Richard, member of Kentucky Legislature, Circuit Judge, thrice Congressman, Presidential Elector, etc. etc.

(3) Stephen, who died young; unmarried—was a lawyer.

(4) Katherine; married Isaac Farrow.

(5) Susan; married Judge Kenaz Farrow.

(6) Olivia; married (first) Walter Cluke, (second) Wm. Prewitt Smith.

(7) Theodosia; married Dr. John W. Hood.

(8) Keziah; married James Prewitt.

Hon. Richard French (above) married Mary Tutt Taliaferro, daughter of Hoy Taliaferro, of Virginia. Their children were: Judge James French who died unmarried; Judge Charles Stephen French, married Margaret Hockaday Moore; Rev. Richard French (my father) who married Mary Taylor Parrish; Joseph William French who died young; Mary Elizabeth who married William Timberlake; and Ann Callaway who married John B. Bright.

BOONE

George Boone, the grandfather of our Daniel, was born in 1666 at the little hamlet of Stoak, near the city of Exeter, in Devonshire, England. His father had been a blacksmith; but he, himself, acquired the weavers' art. He (George) married Mary Maugridge of the village of Bradninch, and they became the parents of nine (9) children—George, Sarah, who married Jacob Stover, Squire, of whom further, Mary, John, Joseph, Benjamin, James and Samuel. All of these, except John, married and left descendants.

The elder Boone, professed Quaker, ambitious for the welfare of his children and chafing under the bitter intolerance encountered by the Quakers in England, determined to move his family to America. Having become interested in the colony previously established by William Penn, family tradition says he sent his three oldest children over on a tour of inspection. At the end of several months, leaving Sarah and Squire in Pennsylvania, George returned for his parents—on the 17th of August, 1717, the Boones, parents and children, set sail for their new home. They arrived safely in Philadelphia on the 10th of October, and settled in what is now Abingdon, twelve or fourteen miles north of the town. In 1718, the elder George took out a warrant for 400 acres in Oley township, and near the end of the year, moved to this neighborhood where his daughter, Sarah, who had married Jacob Stover, a German, had previously settled. Here George Boone died in 1744 at the age of 78. ....

Squire Boone, born November 25, 1696, third child of George and Mary (Maugridge) Boone; married, July 23, 1720, Sarah Morgan, daughter of John Morgan, a Welsh Quaker. Historians tell us that Squire Boone was a man of rather small stature, fair complexion, red hair, and gray eyes—his wife, a woman something over the common size, strong and active, with black hair and eyes.

Squire Boone learned weaving, his father's trade. He purchased in 1730, a grant of 250 acres in Oley township in the valley of the Schuylkill, and it was here that our Daniel Boone, the sixth child, first saw the light of day, November 2, 1734. Children of Squire and Sarah (Morgan) Boone were: Sarah, born 1724; Israel, born 1726; Samuel, born 1728; Jonathan, born 1730; Elizabeth, born 1732; Daniel, born 1734, of whom further; Mary, born 1736; George, born 1739; Edward, born 1744, killed by the Indians in October, 1780; Squire and Hannah, all natives of Oley.

In 1750, after selling their lands and surplus stock, Squire and Sarah Boone of Oley took up their travel southward until they reached the Yadkin Valley in North Carolina—here they chose a claim at Buffalo Lick, where Duchman's Creek joins with the North Fork of the Yadkin. The land here was very fertile, but sparsely settled—always the danger of Indian raids. Squire Boone, in this new home, was farmer, weaver, blacksmith, and justice of the peace for Rowan County. ....

Daniel Boone, fourth son and sixth child of Squire and Sarah (Morgan) Boone, was born November 2, 1734. He had no regular schooling; but in the ways of nature he was well versed—a hunter and herdsman as well as a worker in iron. Since his boyhood in Pennsylvania he had been a woodsman and had known the menace of marauding Indians. His young manhood had been spent on the banks of the Yadkin in North Carolina. Here he married Rebecca, the daughter of Joseph Bryan.

Their children were: James, born 1757; Isarel, born 1759; Susannah, born 1760; Jemima, born 1762, married Flanders Callaway, nephew of Col. Richard Callaway (see Callaway family); Lavina, born 1766; Rebecca, born 1768; Daniel Morgan, born 1769; John B., born 1773; and Nathan, born 1780. The two eldest sons were killed by the Indians, the three younger emigrated to Missouri and the four daughters all married and died in Kentucky.

Daniel Boone was neither the first explorer nor the first settler of Kentucky. Although John Harrod founded Kentucky's oldest settlement, his fame has been eclipsed by that of Boone, who led a small band through Cumberland Gap five years before Harrodsburg was settled. While it was in the summer of 1769 that Boone and his five hunters first viewed the rich fields of Kentucky, it was not until April, 1775, after twice being attacked by Indians, that they began to erect a stockade at Boonesborough—about sixty yards from the Kentucky River. Soon thereafter he brought his family from the Clinch Valley. His wife, Rebecca, and his daughter, Jemima, were the first white women to set foot in Kentucky.

With thirty backwoodsmen he built, through the Cumberland Gap, the Wilderness Road, the perilous highway of colonial migration to the hunting ground of the Indians—the empire beyond the mountains. The many perils and hardships endured by these pioneer settlers of Kentucky is well known history.

Boone was to take an active part in the government of the new territory. As justice of the peace, he performed, early in August, 1776, the first marriage in Kentucky—that of Elizabeth or "Betsy" Callaway, daughter of Colonel Richard Callaway, to Samuel Henderson. He represented Fayette County in the State Legislature at Richmond.

Boone's later life did not reflect the prosperity and the progress for which he helped pave the way. He had been made a major of infantry, then a Lieutenant-General, and a thousand acres of Kentucky land had been given him in recognition of his services. Not knowing how to comply with legal formalities, he did not make his title good and soon lost his holdings.

In 1795, with wife and younger children, he moved to Missouri, then a Spanish possession, and lived until 1804 in the Femme Osage district, where 8,000 acres was given to him and he was made a commandant. When the United States bought this territory from Napoleon he was again dispossessed, this time of all but 850 acres.

Serene and unworldly to the last, he, who had seen so much of adventure and danger, died peacefully in bed, September 26, 1820, at Charette, Missouri, in the home of his son, Nathan, whose house is said to be the first stone house built in Missouri. He was in the 86th year of his age.

Historians tell us Boone was "a man of common stature, of great enterprise, strong intellect, amiable disposition, patient, daring, would neither inflict nor suffer any wrong, fertile in stratagems so that his enemies, the Indians, came to fear and love him."

Thwaite in his "Life of Boone," says: "His sterling integrity; his serene old age—all these have conspired to make for Daniel Boone a place in American history as one of the most lovable and picturesque of our popular heroes; indeed the typical backwoodsmen of the trans-Alleghany region."

BOLLING

Arms—Sable, an inescutcheon ermine
within an orle of eight
martlets, argent.

The above described arms as given by Burke in his Heraldry or General Armory are the same used by the Virginia Bollings.

The Bollings belonged to the English family of Bollings. Robert Bolling, Esq., in the reign of Edward IV possessed "Bolling Hall," near Bradford, in Yorkshire, where many previous generations of his ancestors had lived. Robert Bolling, son of John and Mary Bolling, of the Bollings of "Bolling Hall," who lived in the parish of All-halloway or All Hallows, Barkin Parish, Tower Street, London, the first of the name who settled in Virginia, was born in that city December 26, 1646; arrived in Virginia, October 2, 1660, at the age of fourteen years. Was justice of Charles City County before 1698; high sheriff, 1699; surveyor, 1702; Colonel and County Lieutenant, 1705-09. Married (first) in 1675, Jane Rolfe, the daughter of Lieut. Thomas Rolfe and his wife, Jane (Poythress) Rolfe, and grand-daughter of the Princess Pocahontas (wife of John Rolfe), whose father was Powhatan, the Indian Emperor. Jane (Rolfe) Bolling, wife of Robert died in 1678 and he married (second) in 1681, Anne Stith, daughter of Major Drury Stith, of Brunswick County. They lived at "Kippax" in Prince George County, where he died July 17, 1709.

CHILD BY FIRST MARRIAGE:

(1) John Bolling, born January 27, 1676. (See forward.)

CHILDREN BY SECOND MARRIAGE:

(2) Robert Bolling, born 1682; married Anne Cocke; died 1749.
(3) Stith Bolling.
(4) Edward Bolling.
(5) Ann Bolling.
(6) Drury Bolling.
(7) Thomas Bolling.
(8) Agnes Bolling.

John Bolling, of Cobbs, Chesterfield County, Virginia, son of Robert and Jane (Rolfe) Bolling; born 1676; died April 20, 1729; became a prominent citizen of Henrico, and represented that county in the House of Burgesses in 1714, 1723, and 1726. He married, December 29, 1697, Mary Kennon, daughter of Dr. Richard Kennon, of Conjuror's Neck, Virginia. He settled, lived and died at "Cobbs" on the Appomattox below Petersburg. Engaged in commerce.

CHILDREN:

(1) John, born January 20, 1700. (See forward.)
(2) Jane, born 1703; married Col. Richard Randolph (born at Turkey Island, 1695; died December 17, 1748) of "Curls Neck" on James River, Henrico County, Virginia, in 1720, and died 1766.

CHILDREN:

(a) Richard Randolph, Jr., born 1725; died June 6, 1786; M. H. B.; married, 1750, Anne Meade, born 1731; died December, 1814; daughter of David Meade, of Nansemond County, Virginia.

(b) Mary Randolph, born 1727; died 1781; married, May 31, 1744, Col. Archibald Cary, of Ampthill, Chesterfield County, Virginia, born 1721; died 1787. (Speaker of H. of B., member of Convention of 1766; Speaker State Senate.)

(c) Jane Randolph, born 1729; married, 1750, Col. Anthony Walke, of Princess Anne County, Virginia. M. H. B., son of Anthony and Anne Lee (Armistead) Walke. (One son Rev. Anthony Walke.)

(d) Brhet Randolph, born 1732; died 1759; married in England, Mary Scott, where they both lived and died.

(e) John Randolph, born 1737 at "Curls Neck," removed to Roanoke, Charlotte County, Virginia; married, 1769, Frances Bland, daughter of (Col.) Theodoric and Frances (Bolling) Bland, of "Cawsons," Prince George County, Virginia.

(f) Elizabeth Randolph; married Richard Kidder Meade, aide to General Washington.

(3) Elizabeth, born 1709; married Dr. William Gay.

CHILDREN:

(a) William Gay; married (first) Frances Trent; (second) Judith Scott.
(b) Elizabeth Gay; married Thomas Bolling.
(c) Mary Gay; married Neil Buchanan, of Ettrick Banks; M. Association, 1770.

(4) Mary, born 1711; married Col. John Fleming.

CHILDREN:

(a) Thomas Fleming, Captain in Col. William Byrd's 2nd Virginia Regiment, 1758, and Colonel of 9th Virginia Regiment in the Revolution. Married Miss Randolph. He was killed in the Battle of Princeton, January 12, 1777.
(b) William Fleming, born July 6, 1736; died 1824; M. H. B. from Cumberland County; married Elizabeth Champe, daughter of Col. John Champe, King George County, Virginia.
(c) John Fleming, Major in the Revolutionary Army; killed at the Battle of White Plains; never married.
(d) Charles Fleming, Captain of the 7th Virginia Regiment and Lieutenant-Colonel in the State line.
(e) Mary Fleming; married William Bernard.
(f) Caroline Fleming; married James Drane (or Deane).

(5) Martha, born 1713; married Thomas Eldridge.

CHILDREN:

(a) Jennie Eldridge, born circa 1740.
(b) Mary Eldridge, born 1741; married Thomas Branch.
(c) Judith Eldridge, born 1743; married James Ferguson.
(d) Martha Eldridge, born 1744; married John Harris, of England.

(6) Anne, born 1718; married James Murray.

CHILDREN:

(a) William Murray, born 1742; died 1815; married Rebecca Bolling.
(b) John Murray, born 1744; married Susan Gates.
(c) Anne Murray, born 1746; married Mr. Buchanan.

(d) Margaret or Peggy Murray, born 1748; married Thomas Gordon.

(e) Mary Murray, born 1750; married (first) Alexander Gordon; (second) Col. William Davies, son of Rev. Samuel Davies, President of Princeton College, 1759.

(f) James Murray, born 1755; married Martha Ward.

....

Major John Bolling, son of John and Mary (Kennon) Bolling, of Cobbs, born January 20, 1700; died September 6, 1757. He was county-lieutenant of Chesterfield, commander of the militia; justice of the peace and for thirty years member of the House of Burgesses. Between 1740-51 John Bolling entered 20,000 acres of land in the present counties of Amherst, Buckingham, Appomattox and Campbell for himself and his sons. He married twice; (first) Elizabeth Lewis, daughter of John Lewis, of Gloucester, a member of the Council. No children by this marriage. On August 24, 1728, he married (second), Elizabeth Blair, a daughter of Dr. Archibald Blair, also a member of the House of Burgesses. She died April 22, 1775.

CHILDREN:

(1) Thomas, born July 18, 1735; died August 7, 1804; J. P. of Chesterfield County; married his cousin, Elizabeth Gay, daughter of Dr. William Gay.

CHILDREN:

(a) Elizabeth, born 1760; married William Robertson, of the Robertsons of Strowan, Scotland. He was a member and Clerk of the Council of Virginia.

(b) Rebecca; married William Murray. .

(c) John, educated in Edinburgh, Scotland; deaf mute; died soon after his return to Virginia.

(d) Thomas, educated in Edinburgh, Scotland; died at Gaymont, Caroline County, aged 76 years; deaf mute; never married.

(e) Mary, educated in Edinburgh, Scotland; deaf mute; never married.

(f) William, born May 26, 1777; died July 16, 1845; married Mary Randolph, born July 5, 1775; died August, 1863, a daughter of Richard Randolph, Esq., of Curles.

(2) John, born June 1737. (See forward.)

(3) Robert (Colonel) of "Chillowe," born August 28, 1738; died 1773; member of House of Burgesses; married (first), June 5, 1763, Mary Burton, a daughter of William Burton. She died May 2, 1764. He married (second) Susan Watson.

CHILD BY FIRST MARRIAGE:

(a) Mary Burton, born April 30, 1764; died 1787; married, 1781, Robert Bolling; born 1759, of the Stith Bollings, of Petersburg, Va.

CHILDREN BY SECOND MARRIAGE:

(b) Pocahontas Rebecca; married, 1782, Col. Joseph Cabell.

(c) Elizabeth Blair; married Major Thomas West.

(d) Powhatan, born 1767; died 1802.

(e) Linnaeus, born 1773; died 1836; married Mary Markham.

(4) Archibald, died infant.

(5) Sarah, died infant.

(6) Anne, died infant.

(7) Mary, born July 28, 1744; married, 1761, Richard Bland, of Jordans.

CHILDREN:

(a) Richard Bland, born 1762; died 1806; married Susanna Poythress, daughter of Robert Poythress.

(b) Anne Bland, born 1765; married (first) John Morrison; married (second) Peter Woodlief.

(8) Sarah (2), born June 16, 1748; married John Tazewell, of Williamsburg. Judge of the General Court and Clerk of the Revolutionary Conventions of 1775 and 1776.

CHILDREN:

(a) Elizabeth Tazewell; married Dr. Samuel Griffen, member of Congress, 1789 to 1795.

(b) Littleton Tazewell; married Catherine Nevison, nee Boush.

(c) William Tazewell, M. D.; died 1840; married Mary Page Tanner.

(9) Archibald (2) of "Mount Athos," born March 20, 1749; married
(first), 1770, Sarah Cary, daughter of Col. Archibald Cary;
married (second), in February, 1774, Jane Randolph, a cousin
of John of Roanoke; married (third), 1797, the widow Byrd;
married (fourth), 1802, the widow Clark. Said to have had
thirteen children: seven sons and six daughters—among whom
were the following

CHILDREN:

(a) Sarah; married, 1792, Joseph Cabell Megginson, born
1771; died 1811; a member of the House of Delegates
and son of Captain William and Elizabeth Megginson
(daughter of Col. Joseph Cabell, of "Winton," Amherst
County, near the present town of Clifford).

(b) Anne Everard; married (first) Samuel Shepherd Duval;
married (second), 1804, Joseph Cabell, Jr., son of Col.
Jos. Cabell.

(c) Elizabeth Meade, born ————; died 1823, married,
1801, Archibald Robertson.

(d) Blair, born 1792; died ————; Captain of the State
Guard; married (first), 1824, M. A. Webster; married
(second), 1827, Penelope Storrs.

(10) Anne (2), born February 7, 1752; married William Dandridge,
Sr.

CHILDREN:

(a) John Dandridge; married Miss Underwood.
(b) William Dandridge, Jr.
(c) Nathaniel West Dandridge; married Martha H. Fontaine, a niece of Patrick Henry.
(d) Ann Dandridge; married Frederick James.
(e) Jane Butler Dandridge; married Rev. Jos. D. Logan.

John Bolling, of "Chestnut Grove," second son of Major John
and Elizabeth (Blair) Bolling, of Cobbs; born June 24, 1737; died
179—; married Martha Jefferson, a sister of Thomas Jefferson,
second President of the United States. There were eleven children by
this union of whom we have the following

CHILDREN:

(1) Martha; married Fielding Archer. There were ten children by
this union. Names given of six.

CHILDREN:

(a) Powhatan Archer; married ——— Walthall.
(b) Martha Archer; married (first) John Bolling; married (second) ——— Berry.
(c) Ellen Archer; married ——— Berry.
(d) Mary Archer; married Edward Covington.
(e) Lucy Archer; married ——— Archer.

(2) John; married Miss Kennon and said to have had five children.

CHILDREN:

(a) Evelina Bolling; married Alexander Garrett, Clerk of Albemarle County, Virginia.
(b) Susan Bolling; married John Scott.
(c) ———.
(d) ———.
(e) ———.

(3) Edward, born ———; died 1835; married Dorothea Dandridge Payne, born 1777. Had four sons of whom one: Powhatan Bolling married a Miss Payne.
(4) Archibald; married, November 5, 1801, Catherine Payne. (See forward.)
(5) Mary; married Edward Archer. A son, by this marriage, Peter Jefferson Archer, married (first) M. Michaux; (second) Lucy Gilliam.
(6) Robert; married Jane Payne. There were two children by this marriage.

Archibald Bolling, Sr., fourth child of John and Martha (Jefferson) Bolling; married, November 5, 1801, Catherine Payne, youngest daughter of Archer Payne, of Goochland County, Virginia. There were eight children by this union—six sons and two daughters—the following lived to be grown.

CHILDREN:

(1) (Dr.) Archibald; born ———; died 1860; married Anne E. Wigginton. (See forward.)
(2) Edward, born ———; died 1855; married Anne Crallé.

(3) Alexander, born ————; died 1878; married Susan Gray.
(4) Pocahontas R.; married (first) William G. White; married
      (second), October 10, 1867, Peter J. Hill, of Nelson County,
      Virginia.
(5) ————.
(6) ————.
(7) ————.
(8) ————.

Dr. Archibald Bolling, son of Archibald, Sr., and Catherine
(Payne) Bolling, born ————; married, May 15, 1835, Anne E.
Wigginton, daughter of Benjamin and Harriett B. (Scott) Wigginton,
of Campbell County, Virginia. Dr. Bolling lived on Cheese Creek
between Clay's Crossing and Boonesboro, Bedford County, Virginia,
and here he practiced his profession.

CHILDREN:
(1) John, died in infancy.
(2) William Holcombe, born May 29, 1837; married, September 18,
      1860, Sallie Spiers White, daughter of Col. William Allen and
      Lucy McD. (Reese) White, of Bedford County, Virginia.
      (See forward.)
(3) Harriett W., born ————; married, September 18, 1861, Rob-
      ert H. Waddell, of Attala County, Mississippi, and moved there.
(4) Mary Jefferson, born ————; married, March 31, 1864, Rudolph
      Tuesler, of Petersburg, Virginia—a leading medical missionary
      to Japan. Left issue.

Judge William Holcombe Bolling, born May 29, 1837, son of Dr.
Archibald and Anne E. (Wigginton) Bolling, of Bedford County, Vir-
ginia; married, September 18, 1860, Sallie Spiers White, born January
5, 1843, only daughter of Col. William Allen and Lucy McDaniel
(Reese) White, of Bedford County, Virginia. (See White family.)
[This was Col. White's second marriage, after his death the widow,
Lucy McDaniel (Reese) White, daughter of Joseph T. and Elizabeth
(Tinsley) Reese; married (second), October 23, 1848, Edmund Log-
wood, of Bedford County, Virginia. (See Logwood family.) By this

SALLIE SPIERS WHITE
wife of William Holcombe Bolling

JUDGE WILLIAM HOLCOMBE BOLLING

marriage there were two children. The son died young, and the daughter, Lizzie Logwood, married General James G. Field, of Gordonsville, Va., former attorney-general of Virginia. There were three sons by this marriage: Duncan, Gaven, and Richard.]

Judge William H. Bolling was educated in private schools and at the University of Virginia. He read law under Judge Brockenborough, of Virginia.

Having suffered from the impoverishment of the South, resulting from the Civil War, he started life with rather a poorer outlook, financially, than most his ancestors. However, he had a good mind; and, with the courage of his kind, he did not hesitate to face the world. Soon after the Civil War he removed his family to Wytheville, a little town set among the mountains of southwestern Virginia. Here he resumed the practice of his profession.

He was a lawyer of high standing at the Wytheville bar, and a man of most distinguished personality. For a number of years he was Judge of County Court of Wythe County, Virginia.

He was a member of the Phi Kappa Psi Fraternity. Judge Bolling died July 6, 1899, at Wytheville, Virginia, where he is buried.

His wife, Sallie (White) Bolling, a woman noted for her beauty, was an accomplished musician (piano and guitar), gifted with charm and culture, and a soprano voice of unusual sweetness. She was a splendid homemaker. Their home at Wytheville was the center of delightful hospitality. She died in Washington, D. C., November 21, 1925, and is buried in Wytheville, Virginia. Both she and her husband were members of the Episcopal Church.

CHILDREN:

(1) Rolfe Emerson, born in Bedford County, Virginia, August 22, 1861; married, June 18, 1890, Annie Stuart Litchfield, born in Abingdon, Virginia, February 19, 1869, daughter of George Victor Litchfield and Elizabeth Peirce. He was educated in the private schools of Wytheville and the Episcopal High School near Alexandria, Virginia. He is a banker in Washington, D. C., where he resides. He is a member of the Kappa Sigma Fraternity. Both members of Episcopal Church.

CHILD:

(a) Elizabeth, born in Abingdon, Virginia, December 2, 1891; married at Panama, R. P., August 18, 1915, Dr. Jorge E. Boyd, a graduate of University of Pennsylvania, and of international law of Columbia University, New York, and the University of Paris, France. A lawyer by profession and late Attorney - General of Panama, R. P.

CHILDREN:

(aa) Lola Elizabeth Boyd, born November 24, 1916.
(bb) Mildred Stuart Boyd (triplet), born August 23, 1921.
(cc) Edith Bolling Boyd (triplet), born August 23, 1921.
(dd) Elena Rolfe Boyd (triplet), born August 23, 1921.

(2) Gertrude, born in Bedford County, Virginia, May 16, 1863; married at Wytheville, Virginia, October 14, 1885, Alexander Hunter Galt, born Washington, D. C., December 5, 1860, son of Thomas Jefferson Galt and Mary Ann Hunter.

CHILD:

(a) Alexander Bolling Galt, born Washington, D. C.; July 21, 1890. Now living in Washington, D. C.

(3) Annie Lee, born in Bedford County, Virginia, June 15, 1865; married at Wytheville, Virginia, June 14, 1893, Matthew H. Maury, born in Mt. Sterling, Kentucky, June 9, 1860, son of Joseph Frye Maury and Elizabeth Graves. She died in Roanoke, Virginia, February 26, 1917.

CHILDREN:

(a) Anne Bolling Maury, born September 2, 1900; married John A. Goodloe, of Virginia. Now living at Chester, Virginia.

CHILDREN:

(aa) John A. Goodloe, Jr.
(bb) Anne Goodloe.

(cc) Matthew Maury Goodloe.

(dd) Elizabeth Goodloe.

(b) Lucy Logwood Maury, born April 19, 1903; married, February 23, 1929, John Edward Moeling, of Louisiana. Now living in Chicago, Ill.

(4) William Archibald, born in Wytheville, Virginia, October 11, 1867; married in Louisville, Kentucky, October 21, 1891, Mary Johnson Keller, born in Lexington, Kentucky, March 31, 1870, daughter of John Esten Cook Keller and Frances Weir Berry. After receiving his preparatory training in the private schools of Wytheville, he entered the University of Louisville, Kentucky, from which he was graduated, March 3, 1891, with the degree of Doctor of Medicine. Dr. Bolling is now living in Lexington, Kentucky, where he is a practicing physician and surgeon. He is a member of the American Medical Association, State and County Medical Societies, Ex-President Louisville Society of Medicine, etc.

His public and Military service include A. A. Surg. U. S. M. H. S., Secretary Draft Board U. S. A., Major Med. O. R. C. He is a member of the Episcopal Church.

CHILDREN:

(a) John Esten Bolling, born December 9, 1893; married, April 1, 1918, Edith Marion Bourne, of New York City.

(b) William Holcombe Bolling, born July 31, 1896; married, December 22, 1922, Virginia Gaither, of North Carolina.

(5) Bertha, born in Wytheville, Virginia, October 11, 1869. Unmarried. Living in Washington, D. C. Member of Episcopal Church.

(6) Charles Rodefer, born in Wytheville, Virginia, June 11, 1871; died June 11, 1871.

(7) Edith, born in Wytheville, Virginia, October 15, 1872; married (first), at Wytheville, April 30, 1896, Norman Galt (son of Matthew W. Galt and Mary Jane Galt), a prominent business man of Washington, D. C., where he was born April 30, 1866; died January 28, 1908, Washington, D. C. She married (sec-

ond), December 18, 1915, Woodrow Wilson, President of the United States, born in Staunton, Virginia, December 28, 1856; died in Washington, D. C., February 3, 1924, son of Joseph Ruggles Wilson and Janet (Woodrow) Wilson.

Edith Bolling was educated at Martha Washington College, Abingdon, Virginia, and John A. Powell's School in Richmond, Virginia.

She is a member of the Woman's National Democratic Club, Washington, D. C., and takes an active interest in public affairs. She is a member of the Episcopal Church. There are no children.

(8) John Randolph, born in Wytheville, Virginia, April 11, 1876. He was educated at home and in the local high school at Wytheville. Now living in Washington, D. C., and by occupation he is an Advertising Counsel. Unmarried.

(9) Richard Wilmer, born in Wytheville, Virginia, October 6, 1879; married in Washington, D. C., May 9, 1908, Eleanor Hunter Lutz, born in Washington, D. C., July 8, 1885, daughter of Francis Asbury Lutz and Eleanor Sweeting Galt. He received his education in the private schools of Wytheville. In 1920-21, Richard Wilmer Bolling was Treasurer of the U. S. Shipping Board; now engaged in the real estate business in Washington, D. C. He is an Episcopalian, and a member of the Chevy Chase and Racquet Clubs, Washington, D. C., and the Yorktown Virginia Country Club.

CHILDREN:

  (a) Clara L. Bolling.

  (b) Richard Wilmer Bolling, Jr.

  (c) Sterling Ruffin Bolling.

  (d) Barbara Bolling.

(10) Julian Brandon, born in Wytheville, Virginia, May 7, 1882; married in Bridgeport, Connecticut, June 19, 1906, Viola Roosevelt Belden, born Westport, Connecticut, September 10, 1882, daughter of William Harrison Belden and Elizabeth Roosevelt Jennings. He was educated in the public schools of

EDITH BOLLING
wife of (first) Norman Galt, (second) Woodrow Wilson

Virginia, and at Emerson Institute, Washington, D. C. Living in Washington, D. C. He is a member of the Episcopal Church. They have no children.

(11) Geraldine, born in Wytheville, Virginia, August 12, 1885, died July 6, 1887.

References for early data: Wyndham Robertson's *Pocahontas and Her Descendants; Virginia Historical Magazine.*

ROLFE

The Rolfe family was an ancient one in Heacham, Norfolk County, England. The parish register shows that Eustace Rolfe and Joanne Jener were married, May 27, 1560. They had a son, John, born October 17, 1562; married, September 24, 1582, Dorothea Mason, and died in 1594.

John and Dorothea (Mason) Rolfe had with other issue, (1) Eustace, and (2) John (twins), baptized May 6, 1585; (3) Edward, baptized February 22, 1591; (4) Henry, afterwards a merchant of London. One of the Rolfes of Heacham Hall was Sheriff of Norfolk about 1760. In 1837, S. C. E. Neville Rolfe, Esquire, who took the name and arms, succeeded to the property.

John Rolfe, son of John and Dorothea (Mason) Rolfe, is said to have been educated at an English University; married in England, and in May, 1609, sailed for Virginia. The ship in which he came over was wrecked on the Bermudas, and here his first child, Bermuda, was born. They reached Virginia in May, 1610, and he soon became a prominent member of the colony. His wife having died either at the Bermudas or soon after reaching Virginia, he next married, in April, 1614, Pocahontas, daughter of Powhatan. Two years after their marriage, in 1616, Rolfe and Pocahontas went to England where her beauty, her intelligence and her great personal charm gave her instant social success in aristocratic English circles. She died in England in 1616-17, leaving one child, a son named Thomas. John Rolfe left his infant son at Plymouth under the care of Sir Lewis Stukeley, but he was afterwards transferred to the care of his uncle, Henry Rolfe, of London, with whom he remained until manhood. In 1617, John Rolfe was appointed Secretary and Recorder General of the colony, and in 1619 was a member of the Council. He married for his third wife, Jane Pierce, daughter of Captain William Pierce, of Virginia, and had a daughter, Elizabeth, born 1620. He died March, 1622. Rolfe is spoken of by early writers as an honest and worthy gentleman.

Thomas Rolfe, his son, came to Virginia; in 1646 was a lieutenant; married Jane Poythress, the issue being one child, a daughter named Jane, born 1655.

Jane Rolfe married in 1675, Colonel Robert Bolling, the first of his name in Virginia, son of John and Mary Bolling of Barking Parish, Tower Street, London, and descended from the Bollings of "Bolling Hall," near Bradford in Yorkshire. He was born December 16, 1646; came to Virginia in 1660; settled at "Kippax" (or "Farmingdale"), Prince George County, Virginia, where he died July 17, 1709. Jane (Rolfe) Bolling died in 1678, leaving one child, a son named John, born January 27, 1676. This John Bolling married, December 29, 1697, Mary Kennon. (See Bolling family.)

References: *Pocahontas and Her Descendants,* by Wyndham Robertson; *Virginia Historical Magazine.*

POCAHONTAS

The Princess Pocahontas was the daughter of the Indian Chief Powhatan, the mighty Werowance (chief mystery man) and ruler of all of the Indian tribes of the Potomac region. The great Powhatan lives in the history of colonial times as the ablest and most noted of all the celebrated rulers of confederated Indian tribes. His personal demeanor, his customs and his court were, in fact, little short of regal. All these attributes Pocahontas inherited and adorned with her beauty and her fine personality.

Pocahontas, as her name is in history, and as she was known to the colonists, Matoaka reported to have been her family name, or Rebecca, as she was christened, was born about 1595; married in April, 1614, John Rolfe, first Secretary of the Colony of Virginia. She died at Gravesend, in England, in 1616-17, leaving one child, a son named Thomas. (See Rolfe sketch.) History does not offer, nor has fiction ever portrayed a lovelier character. She was without doubt the loveliest, tenderest, most intelligent, and greatest of all native American Indian princesses. She was her father's favorite daughter, the idol of her tribe, and the admiration of the English. She became the first link between the new continent and the old, and she left her personal history as the ideal romance of unselfish love.

WIGGINTON

Benjamin Wigginton married, December 22, 1806, Harriet B. Scott, of Campbell County, Virginia.

CHILDREN:

(1) Martha J.; married, May 5, 1829, Adolphus Gus Weir.
(2) Anne E.; married, May 15, 1835, Archibald Bolling.
(3) Catharine C.; married, April 11, 1844, Spottswood H. Cox.
(4) Francis M.; married, January 25, 1855, Clara H. Scott.
(5) Emma W.; married, October 25, 1852, William Terry.

The arms on the tomb of Dr. Thomas Clayton at "Warner Hall," Gloucester County, Virginia, are: A cross engrailed between four torteaux; crest: a leopard's gamb erased and erect, grasping a pellet, or torteau. From Mr. Stanards' carefully prepared pedigree, based on Le Neve, Wills at Somerset House &c., printed in Wallace's *Historical Magazine,* for October, 1891. (*William and Mary College Quarterly,* Vol. II, No. 4, April, 1894, page 236.)

Thomas Clayton, of Clayton Hall, County of Lancaster, England, married Agnes, daughter of John Thornell of County of York, England. Had children: (1) a son, died young. (2) William. (See forward.) (3) a son; left issue.

William Clayton, of County of York, England, second son of Thomas and Agnes (Thornell) Clayton, but heir to the family estate, married ————— Cholmeley. He died in 1627, leaving children: (1) John, of Okenshaw, barrister of the Inner Temple, 1660; married Elizabeth Citterne, of Kent. (2) Sir Jasper, of St. Edmunds, Lombard Street, London, mercer, alderman, &c., knighted at Guildhall, 1660; married, May 1, 1624, Mary, daughter of William Thompson, "late citizen and haberdasher," of London, of Tinmouth Castle, Northumberland. They had children as follows: (a) Sir John. (See forward.) (b) George, married Hester, daughter of Sr. Thomas Palmer, baronet. (c) Mary, (d) Prudence, (e) Rebecca.

Sir John Clayton of London and Parson's Green, Fulham, Middlesex County, son of Sir Jasper and Mary (Thompson) Clayton, knighted in 1664; married Alice Bowyer, daughter of Sir William Bowyer, baronet, of Denham, Bucks, England. Had children: (1) John. (See forward.) (2) Jasper, a Lieutenant-General in the English Army; killed at the battle of Dettingen in 1743. (3) Alice. (4) Mary. (5) Elizabeth. (One of these daughters married John Lord Lovelace, and one Thomas Strickland. See Tyler's *Virginia Biography.*)

John Clayton, son of Sir John and Alice (Bowyer) Clayton, was born in England in 1665, died in Virginia, November 18, 1737. He was educated, probably, at Cambridge University, admitted to the Inner Temple, June 6, 1682, and called to the bar. He came to Virginia in 1705, and in 1714, was appointed Attorney-General of the colony, holding this office until his death. He was judge of the Court of

Admiralty, frequently a member of the House of Burgesses, presiding justice of James City County, recorder of Williamsburg, &c. (*Virginia Historical Magazine,* Vol. 4, page 163). He married Anne Page (*The Abridged Compendium of American Genealogy, First Families of America,* Vol. 2, page 187). He had the following children: (1) John, the botanist. (See forward.) (2) Arthur, Clerk of a county on the upper part of York River; died in 1733—not known if he had children. (3) Dr. Thomas, educated at Cambridge, and completing his medical studies in London, he returned to Virginia, where he married Isabella Lewis, of "Warner Hall," Gloucester County, Virginia. Died October 17, 1739, aged 38. He had an only child, Juliana, who died in childhood. (4) James, who married Anne Dawson, sister of Thomas Dawson, President of William and Mary College, and had William Dawson Clayton (Bruton Parish Register). His wife surviving him married (secondly), about 1758, Rev. Goronwy Owen, Welsh poet and preacher. (*William and Mary College Quarterly,* No. 9, page 156.)

Dr. John Clayton, son of John Clayton, the Attorney-General, was born at Fulham, England, in 1685, came to Virginia in 1705, and died in Gloucester County, Virginia, December 15, 1773. He was an eminent botanist, and for fifty years Clerk of Gloucester County, Virginia. At the time of his death (1773), he was President of the Society in Virginia for Promoting Useful Knowledge, author of "Flora Virginica," and had at "Windsor," his estate in Gloucester, a large and highly prized botanical garden. He married, January 2, 1723, Elizabeth Whiting, of Gloucester County, daughter of Henry and Anne (Beverley) Whiting, the latter named a daughter of Col. Peter Beverley, member of the House of Burgesses from Gloucester, and his wife, Elizabeth, daughter of Major Robert Peyton, who emigrated from Norfolkshire, England (Tyler's *Virginia Biography*). Dr. John Clayton had (among children) the following sons and daughters:

——John Clayton (4); married Elizabeth Willis. (See forward.)

——Anne Clayton; married, January 15, 1767, her first cousin, Henry Landon Davies, who was the son of Nicholas Davies and his second wife, Catherine Whiting, daughter of Henry and Anne (Beverley) Whiting. (Nicholas Davies' first wife was Mrs. Judith Fleming Randolph, widow of Col. Thomas Randolph, of Tuckahoe. Nicholas Davies had no children by his first marriage). Henry Landon Davies married, September 11, 1788, for his second wife, a niece of his first wife. She was the widow Manson; but nee' Lucy Whiting Clayton, daughter of John Clayton and his wife, Elizabeth Willis. (The late Miss Ruth H. Early, of Lynchburg, Virginia, author of *Campbell Chronicles and Family Sketches,* was a great granddaughter of Henry Landon Davies, and his first wife, Anne Clayton, daughter of Dr. John Clayton, the Botanist. She kindly furnished data on the Clayton-Davies line for use here.) The deed in Bedford Court from H. L. Davies, February 4, 1797, conveying property to John Willis Clayton and Nicholas Clayton Davies for benefit of Mrs. Mary Clayton and her children (full names given) is herewith published. (See forward, court records.) The John Willis Clayton named was the brother-in-law of Henry Landon Davies, by his second marriage to Lucy Whiting (Clayton) Manson. It further proves that John Willis Clayton and his wife Mary ————, had a son, John Willis Clayton, Jr. This son married in 1797, Lucinda Douglas, daughter of George Douglas. (See Douglas family.)

Henry Landon Davies had nine children—seven being by his first wife, Anne Clayton and two by his second wife, Mrs. Lucy Whiting (Clayton) Manson.

CHILDREN:

(a) Nicholas Davies, born 1769; married Elizabeth, daughter of David Crawford.

(b) Arthur Landon Davies, born 1770; married Miss Pryor, of Gloucester of which county he was clerk.

(c) Catherine E. Davies, born 1772; married, 1793, Francis Thornton Merriwether (born 1768, died 1814), son of Nicholas Merriwether, who married Margaret ("Peggy") Douglas, daughter of Rev. William Douglas. (See Douglas Register.)

(d) Samuel Boyle Davies, born 1774; married, 1802, Elizabeth McCulloch.

(e) Editha Langdon Davies, born 1777; married Rev. Charles Clay.

(f) Henrianne Davies (sometimes written "Henry Ann"), born 1780; married, February 24, 1803, Dr. John Jordan Cabell, son of Col. John and Pauline (Jordan) Cabell,

and grandson of Dr. Wm. Cabell, the founder. and
Elizabeth (Burks) Cabell.

(g) Tamerlane Whiting Davies, born 1782; married Jane
Smith Payne, daughter of Philip and Elizabeth D.
Payne.

(h) Addison Davies, born 1789; married Mary, daughter
of Capt. Robert Coleman.

(i) Dr. Howell Davies, born 1795; married (first) Harriett
Godfrey, of Harrisburg, Pa.; (second) Mrs. Abby
Willing (Byrd) Jackson.

——Elizabeth Clayton; married (first) in 1771, Orlando Jones, (second) William Walker; no children. (See forward suit
"Walker's Administrator vs. Jones' Administrator." Chalkley's
Abstracts and Records of Augusta County, Vol. II, pages 180-181).

——William Clayton; married Elvira ————, and resided in New
Kent County. He was administrator of his brother, Captain
Jasper Clayton (*William and Mary College Quarterly*, Vol.
XII, page 26). Clerk of New Kent County, member of the
New Kent County Committee in 1774, member of the House
of Delegates in 1776, and a member of the Convention of
1776. Later County Lieutenant of New Kent County. His
will dated June 10, 1797, was probated in New Kent County,
December 14, 1797 (Crozier—*Williamsburg Wills*). (See
forward for will.)

CHILDREN:

(a) William Beverley Clayton, Clerk of Charles City
County, Virginia; married Lockey Walker. They had
three daughters: (aa) Catherine; (bb) Elizabeth, married Bartholomew Dandridge, Clerk of New Kent
County; (cc) Mary A., married Robert C. Walker, son
of Wyatt Walker and Elizabeth (Christian) Walker
(*William and Mary Quarterly*, Vol. XVI, page 139,
and Hayden's *Virginia Genealogies*).

(b) Mary Anne Clayton; married Philip Davis who died
about 1800. She died in 1809 (Crozier, *Williamsburg
Wills*). See forward for will of Mary Anne Clayton
Davis.) They had three daughters: (aa) Rebecca

Davis; (bb) Catherine (Davis) Gwatkin; (cc) Mary Anne Davis.

(c) Elvira Clayton, born December 27, 1760; married Armistead Russell. Had one daughter, Elizabeth Armistead Russell.

——Jasper Clayton, deputy clerk of Gloucester County in 1778 (Tyler's *Quarterly*, Vol. V, page 58); died 1779. He had children: (a) Jasper Clayton; (b) Thomas Whiting Clayton; and (c) Catherine Clayton, who married Christopher Pryor, of Gloucester County (*Virginia Magazine*, Vol. II, page 188, and Tyler's *Quarterly*, Vol. VIII, page 140). Thomas Whiting Clayton was a lieutenant in the Revolution.

——Sarah Clayton; married (first) ——— Livingston; (second) Henry Hughes. Had children: (a) Thomas Hughes; (b) Henry Hughes; and (d) Susanna Hughes (Chalkley's *Abstracts and Records of Augusta County*, Vol. II, page 181).

....

John Clayton (4), born about 1725, son of Dr. John and Elizabeth (Whiting) Clayton, married Elizabeth Willis (Tyler's *Virginia Biography*). He served in the Revolutionary War. He was second lieutenant in First Virginia Regiment, October 7, 1775, first lieutenant in the First Virginia Regiment, February, 1776. (Tyler's *Virginia Biography;* Heitman's *Register of Continental Officers.*) John Clayton and Elizabeth Willis, his wife, lived in Charlotte County, Virginia. (See forward—Records from Charlotte County, by W. S. Morton.) They had nine children as follows:

——John Willis Clayton. (See forward.)
——Lucy Whiting Clayton, married (first) Nathaniel Manson, Sr., (second), September 11, 1788, Henry Landon Davies. (His second wife.)
——Henry Clayton.
——Mildred Clayton, married 1775, James Overton. (See Charlotte County Records.)
——William Willis Clayton, moved to Mississippi. His son a judge at Holly Springs. (Miss Early.)
——Elizabeth Clayton.
——Ann Clayton.

——Thomas Lewis Clayton, moved to Kentucky. (Miss Early.)
——Arthur Clayton.

(Miss Ruth Early in her notes states: one daughter married ——— Hays, one married ——— Harvey and a third married ——— North, who had a descendant named Clayton North.)

John Willis Clayton, born about 1750, son of John and Elizabeth (Willis) Clayton, married Mary ———. At the time of his purchase of land in Charlotte County, Virginia, John and his wife, Mary Clayton, were living in Hanover County. (See records of Charlotte County, D. B. 3, pages 451 and 500.) He removed to Charlotte prior to July, 1775. At what date he removed from Charlotte County, am unable to say. In 1793 and 1797, he was a resident of Bedford County, Virginia. (See forward memo. of agreement D. B. "G," page 243, Amherst County, Virginia—Indenture: D. B. "J," page 309, Bedford County, Virginia.) There were nine children as named in deed in Bedford Court from H. L. Davies, February 4, 1797, conveying property to John Willis Clayton and Nicholas Clayton Davies for benefit of Mrs. Mary Clayton and her children. (See forward copy of this Indenture.) Children named are as follows:

——John Willis Clayton, Jr., born about 1774, married, March 21, 1797, Lucinda Douglas, of Bedford County, Virginia. (See forward.)
——Nancy Clayton.
——Jasper Clayton; married 1801, Frances Lesueur.
——Thomas Clayton; married 1803, Theodocia Wright.
——William W. Clayton; married 1800, Clarissa Hales.
——Polly Harrison Clayton.
——Catherine Clayton; married Charles Gwatkin.
——Susanna Pettus Clayton; married, in 1807, John C. Leuseur.
——Rebecca Dabney Clayton.

John Willis Clayton, Jr., born about 1774, son of John Willis Clayton, Sr., and Mary (———) Clayton, his wife, married, March 21, 1797, Lucinda Douglas (marriage bond in Bedford County, Virginia), daughter of George and Mary (Tucker) Douglas, of Bedford County, Virginia, formerly of Amherst County. (See Douglas family.) In 1800, John Willis Clayton, Jr., leased land in Amherst County.

[See forward: Indenture made between Nicholas Clayton Davies and John Willis Clayton in which John Willis Clayton's mother, Mary Clayton, is named. (Deed Book "I," page 103, Amherst County, Virginia.)] The date of the death of John Willis Clayton, Jr., is not definitely known. It was, probably, prior to 1814 since in that year, his wife, Lucinda, signed the permission for the marriage of her eldest daughter, Elvira to Philip Turpin. In 1832, the widow, Lucinda (Douglas) Clayton, married (secondly) Jesse Spinner. She was his third wife. (See Spinner-Burks families.) The three Clayton girls, daughters of John Willis Clayton, Jr., and his wife, Lucinda (Douglas) Clayton, who married the three Turpin brothers, sons of Thomas and Rachel (Cheatwood) Turpin, are as follows:

Elvira Clayton, born December, 1797; married, February 28, 1814, Philip Turpin, of Bedford County, Virginia. She died August 7, 1879. (See Philip Turpin family for descendants.)

Mary Polina Clayton, born October 22, 1802; married, January 2, 1818, Thomas Turpin, Jr. She died January 23, 1875. (See Thomas Turpin, Jr., family for descendants.)

Eliza W. Clayton, born ————; married, June 24, 1822, Captain John Turpin. (See Captain John Turpin's family for descendants.)

———

The following data pertaining to the Clayton family, descendants of Dr. John Clayton, the botanist, has been collected from various sources. The first, "Clayton Deeds from Charlotte County," printed in the *Virginia Historical Magazine*, Vol. XXXVII, No. 2, April 1929, was contributed by Mr. W. S. Morton, of Charlotte Court House, Virginia.

This Indenture made this 10th day of March, 1777, between John Clayton, Senʳ, of Charlotte County, of the first part, and William Clayton, Elizabeth Clayton, Ann Clayton, Thomas Lewis Clayton, and Arthur Clayton, sons and daughters of the aforesaid John Clayton, of the other part: Witnesseth, that the said John Clayton, after the death of him and Elizabeth, his wife, for & in consideration of five shillings sterling by each of the above mentioned children, to him in hand paid, the receipt whereof he doth hereby acknowledge, but more specially for and in consideration of the natural love and affections which he hath and beareth unto the said children, hath given, granted, bargained, sold, enfeoffed & confirmed & by these presents doth give, grant, bargain, sell, enfeoffe & confirm unto the aforesaid children and to each of them the hereafter mentioned negroes now in the possession of the said John Clayton, their father, viz.: To my son, William Clayton, one negro named Davey, and a child that a negro woman, Rose, is with child of; To my daughter, Elizabeth Clayton, one negro girl named Sucky; To my daughter, Ann Clayton, one negro girl named Phillis; To my son, Thomas Lewis Clayton, one negro woman named Judith; and to my son, Arthur Clayton, one negro woman named Rose. But if either of the above mentioned children should die before they arrive to the age of twenty-one years, or have a child lawfully begotten of their body, his or their parts shall be equally divided between my surviving children. In witness whereof the said John Clayton, first above mentioned, hath hereunto set his hand and affixed his seal the day and year first above written.

JOHN CLAYTON (L.S.)

Sealed and Delivered in presence of
JOHN CLAYTON, JR.,
MARY CLAYTON.

At a court held for Charlotte County the 7th day of April, 1777.

The above written Deed of Gift was proved by the oath of John Clayton, Jr., one of the witnesses hereunto subscribed, to be the act and deed of the said John Clayton, and Ordered to be recorded.

Teste: THOMAS REED, *C.*

Deed Book 4, page 2.

The records of Charlotte County show that John Clayton and Elizabeth Willis, his wife, had four other children besides those mentioned in the deed above.

On March 10, 1777, John Clayton (Charlotte), sold to "John Clayton, the younger, eldest son of the aforesaid John Clayton," a negro named Adonis, now in the possession of the aforesaid John Clayton, the elder, at the death of him and Elizabeth, his wife—consideration, five shillings.

Deed Book 4, page 13.

On March 7, 1777, John Clayton gave to "my son, Henry Clayton," a negro, Abraham.

Deed Book 4, page 13.

Among the marriage bonds are found "14 Sept., 1775, James Overton, Jr., Bachelor, & Mildred Clayton, spinster, sec., John Clayton."

"18 August 1775, Nathaniel Manson and Lucy Whiting Clayton, daughter of John Clayton of the Co. of Charlotte."

The above are recognized as daughters of John and Elizabeth (Willis) Clayton.

Nathaniel Manson was living in Halifax County in June 20, 1776, as is shown by a Deed of Trust made to him by John Clayton, Sr. This deed conveyed three tracts of land containing, in all, 536 acres, 3 negroes, 5 feather beds, furniture, 1 double chair and harness, a stand with silver casters, silver sugar dish, 9 silver spoons, "with all the appertenances belonging," etc., to the premises. Deed Book 4, page 52.

James Overton was from Hanover. The settlement of his estate, August, 1784, by John Overton being appointed administrator by the Court of Hanover. (See Deed Book 5, page 198, Charlotte County) dated July 24, 1784. Mildred Overton, the widow of James Overton, made motion, gave bond and become administratrix.

John Clayton, Jr. (wife Mary), lived in Hanover in November 21, 1774, at which date he bought land in Charlotte County. Deed Book 3, page 500. Deed Book 3, page 451. His removal to Charlotte occurred very soon after buying the above lands, as on July 25, 1775, he was living in Charlotte. Deed Book 3, page 530.

On February 5, 1783, power of attorney given to John Clayton, Jr., by his father, John Clayton, Sr., to do business for him in Hanover. This power of attorney was transferred by John Clayton, Jr., to Thomas Price, of Hanover, on July 10, 1784. See Hanover, 1783-1792, part 1, page 43. See Charlotte County Deed Book 5, page 59.

On October 20, 1781, Elizabeth Clayton made a deed of gift to her son, William Willis Clayton. Deed Book 5, page 12.

On December 7, 1782, Elizabeth Clayton made a deed of gift to her son, Thomas Lewis Clayton. Deed Book 5, page 29.

It would appear from the above extracts, taken from the Charlotte County Records, that John[8] Clayton in his deed to his five children giving to each, a negro, did not mention his four older children, three of whom had previously married, viz.: John, Lucy Whiting and Mildred. And he had already provided a negro for his sons, John and Henry. His property had been given in trust to his son-in-law, Nathaniel Manson, for what purpose, we can only conjecture.

Memorandum of an Agreement made this fifteenth day of June, one thousand seven hundred and ninety three, between NICHOLAS DAVIES and JOHN CLAYTON, both of Bedford County, to rent to him for the causes and considerations hereafter mentioned a tract of one hundred acres of land being part of the land the said Clayton purchased of Streets Legatees for said Nicholas Davies in Amherst County the said Clayton is to have the said one hundred acres in any part of said tract that he chuseth running one hundred and thirty poles one way and one hundred and twenty five poles the other for quantity for the sum of ten pounds a year to be paid to the said Davies or his heirs or trustees on or before the twenty fifth of March yearly and the said Clayton and his wife is to have the said land for and during their natural lives and to have peaceable possession on the twentieth day of next November and the said Clayton is within two years from the twentieth of November next to plant a good orchard of one hundred apple trees and two hundred peach trees of the most useful sorts of forward and late fruit and inclose the said orchard in a lawful fence and always keep growing and bearing in said orchard the said number of good bearing fruit trees and to take such care that the said orchard and plantation be after the time aforesaid delivered up to said Davies or his heirs &c. or Trustees if required in good repair and two good sound cabbins sixteen feet square fit for white people to live in and the whole plantation by him made and orchards and cabbins all inclosed in a lawful fence and the said Clayton and all his family is to live peaceable and honestly as long as they reside on said land, if not then to forfeit all their right to said land &c. and be obliged to move from it directly and the said Clayton is not to bargain or sell his lease or right to the said land, &c. without the said Davies' leave in writing nor work on said land more than four tithables in the crop except his own children and for the good honest punctual performance of this agreement the said Davies and Clayton do hereby do bind themselves and their heirs &c. to each other in the penal sum of one hundred pounds current money of Virginia and all damage. In Witness whereof the said Clayton & Davies have hereunto set their hands and seals this day and year above mentioned.

NICHOLAS DAVIES (L. S.)
JOHN CLAYTON (L. S.)

Teste:

JAMES SCOTT,
JOHN W. CLAYTON,
JOSEPH SLAUGHTER.

N. B. The said Clayton has leave to get timber for improving and making buildings on the within mentioned land off any my other lands that may not be rented out. As witness my hand this fifteenth day of June, 1793.

NICHOLAS DAVIES.

Test:

JAMES SCOTT,
JOHN W. CLAYTON.

At a Court held for Amherst County the seventeenth day of June, 1793. This memo. of agreement was proved by the oath of James Scott and John W. Clayton, witnesses thereto, and ordered to be recorded.

Teste:

W. S. CRAWFORD, *Clk.*

Deed Book "G," page 243.
Amherst County, Va.

....

THIS INDENTURE made this fourth day of February in the Year of Christ one thousand seven hundred and ninety seven between Henry Landon Davies of Bedford County of the one part and John Willis Clayton & Nicholas Clayton Davies the former of the said County and the latter of the County of Amherst of the other part Witnesseth. That for and in Consideration of the sum of Seventy five pounds Current Money of Virginia & for divers other Causes & Considerations him the said H. L. Davies thereunto moving doth honestly desire to secure and made over unto Mary Clayton & her

Children called by the following names Viz., John Willis Clayton, Nancy Clayton, Jasper Clayton, Thomas Clayton, William Clayton, Polley Harrison Clayton, Kitty Clayton, Susanna Pettus Clayton, & Rebeccah Dabney Clayton in manner and form hereafter mentioned, & for the farther Consideration of the Sum of five Shillings like money to the said Henry L. Davies in hand paid by the said John Willis Clayton & Nicholas Clayton Davies at and before the sealing & delivery of this, the receipt whereof he H. L. Davies doth hereby acknowledge and thereof and every part thereof doth exonerate & discharge the said John Willis Clayton & Nicholas Clayton Davies their Heirs Exors. & Admors. he the said H. L. Davies hath granted bargained & Sold & by these presents doth grant bargain sell and confirm to the said J. W. Clayton & N. C. Davies their Heirs &c. Forever two Negro. Women Slaves named Juno and Jenny, One Negro Girl named Lucy One feather Bed a bolster, two Sheets One Blanket Bedstead cord & Matt, One feather Bed & Bolster, two Sheets, two Blankets One Rug, One Set of Curtains One Bedstead Rope & mat, One feather Bed & Bolster One Sheet two Blankets One quilt Bedstead cord & Mat, One feather bed & Bolster two Sheets two Blankets, one quilt One Counterpain Bedstead Cord & Mat. One tin Gallon pot, One Dutch Oven, One pair pot Hooks One frying pan, One flesh fork, One Iron Skillet two peuter dishes One Bason Six Plates Six Spoons two water pails two piggins six setting chairs, two Chests One poplar Table two flax Wheels, two Cotton Do. One dark red Cow, One black & White ditto, One red Cow one black Heifer one dark brindle & white Steer, One white & red Cow sawed horns, One Red Yearling, One red & white Yearling, One red Steer white Spot in his forehead, One red & white Yearling, One red Steer, one dark red & white Steer, One pale red Calf, One red & white yearling marked with a smooth Crop in the right Ear each, thirty head of Hogs (that is) One Boar, One Barrow, Six Sows twenty two shoats about Six months old all marked with a smooth crop in the right Ear, with all the appurtenances belonging or in any wise appertaining *the* the premises hereby granted or intended to be granted & all Services benefits & profits of the said Slaves hous–hold furniture & Stocks: To have and to hold the above enumerated property unto the said J. W. Clayton & N. C. Davies their Heirs &c. forever & the said H. L. Davies doth hereby grant for himself & his heirs that he the said H. L. Davies & his heirs & every of them shall and will warrant & forever defend the aforesaid Property & every part & Article thereof unto the said J. W. Clayton & N. C. Davies their Heirs &c. forever against the Claim of him H. L. Davies his heirs &c. & every other person whomsoever. Upon Trust, nevertheless, that they the said J. W. Clayton & N. C. Davies shall hold and Manage the aforesaid Property for Support the said Mary Clayton and those of the aforenamed children that dwell with her until the first day of November in the year 1815, or untill the said Mary Clayton shall depart this life or she said Mary shall desire a division to take place of the property above mentioned which division shall be equal among the several Children herein mentioned after giving twenty days public Notice of such division and out of Money and all other profits arising from the several Articles of Property aforesaid, the said J. W. Clayton & N. C. Davies shall pay the expense attending the recording this Indenture and all other needful & Necessary expenses relative to the intent of this Indenture. And the said J. W. Clayton & N. C. Davies theirs Heirs Exors. & Admors. shall pay or cause to be paid the overplus if any remain of Money or other profits arising from the Property before mentioned unto the Children heretofore named, each a like Sum & devidend of Monies & profits so remaining in their Hands at either of the times nominated for a division and if either of the aforesaid Children should decease before Such division the Survivors shall share equally according to the number of persons then living of those first above mentioned. In Witness Whereof the said Henry Landon Davies hath hereunto set his hand & Seal on the day and Year first above written.

HENRY L. DAVIES (L. S.)

Sealed and delivered
in the presence of

FRANCIS WATERS, SAM. B. DAVIES,
ELIZA MANSON.

At a Court held for Bedford County the 26th day of June, 1797. This Indenture was acknowledged by Henry L. Davies party thereto & Ordered to be recorded.

Teste,

A Copy—Teste: JA: STEPTOE, C. B. C.

V. W. NICHOLS,

Clerk of Circuit Court of Bedford

Deek Book "J," page 309.   *County, Virginia.*

FROM CROZIER'S WILLIAMSBURG WILLS

Clayton, William, Clerk of New Kent County, 10 June, 1797; 14 December, 1797. Son William Beverley Clayton; son-in-law Philip Davis; granddaughter Catherine Clayton; son-in-law Armistead Russell; granddaughter Eliz. Armistead Russell; dau. Mary Ann Davis; dau. Elvira Russell. Exrs. son Wm. B. Clayton. Wit. John Christian, Benjamin Crump, John H. Christian.

Davis, Mary Ann, New Kent County, 10 January, 1809; 9 March, 1809. Daughter Mary Ann; dau. Rebecca; dau. Catherine Gwatkins. Exrs. Wm. H. Macon and my brother Wm. B. Clayton. Wit. William Holt, Henry Holt.

THIS INDENTURE made this fifteenth day of February in the year of our Lord one thousand eight hundred between NICHOLAS CLAYTON DAVIES of Amherst County of the one part and JOHN WILLIS CLAYTON of the other part. WITNESSETH that the said Nicholas Clayton Davies for the causes and considerations hereafter mentioned hath bargained leased and to farm lett and by these presents doth grant bargain lease and to farm let unto the said John Willis Clayton one certain tract or parcel of land containing one hundred and fourteen acres, and bounded as follows, viz.: by a line beginning at an hickory tree and running thence N. 33 W. 60 poles to pointers two black and two white oaks by a line running thence S. 86. W. 48 poles to pointers a double chestnut two red oaks and a dogwood by a line running thence S. 44 W. 194 poles to a soviet tree standing on the point of a ridge by a line running S. 24 E. 26 poles to pointers three black oaks a white oak and a pine by a line running thense S. 60 E. 42 poles to pointers three bushes a poplar a red oak, and an hickory, by a line running thence S. 49 E. 20 poles to pointers, a black walnut, a sycamore and a poplar by a line running thence N. 44 E. 148 poles to pointers, sycamores and walnuts, by a line running thence N. 49 E. 50 poles to a sycamore by a line running thence N. 54 E. 18 poles to the beginning. TO HAVE AND TO HOLD use and quietly possess as a tenant the said one hundred and fourteen acres of land for and during the time and term of six years to be computed from the twenty-fifth day of November last past with the priviledge of working the first year four hands exclusive a negro woman now in possession of his mother Mary Clayton named Juno and a negro boy of his own named Frank, for which quiet tenantable possession of the said land the aforesaid John Willis Clayton doth hereby bind himself, his heirs, &c. to pay the said Nicholas Clayton Davies his heirs or assigns the sum of twenty pounds current money of Virginia for the first year on or before the first day of January eighteen hundred and one, and from that time forward the sum of five pounds like money for each and every hand plow boys excepted under fourteen years of age that shall be worked or employed on the said land on or before the said first day of January of each year, and within two years from the date of the said November last past to plant on the said land one hundred peach and fifty apple trees of good late fruit and the said trees carefully to manage inclose and keep within a lawful fence, separate from the other cleared land, to make no waste nor sell or any way dispose of any kind of trees or timber and to leave the plantation, fruit trees, fences &c. in good tenantable and lawful repair on the twenty-fifth day of November in the year one thousand eight hundred and six not to sell or in any manner convey to another the whole or any part of the said land and to duffer no person or persons to dwell on or occupy the said land and to be peaceable in the neighborhood for which yearly rent fruit trees fences &c. the said Davies his heirs &c. shall and will warrant and defend to the said John Willis Clayton quiet and tenantable posession of the said one hundred and fourteen acres of land. In Witness whereof the said Davies & Clayton do hereby bind themselves, their heirs &c. to each other in the penal sum of five hundred pounds current money of Virginia and hereunto set their hands and seals the day and year above written.

NICHS. C. DAVIES [SEAL].
JOHN W. CLAYTON [SEAL].

Signed, sealed and delivered in the presence of

JAMES GARLAND,
THOS. WOODRUFF,
SAM B. DAVIES,
RICHD. BURKS,
JOSIAH ELLIS, JUNR.

MEMORANDUM that it is understood that the above mentioned John Willis Clayton is not to take or employ on the leased land above mentioned any of those people called mulattoes or free negroes.

NICHS. C. DAVIES [SEAL].
JOHN W. CLAYTON [SEAL].

JAMES GARLAND,
THOS. WOODROOF,
SAM. B. DAVIES,
RCD. BURKS,
JOSIAH ELLIS, JUNR.

At a Court held for Amherst County the 16th day of June, 1800. This lease together with the memorandum endorsed was proved by the oaths of Thomas Woodroof, and Josiah Ellis, Junr., witnesses thereto and ordered to be recorded.

Teste.

Deed Book "I," page 103,
Amherst County, Va.

Deed Book "K," page 745. Bedford County records, dated July 19, 1802. Henry L. Davies and Lucy Whiting, his wife, to John Clayton, Jr., both of Bedford County, "one hundred and two acres—one quarter and twenty-four poles" on the north bank of Battery Creek.

Deed Book "K," page 855, dated December 27, 1802, a deed between John Clayton, Jr., and Mary, his wife, of the one part and Jasper Clayton of the other part, of Bedford County "one hundred and two acres—one quarter and twenty-four poles" on the north side of Battery Creek. (Same land described in above deed Book "K," page 745.)

Deed Book "5," pages 177-189, Amherst County records, dated 26th June, 1807. John P. B. Clayton in account with Joshua Shelton— mentions cash paid Jacob White, Adm'r. of John W. Clayton. Deceased late guardian.

Board of John P. B. Clayton from 26th October, 1805, to 26th June, 1807, @ 20 lb. Joshua Shelton was guardian for James P. B. Clayton.

From Chalkley's *Abstracts and Records of Augusta County, Virginia,* Vol. II, pages 180-181 :

Walker's administrator vs. Jones' administrator — O. S. 226; N. S. 80—Bill, 1810. Bill filed in Albemarle, 1813, by Walter Leake, administrator c. t. a. of Levi Jones, Elizabeth Jones, his widow, and Orlando, Lain and William Jones, infants of Lain Jones. Elizabeth was Elizabeth Clayton. William Walker and Elizabeth conveyed to Lain Jones a tract of land and all their interest in a deed by Orlando Jones to John Clayton, 1771. Lain Jones was only child and heir of Orlando Jones; who died testate. Will dated 4th May, 1804. William Walker and Elizabeth are both dead. Defendants are, viz.: James, Andrew, Francis, Walker, and Sally, his wife; Andrew Laird and Eleanor, his wife (late Walker); Charles Mosly and Jane, his wife, late Walker; Francis, Josephus, Rebecca Walker, and Daniel Couch. Copy of a former bill filed in Albemarle by William Walker and Elizabeth, his wife, shows that on 27 November, 1771, in contemplation of a marriage between Orlando Jones, deceased, and Elizabeth (oratrix), daughter of John Clayton, deceased, a marriage contract was entered into. Conveys 400 acres in Albemarle and certain slaves. In February, 1793, Orlando died without issue by Elizabeth, who married Walker in 1793. Deed 27 November, 1771, by Orlando Jones of Albemarle and John Clayton of Gloucester. Marriage settlement. Recorded in General Court, 30th April, 1772. Deed 19th May, 1795, by William Walker and Elizabeth to Lain Jones, 400 acres in Albemarle. Recorded in Albemarle, June, 1795. Bill of revivor filed by heirs of Elizabeth Walker, viz.: John Clayton, Nicholas Davis, Samuel B. Davis, Timberlake V. Davis, Catherine C. Merriwether, Edith Clay, Thomas Hughes, Henry Hughes, Susanna Hughes, Jasper Clayton, William B. Clayton, Arthur Davis. Deed 30th May, 1795, by Lain Jones of Albemarle to William Walker, mortgage. Recorded in Albemarle, June, 1795. Bill by James Walker, administrator c. t. a. of William Walker of Buckingham County. Will of Orlando (Lain?) Jones dated 4th May, 1804. Sons, Orlando, Lain, and William; wife. Recorded in Albemarle, 1805, 4th February. Joseph Coleman deposes: Orlando Jones died 1793, leaving Lain Jones, father of Orlando, Lain and William.

Marriages of the Clayton family, prior to 1841, from the Bedford County records:

Captain John Clayton and Charlotte Leftwich, daughter of Thomas Leftwich 9 January 1792. Signed: John Clayton, Saml. Mitchell.

Lewis Clayton and Elizabeth Wright, 18th Feby. 1796, by Rev. Jeremiah Hatcher. John Wright, security on license bond.

John Willis Clayton and Lucinda Douglas, 21st March 1797. Rev. Jeremiah Hatcher. Thomas L. Clayton, security.

William W. Clayton and Carissa Hales, 20 March 1800, Robt. Snoody, security.

Jasper Clayton and Frances Lesuer, 28th March 1801. Rev. Jeremiah Hatcher. Fill Lesuer, security.

Thomas L. Clayton and Dicia (Theodocia) Wright, daughter of John Wright, 26 Mch. 1803. Frances Hunter, security.

John Markham and Elizabeth Catharine Clayton, daughter of John Clayton, 19th Jany. 1807. Rev. George Rucker. Elish Dewitt, security.

John C. Lesuer and Susanna Pettus Clayton, daughter John Clayton, 31 March 1807. Rev. Geo. Rucker. Thos. North, security.

Jasper Clayton and Elsa Harris, daughter of Dosia Harris, 24 November 1810.

Pettus C. Clayton and Nancy Jones, daughter of David Jones, 25th Feby. 1811. Edward Hatcher, security.

Phillip Turpin and Elvira Clayton, 28 February 1814. Permission signed by Lucinda Clayton.

Jasper Clayton and Lucinda H. White, 17th Sept. 1817. Rev. Enoch W. Terry. Nelson Sale, security.

Thomas Turpin and Polly Clayton, daughter of Lucindy Clayton, 2nd Jany. 1818. Rev. Enoch Terry. Nelson Sale, security.

John Turpin and Eliza W. Clayton, June 24, 1822. John Turpin, Philip Turpin, security.

Jesse Spinner and Mrs. Lucinda Clayton, 15th November 1832.

Arthur W. Clayton and Eliza Logwood, daughter Alexander H. Logwood, 17th Decr. 1840. Edward H. Hatcher, security.

Jos. Clayton and Paulina Smith, daughter of Samuel Smith, 1 March 1825.

Wm. P. Clayton and Martha H. Robinson. Jos. E. Clayton, security, 11 January 1827.

BEVERLEY

Robert Beverley, the first of the family, who emigrated to this country from Yorkshire, England, about the middle of the seventeenth century, was of the old and highly respectable family of Beverleys of the town of Beverley, in England. He settled in Middlesex County, of which he was a justice in 1673, and was for many years, Clerk of the House of Burgesses.

Mr. W. G. Stanard in his carefully prepared sketch of "Major Robert Beverley and His Descendants" states that he was married twice. His first wife being named Mary—her surname not positively known. (*Virginia Magazine*, Vol. 2, page 405.) His second wife was Madam Katherine Hone, and they were married in "Gloster, March 28th, 1679." That it was possible that Katherine Hone was the widow and not the daughter of Major Theophilus Hone, and a sister of Colonel John Armistead, of Gloucester County (*Virginia Magazine*, Vol. 3, page 169). She married, secondly, Christopher Robinson, of Middlesex, a nephew of John Robinson, Bishop of London.

Major Robert Beverley died in 1686-7, leaving the following children, viz.: Peter; Robert; Harry (married Elizabeth, daughter and heiress of Robert Smith, of "Brandon," Middlesex County—left issue); Mary (married William Jones, of King and Queen); William (married Judith, daughter of Christopher Wormeley); John (died without issue); Thomas (died without issue); Christopher (died without issue); Catherine (married Hon. John Robinson, of Essex County, acting Governor in 1749 when he died, son of Christopher Robinson, of Middlesex and nephew of John Robinson, Bishop of London). (*Virginia Magazine*, July, 1895, page 47 &c., October, 1895, page 169 &c.)

Colonel Peter Beverley, eldest son of Major Robert Beverley, was Clerk of the House of Burgesses, 1691-99 (Hening); Speaker of the House of Burgesses, 1700-14 (Hening); Clerk of Gloucester County, 1702-14; Treasurer of Virginia, 1710-23 (Hening); and appointed a member of the Council in 1719. His wife was Elizabeth Peyton, daughter of Major Robert Peyton, of "Isleham," Gloucester County, Virginia, who was a grandson of Sir Edward Peyton, Baronet (Hayden's *Virginia Genealogies*, 466-68). Colonel Peter Beverley died in 1728, leaving among children the following, viz.:

Elizabeth Beverley, second daughter (*Virginia Magazine*, Vol. 3, page 261), born January 1, 1691; died December 26, 1723; married, June 22, 1709, Colonel William Randolph, Jr., of "Turkey Island," Henrico County (son of Col. William Randolph, Sr., of "Turkey Island," who married Mary, daughter of Henry Isham).

Susanna Beverley, youngest daughter (*Virginia Magazine*, Vol. 3, page 265), born ———; died ———; married Sir John Randolph, of Williamsburg (son of Col. William Randolph, Sr., of "Turkey Island").

Anne Beverley, daughter of Col. Peter and Elizabeth (Peyton) Beverley (*Virginia Biography*, by Lyon G. Tyler), born ———; died ———; married Henry Whiting; her daughter, Elizabeth Whiting, married in 1723, Dr. John Clayton, the Botanist. (See Clayton family.)

Robert Beverley, Jr., second son of Major Robert Beverley, was clerk of King and Queen County; member of the House of Burgesses; author of a History of Virginia published in 1705; married Ursula Byrd, daughter of Colonel William Byrd, of "Westover," on James River. His daughter, Ursula Beverley, married in 1725, John Dudley, of Hanover County; her daughter, Nancy Dudley, married in 1759, John Ragland, of Louisa County; her daughter, Sallie Dudley Ragland, married in 1800, James Davis, of Amherst County. (See Davis family.)

TURPIN

Michael Turpin, the emigrant, came from Yorkshire, England, about 1655, bought lands in 1656 from Col. Wm. Farrar, of Farrar's Island, called "Henrico." He is the emigrant ancestor of the Turpins in Virginia, Kentucky, &c. His will is dated July 4, 1663, or 1673. He had several sons, among them being:

——Philip, born Yorkshire, England, 1655; married Martha Skirm, of Henrico and died 1717. He left issue. (See forward.)

——John, born about 1660.

——Matthew, born 1664; married Sarah Hatcher, daughter of Edward Hatcher and died 1689. He had sons, Henry and Mathew; daughter, Cicely. The widow married, October 16, 1689, Jos. Tanner. Mathew Turpin's estate divided December 2, 1689. (Deed Book 5, page 104, Henrico County Records.)

——Michael; married probably, a Farrar. Sons: Michael and John.

Goochland County was formed from Henrico in 1727.
Cumberland County was formed from Goochland in 1748.
Chesterfield County was formed from Henrico in 1748.
Powhatan County was formed from Cumberland in 1777.

Michael Turpin, the emigrant, settled in Henrico County with his family; but in time, as the counties were cut off from Henrico we find members of the same family, or their descendants, owning property in all the counties mentioned above.

From the early records of Henrico County, Virginia, we have the following notes:

Philip Turpin, born 1655, gave depositions in 1688. Book 5, page 25.)

John Turpin, born 1660, gave depositions in 1685. (Book 4, page 338.) 1689. (Book 5, page 107.)

Will of Mathew Turpin mentions wife Sarah. Eldest son, Henry; son to be named Mathew, also Mr. Thomas Osborne. (January 15, 1688, and April, 1689, pages 41 and 106.)

(Book 5, page 246.)

October 1, 1691—Philip Turpin, a landlord.

1691—Michael Turpin married Elizabeth ———, granted land 1687.

July 4, 1663 or 1677, Michael Turpin's Will: sons, Philip, Michael, and John.

(Book 5, page 189.)

April 1, 1691—Michael Turpin to Wm. Whitley 215 A. granted to Michael Turpin, April 20, 1687. Elizabeth, wife of Mathew Turpin, relinquished her rights April 1, 1691.

(Page 660—October 1, 1696.) Michael Turpin sells to John Davis 200 A. on north side James River.

John Turpin in will dated September 7, 1795, page 343, mentioned children: Betsy Talman, John, Sarah, Beverly, William, and Thomas. Appointed Michael Turpin and Austin Talman, Executors.

Michael Turpin in his will dated May 1, 1796, and proved June 6, 1796, page 377, mentioned wife, Betsy (probably Redford), sons: John, Miles, Elisha, and Henry; daughters: Mary, Martha, and Elizabeth, and brother John. (Note: this Michael and John above were brothers.)

Lusby Turpin, married Martha Bullington, May 8, 1786 (must have been second wife). His will dated January 2, 1791; proved March 7, 1791, mentioned sons: Michael, John, Thomas, Alex., and Lusby; daughters: Mary Goode, Sarah Depriest, Priscilla Vendike, Elizabeth Royster.

(1710-1714, Old Record Book, Part 1, page 51.)

Deed Thos. Turpin & wife Obedience and Joseph Wilkinson & wife Priscilla of Henrico sell to Richard Dennis of Charles City 101 acres on which Mrs. Jane Gower lately lived on south side James River.

From Chesterfield County records:

(Will Book 4, page 454.)

November 25, 1763—appraisement Estate Phil. Turpin.

(Will Book 2, page 211.)

February 19, 1767 — Elizabeth Turpin's will — sons: Phillip, Thomas, Elisha, Josiah, daughter, Mary Winfree, granddaughter, Sally Winfree, granddaughter, Elizabeth Ashurst — "My two daughters, Martha and Mary." Mabel Turpin, wife of Josiah.

(Will Book 2, page 212.)

Will of Josiah Turpin, mentioned wife, Mabel—brothers, Elisha, Philip, Thomas, and daughter, Sally Turpin.

(Will Book 2, page 214.)

Inventory Josiah Turpin—February 8, 1768.

(Deed Book 10, page 1.)

September 24, 1781, Thomas Turpin, of Chesterfield sells to Richard Elam land next to Josiah Turpin dec'd. being now in possession of Thomas Turpin.

(Will Book 3, page 402.)

Will of Henry Turpin, Sr., wife, Ann, made October 18, 1782 (no probate) daughters: Frances Banton, Ann Turpin, Mary Turpin; sons: Hezekiah, Obediah, George, and Jeremiah. "My two sons, George and Jeremiah all my land at Kentucky and my land in Chesterfield." Henry, land I live on. Jeremiah was not 20.

(Hezekiah Turpin married, October 9, 1773, Jane Cheatham, daughter Francis Cheatham.)

(Will Book 2, page 389.)

Will of Philip Turpin, dated August 1, 1794; no probate—wife (no name given) son, Henry (under 15); daughter, Nancy Turner. Executors, Wm. & Philip Turner.

(Deed Book "D," page 368, Bedford County records.)

June 3, 1772—Deed between Thos. Turpin, Sr., of Cumberland County and William Turpin of Bedford County for and in consideration of the natural love and affection which he beareth unto the said William Turpin a certain tract of land containing 2240 Acres, more or less, situated & lying & being on Branches of Ivy Creek of Black Water in Bedford County and bounded by the lands of Thos. Jefferson, Harden Perkins, Sherwood Gaddy and Robert Hardwick.

Survey for James Turpin, March 2, 1774, 120 Acres situated in Bedford on north fork of Blackwater River.

(Deed Book "C," page 173, Bedford County Records.)

October 14, 1765, Thomas Turpin, of Southern Parrish and County of Cumberland sold to Richard Callaway, of Bedford County 700 Acres lying near the Blue Ridge Mountains, crossing Tuckahoe Creek to John Dorson's corner and Samuel Cobbs' line.

(Deed Book "E," pages 168, 169, 170, 171, Bedford County Records.)

November 23, 1773—William Turpin of Cumberland County sold to the following, land situated in Bedford County on Ivy Creek & Wolf

Creek: Micajah Moorman, 210 acres; Charles Moorman, 100 acres; Silas Moorman, 50 acres; Andrew Moorman, 200 acres. (Deed Book "O," page 341.)

December 5, 1815—Wm. Turpin & Sarah, of Cumberland County deed to their son, Edwin Turpin, of Cumberland County, a tract of land lying in the County of Bedford containing 904 acres on Ivy Creek. They also deeded their son Wm. Archer Turpin of the County of Powhatan a tract of 907 acres lying in Bedford County. (These two sons never lived in Bedford County.)

In the census of 1783 we have Henry, Hezekiah, Obadiah and Phill Turpin mentioned as heads of families in Chesterfield County. Horatio, Thos., Jr., and Thos. Turpin, III, in Powhatan, and Wm. Turpin in Cumberland County.

Among early settlers of Prince Edward County, Va., was Thos. Turpin, 25th September 1746—400 acres on Sandy River.

Page 257, *Virginia Historical Magazine,* Vol. 2, 1894, Virginia Troops in Continental Line.
Horatio Turpin, Ensign.

Page 68, *Virginia Historical Magazine,* Vol. 1, 1893, Officers of the Virginia Navy during the Revolutionary War.
John Turpin, Midshipman.

Horatio Turpin was officer in Revolution in 1780 in Cavalry from Powhatan.

John Turpin was Captain of a company from Henrico County in 1781 and Sugly Turpin was Second Lieutenant of same.

William Turpin was sworn in as Ensign of a company from Cumberland County, August 26, 1777.

Martin Turpin was a Revolutionary pensioner residing in Pulaski County, Kentucky, in 1835.

(McAllister's *Virginia Militia in the Revolutionary War.*)

Philip Turpin, born 1655, Yorkshire, England, son of Michael Turpin, the emigrant, married Martha Skirm, of Henrico County, Virginia, and died August 14, 1718. Their children were:

——Thomas (I); married Obedience Branch. (See forward.)

——Philip; married ———— and had Ephriam and Philip.

——Mathew, died in the Barbadoes.

——Elizabeth; married Richard James.

——Martha; married George Carter.

Thomas Turpin, I, son of Philip and Martha (Skirm) Turpin, married, about 1707, Obedience Branch.

CHILDREN:

(1) Thomas, II, born May 9, 1708; married Mary Jefferson. (See forward.)

(2) Obedience; married Benjamin Branch.

(3) William, died young.

(4) Mary, born September 6, 1720; married, 1737, Robert Goode; died March 6, 1765, and was buried at "Whitby." (See Goode's *Virginia Cousins.*)

The following is a copy of the will of Obedience (Branch) Turpin proved June 17, 1746, Goochland County, Virginia.

In THE NAME OF GOD, AMEN. I, Obedience Turpin of Goochland County, Widow, being weak in body but of perfect mind and memory, Blessed be God, do make and ordain this my last will and testament in manner and form following.

Imprimis. I first of all give and bequeath unto my son, John Cocke, and to his heirs forever, one negro boy named Farthing.

Item. I give unto my daughter Martha Friend five shillings.

Item. I give and bequeath unto my grandson William Moseley one negro boy named Pompey but not to be delivered till Christmas next.

Item. I give and bequeath unto my grandson Benjamin Moseley one negro boy named Frank to him and his heirs forever but not to be delivered to him until the said Moseley shall arrive to the age of eighteen years.

Item. I give and bequeath unto my grandson Alexander Trent one negro girl named Dicey to him and his heirs forever.

Item. I give unto my son-in-law Alexander Trent five shillings.

Item. I give unto my daughter Obedience Branch five shillings.

Item. I give unto granddaughter Obedience Branch one negro girl named Sallie to her and her heirs forever.

Item. I give unto my daughter Mary Goode one negro boy named Matt to her and her heirs forever.

Item. I give unto my granddaughter Obedience Turpin three negroes to witt, Amy, a girl, Lucy, a girl, Harry, a boy, to her and her heirs forever.

Item. I likewise give to my said granddaughter Obedience, one feather bed, a pair of blankets, two pair of sheets, one rug, one bed quilt, half dozen new leather chairs which I have now by me, four new dishes, half a dozen new plaits, one chest and one small walnut table.

Item. I give and bequeath unto my son Thomas Turpin three negroes to witt Pompey, Simon and Hannah to him and his heirs forever.

Item. I give unto my daughter Mary Goode five shillings.

Item. All the rest of my estate which I have not before disposed of I give to my son Thomas Turpin and do appoint him sole executor of this my last Will and Testament revoking all Wills by me heretofore made and do order that my estate be not appraised. In witness whereof I have hereunto set my hand and Seal this Twenty sixth day of January 1745/6.

her
OBEDIENCE x TURPIN.
mark

Signed, Sealed and Delivered
in the presence of interlined before signed

BENJ. MOSBY,

PETER BONDURANT,

  her

ANN x BAILY.

  mark

At a Court held for Goochland County, June 17, 1746. This Will was proved by the oaths of Benj. Mosby and Peter Bondurant and ordered to be recorded.

Thomas Turpin, II, born May 9, 1708; married Mary Jefferson, an aunt of Thomas Jefferson.

CHILDREN:

(1) Martha, died young.
(2) Thomas, died young.
(3) Obedience; married John Harris.
(4) Thomas, III, born November 28, 1736; married, April 9, 1767, Martha Ward Gaines, daughter of Bernard and Elizabeth (Ward) Gaines, of Cumberland County, Va.

> CHILDREN:
>
> (a) Thomas IV.
> (b) Lucy Gaines, born July 15, 1774, married (first) Benj. Harris and had Evelyn Harris who married Gen. Wm. Ligon. Married (second), February 15, 1803, Col. Wm. Bently and had Judith Archer Bently who married, January 25, 1825, James Ligon, of Powhatan County. (Dr. James L. Kent, of Pulaski, Virginia is a grandson of James and Judith (Bently) Ligon; and to him I wish to acknowledge my indebtedness for early notes from Henrico County records.)
> (c) Obedience Jefferson; married James Harris.
> (d) Sally Gaines; married Francis Harris.
> (e) Archer, died young.

(5) Mary; married Richard James. (Cumberland County.)
(6) William M., born 1741; married Sarah Harris. Lived in Cumberland County.

> CHILDREN:
>
> (a) Philip.
> (b) William Archer.
> (c) Edwin.
> (d) Polly; married Peter F. Smith.
> (e) Elizabeth; married Dr. Richard P. James.
> (f) Thomas I.; married Martha Gwin.
> (g) Lucy; married (first) Dr. Nice; (second) Reuben Ragland.
> (h) Selina; married Capt. Booker.

(7) Philip, died young.
(8) Lucy, died young.
(9) Dr. Philip, born 1749; married Caroline Rose, of Chesterfield, County, Va.

CHILDREN:

(a) Caroline; married Dr. Edward Johnson.

(b) Mariah, died young.

(c) Philip, adopted son.

(10) Peterfield, never married.

(11) Horatio, born April 13, 1755; married, March 30, 1803, Mary A. Bancroft, died October 8, 1826. He went into the Revolutionary War from Hampden-Sydney College. (See forward.)

The following compilation of the Horatio Turpin family in Kentucky was submitted by his granddaughter, Mrs. Nannie Chambers Abbett, of Louisvile, Kentucky.

Horatio Turpin left Powhatan County, Virginia, shortly before 1820 for Lexington, Kentucky, where he remained a short time before purchasing a large tract of land in Gallatin County, Kentucky, lying between Eagle Creek and Craigs Creek. The home which he called "Beech Park" was about seven miles from the Ohio River. After buying the land he went back to Powhatan County, Virginia, and returned to Kentucky with a large number of slaves in the spring of 1820.

They cleared ground, built cabins, then cultivated the cleared land and burned the brick with which the home at "Beech Park" was built.

The following fall he again went to Virginia to conduct his family to their new home.

His wife, who is referred to as "Pretty Mary Bancroft" in "Reminiscences of Wilmington, Del.," was many years his junior.

Their children were:

Edward Augustus; Philip Osborne; Mary Elizabeth James; William Henry; Horatio Harris; Peterfield; Powhatan Virginius Americus; Harriett; Thomas Jefferson; Anna Cornelia; and two infants William and Thomas, who died and were buried in Virginia.

All of the children were born in Virginia except Thomas Jefferson and Anna Cornelia, my mother, who were born at "Beech Park" in 1823 and 1825, respectively.

The journey from Virginia to "Beech Park" was made overland, Horatio riding his horse while the family, including "Virginius," a child of three years, and Harriett, a babe of three weeks, rode in the carriage. They were accompanied by the house servants and came over the mountains, camping by the way.

Horatio Turpin died in 1826 leaving his widow to raise her ten children, which she succeeded in doing with credit. The home was a center of social life, and the sons were all college men, Edward Augustus attending Transylvania at Lexington, Kentucky, and the others going to Hanover College at Madison, Indiana.

Edward Augustus and William Henry married the Satterwhite sisters of Louisville, Kentucky, and became the owners of a line of steamboats running from Cincinnati to New Orleans. President Buchanan appointed Edward as Minister to Venezuela and he later ran a line of steamboats on the Orinoco River in South America. While at Caracas his daughter, Teresa Langhorne, died of yellow fever. He returned to the States and with his brother, Virginius, amassed a fortune in pork packing in Chicago. Edward later went to Philadelphia to live while Virginius went to New York.

Phillip Osborne married Mary Ellen Butler, of Carroll County, Kentucky, and they had a large family at Carrollton, Ky. The only surviving member of this family is Dr. Thomas Jefferson Turpin of Chihuahua, Mexico.

Mary Elizabeth James married Jesse D. Bright of Shelby County, Kentucky, who had gone to Madison, Indiana, as a young lawyer. He entered political life there and was elected Lieutenant Governor of that state, and afterward United States Senator. While acting as speaker of the Senate he addressed a letter to Jefferson Davis, who had been a classmate at Transylvania as "President Davis" and was expelled from the Senate on this account. Mrs. Lawrason Riggs of Baltimore, Maryland, was their daughter, and Miss Georgie G. Bright of Baltimore, Md., is the only surviving child. Another daughter, Sarah Virginia Bright, married Dr. William Henderson and their daughter Jessie married Hugh P. Colville and still lives in Covington.

Horatio Harris lost his health on a surveying expedition to Washington Territory and died at Carrollton, Ky., shortly after the death of his wife. He had married Mildred Hawkins and they had no children.

Peterfield died at the age of eighteen.

Harriett married Benjamin Murrill and died in less than a year afterward.

Thomas Jefferson married Harriett McIntyre of Madison, Indiana, and went to Indiana to live.

Anna Cornelia, my mother, married Dr. Absalom B. Chambers in March, 1852. In 1853 they went to Peoria, Illinois, to live, taking my brother, Horatio Turpin Chambers, then an infant with them. I was born in Peoria. Illinois was a "free state" and the negroes had been left in Kentucky. They returned to Kentucky and my father bought "Beech Park" and they spent the remainder of their lives there or at Warsaw, Kentucky, where my grandmother Turpin and her son, Horatio Harris were charter members of the Baptist Church.

My grandparents and some of the children are buried at "Beech Park."

My father was a prisoner in the Civil War much of the time, finally finding refuge in Canada until after the troubles were over. He died at the age of 52 years, a prominent and influential citizen of his county and state. My mother died at the age of 67 and a year later her brother, Virginius, died leaving a widow but no children.

My father and mother had four children,

Horatio Turpin Chambers who was older than I, my youngest sister, Mary Bright Chambers, who died at the age of 19, my younger brother, James Whitfield Chambers and myself.

My brother, Horatio Turpin Chambers, died many years ago and his widow, Sallie Bond Chambers and the four grandchildren of Thomas Jefferson Turpin are the only representatives of the family, who still live in Gallatin County. My brother left two daughters, Mrs. J. K. Bannister, of Lima, Ohio, and Mrs. W. S. Corkran, of Milburn, New Jersey.

My younger brother, James Whitfield Chambers, married and has one son, Moreau B. Chambers, who is now 18 years old. They live on their plantation at Clinton, Mississippi.

I married Everett Edwards Abbett at Warsaw, Ky., December 10th, 1878. Mr. Abbett died in 1913. Our children are:

Anna Gibson Abbett, who is not married and who lives with me in Louisville, Ky., Harry Jefferson Abbett, married Jean Tilney Jackson, of Lethbridge, Canada. They lost their only child, Harry, Jr. My son, Harry was graduated from the U. S. Naval Academy, Annapolis in February, 1907, saw service in Mexican waters and commanded a flotilla of destroyers operating out of Brest in the World War. He was awarded the "Distinguished Service Medal" by our Government and the cross of The Legion of Honor with the title of "Chevalier" by the French Government. He is still in the Navy, holding the rank of "Commander" and is the Executive Officer at the U. S. Naval Training Station, San Diego, Cal.

My son, Edward Bancroft Abbett, married Sophie Rogers Lee, of Louisville, Ky. They have two children Ann Preston Abbett, born in 1924 and Mary Bancroft Abbett, born in 1925. Edward is General Manager of The Newport Culvert Co., of Newport, Ky., and they live in Covington, Ky.

My youngest son, Leon Gill Abbett, married Lillian Julian, of Lexington, Ky., and they have one son, Tarlton Julian Abbett who was born in 1925. They live in Clearwater, Florida, where Leon is in the general insurance business.

Both Edward and Leon served overseas in the World War as Captains in the 325th Field Artillery.

Philip Osborne Turpin, son of Horatio and Mary (Bancroft) Turpin, married Mary Ellen Butler, of Carroll County, Ky. Their children were:

(1) Fannie; married Evan Southgate.
(2) Percival Butler; died unmarried.
(3) Sallie; married Edward Southgate.
(4) Dr. Thomas Jefferson; married Sophia C. (Fidie) Buckner.
    Living in Chihuahua, Mexico. One child:
        (a) Katherine; married John N. Goddard.
(5) Virginia, died young.
(6) Philip Bancroft; married Fannie Griffin.
(7) Mary, died young.
(8) William T., died young.

Thomas Turpin, whose will was probated in Bedford County, March 27, 1826, came to Bedford from Chesterfield County, Virginia, sometime after the Revolutionary War. He was born about 1758, a descendant of Michael Turpin, the emigrant, and was, probably, the grandson of Philip and Elizabeth Turpin, of Chesterfield. (The will of Elizabeth Turpin (widow) dated 1769, Will Book 2, page 211, Chesterfield County records, mentions children: Philip, Thomas, Elisha, Mary Winifree, Josiah, Martha.) Thomas Turpin married, about 1779, Rachel Cheatwood, daughter of William Cheatwood, of

Powhatan County, Va. (William Cheatwood's will in Powhatan County, 1777, Will Book "I," page 129, mentions children as follows: John, Daniel, Billy, Lotty, Alexander; nine daughters: Clara, Sillah, Rachel, Beckie, Alice, Patience, Polly, Charity, and Betsy.) (Sillah Cheatwood married Jesse Spinner, and came to Bedford County to live. See Spinner-Burks families.) Thomas Turpin died in 1826, and his wife, Rachel, several years later.

CHILDREN:

(1) Elisha, born about 1782; deceased before 1823. Evidently never married.

(2) Elizabeth, born about 1784; married, January 17, 1801, Sanford Halley. Went West.

(3) Josiah, born about 1785; married, March 6, 1810, Frances Burton. (See forward.)

(4) Philip, born 1787; married, February 28, 1814, Elvira Clayton. (See forward.)

(5) Thomas, Jr., born October 1, 1788; married, January 2, 1818, Mary Polina Clayton. (See forward.)

(6) Roland, born 1790; married (first), March 31, 1831, Margaret Logwood; married (second), September 16, 1841, Elizabeth (Wilson) Reid (widow). (See forward.)

(7) William C., born about 1792; married Alice Smith, of Appomattox County, Virginia. (See forward.)

(8) John, born January 4, 1794; married (first), June 24, 1822, Eliza W. Clayton; married (second), November 12, 1832, Mary M. Lambert. (See forward.)

(9) Vincent, born October 29, 1797; married, January 10, 1826, Sarah A. Lane. (See forward.)

(10) Milly, youngest child, born about 1800, unmarried in 1823.

In Will Book "F," page 313, of the Bedford County records, we find the will of Thomas Turpin as follows:

I, THOMAS TURPIN of the county of Bedford, Va., do make this my last will and Testament, in the form & words following, to-wit: 1st, Immediately after my decease, that my executors hereafter named, do pay my just debts. 2dly, I lend unto my beloved wife Rachel Turpin, my negro woman Rhoda, and one third part of my estate, except a small tract of land which decended to me by the death of my son Elisha Turpin, for & during her natural life. 3dly, My children, Elizabeth Hally (formerly E. Turpin), Josiah Turpin, Thomas Turpin, Phillip Turpin & John Turpin, having received what I consider their portions of my estate, heretofore in advance, I make no further provision for them, or either of them, in this my last will. 4thly, I give unto my daughter Milley Turpin, one third part of my estate, not otherwise disposed of. 5thly, I give to my son William Turpin one sixth part of my estate, not otherwise disposed of. 6thly, I give unto my son Vincent Turpin, one sixth part of my estate not otherwise disposed of. 7thly, I give unto my son Roland Turpin one third part of my estate not otherwise disposed of—and Lastly, I constitute and appoint my friend Martin P. Burk as Executor of this my last will and testament, hereby revoking all other or former wills, heretofore by me made.

In testimony whereof I have hereunto set my hand & affixed my seal this 27 day of January, one thousand, eight hundred and twenty three.

THOMAS TURPIN [SEAL].

Witness:

JESSE SPINNER,
ALBERT A. SHERMAN.

At a Court held for Bedford County, at the courthouse March 27, 1826.

The preceeding last Will and Testament of Thomas Turpin dec'd was proved by the oath of Albert A. Sherman, and ordered to be recorded as a will of personal estate; and on motion of Martin P. Burk, the executor therein named, who made oath & executed a bond with security, according to law, certificate is granted him for obtaining a probate thereof in due form; and afterwards, to-wit, at a Court held for said County, May 23d, 1826, the said will was further proved by Jesse Spinner another subscribing witness, and ordered to be recorded as a will of real estate.

Teste,

A copy,

J. C. STEPTOE, *C. B. C.*

Teste:

V. W. NICHOLS,
Clerk of the Circuit Court of Bedford County, Virginia.

Will Book "F," page 313.

Josiah Turpin, born about 1785, son of Thomas Turpin, Sr., and Rachel (Cheatwood) Turpin, married, in Bedford County, March 6, 1810, Frances Burton (probably, a daughter of Edmund and Cynthia Burton). He lived in Arnold's Valley, Rockbridge County, where he died in 1842 and his will probated in that county December 5, 1842. in Will Book No. 9, page 238.

CHILDREN:

(1) Edwin Madison Turpin.
(2) William Burton Turpin.
(3) Calohill M. Turpin.
(4) Richard Layfaette Turpin.
(5) Caswell Turpin. (See forward.)
(6) Cleopatra A. Turpin.
(7) Brackenridge Turpin.
(8) Frances Burton Turpin.

WILL OF JOSIAH TURPIN:

In the name of God amen I Josiah Turpin of Rockbridge County being of sound mind but infirm health do make this my last will & testament (revoking all others). In form following to wit: My first desire is that all my just debts be paid out of my estate, in the next place it is my wish that my estate both real & personal may be kept together for the benefit of my children till the first day of November, 1852, the small children to be educated out of my said estate. At the expiration of the time aforesaid it is my desire that my said estate be equally divided among my following children, to-wit: Edwin Madison Turpin, Wm. Burton Turpin, Calohill Turpin, Richard Layfaette Turpin, Caswell Turpin, Cleopatra Turpin, Bracken-ridge Turpin, Frances Burton Turpin, & moreover I do hereby con-stitute & appoint my brother John Turpin of Bedford County my executor to this my last will & testament. In witness hereof I have set my hand & affixed my seal this 16th May 1842.

JOSIAH TURPIN [SEAL].

Signed & acknowledged in
the presence of

M. PENDLETON,
JOHN A. REYNOLDS,
HARRISON WRIGHT.

At Rockbridge County Court, December 5th, 1842.

The last Will and testament of Josiah Turpin deceased was produced in Court proved by the oaths of John A. Reynolds and Harrison Wright, subscribing witnesses thereto, and ordered to be recorded, and on the motion of John Turpin the executor therein named, who made oath and together with Thomas Turpin and Vincent Turpin his securities (who justified) entered into and acknowledged a bond in the penalty of fourteen thousand dollars according to law, certificate is granted him to obtain a probat thereof in due form.

A copy from Will Book 9, page 238.

William B. Turpin, Calohill M. Turpin and Richard Layfaette Turpin settled in Pike County, Missouri. Cleopatra A. Turpin married Thomas A. Martin and lived in Warren County, Missouri. Frances Burton Turpin; married, September 5, 1855, P. F. Denton. (Marriage bond found in records of Bedford County, Va.)

Caswell Turpin, born March 4, 1828, son of Josiah and Frances (Burton) Turpin; married (first) Mary O. Layne, of Bedford County, who was born December 12, 1840, and died January 24, 1859, of typhoid fever, six months after her marriage. In June, 1860, he married (second) Willie Howard Carter, of Nelson County. She was born March 25, 1842, and died April 18, 1923. Caswell Turpin served in the Civil War in Company A, Second Virginia Cavalry and was wounded at Manassas, July 21, 1861. He was the father of eleven children as follows:

(1) Robert B., born December 30, 1862; married Rebecca Thomas, of Bedford.

CHILD:

    (a) Goldie M., born April 1, 1888; married, December 18, 1912, Henry R. Hunt, of New York State. They have one child:

        (aa) Elenor M., born October 13, 1913.

(2) Lena A., born April 8, 1864; died October 10, 1895; never married.

(3) Richard L., born March 16, 1866; died March 4, 1887; never married.

(4) Rosalie E., born November 10, 1867; married, in 1889, Addison Norvelle, of Buckingham County, Virginia, who died in 1914.

CHILDREN:

(a) ———————, died an infant.

(b) Helen, born 1898; married, in 1917, Charles T. Smith, of Bluefield, W. Va.

CHILDREN:

(aa) Dorothy, died 1919.

(bb) Nina.

(cc) Anita.

(dd) William.

(5) Mary Willie, born December 11, 1869; married, in 1891, N. O. Hawkins, of Lynchburg, Virginia, who died April 3, 1927.

CHILD:

(a) Ruth, born August 5, 1900; married, in 1920, Lloyd B. Pace.

CHILDREN:

(aa) Mary Louise.

(bb) Sidney B.

(6) John R., born August 5, 1872; married Florence Johnson, of Buckingham County, Va., who died in 1919.

CHILDREN:

(a) Johnson.

(b) Mary.

(c) Gladys.

(d) Harry.

(e) Elizabeth.

(f) Richard.

(7) Otho W., born May 19, 1875; married, August 7, 1924, Mary Lowery.

CHILDREN:

(a) Nancy, born July 2, 1925.

(b) Dorothy, born November 1, 1926.

(c) Infant (deceased).

(8) Edwin Caswell, born April 11, 1877; married, April 27, 1916, Sallie Strother Pendleton, daughter of Col. W. C. Pendleton, of Marion, Virginia.

CHILDREN:

(a) Julia Bittle, born May 6, 1917.

(b) David Howard, born August 10, 1922.

(c) Edwin Pendleton, born May 9, 1926.

(9) Patrick E., born February 10, 1879; died June 16, 1920; never married.

(10) Thomas J., born April 12, 1882; married Lena Rondabush, of Staunton, Virginia. No children.

....

Philip Turpin, of Bedford County, Virginia, son of Thomas Turpin, Sr., and Rachel (Cheatwood) Turpin, was born 1787; married, February 28, 1814, Elvira Clayton, born 1797, daughter of John Willis Clayton, Jr., and Lucinda (Douglas) Clayton, of Bedford County. Philip Turpin was a soldier of the War of 1812, serving in Eastern Virginia. Being unused to the climate of that region he endured many hardships, while rendering distinguished service in Norfolk and vicinity. He owned a large tract of land inherited from his father, part of which still remains in the possession of some of his descendants. He was a man most highly honored by all who knew him.

The following is the epitaph taking from the stone over his and his wife's grave where they rest in the family graveyard at his old home.

PHILIP TURPIN
BORN IN 1787
DIED
NOVEMBER 2, 1881.

ELVIRA TURPIN
BORN IN 1797
DIED
AUGUST 7, 1879.

Their toils are past,
Their work is done
They fought the fight,
The victory won.

CHILDREN:

(1) John Willis; married, December, 1837, Mildred Alba Mosby, daughter of P. W. Mosby, of Bedford; settled in Prairieville, Pike County, Missouri, where he died September 7, 1860, and his wife died January 5, 1861.

CHILDREN:

(a) Ann Judson, born July 7, 1840; died February 14, 1902; married J. R. Powell, who died February 13, 1912, aged 84 years. There were three daughters:

(aa) Anna.
(bb) Mildred.
(cc) Eddie.

(b) Woodson Morris, born August 27, 1841; married Miss Mariam Bell, of Paynesville, Missouri. She died August 16, 1868, and he later married Mrs. Alice Magruder. Woodson Morris Turpin served in the Civil War under General Price—was in prison more than a year. He died April 4, 1928.

CHILD BY FIRST MARRIAGE:

(aa) Morris B. Turpin, living at Vandalia, Missouri.

CHILD BY SECOND MARRIAGE:

(bb) Homer Reid Turpin, now a resident of Cleveland, Ohio.

(c) John Philip, born in Bedford County, Virginia, November 4, 1846, the youngest child of John Willis and Mildred A. (Mosby) Turpin who moved to Missouri when he was only two years old; married Miss Addie Bell, of Paynesville, Missouri (a sister of his brother Woodson's first wife, Mariam Bell). John Philip Turpin died September 29, 1928.

CHILDREN:

(aa) Lula B.; married Fenton J. Fry, Louisiana, Missouri.
(bb) Lemma A.; remained single; died June 4, 1928.
(cc) Ruby B.; married Gilbert X. Henshaw, of Kansas City, Missouri.

(2) Elisha G., born November 11, 1810; married (first) November 25, 1838, Eliza Eldrige Tinsley, born November 15, 1821, daughter of William Tinsley. He married (second) on March 25, 1847, in Lynchburg, Va., Amanda N. Haynes, born October 12, 1822; died August 1902, daughter of Henry E. and Mary (Smith) Haynes, of Amherst County, Va. Elisha G. Turpin died in 1894.

CHILDREN BY FIRST MARRIAGE:

(a) William Henry, born October 10, 1840.
(b) Eliza E., born August 28, 1842; married (first), February 5, 1862, Albert L. Noell. She married (second), January 28, 1868, Monroe Noell.

CHILDREN BY FIRST MARRIAGE:

(aa) Ida Burwell, born November 17, 1862; married, April 16, 1885, Carey Jones.

CHILDREN:

(aaa) Albert, born April 16, 1886.
(bbb) Ruth, born January 15, 1888.
(ccc) Beulah, born January 20, 1890.
(ddd) Harry Lee, born December, 1891.
(eee) Lemma.
(fff) Fannie.
(ggg) Earl.
(hhh) Edward.
(iii) Christine.
(jjj) Lillian.

(bb) Albert Lowry, born August 5, 1864; married, March 12, 1889, Carrie H. Smith, daughter of Rev. Horace P. and Anne Judson (Leftwich) Smith. He is President of The Peoples Bank of Covington, Va., where he lives.

CHILDREN:

(aaa) Albert Lowry, Jr., born January 3, 1890; died in 1895.
(bbb) Horace Wendell, born March 23, 1892;

married, July 31, 1912, Rae Smith. No children.

- (ccc) Corinne, born February 11, 1896; married Dr. C. C. Johnson. One child: Carroll Cullen, Jr.
- (ddd) Herbert Starcos, born June 4, 1898; died October 12, 1901.
- (eee) Catherine Craddock, born September 20, 1900; married, September 14, 1922, Thomas Charlton Cover, and have two children: Anne Judson, born June 17, 1923; Charles Wendell, born July 17, 1925.
- (fff) Geraldine, born June 30, 1903; married, September 8, 1928, A. S. Lancaster.
- (ggg) Terry Edmunds, born December 20, 1905.

CHILDREN BY SECOND MARRIAGE:

- (cc) Judie E., born January 16, 1869.
- (dd) Tinsley Turpin, born December 8, 1874.
- (ee) J. Eldridge, born December 10, 1877.
- (ff) Minnie Haynes, born April 14, 1880; married, in December, 1900, Edward Gilpin Hirons.

CHILDREN:

- (aaa) Edward Gilpin, Jr., born July 29, 1902; married Miss Ruth Rice. They have one child: Patricia Noell Hirons.
- (bbb) James Moorhead, born August 24, 1910.

CHILDREN BY SECOND MARRIAGE:

- (c) John Henry, born August 9, 1848; died November, 1849.
- (d) Mildred M. ("Millie"), born November 20, 1849; married, October 22, 1867, Thomas E. Noell, born 1839, died 1920; son of Cornelius and Ellen (Lowry) Noell.

CHILDREN:

(aa) Edward Turpin; unmarried.
(bb) Marvin Ward; married Bettie Bell. One child:
(aaa) Marvin.
(cc) Nettie; married Rev. O. P. Lloyd.

CHILDREN:

(aaa) Mildred; married, 1922, Dulaney Hammond. Two children: Dulaney, Jr., and Harriet.
(bbb) Novell Owen.
(dd) Henry Judson; married (first) Lillie Wells. She was killed in an automobile accident. He married (second), July 8, 1922, Katherine Sallins Watts, daughter of William Beverley and Edna Douglas (Major) Watts. (See Douglas family.)

CHILD BY FIRST MARRIAGE:

(aaa) Jack Wells, born July 16, 1918.

CHILD BY SECOND MARRIAGE:

(bbb) William Judson, born March 2, 1924.
(ee) Lillian Irene (deceased).
(ff) Triplett Lowry; married Josephine Nolan.

CHILDREN:

(aaa) Lowry.
(bbb) Margaret.
(ccc) Lawrence.
(gg) Frank Tyree; married (first) Ethel Embree; married (second) Ruth Butts.

CHILD BY FIRST MARRIAGE:

(aaa) Harold, born 1918.
(hh) Allie Novell; married Harry L. Keller.
(ii) Hugh Ellis; married Margaret Henley.

CHILDREN:

(aaa) Hugh Ellis, Jr.
(bbb) John Henley, born February 14, 1924.
(jj) Harry Thomas; married Lettie Mae Ayers.

CHILD:

(aaa) Harriet.

(kk) Mary Gretchen; married William Lee Wood.

CHILDREN:

(aaa) Katherine, born 1918.

(bbb) Julia, born 1920.

(ccc) Virginia Lee, born February, 1922.

(e) Mary Herbert ("Hertie"), born October 15, 1851; married Albert Pettigrew, of Lynchburg, Virginia. Both deceased. No children.

(f) Lillian Alice, born November 12, 1853; married Bud Elliott. There were children by this marriage.

(g) Susan E., born August 20, 1855; unmarried. Living in Lynchburg, Va.

(h) Henry Ann, born November 14, 1857; deceased—never married.

(i) Lenna Elvira, born October 3, 1859; married Samuel R. Logwood, born February 27, 1862, son of James A. and Caroline W. (Penn) Logwood, and grandson of Moses and Edna A. (White) Penn. She died 1890. (See Penn family.)

CHILDREN:

(aa) Ruth Logwood; married ———— Doss.

CHILD:

(aaa) Lenna Reid; living in Lynchburg, Va.

(bb) Infant—died in infancy.

(3) Catherine; married J. W. Mosby.

(4) Martha Ann; married (first), 1839, Simon A. White; (second) James W. Stuart.

(5) Elizabeth A.; married (first), October 23, 1844, Jacob White Hatcher (died 1849), son of Thomas and Catherine (White) Hatcher. (See Hatcher family.) Married (second) J. P. Watson. She died August 9, 1883.

(6) Mary P.; married Nelson Wingfield.

(7) James M., born October 6, 1832; married, December 22, 1862, Lucy Mac Penn, born September 8, 1842, daughter of Moses and Edna A. (White) Penn. (See Penn and White families.)

James M. Turpin enlisted in July, 1861, in Company "A," 28th Virginia Infantry and served till the close of the war. Many of his descendants are now living in Missouri.

CHILDREN:

(a) George R., born March 12, 1865.

(b) James W., born September 6, 1867.

(c) Cora E., born August 22, 1869; died July 25, 1870.

(d) Allen W., born August 23, 1870.

(e) Lawrence McD., born September 8, 1872.

(f) Lizzie O., born August 7, 1874.

(g) Sallie D., born November 28, 1876.

(h) Philip C., born January 28, 1879.

(i) Sammie L., born October 31, 1880.

(j) Mattie, born September 3, 1883.

(8) Frances L., born April 22, 1835; died February 15, 1895; married (first), February 8, 1855, George W. Wright; (second), March 25, 1869, Benjamin P. Watson, a native of Botetourt County, Va., born April 9, 1838; died February 11, 1914, son of James F. and Cynthia A. (Wilkerson) Watson, of Bedford County, Va.

CHILD BY FIRST MARRIAGE:

(a) Sarah Elizabeth Wright, born December 8, 1857; married (first), George Turpin, son of Captain John and Mary M. (Lambert) Turpin. (See Capt. John Turpin's family. (Second), William Edward Major, born October 5, 1858, son of Spottswood Alexander and Catharine K. (Douglas) Major. (See Douglas family.)

CHILDREN BY FIRST MARRIAGE:

(aa) Lottie L. Turpin, born July 13, 1877; married Jesse Spinner Douglas; two children. (See Douglas family.)

(bb) George Frank Turpin, born August 7, 1879; married Rachel Main: one child.

CHILDREN BY SECOND MARRIAGE:

(cc) One child died infant.

(dd) Mamie Kathleen; married Ashby Perrow, of Bedford County. Have three children: Jack, Shirley and Louise.

CHILD BY SECOND MARRIAGE:

(b) Alberta Norvel Watson, born December 22, 1870; married, February 14, 1917, Walter Owen Arrington, born December 31, 1872, son of Robert, born in Halifax County, and Virginia T. (Markham) Arrington, born in Botetourt County, now of Bedford County. No children.

(9) Thomas M. ("Tom Phil"), born September 17, 1838; married (first), October 25, 1867, Cleopatra A. Hatcher, born July 3, 1846, daughter of Granville L. Hatcher and Celiste Hatcher; married (second) in Bedford County, December 8, 1874, Caroline W., daughter of Moses and Edna A. (White) Penn, and widow of James A. Logwood. (See Penn family.) Thomas M. Turpin, was a member of Company "E," 34th Virginia Infantry and served with honor during the four years of the Civil War.

CHILDREN BY FIRST MARRIAGE:

(a) Maggie, born April 25, 1869; married Robert H. Noell, born May 19, 1856, son of Palestine W., born October 15, 1815; and Ann Eliza (Jeter) Noell, born October 6, 1822, daughter of Jesse and Susan (Robinson) Jeter, of Bedford County. Susan Robinson was a daughter of Benjamin Robinson, who served with honor in the War for Independence, Robert H. Noell is a grandson of John C. Noell (born in Bedford County, where he died December, 1862), and his wife Nancy Witt (who was born in Nelson County, Virginia, and died September, 1874) and a great-grandson of Thomas Noell who served in the seven years of the Revolutionary War. His father Palestine W. Noell was in the Civil War under Breckenridge.

CHILDREN:

(aa) Lola Otis; married Elmo Thomas Poindexter, of Bedford County.

(bb) Annie Cleopatra; married Jerry Bell Poindexter, brother of Elmo Thomas Poindexter, above.

(cc) Thomas Leonard; married Roma Musgrove.

(dd) William Judson; married Velda Elizabeth Poindexter, of Bedford County.

(ee) Robert Earl (deceased).

(ff) Ruby Evylin (deceased).

(gg) Ruth Jensen; married Ernest Palmer Herndon.

(hh) Robert Marshall.

(ii) Lawrence Raymond.

(b) John Willis, born April 16, 1873; died December 7, 1918; married, November 15, 1904, Sudie Maria Clark, born April 17, 1876, daughter of William Joseph and Pauline R. (Overstreet) Clark, of Bedford County.

CHILD:

(aa) Herbert Moseley Turpin, born March 31, 1906; married, July 7, 1928, Elizabeth Clementine Hatcher, daughter of Samuel H. and Sallie Vaughan Hatcher.

CHILDREN BY SECOND MARRIAGE:

(c) Russell A., born November 6, 1875; married Virgie O. Wilkes, born August 5, 1871, daughter of Benjamin Wilkes, Jr., born May 13, 1844 (son of Benjamin and Matilda (Duffell) Wilkes) and Edna Ann (Penn) Wilkes, born August 3, 1844, daughter of Moses and Edna A. (White) Penn. (See Penn family.)

CHILDREN:

(aa) Loyd Wilkes; married Miss Alice Cridlin.

(bb) Buford Owen; married Miss Louise Key.

(cc) Harry, born October 15, 1905; married Miss Lillian Hatcher.

(dd) Philip Parmer, born February 2, 1914.

MARY POLINA CLAYTON
wife of Thomas Turpin, Jr.

(d) Edna Sale, born February 11, 1877; married, January 29, 1902, George Willis Turpin, born February 12, 1866, son of Spottswood Henry and Lucetta (Lambert) Turpin. (For descendants see Captain John Turpin family—Spottswood Henry Turpin's family.)

(e) Thomas Marvin, born January 29, 1879; married, March 12, 1905, Roberta Leighton Burks, born December 27, 1881, daughter of George Wellington and Harriet Eliza (Hopkins) Burks and a granddaughter of Martin P. and Louisa C. (Spinner) Burks, of Bedford County, Va. (See Burks family.)

CHILDREN :

(aa) Allen Burks, born November 13, 1906.
(bb) Thomas Fredrick, born December 31, 1908.
(cc) Lawrence Wilkes, born November 5, 1911.
(dd) Harriet Caroline, born December 18, 1913.
(ee) Lucy Elizabeth, born June 22, 1917.
(ff) Marvis Cathryne, born November 12, 1919.
(gg) Grace Deen, born September 7, 1922.
(hh) Martin Parks, born January 19, 1925.

Thomas Turpin, Jr., of Bedford County, Virginia, son of Thomas Turpin, Sr., and Rachel (Cheatwood) Turpin, was born October 1, 1788, and married, January 2, 1818, Mary Polina Clayton, born October 22, 1802. She was a daughter of John Willis Clayton, Jr., and Lucinda (Douglas) Clayton, who were married, March 21, 1797, in Bedford County, Virginia. Lucinda (Douglas) Clayton, was a daughter of George and Mary Douglas, of Bedford County (formerly of Amherst County—a Revolutionary soldier from that county) and a sister of David Douglas, who married Sally White, daughter of Captain Jacob and Hannah (Spiers) White. (See White and Douglas families.) John Willis Clayton, Jr., was a son of John Willis and Mary (———) Clayton, Sr., and a direct descendant of John Clayton, the Attorney-General of the Colonies. (See Clayton family.)

Thomas Turpin, Jr., like his father, was a planter by profession, owning large landed estates in Bedford County. He was a man of fine mind, honorable and highly esteemed by all who knew him. He died March 18, 1858, and was buried in the family burying ground. His wife died January 23, 1875, aged seventy-three years. He left a family of worthy sons and daughters. His will dated September 16, 1853, and probated April 26, 1858, Will Book "Q," page 554, of Bedford County records reads:

I, THOMAS TURPIN of the County of Bedford being of sound mind and memory, do make and ordain this my last Will and testament hereby revoking all former Wills by me heretofore made.

Item 1st, I direct all my just debts to be paid.

Item 2nd, I give to my beloved wife during her life or widowhood all of my estate of every kind with the following exception. I wish each of my children, Mary Frances Turpin, Thomas N. Turpin, Paul A. Turpin, America Turpin and George W. Turpin to receive from my estate a Slave as near the value of five hundred dollars as may be, the said slave to be delivered to them by my wife as soon as they severally attain the age of twenty one years to be accounted for by each of them in the final distribution of my estate.

Item 3rd, At the death of my wife I direct that the whole of my estate be equally divided among all my children to-wit, John D. Turpin, Lucy Ackerly, Sarah P. Wilson, Ann Eliza C. Reynolds, Mary Frances Turpin, Thomas N. Turpin, Paul A. Turpin, America Turpin and George W. Turpin, but in such division each of them are to be charged with advancements made to them according to the accounts kept by me against each of them in my book, and that portion of my estate herein given to Ann Eliza C. Reynolds, I hereby direct to be held by my son John D. Turpin in trust for her support and the support of her children, it being intended that her husband Micajah Reynolds shall have no interest therein, and that the same shall not be in any way subject to his debts and contracts, and at the death of my said daughter Ann Eliza C. Reynolds, the same is to be equally divided among all her children then living.

Item 4th, If my wife should marry again, then I give her such portion of my estate as she would be entitled to under the laws of the State of Virginia; and the residue thereof to be equally divided among my children as directed in the third clause to this will, and at her death the portion of my estate held by her for life to be divided in like manner in every case however the portion of my daughter Ann Eliza C. Reynolds to be held by my son John D. as trustee for the purposes and on the terms herein before mentioned.

I constitute and appoint my sons John D. Turpin and Thomas N. Turpin executors of this my last will and testament.

Witness my hand this 16 day of September, 1853.

THOMAS TURPIN.

Witnesses:

JAMES F. JOHNSON,

R. G. TURPIN.

I hereby annex this the 1st Mch. 1858 the following as a codicil to my Will above written, Viz., It is my will & wish that my Grandson Wm. A. Wilson shall inherit all of the *potion* of my estate that was willed to my daughter Sarah it being a childs part and that my son Thomas N. Turpin shall act as Guardian for him and have the control of what may be coming to him till he arrives to the age of twenty one, and in case of his death then it is my wish that all of my estate going to him shall revert back to my children equally.

THOMAS TURPIN.

Witnesses:

GEO. T. SNEAD,

R. G. TURPIN.

At a Court held for Bedford County the 26th day of April, 1858.

This writing purporting to be the last Will and Testament of Thomas Turpin dec'd, together with a codicil thereto annexed, was produced in Court and said will proved according to law by the oath of James F. Johnson and Rowland G. Turpin subscribing witnesses thereto and the said codicil proved according to law by the oath of George T. Snead and Rowland G. Turpin subscribing witnesses thereto and the said will and codicil are ordered to be recorded. And on the motion of John D. Turpin and Thomas N. Turpin the executors in said Will named who made oath and together with Rowland G. Turpin, Lewis C. Arthur, John Turpin & Geo. T. Snead their securities entered into and acknowledged bond in the penalty of fifteen thousand dollars conditioned according to law certificate is granted them for obtaining a probat of said Will in due form.

Teste:

A. A. ARTHUR, C. B. C.

A copy,

Teste:

V. W. NICHOLS,
Clerk of the Circuit Court of
Bedford County, Virginia.

Will Book "Q," page 554.

CHILDREN OF THOMAS TURPIN, JR., AND MARY P. (CLAYTON) TURPIN:

(1) John Dabney; married, November 30, 1842, Celinda Reynolds, a daughter of Jonas Reynolds; one daughter only:

   (a) Martha Turpin; married Charles Tooley.

CHILDREN:

   (aa) Will.
   (bb) Jesse.
   (cc) Ora (girl).
   (dd) Joshua.

(2) Ann Eliza C.; married, October 3, 1836, Micajah Reynolds, who was born August 11, 1811; died August 16, 1888. She died in 1882. He was a son of Charles and Nancy Bright Reynolds, of Bedford County.

CHILDREN:

   (a) Mary V., born June 14, 1838; married, November 22, 1856, Samuel Hutson, born December 18, 1836; died February 3, 1910. He was the son of John S. and Parthenia Hutson, of Chesterfield County and served in the Civil War, C. S. A. Mary V. Hutson is now living at Iron Gate, Va., with some of her children.

CHILDREN:

   (aa) Annie America, born November 29, 1858; married, December 23, 1876, Morgan B. Whitmore. She died in 1926.

(bb) Charles B. R., born September 11, 1860; died 1898; married Mollie Atkinson.

(cc) Cora Parthenia, born October 15, 1862; married Daniel Hoover.

(dd) Lelia A., born April 27, 1865; married David Hoover, in 1880.

(ee) Octavia Mazie, born July 11, 1867; married, December 25, 1884, Syrum Hoover.

(ff) Frank Thomas, born March 22, 1870; married, May 4, 1891, Cora Atkinson.

(gg) Robert Lavert, born January 26, 1872; married Ora Pullen.

(hh) Lula Clarence, born December 31, 1874; married, November 22, 1895, Thomas Lemon.

(ii) Macon Warner, born January 13, 1876; married, April 15, 1899, Mabel Switzer.

(b) John J., born 1839, eldest son, enlisted at the beginning of the war in the Confederate Army, 11th Virginia Regiment, and served till the end. Married Cornelia A. Edwards, daughter of Thomas E. and Anna C. Edwards, of Lexington, Virginia.

CHILDREN:

(aa) Thomas E., born January 8, 1868, in Botetourt, County, Virginia; married Miss Sallie Lowman (she is dead). He makes his home at Eagle Rock, Va.

(bb) Charles W., born July 4, 1873, in Botetourt County, Virginia, educated in the public schools of that county and for past twenty-two years has been a resident of Washington, D. C. Married Miss Maud Johnson, daughter of Sergeant Thadeus C. S. Johnson, of the Confederate Army, and his wife Mollie A. Johnson, of Botetourt County. No children.

(cc) Annie C., born April 7, 1875; married J. M. Brooks, a merchant, of Eagle Rock, Virginia.

One son:

(aaa) Walter R. Brooks, of Eagle Rock.

(dd) Child died infancy.

(ee) Child died infancy.

(c) Thomas E., born 1841; enlisted at the beginning of the war in the Confederate Army, 11th Virginia Regiment, and served till the end of the conflict. He married Belle Myers. Both dead.

(d) Charles Booker, born 1842; died October 31, 1928, in Washington, D. C., aged 86 years. His wife who was Miss Mollie Gilbert died January 7, 1926, and both are buried in Glen Wood Cemetery, Washington, D. C. They are survived by one son: (aa) George H. Reynolds, a retired Captain in the fire department of that city. For more than thirty years, Charles Booker Reynolds was employed at the Bureau of Engraving and Printing, as driver of the horse-drawn currency van which hauled billions of dollars from the Bureau to the Treasury Department; and during the entire period of his service never lost a dollar entrusted to his possession.

(e) Mildred, born 1846; married James Owens. Both are dead.

(f) Lucy; born 1848; married John Leighton. Both dead and are buried in Richmond, where they always made their home. There are two (2) children living there now.

(3) Lucy Douglas, born September 24, 1824; died December 16, 1899; married (first), May 27, 1847, William Ackerly, of Rockbridge County, Virginia. (Two children.) (See Ackerly family.) Married (second) Abraham Lavell. (Six children.)

(4) Sarah P.; married, August 16, 1849, Alexander Wilson, of Amherst County, Virginia. She died June 15, 1854, in Missouri where they lived. One son: (a) William A. Wilson survives. Lives in St. Louis, Mo.

(5) Mary Frances; married, November 26, 1860, John James Ogden, of Amherst County, Virginia. Moved to Troy, Lincoln County, Missouri, where they lived and died.

CHILDREN:

(a) Emmett M., probably living in Troy, Missouri.

(b) Lemma B., married a Mr. Harris. She is dead.

(c) George Edward, probably living in Troy, Mo.

(6) Thomas Nelson, born August 27, 1833; married (first), December 8, 1869, Elizabeth Harrison, born October 17, 1844, daughter of James S. and Nancy (Thomas) Harrison, of Bedford County. She died February 7, 1883. He married (second) Pattie Thomas, born 1845; died August 13, 1914. She was a daughter of Lafayette and Elizabeth (Hake) Thomas. No children by this second marriage. Thomas Nelson Turpin served with rank of second lieutenant in the Civil War; was wounded at Fredericksburg. He owned one of the finest farms near Big Island and devoted his life and interests to farming.

CHILDREN BY FIRST MARRIAGE:

(a) George Penn, born February 8, 1871; married, May 10, 1902, Ethel Milam, born October 29, 1884, daughter of Wm. H. Milam and Mary (Grant) Milam.

CHILDREN:

(aa) Elizabeth Pauline, born November 19, 1904.

(bb) Gordon Keith, born November 29, 1907.

(cc) Mary Maggie, born June 15, 1909.

(dd) Helen May, born October 5, 1911.

(ee) William Winston, born August 5, 1917.

(ff) George Penn, Jr., born November 12, 1922.

(b) Maizie L., born January 23, 1875; married, November 7, 1906, A. J. Trevey. Live at Big Island, Virginia.

CHILD:

(aa) John Turpin, born May 19, 1911.

(c) Thomas Nelson, Jr., born December 27, 1876; married (first) Lucille Trevey, daughter of A. J. and Louisa Burks (Snead) Trevey, of Bedford County, Va.; married (second), January 3, 1910, Mattie Parks, born December 1, 1889, daughter of Robert H. and Edna Frances (Penn) Parks. (See Penn family.) Live at Big Island, Virginia, where he is a successful business man.

CHILD BY FIRST MARRIAGE:

(aa) Thomas Raymond, born March 16, 1903.

CHILDREN BY SECOND MARRIAGE:

(bb) Frances Elizabeth, born November 23, 1910. Teaching in the public schools of Virginia.

(cc) Louis Parks, born February 3, 1912. Student at Washington and Lee University.

(dd) Mattie Teresa, born November 17, 1919.

(ee) Thomas Nelson, III, born August 15, 1921.

(d) James Alonza, born December 17, 1878; died August 5, 1904. Never married.

(7) Paul A.; married Sarah D. Penn, born September 2, 1840, daughter of Moses and Edna A. (White) Penn. (See Penn family.) He enlisted April 20, 1861, Company F, 58th Virginia Infantry; second lieutenant; wounded at Fredericksburg, December 23, 1862.

CHILDREN:

(a) Edward J.; married Mary Riley.

(b) Anna; married Henry Wilkes.

(c) Charlie; never married.

(d) Richard; died young.

(8) America, born July 22, 1838; died October 4, 1884; married, December 7, 1859, James Jacob Penn, born May 22, 1834, son of Moses and Edna A. (White) Penn. (See Penn family.)

(9) George W.; never married. Enlisted in the cause of the Confederacy at the outbreak of the war, joining Company "G," 2nd Virginia Cavalry. Captured at Westminister, June 28, 1863; held at Fort Delaware; died in prison September 14, 1863.

....

Roland Green Turpin, born in 1790, son of Thomas Turpin, Sr., and Rachel (Cheatwood) Turpin; married (first), March 31, 1831, Margaret Logwood, of Bedford County, Virginia. His second wife, whom he married, September 16, 1841, was Elizabeth (Wilson) Reid (widow), (daughter of John Wilson, Sr.), born in Rockbridge County, Va., August 24, 1809; died at Big Island, March 23, 1897, and buried

DORA ANN LAVELL,
wife of Roland Green Turpin, Jr.

ROLAND GREEN TURPIN, JR.

in the Oxford Cemetery in Rockbridge County. She was of Scotch-Irish ancestry; a woman of high character; a loving mother, devoted to her home, her family and her friends. Roland Green Turpin, Sr., was noted for his hospitality; a farmer by occupation, and was substantially successful in life. He died in 1885, age 95 years.

CHILD BY FIRST MARRIAGE:

(1) Sarah, married William Ludwell Davis; born June 22, 1826, son of Charles Lewis Davis, of Amherst County, Va., by his second marriage to Nancy Morris, September 16, 1816. Charles Lewis Davis' first wife was Rebecca White, daughter of Captain Jacob and Hannah (Spiers) White. (See White family.)

CHILDREN BY SECOND MARRIAGE:

(2) Hannah Rachel, born July 19, 1842; married, October 8, 1868, Paul S. Penn, son of Moses and Edna A. (White) Penn. (See Penn family.) She died October 17, 1928.

(3) Roland Green, Jr., born December 15, 1844; married, February 27, 1884, Dora Ann Lavell, born May 14, 1860, daughter of Abraham and Lucy Douglas (Turpin) (Ackerly) Lavell, of Rockbridge County. (See Lavell family.) He enlisted March 1, 1863, in Company G, 2nd Virginia Cavalry, and served with honor until the close of the Civil War, taking part in many of the important cavalry movements. He became a large land holder and influential citizen. Held several county offices; and was elected to the Virginia House of Delegates, 1895-1898 and 1901-1904. He was noted for his kindness and hospitality, a good father and a devoted husband. He was a member of the Baptist Church, the church of his forefathers. He died at Big Island, January 29, 1922.

CHILDREN:

(a) Roland Green, III, born February 9, 1885; died February 9, 1885.

(b) Robert Lucian, born August 27, 1886; died November 24, 1886.

(c) Lawrence Roland, born February 12, 1889; died December 21, 1889.

(d) Lula Buford, born December 29, 1890; died October 30, 1891.
(e) Roland Guy, born February 9, 1893; died February 12, 1896.
(f) Mary Elizabeth, born February 14, 1895; married, June 20, 1917, Robert Watkins Pattillo, born July 6, 1879, son of Robert Henry Pattillo, born December 19, 1847, and Isabella (Nelson) Pattillo, born October 24, 1854, of Chase City, Virginia.

CHILDREN:

(aa) Anabel, born July 11, 1918.
(bb) Roland Watkins, born April 25, 1921.
(g) Ralph Essex, born July 1, 1897; married, August 2, 1924, Edith May Whitlock, of Tobaccoville, Virginia. He is a graduate of V. P. I. and served in the World War.

CHILD:

(aa) Edith May, born November 28, 1925.
(4) Robert Lucian, born in 1848; died November, 1883; never married.
(5) Elizabeth Virginia, born November 17, 1850; married, February 5, 1873, William Thomas Ackerly, born July 23, 1848, son of William and Lucy Douglas (Turpin) Ackerly, of Rockbridge County, Virginia. (See Ackerly family.)

William C. Turpin, son of Thomas Turpin, Sr., and Rachel (Cheatwood) Turpin, born about 1792; married Alice Smith, of Appomattox County, and lived in Amherst County, Virginia. Seven of his sons fought in the Civil War, three of them having met death while serving in the cause of the Confederacy.

CHILDREN:

(1) Henry, died in infancy.
(2) Thomas Edward; married Mary Ogden in 1854.
(3) Robert; married Sallie Reynolds in 1855.
(4) Philip, killed in battle during Civil War.
(5) William, in Company G, Fifty-first Virginia Infantry, promoted corporal; killed at Brucetown, 1864.

(6) John Cheatwood, born April 15, 1842. (See forward.)

(7) Peter Flood, enlisted in 1862; Company F, 28th Virginia Infantry, Hunton's Brigade, Picketts' Division. He married in 1869, Ellen Jones.

(8) George, taken prisoner during Civil War and died while in prison.

(9) James, deceased; never married.

(10) Eliza; married ———— Markram.

(11) Mary; married William Ogden, of Bedford County, Va.

(12) Amanda Melvina; married Robert N. Carter. She died November 24, 1927.

(13) Martha Porter; married Robert Nathaniel Bowles. She died in August, 1927.

(14) Sallie Bettie, died when about eight years of age.

John Cheatwood Turpin, son of William C. and Alice (Smith) Turpin, the former, of Bedford County and the latter, of Appomattox County, and grandson of Thomas Turpin, Sr., and Rachel (Cheatwood) Turpin, was born in Amherst County, April 15, 1842. He saw service in the Confederate cause, having enlisted in Company F, Fiftieth Virginia Infantry, Robert Snead, Captain of the Company. Was in active service one year, then became a member of General Morgan's command and was wounded near Cumberland City in 1864. He later went with the company into Kentucky and was there taken prisoner and held for a period of nineteen months. On January 26, 1870, he married Miss Julia Elizabeth Jones, of Amherst County, daughter of Charles Lewis and Elizabeth Camden Jones. In 1876, he purchased a farm in Nelson County, "Maple Brook Farm," where he lived. He died in 1925. He was a member and trustee of the Jonesboro Baptist Church.

CHILDREN:

(1) Ernest Lynwood, born in Amherst County, November 26, 1870; married Kate Withers, born September 11, 1871, daughter of Dr. Walter Lemon and Frances Elizabeth (Hamilton) Withers. He was a prosperous farmer of Nelson County, where he died January 6, 1929.

CHILDREN:

(a) Susan Alexander, born February 10, 1904.

(b) Julia Elizabeth, born January 17, 1905; married John Raeburn Saunders. Living at Tyro, Nelson County, Va.

    (c) Idell, born June 19, 1907; married, October 4, 1928, Hamilton Cobbs. Living at Wingina, Va.

(2) Bettie Alice; married John T. Nash, of Clifford, Amherst County, Virginia.

CHILDREN:

    (a) Daughter; married ———— Cunningham (deceased).

    (b) Mary Hall, teaching at State College, Memphis, Tenn.

    (c) Daughter; married ———— Mays.

    (d) John Lewis, educated at University of Virginia. Farming at home.

    (e) Minnie Lula, living at home.

    (f) William Linwood; married, living in Lynchburg. One son:

        (aa) William Linwood, Jr., "Billy."

    (g) Dewitt Turpin, living in Charlottesville, Va.

    (h) Susie Watts, student at Sweet Briar College.

(3) Mary Magdaline (called "Lula"); married Andrew Johnson. She is deceased; her husband survives, also, six children. They live in Nelson County.

(4) Lillie Belle; married Nelson R. Phillips, of Nelson County, where they live. Have eight children.

(5) Lottie Cheatwood; married (first) James P. Brent. One son by this marriage. She married (second) Thomas Dameron; live in Nelson County. Two sons and two daughters by this marriage.

Captain John Turpin, born January 4, 1794; son of Thomas Turpin, senior and his wife, Rachel (Cheatwood) Turpin; married (first), June 24, 1822, Eliza W. Clayton, daughter of John Willis Clayton, Jr., and Lucinda (Douglas) Clayton, of Bedford County, Virginia. The Turpin men seemed to have a special fondness for the Clayton girls. Three of the Turpin brothers, having married the three Clayton sisters. By this marriage he had three sons. His second wife was Mary M. Lambert, whom he married, November 12, 1832. She was the daughter of George Lambert.

Captain John Turpin served with honor, four years in the War of 1812. He was a good father, a kind neighbor; beloved and honored by all who knew him. His was a kindly genial nature; and their home was the center of hospitality and good times for the younger people. He died February 17, 1884, at a ripe old age; and his wife in December, 1888, leaving a family of worthy sons and daughters.

CHILDREN BY FIRST MARRIAGE:

(1) Willis Clayton, was in the Civil War; married a Miss Moorman and moved to Missouri.

(2) Spottswood Henry; married, March 12, 1845, Lucetta Lambert, daughter of George Lambert and a younger sister of his step-mother.

CHILDREN:

(a) Sue, called "Sue Henry"; married William Parks, of Bedford County and had several children.

(b) Thomas Mosby, called "Tom Henry" to distinguish him from the other "Toms"; married, February 28, 1882, Annie Marshall Spinner, daughter of Dr. Jesse Frank Spinner and Martha J. (Snead) Spinner, of Bedford County. (See Spinner-Snead family.)

CHILDREN:

(aa) Frank Courtney, born February 14, 1884.

(bb) Irwin Judson, born July 30, 1887; died May 6, 1913.

(cc) Harry Spinner, born July 13, 1891; married, February 26, 1910, Bertha Falls.

(dd) Lambert Marshall, born April 22, 1893; married, December 5, 1923, Reid Eliza Parks, daughter of Robert Henry and Edna Frances (Penn) Parks, of Bedford County. (See Penn family.)

(ee) Mattie Weda, born March 19, 1897; married, November 29, 1922, Guy Judson White, son of Ceril Davis and Gertrude (Spinner) White. (See White and Spinner families.)

(c) Willie; married William M. Ogden, of Bedford County. They have one daughter, Lucy, who married Samuel H. Cornelius, son of William R. and Eliza Susan (Sledd) Cornelius. (See Sledd family.)

(d) George Willis, born February 12, 1866; married, January 29, 1902, Edna Sale Turpin, born February 11, 1877, daughter of Thomas M. ("Tom Phil") and Caroline W., daughter of Moses and Edna A. (White) Penn. (See Thomas M. Turpin's family.)

CHILDREN:

(aa) Connie Louise, born March 10, 1905; married L. T. Neff.

(bb) Spottswood Willis, born September 4, 1907.

(cc) Thomas Robert, born October 13, 1909.

(dd) Edna May, born September 20, 1912.

(ee) Lillian Penn, born November 15, 1915.

(ff) George Lambert, born January 27, 1918.

(gg) Dorothy Elizabeth, born July 5, 1920.

(3) Thomas Pettis; married, November 22, 1854, Mary E. Ogden, daughter of Rev. E. Ogden.

CHILDREN BY SECOND MARRIAGE:

(4) William L., born November 24, 1833; died June 12, 1900; married, May 4, 1858, Marinda J. Hatcher, born December 9, 1839; died May 14, 1894, daughter of Julius H. and Fannie B. (White) Hatcher. He joined Company A, 2nd Virginia Cavalry, first company to go out from Bedford County, and served till close of the war.

CHILDREN:

(a) Walter J., born June 27, 1860; died in Lynchburg, Va., February 9, 1912. Buried at the old family burying ground near Charlemont, Bedford County, Va. A successful business man; having accumulated some wealth. Prominent member of the Elks. Never married.

(b) Sallie Lula, born June 19, 1866; married, November 28, 1888, James Walter Penn, born March 2, 1867, son of James Jacob and America (Turpin) Penn. (See Penn family.)

(c) Georgie M., born August 21, 1869; died June 1, 1918, Marshall Lodge Hospital, Lynchburg, Va. Never married.

(d) Lelia Porter, born January 13, 1875; married, November, 1897; Spottswood A. Major, Jr., born March 21, 1875, son of Spottswood A. Major, Sr., and Cleopatra A. (Harrison) Major, daughter of James S. and Nancy (Thomas) Harrison. Lelia Porter (Turpin) Major, died March 21, 1920. Left one child:

  (aa) Dorothy Frances Major, born May 6, 1903, educated in Lynchburg, Va.; married, April 16, 1927, Gordon H. Warren, son of W. H. Warren.

(e) Viola L., born September 22, 1878; died October 1, 1918; married, October 8, 1908, William Pribble McDaniel, of Lynchburg, Va. No children.

(5) Charles, born July 12, 1835; went to Missouri; killed in the Civil War in 1863; never married.

(6) Sarah Ann, born March 2, 1837; married, January 20, 1863, James T. Noell, son of John C. Noell, born in Bedford County; died December, 1862, and Nancy (Witt) Noell, who was born in Nelson County; died September, 1874.

CHILD:

(a) James Turpin Noell, Jr., a prominent lawyer of Lynchburg, Virginia; married Lucy Dudley Watts, daughter of Ludwell Watts and Nancy Sallings (Davis) Watts (born July 4, 1824); and a granddaughter of Charles Lewis Davis and his second wife Nancy (Morris) Davis. Charles Lewis Davis married (first) Rebecca White, a daughter of Captain Jacob and Hannah (Spiers) White. (See White family.)

CHILDREN:

  (aa) Burroughs.
  (bb) Hortense.
  (cc) Shirley Watts.
  (dd) William Cedric.

(7) Susan Olivia, born May 17, 1839; died September 22, 1893; married, October 26, 1858, Dr. John Jeter, born August 18, 1832; died January 3, 1896, son of Jesse and Susan (Robinson)

Jeter. Dr. Jeter was educated at Richmond College and practiced his profession in Bedford County. (See Jeter family.)

(8) Ellen, born April 16, 1841; died July 23, 1903; never married.

(9) George, born September 28, 1848; married Sarah Elizabeth Wright, born December 8, 1857, daughter of George W. and Frances L. (Turpin) Wright, of Bedford County. He died April 11, 1881. (See Philip Turpin family.)

CHILDREN:

(a) Lottie; married, December 22, 1903, Jesse Spinner Douglas. (See Douglas family.)

(b) Frank; married Rachel Main.

(10) Lucy Jane, born December 25, 1850; married Warren Dulaney Rucker, born April 11, 1848; died February 16, 1920, son of Monroe and Marinda (McDaniel) Rucker.

CHILDREN:

(a) Hugh Clarence, born June 2, 1875; died May 5, 1903; never married.

(b) Edward Lawrence, born September 17, 1880; died April 20, 1911; never married.

(c) Mabel Virginia, born December 18, 1885; married Robert Cary Nichols, son of George Nichols.

CHILD:

(aa) Robert Cary Nichols, Jr., born October 20, 1908.

(d) Lelia Ashby, born September 19, 1892; married Henry Hales Derrick, son of Harry Derrick. No children.

(e) Lou Ella; died infancy.

(11) Laura Porter, born April 13, 1855; married, May 12, 1880, Edward Henry White, born October 18, 1855, son of John Milton and Mary Virginia White, of Bedford County. (See White family.)

....

Vincent Turpin, born October 29, 1797, son of Thomas Turpin, Sr., and Rachel (Cheatwood) Turpin; married, January 10, 1826, Sarah A. Lane, born March 22, 1808, daughter of Henry Lane (Layne). Vincent Turpin was born in Bedford County, Virginia, and married there; later moving to Rockbridge County where he owned land in several sections of the county. He finally settled in the upper part of the county near the Botetourt line. Here he raised his family and died on May 10, 1891. His will dated January 27, 1883; probated August 3, 1891, will be found in Will Book 27, page 398, of Rockbridge County records. His youngest son lived and died at the home place, which is still in possession of the family. He was of a kindly, genial disposition and well liked and esteemed by his fellowman. His extreme deafness in later years, was most unfortunate; but he bore it with Christian fortitude.

CHILDREN:

(1) Susan R., born October 18, 1826; married Elias Daniel. Left Virginia, before the war, in wagons for Missouri.

(2) John R., born March 15, 1830; died April 22, 1853; never married.

(3) Mary J., born March 6, 1832; married, December 23, 1850, Samuel Saville.

(4) James, born October 11, 1834; died 1865. Was a soldier in the Confederate Army; and at the close of the conflict, when returning home was ambushed in Missouri and killed. Was never married.

(5) Elizabeth J., born June 3, 1836; married, September 1, 1858, John E. W. Broughman; and with her eldest sister, Susan, and her family they traveled overland to Missouri.

(6) Nancy P., born November 11, 1842; married, March 6, 1858, Rev. Emmett T. Mason, a Baptist Minister.

(7) Nash, born April 6, 1844. Was a soldier in the Confederate Army. Contracted measles and died in or near Richmond, in 1862. Tablet erected to his memory in Richmond, Virginia.

(8) Samuel Vincent, born January 3, 1848; married (first), January 31, 1872, Sarah M. Rapp, daughter of Mattheas and P. Rapp, of Rockbridge. Married (second), November 25, 1886, Nancy Jane Reed, daughter of John A. T. and M. Reed, of Rockbridge County. He was a farmer by occupation and died at the home of his birth.

CHILDREN BY FIRST MARRIAGE:

(a) Sallie Cassandra, born February 21, 1874; unmarried.
(b) Myrtle Willie, born November 1, 1878; married Edward T. Sizer, of Botetourt County, Va.

CHILDREN:

(aa) Frank.
(bb) William.
(cc) Margaret.
(dd) Jack Phyllis.

(c) Mary Etha, born August 15, 1884; unmarried.

CHILDREN BY SECOND MARRIAGE:

(d) M. Ena Lerissa, born October 22, 1887; married Pat Wingfield. Live in Roanoke, Virginia.

CHILDREN:

(aa) Elizabeth.
(bb) Nancy Hope.
(cc) Pat, Jr.

(e) Ammen Vincent, born March 21, 1889; married, September 4, 1924, Ora Virginia Alphin, born May 2, 1893, daughter of the late William A. Alphin, of Botetourt County, Virginia. A. V. Turpin is successfully engaged in the mercantile business in Rockbridge County.

CHILD:

(aa) William Vincent, born June 28, 1926.

(f) Thurman, born July 2, 1894; married Minnie Saville, daughter of Harry and Josephine (Deacon) Saville, of Rockbridge County.

CHILD:

(aa) Nancy Josephine ("Nannie Joe").

(g) Lorene Virginia, born April 27, 1898; married a Mr. Stevens.

Marriages of the Turpin family, prior to 1867, from the Bedford County records:

Sanford Halley and Betsy Turpin, January 17, 1801. Thomas Turpin, surety.

James Dalton and Sally Turpin, 5th August 1802, Rev. John Ayres.

Daniel Turpin and Betsy Wilson, 27th Novr. 1804, Rev. John Ayres. Joseph Wilson, security, on marriage license bond.

Josiah Turpin and Frances Burton, March 6, 1810. Edmund Burton and Cynthia Burton, security.

Phillip Turpin and Elvira Clayton, 28th February 1814. Permission signed by Lucinda Clayton.

Thomas Turpin and Polly Clayton, daughter of Lucindy Clayton, 2nd Jany. 1818, Rev. Enoch Terry. Nelson Sale, security.

John Turpin and Eliza W. Clayton, June 24, 1822. John Turpin, Philip Turpin, security.

Vincent Turpin and Sarah Layne, 10th Jany. 1826. Henry Layne, security.

Roland Turpin and Margaret Logwood, 31st March 1831, Rev. James Leftwich.

John Turpin and Miss Mary M. Lambert, 12th November 1832, daughter of George Lambert.

Micajah Reynolds and Mary A. E. Turpin, daughter Thomas Turpin, 13 October 1836, Rev. Wm. Harris.

John W. Turpin and Mildred A. Mosby, daughter of P. W. Mosby, 12 Decr. 1837, Rev. Wm. Harris. Simon A. White, security.

Elisha Turpin and Eliza Tinsley, daughter of Wm. Tinsley, 10 Novr. 1838, Rev. Wm. Harris. Simeon White, security.

Siemon A. White and Martha A. Turpin, 27 June 1839, Rev. Wm. Harris. Philip Turpin, security.

John D. Turpin and Celinda Reynolds, daughter of Jonas Reynolds, 28 Nov. 1842, Rev. Wm. Harris. Callohill Turpin, security.

Jacob W. Hatcher and Elizabeth A. Turpin, 23 October 1844, Rev. Wm. Harris.

Spottswood H. Turpin and Lucetta S. Lambert, daughter of George Lambert, 12th March 1845, Rev. Wm. Harris.

William Ackerly (Acholie) and Lucy Turpin, 27 May 1847, Rev. Wm. Harris.

Alexander Wilson and Sarah P. Turpin, daughter Thomas Turpin, 16 August 1849, Rev. Wm. Harris.

Thomas Edward Turpin and Mary E. Ogden, daughter of E. Ogden, 22 November 1854, Rev. E. Ogden. (Son of Wm. C.)

George W. Wright and Frances L. Turpin, daughter of Phillip Turpin, 8th Feby. 1855, Rev. Wm. Harris.

P. F. Denton and Fanny B. Turpin, daughter of Josiah Turpin, 5 Sept. 1855, Rev. Wm. Harris.

Robert Turpin and Sallie Reynolds, daughter of Linwallen Reynolds, 13 Decr. 1855, Rev. Price Woodroof. (Son of Wm. C.)

John James Ogden and Mary F. Turpin, daughter of Thomas Turpin, 26 November 1860, Rev. A. H. Ogden.

Albert L. Noell and Eliza E. Turpin, daughter of Elisha Turpin, 5th Feby. 1862, Rev. Wm. Harris.

James T. Noell and Sallie A. Turpin, daughter of John Turpin, 20th Jany. 1863.

James M. Turpin and Lucy MacPenn, daughter of Moses Penn, 22nd Decr. 1863, Rev. E. D. Dewitt.

Thomas M. Turpin and Patty A. Hatcher, daughter of Granvill Hatcher, 25th October 1867.

Thomas E. Noell and Martha M. Turpin, daughter of Elisha G. Turpin, 22 October 1867, Rev. J. A. Davis.

ACKERLY

The Ackerly family of Virginia trace their ancestry from the German Akerlein, meaning like a field. Aker, field; lein, like.

Paul Akerlein, who appears to be the first of this line to settle in Virginia, came to Augusta County sometime prior to 1786. The following marriage bond is found in the records of Augusta County:

"1788—November 27—Paul Akerly and Stephen Miller, surety, Paul Akerly and Sally Miller. (Meuller.) (Signed)—Paul Akerlein (German)."

Probably the first of the family to come to America settled around Long Island. Records show that the Ackerly family have been residents of Brookhaven Town (Long Island) since 1655. We find the name written Akeley, Ackley, Ackeley, Ackerley, Ackerly, Akerly, Acly, Akely, Akley.

Thomas Akeley married Abigail Wilder, a direct descendant of the William White family that came over in the *Mayflower.*

Paul Akerlein, probably, moved to Augusta County, Virginia, from Pennsylvania directly after the Revolutionary War. His son, Paul (or John Paul) Akerly was a soldier in the Revolutionary War. The old canteen and Revolutionary uniform were in the possession of the family until, some fifteen or twenty years ago, when they were destroyed by fire.

Paul (or John Paul) Akerly owned land in Augusta County, Virginia, prior to 1800. In his will written October 21, 1824, Rockbridge County records, Will Book "6," page 214, he mentions a tract in Augusta County of 195 acres. This same tract of land was sold, February 16, 1829, by his Ex'ors. viz.:—John Paul Ackerly, Jr., and William Ackerly (his sons), of Rockbridge County, Virginia.

John Paul Akerly, Sr., removed with his family to Rockbridge County around 1800. His father Paul Akerlein was also a resident of the county in 1815. The exact date of his death is not known. John Paul Akerly, Sr., died in the year 1827. His will was probated in Rockbridge County Court, September 3, 1827. (See Will Book "6," page 214, Rockbridge County records.) He was a man of thrift and intelligence. Both he and his father were buried in Augusta County.

Sarah (Miller) Akerly, born 1766; married, November 27, 1788, Paul (or John Paul) Akerly; died July 5, 1858, aged 92 years. She was buried in the Ackerly family burying ground at Summers by the side of her daughter Elizabeth and her son William, who had preceded her to the grave. Descendants of the Miller (or Meuller) family are still found in Augusta and other surrounding counties. Adam Meuller, first of the name to settle in the valley, immigrated from Lancester County, Pennsylvania, about 1730. He originally came from Germany.

CHILDREN OF JOHN PAUL AND SARAH (MILLER) ACKERLY:

(1) John Paul, Jr.; married Mary Jane Cobbs, of Campbell County, Virginia, January 16, 1840. They lived in Rockbridge County. There were three children, viz.:

    (a) John Paul, III, for many years, engaged in newspaper work, first, in Lynchburg, Va., later in Portsmouth, Va. Served Rockbridge Grays, Company "H," 4th Virginia Infantry, Stonewall Brigade. Never married.

    (b) Charlie R., died in New Orleans of yellow fever. He left four children, viz.:

        (aa) Lilly.

        (bb) John P.

        (cc) ————.

        (dd) ————.

    (c) Sidney, editor of *Every Saturday,* a newspaper at one time published in Richmond, Va. He married Miss Margaret Lane, of Portsmouth, Va.

(2) William; married Lucy Douglas Turpin, May 27, 1847. (See forward.)

(3) Peter; married Lydia Shafer, November 6, 1828. (See forward.)

(4) Stephen; married Susan McDaniel, February 4, 1830.

(5) Magdalene; married Wiley H. Becket, August 29, 1815. Moved to Ohio.

(6) Mary; married Daniel Carr, June 14, 1817. Went West.

(7) Margaret ("Peggy"); married ———— Almonrode. Moved to Indiana. Returned to Virginia on a visit soon after the Civil War. Nothing further known of the family.

(8) Elizabeth ("Betsy"), died July 7, 1852. Never married.

(9) Anne; married Anthony Martin, April 11, 1844. No issue.

(10) Sarah.

(11) Barbara.

Following is the will of John Paul Ackerly, Sr., found in Will Book "6," page 214, of the Rockbridge County records:

I John Paul Akerly of the county of Rockbridge and State of Virginia in sound mind and memory calling to mind that it is appointed that all men must die do this 21st day of October Eighteen Hundred and twenty four make and constitute this my last will & testament.

1st. I comend my soul to God, and my body to be decently intered, in hopes of a joyful resurrection by the mercy of God, through the intercession & attoning sacrifice of Our Lord & Saviour Jesus Christ: Such of my worldly estate, as it has pleased Almighty God to give me I bequeath in the manner following to wit:

I will and bequeath forever.

1st. To my four sons John Paul, William, Peter & Stephen all my lands & tenements situate & being in the county of Augusta & Rockbridge—viz.: The tract in Augusta of 195 Acres lying on the head of Walkers Creek joining John Armstrong & others and the land I live on 528 acres more or less joining Samuel Walkup & others, to them, their Heirs & assigns forever, on condition however, that they annually pay or deliver to my wife Sarah during her life the third of the crops on the land I live on and provide her a comfortable house and garden, two milch cows of her selection, firewood delivered to her & cut sufficient to make her comfortable, also I will & bequeath to my said wife a good bed & bedding and one third of the cupboard & kitchen furniture—and on condition further that they my sons pay all my just debts and furneral expences, and pay the following legacies.

1st. To my Daughter Mary Kerr I will bequeath the sum of one Hundred Dollars to be paid to her by my executors in five annual payments of twenty Dollars each to commence one year from the death of my wife.

2nd. To my daughter Peggy Almonrode one shilling, she having already been provided for.

3d. To my Daughter Elizabeth I will and bequeath the sum of One Hundred Dollars, to be paid, in the same manner as directed to Mary Kerr, if she should marry, otherwise I direct my Executors to give her a comfortable maintenance at the expence of my said sons, during her life—or until her marriage—also a cow & two sheep.

4th. To my Daughter Sarah I will & bequeath one shilling.

5th. To my Daughter Barbara I will and bequeath the sum of one Hundred Dollars to be paid in the same manner as directed to Mary Kerr also one milch cow & two sheep.

6th. To my daughter Magdelene Becket I will and bequeath the sum of one hundred Dollars to be paid to her in the same manner as directed to Mary Kerr.

7th. To my Daughter Anne, I will and bequeath the sum of one hundred Dollars to be paid to her in the same manner as directed to Mary Kerr. Also one Mil*ch* Cow & two sheep.

8th. It is my wish that my four sons should live & work together or on the same farm, and that the profits of their *labour* together with any property, real or personal, that I may die possessed of, may be equally divided between them they paying the legacies hereby bequeathed and otherwise complying with my directions in this will. But if any of them shall not continue and work as aforesaid, then, and in that case, it is my will, that the property hereby expressed in this clause, shall be divided between those that remain. And as my son John Paul has worked for me some years longer than the others it is my will that a negro girl which he purchased from William McCoy named Sal—shall be paid for out of my Estate either before my death or after, before the said distribution—and that she shall belong to my said son John Paul his heirs and assigns, forever.

Lastly I hereby constitute and appoint my sons John Paul and William, executors of this my last will and testament, and autho*rise* them to sell and convey the first mentioned tract of land lying in Augusta county, and otherwise to carry into effect the provisions of this my will. And I do hereby certify that this is my last Will & Testament, hereby revoking all and every other will or wills hereby by me made. In testimony whereof I have hereby set my hand and seal the date first above written.

Note Before signing the above will I wish it to be understood that it — my will that any bedding and household furniture that my daughters may make during their continuance at my house, shall belong to them and not appraised as my property.

JOHN PAUL AKERLY [SEAL].

*Signed, sealed and
delivered in presence of*

    SAMUEL WALKUP,
    JAMES MILLER,
    JOHN LEECH,
    JOHN FINLEY.

LUCY DOUGLAS TURPIN, WIFE OF WILLIAM
ACKERLY, AND HER SONS JOHN PAUL
AND WILLIAM THOMAS ACKERLY

At Rockbridge county court September 3, 1827.

This writing purporting to be the fast Will and Testament of John Paul Aker*ley* Deceased was produced in Court, proved by the oaths of James Miller, and John Finley two of the subscribing witnesses thereto and ordered to be recorded. And on the motion of John Paul Akerley and William Akerley the executors therein named, who made oath thereto, and together with Robert White, Richard Morris, William Zollman and James Hall their securities entered into and acknowledged bond in the sum of six thousand Dollars conditioned according to law, certificate was granted them for obtaining probat thereof in due form.

Teste: SAML McD REID, *D. C.*

A Copy,

Teste:

A. T. SHIELDS, *Clerk.*

William Ackerly, second son of John Paul and Sarah (Miller) Ackerly, of Augusta and Rockbridge counties, was born in 1804. He lived in Rockbridge County, Virginia, where he owned a large estate and was a prosperous planter and stock raiser of that section. He was a man of fine character, well educated, loved and respected by all for his many sterling qualities, kindness of heart, and generosity to the poor. He married, May 27, 1847, Lucy Douglas Turpin, born September 24, 1824, daughter of Thomas Turpin, Jr., and Mary Polina (Clayton) Turpin, of Bedford County, Virginia. (See Turpin and Clayton families.) Their married life was a singularly happy one. William Ackerly died August 4, 1853, aged 49 years. He was survived by his widow and two young sons.

The widow married, January, 1856, Abraham Lavell, son of Abraham and Ann (Beard) Lavell, of Augusta County, Virginia. (See Lavell family for descendants by this marriage.) She was a woman of great simplicity of character, but firm in her conceptions of duty, a sincere Christian, a faithful wife, and devoted mother, who lived for her home and her children. She died December 16, 1899.

Like many southern women she had some thrilling experiences during the Civil War. One occurred during Hunter's raid through the valley. About twenty-five or thirty soldiers, in their search for whiskey, came to her home which was situated a mile off the main highway. After searching her house from cellar to attic, raised their swords, threatened her life and to burn the house if she did not tell them where whiskey could be found. This, however, she would not do; but instead, gave them meat (hams and shoulders), flour, and other things to eat—bade her servants prepare a meal for the officers. They were served in her dining room, while the other soldiers cooked and ate their food on her front lawn. They left without taking anything except food.

When she first heard of Hunter's approach she had some highly prized silver and jewelry, the gift of her first husband, buried in the garden. The exact location where the silver was buried was lost. It was several years afterwards before the silver was finally plowed up. It is now the prized possession of two of her granddaughters.

The soldiers were not wrong in suspecting whiskey concealed somewhere. Like all large plantations in those days, this one, too, had its small distillery. Upon warning of the approach of soldiers several barrels of whiskey had been hauled to as many blackberry thickets on the plantation and safely concealed.

All the live stock had been driven either across the mountains into Bedford County or to a mountain farm nearer the mountains (Short Hills).

One incident connected with this same raid which was rather amusing, occurred at a tenant house known as the Hamilton place. This place belonged to the family and was located on the main highway—in the path of the raiding soldiers. Over the front porch of this house was a secret room and here, too, had been stored quantities of meat and flour from the manor house more than a mile away. The opening leading to this room was by means of a sliding panel or door, which was concealed by a large chest of drawers. The soldiers searched this house upstairs and down; but, through their failure to move the huge chest, they never discovered the sliding panel. This meat and flour was saved.

CHILDREN OF WILLIAM AND LUCY DOUGLAS (TURPIN) ACKERLY:

(1) William Thomas, born July 23, 1848; married Elizabeth Virginia Turpin, of Bedford County, Va. (See forward.)

(2) John Paul, born August 3, 1850; married Conna Blount White, of Bedford County, Va. (See forward.)

William Thomas Ackerly, born July 23, 1848, eldest son of William and Lucy Douglas (Turpin) Ackerly, of Rockbridge County, Va.; married, February 5, 1873, Elizabeth Virginia Turpin, born November 17, 1850, youngest daughter of Roland Green Turpin, Sr., of Bedford County and his second wife, Elizabeth (Wilson) Reid (widow), daughter of John Wilson, Sr., of Rockbridge County, Va. (See Thomas Turpin and Roland Green Turpin, Sr., families.)

William T. Ackerly received his education from private tutors and the Fancy Hill Academy. In early life he was, for a short period, in the mercantile business in Bedford County, Va. Later returning to Rockbridge he engaged in farming, an occupation in which he was materially successful. He was a devoted father, a kind and generous husband, respected and honored as one of the most substantial citizens of his community. He was an elder in the Broad Creek Associate Reformed Presbyterian Church. He died August 2, 1909; and his wife died March 31, 1914.

CHILDREN:

(1) Harry Reid, born January 25, 1874. With his two unmarried sisters, he lives at the old home place where he is successfully engaged in farming.

(2) Mary Lucy, born September 18, 1875. Unmarried.

(3) Annie Eliza, born July 28, 1878; married, December 23, 1908, James Floyd Mohler, born October 1, 1876.

CHILDREN:

(a) William Floyd, born May 9, 1911.

(b) Lois Elizabeth, born July 30, 1913.

(4) Alice Blanche, born January 9, 1881. Unmarried.

(5) John Taney, born February 8, 1883; married, January 29, 1913, Annie Pattillo, daughter of Robert Henry Pattillo, born December 19, 1847, and Isabella (Nelson) Pattillo, born October 24, 1854, of Chase City, Virginia. (See Roland Green Turpin, Jr., family.) They have one child:

(a) Robert Nelson Ackerly, born August 17, 1914.

(6) Bessie Turpin, born May 29, 1885; married, October 31, 1909, Emmet Agarin Swartz, son of Prof. Joseph G. and Margaret Jane (Ochiltree) Swartz, of Rockbridge County, Va.

CHILDREN:

(a) Roy Edward, born December 2, 1910. Now a student at V. P. I.
(b) Margaret Elizabeth, born March 7, 1915.
(c) William Emmet, born September 26, 1917.

....

John Paul Ackerly, Sr., born in Rockbridge County, Virginia, August 3, 1850, was the second son of William Ackerly and Lucy Douglas (Turpin) Ackerly, daughter of Thomas and Mary Polina (Clayton) Turpin, of Bedford County, Virginia. (See Turpin, Douglas, and Clayton families.) He married, February 21, 1883, Mary Conna Blount White, born May 12, 1862, daughter of John Milton and Mary Virginia White, of Bedford County, Virginia. Her maternal grandparents were Captain Henry Milton and Mary Ann (Gwatkin) White, and her paternal grandparents, Col. William Allen and Caroline (Poindexter) White, of Bedford County, Virginia. (See White, Gwatkin, Clayton, Callaway, Slaughter, and Poindexter families.)

When John Paul Ackerly, Sr., was only three years old his father died. He was educated in private schools and at the Fancy Hill Academy, a classical school established, probably in the early sixties, and conducted for many years for the education of the youth of the county.

On becoming of age he inherited property from his father's estate that had belonged to his family for several generations. He was a dealer in live stock, and for a number of years in addition to this business and the management of his farm, he conducted a mercantile business at Summers Post Office. He early became prominent in the Republican party in Rockbridge and was one of its leaders. In 1897 he was appointed postmaster at Lexington, Virginia, by President McKinley, a position he held during this administration, giving entire satisfaction to the public. Following his retirement from the postmastership, he engaged actively in the handling and shipping of cattle. Few men were better known or more highly esteemed than he was throughout Rockbridge and adjoining counties. The five-year assessment of real estate in Lexington District was made by him twice as deputy assessor, in 1920 and 1925.

MARY DENHAM ACKERLY

JOHN PAUL ACKERLY, SR., AND WIFE
CONNA BLOUNT WHITE

By both inheritance and association John Paul Ackerly, Sr., was the possessor of an old and fine tradition, and he lived its code in his daily life. He was a man of keen intellect, broad vision and exemplary habits. He took an active interest in all public affairs, being the possessor of great executive ability and a wide fund of information. He had a cheerful disposition, a keen sense of humor, a warm and genial manner, full of simple, unconscious charm, was loyal in his friendships and quick to sympathy. He could not be tempted to sacrifice principle or to scheme for reputation. His numerous activities gave him a wide acquaintance and his qualities rendered him popular with all classes. He was devoted to his family and was never so happy as when at his own fireside surrounded by his loved ones. He lived a quiet but unswerving Christian life, and his example is a priceless legacy and inspiration to his children. He was a member of the Lexington Presbyterian Church.

For several years before his death he was an invalid and bore his sufferings with patience and fortitude. He died August 4, 1927, and is buried in Lexington, Virginia.

> "When good men die their goodness does not perish,
> But lives though they are gone."

Conna B. White was educated in private schools of Bedford County and Petersburg, Virginia. She possessed a musical talent of marked degree, and in her girlhood was one of the belles of Bedford County. She possesses a charming personality, and is a true friend, a generous neighbor, and a devoted mother, who lives for her home and her children. From girlhood she has been a member of the Methodist Episcopal Church.

CHILDREN:

(1) Mary Denham, born at Summers, Rockbridge County, Virginia, May 29, 1885. Educated in the Lexington Public and High Schools, attended State Teachers' College, Farmville, Va., and for five sessions taught in the public schools of Rockbridge County. Owing to ill health gave up teaching in 1915. Accepted the position as assistant to the commissioner of the revenue of Lexington Magisterial District in the Spring of 1917, and was appointed deputy commissioner of the revenue of that district

on February 24, 1921. In connection with which appointment the *Rockbridge County News* of March 3, 1921, said:

"Before Judge Henry W. Holt in the circuit court last week there qualified several deputy commissioners of the revenue. Among them was Miss Mary D. Ackerly appointed deputy commissioner of the revenue of Lexington district by Major Thomas M. Wade. This is the first time that a woman ever qualified for office in the circuit court of this county. She has demonstrated how well qualified she is for the position. For some years she had been the efficient clerk of Major Wade as commissioner and would have been a deputy had the law permitted. She had already held a federal office. A year ago, as a federal official, she took the census for the town of Lexington."

Since January 1, 1928, she has held the position of deputy commissioner of the revenue for Rockbridge County. She is a member of the Board of Trustees of the Stonewall Jackson Memorial Hospital, Lexington, Va., Mary Custis Lee Chapter, United Daughters of the Confederacy, American Legion Auxiliary and the National Society of the Daughters of the American Revolution. Unmarried.

(2) William White, born at Summers, Rockbridge County, Virginia, June 15, 1890; graduated Lexington High School, June 4, 1908, and awarded the scholarship to Washington and Lee University, where he graduated with Bachelor of Laws degree, June 12, 1912, having been Vice-President of his Senior class. Admitted to the Virginia Bar, June, 1912; accepted position as Associate Editor, Editorial Staff, The Lawyer's Co-operative Publishing Company, Rochester, N. Y., October, 1912, which he resigned in Spring of 1917 to enter military service. Appointed land assessor of Lexington District for 1920 and 1925; elected Commonwealth's Attorney of Rockbridge County on Democratic ticket, November 8, 1927; author of following special legal articles:

"Design Patents," *Case and Comment*, September, 1914; "Law and Apparitions," *Case and Comment*, November, 1914; "Unneutral Service," *Case and Comment*, January, 1915; "Constitutional Freedom of Speech and of the Press," *Case and*

Comment, November 1915; "Legal Responsibility of Obedient Soldier or Militiaman," *Case and Comment,* February, 1916.

Captain Ackerly is a Past Master of Mountain City Lodge No. 67, A. F. and A. M., Lexington; a member of Rockbridge Chapter No. 44, Royal Arch Masons; Lexington Lodge No. 66, Knights of Pythias; Lexington Lodge No. 1364, Loyal Order of Moose; Rockbridge Post No. 95, The American Legion (past post commander); 40 Hommes and 8 Cheveaux; 27th (N. Y.) Division Veterans Association; Virginia State Bar Association; honorary member Square and Compass Fraternity and Iota Chapter, Sigma Delta Kappa law fraternity at W. and L. U.; Past Department Judge Advocate, The American Legion, Department of Virginia; Secretary, Rockbridge and Buena Vista Bar Association; Secretary, Lexington Kiwanis Club (charter member); Captain Cavalry, O. R. C., U. S. A., 1923-1928; Scout Master of Troop 2, Stonewall Jackson Council, Boy Scouts, for two years; Secretary, Board of Fire Commissioners (1929—) Town of Lexington, Va.

While at Rochester, Wm. W. Ackerly enlisted, January 22, 1915, in Troop "H," 1st Cavalry N. G. N. Y.; promoted to corporal, June 17, 1915, and to Sergeant, October 25, 1915. Served with Troop "H," on Mexican Border, June 19, 1916, to March 15, 1917. Discharged from Troop "H," July 24, 1917, to accept commission as First Lieutenant, 102nd Am. Train. He served throughout the period of the World War with 27th (New York) Division, participating in all of its operations in the A. E. F. from May 30, 1918, to March 11, 1919. Commissioned First Lieutenant, July 24, 1917, and promoted to Captain, March 3, 1918. His discharge from the service on April 3, 1919, at Camp Upton, New York, with the rank of Captain, Field Artillery, officially credits him with the following battles, engagements, etc.:

Battles—Hindenburg Line (vicinity Bony), France, September 29-30, 1918; La Selle River (vicinity St. Souplet), France, October 17, 1918; Jonc de Mer Ridge (vicinity Ar du Guermon), France, October 18, 1918.

Engagements—Vierstraat Ridge (vicinity Mont Kemmel), Belgium, August 31-September 2, 1918; The Knoll, Guille-

ment Farm, Quennemont Farm, France, September 27, 1918;
St. Maurice River (vicinity Cattilon), France, October 19-20,
1918.

Minor Actions—East Poperinghe Line, Belgium, July 9-
August 20, 1918; Dickebusch Sector, Belgium, August 21-30,
1918.

Served with 102nd Am. Train, July 24, 1917, to March 11,
1918, 102nd Supply Train, March 11, 1918, to April 28, 1918,
102nd Military Police, April 28, 1918, to October 14, 1918.
27th Division Headquarters Troop, October 14, 1918, to
November 1, 1918—Transferred to 102nd Am. Train, November 1, 1918. Acting Motor Transport Officer, 27th Division,
November 1, 1918, to December 28, 1918. Assistant Division
Motor Transport Officer, December 28, 1918, to February 21,
1919, at which time returned to duty with 102nd Am. Train,
and placed in command of Company "G" to date of discharge,
April 3, 1919. Organized, and was Senior Instructor in Motor
Transportation Section, 27th Division School of the Line, Jan-
uary 5, 1918, to April 6, 1918, Camp Wadsworth, S. C.

The following commendations are noted in his "Officer's
Record Book."

"Captain Ackerly is an able, efficient and conscientious
officer. His work as a Motor Transport officer was entirely
satisfactory.   (Signed) WM. A. TAYLOR,
                                        Colonel, Inf."

"The services rendered by this officer, first in organizing
and commanding one of the companies of the Motor Battn. of
this Amm. Train, later commanding a company of the Military
Police of this Division during all the time the Division was in
active service in Belgium and Northern France—1918—(at all
times under my personal observation) have at all times been of
the highest type.

"Captain Ackerly has repeatedly demonstrated his coolness
and courage under enemy fire and has at all times had the
complete confidence of the men under his command.

(Signed) WALTER L. BELL,
              Lieut.-Col. F. A., Comdg. 102 Am. Train,
                  27th Div., A. E. F."

CAPTAIN WILLIAM WHITE ACKERLY

The following commendation was received in connection with the operations of the 27th Division in the Battle of the Hindenburg Line:

"3rd Australian Division,
4-10-18.

"A. P. M.

Australian Corps.

"A. A. & Q. M. G.,

3rd Australian Div. (For information.)

"In connection with the recent operations of the Div. from 28/9/18 to 2/10/18, during which time the 27th American Division was operating in conjunction with this Division, I beg to bring to your special notice the very valuable assistance rendered to me by the A. P. M., 27th American Division (Major Shanton) and his two assistants Capts. Ceballos and Ackerly.

"Their Military Police and traffic arrangements were perfect and the business-like, cool and tactful manner in which the whole of the American personnel went about their duties was very noticeable and certainly deserves commendation.

"Altho at times the traffic was most congested and the roads not infrequently being shelled heavily, both officers and men carried on admirably throughout, and I feel it to be my bounden duty to bring their praiseworthy conduct to your notice.

(Signed)   J. WATSON CORPITTO,
Major Asst. Provost Marshal,
3rd. Australian Div.

"Ist Ind.

"P. M. II. Corps, A. E. F., 11/10/18——To Commanding General, II. Corps, A. E. F.

"I Forwarded.

H. A. C. DE RUBIO,
Major, N. A., A. E. F.

"2nd. Ind. Cofs.

"Headquarters II. Corps, American E. F., France, October 11, 1918:

To the Commanding General, 27th Division.

"The Corps Commander is pleased to forward to you this evidence of the efficiency of your Military Police.

(Signed) STEPHEN C. CLARK.
Adjutant General.

201.1 3rd Ind. A/hme

Hq. 27th Div., U. S. A., A. E. F., 16, October, '18, To Commanding Officer, 102nd Military Police, to note and return.

The Division Commander desires to add his personal appreciation of the valuable services rendered by the Military Police on the occasion mentioned.

By Command of Major-General O'Ryan:

(Signed) H. B. BATTENBERG,
Adjutant General Division Adjutant."

(3) Lucy Pauline, born at Summers, Rockbridge County, Virginia, November 8, 1892. Graduate of the Lexington High School; attended State Teachers' College, Farmville, Va., and William and Mary College. She is a successful teacher in the primary department of the Lexington Public Schools, where she is loved and respected by her pupils for her ability as a teacher and her interest at all times in their welfare. She is a member of the Mary Custis Lee Chapter, United Daughters of the Confederacy, American Legion Auxiliary, Woman's Club, of Lexington, Va., National Society of the Daughters of the American Revolution, and the Virginia State Teachers' Association. Unmarried.

(4) Kate Thelma, born at Summers, Rockbridge County, Virginia, October 17, 1895; died February 7, 1897.

(5) John Paul, Jr., born at Lexington, Virginia, December 28, 1899; married, November 9, 1929, Marguerite Emmetta Clarkson, born April 2, 1905, daughter of Benjamin Walton and Lily

(Burns) Clarkson, of Bath County, Virginia. He was educated in the public schools of Lexington and at Washington and Lee University. Volunteered for service in the World War and entered, October 1, 1918, Students Army Training Corps, a branch officers training camp at Washington and Lee University. Discharged from U. S. Army, December 14, 1918. He is District Manager of the Sun Life Assurance Company of Canada, and is also, a member of the firm, Morrison and Ackerly, General Insurance, Lexington, Virginia. He is a member of the Blue Lodge Chapter, and the Moomaw Commandery of Masonic Lodge, at Lexington, Virginia. A reserve member of the Lexington Volunteer Fire Department and a member of Lexington Lodge No. 1364, Loyal Order of Moose.

(6) Eugene Glasgow, born at Lexington, Virginia, July 11, 1903. He was educated at home and in private schools. Now living in Lexington, where he is employed as an automobile salesman. He is an active member of the Lexington Volunteer Fire Department and of Lexington Lodge No. 1364, Loyal Order of Moose. Unmarried.

(7) Frank Douglas, born at Lexington, Virginia, May 13, 1911; died June 30, 1911.

The following is a copy of the letter written by Captain Wm. W. Ackerly, from Corbie, France, to his father on "Dad's Letter Day."

Corbie, France,
Nov. 24th, 1918.

Dear Father,—

This is "Dad's Letter Day" in the A. E. F. The war is over; and this day we are allowed to tell the story with practically no censorship restrictions. About the only requirement is that we tell the truth, the whole truth, and nothing but the truth. This I shall do!

Six months ago the 17th of this month, I left the shores of Virginia on what has been the greatest experience of my life. I sailed with my company on a former German liner, The Koenig Wilhelm, II, refitted as a troop transport, and re-named "The Madawaska." This ship was one of a convoy of nine. My ship-mates were some two thousand national army men, my company being the only National

Guard unit on board. I was the only officer in my company, but my men were most loyal to me, and made a name for themselves for good discipline, fine courtesy, and excellent bearing. Every one of the one hundred and forty-seven seemed to appreciate the task that confronted me, and did his best to make it easier for me.

It was late in the afternoon that we slipped away from the dock at Newport News and drifted out to mid-stream. Then, when the sun was low in the west, we moved slowly down through Hampton Roads, where we lay at anchor until sometime in the night, when we stole out to sea. I was dead tired and went to bed early. I was awakened in the early morning by the gruff tones of a fog-horn. A dense fog was on the sea. Visibility was practically impossible; and I was told that our ship had barely avoided a collision. So began a voyage filled with thrilling experiences.

For, it was our fortune to be favored with three submarine attacks before arriving at our destination. The most important one took place on the afternoon of May 30th, just as we were coming in sight of land. It lasted for more than an hour and a half, and there was all the excitement anyone could crave. The Huns seemed to know we were coming, and just where we were going a good deal better than many of us, and were ready all along the line with a warm reception. However, we were not taken by surprise, and before the party was over at least two subs had passed out of existence; and the others, I can't say how many, had made a practical application of the theory that "he who fights and runs away lives to fight another day." That evening we dropped anchor in the river opposite St. Nazaire, France. The next morning we debarked and were, at last, "OVER THERE."

Then followed weeks of training and re-equipping, for we were sent to fight with the British. There were drills and long hikes, and journeys by rail and by bus, and finally we landed in Flanders on the Ypres front. Before leaving there, our division, along with the 30th took a fling at "Jerry" in front of Mont Kemmel, and the evacuation of that important point by the enemy followed.

After that, we came back to France and rested near Doullens for four or five weeks. During this time I was acting A. P. M. of that town. Then, we got orders to move up to Peronne. We "took over" from the British near there, and on the 28th and 29th of September, the battle of Ronssoy was fought. It was here that the 27th and 30th

Divisions broke through the Hindenburg Line at what was probably its strongest point. I afterwards went over the greater part of this battlefield, and it is nothing short of marvelous that our men were able to accomplish what they did here. You have probably already read what Sir Douglas Haig said about this operation. It was a great achievement for American arms, as it broke the back of the Hun's resistance, and made further victories possible all along the line.

During this battle I was in charge of a line of traffic posts on a road exposed to heavy shell fire, and had one or two rather narrow escapes. I had practically no sleep to speak of for about seventy-two hours, and was in the saddle most of the time. When it was all over I felt like a well squeezed lemon!

After a short rest, we again went into the line, and on the 17th of October gave the Huns another blow that started him reeling; and for about five days we kept at him, always gaining our objectives, frequently taking many prisoners and guns. I now am operating a German truck that we captured in this fighting.

When we came out of the line after this fight, we came to Corbie; and somehow I felt when we were moving back that we would never have to go in the line again. And sure enough the end did come while we were here resting and filling up with replacements, for we had had quite a few casualties in the fighting we had been through.

Today our Division began to move back to La Mans, which is not far from St. Nazaire where we landed. Just what this means, I cannot say. It may mean HOME SOON, or most anything. I will let you guess what we are hoping it means!

It is impossible to adequately describe the conditions that exist here in the area where the heaviest fighting has been done. There is hardly a house that is not in ruins. Many a Frenchman must be broken hearted to return and find HOME but a mass of wreckage. We can all thank God that we have not had to fight the war in our own country.

In four more days we will all be celebrating Thanksgiving Day. How much all of us will have to be thankful for! I don't know just where I will be that day. Probably somewhere on the road with a truck train. Wherever I am, I will be happy and thankful that I have been spared, and that all of you are well and happy.

It will be Christmas when you receive this. Thus far I have not made any attempt to send you any Xmas presents. If you got them there would be duty to pay. I will try and send some cards if I am where I can get them, and I will also send some souvenirs as soon as I can. I hope that you will all have a wonderful Xmas, and I am sure you will. I will think about you and wish you all a Merry Xmas and a happy New Year that morning when I wake up!

Trusting that this finds all of you in good health I will attempt to write no more this time. Write soon. Take good care of yourself. With lots of love to each and all, I am ever

Fondly your son,

WM.

Wm. W. Ackerly,
    Capt. U. S. A.

———————

Peter Ackerly, son of John Paul and Sarah (Miller) Ackerly, of Augusta and Rockbridge Counties, was born June 30, 1807. In Chataigne's Virginia Business Directory and Gazetteer, 1880-81, he is listed, from both Botetourt and Rockbridge Counties, as one of the principal farmers of the county. In addition to his inheritance, he accumulated, by his natural thrift and ability, a great deal of property, owning large tracts of land in both counties. He was a man of fine character and held the esteem and confidence of all who knew him. On November 6, 1828, he married Lydia Shafer, born October 12, 1805; died June 7, 1880. He died June 18, 1880.

CHILDREN :

(1) Elizabeth, born August 5, 1829; married, November 2, 1848, Moses H. Patterson; died May 17, 1896.

(2) John S., born November 1, 1830; died May 20, 1863. Never married. In War, C. S. A.

(3) George W., born March 30, 1832; died June 30, 1871. Second Sergeant Company "E," 52nd Virginia Infantry, 4th Brigade, C. S. A. Never married.

(4) Mary Margaret, born May 31, 1833; married, July 28, 1853, Matasine (Madison) Zollman.

(5) Sarah Ann, born November 14, 1834; married, November 17, 1853, Richard Pettigrew; died March 19, 1870.

(6) William, born February 25, 1836. Belonged to Company "E," 27th Virginia Infantry, C. S. A.

(7) James P., born November 19, 1837; died June 1, 1852.

(8) Elvira Jane, born February 10, 1840; married, May 13, 1858, William Pettigrew.

(9) Lucinda Agnes, born September 11, 1841; married in 1863, James William Poague, born October 26, 1836, died December 10, 1892, son of James Moore Poague and Sarah B. Poague. She died December 9, 1920. Her home, "Willow Spring," was always the center of hospitality.

CHILDREN:

(a) John Sandy Moore Poague, born April 14, 1867; married, December 11, 1901, Lillian Sophia Houser.

CHILDREN:

(aa) Lillian Virginia, born December 29, 1902. Unmarried.

(bb) Mary Agnes, born August 3, 1904; married, May 19, 1922, Dorsey Grey Shorter. They have three children.

(cc) Pauline Houser, born July 10, 1906. A teacher in the public schools of Virginia.

(dd) George William, born February 5, 1908.

(ee) Cornelia Moore, born October 24, 1909. A teacher in the public schools of Virginia.

(ff) John Robert Eugene, born October 14, 1912; died December 8, 1913.

(b) Ollie Margaret Poague, born December 27, 1870; married, September 29, 1897, Thomas Davis Parsons.

CHILDREN:

(aa) Harry Poague Parsons.

(bb) George Moore Parsons; married, July 4, 1923, Bessie Irene Lotts. They have two children.

(cc) Mabel Agnes Parsons.

(c) William Franklin Poague, born August 28, 1872; married, September 17, 1902, Macie Lee Logwood, daughter of William Logwood. No children.

(10) Meriah W., born July 23, 1843; died April 14, 1855.
(11) Shanklin M. (twin), born January 23, 1846; died April 16, 1922. Private Company "C," 14th Virginia Cavalry, C. S. A.
(12) David G. (twin), born January 23, 1846; married, February 23, 1868, Eckalene C. Zollman. Private Company "C," 14th Virginia Cavalry, C. S. A.
(13) Edmonia T., born October 11, 1849; married, January 14, 1869, John W. Zollman.
(14) Andrew Jackson, born September 15, 1852; died October 28, 1927; never married.

LAVELL

Abraham Lavell (or Lavelle), born July 21, 1832, son of Abraham and Ann (Beard) Lavell, of Augusta County, Virginia; married (first), January, 1856, Lucy Douglas (Turpin-Ackerly), widow of William Ackerly, of Rockbridge County, Virginia. (See Ackerly family.) She died December 16, 1899. He married (second), February 22, 1901, Miss Lucy Hudson, daughter of Robert Jackson and Sarah Jane (Rucker) Hudson, both of Amherst County, Virginia. There were no children by the second marriage.

Abraham Lavell was a Confederate soldier and fought bravely under General Stuart in the First Virginia Cavalry, C. S. A. He was, by occupation, a prosperous farmer and stock dealer. He died October 29, 1921, and was buried in the Ackerly family burying ground at Summers, Va.

CHILDREN BY FIRST MARRIAGE:

(1) Infant, born May 6, 1857; died May 7, 1857.

(2) Robert Walter, born July 22, 1858; married, November, 1900, Fanny Ruth, daughter of Rev. A. F. Persley, of Botetourt County, Virginia. He was engaged principally in farming, and was a man of many sterling qualities. He died October 28, 1925, and was buried in the Ackerly family burying ground. No children.

(3) Infant, unnamed.

(4) Dora Ann, born May 14, 1860; married, February 27, 1884, her cousin, Roland Green Turpin, Jr., born December 15, 1844, son of Roland Green and Elizabeth (Wilson-Reid) Turpin, of Bedford County, Virginia. (See Turpin family for descendants.) She was a beautiful girl of the brunette type. She is a devoted mother, a kind neighbor, and in her home she is a charming hostess.

(5) Mary Lee, born October 22, 1864; married, June 9, 1887, Graham Montgomery Leech, born February 12, 1858; died January 30, 1920, son of William and Mary (Montgomery) Leech, of Rockbridge County, Virginia. She possessed both beauty and a charming personality—was greatly loved by all who knew her for her many deeds of kindness and her sincere

Christian character. She died May 25, 1926, and was buried by the side of her husband in the family plot at High Bridge Church.

CHILDREN:

(a) Emmett Russell Leech, born October 28, 1888; married, April 7, 1915, Mabel Burks Stoner, born July 8, 1891, daughter of John Harden Stoner, born March 8, 1863, and Mary Elizabeth (Braford) Stoner, born September 19, 1865, daughter of Hugh White Braford, of Rockbridge County and Adelade (Abbitt) Braford, of Appomattox County, Virginia. Emmett R. Leech received his education in the public schools of Rockbridge County and at Virginia Polytechnic Institute. Now owns and operates successfully the farm he inherited from his father.

CHILDREN:

(aa) Graham Stoner, born September 3, 1916.

(bb) Elizabeth Lee, born March 13, 1918.

(cc) Edna Earle, born October 18, 1920.

(dd) Malcom Russell, born July 21, 1923.

(ee) Mary Douglas, born April 20, 1927.

(ff) Jean Hortense, born May 15, 1929.

(b) William Lavell Leech, born in 1889; married, September 22, 1915, Margaret Wilson Stark, daughter of Walter E. L. Stark, born in Scotland and Margaret (Wilson) Stark, of Rockbridge County, Virginia. He was killed, April 25, 1922, by the over turning of a farm tractor. By his fidelity, intelligence, and genial personality he won for himself the respect of all who knew him.

CHILD:

(aa) William Stark Leech, born July 24, 1916.

(6) George Edward, born 1867; died infancy.

POEMS BY "OUR KIN"

THE CHILDREN

Benjamin Sledd

from "The Watchers of The Hearth"

No more of work! Yet ere I seek my bed,
   Noiseless into the children's room I go,
   With its four little couches all a-row,
And bend a moment over each dear head.

Those soft, round arms upon the pillow spread,
   These dreaming lips babbling more than we know,
   One tearful, smothered sigh of baby woe—
Fond words of chiding, would they were unsaid!

And while on each moist brow a kiss I lay,
   With tremulous rapture grown almost to pain,
   Close at my side I hear a whispered name:—
   Our long-lost babe, who with the dawning came,
And in the midnight went from us again.
And with bowed head, one good-night more I say.

GLORIA IN EXCELSIS

Georgie Tillman Snead

in "Lyrics of Hope"

The gates of Heaven swung wide!
Forth flashed bright wings through all the high, ethereal dome.
A host of cherubim and seraphim in glistening white—
Their faces shining as the sun—
With gentle, undulating motion,
With pinions flashing radiant,
Moved down from Heaven's high battlements
To lowly earth.

Millions upon millions of stars shone
In the blue depths of ether far below,
And as the lustrous throng drew near
They paled, abashed at the seraphic glory.
There was a hush o'er all earth's realms—
Nature in homage to her Lord stood silent in speechless awe.

Oh, mystery infinite! Oh, thought beyond all thought!
The great Creator had become a creature,
And now with all a creature's limitations
Lay helpless in a manger.
On a lone hill in Judah's realm
Shepherds were abiding their flocks to keep;
Weary with long watching, they lay asleep
Unconscious of the radiance round about them.

"Glory, glory, glory!
Glory in the highest,
Peace on earth, good will to men."

Myriads of angelic hosts
With strains divinely sweet,
Filled all the earth with symphonies supernal.
The shepherds rose upon their feet,
And dumb with a great astonishment,
Looked up into the fathomless abysm.
Where millions of gleaming wings
Made luminous the darkness.

The light grew brighter and more bright
Till night in terror fled amazed
Henceforth to know that Day
Her reign eternal had begun.

"Glory, glory, glory,
Glory be to God in the highest,
Peace on earth, good will to men!"

There was a sound of rushing hosts—
A harmony infinite to mortal ears—
Highest Heaven caught up the strain,
And from the Eternal Throne was echoed:

"Glory, glory, glory,
Glory be to God in the highest,
Peace on earth, good will to men.
Amen! Amen! Amen!"

GOD OF THE FLOWERS

J. E. GWATKIN

Every lily on the planet
    Breathes an odor born of God.
He is crystaled in the granite
    He is moulded in the sod.

Every ivy leaf that trembles
    In His breath, the mountain air,
Speaks His glory nor dissembles
    But proclaims His constant care.

In the meadow bright with daisies,
    In the dog-wood's open cup,
Where the primrose upward raises,
    Or bees from clover nectar sup:

Where the roses, queen of flowers,
    Nod upon their stately stems
In the scented summer hours,
    Flashing with their dew-drop gems:

In and over all their beauty
    Broods the great Creator's care,
Urging us to holy duty,
    For our God is everywhere.

Let thy flowers teach this nation!
    Teach endurance by Thy trees!
'Till the crown of thy creation
    Glorify Thee as do these!

APRIL IN VIRGINIA

BENJAMIN SLEDD

April in Bedford . . . and again
To leave behind the ways of men,
To wander as of old
Down the wildwood brook and glen;
Violets there how fresh, how sweet,
Earliest touched by April's feet,
How pure the kingcup's gold!
Catbirds wrangling in the thorns,
And in the alders twinkling horns;
And near or far, no ear can tell,
The shy clink-clank of vagrant bell;
The brook that babbles up to me
Its wonderings of a far off sea;
Heaven itself down bending low
And winds flinging me, as they go,
Raptures and longings never told.

AFTER THOUGHT

O brook that babbles up to me
Your wonderings of a far off sea,
I know, I know
Whither at last your windings go,
But you can tell naught of the sea
Which somewhere, somewhere, waits for me.

EVENTIDE IN SUMMER

By Georgie Tillman Snead

The long, low line of the foothills, the azure of the mist,
The dewy grass of the meadows, a vault of amethyst;
An orb of gold slow sinking low in the roseate west,
And over all is brooding the dove of peace and rest.

Golden sheaves of the wheat field in graceful outlines stand,
The song of the homeward reaper resounding through the land,
The answering call of a ricebird to his mate on the distant hedge,
The chirp of a timid nestling anear in the waving sedge.

A lengthening of the shadows on mountain, hill and dale,
The dolorous hum of insects, the whippoorwill's weird wail,
The slow sweet hush a falling o'er earth and sky and sea,
A music full of longing—of nature's melody.

The roseate flush now fading, the gates of night ajar;
A crescent moon now rising, the twinkling of a star;
And little children weary with the long day's merry play
In slumber bound are dreaming their childish cares away.

An hour of retrospection as the vanished past returns,
The touch of a hand so tender that all my being yearns
For the day of the old time sweetness, of the well-remembered voice
For the angel-smile of welcome that made my heart rejoice.

Then I lift my eyes above me to the starred and gleaming dome,
And I see beyond the shadows the lights of my distant home!—
Where in their radiant beauty I shall clasp my own again,
In the realms of bliss undying, amid the glad amen!

THE WHY OF LITIGATION

By Wm. W. Ackerly

in "Case and Comment"

Why is folks all de time a-suin',
Each seekin' sum 'vantage ob de uddeh,
When da's things dey might be doin'
Dat would get dem 'long a good deal fuddeh?

But dey jes' seem to r'ar and fuss
And fill de cote as full of liddigation
As, from thinkin' deir cause is jus',
Dey, demselves, is full ob indignation.

One is claimin' lots ob damages,
All de jury will allow,
'Cause, he says, all his cabbages,
Done been et up by his neighbor's cow.

Anuddeh's filed a 'junction bill,
'Cause his tenant's committin' waste
By cuttin' all de timbeh on de hill
And sellin' it in a-mighty haste.

And anuddeh wants a separation
As quick as she can land it,
'Cause her ole man cusses like de nation,
And she don't intend to stand it.

But why do folks purfur to liddigate,
And all deir money spend,
When dey can simply a'bitrate,
And hab a little left to lend?

Well, I don't know what uddehs say,
Dat to dem a'pear de causes;
But to me, it jes' Gawd's own 'pointed way
Ob takin' care de lawyehs!

AT EVENING TIME AFLOAT

J. E. GWATKIN

As ships pass in the gloaming
    Bound for a distant shore,
So my soul in its homing
    Shall soon be here no more.

As one on some great river,
    In just a shell of a boat,
I am by the grace of its Giver
    On life's deep tide afloat.

And, as the tides of the river,
    Fast ebbing at close of day,
Would bear my frail bark ever
    Farther and farther away;

So the cruel years, swift passing,
    Are bearing my life's frail bark
Out where the clouds are massing,
    Out, still out to the dark.

But, as when storm clouds fading
    Before the setting sun
Furnish a rainbow shading
    Before the day is done;

So, Lord, your bright smiling
    Irradiates life's gloom,
As, by your love beguiling,
    You lighten e'en the tomb.

Then shall I float on gladly
    O'er life's resistless tide,
Nor cast my anchor sadly
    When I reach the other side;

For peace and calm attend me,
    As I float alone in my boat,
And from all fears defend me
    At evening time afloat.

SEPTEMBER IN VIRGINIA

Benjamin Sledd

September! and once more to lie day long
Stretched on my Bedford hills, while all around
A thousand voices drone a drowsy sound
Which to the silence is as word to song;
And dreaming watch, from depths of bearded grass,
Over field and wood the trailing shadows go,
From clouds that float on folded wings, how slow,
Gathering above old Otter's far blue pass.

Cloud-ships becalmed, all day they drift asleep,
Their shadows drifting on the mountain-side;
But when the wind in full, deep undertone
Pours from the sunset-ridge its freshening tide,
Close over me with kindling sails they sweep,
My argosies from Eldorado blown.

—(Published in *Virginia Quarterly*.)

The following poem was taken from the fly leaf of a notebook carried by John Milton White during the four years of the Civil War and "a prisoner on Lake Erie" from early in April, 1865, to June 17, 1865.

THE PRISON ON LAKE ERIE

The full round moon, in God's blue bend
Glides o'er her path so queenly;
Dark shadows creep, fade into light
And stars look down serenely.
A captive looks out on the scene
A scene so sad; so dreary,
And thinks a weary captive's thoughts
In prison on "Lake Erie."

The happy, happy days of youth
Fleet by him fast and faster,
The days which give no warning note
Of manhood's dire disaster.
The days when joys, and peaceful home
And firesides bright and cherry,
Come back to find him sad and wan
A prisoner on "Lake Erie."

A passing cloud flits o'er the scene
The light a moment banished,
Returns again but now alas
The vision bright has vanished.
The happy views of childhood gone
Leaves but a picture dreary,
To rest the aching eyes upon
The prison on "Lake Erie."

How many moons will rise and wane
How many months will languish,
Ere peace, the "white winged angel" comes
To soothe the peoples anguish.
God speed the long'd and pray'd for day
When loved ones bright and cheery,
Shall welcome us among the hearths
From prison on "Lake Erie."

Johnson's Island, Ohio.
June 9th, 1865.

Song Without Words, To Her.

J. R. BOLLING.

Moderato con moto.

con passione portamento

JETER

Very little was known of the origin of the Jeters of America up to the time this work was begun (1922), but in the last few years members of the family in many states have become interested in their ancestry and it has only been necessary to inform them that an effort was being made to collect data for a history of the Jeters of America to enlist their co-operation and support. But for this co-operation it would never have been possible to have worked out so many branches of the family, nor to have secured such detailed information.

From every section has come the tradition that the Jeters were Huguenots who refugeed in England for many years, and came from there to Virginia early in the eighteenth century, settling in what is now Caroline County.

The name is undoubtedly French and means "to throw," but the French ancestry has not yet been proved unless the following statement made by Bishop Meade in his "Old Families and Churches" (Vol. I, page 468) can be considered proof:

"From the family of Du Puys I have gotten the old church register which, though rotten and torn and in fragments, has been kept so as to enable me to obtain the statistics given in this article.

"The foregoing account of the escape of Bartholemew Du Duy and his wife is a true picture of the methods resorted to by the persecuted Huguenots to fly from the kingdom. Nothing now remains but that I mention the names of those families still remaining in Virginia who derive their descent from the Huguenots. From information coming through books and individuals they are as follows: Marye, Fontaine, Du Puy, Harris, Sublett, Watkins, Markham, Sully, Chastain, DuVall, Bondurant, Flournoy, Potter, Michaux, Pemberton, Munford, Hatcher, Jacquelin, Bernard, Barrand, Latane, Moncure, Agie, Amouet, Chadouin, Dibrell, Farrar, Fuqua, Jeter, Jordan, Jouette, LeGrand, Ligon, Maupin, Maxey, Pasteur, Perrow, Thweatt, Maury, Boisseau, Fouche, Lanier, Le Neve. Concerning a few of these it may be questioned whether they be not of Welsh descent, while there are doubtless others who might be added."

REV. JEREMIAH BELL JETER, D. D.

QUARTERING JUSTICE (upper right) AND
BENNETT (lower left)

The English pedigree of the family, as taken from "The Visitations of Suffolk, 1561, 1577 and 1612," edited by Walter C. Metcalf, 1882, page 147, is as follows:

"JETER OF LOWESTOFT

"John Jeter of Laystolfe in Suff. Gent., mar. and had issue—Edmond, son and heir.

"Edmond Jeter of Laystolfe, son and heir of John, mar. Frances, dau. and coheir of ———— Justice of Berks and of his wife, the da. and heir of ———— Benet, and had issue—James, obiit; Robert, son and heir; William, obiit; George, John, and Edmond, ob.; Margaret, mar. to Edmund Walle of Aldeby in Norf.; Ellen—obiit unm.

"Robert Jeter of Laystolfe, second son and heir of Edmond, mar. Ann, da. Clement Herward of Booton in Norf. and hath issue—Robert, son and heir; John, second son; Henry, third son; Christopher, fourth son; Francis, fifth son; Ann; Mary; Mawdelyn; and Elizabeth.

"Robert Jeter, son and heir of Robert, mar. Katherine, da. of George Cotton of Warbleton in Hants, and as yet hath no issue, 1612."

And from the publications of the Harleian Society, Vol. 61, 1890, pages 63 and 13, the following:

"Henry Jetter, third son of Robert, of Mutford in Com. Suff. mar. Anne, da. of ———— Flowerdew.

"George Jetter, son of Henry, of Ellow in Co. Suff. gt. 1664. mar. Uuica, da. of Robert Spencer of Backton in Com. Suff.

"Robert Jeter, sonne and heire of George aet.: 10 An° 1664.

"Henry Jetter, son of George.

"Christopher Jeter, fourth son of Robert, mar. Jane, da. of John Druery of Dry Docken in Com. Norf.

"Their dau. Mary vx. Tho. Burton."

Neither has it been possible to verify the tradition—though it is no doubt correct—that "the first Jeter settled near Port Royal in Caroline County, Va., in the early days of the eighteenth century" because Caroline was not formed until 1728, and the records of the counties from which it was taken contain (so far as we have been able to find) no mention of the name. The earliest records of Caroline have been destroyed and the later ones are in such bad condition and so many of them missing that it has been very difficult to find data of the early Jeters sufficient for any sort of history, or from which to draw definite conclusions.

In a book, recently published, called "Bristol and America. A Record of the First Settlers in the Colonies of North America, 1654-1685," Thomas Geter is listed on page 78 with Virginia as his destination. Whether or not he ever reached his destination is not known, for no mention of the name has been found in Virginia until 1738, when in the List of Tithables of Orange County is given "Geor. Jeter—1 tithe." Nothing more is known of him.

A memorandum, found in the branch of the family which settled in Kentucky, says the immigrant was John Jeter; that he settled about eight miles from Port Royal in Caroline County, Va.; that he married twice and had eleven children by each marriage. (See page 579.) This is very probably correct, though it has not been verified for reasons already stated. Certain it is that there were many of the name in Caroline during the eighteenth century whose parentage was very uncertain up to the time this memorandum was found (1929).

Some of the old Order Books of Caroline County have been deposited in the Archives Department of the Virginia State Library at Richmond, and a careful examination of these has produced the following:

"Order Book 'B'—1741-46, page 259—

"Upon the petition of John Jeater it is ordered that he have administration of the estate of Henry Jeater, Dec'd., with Nicho' Jeater as security, who acknowledged their bond for the same.

"It is ordered that James Lewis, Jon. Mitchell, Kemp Taliaferro, and Sherwood James or any three of them to appraise the estate of Henry Jeater, dec'd., in money, etc., and return their statement to the next court, 9 March 1743."

At first we were inclined to believe that Henry was the immigrant, and father of the others, because his was the first death recorded, but since studying the record more closely and noting that the appraisers were ordered to appraise his estate "in money, etc.," we think it probable that he had little else than money, and was the son rather than the father of John. So, adopting the memorandum of the Kentucky Jeters, we have concluded—without positive proof, however—that John was the immigrant.

THE EARLY JETERS OF AMERICA

The name of John Jeter continues to appear in the fragmentary records of Caroline until 1762, and the items show that he was a public spirited citizen and a man of integrity and ability. The date of his death is unknown.

From "Public Claims"—Caroline County—in the State Archives is taken the following:

"Nov. 14, 1782. John Jeter's Est. 17£—18s—9d. U. S.

"John Jeter's Est. #185—Caroline 1782. Entered there. #5017. #185.

Caroline County.

"I hereby certify I have received of John Jeter's Estate One grass fed beef—adjudged to weigh three hundred and twenty-five pounds, taken for publick use, pursuant to Act of Assembly, and to be paid for at two pence per pound specie in . . . paper money at such rate of depreciation as shall be settled by Governor and Council at the time of payment, the present rate being six hundred for one. Oct. 17, 1781. £1625—325 Beef.

14£	: 1s	: 3d	#1
3	: 2	: 6	2
	15	: 0	3

17£   18s   9d
JOHN BROADDUS."

No record has been found of either of the marriages of John Jeter, but the name of his wife, Elizabeth—no doubt his second wife—is signed to a deed of gift made to his son, John, Jr., in Amelia County in 1756.

The following are believed to have been his sons:

(1) George; living in Orange County, Va., in 1738.

(2) Henry; died in Caroline County in 1743.

(3) Nicholas; died in Caroline County in 1785. Elijah Jeter administrator of his estate.

(4) Thomas; married about 1740; died in Amelia County in 1765. (See forward.)

(5) William; married about 1741; died in South Carolina in 1797. (See forward.)

(6) John, Jr.; died in 1807; said by his descendants to have been nearly one hundred years old. (See forward.)

(7) James; married 1756 in Amelia County, Priscilla Yarbrough-John Jeter, security; went to Province of Onslow, North Carolina, before 1760.

(8) Edmund, Sr.; living in Greensville County, Va., in 1782—ten whites in his family.

(9) Ambrose; married 1760 in Amelia County, John Jeter, security. (See forward.)

(10) Elijah; married 1768. (See forward.)

(11) Burrell; went to Tennessee.

(12) Littleton; married 1786; went to Kentucky. (See forward.)

(13) Horatio; married 1786; died in Caroline County. (See forward.)

(14) Fielding; died in Kentucky. (See forward.)

(15) Elisha; married 1797; died in Kentucky. (See forward.)

No names of any of his daughters have been found unless Jane who married Moses Higgins was his child. We have had the pleasure of reading a very remarkable family letter written October 16, 1872, by H. H. Higgins of Athens, Ala., to his cousin, Wm. J. Higgins of Kentucky, from which we quote the following extracts:

"Moses Higgins married Jane Jeter at a place called Hobb's Hole on James River. Children: James Jeter, Catherine, Betsy, Nancy, Matilda, William Young, and America.

"Moses Higgins was about five feet eleven inches, or probably six feet high, well made, large but no surplus flesh, rather thin visaged, fair skin and fair hair, blue eyes, and a very dignified, commanding looking old gentleman, just such a looking man as would command attention and respect in any company. Jane, his wife, was a large woman, moderately corpulent, weight when in health about 260 or 270 pounds, tall and stately, coal black hair, fair complexion, regular features, very small feet and hands for one of her size. I presume she must have been very good looking when young, as she was a very fine looking old lady. She outlived my grandfather twelve or fourteen years, and finally died at her daughter's house (America Fortune) in Greensboro, Ala., having left her Kentucky home in October, 1835, to visit her relatives in Alabama, and to make her future home with her daughter."

The name of Thomas Jeter, who is believed to have been the son of John, the immigrant, occurs at intervals in Caroline County, until about 1760, and also in Amelia County in 1752, when he bought land from William Jeter. The deed (Deed Book No. 4, page 397) reads, "Thomas Jeter of Caroline County" and "William Jeter of Lunenburg, County," and conveys 404 acres of land in Amelia. He died in Amelia in 1765. His will follows:

Thomas Jeter's Nuncupative Will, August 29, 1765.

Memorandum

Thomas Jeter about an hour or two before he died and at two different times called up his boys that was present, which was Oliver, Henry, and Samuel Jeter, and then proceeded to mention what was his will. And desired Thomas Payne to take notice that if he died, his desire was that his wife should have his whole estate during her life, or widowhood, after which his desire was that his whole estate should be equally divided among his children, that out of his estate he desired his young children should have their schooling.

At a Court held for Amelia County the 24th day of October, 1765.

This writing purporting the nuncupative will of Thomas Jeter, Dec'd was presented in Court, and Winifred Jeter, the widow, and Oliver Jeter, heir-at-law of the said Thomas Jeter, appeared in Court, and having no objection to the proof thereof, and refusing to take on them the administration of the said Decedent's Estate, the said will was prov'd by oaths of Oliver Jeter and Samuel Jeter, who deposed that the said Thomas Jeter desired them a few hours before his decease, to take notice that such as contained in the said writing was his last will.

And thereupon, at the motion of Henry Jeter, second son of the said decedent, who took oath, and entered into and acknowledged bond with security as the law directs.

Certificate was granted him for obtaining Letters of Administration on the Estate of the said Thomas Jeter with the will annexed.

Teste

T. G. PEACHY, *Clk.*

A Copy—Teste,

S. L. FARRAR, *Clerk of the Circuit Court of Amelia County, Virginia.*

We cannot be sure of his "young children," but the will of James Vaughan—recorded in Amelia—mentions his second wife, Mary, and Thomas Jeter as the grandfather of her children. Mary's daughter, Matilda Vaughan, married Sovereign Jeter, and is mentioned in the will of Presley Jeter as "my niece, Matilda Jeter." His will also mentions his sister, Docey Bradshaw. So Mary, the wife of James Vaughan, Docey, the wife of ———— Bradshaw, and Presley Jeter must have been three of the "young children" of Thomas Jeter. Presley Jeter's Bible, which descended to Matilda (Vaughan) Jeter, gives the following items on the fly leaf:

"Presley Jeter was born May 7, 1754.
Phebe Jeter was born Dec. 1, 1751.
They were married Oct. 29, 1783."

His Bible contains this record also:

"Ransom Carter Jeter, our Dear beloved son was born The 5th day of August in the year of our Lord Christ 1790 and departed this life the 8th day of December, 1790."

This must have been their only child for no mention of any other is made in his will, and none has been found elsewhere.

The marriage bond of Presley Jeter and Phebe Carter is in Amelia County, and also the record of his being commissioned Ensign in the Amelia County Militia.

THE TENNESSEE JETERS

Oliver Jeter, son of Thomas and Winifred Jeter, was born in Caroline County, Va., about 1742. He married Mary Jennings, daughter of William, Jr., and Agnes (Dickerson) Jennings, of Amelia County, Va., and Wilkes County, Ga. He lived in Amelia County until after 1790, when he moved his family to Edgefield District, S. C.

CHILDREN:

Samuel, Robert, Thomas, William, James, and Virginia (Jincy), who married ———— Harding.

Thomas Jeter, son of Oliver and Mary (Jennings) Jeter, married and had children, one of whom was—

Fielding Jeter, born in Georgia in 1804; married in 1824, Nancy Goodman of South Carolina, who was born in 1809; died 1896; daughter of Charles Goodman (born 1785) and Mary King (born 1787). They went to Shelby County, Tenn., in 1828, and he died there in 1852.

CHILDREN :

(1) Sarah Ann, born 1825; died 1870.
(2) Charles Whitfield, born 1827; died 1880. (See forward.)
(3) Mary Elizabeth, born 1830; married William A. J. Gift in 1848, and moved to Martinez, California in 1855, where she died in 1885.

CHILDREN :

(a) Janie, born 1849; married ———— Brown.
(b) Mary Louisa, born 1851; married I. E. Marshall.
(c) Georgia, born 1853; married Charles Sickal and had one daughter, Gertrude.
(d) Nancy Ann; married W. F. Pitts.
(e) Rachel.
(f) Kate; married Charles O'Neil.
(g) William A. J., Jr.
(h) Robert.

(4) Susan Wesley, born 1833; died 1881; married in 1857, T. Oldham.

CHILDREN :

(a) Estella, born 1858.
(b) Nancy, born 1860.
(c) Georgia, born 1866.
(d) William A., born 1870.
(e) Ruth, born 1873.

All of these are now dead except Estella and William.

(5) William Andrew, born 1841; died intestate during the Civil War, in 1862.

Charles Whitfield Jeter, son of Fielding and Nancy (Goodman) Jeter, of Shelby County, Tenn., was born in South Carolina in 1827. He married Martha Garvin of Georgia, who was born in 1832 and died in 1920. She was the daughter of James and Mary (Johnson) Garvin.

CHILDREN :

(1) Mary Ann, born 1851; died 1922; married Thomas Bland in 1877.

CHILDREN:

(a) Charles Bascom, born 1880; married Mary Jo Johnson of Pine Bluff, Ark.

CHILDREN:

(aa) Mary Jo.
(bb) Evangeline.
(cc) Charles Bascom, Jr.

(b) Addison Jeremiah, born ————; died 1926.
(c) Lottie; died in youth.
(d) Lucy Beckner; married George Pease of Gunnison, Miss., and had one child.

(a) Ora Lynn.

(e) Williford Daniel; married Ruby Pennington, daughter of Edward and Mittie (Fete) Pennington, of Millington, Tenn.

CHILDREN:

(aa) Williford D., Jr.
(bb) Edward Early Bland.

(2) Lula Virginia, born 1852; died 1910.
(3) Charles Fielding, born 1855; hale and hearty in 1929.
(4) James Edward, born 1857; died 1917; married Margaret Elizabeth Stovall (born 1863) daughter of Berry and Sue (Robinet) Stovall.

CHILDREN:

(a) Charles Edward, born 1889; married Rose Burk in 1913.

CHILDREN:

(aa) Charles Edward, Jr., born 1914.
(bb) James Edward, born 1917.
(cc) Margaret Nell, born 1920.
(dd) Billie Burk, born 1926.
(ee) Ben S., born 1927.

(b) James Stovall Jeter, born 1892; married Ann Kindred Prescott of Memphis, Tenn., in 1917.

CHILDREN:

(aa) Ann Kindred, born 1917.
(bb) Jean Stovall, born 1920.
(cc) Margaret Louise; died in infancy.

(5) Martha Elizabeth, born 1859; died 1884.

(6) Nancy Ann, born 1861; married Jesse P. Walt (died 1929), son of James R. and Mary (Bateman) Walt, of Memphis, Tenn.; died in Little Rock, Ark., in 1917.

(7) Donie May, born 1866; died 1892; married Albert Forest Bateman (born 1865; died 1896), son of Ben and Lucy (Massey) Bateman, of Shelby County, Tenn.

CHILDREN:

 (a) Ben Forest, born 1888; married in 1923, Letitia Walsh, daughter of Hugh R. and Emmie (Jones) Walsh, of Kerrville, Tenn.

CHILDREN:

  (aa) Ben Forest, Jr., born 1924.
  (bb) Henry Fielding, born 1926.
  (cc) Edward Chamberland, born March, 1928; died October, 1928.

 (b) Donie Vashti, born 1889; married L. M. Scott.

CHILDREN:

  (aa) Luther Edward, born 1911.
  (bb) Francis Bateman, born 1916; died 1917.
  (cc) Jessie M., born 1919.
  (dd) Ben Jeter, born 1921.
  (ee) Donie Jeter Bateman, born 1892; died in infancy.

(8) Fannie, born 1869.

(9) Ora, born 1871; married L. Berry Stovall (died 1894), son of Berry and Sue Stovall of Shelby County, Tenn. They had one child:

 (a) Lillian Berry, born 1895; married in 1920, Robert Wharton Thweatt, son of Joseph and Fannie (York) Thweatt of Shelby County, Tenn.

(10) Emmett Early, born 1874; married (first), September, 1900, Mary Louise Walt (died in 1902), daughter of James R. and Mary B. Walt of Memphis, Tenn. One child:

 (a) James Walt, born January, 1902; died August, 1902. He married (second) in 1904, Ada M. Smith, daughter of Obion and Mary (Ward) Smith, of Millington, Tenn.

CHILDREN:

(aa) Martha Elizabeth, born 1905; married in 1925, William Harold Carleton of Knoxville, Tenn.

CHILDREN:

(aaa) Ann Jeter, born 1926.
(bbb) William Harold, Jr., born 1929.
(bb) Emmett Early, Jr., born 1906; married February, 1929, Dixie Evelyn MacFarland, daughter of A. F. MacFarland of Ellendale, Tenn.
(cc) Paul Allen, born 1910.
(dd) Marion Francis (infant) died 1914.

The Commercial Appeal (Tenn.), in the issue of August 25, 1929, has this to say of "Squire" Emmett Early Jeter, who was being urged by his friends to run for the office of Sheriff of his county:

"The Squire's history is probably the most unusual of any man at the courthouse and can really be said to have begun in 1901 when he cleared away a tract of virgin timber land near Locke, Tenn., where he was born, and built his own home.

Left Store for Politics

"For years—until 1918, in fact—he conducted a general merchandising store and then, with his children approaching school age, the idea occurred to him that the county school system was all wrong. And to rectify it he got into politics, woke up in the Legislature and opened his eyes again to see that he was chairman of the county court.

" 'I never had the advantages of a thorough education myself,' Squire Jeter said yesterday. 'In fact, I didn't go past the seventh grade. But I didn't want my children to be at the same disadvantage. And yet, when I went to inspect the school at Locke, where I intended to send them, I found that it had an average attendance of twenty and one teacher.

" 'There were schools at Ramsay and at Cuba, too, and in much the same condition and I got the idea that it would be a fine thing to consolidate all three schools into one that was really a school.'

"The Squire eventually succeeded in doing this but it was a stormy course. He found opposition everywhere, as each community wanted its own school regardless of how lax it was conducted. He sold the home he had built himself and paid $10,000 for a farm nearer the center of the population so he could mix with the citizenship of all three communities to get this idea over.

"And when he finally won out, and the schools were merged into what is now the E. E. Jeter Junior High, those who had bitterly opposed his plan took the case into chancery and finally to the supreme court in a determined but futile effort to block it.

Elected, Hands Down

"His fight for the consolidation put him first in the public eye of his neighborhood and the same year he was induced to run for magistrate, winning easily over four candidates. This was in 1918.

" 'But I only tried one case,' he said, ' and this cost me the friendship of a life-long acquaintance, so I gave up being an official magistrate and became an unofficial one. From then on I tried my remaining cases out of court.'

"In 1921 and again in 1923 Squire Jeter was a member of the State Legislature and there he carried on his fight for further consolidation of schools, working with the county board of education.

"On his return from the General Assembly of 1923 he ran again for magistrate and again showed his heels to a field of four.

Gets Every Vote

"In 1927 the Squire was unanimously elected chairman of the county court. In 1928 the same course was duplicated and again this year. In none of the elections was a dissenting vote cast for the first time in the 109-year history of the county court.

"The Squire is a Mason and an Elk, but his particular pride, aside from giving barbecues for his friends and daily admiring the E. E. Jeter High School, which is situated across from his home, is that for twenty-seven consecutive years he has been elected chairman of the board of stewards of the Embury Methodist Church, South."

....

James Jeter, youngest son of Oliver and Mary (Jennings) Jeter, died in Georgia in 1830. He married ————.

CHILDREN:

(1) Presley, born September 16, 1794.
(2) Nancy, born February 29, 1796.

(3) William, born June 4, 1798.
(4) Docy, born March 8, 1800.
(5) Wiley, born February 8, 1802.
(6) Mary (Polly), born November 5, 1808.

Wiley Jeter, son of James Jeter and grandson of Oliver and Mary (Jennings) Jeter, married ————.

CHILDREN:

(1) Martha Palmer, born February 9, 1821.
(2) John S., born October 11, 1825.
(3) Wm. P., born March 27, 1828.
(4) Dolphus, born November 7, 1830.
(5) Augusta, born April 5, 1832.
(6) Wiley, born May 2, 1834; died without issue.

JENNINGS

There was born in Yorkshire, England, on November 10, 1676, one William Jennings, who came to Virginia in 1700, and settled in Nottoway County, where he died in 1775. He married Mary J. Pulliam in Hanover County Va., in 1724. She died, 1774, in Nottoway County.

CHILDREN:

(1) William, Jr., born 1726; died 1793.
(2) Agnes, born 1727.
(3) Elizabeth, born 1729; married George Walton.
(4) Sarah, born 1730; married John Fowlkes.
(5) Mary, born 1732.
(6) Robert, born 1733; died 1797; married Elizabeth Childs.
(7) John, born 1735; died 1783.
(8) Nancy, born 1736.
(9) James, born 1737.
(10) Joseph, born 1739; died 1804.

William Jennings, Jr., married Agnes Dickerson.

One of their children was Mary, who married Oliver Jeter, son of Thomas and Winifred Jeter of Amelia County, Va.

THE WILL OF WILLIAM JENNINGS, JR.

Wilkes County's Record of Wills, 1792-1801, page 56:

In The Name of God Amen. I, William Jennings of the state of Georgia and county of Wilkes being weak in body but of a sound memory for which I bless God for, do make this my last will and testament, and revoking all other wills—

and as touching my worldly state I dispose of it in the following manner, (viz.):

Item, I give and bequeath unto my grandson Garland—five pounds in property to be received out of my estate at the discretion of my executors.

Item, I have given and delivered in possession to my son Dickerson Jennings all his part of my estate to him and his heirs and assigns forever.

Item, I have given and delivered in possession to my son John Jennings all his part of my estate, except ten pounds to be received in property, as it may be best raised to him and his heirs and assigns forever.

Item, I have given and delivered in possession to my son William Jennings all his part of my estate except ten pounds to be raised in property to balance amounts with him, to him and his heirs and assigns forever.

Item, I give and bequeath unto my son Moody Jennings two hundred acres of land including his plantation and two negroes, David and Phillis to him and his heirs and assigns forever.

Item, I have given and delivered in possession to my son James Jennings all his part of my estate, except ten pounds to be raised in property as it may be best raised to him and his heirs and assigns forever.

Item, I give and bequeath unto my son Joseph Jennings one negro named Dick to him and his heirs and assigns forever.

Item, I do give and bequeath unto my son Robert Jennings one negro named Jack, one feather bed and furniture to him and his heirs and assigns forever.

Item, I do give and bequeath unto my son Thomas Jennings, two hundred acres of land, including the plantation where he lives, one negro named Hanner, one feather bed and furniture to him and his heirs and assigns forever.

Item, I do give and bequeath unto my son Henry Jennings two hundred acres of land including the plantation whereon I now live, beginning at Moody Jennings' line on north of the branch, then up the river to include his two hundred acres and one negro named Peter, one feather bed and furniture to him and his heirs and assigns forever.

Item, I have given and delivered in possession to my daughter Elizabeth Anderson all her part of my estate to her and her heirs and assigns forever.

Item, I have given and delivered in possession to my daughter Sarah Roberson all her part of my estate except ten pounds to be raised in property as it may be best to her and her heirs and assigns forever.

Item, I do lend unto my daughter Mary Jeter during her life one negro named Lucy and after her death to be equally divided among her children to them and their heirs and assigns forever.

Item, I do lend unto my daughter Nancy Hix during her life and after her death to her children one negro named Milley to them and their heirs forever.

Item, I will that the remaining part of my land not given out be equally divided between my two daughters Mary Jeter and Nancy Hix.

Item, I will that the remaining part of my estate be it whatever nature or quality soever which I have not given out after what is to be raised out of the estate in property to be equally divided among my five sons (viz.) Moody Jennings, Joseph, Robert, Thomas and Henry Jennings, provided nevertheless that if any of my sons should die before they marry then and in that case their estate given to them should be equally divided among the five youngest boys then living. I will nothing herein contained be misconstrued for want of them or form in law. I do appoint Robert Walton and my son Moody Jennings my executors of this my last will and testament in witness whereof I have hereunto set my hand and seal this nineteenth day of October Anno Domini 1793.

N. B.—Robert and Thomas Jennings have already had their parts beds and furniture before the signing of this.

his

WILLIAM x JENNINGS [SEAL].

mark

Test

OLIVER JETER
ROBERT JENNINGS
HENRY JENNINGS

THE JETERS OF BEDFORD COUNTY, VIRGINIA

Henry Jeter, 2nd son of Thomas and Winifred Jeter, was born in Caroline County, Va., about 1744, and went with his parents to Amelia County about 1760. His father died in 1765 and Henry was made administrator of his estate. He settled this estate in 1775—no legatees mentioned in the settlement.

In 1770 he received from his brother, Oliver Jeter, 304 acres of land in Amelia County, on Cold Water Run, and in 1775, while still living in this county, he sold a part of it to Francis Belcher. In 1783, he sold the remainder to his brother, Presley Jeter, and the records show that at this time he was a resident of Bedford County.

He most probably married in Amelia—certainly, while he was living there—but no marriage bond has yet been found. His wife was Elizabeth Bell, called "beautiful Betsy Bell," who was born in 1747, and died, in Bedford County, Va., in 1833.

In 1781, Henry Jeter was made First Lieutenant of the Bedford County Militia, so he must have changed his place of residence during the Revolutionary War.

On May 30, 1789, a large boundary of land was granted to him on the north side of Bedford County, running north from what is now Centerville, and east of the road to Big Island, and the residence that he built upon it still stands. The basement of this house is brick-lined, and the brick for this and the chimneys, which are still in perfect condition, were made right near the house. Osage orange trees, two feet in diameter, stand in the yard, and handsome old boxwoods line the walk, while here and there a perfect specimen of the tree box, in beautiful pyramid shape, points heavenward, entirely unmindful of the passing years. This place has been in the Jeter family continuously since the grant was made in 1789, having descended each time to the youngest son, and is now owned and occupied by R. Kemper Jeter, youngest son of Robert H., and grandson of Jesse, who was the youngest son of Henry, the original owner.

The story has been handed down in the family that Henry Jeter gave two hundred acres of this land for a yoke of oxen, and another two hundred for an old stallion, blind in one eye.

He and his wife, his son, Jesse, and his wife, and others of the family, are buried in the old graveyard near where the road to the house leaves the main road.

CHILDREN OF HENRY AND ELIZABETH (BELL) JETER WERE:

(1) Nancy; married (first), October 4, 1787, Stephen Phillips; (second), ———— Overstreet.
(2) Jenny; married Josiah Lockett, January 17, 1793.
(3) John; married Mary Hardy. (See forward.)
(4) Pleasant; married Jane Hatcher. (See forward.)
(5) Betsy; married Jeremiah Hatcher. (See Hatcher family.)
(6) Sovereign; married (first) Matilda Vaughan; (second) Nancy Overstreet. (See forward.)
(7) Henry.
(8) Elliott; married Polly Harris, November 15, 1810.
(9) Ransom; married Patsy H. Claybrook, December 2, 1807. They lived near Hollins Institute, in Botetourt County, Va. His ambition is said to have been to live long enough to see another Democrat elected President of the United States. This wish was gratified. He died in 1884, after the election of Grover Cleveland, but before his inauguration. He was ninety-nine years old. Their daughter, Mary M., married William Jeter, son of John and Mary (Hardy) Jeter.
(10) Caleb; married Sarah Cobb. (See forward.)
(11) Jesse; married Susan Robinson. (See forward.)

Dr. Wm. E. Hatcher, in his "Life of J. B. Jeter" (grandson of Henry and Elizabeth (Bell) Jeter), says:

"The Jeter family hold a large and respectable place in the County of Bedford, as well as in other portions of Virginia. They have always seemed to be wedded to rural life, and fond of agricultural pursuits. While never distinguished for wealth or genius, they have usually stood above the average of their neighbors in intelligence and self-respect. A few of them have taken rank in professional life, though not in those professions which depend for success upon public speaking. Now and then some of them have sought their fortunes on the treacherous sea of politics, but, owing either to the madness of the waves, or to the piratical character of rival crafts, they have never ventured very far from shore.

"In an autobiographical sketch which Dr. Jeter commenced, but never finished, he has this to say of the Jeters—

" 'Of my family-name I have not been able to learn the history. It is obviously a French name. The first Jeter, according to the family tradition, settled near Port Royal, in Caroline County, in the early colonial days. From all that I can learn I deem it probable that the family was of Huguenot origin, was settled a while in England, and thence emigrated to this country. . . .'

"There is something characteristic in the foregoing description which Dr. Jeter furnishes of his family. He mentions that the Jeters are French in their origin, and it is an interesting fact that after the changes of many generations and the intermingling of other blood they still possess, in a marked degree, the buoyancy and volatility of their fore-fathers. Even to the present day they are remarkable for their impulsiveness and their easy and hopeful views of the future. They never cease to dream of the good day that is to come, and often they dream of good days that never come. The sun of hope rarely sinks below the Jeter horizon."

Dr. Hatcher quotes Dr. Jeter further:

"My father's grandmother, named Miller from her third marriage, died after I commenced my ministry, in the ninety-sixth year of her age. I heard her say that she kept a register of her descendants until they numbered one hundred and fifty, and that they then multiplied beyond her knowledge, but that she supposed that they amounted to three hundred. Shortly after that time I know that I had one hundred and twenty-five living first cousins, eighty of whom were her descendants."

He says, also, that Dr. Jeter represented his grand-mother, Elizabeth (Bell) Jeter, as a woman of strong character, and said that he once heard his father, Pleasant Jeter, say, after her death that he had never in all his life "seen her angry," though she did not die until she was in the eighty-seventh year of her age.

Elizabeth Jeter died in Bedford County in 1833. Her will is recorded in that county. From the above statement of her grand-son she was born in 1747.

Henry Jeter was no doubt twenty-one years of age when he was made administrator of his father's estate in 1765, so he must have been born not later than 1744. He died in Bedford County in 1821. His will follows:

In the name of God, Amen, I, Henry Jeter, of Bedford County being in a perfect mind, memory and understanding, knowing it is appointed for all men once to die, and knowing the uncertainty thereof do make and ordain this to be my Last Will and Testament. First of all I recommend my soul to Almighty God who gave it and my body to the dust from whence it came, to be buried in a Christian-like Manner. And as for such worldly goods as it has pleased God to bless me with in this life I dispose of in the following manner, to-wit: I lend to my beloved wife Betty Jeter all my estate both real and personal (that is to say whereon I now live) which estate I lend to my beloved Wife as long as she continueth my widow. Then to be equally divided between all my children and their heirs, either by sale or division as shall be thought most expedient at that time, only to be observed that there is several of my children married and has got things given to them to the amount of (£) which may be seen in their accounts left against them by me. (To-wit) Some of them 80 acres of land and other things— John Jeter, Sovereign Jeter, Nancy Overstreet and Gincy Lockett and Betty Hatcher one negro girl, Nicey, at (£40) has 80 acres, my sons Henry Jeter, Elliott Jeter, Caleb Jeter, Ransom Jeter, and Jesse Jeter must have as much money as 80 acres of the land will fetch when sold, and as much of the other things as the other children. The balance of my estate to be equally divided among them all. My land in Montgomery County to be sold for the best price and the money after my just debts are paid to be divided as above mentioned. And I do hereby empower my sons hereafter named to make a good and lawful right to the purchaser of said lands. And I do hereby appoint my beloved wife

Betty Jeter and my sons Henry Jeter and Caleb Jeter Exors. of this my last will and Testament. In witness whereof I have hereunto Set my hand and Seal this 27th day of May in the Year of our Lord 1807.

HENRY JETER [SEAL].

Signed in
presence of

         his
EDM'ND x POWELL
    mark
     his
JNO. x POWELL
   mark

Memorandum—Pleasant Jeter is to have 80 acres of Land where he lived to run near the back fence to the lower end, if any lacking to run to my back line, adjoining the line of Bondurants.

H. JETER.

This will was probated September 24, 1821. His wife, Betty Jeter, and Henry Jeter, Jr., refused to be executors and Jesse Jeter was made administrator. No mention of Caleb Jeter.

In Henry Jeter's List of Sales his land in Montgomery County is mentioned as being 864 acres.

....

John Jeter, eldest son of Henry and Elizabeth (Bell) Jeter, was born in Amelia County and came to Bedford with his parents while still a small boy. He married November 16, 1796, Mary (Polly) Hardy, daughter of Joseph and Margaret (McKenzie) Hardy.

CHILDREN:

(1) Mahala.
(2) Elizabeth; married Pleasant Bond. (See Bond family.)
(3) Susan.
(4) Sarah; married James Valentine Cobbs. (See forward.)
(5) Henry; married Chelessie Dent. (See forward.)
(6) Allison; married (first) Lucy W. Hunter; (second) Elizabeth Ann Peters. (See forward.)
(7) William; married (first) Eliza Noell; (second) Mary M. Jeter.
(8) Margaret P.; married ———— Bowling.

John Jeter died in 1858 and his will, which was made July 13, 1848, and recorded in Bedford County (Will Book "O," page 165) mentions: wife, Mary Leak Jeter; daughters, Mahala, Elizabeth, Susan, and Sarah; sons, Henry, Allison, and William; grandfather of his children, Joseph Hardy; daughter Margaret P. Bowling.

....

Sarah L. Jeter, daughter of John and Mary (Hardy) Jeter, was born February 24, 1819, and died February 8, 1907. She married James Valentine Cobbs, who was born June 10, 1821, and died April 4, 1884.

CHILDREN:

(1) John H., born in Bedford County, May 22, 1846; died in Lynchburg, Va., April 24, 1929; married Edmonia Offutt in 1888.

CHILDREN:

(a) Josephine; married Jesse L. Jones; had two children: Elinor and Josephine.
(b) W. Offutt; killed in World War. Was member of Company L, 116th Infantry.
(c) J. Madison; married Marjorie Jerkins; lives in New York City.

(2) Molly E., born November 17, 1847; died December 20, 1896; married William S. Allen.

CHILDREN:

Lula, Melvin, Girther, Bernard, and Coral.

(3) Charles E., born March, 1845; died, unmarried, March 4, 1911.
(4) Ann Stitira; married February 16, 1871, John Calvin Hatcher, Jr. (See Hatcher family.)
(5) Fannie R., born February, 1856; married March 28, 1883, Edward Perkins Hatcher, son of J. Calvin and Rebecca (Hatcher) Hatcher. (See Hatcher family.)
(6) James Valentine; married Judson Jeter, daughter of Robert H. and Lucy (Hatcher) Jeter. (See Jeter family.)

CHILDREN:

(a) Robert Valentine; married Mary Crute. Two children Robert Valentine, Jr., and Mary Elizabeth.

(b) Sara; married Charles Bates. Children: Charles, Jr., and James Oakey.

(c) Sallie Lee; married Jean Matthews. One child: Robert.

....

Henry Jeter, son of John and Mary (Hardy) Jeter, was born in 1804, and died in 1883. He married Chelessie Dent.

CHILDREN:

(1) William Peter, born February 4, 1837. (See forward.)
(2) Joseph; married Frances Thomasson.
(3) Robert; unmarried; killed in Civil War.
(4) Virginia Frances, born May 1, 1847; died April 18, 1921; married, John Clay Dickerson.
(5) Victoria Alice, born March 1, 1849; died January 23, 1924; married November 24, 1872, James Kent Richardson.
(6) Mary; married John Barbour; died in 1890.
(7) Sarah Ann; married Jonathan Neighbors; died in 1905.
(8) Griffin D., born December 27, 1857; died March 1, 1929; married Fannie Basham.

....

William Peter Jeter, son of Henry and Chelessie (Dent) Jeter, was born February 4, 1837, in Bedford County; died June 29, 1918; married May 16, 1858, Sallie Agnes Meador of Franklin County, Va.

CHILDREN:

(1) John Calvin, born April 9, 1859; died February 7, 1910.
(2) James Garrett, born August 13, 1861; married, June 17, 1896, Annie Maria Smith.
(3) Nannie Alberta, born June 8, 1864; married, April 14, 1886, James D. McLain.
(4) Cornelia Ann, born July 28, 1868; married, October 10, 1889, John W. Ayers.
(5) Jerry Camlin, born August 31, 1872; married, September 16, 1903, Elizabeth G. Hartwell.
(6) Willie Esther, born June 26, 1875; married (first), June 12, 1898, John Fitz Willie Huddleston; (second) June 26, 1920, Robert L. Meador.

(7) Rowena Mae, born December 11, 1878; died October 14, 1910; married, September 15, 1903, John C. McGuire.

(8) Grover Cleveland, born August 13, 1881; married, September 13, 1905, Elsie Franklin Turner.

(9) Minnie, born August 13, 1883; died June 24, 1884.

Allison Jeter, son of John and Mary (Hardy) Jeter, married (first) Lucy W. Hunter, March 26, 1827.

CHILDREN:

(1) Paulina; married Hayden Peters.

(2) Elizabeth; married Wesley Peters.

(3) Diana; married Zachariah Gallion.

(4) Amanda; married William Morgan.

(5) Catherine; married Henry Hines.

Allison Jeter married (second) Elizabeth Ann Peters, December 9, 1844.

CHILD:

(6) John, who married Judith Dickerson, and had two children:

    (a) Eula; married Cham St. Clair.

    (b) James; married Belle Wright, daughter of Peter M. and Sarah (Dearing) Wright.

William Jeter, son of John and Mary (Hardy) Jeter, married (first) in 1838, Eliza Noell of Bedford County, Va.

CHILDREN:

(1) Frances Doiliska, born March 4, 1839; died February 16, 1888.

(2) James Nathaniel, born March 16, 1841; died May 3, 1862, from wounds received in Civil War.

(3) Alwilda Virginia, born May 22, 1845; died April, 1923.

(4) Alonza Travis, born December 20, 1850. (See forward.)

(5) Fernando, born June 27, 1852; went to Mobile, Mo.; left one son, Ira.

William Jeter married (second), August 29, 1854, his first cousin, Mary M. Jeter, daughter of Ransom and Patsy (Claybrook) Jeter.

CHILDREN:

(1) Wilbert Thisco, born August 28, 1855; lives at Lexington, Va.
(2) Ida Alice, born June 23, 1857; died November 24, 1878.
(3) Grovella Gertrude, born April 8, 1860; died March, 1915.
(4) Warren, born October 7, 1861; died in infancy.
(5) Florence, born August 8, 1863; died August 7, 1907.
(6) Lillie Mary, born October 7, 1866; died December 16, 1927.

Alonza Travis Jeter, son of William and Eliza (Noell) Jeter, married, November 17, 1872, Ida Olivia Reynolds of Rockbridge County, Va.; now living in Roanoke, Va.

CHILDREN:

(1) Corrie Etta, born August 26, 1873; married, September 29, 1897, Charles Evans, who is now deceased.
(2) Walter Raleigh, born January 27, 1876; married, August 27, 1902, Eula Haeberlet.
(3) Alice Noell, born October 8, 1878; married, March 23, 1898, F. L. Koontz, who is now deceased.
(4) Fernando, born March 2, 1881; died July 18, 1915; married, October 2, 1901, Etta Hoal.
(5) Lelia Estelle, born September 22, 1884.
(6) Alwilda Frances, born July 3, 1887.
(7) Warren Alonza, born November 23, 1889.
(8) Mable Viola, born July 5, 1892.
(9) Anna Eliza, born April 30, 1894; married, March 7, 1917, Frederick Nover.

BOND

Wright Bond, founder of the family in Bedford County, came from Cumberland County before the Revolutionary War, and was a member of the Bedford County Militia.

He married Martha ——— and their son—

Pleasant Bond, married, March 21, 1826, Elizabeth Hardy Jeter, daughter of John and Mary (Hardy) Jeter. (See Jeter family.)

CHILDREN:

(1) William Pleasant, born December 25, 1826; died September 12, 1916; married, December 24, 1858, Bettie Ann Smith (born October, 1831; died October 1, 1907), daughter of Steven and Rebecca (Morgan) Smith.
(2) Mary Jane; married William N. Preas.

CHILDREN:

(a) Ferdinand; drowned in childhood.

(b) Thomas Pleasant; married Ann Henry Stiff.

(c) John Robert; married (first) Judith Noell; (second) Etta French.

(d) Olivia Alberta (twin); married John Henry Moore.

(e) Dora Gertrude (twin); married William Hayden Bush.

(f) William Alpheus; married Jennie Keller.

(g) James Clay; married Fannie Cundiff.

(h) Mary Magdaline; married James Rosser Noell.

(i) Sallie Elizabeth; married Gustavus Beauregard Williams.

(j) Anna Harris; married Richard D. Carlysle.

(k) Virginia Belle; married Abraham Smith Wood.

(3) Henry; married Elizabeth Board, daughter of John Board. (See Board family.) He died of wounds received in the Civil War and was buried in Norfolk, Va.

CHILD:

(a) Joseph Wright, born December 8, 1858; died December 13, 1922; married, June 11, 1890, Mary J. Gardner (born April 3, 1869), daughter of John B. and Sarah (Goggin) Gardner. (See Goggin family.)

CHILDREN:

(aa) Gardner Wright, born February 14, 1893; married, September 2, 1922, Effie Golden Luck, daughter of Hugh and Lillian (Hatcher) Luck, of Montvale, Bedford County, Va. Now cashier of the Bedford Trust and Savings Bank, Bedford, Va.

CHILD:

(aaa) Gardner Wright, Jr., born March 22, 1929.

(bb) Elizabeth Clark, born April 21, 1895; married, August 22, 1919, George Edward (Fritz) Heller, popular druggist of Bedford, Va.

CHILDREN:

(aaa) Gardner Parrish (Fritz), born December 20, 1920.

(bbb) Betty Bond, born February 20, 1928.

(cc) Sarah Virginia, born September 8, 1904; married, September 14, 1927, Dr. Sterling Kennedy Wallace of Blackstone, Va., who is now a dentist in Bedford, Va.

(dd) Mary Catharyn, born February 3, 1907.

(4) Julia Benson, born February 29, 1836; died September 9, 1896; married, September 25, 1857, Thomas Robertson Burroughs (born February 8, 1827; died February 19, 1902), son of James and Elizabeth (Robertson) Burroughs. (See Robertson family.)

CHILDREN:

(a) Minnie Eugenia, born August 14, 1862; married, November 21, 1881, Charles Warfield Price (born February 5, 1852); now living in Bedford,

Va., where, for many years, she has been a loyal and enthusiastic leader of the Woman's Christian Temperance Union.

CHILDREN:

(aa) Claude Thomas, born September 25, 1883; died May 23, 1903.
(bb) Horace Benson, born November 27, 1884; married, January 15, 1920, May Stella Arnn; now living in Hurley, Buchanan County, Va.

CHILD:

(aaa) Horace Benson, Jr., born July 31, 1926.

(cc) Norma Alice, born August 18, 1886; married, June 3, 1908, Thomas Carlysle Lavinder; now living in Abingdon, Va.

CHILDREN:

(aaa) Evelyn Carlysle, born March 7, 1909; graduated from Abingdon High School in 1925; from Stonewall Jackson College in 1927; now a student at Duke University, N. C.
(bbb) Thomas C., Jr., born April 18, 1914.
(ccc) Douglass, born September 6, 1917.
(ddd) Beverly Routh, born September 25, 1920.
(eee) David Richard, born May 25, 1929.

(dd) Bessie Eugenia, born June 28, 1888; married, November 16, 1919, Shirley S. Lynn; now living at Villamont, Bedford County, Va. No children.
(ee) Cora Lee, born September 12, 1890; married, November 15, 1918, Eugene Gifford Cullings of Wilmington, Del.; now living in Charlotte, N. C. No children.
(ff) Charles Benjamin, born April 3, 1893; married, September 12, 1914, Nellie Reinier.

CHILDREN:

(aaa) Anna Elizabeth, born September 11, 1915.
(bbb) Mary Virginia, born March 3, 1917.
(ccc) John Edward, born June 14, 1919.

(gg) Julia Bond, born March 14, 1897; married, September 15, 1921, Thomas Christian Armstrong of Richmond, Va.; now living in Richmond.

CHILDREN:

(aaa) Thomas Christian, Jr., born November 11, 1922.
(bbb) Cary Warfield, born April 6, 1929.

(hh) Herbert Vance, born May 19, 1900; married, April 15, 1922, Ruth Grimm of Detroit, Mich.; now living in Detroit.

CHILDREN:

(aaa) Herbert Vance, Jr., born April, 1923.
(bbb) Donna Lee, born August 31, 1925.

(b) Frank Emmett, born November 27, 1865; married, September 2, 1891, Mary Washington Reese. (See Reese family.)

CHILD:

(aa) Mary Julia, born 1892; married, January 14, 1914, Lewis Waid.

(c) James Pleasant, born November 25, 1866; died December 2, 1907.

(d) Herbert Eustace, born July 18, 1869; married Mary Linda Mead. Now living at Drake's Branch, Va.

CHILDREN:

Doris, Thomas, William, Walter, and Julia.

(e) Robert Edward Lee, born August 18, 1872; died unmarried, February 24, 1917.

(f) Charles Percy, born October 12, 1874; unmarried; still lives at the old Bond homestead near Hendrick's Store.

(g) Thomas Nicholas, born April 18, 1876; died unmarried, November 6, 1901.

(5) Ann Mahaley; married James G. Board, captain in the Civil War. (See Board family.)

(6) Fannie; married James E. Witt.

(7) Susan Elizabeth, born July 7, 1847; died November 18, 1915; married, November 27, 1867, William Lowry Bush (born October 31, 1842; died June 24, 1917), son of William and Sarah (Lowry) Bush.

CHILDREN:

(a) William Pleasant, born December 18, 1869; died March 14, 1909; married (first) Alma Hopkins; (second) Lula Bondurant.

CHILD:

(aa) Howard.

(b) Sarah Elizabeth, born April 18, 1870; married, July 11, 1888, Ellis Brown Bibb (born June 28, 1860), son of Horace Branham and America (Lipscomb) Bibb of Louisa County, Va. He has been a merchant in Bedford, Va., since his marriage.

CHILDREN:

(aa) Helen Elizabeth.

(bb) Merrie Louise; married Charles William Wharton, son of Charles William and Estelle (Steptoe) Wharton of Bedford.

(cc) Eula Pleasant; married Robert Quarles Lowry, vice-president of Citizens National Bank, Bedford, Va.

CHILD:

(aaa) Robert Quarles, Jr.

(dd) Ellis Brown, Jr.; married Inez Carolyn Reese of Greensville County, Va.

CHILD:

(aaa) Ellis Brown, III.

(ee) John Sale; educated at Virginia Polytechnic Institute; now electrical engineer for the Westinghouse Company, Newark, N. J.

(ff) Josephine Rucker, twin of John Sale; A. B. of Randolph-Macon Woman's College, Lynchburg, Va.; now teaching in Bedford High School.

LOWRY

William Lowry, the first of the name in this section of the state, married Elizabeth Pullen in Lunenburg County, Va. Their son, William Lowry, Jr., married Nancy Hoard, daughter of William Hoard, of Caroline and Prince George Counties, and his wife, Mary Thorpe, daughter of Thomas and Sarah (Triplett) Thorpe.

CHILDREN:

(1) Triplett; married Sallie Noell.

(2) Milton; married Mildred Key, daughter of Martin Key. (See Key family.)

CHILDREN:

(a) Almira; married John Lowry, son of Triplett and Sallie (Noell) Lowry. Two sons: Julius and Augustus.

(b) Henry Clay; married Elizabeth Quarles. Children: Francis Scott Key; Landon, who married Ruby Hamner, and has three children: Henry Clay, Cordelia, and Edith; Robert Quarles, who married Eula Bibb, and has one child: Robert Quarles, Jr.; and Annie.

(c) Judith; married Edward Beale. Children: Mary and Mildred.

(d) Robert; married ——— Davis of Texas.

(3) Ellen; married Cornelius Noell.

(4) Mary Isabel; married Alfred A. Bell. (See Bell family.)

(5) Nelson; married Sarah Rucker, daughter of Barnett Rucker.

(6) Albert; died unmarried.

(7) Thomas; died unmarried.

(8) Howard; married Cicely Key. One child: Judith, who married ——— Puckett of Tennessee or Kentucky.

(9) Richard Warren; married Cicely M. Patteson, and had children: Nannie J., Patteson, Virginia Warren, Lucie Bell, Edward Scruggs, Mollie Burwell, Willie Augusta, and Samuel Anderson who married Alice King and had children: Warren Lee who married Nora Templeton, and Charles King.

(10) Nancy; married George Grounds of Roanoke County, Va.

(11) Sarah; married William Bush and died at the birth of her only child, William Lowry Bush.

William Lowry Bush became a captain in the Confederate Army and married Susan Elizabeth Bond, youngest child of Pleasant and Elizabeth (Jeter) Bond. (See Bond family.)

Pleasant Jeter, son of Henry and Elizabeth (Bell) Jeter, married in Bedford County, December 15, 1800, Jane Hatcher, daughter of Jeremiah, Sr., and Edith (Logwood) Hatcher. (See Hatcher family.)

CHILDREN:

(1) Jeremiah Bell, born July 18, 1802.
(2) Andrew.
(3) Margaret (always called Peggy).
(4) Edith.
(5) Betsey.
(6) Sarah.

All of these except the first lived and died in Missouri.

"By the generous assistance of his older brother, Andrew was well educated, entered the medical profession and won distinction as a practitioner and teacher. He died before he reached the meridian of life, and was at the time of his death a professor in the Medical University of Missouri." (Hatcher's *Life of J. B. Jeter.*)

Jeremiah Bell Jeter, familiarly known as "Jerry Bell," became one of the greatest preachers the Baptist Church has ever had in the South. After serving a long pastorate in the Northern Neck of Virginia he accepted a call to the First Baptist Church of Richmond, Va., in 1836, where he remained thirteen years.

From Richmond he went to St. Louis, Mo., in 1849, to become pastor of the First Baptist Church of that city. In 1852 he resigned this church and returned to Richmond to begin a pastorate of Grace Street Church which lasted seventeen years.

From 1865 until his death in 1880 he was editor of the *Religious Herald,* the organ of the Baptist church in Virginia, and published in this paper from time to time his "Reminiscences of a Long Life," which have since been published in book form, and extracts from which are still being published by the press of today, and enjoyed by admirers of this quaint and gifted son of Bedford County.

Dr. Jeter was married four times. First, to Miss Margaret P. Waddy of Northumberland County; second, to Miss Sarah Ann Gaskins of Northern Neck; third, to Miss Charlotte Wharton of Bedford County; and fourth, to Mrs. Mary C. Dabbs of Richmond, Va.

His second wife bore him one son, which died in infancy. This was his only child, but so fond was he of children that after his third marriage he adopted an orphan girl, Bessie Bradley, and gave her his name. She married J. B. Woodard and had one son, whom she named "Jeter."

When he married Mrs. Dabbs, she too had an adopted child—a little boy named Phillip Stratton. Dr. Jeter adopted him also and educated him for a doctor. He and his family also bear the name of Jeter.

Dr. Jeremiah Bell Jeter died in Richmond, Va., in 1880, and is buried in Hollywood Cemetery. The *Life of J. B. Jeter*, written by his cousin, Dr. William E. Hatcher, also a Baptist preacher from Bedford County, is a most interesting story of the characteristics and experiences of this remarkable man.

————o————

SOVEREIGN JETER AND HIS FAMILY

Sovereign Jeter, son of Henry and Elizabeth (Bell) Jeter, married first, Matilda Vaughan of Amelia County in 1806.

CHILDREN :

(1) Lucy Carter, born August 25, 1807. (See forward.)
(2) James Milton, born January 27, 1809; died young.
(3) Fielden Harris, born December 29, 1810. (See forward.)
(4) Julia Ann, born February 17, 1813; married Joel Walker, December 15, 1831; died soon after.
(5) Allen Presley, born July 31, 1815; married Martha A. J. Cooper. No children.
(6) Beverly Ryland, born August 22, 1817; married Mary Cofer. No children.
(7) Thomas Archer, born July 12, 1823. (See forward.)
(8) Samuel Henry, born March 26, 1827; married Elizabeth Williamson. No children.

Matilda (Vaughan) Jeter was born about 1785, and was the daughter of James and Mary (Jeter) Vaughan of Amelia County.

She died in Bedford in 1833.

————

VAUGHAN

James Vaughan was a private in the Amelia County, Va., Militia, during the Revolutionary War. (McAllister's Data, Sec. 252, page 180.)

His will, recorded in Amelia County, Will Book No. 7, pages 15-16, follows:

I, James Vaughan of the County of Amelia being of a sound disposing mind and memory do make and ordain this my last Will and Testament in manner and form following: To-wit:

Imprimis: It is my will and desire that all my just debts be paid and for that purpose my Executor hereinafter named is hereby authorized to sell any part of my personal estate which in his opinion can best be spared for the interest of my estate.

Item: It is my will and desire that my loving wife, Mary Vaughan, do enjoy the profits of my land whereon I now live during her natural life ———. I also lend her for the purpose of cultivating of the said lands the following negroes, to-wit, Davey, Winnie, Sukey, Nancey and Patt during her natural life ———. Also I lend her 3 bedsteads, beds, and furniture during her natural life ———. Also I give to her and her heirs forever all the property in this clause of my Will hereafter mentioned: To-wit: 2 horses, one a bay horse known by the name of Tom, and one sorrel mare called the Celer Filley, and a side saddle, and bridle, 5 hilling hoes, 2 axes, one set of maulling wedges, 2 ploughs, four cows and calves, 1 yoke of oxen, 6 yews, 3 iron pots (her choice) and 1 frying pan, and as many hogs that will be sufficient to supply her with pork the next year and two sows and pigs—and such other of my household and kitchen furniture as my Executor, hereinafter named may think necessary.

Item: It is my will and desire, that as my daughter Obedience Mitchell hath already been provided for by her Grand Father Hill that she come in for no part of my estate.

Item: It is my will and desire that my children, James Vaughan, Wilkes Vaughan, Francis Vaughan, and Nancy Haskins, who have also been provided for by their Grand Father Hill, come in for no part of my Estate.

Item: It is my will and desire that after the payments of my just debts as aforesaid and after my loving wife has what is given her above that then my 4 children, Milton Vaughan, Matilda Vaughan, Billy Vaughan and Thomas Vaughan, do have to them and their heirs forever, the rest and residue of my personal estate to be possessed and enjoyed by them as they severally attain the age of twenty-one years or marry.

Item: It is my will and desire that after the death of my living wife, Mary, the negroes which I have lent her for life, and the bed steads, beds and furniture which also I have lent her for life—to be equally divided between my children, Milton, Matilda, Billy, and Thomas, to them and their heirs forever—to be passed as they attain the age of twenty-one years or marry.

Item: It is my will and desire that after the death of my loving wife, Mary, the tracts of land whereon I now live, which is lent unto my wife during her natural life be sold by my Executor, and that the money arising from such sale be equally divided between my sons, Milton, Billy, and Thomas to be paid them as they attain the age of twenty-one years or marry.

Item: Whereas my children Milton and Matilda have had left, them, about the sum of seventy-five pounds each by their grand father Thomas Jeter, which money I have received—Now my will and desire is that the legacies given by me to my said children, be considered and understood to be as well in discharge of the said sums of money, as in consideration of my natural love and affection for them my children.

Item: It is my will and desire that no appraisment nor inventory be made of Estate.

Item: It is my will and desire that all the rest and residue of my Estate, not hereinbefore particularly mentioned, be equally divided between my sons, Milton, Billy, and Thomas to them and their heirs forever to be possessed when they attain the age of twenty-one years or marry.

Lastly—It is my will and desire that my friend Bennett Brown be whole and sole Executor to this my last Will and Testament, and also Guardian to my sons, Milton, Billy, and Thomas till they attain the age of twenty-one years. Dated this 18th day of October in the year One Thousand Eight Hundred and One.

JAMES VAUGHAN [SEAL].

In presence of:
WILLIAM BURTON
BENNETT BROWN

Amelia County Court, July 28, 1803.

This the last Will and Testament of James Vaughan deceased was exhibited into Court and proven by the oath of William Burton, one of the subscribing witnesses thereto who also proved that he saw Bennett Brown the other subscribing witness thereto subscribe the same by the request of the Testator and in his presence who is since dead and was ordered to be recorded. And at another Court held for the said County the 22nd day of September following. On the motion of Mary Vaughan widow and relict of the said James Vaughan deceased letters of administration is granted her on the said estate with the will annexed who accordingly entered into and acknowledged bond with Joshua Chaffin, John Foster, Booker Foster and William Burton, her securities in the penalty of fifteen thousand dollars.

Test:
JAMES TOWNES, *C. A. C.*
A copy—Teste,
S. L. FARRAR,
Clerk Circuit Court of
Amelia County, Va.

Sovereign Jeter, married (second), November 10, 1834, Nancy Overstreet of Bedford County. She died in 1843.

CHILDREN:

(1) Martha Ann, born August 11, 1835. (See forward.)
(2) Mary Bell, born November 17, 1836; married (first) John Crouch.

CHILDREN:

(a) Robert; married ———— Gill.

(b) John, Jr.; married ———— Motley.

She married (second) Benjamin Goff.

CHILDREN:

(a) James.

(b) Lizzie; married ———— Bell of Michigan.

(c) Saluda; married William Smith of Michigan.

(d) Thomas; married ———— Maxey.

(e) Sales; unmarried.

(3) Frances Parkey, born January 21, 1839; died young.

(4) Saluda Elliott, born July 20, 1840. (See forward.)

(5) George Washington, born September 11, 1842; died young.

Judging from the records of Bedford County, Sovereign Jeter was not a successful business man. He owned considerable land from time to time but mortgaged it heavily, and finally settled upon a plantation, consisting of three tracts of land, given to him and his heirs by Thomas J. Vaughan and Martha P. Vaughan, his wife—deed dated November 11, 1828. On November 12, 1828, he gave a Deed of Trust to Robert Campbell, Trustee, on this land to secure a debt which he owed to Thomas J. Vaughan, and on May 29, 1832, it was sold to satisfy this debt.

Sovereign Jeter's son, Fielden—the oldest to live to be grown—bought back the greater part of this land in 1837, and later sold the portion upon which the residence stood to his brother, Ryland Jeter. Fielden built a small house in the yard of his own home for his father and his young family, and there Sovereign Jeter spent his last days.

He and both of his wives and three small children are buried on his old home place, near the residence. The burying ground is enclosed with a rock wall and periwinkle covers the graves.

Two small children of Fielden H. Jeter, by his first marriage, and Ryland Jeter and his wife are also buried here.

Lucy Carter Jeter, daughter of Sovereign and Matilda (Vaughan) Jeter, married, October 16, 1830, John H. Turner (born May 16, 1807; died November 11, 1861).

CHILDREN:

(1) William H., born June 22, 1831; married (first) Sarah Julena Shoon in 1857; (second) Louisa Luken in 1861.
(2) Frank Jeter, born March 17, 1833; married Nancy Emeline Saunders, July 23, 1856; died July 26, 1921.
(3) Matilda Vaughan, born January 27, 1835; married James Richard Metts in 1852; died June, 1916.
(4) James Monroe, born July 1, 1836; married (first) M. A. Elizabeth Hepinstall, December 6, 1865; (second) Deborah E. Wright, February 9, 1871; (third) Mrs. Virginia A. Tucker, March 11, 1891, in Missouri; died March 24, 1914.
(5) Milton J., born October 7, 1838. (See forward.)
(6) Letitia, born January 25, 1842; married Thomas Hammett Fitzpatrick, February 16, 1865; died August 28, 1905.

Lucy (Jeter) Turner died near Booneville, Cooper County, Mo., while visiting her son James, and was buried there. Her death occurred April 18, 1889.

Milton J. Turner, son of John H. and Lucy (Jeter) Turner, married Sallie Ann Craton Snow, November 15, 1865.

CHILDREN:

(1) George Gideon, born October 19, 1866; married July 5, 1891, Sallie Susan Nichols (born March 8, 1871; daughter of Jesse Cumberland Nichols and Almira Susan Johnson).

CHILDREN:

(a) Milton Jeter, born July 25, 1892; married Ida L. Martin, January 13, 1921.
(b) Rufus Shelton, born August 9, 1894; married, December 4, 1926, Lucille May Burroughs (born October 16, 1899; daughter of Samuel Nicholas and Emma (Hancock) Burroughs).
(c) Bryan Nichols, born January 18, 1897; married, October 28, 1920, Lillie Hancock Burroughs (born August 31, 1898; daughter of Samuel N. and Emma H. Burroughs).

CHILDREN:

(aa) Bettie Burroughs, born September 6, 1922.

(bb) Sarah Hancock, born February 7, 1928.

(d) Reva May, born February 15, 1899.

(e) Sallie Snow, born June 26, 1902; married Emmett L. Weddle, May 28, 1925.

(f) George Gideon, Jr., born September 23, 1904; died July 27, 1908.

(g) Evelyn Irene, born August 30, 1910.

(h) Margaret Louise, born October 16, 1913.

George G. Turner represented his county in the State Legislature four consecutive terms, 1916-1924. In 1920 he entered the ministry of the Baptist Church and served as pastor of a number of churches in his vicinity. He died June 25, 1926.

(2) Celestia May, born September 15, 1868; married Walter A. Fitzpatrick, April 5, 1893; died October 7, 1896.

(3) Vaughanie Kate, born April 26, 1870; married, December 6, 1899, Dr. William O. Smith, son of Oliver C. and Laura (Reese) Smith.

CHILDREN:

(a) Albert Gordon, born September 13, 1900.

(b) Mamie Turner, born February 7, 1902.

(c) William Royal, born March 12, 1904.

(d) Dorothy Snow, born November 3, 1908.

(4) Milton Davis, born August 13, 1872; married Birdie J. Hughes, January 7, 1894.

CHILDREN:

(a) Susie Ethelyn, born November 28, 1898.

(b) Ruby Kate, born April 8, 1903.

(c) James Milton, born April 22, 1908.

Four others died in infancy.

(5) Lizzie Snow, born December 7, 1876; died October 21, 1905.

(6) William Rufus, born January 13, 1879; married Fannie ———; born at Bedford, Mo., September 8, 1879.

CHILDREN:

(a) Carrie Vaughan, born June 13, 1902; married Houston Lively, August 3, 1920.

(b) Rufus Lee, born August 9, 1903.

(c) Alma Virginia, born February 27, 1909.

(d) William Augustus, born March 13, 1915.

(e) Frances Corinne, born April 10, 1916.

William R. Turner spent many years in Missouri, but is now living in Crockett, Texas.

Milton J. Turner was a member of Board's Company, 58th, Virginia Regiment in the Confederate Army. He was wounded in the Second Battle of Manassas, the bullet passing through his left arm into his left breast, within an inch of his heart, through his left lung, and lodged by the side of his spine, where it remained as long as he lived. He lay on the battlefield three days without attention of any kind, and when he was finally carried to a house and given such care as was possible, no one thought he could survive the severe wound and the hardships he had endured, but many years of usefulness were in store for him. He lived until February 11, 1891, and died of pneumonia at his home on the south side of Bedford County.

SNOW

George W. Snow, grandson of George and Frances (Oaks) Parker, married Nancy Catherine Mattox.

CHILDREN:

(1) Sallie Ann Craton, born September 15, 1845; married Milton J. Turner; died April 26, 1919.

(2) Frances; married Britt Strong.

(3) Catherine; married Andrew B. Stone.

(4) Valeria Jennie; married Thomas H. Turner.

(5) George Thomas; married Addie Ware.

(6) Mattie Vilanti; married John Summers.

(7) Emma Parker; married (first) Henry Ware; (second) ———— Morrow.

FIELDEN H. JETER AND HIS FAMILY

Fielden Harris Jeter (why he changed the spelling of his name from Fielding, as the older members of the family had spelled it, we do not know), son of Sovereign and Matilda (Vaughan) Jeter, was, like his brothers, small of stature, but strong in body, and bright in intellect. His good health was remarkable, and when he died, at the age of eighty-four years, his teeth were all in a perfect state of preservation.

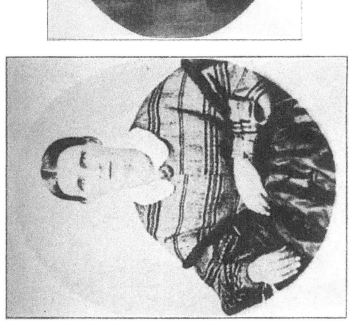

TILGHMAN B. JETER   WALTER P. JETER
EDWIN E. JETER   JAMES S. JETER

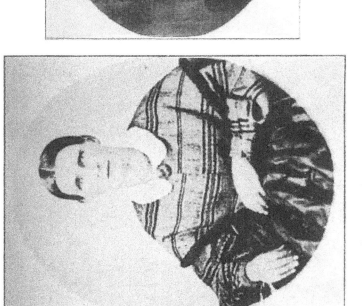

VIRGINIA ANN WHITE
wife of Fielden H. Jeter

He was a great lover of music, and played the violin even down to his last days. His grandchildren considered it a mark of special favor for "Grandpa" to get out his "fiddle," which he kept in the top drawer of his bureau, and play for them.

He was an old-fashioned, country gentleman, courteous and kind, honest and upright in his dealings with his fellowmen, and greatly respected by all who knew him. He held many positions of trust in his county and was a member of the sub-committee of his magisterial district for the distribution of supplies to needy families of volunteer soldiers during the Civil War. He was one of the magistrates of the county for many years and was known as "Squire" Jeter.

He married (first) Virginia Ann White, January 4, 1837. (See White family.)

CHILDREN:

(1) William Jacob, born October 27, 1837. (See forward.)
(2) Tinsley White, born May 4, 1839. (See forward.)
(3) Thomas Alexander, born July 16, 1841. (See forward.)
(4) Matilda Frances, born October 20, 1843; married W. R. Johnson. (See Johnson family.)
(5) Lucy Ella, born July 26, 1846. (See forward.)
(6) Tilghman Buford, born May 3, 1848. (See forward.)
(7) James Sovereign, born September 23, 1850. (See forward.)
(8) Infant; died April 17, 1853.
(9) Walter Presley, born May 26, 1855. (See forward.)
(10) Edwin Everett, born February 10, 1857; died in Kansas; unmarried.
(11) Infant, died January 22, 1861.
(12) Jesse, born April 23, 1862; died October 19, 1862.
(13) Gilbert Carey, born April 20, 1864. (See forward.)

Virginia Ann (White) Jeter, born July 28, 1820, was the daughter of Jacob W. and Matilda (Buford) White. She died April 9, 1877.

Fielden H. Jeter married (second), Mrs. Mary (Wright) Stewart, widow of William R. Stewart, November 20, 1879. They had one son:

(1) Ernest Stewart, born April 17, 1881. He lives in Alden, Kansas. Unmarried.

Fielden H. Jeter died at his home in Bedford County May 2, 1894, and was buried by the side of his first wife in his family burying ground.

His second wife, Mary (Wright) Stewart Jeter, went to Kansas soon after the death of her husband and spent her last days in Alden, near her only daughter, Alice, who had married Walter P. Jeter, the son of her husband by his first marriage. She died in Alden, April 5, 1919.

....

William Jacob Jeter, son of Fielden and Virginia Ann (White) Jeter married Nannie Compton in 1861. One child was born to them which died in infancy. (See Wright family.)

He enlisted in the Confederate Army at the outbreak of the Civil War and was killed in the Battle of Cedar Run, Culpeper County, Va., August 9, 1862.

His widow, Nannie (Compton) Jeter, afterwards married Edward Brugh of Botetourt County and raised a large family of children. They were a model host and hostess, and their home was noted for its lavish old Virginia hospitality.

....

Tinsley White Jeter, son of Fielden and Virginia Ann (White) Jeter, married his first cousin, Matilda Jane White, May 28, 1873, in Missouri.

CHILDREN:

(1) Sarah Ann, born April 17, 1874; died March 14, 1919.
(2) Edna Earl, born November 7, 1875; married G. B. Dodson, January 14, 1897, in Belton, Mo.

CHILDREN:

    (a) Helen Irene, born November 30, 1897; died February 18, 1899.
    (b) Marie M., born April 10, 1900; married Chester R. Meador, June 18, 1921. One child:
        (aa) Chester LeRoy, born May 4, 1922.
    (c) Faustina Opal, born December 12, 1901.
    (d) A. LeRoy, born December 15, 1915.

(3) Tinsley White (daughter), born September 21, 1877; married Herman R. Hipsher, December 17, 1901, in Belton, Mo.

CHILDREN:

    (a) Milton R., born September 28, 1903.
    (b) Freddie M., born December 24, 1906.

Tinsley W. Jeter was a member of "The Old Dominion Rifles," which later became Company "C," Twenty-eighth Virginia Infantry of the Confederate Army. This company fought throughout the war, surrendering with Lee at Appomattox. Tinsley Jeter was in every battle in which his company was engaged, but never wounded.

He died at his home August 15, 1877, from the effects of inhaling foul gas while being lowered into his well, to inspect it after having it cleaned out. He was buried in Cass County, Mo., where he had spent all of his married life.

Matilda (White) Jeter, born August 16, 1845, was the daughter of William A. B. and Sarah (Leftwich) White. She died of influenza during the epidemic of 1918-1919, on March 15, 1919—the day after her daughter, Sallie, had succumbed to the same malady, in the same house.

....

Thomas Alexander Jeter, son of Fielden H. and Virginia Ann (White) Jeter, was educated at Mt. Pleasant Academy in Bedford County and taught for many years in the public schools. He had a keen sense of humor, even though his manner was often gruff in the school room, and used to enjoy telling of a little incident that occurred while he was teaching at Chamblissburg. John H. Preas, who was afterwards proprietor of the Palace Hotel in Bedford and a good business man, was not a brilliant pupil, and one day in his spelling class he was given the word "gun" to spell. He spelled it "g-u-n-n." "Now why did you put a double n to it, Sir?" asked the teacher. John replied, as quick as a flash, "I thought maybe it was a double barrel gun."

He left Mt. Pleasant Academy to enlist in the Confederate Army but was refused on account of a stiff right arm, which was caused by having the flesh torn from it while threshing wheat. He was accepted for service in the Commissary Department.

He married Laurie Cornelia Mays, October 16, 1872, at Beaverdam Baptist Church, Chamblissburg, Bedford County, Virginia. (See Mays family.)

CHILDREN:

(1) Lula Eastman, born August 3, 1873.
(2) Laura Erminia Morna, born November 13, 1875.

Laurie Cornelia Mays, born February 2, 1851, was the daughter of Joseph W. and Malinda (Wright) Mays. She died February 22, 1876, leaving her babies to the care of her husband and her parents, with whom she had always lived.

After her death Mr. Jeter was elected Commissioner of Revenue in Chamblissburg District, which office he held for several years. Later he went to Liberty and engaged in the tobacco business with Major D. M. Newsom, conducting a large warehouse for the sale of leaf tobacco until the time of his death.

Thomas A. Jeter (called "Pomp" Jeter from childhood by his family and intimate friends), was one of the most popular men that Bedford County has ever produced. He had a big heart and pleasing personality and his business brought him into daily contact with all classes of people—both black and white—and also placed him in position to befriend many who needed assistance, by advancing money on their crops of tobacco. These kindnesses were never forgotten, and for decades after, were recounted to his children whenever occasion permitted.

He was assassinated May 16, 1885, at his place of business by Hairston H. Terry, son of General William R. Terry, who, in a temporary fit of insanity and without the slightest provocation, shot him through the heart—death resulting instantly. Terry, for years, had been one of his most intimate friends, had never shown any ill feeling toward him, and often came in town and visited him at the warehouse in a most pleasant manner. The following account was sent by the Liberty correspondent to a New York newspaper:

"SLAIN FOR A DOG'S NAME

"T. A. JETER SHOT FOR CALLING HIS PUP AFTER H. H. TERRY'S SISTER

"And Mr. Terry Promptly Lynched by Mr. Jeter's Relatives and Friends—Repenting When Too Late—Was the Murderer Insane?

"LIBERTY, Va., May 16.—Thomas A. Jeter, an inoffensive and very popular man of this place, was, without any sufficient provocation, shot by H. H. Terry about 11 o'clock this morning. There had been no quarrel, no misunderstanding of any kind between them, as far as known. Some time ago Terry gave Jeter a dog, and Jeter named it after Terry's sister. Terry lived in Richmond, his father, Gen. W. R. Terry is Superintendent of the Virginia Penitentiary. Terry was on a visit to his sister, Mrs. E. T. Walker, in this county and a short distance from this town. Terry was in bad health. He came to town this morning and attended to some business, among other things writing a letter to his people in Richmond. He went from the Windsor Hotel, where he wrote the letter, to Jeter's tobacco warehouse, and was standing in the warehouse yard in front of the door.

"Jeter came to the door and asked in a perfectly friendly manner how his father was. Terry's father, Gen. Terry, had been stricken with paralysis and was one of Jeter's warm friends. Terry said he was dying. Mr. W. S. Jones, who went with Terry to the warehouse, said: 'No, he is better.' Terry said: 'No, he is dying.' Jeter then playfully said: 'Why don't you come up to see your kinfolks?' meaning, it is inferred, why he did not come up to see the dog which he had given him. Terry immediately drew his pistol and fired before Jones, who was standing near Terry, could interfere. The first shot took effect just below the point of the breastbone and ranged upward. Jeter screamed and turned to go to the office in his warehouse, and the second shot was fired and took effect just above the left lung. Jeter did not speak after he was shot and only lived a few moments. Terry was arrested, but threatened to shoot Jones if he did not get out of his way.

"Mr. Knight, who was standing near, says Terry said immediately after he did the shooting:

" 'I have been up here a month to do that and I have done it.' To another person he said: 'He (meaning Jeter) knows why I shot him,' and to another, that it was because he named the dog after his sister. Terry expressed great sorrow at his deed and wished it had been he that was killed instead of Jeter. The murdered man was about forty years old, a widower, and leaves two children. Terry is about twenty-two or twenty-three and was educated at the Virginia Military Institute.

"LIBERTY, Va., May 18.—The terrible tragedy of Saturday—the killing of Thomas A. Jeter, in cold blood, by Hairston Terry—was followed this morning by the lynching of Terry.

"About 2:30 o'clock this morning a band of mounted men rode up to the Bedford Jail in Liberty, and one of the number knocked at the front door. The jailer asked who was there, and the party said they had a prisoner to put in. The door was opened, and the leader, a large man, masked, presented a pistol to the head of the keeper, Kirkwood

Bell, demanding the keys. He told them he did not have them, but when asked if they were in his room answered yes. They procured the keys and then demanded that he should show them the cell where Terry was confined, but Bell refused. They found out by searching the jail, and without any fuss or alarm of any kind brought Terry out without coat or hat, put him on one of the horses, filed out from the jail and down Main Street. Just outside the corporate limits and south of the town they hanged him to an apple tree on an embankment by the side of the main road, and his body was found swinging there this morning. The jailer and his assistant guard gave the alarm as soon as possible, but it was too late. The mob were not fifteen minutes in entering the jail and taking the unfortunate man away. Not a word was spoken by any of the party except those who went into the jail. Terry, it is believed, was gagged, as he was not heard to speak at all. It is supposed that the party came from the country and probably from that part where Jeter was born and brought up.

"There was an immense crowd at Jeter's funeral yesterday. It took place at his old home eighteen miles south of here. About two hundred persons from this place attended. Jeter was a prominent Mason, Knight of Honor, and President of the Liberty Tobacco Association, all of which organizations attended the funeral services.

"It is believed that the cause of the lynching was the recital of the circumstances attending the cold-blooded deed, which caused great indignation on account of the esteem in which everyone held him and his kindness to the tobacco planters, to all of whom he advanced money on their crops. It seemed to be the firm belief, too, that the plea of insanity would be set up and that Terry would escape. It is said that it was at the funeral that the idea of organizing and taking the law in their own hands was formed by the band. Terry evidently expected something of the kind, as he sent to know, Saturday evening, if there was any danger. Terry said to a friend, Saturday evening after the shooting, that he expected he would be sent up for twenty years or they would swing him, and that he believed he preferred the latter. When asked by his sister if he had anything against Jeter he said no, that he loved him. When asked why he shot him he said he could not help it.

"The body of Terry was cut down by the Coroner this morning after sunrise in the presence of the jury. The rope used to hang Terry

GILBERT CAREY JETER

THOMAS ALEXANDER JETER

was the one which belonged to the Jeter warehouse well, part of which had been unravelled and with which his hands and feet were tied. It is supposed there were some ninety or a hundred men in all, but only forty or fifty were in the party that went to the jail to take him out. They were all well armed and prepared to accomplish their designs. The whole community is saddened by these calamities. None of the lynching party were recognized. All were masked by tying a handkerchief over the face. As they came from the neighborhood of Jeter's old home, it is thought pretty certain that some of his many relatives were in the crowd. It is said the men declared that too many murderers had escaped of late on the plea of insanity.

"The name of the dog over which so much blood has been spilled is Lettie."

Lula Eastman Jeter, daughter of Thomas A. and Laurie (Mays) Jeter married George Pleasant Parker, November 11, 1903, in Bedford, Va. (See Parker family.)

She was educated at Belmont Seminary, Bedford, Va., and at Hollins Institute, Hollins, Va.

During the World War she served as County Chairman of the Woman's Liberty Loan Committee; as Director of Home Economics for the county; and as Chairman of the Supply Committee of the Red Cross Chapter of Bedford County.

She was President of the Bedford County Federation of Clubs in 1917 and 1918, and Chairman of the Woman's Department of the Bedford County Fair Association from its organization in 1911 until 1921.

In 1919 she was appointed County Chairman of the War History Commission of Virginia by Governor Westmoreland Davis and collected much valuable data concerning Bedford's part in the World War.

In 1922 she was appointed Chairman of the Bedford Historical Pageant Committee which did much research work among the old records of the county and published historical articles of great value in the local papers. This pageant was written by Dr. James Elliott Walmsley, who was at that time, Professor of History in Winthrop College, S. C., and was produced on the beautiful grounds of the Elks National Home, May 18, 1922, those taking part being descendants, as far as possible, of the characters in the pageant.

When the State Highway was being constructed through Bedford County from Lynchburg to Roanoke in 1927-1928, her knowledge of the history of the county was sought by the Bedford Chamber of Commerce and she wrote sketches of historic places along its route for the State Guide Book; and in 1929 her services were secured by the Conservation and Development Commission of Virginia to furnish data for historical markers in the county.

She is a member of the Daughters of the American Revolution and of The Huguenot Society of the Founders of Manakin in the Colony of Virginia.

Laura Erminia Morna Jeter, daughter of Thomas A. and Laurie (Mays) Jeter, married, November 7, 1900, Jesse Thornhill Davidson in Bedford, Va.

CHILDREN:

(1) Joseph Mays, born December 12, 1904; graduated from Virginia Military Institute in 1925; taught two years at Randolph-Macon Academy, Bedford, Va.; married, October 6, 1928, Mildred Mitchell Thomas, born December 18, 1903, daughter of Cabell Whitfield Thomas (born May 13, 1873; died November 20, 1906; son of Joshua W. and Mildred Otey (Hopkins) Thomas) and Mildred Ormond Humphreys (daughter of James and Mildred Otey (Mitchell) Humphreys). He is now Business Manager of the Piedmont Label Company.

(2) Jesse Thornhill, Jr., born September 18, 1907; graduated from Randolph-Macon Academy in 1926; now a senior at V. M. I.

(3) Dorothy, born May 24, 1914; now a junior in the Bedford High School.

Laura E. M. Jeter was educated at Belmont Seminary and Jeter Institute, Bedford, Va. During the World War she rendered distinguished service as Chairman of the Knitting Committee of the Red Cross Chapter of Bedford County. She was President of the Bedford Library Association from 1917 to 1919, and was elected to that position again in 1928 and re-elected in 1929.

Jesse Thornhill Davidson, born in Appomattox County, Va., June 10, 1867, is the son of Jesse Thornhill Davidson (born 1814; son of Samuel Davidson (born 1777) and Elizabeth Thornhill (born 1789)) and his second wife, Mrs. Elizabeth (Robertson) Martin.

He came to Bedford, August 1, 1891, to be agent for the Norfolk and Western Railway and held that position until November 15, 1925, when he resigned to become President of the Bedford Can Company, one of the largest business enterprises in Bedford.

In 1928 this company sold out to the Continental Can Company and he was made District Manager of that organization, with headquarters at Bedford. He is also President of the Town Council and Chairman of its Finance Committee, Vice-President of the Piedmont Label Company of Bedford, a Director of the People's Bank of Bedford, Chairman of the Board of Stewards of the Methodist Episcopal Church, South, a member of the Rotary Club, and an enthusiastic Shriner, member of Kazim Temple, Roanoke, Va.

MAYS, MAYES, OR MAYSE

In "Extracts from a letter from John Rolfe to King James, while he was in England with Pocahontas (1617), concerning plantations and settlements in the Colony," in Vol. 2, of Meades "Old Churches and Families," William Mays is mentioned as minister in a settlement of twenty farmers at "Kecoughtan" (being not far from the mouth of the river, thirty-seven miles below James Towne on the same side).

....

Patents issued during the Regal Government in Charles City County. From Book No. 6:

John Maise, sonne of William Maise, tract, August 7, 1667. 293 acres 2R. 33po. On the south side of Appomattox River, 125 acres, part thereof being part of a patent of 250 acres granted to Ed Townstall and by him sold to Wm. Maise, father of the said John Maise, adjoining the said Maise land next the river. (*William and Mary Quarterly*, Vol. 13, p. 117.)

John Maise. October 27, 1673. 89 a. 23 ps. On the south side of Appomattox River, beg'g &c. at Easterly end of ye long slash, neigh Samuel Woodwards head line. (Same as above, p. 119.)

....

In the records of Prince George County, the names of William, Matthew, and John Mayes appear in separate places in 1715; Mary, the wife of Samuel Mayes, in 1717; and Henry Mayes in 1719.

In Chamberlayne's Bristol Parish Register (which Parish covered Prince George County until 1740) it is recorded that John Mayes was made Clerk of the Vestry, February 20, 1725, at 400 pounds of tobacco per year, which office he held until 1734.

October 23, 1739, Joseph Mayes mentioned in bills paid by the Vestry.

In returns of Processional for the year 1739, Joseph Mayes is mentioned as not appearing.

Among the births of the Parish Register are those of Drury, son Matthew and Elizabeth Mayes, born 1727; Henry, slave of Wm. and Mary Mayes, born 1729; Johanna, daughter of Wm. and Elizabeth Mayes, born 1732.

Henry Mayes received a patent in Henrico County, April 24, 1703; Joseph Mayes received 400 acres in Brunswick County, August 20, 1741, and 200 acres in Lunenburg County in 1755, on the south side of Staunton River, adjoining Mattox Mayes.

In Lunenburg County is recorded the will of William Mayes, under date of November 8, 1748, which mentions his wife, Mary; sons, Joseph, Mafia (Matthew), and William; daughter, Jeanie White; and grandson, William Childrey.

At a Court held in Bedford County, July 22, 1754, Joseph Mays appeared as security for Joseph Ray, Sheriff. He lived in Pittsylvania County.

The first of the name in Bedford County were John and James, who bought land on Cate's Creek in 1776 and 1777, respectively. At that time there were branches of the family in Augusta, Amherst, and Pittsylvania counties, and in each of these branches occur the names John, James, Joseph and William, and so far it has not been possible to link the Bedford Mayses up with their immediate ancestors, though it is certain that they are all descended from the same stock. Inaccuracy of spelling is another great stumbling block in the way of tracing the early families. So few of them had any educational advantages, and were entirely at the mercy of the clerks as to how their names should be spelled. In Pittsylvania, for instance, we find the marriage bond of John May and Susannah Porter. In the will of John Mayse of Bedford he mentions his wife, Susannah. It is most probable that they were one and the same, and if so, that would indicate that the Bedford Mayses came from Pittsylvania County; but, on the other hand, they settled near Thomas Wright, who had come from Augusta County in 1748, and from the number of intermarriages between these families and the fact that some of the later Mayeses were married in Augusta, while visiting relatives there, lead us to the conclusion that they might have come to Bedford by way of Augusta.

The will of John Mayse, made May 30, 1817, and probated in Bedford County, November 26, 1821 (Will Book "E," page 314) mentions wife, Susannah; children: Elijah, Richard, Elizabeth Jordan, Sarah Board, Nancy Babit, John, Susannah Gibbs, Rhoda Jordan, and Jesse. Elizabeth married Vincent Jordan, Rhoda married LeRoy Jordan, and Susannah married William Gibbs.

The will of James Mayse, made December 15, 1792, and probated in Bedford County, June 22, 1795, mentions wife, Mary; daughters: Sinthey Wright, Elizabeth Wright, Ann, Milly, and Mary; sons: Sam'l, James and Joseph. He gives land on which he lives to son, Samuel. Witnesses, John Mays, Elijah Mays, Richard Mays.

Samuel Mayse, son of James and Mary Mayse, married Agnes Wright, October 22, 1792; went to Davidson County, Tenn., before 1820.

James Mayse, son of James and Mary Mayse, married, January 3, 1802, Patsey Wright, daughter of Joseph and Elizabeth (Kemp) Wright, in Bedford County. (See Wright family.)

CHILDREN:

(1) Samuel C.; went West and was lost sight of.

(2) Polly; married William Worley; had one son, killed in Civil War.

(3) Charlotte; married ———— Dowdy.

(4) Martha (Patsey); married ———— Carter; lived and died in Santa Fe, N. M.; had son, Judge Joseph N. Carter, of Quincy, Ill.

(5) Joseph Wright, born January 6, 1811. (See forward.)

(6) Agnes; married Jubal A. Anderson; lived and died in Floyd County, Va.

(7) Judith; died unmarried.

(8) Parmelia.

(9) William S.; went to Kentucky.

(10) James David Kyle; married Sarah Lloyd; died in Richmond, July 1, 1862, while in Civil War.

James Mayse died September 18, 1847. His will mentions his wife, Patsey; children: Joseph W., Samuel C., Charlotte Dowdy, Martha Carter, William S., Agnes Anderson, James D. K., Judith, Polly, and Parmelia. He gives land on which he now lives to his wife, and mentions lots in the town of Liberty to be disposed of.

(The present Baptist Church in Bedford is built upon one of these lots, purchased from his estate for this purpose.)

Patsey (Wright) Mayse died June 28, 1850.

"King, William Montgomery. January 7, 1833—born about 1755; enlisted in Bedford County, Va., 1778. . . .

"About 15 days later went as substitute for James Mayes, serving under Capt. Nathaniel Tate, Lieutenant Stephen Goggin and Ensign Richard Edmundson, and marched to join General Gates at Charlotte, N. C." (*McAllister's Militia*, Section 153, pp. 134-135.)

....

Joseph Wright Mays, son of James and Patsy (Wright) Mays, was educated in the "Old Field" schools of Bedford County and taught for several years. He traveled over ten states on horseback and taught one term on top of the Ozark Mountains in Missouri, but finding "no place like home," he returned to his native county and married, February 11, 1841, his first cousin, Malinda Wright, daughter of Anthony and Betsy (Mayse) Wright.

They had only one child—the idol of their hearts—Laurie Cornelia, born February 2, 1851, ten years after their marriage. They settled on a plantation, near what is now Chamblissburg, part of which was given to him by his father.

Joseph W. Mays was a man of influence and great usefulness in his community, and a deacon of the Beaver Dam Baptist Church for many years. He was noted for his high ideals, his hospitality and his kindness of heart, and his sense of humor made him always a delightful companion.

His wife died August 10, 1879, and his sister, Polly—Mrs. Wm. Worley—whose husband and only child were dead, assumed control of his household, and continued to live with him until her death, October 14, 1893.

Laurie Cornelia Mays, daughter of Joseph W. and Malinda (Wright) Mays, married, October 16, 1872, Thomas A. Jeter, son of Fielden H. and Virginia Ann (White) Jeter. (See Jeter family.)

CHILDREN:

(1) Lula Eastman, born August 3, 1873.

(2) Laura Erminia Morna, born November 13, 1875.

She was educated at Piedmont Institute in Liberty, Va., and taught one or two terms in the schools of the county. She was a person of unusual amiability, gentleness of manner, and purity of heart, making friends of all with whom she came in contact; a shining light in her church (Baptist) and a leader in the social life of her community. She was never strong, physically, and soon after the birth of her second child she contracted a cold, from the effects of which she died, February 22, 1876. She was buried near her father's home, from which she had never been separated, on a little hill just east of the residence, where now sleep also her parents and her husband.

The following is an extract from a letter written to her daughter, Lula, author of this sketch, February 12, 1929, by Mrs. O. B. Barker of Lynchburg, Va., who was a neighbor and cousin of Laurie (Mays) Jeter.

"My mind often reverts to your grandparents and 'Aunt Polly'; your mother's girlhood and young ladyhood when she attended the Piedmont School in Liberty; her having the only piano in the neighborhood; the belle of that community—once when a gentleman from Big Lick (now Roanoke), or it may have been Gish's Mill (now Vinton), escorted her to church and sat with her—a thing almost unknown in country churches at that time; my beloved Sunday School teacher; then her marriage in a blue silk dress in the church—the first in that church; how my brother John and I rode horseback to witness the ceremony—well do I remember how they looked as they drove off in your father's single buggy; your father the scholar of that section; the imprints of your mother's baby foot in bricks in the chimney near the side entrance to your grand father's home; the coming of you two baby girls; your mother's death soon after Laura's advent—Countless memories arise!"

After the death of Laurie (Mays) Jeter her two little girls lived with their grandfather (Mays) at his home until 1884, when their father built a residence for them in Liberty and took them to live with him—so that they might have better school advantages—their grandfather and "Aunt Polly" going also. They had enjoyed only one short year of comradeship with him when his life was snuffed out by an assassin's bullet, May 16, 1885. They were again thrown upon the care of their grandfather, who, with the help of "Aunt Polly" and "Miss Mary" (Thomas), the faithful housekeeper, lavished upon them his fondest affection, and guided their footsteps until they were grown and educated. Laura, the younger, was his pet and constant companion, going with him wherever he went, even to riding on his rake on a hot summer's day as he raked the hay, with her little parasol sheltering her from the sun—nothing daunted when he drove into a rut and she fell off, but got up and resumed her seat, with her parasol still in position.

He died March 5, 1900, from the infirmities of old age, retaining to the very last all of his faculties and his sunny disposition.

JOHN A. COOPER AND WIFE, LUCY ELLA JETER

JOSEPH W. MAYS, WIFE AND DAUGHTER,
LAURIE—WIFE OF THOMAS ALEXANDER JETER

Lucy Ella Jeter, daughter of Fielden H. and Virginia Ann (White) Jeter, married John A. Cooper, October 7, 1869.

CHILDREN:

(1) Virginia Frances, born August 7, 1870; married Thomas Board Kemper, September 6, 1893.

CHILDREN:

(a) Corinne, born January 19, 1895; educated at Farmville State Normal School, taught several terms in schools of Roanoke; married William Theodore Dent, Jr., October 14, 1916. "Ted," as he is familiarly called, was born in Tennessee, February 20, 1892, and is a son of William Theodore and Elizabeth Emma (Rogers) Dent of Tennessee. He came to Virginia when a young man and accepted a position with the Norfolk and Western Railway in Roanoke. Here he met and married his wife. They have three children:

(aa) Lucile Milnes, born January 6, 1918.
(bb) Dorothy Kemper, born December 1, 1919.
(cc) John Robert, born May 18, 1926.

(b) Verna, born June 25, 1899; died February 19, 1905.

Thomas Board Kemper, born October 8, 1868, is the son of George Edward Kemper and Martha America Wright of Bedford County. He and his family live in Roanoke, Va.

(2) Mary Ella, born October 19, 1872; unmarried; lives in Roanoke.

(3) Martha Elizabeth, born May 21, 1874; married Ashby Scott, November 27, 1901.

CHILD:

(a) Wallace Cooper, born April 24, 1906; now a student at Georgia Polytechnic Institute.

Ashby Scott, born May 25, 1875, is the son of John Pleasant and Sarah Georgia (Garrett) Scott. He and his family lived at Thaxton, Va., until 1916, when they too moved to Roanoke, and settled in Wasena.

(4) Anna White, born November 11, 1875; teaches in the city schools of Roanoke. Va.

(5) Lura Edna, born March 8, 1878; married, December 24, 1913, James Thomas Wood, born September 15, 1881; son of Samuel Harvey and Virginia Deven (Cowherd) Wood. One child:

    (a) Claibourne, born October 12, 1914.

(6) William Tinsley, born October 26, 1879; married in Washington, D. C., February 21, 1906, Mary Wilhelmina Byrnes, born October 13, 1886; daughter of James Joseph and Augusta Theresa (Fritch) Byrnes. They live in Washington, D. C.

CHILDREN:

    (a) Genevieve Evelyn, born December 9, 1906.

    (b) John Maurice, born December, 1908.

(7) John James, born November 13, 1882; married August 14, 1912, Ella Wood Teass, born October 15, 1888, daughter of John Thomas and Annie (Boswell) Teass. J. J. Cooper is connected with the Post Office in Bedford, Va.

CHILD:

    (a) James Edward, born November 10, 1913.

(8) George Gilbert, born May 19, 1884; married, June 4, 1917, Judith Irene Preas, daughter of Thomas Pleasant and Ann Henry (Stiff) Preas. They live in Washington, D. C.

CHILDREN:

    (a) Annie Loraine, born June 4, 1918.

    (b) Gladys Eloise, born November 11, 1922.

(9) Thomas Henry, born April 23, 1886; married, December 17, 1912, Rosa Lurline Old, born October 30, 1892, daughter of William Peterson and Lenora Teressa (Richardson) Old; lives at the old Cooper home near Thaxton, Bedford County, where he is successfully engaged in farming.

CHILDREN:

    (a) John William, born September 29, 1913.

    (b) Gilbert Glenwood, born July 2, 1915.

    (c) Frances Irene, born May 8, 1919.

    (d) Carlton Duvall, born August 20, 1921.

    (e) Doris Ella, born September 24, 1924.

John Adam Cooper, born April 7, 1833, was the son of Adam Cooper (born July 27, 1792; died January 29, 1850) and Fannie Hudnall St. Clair (born July 9, 1796; died January 27, 1892), who were married April 5, 1821.

He was raised on a farm on Goose Creek near Thaxton, Va. He enlisted in the Confederate Army at the beginning of the Civil War and served throughout the time.

His Discharge reads:

"TO WHOM IT MAY CONCERN

"KNOW YE, that John A. Cooper, a private of Captain N. C. Luck's Company, thirty-fourth Regiment of Virginia Infantry who was enlisted the twenty-ninth day of June to serve one year (Re-enlisted 14th, May 1862, for the war) is hereby HONORABLY discharged from the Army of the Confederate States.

"Said John A. Cooper was born in Bedford County in the state of Virginia, is Thirty-one years of age, Five feet ten inches high, dark complexion, Gray eyes, Dark hair, and by occupation, when enlisted, a Planter.

"Given at Askeo (?), South Ga., this Seventeenth day of April, 1864.

N. C. LUCK,
Capt. Commanding Company.

"Approved
RANDOLPH HARRISON,
Lt. Col. Com'd'g Reg't.

John A. Cooper was a man of stern integrity and strong religious convictions, and lived a long and useful life in the community in which he was born. He died August 15, 1912, respected by all who knew him, and is buried in Fairview Cemetery, Roanoke, Va.

Lucy Ella (Jeter) Cooper was injured in an automobile accident February 22, 1925, from the effects of which she died the next day. She is buried beside her husband in Fairview Cemetery.

James Sovereign Jeter, son of Fielden H. and Virginia Ann (White) Jeter, married in Franklin County, Va., January 25, 1888, J. Annie Zeigler (born October 25, 1868; daughter of Charles M. Zeigler (born December 24, 1839) and Charlotte C. Morgan (born December 23, 1844) who were married October 2, 1862).

CHILDREN:

(1) Carrie Virginia, born February 17, 1889; married (first), November 6, 1907, George R. Shumate (born November 17, 1872; died September 12, 1908; son of Nusom J. Shumate and Martha Turner, who were married December 29, 1868).

CHILD:

(a) Georgea Clark, born October 24, 1908.

After the death of her husband, Carrie (Jeter) Shumate married, August 28, 1912, Henry G. Doss (born January 22, 1878; son of George Z. Doss (born November 9, 1848) and Elizabeth A. Boothe (born October 14, 1856) who were married February 3, 1875).

CHILDREN:

(a) Jeter, born August 19, 1914.
(b) Anna Elizabeth, born September 24, 1922.

Henry G. Doss and family live at Penhook, Franklin County, Va.

(2) Chesley Gilbert, born August 16, 1893. Enlisted for service in the World War at Tazewell, Va., September 21, 1917.

The following is taken from his Discharge papers: "Chesley Gilbert Jeter. Grade, 1st; Class, Private. Trained at CAMP LEE, Va., in infantry. Company "D," 318 Infantry of 80th Division. Left Camp Lee for France, May 20, 1918, via Hoboken, N. J., on the ship 'Leviathan'; arrived at Port Brest, May 30, 1918. Was in battles: 'Artois Sector,' 'St. Mihiel Offensive,' 'Meuse-Argonne Sector.'

"While in France, he was an observer and a scout under the command of Major Charles Sweeney.

"Left France for home, May 17, 1919; arrived at Newport News, May 27, 1919; was Honorably Discharged from duty, June 3, 1919."

James S. Jeter spent the greater part of his life merchandising in the counties of Bedford, Pittsylvania and Franklin. For a few years he was connected with some of the coal operations in West Virginia, but his health became poor and he returned to Franklin County. In 1907, his brother, Walter, who was visiting in Virginia, persuaded him to return with him to his home in Kansas, thinking the change of climate might prove beneficial to him; but it did him no good whatever—on the contrary, he steadily declined, and died in Kansas, January 22, 1908. His body was brought back to his home in Virginia, and interred in the Zeigler burying ground in Franklin County.

THE KANSAS JETERS

Tilghman Buford Jeter, son of Fielden H. and Virginia Ann (White) Jeter, married Mary William Wren, January 16, 1878.

For several years he engaged in the milling business at Coonsville, Va., near his father's home where he lived, but not finding this profitable, in 1888, he took his family and joined his brother, Walter Jeter, in Alden, Kansas. It was a brave wife who was willing to take their six little children and go with her husband into an unknown land and make a home for them, but not once did she flinch from it, nor has she ever failed to be a faithful wife and mother. Much of their success in life is due to her executive ability and good judgment.

Three more children were born to them in Kansas and all but one have settled near their parents.

Mary William (Wren) Jeter was born January 29, 1850, and is the daughter of Charles Carter Wrenn (born June 27, 1817; died February 26, 1911) and Virginia Foster Garrett (born February 3, 1823; died September 22, 1876), who were married, October 3, 1852.

CHILDREN OF TILGHMAN B. AND MARY W. (WREN) JETER:

(1) Ann Virginia, born November 24, 1878; died July 13, 1909.

(2) Thomas Herbert, born April 28, 1880; married August 18, 1909, in Alden, Kansas, Dessie Estabrook (born September 14, 1888; daughter of Edwin Estabrook (born January 11, 1866) and Rebecca Ann Mullikin (born December 1, 1871; died October 17, 1910), who were married February 17, 1886).

CHILDREN:

(a) Virginia, born August 17, 1910.

(b) Geraldine, born October 3, 1912.

(3) Julia Myrtle, born November 6, 1881; married, June 20, 1905, Joseph D. Zimmerman (born January 9, 1878; son of Isaac Zimmerman (born January 17, 1838; died at Phoenix, Arizona,

December 30, 1903) and Mary Stuckey (born at Sterling, Kansas, August 30, 1847; died April 19, 1901), who were married at Fayette, Ind., February 6, 1868).

CHILDREN:

(a) Julius Buford, born April 13, 1907.

(b) Helen Mary, born April 4, 1913.

Joseph D. Zimmerman and family live at Sterling, Kansas, where he is a popular banker.

(4) Matilda Buford, born October 23, 1883; married, March 26, 1905, Garfield Read (born November 11, 1880; son of Robert Read (born September 11, 1843; died July 11, 1915) and Sarah Elizabeth Chaffin (born July 31, 1848; died June 9, 1890), who were married in Harrison County, Ind., May 20, 1886).

CHILD:

(a) Josephine, born February 23, 1909.

Garfield ("Jean") Read and family live near Alden, Kan.

(5) Mary Ethel, born February 15, 1885; married April 3, 1920, James Elmer Brown, born March 27, 1892; son of James Brown (born August 28, 1860; died October 14, 1893) and Hattie Mardis (born May 6, 1860), who were married in September, 1881.

CHILD:

(a) Harriett Jeter, born December 2, 1922.

James E. Brown and family live at Pratt, Kansas.

(6) Ella Hervey, born August 23, 1887; married December 15, 1909, George Murray Ross (born December 19, 1887; son of George B. Ross (born August 12, 1864) and Lydia Stout (born October 13, 1865), who were married February 2, 1886).

CHILDREN:

(a) Murray Fleming, born November 6, 1910.

(b) Genevieve Evelyn, born June 11, 1912.

George Murray Ross and his family live at Ottawa, Kan., where he is manager of a large mill.

(7) Charles Harris, born April 16, 1888; married, July 20, 1911, Bessie Ross (born October 18, 1887; daughter of John Ross

Hugh Gilbert Jeter, M. D.

William Stewart Jeter

(born August 29, 1848) and Sarah Ellen Fair (born May 4, 1851; died July 29, 1915) who were married June 5, 1870).

CHILDREN:

(a) Norman Wren, born June 26, 1912.

(b) Cleta Maxine, born June 1, 1915.

Charles H. Jeter and his family live near Alden, Kan., where he owns and cultivates a large farm.

(8) Lena Evelyn, born April 25, 1890; lives at home with her parents.

(9) Hugh Gilbert, born May 8, 1895; married, June 30, 1920, Josephine Ruth Houoni, daughter of Joseph Jefferson Houoni (born November 27, 1872) and Nora Lee Yeckey (born August 21, 1876), who were married January 1, 1896.

CHILD:

(a) Patti Jo, born August 15, 1928.

Hugh Gilbert Jeter, after receiving his diploma from the Alden High School, spent four years at the University of Kansas, taking the degree of A. B. in 1919. He attended the University of Scotland for one term, while overseas with the American Expeditionary Forces, taking courses in Tropical Medicine and Pathology. From 1919 to 1921 he was Bacteriologist for the State Board of Health of Montana.

In 1921 he entered the University of Louisville (Ky.) Medical Department, as a student-instructor, acting as Seralogist for the University, and at the same time working up to an M. D. degree, which he received in 1925. He is now (1929) a practicing physician in Oklahoma City.

He says of his war experiences:

"In the spring of 1918 I began the study of medicine at the University of Kansas and was automatically made a member of the enlisted Medical Reserve Corps; but in a few months I discontinued my studies to enlist in a more active branch of the service.

"In May, 1918, I made arrangements with officers of the Medical Corps at Fort Riley to take an examination for a commission in Sanitary Engineering. While preparing for this examination, I received a notification from my County Board that I was in the next conscription quota into the U. S. Army, and therefore could not enlist. I was consequently drawn into the service on June 24, 1918, at Lyons, Rice County, Kansas.

"I was assigned to Camp Cody, Deming, N. M., and arrived there June 26th. For five weeks I remained in Casual Camp, and then was assigned to 135th Infantry, Company L of the 34th Division. A few weeks later I was transferred to Field Hospital, Company 135 of the same Division, because of my previous training as a medical student.

"About September 6th our entire Division moved to Camp Dix, New Jersey, to await transportation overseas. Soon after our arrival at Camp Dix an epidemic of influenza spread throughout our camp and we lost a thousand men. This, of course, delayed our embarkment several weeks.

"On Friday, October 13th we sailed from Hoboken with thirteen transports in our convoy and arrived at Liverpool October 24th, after an uneventful voyage. It was my pleasure to be a passenger on the 'Baltic,' which is noted for having carried over General Pershing and the first American troops.

"Passenger trains were waiting for us at the pier, and we went immediately to Camp Winchester, a rest camp near South Hampton. From here, a few days later, we took a small freight boat for L'Havre, and from there by cattle cars to Le Mons, which, at that time, was a forwarding camp.

"We remained at Le Mons for some time and our Division was disorganized and our Company changed from Field Hospital 135 to Casual Unit No. 1. Meanwhile preparations were being made to go to a First Aid Station somewhere near Metz; but on November 9th we were ordered to the front. Transportation could not be furnished at this time, so we had to remain here with approximately one hundred thousand men in a steady downpour of rain for days, and not a shelter except our 'pup' tents. We slept on one blanket in mud ankle deep. We ate our two meals a day in the rain, and for shaving purposes, used coffee instead of water, of which there was a great scarcity. We could not train under these circumstances, so lay in our tents eagerly awaiting our turn to go to the front.

"It was here that we received our first mail from home since we left Camp Dix, a month previously. One of the boys, whose bride lay dangerously ill with 'flu' when he sailed, received only one letter which notified him that he would not receive his copy of the *Literary Digest* for that week. It was under these circumstances that we received the news on November 11th that the 'War is ended.'

"But on the same day we received our transportation to the front and our orders had not been cancelled, so we loaded on freight cars and started. When we reached Revigny, a village on the River Marne the scene of the early battle of the Marne, we had orders to stop. We were then temporarily attached to Division 40, and helped in their hospital—our principal duty being to saw wood for fires.

"Upon our arrival there I was taken with influenza and was confined to my bed in the hospital for three weeks, having excellent care. When I was able to go on duty again we were ordered to Camp Hospital 48, at Recey sur Rouce. Having no transportation furnished us, we bummed our way—some on one train and some on another; but all of us, seventy in number, arrived safely at Camp Hospital 48, which was a unit of the Service of Supply (S. O. S. Division). Here we were permanently attached.

"The first two nights in this camp I spent as ward master, and the next night I was on the ward as a patient with mumps. I recall that on Christmas Day I was again able to sit up and write to my mother. I also remember that on this day there was a little flurry of snow, which was the only snow I saw while in France.

"When sufficiently recovered from mumps, I was assigned to the laboratory as bacteriologist. Here I was made a Private First Class. My service was uneventful until about the first of March, when I received an appointment to go to a British University. (The U. S. Army provided for a limited number of A. E. F. college graduates to go to universities while they were waiting for their transportation to the United States.) My ticket permitted a stop-over in Paris of which I availed myself, going from there to L'Havre and on to Southhampton by boat, and thence to Camp Knotty Ash, near Liverpool.

"At my request I was assigned to the University of Aberdeen, where I enrolled in the Medical School in the Spring Session, 1919.

"I had been granted a permanent pass and one-half reduction in railroad fare, so I took many trips to places of interest in England, Ireland, Scotland, and Wales. My time at the University of Aberdeen was most enjoyable and profitable to me and an experience which I shall never forget. I left on July 4th with the greatest respect for Scotland and her splendid people, and sailed the next day on a cattle boat, from South Hamption, arriving the next morning after a stormy voyage, at Brest, France, to await transportation to the United States.

"We sailed from France, July 14, 1919, on the Battleship 'Minnesota,' and arrived at Newport News, Va., on July 28th. On July 29th, we arrived at Camp Lee, and on the following day, July 30th, I was discharged from the service."

....

Walter Presley Jeter, son of Fielden H. and Virginia Ann (White) Jeter, married Alice Pinkney Stewart at Stewartsville, Va., November 2, 1882. Immediately after their marriage, Walter P. Jeter took his wife to live at his father's home—his father having married her mother, Mrs. Mary Jane (Wright) Stewart, just three years before.

About that time there was a migration from this part of the state to Kansas, which was then just being opened up for settlement. Many Bedford people were already there, and Mr. Jeter decided to cast his lot with them, and in February, 1885, left his wife and baby with their parents and went to Rice County, Kansas, buying land near the village of Alden.

As soon as he could provide shelter for them, his wife and child joined him, and together they faced the hardships of frontier life, many times longing for the comforts of the home they had left behind, but ever determined to succeed in the land of their adoption.

Four other children were born to them after going to Kansas, all of whom they have educated and started safely on life's journey. Their home is just out of Alden, where they are spending their ripe years in well deserved ease and comfort.

Alice Pinkney (Stewart) Jeter, born November 2, 1862, in Bedford County, Va., is the daughter of William Reynold Stewart (born April 19, 1826; died May 16, 1864) and Mary Jane Wright (born December 25, 1838; died April 5, 1919), who were married January 17, 1860.

CHILDREN OF WALTER P. AND ALICE (STEWART) JETER:

(1) Anne Elizabeth, born June 4, 1884; married January 5, 1913, Samuel Calvin Hair (born July 3, 1879; son of William T. Hair (born in Claysville, Washington County, Pa., September 26, 1848) and Hester Luella Dixon (born in Pierceville, Ripley County, Ind., August 6, 1856).

CHILDREN:

(a) Joyce Virginia, born August 9, 1913.
(b) Jeter Kemper, born November 16, 1918.

Samuel Calvin Hair and family live in Nickerson, Kansas.

(2) Mary Alice, born July 25, 1886; married, October 2, 1907, Frank Edward Vincent (born February 15, 1884; son of Harvey B. Vincent (born November 10, 1822; died April 15, 1906) and Mary Whitaker (born February 11, 1856) who were married November 23, 1878).

CHILDREN:

 (a) Neta Claire,.born September 26, 1908.
 (b) Doran Jeter, born April 12, 1911.
 (c) Harvey Fielding, born March 9, 1914.
 (d) Walter Presley, born May 10, 1919.
 (e) Helen Virginia, born June 16, 1922.

Frank E. Vincent and family live near Alden, Kansas.

(3) William Stewart, born July 24, 1888; lived on the farm with his parents until the beginning of the World War. His interesting experience as a soldier, follows:

"On May 10, 1918, I left Lyons, Kansas, for Jefferson Barracks at St. Louis, Mo. After a physical examination, I was sent to Camp McArthur at Waco, Texas, and put into the 7th Division, Headquarters Company, 34th Infantry, and I remained in that division until the close of the war. I was trained in the very beginning for a messenger boy.

"From Camp McArthur, I was transferred to Camp Merritt, New Jersey, on July 31st, from which place we sailed for France, landing at Brest on August 28th.

"The next day I was sent to the front, and was in three heavy battles—one of them on the Argonne front.

"On one occasion I was in the trench doing some washing and had hung my watch on a twig, when our Lieutenant rushed in and said we were in our heaviest battle, and to make ready. In a few minutes I saw him fall—he had made the supreme sacrifice. In my hurry I left my watch hanging on the tree.

"On the day after this terrible battle, I was put on police duty, which duty was to gather up the lifeless bodies of my comrades and take them to their final resting places in Flanders Field; and then to collect bombs, shrapnel and articles of war, which were strewn on the battle ground.

"After this I was made Mess Sergeant—serving meals to officers.

"Finally, I was placed in the Army of Occupation and remained there until my return home.

"One of our red letter days was March 14th, when our Division was sent to Paris for the inspection of General Pershing.

"When the order came for my return home I was in Treves, Germany. I went first to Italy and then sailed from Marseilles on an Italian vessel. The boat was dirty and the food very poor—a number died en route. We had to wait seven days in Strait of Gibralter for Spaniards to coal the ship, the soldiers not being allowed to help. All the coal was carried in baskets.

"We were twenty days reaching Camp Mills, New Jersey, where I received my Discharge on June 30, 1919."

(4) Lillian Claire, born March 20, 1891; was educated at Mehellan College, Kansas, and Columbia University, New York, receiving the degree of A. B. at Mehellan and that of A. M. at Columbia. She was for several years head of the Home Economics Department of the M. E. University at Lincoln, Nebraska, now teaching at Menomonie, Wis.

(5) Esther Priscilla, born February 5, 1899; was educated at Cooper College, Sterling, Kansas, and at Lawrence, Kan., where she received the degree of A. B. She taught in the Junior High School at Junction City, Kan., and is now (1929) teaching in the city schools of Kansas City, Mo.

———

Gilbert Carey Jeter, youngest son of Fielden H. and Virginia Ann (White) Jeter, married Ann Pannill Ficklen, October 5, 1892, at "Woodburn" in Campbell County, Va.—the home of her aunt, Mrs. Ruth (Pannill) Gordon. (Her sister, Ellen Douglass Ficklen, was married at the same time to Louis C. Arthur.)

CHILDREN:

(1) Fielding Ficklen, born July 14, 1893; educated at Randolph-Macon College, taking the degree of A. M.; taught four years in the State College of North Carolina, giving up his position there to enter a training camp for the World War. He entered the service July 22, 1918, at Raleigh, N. C.; was assigned to

Fielding Ficklen Jeter

Chesley Gilbert Jeter

Company 54, 5th Group Regiment, at Camp Hancock, Ga.; was transferred to Company 12, C. M. Regiment, G. O. T. S. Division, Camp Hancock, Ga.

He was promoted to rank of Corporal, October, 1918. He did not go over seas but was retained in camp as a Machine Gun Instructor, and was discharged from service January 29, 1919.

He is now manager of a branch house of the F. S. Royster Guano Co., of Norfolk, Va., which is located at Tarboro, N. C.

(2) Frances Louise, born September 10, 1894; received the degree of A. B. at Randolph-Macon Woman's College; taught five years in the High School of Huntington, W. Va.; married in Lynchburg, Va., June 30, 1923, Charles Andrew Anderson, of Prince Edward County, Va. They live in Richmond, Va., where he is connected with the Mutual Life Insurance Company.

(3) Gilbert Carey, born May 21, 1896; educated at Farmville State Normal School and Columbia University; taught in the public schools of Virginia and North Carolina; was instructor in Home Economics at Radford State Normal and later at Farmville State Normal; and still later at Winthrop College, S. C. She married, June 23, 1927, in Lynchburg, Va., William Gist Finley of York, S. C. They now live in York, S. C.

Gilbert Carey Jeter was educated at Hale's Ford Academy, Franklin County, Va., and taught several terms in the public schools of Bedford before entering the hardware business in Liberty (now Bedford). He was senior partner of the firm of Jeter and McGhee, hardware merchants. He was prominent in church, fraternal and social circles, and was a man of high ideals and sterling worth.

In the fourth year of his married life he was stricken with typhoid fever and died September 14, 1895, after only one week's illness.

Ann (Nannie) Pannill (Ficklen) Jeter, born April 6, 1870, is the daughter of James Burwell Ficklen and Frances Augusta Ann Pannill. She was educated in the public schools of Lynchburg, Va., and taught in the schools of Amherst and Bedford counties.

After the death of her husband she continued to live in Bedford until her children were old enough to enter a boarding school, when she went to Danville, Va., and took a position as housekeeper in Randolph-Macon Institute, placing her little girls in that institution, and leaving her son with relatives in Bedford to attend Randolph-Macon Academy. By persistent effort and rare determination she succeeded in educating all three of them. She is now head of the Home Economics Department of the East Carolina Training School, Greenville, N. C.

FICKLEN

James Burwell Ficklen was born near Winchester, Va., October 1, 1831, and died in Buckingham County, Va., January 31, 1883. July 11, 1860, he married Frances Augusta Ann Pannill, born at Chalk Level, Pittsylvania County, Va., May 3, 1839, and died in Richmond, January 9, 1888.

James B. Ficklen was a member of the "Richmond Howitzers" before the Civil War, and was with his company at Harper's Ferry at the time of John Brown's Raid. He entered the Confederate service with the Howitzers, and was later relieved of active service on account of physical disabilities and instructed to raise supplies for the Confederate Army. For this purpose he purchased the "Red House" estate on James River, in Buckingham County, and moved his family there, contributing to the Confederate cause all crops raised on his plantation during the period of the war.

FINLEY

The Finleys of South Carolina are of Scotch-Irish extraction and settled first in Pennsylvania. From there they came to Augusta County, Va., in 1736. John, Robert and William Finley are mentioned in the list of early settlers in that section. John married Thankful Doak and had sons, John, Robert, James, William, Joseph, David and others.

John Finley, son of John and Thankful (Doak) Finley, born in Carlisle, Penn., 1727, was with Dr. Thomas Walker's expedition to Cumberland Gap in 1748. He served under Captains Evans Shelby and Preston in the French and Indian Wars; was trustee and elder of Tinkling Springs Church, 1747; died 1791; buried in Tinkling Springs Churchyard; married, 1746, Mary Caldwell, born 1730, daughter of Major John Caldwell, who led the way in colonizing Prince Edward County, Charlotte County, and Campbell County, Va. He was major in the Revolution and was murdered by the Tories in cold blood in his own yard, after they had set fire to his house.

Children of John and Mary (Caldwell) Finley: John Caldwell, David, George, Robert Osborne, Thomas C., Margaret, Mary Thankful, and Jean.

John Caldwell Finley, born June 16, 1747; married, 1767, Ann Miller, daughter of Thomas Miller of North Carolina—Revolutionary soldier. Children: John, Agnes, James, David, William, and Robert Miller.

Robert Miller Finley; died May 24, 1869, age 86 years and 9 months; married Nancy Bryant, daughter of James Bryant—Revolutionary soldier. She died 1854 age 70 years. Children: John, Robert, Alexander, James, Isabella, David Miller, born 1816 in Gaston County, N. C.; died in Trenton, Ark., 1863; married, February, 1841, Elizabeth McIlwaine, born in York County, S. C., October 22, 1816; died in Arkansas, November 2, 1861.

Children of David Miller and Elizabeth (McIlwaine) Finley: Margaret Jane, Nancy Elvira, Zachary Taylor, John Alexander, Charles Robert, James William, Stern Calhoun, and David Edward.

David Edward Finley, son of David M. and Elizabeth (McIlwaine) Finley, was born February 28, 1861. He married Elizabeth Lewis Gist, 1889. In 1892 he was elected to the State Legislature, in 1894 to the State Senate where he served four years. In 1898 he was elected to the Fifty-sixth Congress and was re-elected nine successive times, dying in office, January 26, 1917. His name is more closely associated with the Postal Service than any other activity with which he was connected in Congress. No other member contributed more than he to the permanency and success of the Rural Free Delivery System.

Children of David E. and Elizabeth (Gist) Finley: David Edward, Jr., Elizabeth, Frances, William Gist, Robert McIlwaine, States Rights, Margaret Adams, and John Campbell.

William Gist Finley, born September 10, 1895; married, June 23, 1927, Gilbert Carey Jeter, born May 21, 1896, daughter of Gilbert Carey and Nannie (Ficklen) Jeter. He is a rising young lawyer of York, S. C.

GIST

Christopher Gist, colonist, came from England to America and settled in Baltimore County, Md., prior to 1682. In 1683 he married Edith Cromwell, and they had one child, Richard Gist, born in 1684.

Capt. Richard Gist represented Baltimore County in the Provincial Assembly, 1740-41, and was one of the seven commissioners who laid out Baltimore City. He married, December 7, 1704, Zipporah Murray, daughter of James Murray, Gent., of Baltimore County, and Jemima Morgan, his wife, daughter of Capt. Thomas Morgan (died 1698). (Friends record.)

CHILDREN:

(1) Capt. Christopher; surveyor—Washington's friend and guide; married Sarah Howard.

(2) Nathaniel; married Mary Howard.

(3) William, born 1711; died 1794; married Violetta Howard, October 22, 1737.

(4) Thomas; born 1711; died 1788; married Susan Cocky. Four daughters.

William Gist, son of William and Violetta (Howard) Gist, was born September 23, 1743 (Records St. Thomas' Church), and went to South Carolina, where he married Sarah Fincher of Union County. He died in Charleston, S. C., in 1802, and is buried in St. Michael's Churchyard. They had five sons—among them:

Nathaniel; wealthy planter of Union County, S. C.; married Elizabeth Lewis McDaniel, and had eight sons and two daughters.

William Gist, son of Col. Nathaniel and Elizabeth Lewis (McDaniel) Gist, married Frances Caroline Dorothy Crenshaw and had three daughters and one son. The eldest daughter, Elizabeth Lewis Gist married Hon. David E. Finley.

To the Gist family belong Major General Mordecai Gist of the Revolution, States Rights Gist, killed at Battle of Franklin, Tenn., and Governor William H. Gist, secession Governor of South Carolina, 1859-60.

THE TEXAS JETERS

Thomas Archer Jeter, son of Sovereign and Matilda (Vaughan) Jeter, went to Pulaski County, Va., soon after he was of age and entered the mercantile business, afterwards becoming postmaster at Dublin, Va.

About this time Susan McCampbell of Tennessee, daughter of James and Jean Cunningham (Boyd) McCampbell, came up to Draper's Valley, in Pulaski County, to visit her uncle, Andrew Boyd, and was secured by Dr. Moses Hoge as governess for his children and his small grandson, Hoge Tyler (afterwards Governor of Virginia), whom she taught to read. She met Thomas A. Jeter at the home of Dr. Hoge.

At the end of her school term she returned to her home in Tennessee, and in a short time her father moved his family to Goliad, Texas. In about eighteen months the young Pulaski merchant found himself, also, on the prairies of the Lone Star State, and on January 25, 1860, he married Miss McCampbell, and brought her back to Virginia. They made their home in Dublin, Pulaski County, until after all their children were born, and in 1877, when his health began to fail, he moved his family back to Texas, settling in Goliad County, near Berclair.

He never regained his strength, but lived to see all of his children grown. He died at Aransas Pass, Texas, March 31, 1892.

Susan (McCampbell) Jeter was a woman of superior mental attainments, strong convictions and high Christian character—a devout Presbyterian. She was born in Knox County, Tenn., June 26, 1830, and died in Refugio, Texas, September 4, 1903.

CHILDREN:

(1) Virginia Vaughan, born November 12, 1860; died October 25, 1929; married, January 4, 1881, in Bee County, Texas, Conizene Hamilton Heard, who was born in Refugio, Texas,

November 10, 1857; son of Thomas Clinton Heard (born in Clark County, Ala., January 4, 1829; died in Refugio, Texas, June 4, 1905; son of Joel and Nancy (Gilmore) Heard) and Mary Caroline Busby (born in Sumpter County, Ala., September 8, 1835; died in Refugio, June 8, 1916; daughter of John Flowers and Penelope (Jones) Busby).

"Benie" Heard, as he was familiarly called, was a wealthy stockman, and spent all his life, except the last year or two, in the town of Refugio, where he was born. He was a man of great influence in his community; of charming personality; and greatly beloved by his fellow citizens for his purity of life, kindness of heart and noble Christian character.

He died in San Antonio, Texas, March 30, 1923, and was carried back to Refugio and buried in the cemetery there.

CHILDREN:

(a) Aletha Maud, born July 29, 1884; educated at Mary Baldwin Seminary in Va.; married (first) in Beeville, Texas, December 27, 1903, Dr. Earl Stafford, son of William Maner and Emily (Vedder) Stafford.

CHILDREN:

(aa) Conizene Earl, born November 10, 1904; married, January 24, 1925, Catherine Speir. They live in San Antonio, Texas, and have two little girls:

(aaa) Geraldine Jane, born June 11, 1926.

(bbb) Cathryn Vaughan, born August 7, 1928.

(bb) Gerald Maner, born February 15, 1906; married, September 22, 1929, Emily Murray. Both are students at the University of Texas, where he expects to get the degree of A. M. in June, 1930.

Maud (Heard) Stafford married (second), February 4, 1913, in San Antonio, Texas, Julius F. Leisering, son of Charles Frederick and Susan (Dorsett) Leisering. Their home is in Kerrville. Texas.

CHILDREN:

(aa) Julius F., born November 11, 1915.

(bb) Virginia Elizabeth, born March 16, 1918.

(b) Thomas Henry, born September 23, 1887; married, June 10, 1908, in Refugio, Texas, Edna Earle Adkins, daughter of Dr. John James and Emma Josephine (Trice) Adkins. He has followed in the steps of his father in business, and is a successful stockman of Refugio, Texas.

CHILDREN:

(aa) Alta Earle, born April 22, 1909.

(bb) Thomas Henry, Jr., born October 15, 1917.

Four other children of Conizene and Vaughan (Jeter) Heard died in infancy.

(2) Maud Houston, born September 29, 1864; married, December 6, 1893, in Aransas Pass, Texas, Elijah Robert Porter, son of Joseph Marion and Sarah Elizabeth (Baugh) Porter. They now live at Gregory, Texas.

CHILDREN:

(a) Robert Clifton, born September 22, 1894; married September 14, 1927, Inice Hogan.

(b) Della Vaughan, born May 14, 1900; married, June 14, 1927, Bradley Nutt.

(3) Della Archer, born October 26, 1866; married in Patricia County, Texas, June, 1886, Charles Norton Bailey, son of Charles Franklin and Fannie (Reeves) Bailey.

(aa) Norton Henry, born August 14, 1887; married in Dallas, Texas, Laura Seaton. They live in Dallas and have three children:

(aaa) Charles Edwin, born October 19, 1909.

(bbb) Ethel, born May 8, 1911.

(ccc) Dorothy Lee, born December 11, 1912.

(bb) Claude Archer, born August 24, 1889; married in Georgia, November, 1914, Marguerite Wilson, daughter of Dr. Charles A. and Ilda (Corey) Wilson. Their children are Claude Wilson, and Malcolm.

(cc) Vivian Vaughan, born June 29, 1896; married in Lovelady, Texas, August 24, 1922, Norma Shaw, daughter of Mitchell Lafayette and Elizabeth Caroline (Hooper) Shaw. They live in Refugio, Texas, and have two children:

(aaa) Virginia Elaine, born August 29, 1923.

(bbb) Charles Pat, born January 1, 1929.

(dd) Edwin Houston, born May 4, 1905; married, 1929, Genelle Howell.

(4) Allen McCampbell, born August 19, 1868; married in Refugio, Texas, June 24, 1903, Ellen Bridgett Fox, daughter of John Darrell and Maggie (Murphy) Fox. Both now deceased.

(a) Clarence Archer, born June 13, 1904.

(b) Gertrude Vaughan, born May 23, 1906.

(c) John Darrell, born May 20, 1909.

(5) Thomas Edwin, born February 10, 1870; married in Goliad, Texas, June 20, 1911, Jennie Porterfield, daughter of Isaac and Jane (Eaton) Porterfield. They live at Tivoli, Texas, and have no children.

(6) Leonard Ramsey, born October 6, 1871; married in Refugio, Texas, December, 1897. Annette Rogers, daughter of Licucn M. and Emma (Stribling) Rogers.

CHILDREN:

(a) Lenette Blanche, born July 17, 1899; married at Tivoli, Texas, February 27, 1923, James Clark Adkins, son of Dr. John James and Emma Josephine (Trice) Adkins. They live at Heardsdale, Texas, and have two little girls:

(aa) Clark, born December 5, 1923.

(bb) Aline Annette, born May 23, 1925.

(b) Gentry Archer, born September 7, 1901.

(c) Leonard Ramsey, born April 17, 1910; married, June 2, 1929, Edward Jones.

(d) Leslie Rogers, born December 10, 1913.

Martha Ann Jeter, daughter of Sovereign Jeter and his second wife, Nancy (Overstreet) Jeter, married William B. Craghead, who was born December 11, 1832, and died in August, 1860. She died in October, 1928.

CHILDREN:

(1) Virginia Roberts, born December 11, 1854; married, December 11, 1879, James A. Dinwiddie (born February 8, 1855), son of James and Sarah A. (Holland) Dinwiddie, who were married, October 10, 1850.

CHILDREN:

(a) Willie Blanche, born October 3, 1880; married June 18, 1902, Robert Edward Lazenby, son of Henry L. and Elizabeth (Grounds) Lazenby.

CHILDREN:

(aa) Willie Ruth, born March 1, 1903.
(bb) Margaret Elizabeth, born January 27, 1905.
(cc) Virginia Dinwiddie, born December 13, 1906; married Dr. Frank Jackson Holroyd, son of Dr. Frederick Fairfax and Hettie (Shumate) Holroyd.
(dd) Lois, born March 18, 1909.
(ee) Mary, born June 15, 1911.
(ff) Martha Jeter, born March 8, 1915.
(gg) Blanche, born March 28, 1917.
(hh) Robert Edward, born August 22, 1920.
(ii) Nancy Grey, born April 16, 1924.

(b) Everette Hunt, born January 17, 1882; died August 8, 1908.
(c) Mary Virginia, born October 13, 1883.
(d) Sarah Martha, born September 7, 1887.
(e) Eva Acree, born January 19, 1890; married, July 9, 1917, Clifford Abraham Lilly.
(f) James William, born January 11, 1892; married Harriet Leah Brown, born August 25, 1894, daughter of Glyndon and Leah (Laugevin) Brown.

CHILDREN:

(aa) James Fearing, born August 20, 1924.
(bb) William Frank, born July 5, 1927.

(g) Evelyn Bowker, born July 31, 1894.

(2) Sarah Frances, born January 23, 1856; died February, 1927; married, March 1, 1876, Charles F. Thomas.

CHILDREN:

(a) John Walton, born June 9, 1877.

(b) Frederick Reed, born April 9, 1879.

(c) James Emmett, born November 26, 1880.

(d) Clelia Irene, born August 18, 1882.

(e) Lillian Frances, born August 11, 1884.

(f) Charles Herbert, born October 28, 1888.

(g) Marguerite, born April 26, 1894.

(3) Robert Emmett Craghead, born February 17, 1858; died May 3, 1915; married, April 8, 1891, Hettie Susan Dinwiddie.

CHILDREN:

(a) William Dinwiddie, born September 24, 1924; married Ethelyn Virgie Turner, born January 7, 1902, daughter of Samuel Clayborn and Bessie Eva Turner.

CHILD:

(aa) Billy Douglass, born March 29, 1921.

(b) Jessie Clair, born July 4, 1894; married Hubert Gill Johnson, born October 10, 1893, son of Samuel D. and Emma Johnson,

CHILDREN:

(aa) Clemantine Jayne, born September 12, 1922.

(bb) Sinward Samuel, born March 21, 1927.

(c) Irma Virginia, born October 30, 1896; married William Wesley McGeorge, born February 28, 1892, son of Thomas Judson and Fannie Kate McGeorge.

CHILDREN:

(aa) Emogene Virginia, born March 14, 1923.

(bb) Nancy Leigh, born March 10, 1924.

(cc) Peggy Adeline, born September 12, 1925.

(dd) Jacqueline Susan, born January 27, 1928.

(d) Mary Blanche, born April 8, 1899; married David Strousse Blount, born November 4, 1895, son of Charles Robert and Sallye Frances Blount.

CHILD:

(aa) Strousse David, born February 16, 1927.

(e) Edna Irene, born October 29, 1901.

(f) Robert Emmette, Jr., born February 4, 1904; married Della Lancaster Dillon, born April 29, 1906, daughter of Davis and Julia Adeline Dillon.

CHILD:

(aa) Robert Eugene, born March 10, 1926.

(4) John Tinsley, born March 28, 1860; died September, 1929; married, January 14, 1886, Linnie White, born April 30, 1860, daughter of Archie and Cynthia White. Lived and died in Texas.

CHILDREN:

(a) George Leonard, born June 11, 1888; married, October 6, 1907, Bertha Mae Culwell, born December 3, 1888, daughter of John Wesley and Mollie Culwell; lives in Texas.

CHILDREN:

(aa) Archie Leonard, born September 10, 1909.

(bb) John Lloyd, born August 11, 1911; married, November 5, 1928, Flora Lou Mauney, born May 20, 1908, daughter of Jack and Elizabeth Mauney.

(cc) J. B., born April 27, 1926.

(b) William Cathie, born October 6, 1889; unmarried.

(c) Roy Spencer, born March 17, 1891; married, August 29, 1909, Nannie Ferguson, born June 17, 1891, daughter of James and Voda Ferguson.

CHILDREN:

(aa) Willard Lee, born November 21, 1910.

(bb) Collins Bryan, born July 8, 1914.

(cc) Roy Spencer, Jr., born November 23, 1923.

(d) Winnie Alma, born October 9, 1893; unmarried.

(e) Jeff Bryan, born October 30, 1896; married, December 22, 1915, Texas Reed, born August 10, 1894, daughter of David and America Reed.

....

Saluda Elliott Jeter, youngest daughter of Sovereign Jeter and his second wife, Nancy (Overstreet) Jeter, was only three years old when her mother died. Mr. and Mrs. Henry Terry lived near the Jeters, and, having no children of their own, besought her father to let them have little Saluda. He was now old and had two other small children to care for, so knowing that the Terrys were people of means and believing that they would be kind to the child, he allowed them to take her. She soon won their affection and became the joy and sunshine of their home. They reared her as their very own, providing for her every luxury within their power.

On June 18, 1862, she married James Armistead Dooley (born January 1, 1829; died May 17, 1914).

CHILDREN:

(1) Albert Harrison, born January 20, 1864; married, October 24, 1900, Lelia Anne Moomaw. No children.

(2) Waverly Henderson, born May 19, 1866; married, December 11, 1895, Lizzie Jane Lockard.

CHILDREN:

  (a) Nettie Marie, born September 25, 1896; married Alfonso Tyndall; died November 3, 1925.

  (b) Floyd Harrison, born August 9, 1898; married July 24, 1924, Elsie Pollen.

CHILD:

    (aa) Bettie Marie, born October 21, 1928.

  (c) Norma Leora, born April 26, 1900; married, November 9, 1927, George W. Mills.

  (d) James Rice, born June 24, 1902; died in infancy.

  (e) Beulah Celosia, born May 7, 1906.

  (f) Waverly E., born June 4, 1909; died in infancy.

  (g) Lula Elizabeth, born September 7, 1912.

(3) William Ryland, born February 11, 1868; married (first) Laura James Ferguson, September 25, 1895.

CHILDREN:

  (a) Mabel Ruth, born September 7, 1896.

  (b) William Paul, born October 5, 1898.

  (c) Marvin Ryland, born June 28, 1900; died April 8, 1924.

  (d) James Warren, born May 21, 1903.

(e) Laurie Lyle, born August 6, 1908; died March 26, 1919.
William R. Dooley married (second), May 11, 1915, Florence
Sampson.

CHILDREN:

(a) William Ryland, Jr. (Jack), born December 2, 1916.
(b) Nina Beth, born January 9, 1918.

(4) Frederick James, born March 31, 1870; married, August 29, 1899,
Pearl Dooley.

CHILDREN:

(a) Sadie K., born August 29, 1900; married, June 8, 1929,
Alfred Kyle Tuck, born September 5, 1891.
(b) Lois J., born May 24, 1902.
(c) James W., born February 28, 1904.
(d) Bertram B., born September 28, 1905.
(e) Levia L., born July 15, 1909.
(f) Harriett D., born July 9, 1911.
(g) Claudine T., born July 24, 1914.
(h) Hazel S., born September 22, 1917.
(i) Leon P., born April 27, 1920.
(j) Alfred Alton, born July 30, 1923.

(5) Elma Lou, born January 20, 1872; married, December 6, 1899,
Charles Richard Walker, who is now deceased.

(6) Addison Maupin, born May 20, 1874; unmarried; has always
lived on the farm, near Bedford, with his mother.

(7) Lillian Mattie, born May 2, 1877; married, May 5, 1901, William
Emmett Arrington.

CHILDREN:

(a) Glen Nelson, born December 3, 1902.
(b) James Berkley, born June 4, 1904.
(c) Frank Emmett, born June 3, 1906; died in infancy.
(d) William Richard, born October 10, 1907.
(e) Gladys Virginia, born October 18, 1909.
(f) Saluda Jeter, born September 11, 1911.
(g) Earl Dooley, born December 3, 1913.
(h) Clarence Gibbs, born May 8, 1916.
(i) Edison Bernard, born January 28, 1919.
(j) Lula Ruth, born September 30, 1921.
(k) Ralph Moorman, born June 18, 1923.

(8) Lelia Virginia, born April 26, 1880.; married, June 11, 1902, Walter G. Ramsey, a hardware merchant of Bedford, Va.

CHILDREN :

(a) Irene, born August 17, 1903.

(b) Ruby May, born May 25, 1906.

(c) Mary Virginia, born October 17, 1908.

(d) Glenwood A., born July 11, 1912.

(e) Albert Harrison, born July 4, 1919.

————o————

THE MISSISSIPPI JETERS

Caleb Jeter, son of Henry and Elizabeth (Bell) Jeter of Bedford County, Va.; married Sarah Cobbs, October 2, 1806, in Chesterfield County, Va., according to family tradition, which doubtless is correct, since their marriage bond is not in Bedford County. They lived in Bedford, however, for a few years, and all of their children were born there. About 1815 they moved to Raleigh, N. C., and bought the City Hotel, which they ran until his death, August 4, 1819. His wife continued to live in Raleigh until after the marriage of her youngest child, and then went to Gainesville, Alabama, where she spent her remaining days with her daughters, who had already established homes there. She died about 1840.

CHILDREN OF CALEB AND SARAH (COBBS) JETER:

(1) Harry Munford, born September 10, 1807; went with his parents to Raleigh; studied medicine and began his career as a physician in Waynesboro, N. C. In 1840 he left Waynesboro and went to Hernando, Miss., where he remained only one year, and then settled in Coldwater, Miss. He married Mrs. Evalina Blackman and they had three children: Sally, Anna, and Eliza. He died August 2, 1883.

(2) Cynthia Cobbs, born December 15, 1808; died unmarried.

(3) Eliza Ann, born August 6, 1810.

(4) Julia Bell, born March 5, 1812; died September 28, 1812.

(5) Emelia Robinson, born December 21, 1814.

(6) Lavenia Sarah, born October 23, 1815.

Eliza Ann, daughter of Caleb and Sarah (Cobbs) Jeter, married, August 21, 1834, John Alexander Minniece, who was born October 26, 1810, in Belfast, Ireland, and who was the son of William and Margaret (Alexander) Minniece.

CHILDREN:

(1) Sidney, born May 31, 1835; practiced law in Hernando, Miss.; was a soldier in the Confederate Army; contracted tuberculosis and died, unmarried, October 31, 1862.

(2) Walter Russell, born July 31, 1837; married, May 21, 1868, Mary Frances Gresham.
CHILDREN:

    (a) John Gresham (twin), born August 14, 1869.
    (b) Sidney (twin), born August 14, 1869.
    (c) Walter Russell, Jr., born August 14, 1873; unmarried.
    (d) Jennie Leatherbury, born February 14, 1878.

(3) Sara Evelyn, born February 6, 1839; married James Moore.

CHILDREN:

    (a) William McDow, born March 26, 1863.
    (b) Eliza; died in childhood.
    (c) Evie; died in childhood.
    (d) Infant; died.

(4) Alice, born November 7, 1840; married Thaddeus W. Westbrook.
CHILDREN:

    (a) William Henry, born April 2, 1864; died young.
    (b) John Minniece, born July 7, 1865.
    (c) Thaddeus Phillips, born July 20, 1867.
    (d) Sidney Ivey, born April 25, 1869; died August 26, 1869.
    (e) Lizzie Alice, born January 11, 1872; died September 23, 1872.
    (f) Polk, born August 20, 1873.

(5) William Henry, born June 22, 1843; killed in Battle of Chickamauga, September 20, 1863.

(6) Mary, born December 12, 1844; died June 1, 1846.

(7) Anna Roberts, born December 9, 1846; married, October 6, 1869, George Henry Kimbrough (born July 10, 1845; died February 23, 1924; son of George Henry and Esther Love (Steele) Kimbrough of Scooba, Miss.).

CHILDREN:

(a) Alice, born October 3, 1870; died October 6, 1872.

(b) Bettie, born April 3, 1872; married, December 19, 1906, Thomas Reeves Moseley.

(c) Ormond Patillo, born January 24, 1874; married Henry Tharp, November 30, 1904.

(d) Walter Minniece, born January 7, 1876; unmarried.

(e) Anna Eliza, born February 11, 1878; unmarried.

(f) George Alexander, born November 1, 1879; died July 7, 1900.

(g) Essie Love, born August 4, 1882; died April 18, 1906.

(h) Sidney Jeter, born July 3, 1885; married Eleanor Mc-Creight; died August 16, 1925.

(8) Lizzie, born January 28, 1849; married, January 30, 1879, Thomas P. Bannerman (born January 27, 1842; died March 31, 1895).

CHILDREN:

(a) Charles Alexander, born February 11, 1880.

(b) Mary Evelyn, born October 8, 1882.

(c) Thomas Percy, born December 20, 1886; died November 18, 1914.

(d) Alice Dawson, born October 31, 1888; married, July 4, 1907, William Guy McDowell of Oklona, Miss.; died July 11, 1913.

Emelia Robinson Jeter, daughter of Caleb and Sarah (Cobbs) Jeter, married William Pettus, brother of John Pettus, War Governor of Mississippi.

CHILDREN:

(1) William O.; married Hallie Day.

(2) Sarah.

(3) Martha; married ———— Cox.

(4) Edward; killed in Battle of Gettysburg.

(5) Henry; owned and lived at Healing Springs, Miss.

(6) Emma; married ———— Pettus.

(7) Dabney; thrown from a horse and died from injuries.

(8) Winston.

Lavenia Sarah Jeter, daughter of Caleb and Sarah (Cobbs) Jeter, married Calvin High, August 21, 1834.

CHILDREN:

(1) Susan; married ———— Darby.
(2) Jennie.
(3) Anna; married ———— Davis.
(4) Jeter.
(5) Mary.
(6) Ella.

....

Jesse Jeter, youngest son of Henry and Elizabeth (Bell) Jeter of Bedford County, Va., married, December 17, 1821, Susan Robinson, daughter of Benjamin Robinson, also of Bedford County. Jesse Jeter died in 1862.

CHILDREN:

(1) Anna Eliza, born October 6, 1822; died January 6, 1907; married, December 19, 1839, Palestine W. Noell (born October, 1815), son of John C. and Nancy Noell of Bedford County.

CHILDREN:

(a) Thomas Benjamin, born March 30, 1841; married Ellen Noell; both now deceased.
(b) Dematris Ann, born July 6, 1844; married John Ferrell; both now deceased.
(c) Jennie, born October 21, 1846; unmarried.
(d) Mary Elliott, born July 21, 1849; married Peter Noell.
(e) William Alonza, born July 21, 1853; married Alice Hogan.
(f) Robert Hall, born May 19, 1856; married Maggie Turpin; now deceased.
(g) Jesse Callaway, born July 21, 1859; married Lula Collins; now deceased.
(h) Paul Cary, born January 17, 1862; married Mattie Logwood; both now deceased.
(i) Ida Florence, born February 11, 1865; married Melvin Hatcher; now deceased.

(2) Benjamin Elliott, born November 28, 1824; educated in private schools; took M. D. degree at University of Pennsylvania;

practiced medicine at Bonsack, Roanoke County, Va., from 1850 until his death January 31, 1903. He married, September 6, 1852, Susan Ann Bonsack (born August 14, 1834; died July 16, 1906), daughter of John and Susan Bonsack.

CHILDREN:

(a) J. Albert, born July 8, 1854; married Carrie Musser of Marietta, Penn., January 11, 1887. They live in Salem, Va.

CHILDREN:

(aa) Victor Benjamin, born November 11, 1889; died October 16, 1907.
(bb) John Paul, born September 17, 1890; lives at Welch, W. Va.
(cc) Carrie M., born January 31, 1898; married Graydon Robertson, October 3, 1924.

CHILD:

(aaa) William Graydon.
(dd) Mary Hazel, born January 25, 1903; now teaching at Wilson, N. C.
(ee) Gwynhilda, born February 8, 1907; trained nurse.

(b) Jesse W., born August 11, 1855; killed October 30, 1876, when a steam locomotive, on which he was making his first run, exploded near Abingdon, Va.

(c) Edward M., born August 11, 1859; married Jennie McWhorter of Millington, Md., February, 1889; graduated in medicine at University of Maryland; practiced on Eastern Shore of Virginia; died 1912(?).

CHILDREN:

(aa) Allen, living at Atlantic City, N. J.
(bb) Julian, living at Atlantic City, N. J.

(d) Alice Cary, born March 1, 1861; died July 24, 1862.

(e) Laura Susan, both June 6, 1863; married James Meade Harris, October 22, 1889.

CHILDREN:

(aa) Eugene Jeter, born in Roanoke, Va., August 17, 1890; was graduated from V. P. I. in 1913; married Lois Agnew, April 30, 1919. Now a member of the firm of J. M. Harris and Co., Roanoke, Va.

CHILDREN:

(aaa) Elizabeth, born August 24, 1921.
(bbb) Ann, born March 14, 1924.

(bb) Fred Bonsack, born June 19, 1893; educated at V. P. I.; served in the World War in France; married Marie Vogenthaler, August 19, 1925.

CHILD:

(aaa) Marie Louise, born April 14, 1927.

(cc) Louise Virginia, born June 19, 1893; married Stanford L. Fellers, attorney-at-law, Roanoke, Va.

CHILDREN:

(aaa) Catherine, born April 21, 1922.
(bbb) Stanford, Jr., born May 25, 1928.

(dd) James Meade, Jr., born July 2, 1897; educated at Washington and Lee University and married Madeline Reader of Delevan, Wis. In business in Roanoke, Va., with his two brothers—all members of the firm of J. M. Harris and Co.

(f) Charles Elliott, born October 7, 1865; married Elizabeth Royer of Reading, Penn.; died June 8, 1916.

CHILDREN:

(aa) Frederick.
(bb) Elizabeth.
(cc) Franklin.

(g) Reuben R., born December 3, 1867; died September 20, 1890.

(h) Dillie, born July 1, 1872; married George S. Strader of Bluefield, W. Va., October 10, 1901. Mr. Strader was born at Bane, Giles County, Va., March 2, 1870, and is now a prosperous business man of West Virginia.

CHILDREN:

(aa) George Stewart, Jr., born February 24, 1903; educated at Randolph-Macon College, taking his A. B. degree in 1924; member of Phi Delta Theta Fraternity; now employed in his father's office in Bluefield, W. Va.

(bb) Benjamin Jeter, born June 16, 1904; educated at Randolph-Macon College, A. B. degree in June, 1924; member, Kappa Sigma Fraternity; now engaged in real estate business in Bluefield.

(cc) William Robinson, born January 19, 1909; now a student at Randolph-Macon College; member, Phi Delta Theta Fraternity.

(i) Jacob, born April 2, 1864; married Hattie Brugh in 1914; is a farmer and lives at Bonsack, Va., at the old Jeter home place. Children: Max, Richard, Josephine, and Anne.

(3) Jesse R., born June 10, 1830; married Susan B. Poindexter, December 4, 1851.

CHILDREN:

(a) Emma Ann, born September 23, 1852; married Osson P. Knight, February 1, 1871; died August 16, 1921.

(b) Samuel Cary, born February 12, 1855; unmarried; lives at Coleman Falls, Va.

(c) John Slaughter, born March 16, 1857; married Emma F. Wilson, December 3, 1879. They live at Leon, Iowa.

(d) Jesse Elliott, born June 27, 1859; died December 15, 1859.

(e) Mary Elizabeth, born July 9, 1861; married William Dabney Poindexter, December 3, 1879. (See Poindexter family.)

(f) Jessie C., born May 18, 1864; married Sterling L. Knight, December 21, 1887. They live at Coleman Falls.

(g) Rosa Bell, born December 3, 1866; married Albert W. Milliner, December 23, 1896. They live at Coffee, Va.

(h) James Perry, born May 28, 1871; married Annie I. Adams. Their home is in Roanoke, Va.

Jesse R. Jeter died April 20, 1921.

Susan (Poindexter) Jeter died August 12, 1909.

(4) John Abraham Jeter born August 18, 1832; died January 3, 1896; married, October 26, 1858, Susan Olivia Turpin (born May 17, 1839; died September 22, 1893; daughter of Captain John and Mary M. (Lambert) Turpin). (See Turpin family.)

CHILDREN:

(a) Hettie Orelia, born February 1, 1860; married Charles L. Moorman, January 1, 1884. Children: Curtis C.; Leona, married ———— Cross; Sallie Olivia, married Joseph M. Hawkins.

(b) Charles Lambert, born April 4, 1861; married Lizzie Collins. One child: Helen, who married ———— Crow.

(c) John Waller, born May 4, 1863; married Lucy Richards of Bedford, Va., December 2, 1903. Children: Winnie May, Florrie Maddox, Robert Edwin, Allie Almond, Ruby Vernella, and Hazel Braswell.

(d) Robert Edwin, born December 7, 1864; died October 3, 1928.

(e) William Winfree, born April 18, 1866; married Ella Hunley of Richmond, Va. Children: William Winfree, Jr., and Aubry. They now live in New Jersey.

(f) Jessie M., born March 1, 1868; died January 27, 1888.

(g) Louie Clifford, born January 8, 1874; married Kate Myers. No children. Live in Cleveland, Ohio.

(h) Richard, born September 5, 1871; died December 9, 1873.

(i) Sallie May, born March 4, 1874; married Invin Bininger. No children.

(j) Laura Vixella, born January 8, 1876; married George Echols. Children: four. Live in Richmond, Va.

(k) Kate, born February 17, 1877; married Dr. Thomas Wisdom Repass, January 12, 1899, of Bland County, Va. Children: Robert Jeter, born April 19, 1900; Thomas Harold, born April 15, 1902; Rufus Brown, born March 16, 1906. Dr. Repass died November 8, 1927.

(l) Ida Blanche, born November 12, 1879; married Dr.
Ralph Waldo Emerson. Children: Ralph and Donald.
Live in Plainfield, New Jersey.

(m) Georgia Turpin, born August 17, 1882; married Leone
John Cutler (born February 20, 1882), November 29,
1913. One child: Mary Katherine, born February 21,
1916.

(n) Mary Gay, born February 15, 1884; married Harry D.
Garst, September 26, 1906. One child: Harry Latane.
Live in Huntington, W. Va.

Dr. John Abraham Jeter was educated at Richmond Medical
College and practiced medicine on the north side of Bedford
County.

(5) Robert Hall, born April 19, 1835, married Lucy Ann Hatcher,
November 10, 1857.

CHILDREN:

(a) Cora Frances, born September 6, 1858; married J. S.
Thomas, December 12, 1877.

(b) Lelia Judson, born February 27, 1860; married James
V. Cobbs, November 3, 1886.

(c) Sallie Robert, born November 20, 1861; married Jessie
B. Falls, December 22, 1882.

(d) Nettie Lucy, born October 29, 1864; married D. S.
Lankford, October 12, 1887.

(e) John E., born September 26, 1866; married Luella Noell,
February 13, 1901.

(f) Mary James, born February 19, 1869; married A.
Fuqua Bowles, October 9, 1895.

(g) Ossie Bell, born August 29, 1871; married John E. Key,
June 6, 1894.

(h) Robert Kemper, born January 15, 1873; married Champie Spencer, April 28, 1910.

(i) Lucy Mc., born August 4, 1876; married C. E. Ramsey,
November 10, 1907.

Robert Hall Jeter was a soldier in the Confederate Army, enlisting in Company "A," 2nd Virginia Cavalry. He was made
prisoner near Stannardsville, Va., and was held at Washington
for several months. and then thirteen months at Fort Delaware.

After the War he was Commissioner of the Revenue of Bedford County for many years. He died January 10, 1922, in the home in which he had spent his long life, and which had descended to him from his grandfather, Henry Jeter. He was a Confederate soldier, his father a Captain in the War of 1812 and his grandfather, a Lieutenant in the Revolutionary War. His descendants have every right to be proud of the patriotism of their ancestors, who have answered their country's call whenever the alarm has been sounded.

Lucy (Hatcher) Jeter was the daughter of Julius H. and Fannie (White) Hatcher and died June 16, 1906.

(6) Susan E., born December 8, 1837; married (first) Samuel Poindexter in March, 1854.

CHILDREN:

(a) Susan; married Purnell Coffee.
(b) Willie; married Jennie Noell.
(c) Emmett; married Pearl Hunter.
(d) Thomas; married ——— Waldron.
(e) Jerry; killed on Railroad.
(f) Samuel; married Samuel Callahan.

Susan Jeter Poindexter married (second) James T. Leftwich.

CHILDREN:

(a) Gilmore; married Lucy Watts.
(b) Ruth; married ——— Lacy; now dead.
(c) Jeter; unmarried.

(7) Mary Bell, born 1841; married J. B. Crenshaw and lived in Lynchburg, Va.

CHILDREN:

(a) Cary J.; married Mabel Beck.
(b) Lucy Jordan; married W. I. Daugherty.
(c) Warren; married twice.
(d) Ottie; married (first) Nathaniel Eubank; (second)
——————.
(e) Jessie; married Samuel Hudson.
(f) Eliza; married Frank Monell.
(g) Samuel; died unmarried.

(h) Mary Will; married (first) Steven Pattee; (second) Frank Erb.

(8) Cary Robinson, born 1843; killed in the Battle of Seven Pines, during the Civil War.

....

Samuel Jeter, third son of Thomas and Winifred Jeter, of Amelia County, Va., married (first) —————; (second) "Mene(?) Moody (alias Ellison)," April 4, 1777, in Chesterfield County, Va.

He died in Amelia County in 1793. His will, made June 8, 1793 (Will Book No. 4, page 343), mentions: Olive Jeter (when single called Olive Craddock); daughter, Frances Parkes Jeter; sons, Tilman Jeter, Ellison Jeter, Thos. Ellett Jeter, and Samuel Beverly Jeter. It also mentions his brother Oliver Jeter.

THE SOUTH CAROLINA JETERS

William Jeter, believed to have been the son of John Jeter, the immigrant, bought land in Amelia County, Virginia, in 1751. The deed to this land, dated October 24, 1751, reads, "William Jeter of Caroline County." When he sold this land the following year to his brother, Thomas Jeter, his deed reads, "William Jeter of Lunenburg County," so we know that he removed from Caroline to Lunenburg between October of 1751 and June of 1752.

He married, about 1741, Margaret Vaughan, daughter of Martin and Elinor Vaughan of Caroline County, and grand-daughter of Cornelius and Elizabeth Vaughan of Spotsylvania County, Virginia.

Cornelius Vaughan died in Spotsylvania before 1750, and two of his sons, Cornelius and Martin, are mentioned in the records of that county. His wife, Elizabeth, died in Spotsylvania, November 14, 1775. Legatees mentioned in her will are, "my four children which are now alive, and my son Martin's four children, his part to be equally divided amongst them, Cornelius Vaughan, Bridget Broadus, Elizabeth Pemberton, and Margaret Geter." (Will Book "E," 1772-1798, page 251.)

On April 6, 1761, Martin Vaughan of Caroline County and Elinor, his wife, sold to John Bullard of Spotsylvania County, 233 acres of land in Spotsylvania, this being a part of a tract purchased by Cornelius Vaughan, Sr., of John Foster and conveyed by said Foster to Cornelius and the said Martin Vaughan, sons of Cornelius Vaughan, dec'd, as by deed of June 5, 1750.

A deed, recorded in Spotsylvania County, made by Cornelius Vaughan (Jr.) in 1750, is signed also by his wife, Frances Vaughan.

The names of William Jeter and his wife, Margaret, appear frequently in the records of Lunenburg County until 1769. Those of his son, William, Jr., and his daughter, California, who married Bartholemew Baker, are likewise mentioned, and Craddock Vaughan and his wife, Parthenia, appear in the records of Halifax County, which county was formed from Lunenburg.

From Lunenburg, William Jeter, took his wife and those children, who were not already married and settled in Virginia, to South Carolina and established a home in Edgefield District, where he died in 1797.

The story of the bravery of his wife, Margaret, has been handed down, from generation to generation, in his family, and has been contributed to this sketch by his great-great-grand-daughter, Mrs. Virginia (Jeter) Wilson, of Union, South Carolina.

MARGARET JETER AND THE BRITISH SOLDIERS

At the outbreak of the Revolutionary War, William Jeter and his wife, Margaret, were living in Edgefield District, South Carolina. They and their youngest children had come from Virginia some years before and had prospered greatly, owning much land, many slaves and a large sum of gold.

A young couple who lived near them had died a number of years before the war, leaving an only child, a little boy, whom his mother had given to Margaret, who had loved him as her own. He was now old enough to bear arms and was with the American forces. However, he soon sold himself to the British as a spy.

It was an easy matter for him to make frequent visits to the home of his foster parents, to whom he seemed most deeply attached, always appearing most solicitous concerning the welfare of "Father." On learning that the British Soldiers were nearing that part of the country William placed his gold in kegs, said to be seven of them, and, with the assistance of a faithful African slave, Toby, they carried it and buried it, at midnight, in a cluster of five oak trees near the house. The British had heard of William's gold and had determined to possess it.

A squad of soldiers in charge of an officer came to the Jeter home to search for the gold. They prowled through the entire dwelling and every outbuilding on the plantation, ripped open all the beds and quilts, and burned the pillows. Finding nothing of value they were much enraged and seizing Toby, who was always to be found near his mistress, they handled him very roughly, commanding him to show them where the gold was hidden, and to lead them to his master. Toby stoutly denied any knowledge of the money or of his master's whereabouts. They then built a huge fire, and placing his feet to it, kept them there until the soles were baked. Their efforts proving fruitless, they left, vowing to come again and not leave until the treasure was found.

The young man made another visit to "Mother," who told him that "Father" hoped for an opportunity to come home about a certain time. This was told, also, to the British, who, secretly, kept a watch over the premises.

William came, was surprised and captured in his own home. Threats of torture and death had no effect on the courageous American, so, as in Toby's case, they resorted to torture by fire. Taking two forked sticks and implanting them firmly in the ground, they built a fire between them, and, binding William hand and foot, hung him over the blaze.

When Margaret saw what the villains were about fury possessed her soul. Looking quickly for some weapon with which to defend her husband, she seized a reap hook, which was hanging on a wall nearby, and rushed to his assistance. In desperation she threw herself in the midst of her enemies, cutting and slashing, right and left, with all her might. The British were terrified and, in their agony, ran from the avenging fury, as if all the American soldiers were at their heels. William was released from his perilous position and, in a short while, was entirely recovered from the effects of his ordeal.

A few days after this occurrence Cornwallis went to the Jeter home. Margaret saw him coming, and, nothing daunted, met him at the door. Removing his hat, he made a low bow, and, extending his hand, said, "My respects to the bravest woman I ever saw." Stepping back, Margaret put her hands behind her, saying, "My hands are for my friends, and not for robbers and murderers." Cornwallis showed no displeasure at this thrust, but continued, "Had I an army of such soldiers as you, I had quelled this rebellion long since." With a look of defiance she replied, "Then you would have the women to reckon with."

Cornwallis must have greatly admired her indomitable spirit for he gave orders that she should never more be molested.

CHILDREN OF WILLIAM AND MARGARET (VAUGHAN) JETER WERE:

(1) William. (See forward.)
(2) Parthenia; married Craddock Vaughan; died in Halifax County, Virginia.
(3) Ancridge; married ———— Howlett; son, Seth.
(4) California; married Bartholemew Baker; lived in Lunenburg County, Virginia.
(5) Hal.
(6) Joseph; Ensign in Revolutionary Army under Captain Street; appointed in Lunenburg County, Virginia.
(7) Cornelius. (See forward.)
(8) James. (See forward.)
(9) Argulus.
(10) Eleazer. (See forward.)
(11) Elizabeth; married ———— Cruze; son William.
(12) Sarah; married ———— Crosby.
(13) Nancy; married ———— Moseley; son, George.
(14) Delilah; married ———— Garrett.
(15) Priscilla; married ———— Moseley; daughter, Sallie.
(16) Margaret (Peggy); married Minor Kilcrease.

The will of William Jeter follows:

Last will and testament proved in open Court by the oath of Edmund Holeman and ordered to be recorded, March Term, 1797. Rd. Tutt, O. E. D.

In the name of God amen the twenty fifth day of November in the year of our Lord one thousand seven hundred and ninety three, I William Jeter of Edgefield County and Ninety Six District in the State of South Carolina, planter, being aged and feeble of body but of perfect mind and memory, thanks be to God for the same, and therefore calling the mortality of my body and knowing that it is appointed for all men once to die do make and ordain this my last will and testament, that is to say:

Principally and first of all I recommend my sould into the hands of Almighty God that gave it and my body I recommend to the earth to be buried in a decent like Christian like burial at the discretion of my executors nothing doubting but at the general resurrection I shall receive the same again by the mighty power of Almighty God and receive the salvation through the merits of blessed Lord and Savior, Jesus Christ, and as touching such worldly goods wherewith it has pleased God to bless me in this life, I give demise and dispose of the same in the following manner and form. . . .

IMPRIMIS

Item. I lend my beloved wife, Margaret Jeter, all my whole estate both real and personal that I am now possessed with her life time or widowhood.

Item. I will and bequeath unto Margaret, my dearly beloved wife, one feather bed and furniture—being the bed we now usually lie upon or in, one dark bay mare known by the name of Fancy, one cow and calf and three head of sheep.

Item. I give and bequeath unto my well beloved son, William Jeter, four hundred acres of land, one negro man named Ned, one feather bed and furniture, all which being put into his possession with other household furniture as likewise to him and his heirs forever.

Item. I give unto my daughter, Partheny Vaughn, one hundred acres of land, one feather bed and furniture, one mare, saddle and bridle with all which I had formerly given her and put into her possession unto her and her heirs forever.

Item. I give and bequeath unto my daughter, Ancridge Howlet, the goods and chattels that I formerly lent her as also a debt of twenty one pounds, two shillings & eight pence half penny Virginias currency now due to me by Cradock Vaughn, unto her and her heirs forever, as also one hundred acres of land which I give to my grandson Seth Nowlet lying between the mire branch and the red lick branch.

Item. I give and bequeath unto my daughter, Calpharna Baker, one tract of fifty acres of land, two mares, seddale and bridle and other household furniture which I have formerly given and put into her possession to her and her heirs forever.

Item. I give and bequeath unto my son, Hal Jeter, a wagon and horse which I now have lent him all my lands lying from the back line to the old road running by Samuel Hills on both sides of Gunnells Creek to him and his heirs forever.

Item. I give and bequeath unto my son, Joseph Jeter, one negro girl called Edy to him and his heirs forever.

Item. I give and bequeath unto my son, Cornelius Jeter, one mulatto boy called Boson and one cow and calf which he now has in his possession, to him and his heirs forever.

Item. I give and bequeath unto my son, James Jeter, two negroes known by the name of Jack and Hannah one hundred acres of land and plantation whereon he now lives together with a negro boy named Phill, which land and boy he now has in possession, to him and his heirs forever.

Item. I give and bequeath unto my son, Argalus Jeter, one negro boy known by the name of Isaac, one sorrel stallion, called Spiddill which he hath now in possession, to him and his heirs forever.

Item. I give and bequeath unto my son, Eliazer Jeter, the plantation and land whereon I now live up Gunnels Creek to the road dividing between Hal Jeter that has been heretofore mentioned, one negro boy named Sam, one cow and calf, one black stallion colt, three head of sheep and one feather bed and furniture to him and his heirs forever.

Item. I give and bequeath unto my daughter, Elizabeth Cruze, one negro girl called Jude, one negro boy I give to my grandson, William Cruze, named Bob, to them and their heirs forever.

Item. I give and bequeath unto my daughter, Sarah Crosby, one negro girl called Edy which she now has in possession, to her and her heirs forever.

Item. I lend unto my daughter Nancy Moseley, during her life one hundred Acres of land adjoining Jno. Kilcrease and Henry Key surveyed for & granted to me by the Honble at her death, I give unto my grandson George Moseley, son of Nancy Moseley, all the aforesaid land of one hundred acres and fifteen pounds sterling after the death of my wife which I desire may be put at lawful interest til his arrival to twenty one years of age.

Item. I give unto my daughter, Delilah Garret, one feather bed which she has received to her and her heirs forever.

Item. I give and bequeath unto my daughter Priscilla Mosely, one cow and calf to my granddaughter Sallie Mosely, daughter of Priscilla Mosely, one hundred and twenty acres of land lying on the upper side of red lick branch waters of Gunnels Creek.

Item. I lend unto my daughter Peggy Kilcrease, one negro girl called Tamer and one feather bed which she now has in possession and one bay stallion colt by the name of Jubiter and if she dies without living issue to be divided as hereinafter mentioned and I give unto my daughter Peggy Kilcrease One Hundred and Fifty Acres of land whereon she now lives provided that there should not be a charge of a certain sorrel horse by Minor Kilcrease husband of my daughter Peggy against my estate.

Item. I leave all my estate that has not been heretofore mentioned to be divided in the following manner, viz.:

One sixth part to Hal Jeter, one sixth part to Cornelius Jeter, one sixth part to Eliazer Jeter, one sixth part to Geo. Moseley, sone of my daughter Nancy Moseley, one sixth part to Sallie Moseley, daughter of my daughter Priscilla Moseley, and one sixth part to my daughter Peggy Kilcrease.

Item. I do constitute and ordain Margaret Jeter, my beloved wife, my friend John Martin and my son, Hal Jeter, the sole executors of this my last will and testament & I do utterly disallow, revoke, disannul all and every other former testament, wills, legacies, bequeaths, executed by me at any wise before named, willed, bequeathed, and confirming this and no other to be my last will and testament.

IN WITNESS whereof I have set my hand and seal the day and year first above written.   (Signed) WM. JETER [SEAL].

Signed, sealed and acknowledged
in the presence of

EDMUND HOLLEMAN
MERRYMAN COOK . . . his mark.
ELEANOR COOK . . . her mark.

Interlined before assigned the words and if she dies without leaving issue to be divided as is hereafter mentioned of a certain sorrel horse.

Recorded in Will Book A, pages 114-117.

A True Copy:

W. T. KINNAIRD [SEAL],
Judge of the Court of Probate in and
for the County of Edgefield,
State of South Carolina.

Edgefield, S. C., January 10, 1929.

William Jeter, Jr., son of William, Sr., and Margaret (Vaughan) Jeter, was born about 1743, no doubt, in Caroline County, Virginia. The first authentic record that has been found of him is his marriage bond in Mecklenburg County, Virginia, to Lucy Speed, dated December 12, 1780, and signed by Dabney Phillips as security. Then, in 1781, a grant of 401 acres of land was made to him in Lunenburg County, but he did not remain much longer in Virginia, for the South Carolina Census Report of 1790 shows that he had already followed his father into Edgefield District, and lists him with "2 males over 16, 3 under 16, 6 females and 12 slaves."

In the Caroline County records, now in the Archives Department of the Virginia State Library (Public Claim No. 3998), William Jeter is allowed payment at the October Court, 1781, for "One grass fed beef—adjudged to weigh two hundred and fifty pounds—taken for Public use" etc. No proof has been found that this is William who married Lucy Speed, but no other William is known at that time except his father, who was then living in Lunenburg County.

William Jeter, Jr., died in Edgefield District, South Carolina, September 7, 1820. His will, recorded there, mentions heirs: Jos., Thos., Jno., and Martin Phillips, children of Charlotte Phillips; Edmund Martin and wife; Wm. Williams and wife; W. C. Mantz and wife; 2 Glover grandchildren; grandchildren, Lucy and Charles Jeter.

Sally Jeter, daughter of William, Jr., and Lucy (Speed) Jeter married, January 28, 1810, Edmund Randolph Martin of Edgefield District, South Carolina, who was born December 28, 1784.

FROM THE BIBLE OF LUCY SPEED:

Lucy Speed's book, the gift of her Father, March 1, 1772, with his register transcribed. James Speed and Mary Pulley, our Grandfather and Grand-mother, were married the 6th of September, 1711, by the Rev. John Cargill in Surry Co., Va., and both died in the same county. He was born in old England and died March 5, 1719—aged 39 years, 5 months and 6 days. She was born in Virginia and died June 3, 1733, aged 40 years and 19 days.

They had four sons, viz.: James, born June 16, 1712; John, born Feb. 5, 1714; William, born Feb. 19, 1716; and Thomas, born Apr. 29, 1719.

John Speed and Mary Taylor, our Father and Mother, were married Oct. 6, 1737, by Rev. Henry Wilbeck in Surry Co., Va. They had seven sons and four daughters, viz.: John, born Aug. 3, 1838; James, born Mar. 4, 1739; Henry, born Mar. 28, 1742; Sarah, born Feb. 14, 1743; Lewis, born Jan. 26, 1745; Martha, born Aug. 11, 1748; Joseph, born May 27, 1750; Lucy, born Apr. 11, 1752; Matthias, born June 18, 1754; one son born dead July 29, 1756; Mary, born Sept. 30, 1758; lived two months.

William Jeter and Lucy Speed were married Dec. 12, 1780, by the Rev. John Cameron in Mecklenburg County, Va. One son born Nov. 9, 1781, lived a half hour. William Jeter, born Feb. 18, 1783; Sallie Jeter, born Dec. 8, 1785; George Jeter, born Nov. 27, 1786; died Sept. 15, 1789; John Speed Jeter, born June 20, 1789; died Apr. 14, 1847; Martha M. Jeter, born July 31, 1791.

Sally Jeter married Edmund Martin.

John Speed Jeter married Sabra Simkins of Edgefield, S. C., Sept. 8, 1814.

Martha M. Jeter married William Williams.

Descendants of John Speed Jeter and Sabra Simkins: Sarah Jane, married William A. Harris; John, Virginia, Eliza, Martha, Caroline Simkins; married Rev. C. Bruce Walker of the Episcopal Church; Maria Louise and John—twins.

Register copied by Mrs. Caroline S. Walker from her Grandmother's Bible.

································

By comparing the Bible records of Lucy Speed with the Census Report of 1790 and the will of William Jeter, Jr., we see that Lucy must have been his second wife, for they had only been married ten years in 1790 when he was listed with "2 males over 16, 3 under 16, and 6 females" in his family. All of these could not have been Lucy's children. Then his will mentions "children of Charlotte Phillips and two Glover grand-children." Charlotte does not appear in the Bible records, and neither does the daughter who married ——— Glover. The grandchildren, Lucy and Charles Jeter, were doubtless children of Charles P. Jeter, who married in Mecklenburg County, Virginia,

December 22, 1802, Mary Phillips, daughter of Dabney Phillips. Charles and Mary (Phillips) Jeter also went to Edgefield, South Carolina. The wife of Wm. Mantz, mentioned in the will of William Jeter, Jr., was another daughter by the first wife, no doubt. So it is very probable that he married first in Caroline County and lived there until his second marriage, in 1780.

....

Cornelius Jeter, son of William, Sr., and Margaret (Vaughan) Jeter, was born in Lunenburg County, Virginia, about 1756; and married Sarah Lovelace, daughter of Sir William Lovelace, who came from England and settled first in Maryland, going from there to Georgia during the latter part of the eighteenth century.

Their son, Jesse Lovelace Jeter (born June 4, 1793; died March 10, 1868), married, January 15, 1829, in South Carolina, Sarah Crosby Jeter, youngest daughter of James and Mary (Crosby) Jeter.

CHILDREN:

(1) William Lovelace; died in infancy.
(2) Mary Crosby; died in infancy.
(3) David Eliezer, born February 14, 1832; married Elizabeth Lee.
(4) James Jefferson, born October 3, 1833. (See forward.)
(5) Laura Ann, born July 4, 1835; married (first) Wesley Busby;
    (second) T. J. Whittle.
(6) Mary Louise, born October 6, 1836; died unmarried.
(7) Thomas Berry, born January 18, 1838. (See forward.)
(8) Sara Elizabeth Lovelace, born February 4, 1839. (See forward.)
(9) Jesse Lovelace, born November 22, 1840; died unmarried.
(10) Araminta Brooks; died in infancy.
(11) Antoinette Rebecca; died in infancy.
(12) John Brooks, born April 8, 1844. (See forward.)
(13) Charles Washington, born December 13, 1845; died unmarried.
(14) Cornelius Burwell, born August 7, 1847.
(15) Aletha Eugenia, born June 22, 1849; married W. Dexter Groves.
    No children.
(16) Jane Bruce; died in infancy.

All of these seven brothers who grew to manhood were Confederate soldiers. All were wounded in battle, but none died during the War.

James Jefferson Jeter, son of Jesse L. and Sarah Crosby (Jeter), married, August 10, 1866, Julia Frances Eison (born November 30, 1838; died April 8, 1927), daughter of Jacob Eison (born January 1, 1800; died April 25, 1872) and Amelia Stokes Getzen Danner (born October 28, 1810; died September 27, 1853), who were married, March 10, 1831. James J. Jeter died October 27, 1872.

CHILDREN:

(1) Edgar Montrose; died in infancy.
(2) Virginia Lovelace, born May 10, 1868; married Edwin Morgan Wilson in 1886.

CHILDREN:

(a) Eloise; died in infancy.
(b) Charles Eugene, born September 13, 1894; married Geraldine Bell of Mississippi in 1916.
(c) Molina Calvert, born October 25, 1897; married Rev. John C. Neville in 1926.

CHILD:

(aa) John C., Jr., born, May 14, 1928, in Union, South Carolina.

(d) Maude Arundel, born October 8, 1899; married Edward R. de Mucci, of New York, in 1917.
(e) Edwin Morgan, II, born September 14, 1902; married Icely Butler, of Mississippi, in 1925.

CHILD:

(aa) Edwin Morgan, III, died in infancy.

(f) Cecil Calvert, born January 22, 1911.
(3) Ernest Linwood, born July 21, 1869; died August 1, 1905.
(4) Eugene Mumford, born April 17, 1871; died September 11, 1892.
(5) Eula Claude, born January 26, 1872; married Janie Allen in 1893.

CHILDREN:

(a) Virginia Pearl, born August 10, 1894; married Horace Kimbrell in 1912.

CHILDREN:

(aa) Madeline, born October, 1913.
(bb) Lilah, born 1915; died 1917.

(cc) Margaret, born 1917; died 1919.
(b) Eula Eugene, born June 26, 1896; married Ruth McCain
     in 1915.

CHILDREN:

(aa) Mozelle Ruth, born 1916.
(bb) Eula Eugene, born 1918.
(cc) William Elias, born 1923.
(dd) James, born 1925.
(ee) Sarah Elizabeth, born 1927.

(c) Ethel Ferrol, born August 8, 1898; married Lamont De
     Young in 1917.

CHILDREN:

(aa) Ferrol Lamont, born October, 1919.
(bb) Frances Jeter, born January, 1921.

(d) Julia Grace, born November 19, 1900; married Ansel A.
     Vaughan in 1917.

CHILDREN:

(aa) Vera Jeter, born 1918.
(bb) Harry James, born 1920.
(cc) Ansel, Jr., born 1925; died 1928.

(e) Lily Maude, born April 17, 1902; married Isadore
     Vaughan in 1918.

CHILDREN:

(aa) Janie Elizabeth, born 1921.
(bb) Mary Louise, born 1924.
(cc) Isadore, Jr., born 1928.

(f) William Ernest, born July 15, 1904; married Lella
     Roberts in 1923.

CHILDREN:

(aa) Heyward, born 1924.
(bb) Leon, born 1926.
(cc) Geraldine, born 1928.

(g) Dexter Groves, born January 28, 1910.
(6) Agatha Maude, born June 11, 1873; married Harry Eugene
     Mabry in 1903.

CHILD:

(a) Maude Harry, born October 12, 1904; married Simon A. Dixon in 1924.

CHILD:

(aa) Harry Aubrey, born November, 1924.

································

Thomas Berry Jeter, son of Jesse L. and Sarah Crosby (Jeter) Jeter, married, March, 1864, Mary Catherine Busby (born 1842; died 1910), and died in 1889.

CHILDREN:

(1) Jesse Benjamin, born 1878; died 1899.
(2) John Broxie, born February 19, 1880; married, 1912, Corinne Owens (born 1881).

CHILD:

(a) James Reginald, born 1914.

(3) Jacob Busby, born February 19, 1882; unmarried.
(4) Sarah Eva, born 1887; died 1915; married (first), 1904, Jack Hodges, (died in 1906); (second) C. D. Shealy.

································

Sara Elizabeth Jeter, daughter of Jesse L. and Sarah Crosby (Jeter) Jeter, married Laurie M. Groves (born 1846; died 1912), and died in 1900.

CHILDREN:

(1) Sarah Maude, born June 12, 1873; married in 1897, De Leon Lynch. No children.
(2) Nina Josephine, born December, 1874; married, 1897, Pierre C. Mellichamp.

CHILD:

(a) Pierre C., Jr., born 1904; married Grace Layton, 1923.

CHILD:

(aa) Laurie M., born 1924.

(3) Annie Laurie, born January 6, 1878; unmarried.

································

John Brooks (Broxie) Jeter, son of Jesse Lovelace and Sarah Crosby (Jeter) Jeter, of Santuc, South Carolina, married, March 25,

1874, Augusta Ann Glen (born October 14, 1840; died February 23, 1885), daughter of Thomas Cole and Margaret Eliza (Artman) Glen of Charleston, South Carolina.

CHILDREN:

(1) Herbert, born 1875; died in infancy.
(2) Grace Augusta, born July 30, 1877; married in Charleston, South Carolina, June 13, 1911, Jesse Marcellus Cooper.

CHILDREN:

(a) Mable Louise, born June 4, 1914.
(b) Ruth Augusta, born March 23, 1918.
(3) Mable Broxie, born July 9, 1879.

James Jeter, son of William, Sr., and Margaret (Vaughan) Jeter, was born January 15, 1759, and died in Union County, South Carolina, March 16, 1840. (Dates taken from his tombstone.)

He was a soldier in the Revolution, serving under Colonel Brandon in South Carolina Militia, his immediate officers being Major Otterson, and Captains Hopkins and Winn. He served thirteen months and three days. He was at the Siege of Ninety-six and Battle of King's Mountain. (This information was obtained from the War Department in Washington, D. C.)

James Jeter married in 1782, Mary Crosby, daughter of David Crosby of Fairfield District, S. C.

This interesting story was also contributed by Mrs. Virginia (Jeter) Wilson:

MARY CROSBY, POCAHONTAS OF SOUTH CAROLINA

James Jeter, son of William and Margaret Jeter, was wounded in the shoulder while engaged in the Siege of Ninety-six. While his wound was not serious, he was unable to engage in active duty, but was, for the time being, detailed as a scout. While acting in this capacity, he, with two other American soldiers, was captured by a band of English bushwhackers just after crossing Broad River into Fairfield County, in 1781.

The English soldiers took the three Americans to the home of David Crosby, a farmer of Fairfield County, where they demanded food and shelter for themselves and captives.

It is not known what stand David Crosby had taken in the fight for freedom from England's hated rule, but his daughter, Mary, hated with intense vehemence every redcoat on American soil.

After partaking of the evening meal the American soldiers were bound hand and foot and locked in a room, the English occupying another. Mary noiselessly crept from the house and placed herself underneath a window of the room occupied by the British, and stood there—eavesdropping.

They were calmly discussing plans for the next day, chief among them being the execution of the three American prisoners. They decided to shoot them the next morning at sunrise.

Terror filled Mary's heart, and, falling on her knees, she prayed God to help her save James Jeter, if no one else. Going to her father she told him what she had overheard and implored him to do what he could for the young men to prevent the British from carrying out their terrible plan. "O, Father," she said, "you must save James Jeter! He is too young to be shot; he has such beautiful black eyes; such pretty black curly hair—he is too pretty to be shot! O, Father, don't let them shoot him! Father! Father! Save him! You must not let him die!"

David Crosby undoubtedly had some influence with the British, for the next morning, before daylight, they and James' two companions quietly left David Crosby's house, leaving James behind, unmolested. Nothing more was ever known of the two American patriots or their captors, but James returned in about a year and married sweet Mary Crosby. A long, happy and prosperous life together was theirs, and many of their descendants, even to the seventh generation, are able to move hearts with a look from sparkling "black eyes" and a toss of "beautiful black curls."

Note.—I have no record of this occurrence or of that of Margaret (previously given) to prove them either true or false.

They have been handed down from generation to generation, and I have never heard them questioned. Margaret's experiences were well known to her children, and by them told to their children, and so on, 'til now the seventh generation is hearing the story of the bravery of "Grandmother Margaret."

Mary, James' wife, told her story to her children and grandchildren, and two of her grand-daughters—Mrs. Dora Jeter Johnson, and Mrs. Aletha Jeter Groves, my father's youngest sister—told it to me.

VIRGINIA JETER WILSON.

Union, South Carolina,
June 6, 1929.

THE WILL OF JAMES JETER:

South Carolina,
    Union County.

I, James Jeter, being as I hope in some measure thankfull to God for the portion of the goods of this world with which it has pleased him to bless me, and deeming it my duty so to do, for reasons which are satisfactory to myself, to declare how my estate shall be disposed of after my death, I therefore make my will as follows, that is to say:

Imprimis, or in the first, I desire all my just debts, if any, shall be paid.

Secondly. I give and bequeath unto my dearly beloved wife, Mary Jeter, the one tenth part of all my estate, both real and personal to her and her heirs forever. I had intended to have given her more but this she assures me is all she desires.

Thirdly. I give to my Grand-son, William Jeter, son of Eleazer Jeter, one dollar, and *no more of my estate.*

Fourth. I give unto my grand-daughter, Mary Ann Fuller, six hundred dollars ($600.00), and no more.

Fifth. I give to my Grand-son, Francis C. Jeter son of John C. Jeter, one colt called Hemlock, as he has been some time in the company of his grandmother and myself.

Sixth. And all the rest, residue and remainder of my estate of what kind or nature soever, and wheresoever situated I give and bequeath to be equally divided amongst my nine following named children, and these only. That is to say, A. V. Jeter, James Jeter, Elizabeth Gregory, wife of Benjamin J. Gregory, L. B. Jeter, John C. Jeter, Richard C. Jeter, Thomas C. Jeter, David S. Jeter and Sally Jeter the wife of Jesse Jeter.

Seventh. I do hereby revoke all former wills by me made, and declare this as my true last and testament, and appoint my sons, James

Jeter, L. B. Jeter and David Jeter, my executors not doubting they will faithfully execute the same, which I have this day acknowledged as my act before these witnesses.

JAMES JETER [SEAL].

We hereby testify that Jas. Jeter acknowledged his
name to this paper and assured us he heard it read,
and that we signed our names in his presence, at his
request and in presence of each other, done this 4th, July, 1839.

B. ELLIS.
JNO. JENNINGS.
R. G. HOBSON.

South Carolina,
Union County.   By J. J. PRATT, *Esq., Ordinary.*

Personally appeared before me R. G. Hobson who being duly sworn on the Holy Evangelist of Almighty God, doth make oath and say that he heard James Jeter acknowledge the signature and herewith pronounce and declare this same to be his last will and testament. That he, the said James Jeter was then of sound and disposing mind, memory, and understanding to the best of this deponent's knowledge and belief, and that B. Ellis and John Jennings together with this deponent did sign their names thereto as witnesses at the request and in the presence of the testator and in the presence of each other.

Given under my hand this first day of June, 1840.

J. J. PRATT, *O. U. D.*

CHILDREN OF JAMES AND MARY (CROSBY) JETER WERE:

(1) William, born 1783; died in early manhood.
(2) Eliezer, born 1785; married and had two sons: Frank and William.
(3) Argulus V., born December 23, 1786; died August 6, 1849; married Mrs. Matilda (McDaniel) Dugan, widow of James Dugan.

CHILDREN:

(a) James B.; married Elizabeth Harden.
(b) Singleton A.; unmarried; was mortally wounded in Battle of Cold Harbor in 1864.

(c) Thomas C.; married Julia Sartor.

(d) Jane; married (first) Capt. Jack Giles; (second) Capt. James Douglass.

(e) Frances; married Col. Robert W. Beaty.

(4) Elizabeth, born January 2, 1791; died May 18, 1851; married Benjamin Gregory.

CHILDREN:

Harrison, John, Thomas, Andrew, Frank, Pickens, Adolphus, Starks, and Elvira who married Dr. James Gregory.

(5) James R., born 1792; died January 26, 1867; married Elizabeth Hobson. (See Hobson family.)

CHILDREN:

(a) Antoinette; married Dr. J. P. Knight.

(b) Gilliam Hobson; married Leonora Hamilton. (See forward.)

(c) Martha N.; died unmarried.

(d) Mary Anne; died unmarried.

(e) John Randolph; married Ophelia Hamilton. (See forward.)

(f) Cicely Sarah Jane; married Reuben Gilliam Thomas. (See forward.)

(g) Susannah; died unmarried.

(6) Little Berry, born February 1, 1793; died January 19, 1874. (See forward.)

(7) John Crosby, born December 15, 1795; died September 12, 1845. (See forward.)

(8) Mary Crosby, born April 6, 1797; died 1835; married Messer Fuller.

CHILD:

(a) Mary Ann; married Robert Knight.

(9) Richard Crosby, born March 3, 1799; went to Mississippi and married Augusta Ann Mitchell.

CHILDREN:

(a) Buck.

(b) Elvira.

(10) Thomas Crosby, born October 6, 1801. (See forward.)

(11) David Sims; died unmarried; was a man of substance and influence in his community.

(12) Sarah Crosby, born November 5, 1805; died January 26, 1875;
married Jesse Lovelace Jeter, son of Cornelius and Sarah
(Lovelace) Jeter.

Gilliam Hobson Jeter, son of James R. and Elizabeth (Hobson)
Jeter, was born January 7, 1830, and died April 23, 1903. He served
in Company "C," 7th South Carolina Cavalry Regiment, of the Confederate Army; was promoted to First Lieutenant, and at the end of
the war was serving as Captain of his company, the Captain having
been promoted to rank of Lieutenant Colonel. He married, November
24, 1863, Lenora Frances Hamilton, who was born April 7, 1841;
died April 21, 1883; was a graduate of Spartanburg Female College,
South Carolina.

CHILDREN:

(1) Paul Hamilton; married, November 22, 1891, Mary Eva Jeter,
daughter of William Tecumseh and Nannie (Coleman) Jeter.
Their home is at Carlisle, S. C.

CHILDREN:

(a) Gilliam Hobson, born October 31, 1892; married,
November 10, 1915, Genie Marion Crowder.

CHILDREN:

(aa) Mary Frances.
(bb) Jean Crowder.

(b) William Tecumseh, Jr., born May 10, 1894; married
Minnie Fleming.

CHILDREN:

(aa) Mary Fleming.
(bb) Nancy Evelyn.
(cc) Elizabeth.

(c) Robert David, born December 24, 1895; died October
14, 1906.

(d) John Randolph, born October 15, 1898; married Dorothy Sullivan.

CHILD:

(aa) John Randolph, Jr.

(e) Nannie Leonora, born September 10, 1899; died June 13, 1900.

(f) Nancy Coleman, born February 28, 1901; married Luke J. Wilburn.

(g) Paul Hamilton, Jr., born September 24, 1903.

(h) Mary Evelyn, born April 6, 1906; married Earl Patrick.

(i) Joseph Hampton, born January 27, 1908.

(2) Mattie.

(3) Annie Gilliam, born December 12, 1868; died December 30, 1914; educated at Clifford Seminary, South Carolina, and Williamston Female College (now Lander College), South Carolina; married (first), June, 1889, Summer S. Smith, who died in 1897, leaving no children.

She married (second), June 29, 1904, George W. Going.

CHILDREN:

(a) James Clyde, born July 5, 1905; educated in schools of Union, South Carolina, Wofford Fitting School, College of Charleston, and University of South Carolina where he received the degree of LL. B. in 1927. Member of Pi Kappa Phi Fraternity at College of Charleston, and Phi Delta Phi Legal Fraternity at the University.

In July, 1927, he began the practice of law in his home town, Union, as junior member of the firm of Thomas and Going.

He married, November 28, 1928, Sarah Elizabeth Bell, of Spartanburg, South Carolina, who graduated from Converse College, South Carolina, in 1926.

(b) George Washington, Jr., born April 1, 1909; educated at schools of Union, South Carolina, and at Carlisle School, Bamberg, South Carolina, where he graduated in 1929. He was Captain of Cadet Company "B," while at Carlisle.

(4) Ophelia Parham, born September 15, 1873; attended Clifford Seminary and other private schools; married, December 25, 1904, Joseph Gary Going, M. D.

CHILDREN:

(a) Cleo, born June 12, 1907; now a student at Brevard Institute, N. C.

(b) Joseph Gary, Jr., born December 7, 1913; now a student in the Union High School.

....

John Randolph Jeter, son of James R. and Elizabeth (Hobson) Jeter, was born December 10, 1836, and died October 15, 1891. On November 30, 1859, he married L. A. Ophelia Hamilton, who was born May 3, 1837, and died January 27, 1907. (See Hamilton family.)

CHILDREN:

(1) Gilliam H., born October 27, 1860.

(2) James Parham, born January 2, 1862; died June 22, 1926; married, April 23, 1890, Mary Elizabeth Jeter, daughter of James Thomas and Catherine Elizabeth (Mobley) Jeter. Mrs. Jeter lives at Santuck, S. C.

CHILDREN:

(a) Kathleen, born July 20, 1891; married, November 9, 1915, Oscar Thornwell Culp.

CHILDREN:

(aa) Elizabeth, born December 12, 1918.

(bb) Oscar Thornwell, Jr., born November 19, 1925.

(b) John Randolph, born March 8, 1893; died April 6, 1893.

(c) James Parham, Jr., born September 1, 1894.

(d) Robert Russell, born November 26, 1896; married, December 15, 1926, Blanche Redditt.

CHILD:

(aa) James Parham, III, born October 8, 1927.

(e) John Mobley, born October 25, 1898.

(f) Mary Elizabeth (Polly), born April 7, 1901; married April 20, 1922, Curran Sloan Easley.

CHILD:

(aa) Curran Sloan, Jr., born March 11, 1923.

(g) Douglass DeLashmette, born October 26, 1905.

(h) David Hugh, born December 10, 1908.

(3) Edwin Hugh, born December 26, 1863.

(4) Robert Russell, born December 13, 1865; died May 7, 1921; graduated at "The Citadel," Military College of South Carolina (1887); at Medical College of South Carolina (1889); located at Whitmire, South Carolina, in 1889, and practiced his profession (M. D.) for a number of years; later Secretary-Treasurer of Glenn-Lowry Manufacturing Co., of Whitmire, and at one time also Business Manager for same. He married, April 26, 1899, Agnes Morgan Coleman (born July 16, 1872).

CHILDREN:

(a) Robert Coleman, born July 15, 1900.
(b) Victoria Rice, born January 6, 1902; married, January 11, 1927, George Dexter Sherrill, Jr.

CHILDREN:

(aa) Patricia Ann, born January 3, 1928.
(bb) George Dexter, III, born April 3, 1929.
(c) John Randolph, Jr., born January 8, 1904; married, July 23, 1929, Sara Latimer Rasor.
(d) Agnes Morgan, born February 22, 1908.
(e) Ethel Antoinette, born November 22, 1909.
(f) Russell, born September 17, 1912.

(5) Mary Elizabeth, born March 9, 1868; married Clarence A. Jeter.

CHILDREN:

(a) Adele Coleman, born April 14, 1895; married, February 24, 1916, George W. Thomas. No children.
(b) Jane Antoinette, born October 2, 1897; married, November 24, 1920, Dr. Charles T. Sowell.

CHILDREN:

(aa) Betty Ann.
(bb) Dot Jeter.
(c) Ireneus P., born July 12, 1899; married, June 4, 1923, Florence Parratt.

CHILDREN:

(aa) Jack Hamilton.

(bb) Allen Parratt.

(d) Clarence A., Jr., born March 22, 1902.

(e) Mary Elizabeth, born October 5, 1905; died December 23, 1915.

(f) Grace Muriel, born April 27, 1907.

(g) Bill, born May 27, 1909.

(6) Sue Nora ("Snow"), born June 30, 1871.

(7) Janie Antoinette, born December 15, 1874.

(8) Gary Hamilton, born December 25, 1876.

Cicely Sara Jane Jeter, daughter of James R. and Elizabeth (Hobson) Jeter, married in 1859, Reuben Gilliam Thomas.

CHILDREN:

(1) Elizabeth Frances; married in 1885, W. Fowler Bobo; now deceased.

CHILD:

(a) Minnie Lou; married T. B. Wilkes.

CHILDREN:

(aa) Frances.

(bb) Thomas Lee.

(cc) Malcolm.

(b) William Yancey; married Lillian O'Neal.

CHILDREN:

(aa) Yancey Fowler.

(bb) Ruby.

(cc) Infant.

(c) Eva Grace; married Lt. R. C. Greer.

CHILDREN:

(aa) Robert.

(bb) Betty.

(cc) Donnie.

(dd) William.

(ee) Mary Payne.

(ff) Curtis.

(gg) Infant.

(d) John Kemper Hobson; married Mae Nance.

CHILDREN:

(aa) Angus.

(bb) James Haskell.

(e) James Curtis.

(f) Gilliam.

(2) Annie; deceased.

(3) James Haskell; unmarried.

(4) John Kemper; married, August, 1901, Agnes Louise Thomas. No children.

(5) Lula (deceased).

(6) Woodley Robert (deceased).

(7) Mattie Agnes; married in July, 1900, Thomas M. Sims.

CHILDREN:

(a) Reuben Kemper.

(b) Sara Louise; married in May, 1926, William J. Sparks.

CHILD:

(aa) Bettie Jo.

(c) Mattie Lucile.

(8) Susan; married in December, 1905, Eugene Edwards.

CHILD:

(a) Mary Antoinette; married in August, 1926, Charles William Cooper.

CHILD:

(aa) Charles William, Jr.

(9) Reuben Gilliam (deceased).

....

Little Berry Jeter, son of James and Mary (Crosby) Jeter, married Sarah Hobson, daughter of R. G. Hobson.

CHILDREN:

(1) James Thomas. (See forward.)

(2) Richard Gilliam Hobson; married Kate McJunkin.

(3) John Calhoun Pinckney; married Luella Coleman.

(4) William Hobson; killed in Battle of Cold Harbor—1864.

(5) Sara Jane; married Robert McJunkin.

(6) Cicely; died unmarried.

James Thomas Jeter, born November 28, 1821; died February 25, 1893; son of Little Berry and Sarah (Hobson) Jeter; minister of Baptist Church; married, April 25, 1848, Catherine Elizabeth Mobley (born January 14, 1827; died April 17, 1894).

CHILDREN:

(1) Catherine Mobley, born September 6, 1849; died October 25, 1888; married, May 20, 1869, William Cornwell.

CHILDREN:

(a) William Ely, born April 1, 1871; married Nellie Cornwell.

(b) James Jeter, born April 10, 1873; married Love Jackson.

(c) Lily, born July 6, 1875.

(2) Little Berry, II, born March 13, 1851; married (first), January 3, 1878, Janie Hamilton (born April 1. 1855). (See Hamilton family.)

CHILDREN:

(a) Essie Sims, born January 3, 1879; died October 21, 1879.

(b) Joseph Hamilton, born February 26, 1880.

(c) John Mobley, Jr., born September 7, 1881; married, October 5, 1911, Louise McKissick, who was born February 25, 1891.

CHILDREN:

(aa) Lillian Gilliam, born August 8, 1912.

(bb) Janie Hamilton, born August 12, 1914; died in infancy.

(cc) Joseph McKissick, born July 22, 1915.

(dd) Robert Bothwell, born April 25, 1918.

(ee) Mobley Lewis, born August 18, 1925.

(ff) Louise Fant, born May 17, 1929.

(d) Ethel Lenora, born March 13, 1883; died November 13, 1909; married, June 26, 1907, John Graham O'Keeffe.

CHILD:

(aa) John Jeter, born October 21, 1909.

(e) Little Berry, III, born October 13, 1885; married, April 21, 1914, Nannie Louise McDow, who was born February 5, 1890.

CHILDREN:

(aa) Little Berry, IV, born March 29, 1916.
(bb) Richard Parham, born September 2, 1918.
(cc) John McDow, born July 4, 1921.

(f) Robert Parham, born December 31, 1888; married, June 6, 1921, Sara Little.

(g) Frank Hamilton, born May 2, 1891; educated at Clemson College, from which he graduated in 1911; since 1914, editor for School of Agriculture of North Carolina State College; contributor to *Southern Planter* (Virginia), oldest farm journal in America; married, June 8, 1915, Irene Annie Albert; lives in Raleigh, North Carolina.

Little Berry Jeter, II, married (second), March 24, 1807, Addie Crosby, who was born August 31, 1866.

CHILDREN:

(h) Malcolm Crosby, born February 4, 1899; married, October 23, 1924, Mary Earline Wilson.

(i) Sarah Mildred, born March 16, 1900; married, December 25, 1925, Francis Marion Strock.

CHILD:

(aa) Francis Marion, Jr., born October 4, 1926.

(j) Kate Mobley, born March 21, 1901; married, May 25, 1928, Lewis Talmadge Strother.

CHILD:

(aa) Jean Bergen, born July 17, 1929.

(k) Flournoy Belle, born September 27, 1902.

(l) Stephen Louis (twin), born June 8, 1905; died September 23, 1905.

(m) Mary Louise (twin), born June 8, 1905.

(n) Ida Christine, born December 28, 1906.

(o) Nancy Gillespie, born February 22, 1910.

(3) Sarah Hobson, born October 23, 1852; died November 9, 1874; married, April 21, 1874, J. T. Walker.

(4) John Mobley, born August 17, 1854.

(5) Nancy Thompson, born March 17, 1856; died January 7, 1884.

(6) William Hobson, born April 26, 1863; married, December 13, 1892, Margaret Lucy Farr.

CHILDREN:

(a) Esther Mae, born January 12, 1894; married, August 12, 1913, Arnold Miller Siler.

CHILDREN:

(aa) William Weimer, born August 27, 1914.

(bb) Arnold Jeter, born December 27, 1916.

(b) William LeRoy, born November 28, 1895; died June 22, 1914.

(c) Harold Hubert, born February 2, 1898; married, September 3, 1923, Elizabeth Brown Scott.

CHILD:

(aa) Harold Hubert, Jr., born July 13, 1925.

(d) Margaret Roberta, born April 9, 1900.

(e) William Hobson, Jr., born August 20, 1905.

(7) Mary Elizabeth, born August 14, 1865; married, April 23, 1890, James Parham Jeter, son of John Randolph and Ophelia (Hamilton) Jeter.

(8) James Thomas, Jr., born August 2, 1867; Captain of Medical Corps during World War; now Senator from Union County, South Carolina; married, January 6, 1895, Corrie Belle Jeter, daughter of Rev. Camillus and Elizabeth (Atkinson) Jeter.

CHILDREN:

(a) James Ryan, born December 18, 1895; married, February 20, 1922, Cornelia Caveney.

CHILDREN:

(aa) June, born November 17, 1923.

(bb) Mary Elizabeth, born February 11, 1926.

(cc) James Ryan, Jr., twin of Mary Elizabeth, born
February 11, 1926.

(b) Catherine Elizabeth, born September 1, 1897; married,
June 10, 1926, Ball Edgar Wilkins, Jr.

(c) Manning Thomas, born November 13, 1898; married,
July 20, 1922, Martha McBryde.

CHILD:

(aa) Manning Thomas, Jr., born November 22, 1924.

(d) Camillus Bothwell, born July 4, 1900.

(9) Marion Russell, born April 5, 1869; married Octavia McKay,
November 4, 1889.

CHILDREN:

(a) Marion Russell, Jr., born August 4, 1890; married,
November 4, 1919, R. E. Trotter.

CHILD:

(aa) Grace Elizabeth, born October 17, 1920.

(b) Robert McKay, born September 2, 1891.

(c) Marie Louise, born August 26, 1892; died November 18,
1899.

(d) Rebecca Elizabeth, born May 8, 1894; died December 3,
1894.

(e) Edwin Reuben, born September 21, 1895; married Anna
Roddey Miller, April 26, 1922.

CHILDREN:

(aa) Mary Miller, born February 17, 1923.

(bb) Edwin Russell, Jr., born January 25, 1927.

(f) Alfred B. Williams, born March 10, 1897; died February 18, 1903.

(g) Hugh Donald, born October 9, 1898.

(h) Octavia, born December 14, 1902.

(i) Lois Constance, born December 16, 1905.

(j) Rene Saxby, born December 5, 1908; died February 26,
1910.

(10) Reuben Edward, born April 15, 1871; married Beatrice Winters.

M. Russell Jeter is a farmer and dairyman of Union County, S. C.,
and an elder in the Cane Creek Presbyterian Church. His grandfather,

Little Berry Jeter, Sr., was also an elder in this church. The following story is taken from a sketch of the Cane Creek Church, recently published in *The Union Daily Times:*

"In 1884 it was thought best to move this church from the country to the village of Santuck, where it now stands, and Russell Jeter, then a mere boy, did some of the hauling. The moving spirit in the enterprise was 'Aunt Mary' Russell, the school teacher at forty dollars a month, who spent her last dollar in getting the task done. Her faith was great in the fact that 'the Lord will provide.'

"Much of the work was contributed, but carpenters had to be hired and money was very scarce, the community apparently had dug up the last dollar and Saturday was here when the carpenters had to be paid. Aunt Mary found the situation critical, her last dollar gone, she made another hurried canvass with no success; coming back, she carried Russell in the room and told him they were going to pray over this situation, 'for I know the Lord can provide.' They knelt down and prayed and Russell said he could feel the fifteen dollars he had been saving up all the year to get himself a shotgun slipping away from him. After the prayer was over he told Aunt Mary that he had fifteen dollars she could use. 'There, now. Didn't I tell you the Lord would provide?' Such self-denial must have been a bitter pill at the time but when Christmas came someone sent him a present that covered the situation and we wonder if the influence of that self-denial has not helped him over many rough places since that time."

John Crosby Jeter, son of James and Mary (Crosby) Jeter, was born December 15, 1795, and died September 12, 1845. He was a minister of the Baptist Church, and married, December 23, 1823, Elizabeth Gallman (born March 3, 1803; died October 1, 1852).

CHILDREN:

(1) Camillus, born February 27, 1825; died September 26, 1891; a minister of the Baptist Church; married, February 6, 1849, Margaret Elizabeth Atkinson.

CHILDREN:

(a) Ealetha Eugenia, born February 2, 1851; died April 4, 1860.

(b) John Erastus, born April 9, 1853; died October 10, 1881; married Clara Tucker.

CHILD:

(aa) Daisy Erastus, born February 14, 1881; died October 13, 1914; married, October 23, 1906, Richard Pride Morgan.

CHILD:

(aaa) Richard Erastus, born April 16, 1914.

(c) Margaret Elizabeth, born June 26, 1862; married Rev. Alexander McA. Pittman.

CHILDREN:

Roland, Elizabeth, Jeter, Arthur, Annie Belle, Pearl, and Margaret.

(d) James Woods, born September 20, 1856; died September 21, 1905.

(e) Corrie Belle, born March 29, 1872; married, January 6, 1895, Dr. James Thomas Jeter, Jr., son of James Thomas and Catherine Elizabeth (Mobley) Jeter.

(2) Thomas Bothwell, born October 13, 1827; died May 20, 1883; married Ann H. Thomson (born April 22, 1832; died May 22, 1918), daughter of Wallace and Nancy (Henderson) Thomson. They had no children.

The following sketch of his political career appeared in *The State*, Columbia, S. C., March 2, 1928:

"The governor's office yesterday morning received from Lieutenant Governor T. B. Butler, the portrait of his uncle, Thomas Bothwell Jeter, a former governor of South Carolina, who occupies an unique position in the history of South Carolina, both in the manner in which he became governor and the length of his administration, which was about three months.

"Thomas Bothwell Jeter was elected senator from Union County in 1876, defeating June Mobley, two years after Wade Hampton became governor of this state. Serving as lieutenant governor under the Hampton administration was W. D. Simpson of Laurens.

THOMAS BOTHWELL BUTLER
Lieutenant Governor of South Carolina (1927—)

THOMAS BOTHWELL JETER
Governor of South Carolina (1878)

"A year after his election to the state senate, Thomas B. Jeter was elected president pro tempore of the senate, serving under Lieutenant Governor Simpson who by virtue of that office was president of the senate. In 1878 the Hampton-Simpson ticket again carried in South Carolina, for a second term.

"In February, 1879, however, Governor Hampton resigned his office to take the office of United States senator to which he had been elected shortly after the beginning of his second term. Whereupon Lieutenant Governor Simpson assumed the duties of governor and Mr. Jeter became president of the senate, advancing from the office of president pro tempore.

"Governor Simpson resigned the office of governor in 1880 to take up the duties of chief justice of the supreme court, to which he had been elected the preceding year. Before the election of Governor Simpson, however, as chief justice, Judge Henry McIver, an associate justice, had on December 11, 1879, been unanimously chosen as chief justice. December 15 of the same year, he declined to accept the office, and December 18, Governor Simpson was chosen.

"Nearly a year later, September 1, 1880, Governor Simpson assumed the duties of chief justice, and was succeeded in the governor's office by Governor Jeter, who by virtue of his office as lieutenant governor to which he had advanced from president pro tempore of the senate, filled the unexpired term, a matter of some three months. He retired from the governorship, November, 1880.

"Then developed a question as to whether his office as senator from Union County had been vacated. By a vote of 17 to 9, the judiciary committee decided that the seat had not been vacated and Governor Jeter again assumed the role of senator

"Relative to the question of the vacancy of the Union County senatorship, Governor Jeter addressed the following letter to the senate:

" 'It is a question whether the office of senator from Union County is vacated by my exercising the office of governor of the state.

" 'If the office is vacant, an election should be ordered as soon as practicable, so that Union County may be represented in the senate.

" 'Your body is, by the provisions of the constitution, the proper tribunal to decide the question.

" 'I could not resign the office of senator at the time I assumed the duties of the executive of the state, for the resignation would, of necessity, have included the office of president pro tempore, and by virtue of this office the duties of governor devolved upon me.

THOMAS B. JETER.'

"In 1882 Governor Hagood, who had succeeded him as chief executive of the state, appointed Governor Jeter as a member of the state railroad commission. Prior to his election as senator, Governor Jeter was president of the Spartanburg & Union Railroad Company. He died May 20, 1883.

"Facts on the life of Governor Jeter were provided by Lieutenant Governor Butler, and W. J. Stricklin, secretary to Governor John G. Richards."

(3) Berry Argivis, born April 11, 1829; died 1872; Captain in Confederate Army; married Mary Hill.

(4) Aletha Adelina Eugenia, born August 24, 1831; died September 12, 1850; married Dr. Daniel Sartor.

(5) Mary Adella, born June 9, 1836; married Robert Garlington.

(6) Arsinoe Marcella, born July 25, 1841; died November 20, 1917. (See forward.)

(7) Aurelia Rufena, born January 6, 1843; died October 10, 1867; married Dr. A. Wallace Thomson.

CHILD:

(a) A. Wallace, Jr.

Arsinoe M. Jeter, daughter of Rev. John C. and Elizabeth (Gallman) Jeter, married, October 18, 1860, Dr. Pierce Pickens Butler, a practicing physician of Union, S. C.

CHILDREN:

(1) Janie Perry, born July 23, 1861; died December 17, 1862.
(2) Elise, born November 14, 1862; died May 22, 1924; married, February 26, 1884, Richard Marlborough Foster (born February 6, 1852; died December 17, 1926).

CHILDREN:

(a) Guy Butler, born January 22, 1885; married Katherine Clark.

CHILDREN:

(aa) Floyd Clark.
(bb) Elizabeth.
(cc) Katherine.

(b) Olga Adella, born February 10, 1886; married Stephane Frisard.

CHILDREN:

(aa) Marie Elise.
(bb) Olga Foster.

(c) Arsinoe Belmont, born May 18, 1887; married Harry H. Geiger.

CHILDREN:

(aa) Harry Butler.
(bb) Frances Foster.
(cc) Helen Perry; married O. Stanton Luthi, March 3, 1929.

(d) Richard Columbus, born February 9, 1889; single.
(e) Bothwell Jeter, born April 23, 1890; married Julia McCarroll.

CHILDREN:

(aa) Jack.
(bb) Frank.
(cc) William.
(dd) Mary Jane.

(f) Mary Butler, born November 15, 1892; married Erastus T. Crawford.

CHILD:

(aa) Mary Butler.

(g) Calbraith Perry, born October 2, 1893; married Estella Alverson.

CHILDREN:

(aa) Mary Elizabeth.

(bb) Calbraith Perry, II.

(cc) Earle.

(h) William Leontine, born March 12, 1895; married Ruth Hellams.

CHILDREN:

(aa) Dorothy.

(bb) William Leontine, II.

(i) Robert Pierce, born July 13, 1898; married Cordelia Budgers. No children.

(j) Annie Elise, born July 26, 1903; married Palmer T. Jones.

CHILD:

(aa) Carolyn.

(k) Minnie Ethelind, born October 7, 1905; married Frank C. Cunningham.

CHILD:

(aa) Marjorie.

(3) Perry Pickens, born January 25, 1864; died, unmarried, November 23, 1898.

(4) Thomas Bothwell, member of firm of Butler and Hall, Attorneys-at-law, Gaffney, South Carolina; born January 11, 1866, in Union, South Carolina; educated at South Carolina College; married, November 7, 1899, Annie Wood of Gaffney, who died April 18, 1926; served as Alderman at Union and as Mayor of Gaffney; National Democratic Elector-at-large; County Chairman Democratic Committee; United States Commissioner; member Gaffney Board of Public Works; State Democratic Executive Committeeman for last twenty-five years; vice-president for South Carolina National Council of State Legislatures; in House of Representatives, 1901-1902; in State Senate, 1903-1907, 1919-1926; elected Lieutenant Governor, 1926; inaugurated January 18, 1927.

CHILDREN:

(a) Thomas Bothwell, Jr., born January 18, 1903; graduated with honors from Vanderbilt University before he was twenty-one; now practicing law in Spartanburg, South Carolina.

(b) Ann Jeter, born February 3, 1907; graduated from Converse College, South Carolina, in 1928.

(5) James Leontine, born March 25, 1868; died unmarried, April 17, 1912.

(6) William Matthew, born February 23, 1870; married Ethelind L. Davis.

(7) Jeter, born December 24, 1876; was Member of House of Representatives for one term; unmarried.

Dr. Pierce Pickens Butler, born March 24, 1836; died November 1, 1910; was a son of Dr. William Butler, who was a member of Congress from Greenville District, South Carolina, and died in Arkansas, while there as Indian Agent, and Jane T. (Perry) Butler, sister of Commodore M. C. Perry, who opened the ports of Japan, and of Commodore Oliver H. Perry, who won the famous Battle of Lake Erie.

Dr. Pierce Pickens Butler had six brothers in the Confederate Army, among them General M. C. and Col. William Butler. General Butler, Democrat, represented South Carolina in the United States Senate for eighteen years; was first elected in 1876, just after the overthrow of the Carpet-baggers, making the fight with Gen. Wade Hampton. He was appointed Major-General in the Spanish-American War by President William McKinley.

Dr. P. P. Butler was a Surgeon in the Confederate Army. Another brother, Capt. O. Nathaniel Butler, lost an arm in the service, and General M. C. Butler lost a leg, but both went back into active service and served throughout the remainder of the war.

Thomas Crosby Jeter, son of James and Mary (Crosby) Jeter, was born October 8, 1801; died September 28, 1878; married, December 16, 1830, Mary Tucker, who was born March 11, 1806, and died July 29, 1891.

CHILDREN:

(1) Frances Elizabeth Helen, born December 14, 1831; died May 2, 1912; married, December 14, 1854, Reuben Sims Thomas, son of John and Jemima (Sims) Thomas.

CHILDREN:

(a) Ida Jemima, born August 25, 1858; died in childhood.

(b) Mary Irene, born December 21, 1859; married James Lyles.

(c) Florence, born March 25, 1861; died June 16, 1888; married Elisha Rogers.

(d) Eugene Gadsden, born December 2, 1862; died March 29, 1929; married Elise McGowan.

(e) Reuben Walter, born May 23, 1864; died in infancy.

(f) Claude Jeter, born June 25, 1866; married Zilla Holcombe.

(g) Nettie Camilla, born July 28, 1868; died November 16, 1915; married Walter Harlock Harvey.

(h) Maud Angelina, born February 10, 1871; married R. Preston Redick; lives at Hodges, S. C.

(i) Herbert Jeter, born November 1, 1872; married Essie Harvey; lives at Hodges, S. C.

(j) Lovie Pierce, born July 17, 1875; married, January 16, 1900, Caroline Nora Gibbs, daughter of Jasper and Frances Elizabeth (Smith) Gibbs.

CHILDREN:

(aa) Infant; died 1901.

(bb) Sadie Irene, born July 12, 1903.

(cc) Lovie Pierce, II, born August 7, 1908.

(dd) Reuben Jasper ("Jack"), born April 24, 1910.

(ee) Helen Caroline, born April 21, 1914.

(2) Infant; died 1833.

(3) John Ludolphus, born July 25, 1834; died May 2, 1855.

(4) William Tecumseh, born August 6, 1835; died April 24, 1914; married (first) Eliza Richards. No children. He married (second) Nannie D. Coleman.

CHILDREN:

(a) Ireneus P.; married Nannie Fleming of Raleigh, N. C.; now a dentist at Morganton, N. C.

CHILDREN:

(aa) Nan Fleming.

(bb) Mary Tucker.

(b) Mary Eva; married Gilliam Hobson Jeter.

(c) Thomas Crosby, Jr., born July 25, 1879; died February 3, 1918; married, February 24, 1904, Sallie Henderson Whitney, who was born March 9, 1882.

CHILDREN:

(aa) William Whitney, born February 16, 1905; died in childhood.

(bb) Sadie Coleman, born September 17, 1907; married, August 14, 1927, James Caldwell Hall, who was born May 22, 1899.

CHILDREN:

(aaa) Sadie Jeter, born February 24, 1928.

(bbb) James Caldwell, Jr., born June 6, 1929.

(cc) Thomas Crosby, III, born September 17, 1917.

(5) Ireneus, born August 25, 1837; member of Company "D," 5th Regiment, South Carolina Volunteers; wounded at Battle of Seven Pines, May 31, and died in Richmond, Va., June 6, 1862. His remains were brought back to South Carolina and interred in Tucker's Cemetery, near Carlisle, South Carolina.

(6) Mary Lou, born March 29, 1839; married David Thomas, son of John and Jemima (Sims) Thomas.

(7) James R., born October 16, 1841; died July 23, 1847.

(8) Elmira R., born March 5, 1844; died in 1921 (?).

(9) Aletha Angelina, born November 23, 1847; died December 13, 1926; married, November 19, 1873, Peterson Parham Hamilton. (See Hamilton family.)

CHILDREN:

(a) Mary Helen, born October 1, 1874; married, January 4, 1903, Samuel S. Wood. No children.

(b) Reuben Gilliam, born February 7, 1876; educated in public schools of Union County, South Carolina; Spartanburg graded schools; Clemson College, B. S., 1896; Medical Department, University of Georgia, M. D., 1902.

Volunteered for service in World War in April, 1917; inducted into service June, 1917, as Lieutenant

M. C.; France, 1917-1919; gassed November 7, 1918; discharged November, 1919. Major M. C.

Decorations: Division citation for heroism in action, 26th Division; Distinguished Service Cross for heroism in action, September 25-26, 1918.

Retired as Major M. C., U. S. Army, 1928.

Practiced medicine in Union and Spartanburg counties, South Carolina, 1902-1910; Fairfield County, 1910-1917.

With South Carolina State Board of Health from March, 1920, as County Health Officer of Fairfield County to 1923; from 1923 to present time (1929) as Malarialogist of Board of Health of Columbia, South Carolina.

Married, October 26, 1897, Flora Setzler, who was born December 25, 1876.

CHILDREN:

(aa) Laurens Adams, born July 31, 1898; Lieutenant of Infantry in World War; volunteered in September, 1917, from North Carolina State College, where he was then a student.

(bb) Helen Louise, born January 14, 1904.

(c) Frank Watson, born April 30, 1877; died in childhood.

(d) Thomas Laurens, born February 6, 1879; died June 29, 1897.

(e) Frederick Parham, born April 7, 1881; married, December, 1908, Mattie Louise Littlejohn.

(f) Bertha Leonora, born June 22, 1890; married, February 14, 1911, John William Wallace.

CHILDREN:

(aa) Hamilton, born June 5, 1914.

(bb) Dorothy, born March 8, 1917.

(cc) James Reuben, born December 3, 1920.

(dd) John William, Jr., born September 22, 1924.

(ee) Bert, born June 4, 1927.

(g) Anne Adele, born December 10, 1892; married, October 26, 1915, George Maxcy Perry. No children.

(10) Martha Madora, born March 6, 1851; died 1928; married David Johnson.

HOBSON

Nicholas Hobson of Virginia was a captain in the Revolutionary War, and wounded in the face, from the effects of which he lost his eyesight. For his services in the war he was granted about four thousand acres of land in Green County, Alabama. He took six of his children—Archibald, Matthew, Frank, William, Agnes, and Regina—and started to Alabama to take possession of this land.

They stopped in Chester County, S. C., just across Broad River from Fish Dam, Union County, to stay from Saturday night until Monday morning at the home of Allen De Graffeureid. William was offered a position as clerk in the business of Mr. De Graffeureid and this, together with the charms of his young niece, was more than he could resist, and he remained in Chester County, while his father and brothers and sisters went on to Green County, Alabama. Among their descendants is Richmond Pearson Hobson of Spanish War fame. He was born in Greensboro, Alabama, August 17, 1870; graduated from U. S. Military Academy, 1889; commanded collier "Merrimac" and sunk her in Santiago harbor during Spanish-American War, 1898; resigned from U. S. Navy in 1903, and elected to Congress in 1907 from sixth Alabama district. He is author of many naval books.

William Hobson married Cicely Thomas, the niece of his employer, before she was fifteen years old, and their children were:

(1) Sarah; married Little Berry Jeter, I. (See South Carolina Jeter family.)
(2) Jane; married Archibald Gordon.
(3) Elizabeth; married James R. Jeter. (See South Carolina Jeter family).
(4) Gilliam; married Sarah Ann McDaniel.
(5) Susan; married Jeremiah Hamilton.
(6) Evelyn; married James McJunkin.
(7) Regina; married William Hamilton.
(8) Franklin; married Margaret Beatty.
(9) Cicely; died unmarried.

HAMILTON

Jeremiah Hamilton came from Dublin, Ireland. He married Anne Hampton, a kinswoman of General Wade Hampton, and their son, Joseph Hampton Hamilton, born February 28, 1788, married Nancy Parham, who was born in Mecklenburg County, Va., May 30, 1793. When she was about fourteen years old, she and her father went to South Carolina en route to Tennessee. He was taken ill, and before he was able to resume his journey Nancy had married. They settled in South Carolina and among their children was a son—

Peter Parham Hamilton, who was born August 26, 1810, and married, 1833, Annie Simms Gilliam, who was born in 1819,. and was the grand-daughter of Patrick Simms and Lucy Beaufort.

CHILDREN:

(1) Infant; died 1834.

(2) Mary C. Simms, born July 29, 1835.

(3) Laura Ann Ophelia, born May 3, 1837; married John Randolph Jeter. (See South Carolina Jeter family.)

(4) Reuben Gilliam, born February 5, 1839.

(5) Leonora Frances, born April 8, 1841; married Gilliam Hobson Jeter. (See South Carolina Jeter family.)

(6) Nancy Drucilla Elizabeth, born October 25, 1843.

(7) Jeremiah Alexander, born December 25, 1845.

(8) Peterson Parham, born January 13, 1848; married Aletha Angelina Jeter. (See South Carolina Jeter family.)

(9) Robert W., born August 11, 1850.

(10) Joseph Hampton, born February 24, 1852.

(11) Rosa Jane, born April 1, 1855; married Little Berry Jeter, II. (See South Carolina Jeter family.)

(12) Beaufort Ann, born February 10, 1857.

THE ALABAMA JETERS

Eleazer Jeter, youngest son of William and Margaret (Vaughan) Jeter, of Virginia and South Carolina, born in Lunenburg County, Virginia, about 1763; married Ann ——— (died 1847), and went to Mobile County, Alabama, in 1818, where he was one of the Justices from 1818 to 1820. He died in Montgomery, Alabama, in 1821.

CHILDREN:

(1) George Washington, born 1800; died 1866; married three times— (first) Mary Oats; (second) Boley ———; and (third) Malinda Ann Dean. He was a Primitive Baptist preacher. He took his family to Panola County, Texas, in 1846.

CHILDREN:

Eleazer, William, Mary, Shackelford, Belle, John, Charlotte, Frank (born 1844), and Sallie. Frank now lives at Fort Worth, Texas.

(2) Mary; married ——— Hartley.

(3) Penelope; married Theophilus Harrison.

(4) Melville; married Mary Ann Armstrong; was a Primitive Baptist preacher; went to Panola County, Texas, in 1846.

CHILDREN:

James, Melville, Edmund, Julia, Mattie, and Simeon.

(5) Annette, born 1806; died 1870; married (first) George Shackleford (1779-1852); (second) Alexander Robert Hutchinson. Her children (all by her first marriage) were:

(a) Rebecca, born 1825; died 1896; married Nathaniel Williams.

(b) George Washington, born 1827; died 1867; married Amanda Delbridge.

(c) Penelope, born 1828; died 1847; married Christopher Rives.

(d) Francis, born 1830; died 1905; married Parmelia Jane Watts.

(e) Mary, born 1832; died 1907; married William La-Fayette Allen.

(f) James, born 1834; died in infancy.

(g) Joseph, born 1835; died 1902; married Mary Tanner Sales.

(h) Madison, born 1838; died 1905; married Sofronia Jane Ledbetter (1843-1895).

(i) Ann, born 1842; died 1895; married William Wert Walker.

(j) Martha, born 1845; died 1901; married Walter Scott Stokes.

(6) Mira Ann; married Edmond Lewis.

CHILDREN:

(a) Elizabeth Ann; married (first) ———— Reeks; (second) ———— Williams.

(b) Penelope; married ———— Shoemaker.

(c) Harrison.

(d) Benjamin Eleazer; married Elizabeth Talley.

(e) William Worth; married Janes Stokes.

(f) Jasper.

(g) Washington.

(h) Elmira; married Robert Pool.

(7) Eleazer; married ————.

CHILDREN:

Hamp, Mary, Elie, Ann, Mattie, and Allen.

(8) James; married ————.

CHILDREN:

Rebecca, Vaughn, Frank, William, George, and Queenie.

(9) William; married ————.

CHILDREN:

Elijah and David.

(10) Jesse; married ————.

CHILDREN:

Mollie Ann, Anderson, Thomas, and Alfred.

John Jeter, Jr., son of John Jeter, the immigrant, said, by his descendants, to have died in 1807, when nearly one hundred years old, married Lucy Robinson, perhaps in Caroline County, Va.

On June 19, 1747, John Jeter, Sr., of Caroline County, bought a certain tract of land on the south side of Whetstone Creek in the fork of Nottoway River in Amelia County from John Tomlinson and Mary, his wife, of Surry County, and December 22, 1756, the same John Jeter and his wife, Elizabeth, conveyed this land to "John Jeter, Jr., of Amelia County, for natural love and affection and 5 pounds." A witness to the deed was Ambrose Jeter, believed to have been another son of John, Sr.

The following year John Jeter, Jr., and his wife, Lucy, sold a part of this land, and in 1760 they sold the remainder of it, and evidently left the county. (Amelia County records.)

We find him in Greensville County, Va., in 1785, as "John Jeter, Sr.," when he consents to the marriage of his daughter, Clara, to Absalom Jeter. His son, John, has now become "John, Jr." Which of them married the widow Tomlinson in Brunswick County we do not know, for the marriage bond reads, "January 4, 1781. John Jeter, Jr., and Elizabeth Tomlinson, widow. Security, Edmond Jeter."

In a list of Greensville County, Va., marriages, in Tyler's *Historical Quarterly*, we find, in Vols. II and III, the following Jeter marriages:

Thomas and Martha Jeter—April 22, 1805. Edmund Jeter, security.

Absalom and Clara Jeter—December 14, 1785. John Jeter, Sr., consents.

John Jeter, Jr., and Mary Rives—January 3, 1786.

Edmund Jeter and Rebecca Rives—January 13, 1791. Sarah Rives (mother), consents.

Henry and Rebecca Jeter — November 11, 1796. John Jeter, security.

William D. and Lucy Jeter—February 25, 1803.

John and Elizabeth Jeter—August 29, 1809.

In "Heads of Families in Virginia in 1782," Edmund Jeter, Sr., is listed in Greensville County with ten whites in his family, so these are evidently his children who have married those of John.

(Data for the following sketch of the descendants of John, Jr., and Lucy (Robinson) Jeter have been furnished us by their great-great-great-grand-daughter, Mrs. John W. Bradshaw (Elloie Evans Jeter), of Ensley, Alabama.)

John Jeter, Jr., died in 1807 or 1808, nearly one hundred years old. He married Lucy Robinson. Their son—

John Jeter, III, born May 1, 1751; died October 19, 1822, in Green County, Georgia; married Mary Rives, born March 20, 1758, died September 9, 1826. Their son—

Samuel Jeter, born in Halifax County, North Carolina, September 29, 1796; died in Chambers County, Alabama, July 15, 1881; married (first) in Green County, Georgia, October 1, 1822, Winifred Cone, born in Green County, Georgia, May 8, 1800, died in Chambers County, Alabama, October 29, 1850. Their son—

Richard Cone Jeter, born October 29, 1827, in Rowan County, North Carolina; graduated at University of Alabama; married, May 18, 1852, in Chambers County, Ala., Sarah Matilda Clayton, daughter of Nelson and Sarah (Carruthers (?)) Clayton, and grand-daughter of James Clayton, the immigrant, who settled in Maryland about 1700.

CHILDREN:

(1) Joseph Henry, born in Lee County, Alabama, May 28, 1857; married, December 12, 1900, Rennie Elise Burton in Opelika, Lee County, Ala.

CHILDREN:

(a) Rennie Burton, now secretary to Dean of Agricultural Department of Alabama Polytechnic Institute.

(b) Joseph Henry, Jr.; now living in California.

(c) Mary Dalene; secretary in Agricultural Department of Alabama Polytechnic Institute, Auburn, Ala.

(2) Lelia Winny, born July 28, 1861; died October 4, 1866.

(3) Sarah Clayton, born in Russell County, Alabama, September 12, 1863; died October, 1892.

(4) Richard Cullen, born in Lee County, Ala., February 2, 1867; educated at University of Alabama and at Sewanee University, Tennessee; died in San Antonio, Texas, November 30, 1916; was first a lawyer, then a clergyman of the Protestant Episcopal Church. He was for ten years Chaplain of the Alabama National Guard; later, Chaplain of the First South Carolina Regiment, National Guard; still later, rector at Aiken, S. C.

He married, April 27, 1892, Mary Lee Powers, of Florence Alabama, daughter of Thomas R. and Mary (Evans) Powers.

CHILDREN:

(a) Richard Cullen, Jr., born in Dee County, Ala., January 14, 1893; educated at Porter Military Academy, Charleston, S. C.; Marion Institute, Marion, Ala.; and University of Michigan, where he specialized in metallurgy. He is now superintendent of the casting department of the Scoville Manufacturing Company of Waterbury, Conn.

He married, September, 1917, Martha Brewer Alston, of Florence, Alabama.

CHILDREN:

(aa) Elloie Evans, born November, 1918, in Florence, Alabama.

(bb) Mary Lee, born February, 1921, in Waterbury, Connecticut.

(b) Elloie Evans, born in Florence, Alabama, November 16, 1895; married, October 5, 1920, John William Bradshaw. For the past five years she has been Director of the Bradshaw Kindergarten of Ensley, Ala.

CHILDREN:

(aa) John William, Jr., born August 2, 1921.

(bb) Richard Jeter, born May 15, 1924.

(c) Thomas Powers, born in Florence, Ala., August 25, 1893; graduated in Annapolis; studied aviation at Pensacola, Fla.; graduated from Bureau of Aeronautics, Air Service, Engineers Army School at Dayton, Ohio; won the Curtiss Marine Trophy for 1926; now in the United States Air Service at San Diego, California.

(d) Sarah Clayton, born in Florence, Alabama, May 15, 1901; graduated at Ward-Belmont College, Nashville, Tennessee; taught dancing, swimming, and athletics at Ward-Belmont; now head of dancing school at Nashville Conservatory. She studied with Vestoff Sarova at his Russion school in New York, with Nikolas Tsukalas in Chicago, and with Alexis Kosloff in New York.

(5) Froebel, born February 18, 1869; died September 20, 1870.

Samuel and Winifred (Cone) Jeter and their little son, Richard Cone Jeter, settled in Chambers County, Alabama, in 1836, on a plantation of 640 acres, near LaFayette. (In 1926, Oscar Jeter, son of Samuel and his second wife, still owned this entire estate.)

In 1850, Winifred (Cone) Jeter died, and in 1852, her son, Richard, married and brought his bride to his father's home. The next year his father, Samuel Jeter, announced his intention of marrying Sallie Taylor, a young girl, still in her twenties, whose family had just moved to that section from Georgia. This step was vigorously opposed by the young couple, but they could not prevent it, and in 1853, Samuel Jeter married Sallie Taylor.

They had one son, Oscar, born April 25, 1854. After his birth, his parents had a disagreement over giving Richard his birthright—a plantation of 670 acres near that of his father—and his mother took her young son and went back to live with her father, who had advised her not to sign the deed of gift to Richard, thus causing the trouble which resulted in the separation of Samuel and Sallie Jeter.

She died in 1860, and Mr. Jeter demanded his son. This was refused and a lawsuit ensued, which was won by Mr. Jeter. The Taylors then kidnapped the child and a feud began. Detectives were employed, and little Oscar was recovered, but bitter animosity was engendered, and the Taylors fired from ambush upon members of the Jeter family upon several occasions.

Samuel Jeter and his son, Richard, were attending a political barbecue in a nearby town, when one of the Taylors attacked Mr. Jeter. Richard ran to the assistance of his father just as Taylor was raising his knife to stab him in the back. Richard drew his pistol and fired, killing Taylor instantly. The case was never brought to trial, which aggravated the feeling among the Taylors and they threatened to shoot at sight.

Some time after this Richard Jeter was in another small town in the state, and upon going into the hotel he discovered Dave Taylor sitting facing the door, asleep, with his pistol across his knees. Richard stood looking at him a few minutes, and then, walking over to the clerk, he said, "Do you see that man? He is Dave Taylor. When he awakes, tell him that Dick Jeter was here and let him live." Then turning on his heels, he walked out. A day or two later he received a letter from Dave Taylor, saying that he had heard the story from the hotel clerk, and that he could not continue to be the enemy of a man with such a sense of honor, and hoped that they might now be friends. Richard replied that he could never consider any man his friend who had sought the life of his father, but that he would be glad to call off hostilities. And thus the feud ended.

The following is quoted from Mrs. Bradshaw's account of a visit to the home of Oscar Jeter in 1926:

"He had lost his second wife only a few months before, and was living alone, except for his servants. We found a beautiful plantation, excellently cared for, with house and grounds in perfect order and so clean that they put some of us, housekeepers, to shame. A wonderful dinner—a really, truly old-fashioned southern dinner—was served us by Kate, the cook who had been with the Jeters for years. Uncle Oscar, himself, was true to Jeter type—every inch a gentleman, gentle, humorous, hospitable, and altogether lovable."

Oscar Jeter married (first) in 1873, Clara Morefield; (second) in 1907, Mrs. Jennie (Wyche) Jones, who died in 1926.

THE KENTUCKY JETERS

Elijah Jeter of Caroline County, Va., believed to have been the son of John Jeter, Sr., married in 1768, in Caroline County, Elizabeth ————. He died in 1786, and his wife, Elizabeth, was made administratrix of his estate. (Order Book of Caroline County, 1746-1754, page 466.)

CHILDREN:

(1) Sabrina, born November 6, 1769.
(2) Sarah Dozier, born August 31, 1771; died in Jessamine County, Ky., in 1850. (See forward.)
(3) Ann, born August 17, 1773; married, October 20, 1792, George White.
(4) Elizabeth, born December 28, 1775; died 1740-45. (See forward.)
(5) Jane, born August 15, 1777; married Nathan Marders.
(6) Mary Graves, born December 23, 1779.
(7) Neggy, born June 19, 1784.
(8) Elijah, Jr., born April 27, 1786; died in Jefferson County, Ky., January 7, 1832. (See forward.)

In the closing years of the eighteenth century and the early years of the nineteenth there was a strong migration from Caroline and adjoining counties of Virginia into Central Kentucky. One large colony, consisting of families who were closely allied by blood and other ties, settled in Fayette County—from which Jessamine County was later taken. Among them were several families of Young, Jeter, Dozier, Marders, and others, who, by marriage with other families from Virginia, have made a strong and worthy contribution to the citizenry of Kentucky.

In this migration—perhaps about 1802—were two daughters of Elijah Jeter who had married brothers, James and John Young of Caroline County, Va.

Sarah Dozier Jeter married, December 20, 1792, James Young (born 1766; died in Jessamine County, Ky., January, 1842).

CHILDREN:

(1) Laurence, born December 6, 1793; died December 23, 1872, in Jefferson County, Ky.; married, March 27, 1823, Eliza Johnson White (born April 27, 1803; died April 9, 1891).

CHILDREN:

(a) Richard, born June 1, 1824; died February 21, 1878.
(b) William Worsley, born June 24, 1828; died June 11, 1903. (See forward.)

(c) Hiram Clay, born April 30, 1831; died May 29, 1846.

(d) Sarah Virginia, born October 1, 1834; died January 13, 1906; married T. W. Chamberlin.

(e) Benjamin Lee, born July 27, 1840; died November 15, 1888.

(2) Richard, born 1795; died in Jessamine County, Ky.

(3) Walker Preston; died 1868.

(4) Lucy; married ———— McCampbell. No descendants.

(5) Parthenia; died, unmarried, September 14, 1872.

....

William Worsley Young, son of Laurence and Eliza Johnson (White) Young, married November 22, 1853, Ann Amelia Chamberlin (born November 13, 1834; died December 17, 1909).

CHILDREN:

(1) Emma Virginia, born October 4, 1854; married, May 20, 1874, Edward Shinkle Porter (born May 12, 1850; died June 13, 1902).

CHILDREN:

(a) Amelia Finnie, born August 13, 1875; married, July 9, 1895, Wible Lawrence Mapother (born September 28, 1872; died February 3, 1926).

CHILD:

(aa) Helen Marie, born December 9, 1896; married, August 18, 1917, Leonard Godfrey Strater.

(b) Evelyn, born March 17, 1880; married, September 27, 1913, Richard Dorsey Blair.

(c) Florence Virginia, born July 30, 1885; died February 14, 1923; married, June 11, 1907, William Bridges Hunter.

CHILDREN:

(aa) William Bridges, Jr., born June 7, 1915.

(bb) Edward Porter, born June 8, 1918.

(d) Alice Nones, born May 20, 1891; married, October 14, 1913, Walter Smyth Moore.

CHILDREN:

(aa) Virginia Duncan, born September 3, 1914.
(bb) Evelyn Porter, born August 6, 1916.
(cc) Mary Susan, born November 8, 1918.
(dd) Martha Rutherford, born March 9, 1920.

(2) Laurence Chamberlin, born July 28, 1856; married (first) Arabella Harris; (second) Annie Williams.
(3) Edward Payson, born February 10, 1858; died September 13, 1883.
(4) Hiram Clay, born March 6, 1860; married Kate Frederick.
(5) William Worsley, Jr., born June 28, 1862; died October 7, 1892; married Medora Cravens.

Elizabeth Jeter, daughter of Elijah and Elizabeth Jeter of Caroline County, Va., married, May 17, 1796, John Young (born June 10, 1764; died December, 1841, in Jessamine County, Ky.).

CHILDREN:

(1) William Dudley, born in Caroline County, Va., May 16, 1797.
(2) George, born in Caroline County, October 30, 1798.
(3) Elijah, born in Caroline County, September 21, 1800; died in Jefferson County, Ky., 1865; married Mrs. Celia Pendleton Taylor.

CHILDREN:

(a) Jessamine Medora; married George D. Sherwin.
(b) Elizabeth Lucy; married Walter P. Mayo.
(c) Eugene; died in early life.

(4) Frances, born October 4, 1803, in Jessamine County, Ky.
(5) Nancy, born January 19, 1806; married (first) ———— Baker; (second) ———— Bradshaw.
(6) Leonard, born April 25, 1808; died October 28, 1825.
(7) Elizabeth Sabrina, born May 6, 1813; died October 1, 1851; married her cousin, William Jeter, of Jessamine County, Ky., May 18, 1842.

CHILDREN:

(a) John E. (twin), born April 3, 1843; died in early life.
(b) Leonard D. (twin), born April 3, 1843; married Agnes ———— and has several children living in Lexington, Ky.

Elijah Jeter, Jr., son of Elijah and Elizabeth Jeter of Caroline County, Va., went to Kentucky and married (first), December 25, 1810, Susan Sanford.

CHILDREN:

(1) John Dozier, born September 22, 1814.

(2) Ragsdale E., born May 17, 1820; married, November 14, 1844, Katherine Hoke.

Elijah Jeter, Jr., married (second), May 5, 1821, Barbara Liter, and had one child:

(3) Mary E., born November 25, 1823; married, April 30, 1844, Wesley Whips, of Jefferson County, Ky.

....

Mrs. Edward Shinkle Porter (Emma Virginia Young), of Louisville, Ky., has contributed all the data from which the above sketch of Elijah Jeter's family has been written, and when we appealed to her for "just a little more than names and dates" she sent us her "Reminiscences," which she has written for her grandchildren. We have found it so interesting that, instead of condensing it—as, perhaps, she thought we would—we are quoting entire pages, because it gives an insight, not only into the everyday life of the Kentuckians who went from Virginia, but also of the Virginians who were left behind.

Extracts from "Reminiscences," by Mrs. Emma Young Porter:

"I shall begin with the YOUNG family—since I was born in my grandfather Young's home, grew up under his influence and training, and the memories of my childhood are centered there. . . .

"Our branch of the Young family were of Scotch-Irish descent; but unfortunately the early records of those days have been destroyed by fire, both before and during the Civil War, consequently all data relating to them have been lost, except such fragmentary bits as are preserved in family traditions, etc. Our great-grandfathers were too much engrossed in clearing forests, building their early homes, and laying the foundations of this great country, to have much time for diaries or notes.

"Caroline County, Virginia, was the home of our 'clan,' and sometime during the closing years of the eighteenth century, my great-great-grandfather, Richard Young, with his wife, Nancy, and their two daughters, Jane and Nancy (married ———— Proctor), crossed the mountains and settled in what was then Fayette, but is now Jessamine County, Kentucky. About 1802, the two sons, James and John, having married two sisters, Sarah and Elizabeth Jeter, in Caroline County, Virginia, also came into Kentucky, bringing with them several children, their servants, stock, and such possessions as were portable. There is a tradition that the first land they bought—a tract of about 300 acres— was paid for, not in 'the coin of the realm,' but in log chains, and little imagination is required to realize that in those days of clearing forests, and taming of the wilderness, the chains were of far greater value than the money would have been. This land was bought from Flanders and Jemima Boone Callaway. Jemima, daughter of Daniel Boone, was one of the three young girls who were captured by the Indians, just outside the fort at Boonesboro, and Flanders was one of the rescuing party in that interesting and exciting episode. (See Callaway family.)

"Another story which has come down to us, is that in the first log house built by our ancestors, only one side of the flooring was dressed, the other side being rough and unfinished. On Saturday afternoons the young people would turn the boards, smooth side up, for the Sabbath use, and on Monday morning they were again reversed. . . .

"Springdale, the home of my grandfather, Laurence Young, was an estate of almost a thousand acres, in Jefferson County, Kentucky, about seven miles from Louisville, on the Brownsboro road—so-called because of a very remarkable spring of water. . . .

"The story is told that when the farm was bought, my grandfather and his brother-in-law (great Uncle Lee Ehite), were for a time business partners and joint owners of the estate. Grandfather wished to build on one hill—Uncle Lee preferred the one opposite, so they compromised by building the house in the valley, which lay between the two—the house being built directly over the spring. . . .

"The foundation of the house was of stone masonry, and what would have been a cellar or basement was first a walled basin, into which the spring emptied itself—thence it flowed into a large room, with solid floor of stone and cement, which was the milk room. Here row after row of stone jars, or crocks, stood in this great pool of cool, running water, while at one side, upon a raised level, was the long, polished marble table, upon which the butter was washed and molded. Flowing out from the house, this strong stream filled a large basin in a stone-flagged court-yard, into which the kitchen also opened, and then became a stream and pond for fowls and stock—to say nothing of the wonderful place for wading and other water sports for the children. . . .

"To go back to the home life of those early days: Hospitality was indeed a grace which abounded in the superlative degree, and no guest was ever unwelcome. The table was always ample in its provisions for almost any number of unexpected visitors—no visit was complete unless a meal had been shared, and I often wonder what the contents of pantry and store house must have been. Of course the year's supply of ham, bacon, and lard was cured on the place, supplemented by fresh meats and fowls of every kind, even the royal peafowl. Fruits and vegetables were dried, preserved, and canned, and many varieties kept by storing in trenches in the earth.

"Aside from the hospitality as it related to temporal things, there was a spirit which characterized the home life of that period, which I believe can never be experienced again, a leisure to enjoy and cultivate the worth while things of life, and a neighborliness which extended far beyond all ordinary boundaries."

Other Jeters in the above mentioned migration from Caroline County, Va., to Kentucky were Littleton, soldier of the Revolution, who married Jane Alsop before leaving Caroline; Fielding, another soldier of the Revolution, whose marriage bond has not been found; and Elisha, who married Rebecca Martin before going to Kentucky. It is probable that all of these were sons of John, Sr., though this fact has not been proved.

The following are extracts taken from applications for pensions, certificates of pensions, and letters pertaining to same which have been obtained from The Bureau of Pensions, Washington, D. C.:

Service	Littleton Jeter	Number
Va.	wife—Jane Alsop	W-9077

of Fayette Co. in the State of Ky. was a private in the Company commanded by Cap. Talliaferro of the Regiment—commanded by Col. Woodford in the Va. line—for the term of one year from Sep., 1776, to Sep., 1777.

A letter in which is stated:

"Littleton Jeter, aged 67 years, resident of Fayette Co., Ky. Enlisted first Sep., 1776," etc.

Littleton Jeter

Inscribed on the Roll of Ky. at the rate of $8.00 per month—to commence on 10th Day of Dec., 1828.

One son—Hugh Jeter—mentioned.

Certificate of Pension issued the 11th of Dec., 1828—and sent to Hon. R. M. Johnson. Senate of United States.

Arrears to 4th of March, 1829—$22.70.

Revolutionary Claim Acts March 18, 1818, and May 1, 1820.

Littleton Jeter died May 20, 1842.

Jane Alsop Jeter died Nov. 11, 1843.

Service	Jeter-Fielding	No.
Va.	Private Rev. War	S.36629

asked for pension June, 1818. Admitted 8 June, 1820.

Fielding Jeter of Fayette Co. Ky., private in the Regiment commanded by Col. Campbell for term of 1 yr. and six months.

Inscribed on the Roll of Ky. at rate of $8.00 per month to commence on the 20th day of June, 1818.

Certificate of pension issued the 9th of June, 1820, and sent to Daniel McC. Payne, Esq., Lexington, Ky.

District of Ky.

June 20, 1818.

Fielding Jeter, aged 56, personally appeared and was sworn according to law. He enlisted in 1779 in the State of Va. for 1 yr. and 6 mos. in the Company commanded by Cap. Denham of the 1st Va. Regiment —commanded by Col. Richard Campbell. He continued to serve in said corps—or in the service of the U. S. until 1782. When he was discharged from service in the vicinity of the Town of Ninety-six, State of South Carolina, he was in the battles of Guilford, under General Green—and Camden against Lord Rodney—also under Gen. Green—that he is in reduced circumstances and in need of assistance for support.

BENJAMIN JOHNSON, *Circuit Judge.*

Benjamin Johnson Submitted the above testimony to the Sec. for the Department of War pursuant to the directions of the aforementioned Act of Congress.

Given under my hand this the 20th Day of June, 1818.

(Signed) BENJ. JOHNSON, *Circuit Judge.*

At the time of application he (Fielding Jeter) had a wife and three children dependent for support—two daughters and one son, John Jeter—from old age and wounds rec. in Rev. War is almost incapable of bodily labor and even now measurably dependent upon the charity of the world for support.

Sworn to on the 17th day of July, 1820, before

WM. WARREN, *Judge of Circuit Court.*

Fielding Jeter was still living in 1843, when he certified that he was present at the marriage of his brother Littleton Jeter, and Jane Alsop in Caroline County, Va., September 7, 1786. This certificate was filed with Jane Jeter's application for pension, after the death of her husband.

Elisha Jeter, believed to have been the son of John Jeter, the immigrant, was born in Caroline County, Virginia. He married, October 12, 1797, Rebecca Martin, of Caroline County, and went to Kentucky. Only two of their children are known—Elbert and Horatio —and these may have been all, for Rebecca did not live many years, and we find Elisha marrying again in Jessamine County, Kentucky, after 1806 (date of his marriage bond not given). His second wife was Isabella Long.

Elbert Jeter, son of Elisha and Rebecca (Martin) Jeter, was born in Kentucky, November 26, 1798; married in Lexington, Ky., January 6, 1820, Sarah Irvine, born in Lexington, Ky., in 1796 daughter of William Irvine, who was an officer in the Revolutionary Army from Halifax County, Va., and who went to Kentucky soon after the Revolutionary War.

CHILDREN:

(1) William Oliver, born near Lexington, Ky., October 23, 1820; died February 28, 1905; married in Lexington, Ky., January 24, 1850, America Ann Maxwell of Orleans, Indiana.

CHILDREN:

    (a) Maxwell Pembroke, born February 5, 1851; married, September 1, 1880, Louisa Moulder.

    (b) Osman Dixon, born February 7, 1853; died August 8, 1926.

    (c) Zeno Erwin, born December 16, 1855; died in Tampa, Florida, July 12, 1904; married, April 18, 1888, Nora E. Andrew.

    (d) Eliab Sales, born November 21, 1859; married, August 3, 1882, Araminta E. Bishop.

    (e) Sarah Eliza, born April 21, 1863; married, January 3, 1906, William Foley Gordon.

(2) Elisha.

(3) Jeptha.

(4) Elbert, Jr., born May 28, 1829, in Laurence County, Indiana; died February 5, 1899, at Worthington, Greene County, Indiana; married (first) in 1856, Louisa Harvey (died 1870).

CHILDREN:

    (a) Edwin.

    (b) Charles.

    (c) George.

    (d) Edward.

    (e) Francis.

    (f) Harry.

        Of these, only Francis was married. His wife was Clarinda E. Wood, and they had two children:

    (aa) Anna Louisa.

    (bb) Elbert.

Elbert Jeter, Jr., married (second) in 1872, Elmira Jane Harmon.

CHILDREN:

(g) Elbert, III.

(h) John; married Emma Haddix.

CHILDREN:

(aa) Ruth.

(bb) John, Jr.,

(cc) Theodore.

(dd) Elbert.

(ee) James N.

(i) Bertrand; married Jessie M. Gerhardt. No children.

(j) Mary; married Benjamin F. Haton.

(k) Fred; married Lorene Walker.

CHILDREN:

(aa) Lena Jane.

(bb) Mary Carolyn.

(5) James Newton, born February 14, 1834, at Orleans, Indiana; died October 20, 1919; married, 1857, Mary Ann Payne, who died July 20, 1890.

CHILDREN:

(a) Hester Jane, born September 10, 1858; died August, 1868.

(b) Edward Everett, born October 5, 1860; lives in Pueblo, Colorado.

(c) Theodore, born June 13, 1865; lives at Champaign, Illinois.

(d) James Newton, Jr., born February 28, 1868; lives at Glendale, California.

(e) William Jeptha, born January 2, 1870; lives at Eagle Rock, California.

(f) Maud, born December 22, 1872; died August 10, 1912.

(6) John.

(7) Henry.

(8) Theodore.

(9) Mary; and two other daughters, names not known.

The following memorandum, made by William Oliver Jeter, oldest son of Elbert, Sr., and Sarah (Irvine) Jeter, was furnished us, along with all the data of this branch of the family, by Mr. Bertrand Jeter of Brookfield, Illinois, who assures us that we "can depend upon this memorandum of my uncle, William O. Jeter, because my grandfather was a very intelligent man, had a good education, for his time, and a good memory, and Uncle Will says he heard his father and grandfather discuss the family often":

MEMORANDUM

"My great-grandfather, John Jeter, emigrated from England early in the eighteenth century and settled in Caroline County, Virginia, eight miles from Port Royal. He was twice married, and was the father of 22 children, 11 by each wife.

"At his death he left $1,000.00 and a negro man slave to each of his children.

"Most of the family left Virginia, going South, except three brothers, Littleton, Fielding and Elisha, who went to Kentucky, and Burrell to Tennessee. The others, who did not remain in Virginia, went to North and South Carolina and Georgia.

"My grandfather, Elisha Jeter, settled in Franklin County, Ky., where my father, Elbert Jeter, was born November 26, 1798. My grandfather, Elisha Jeter, afterwards moved to Fayette County, Ky., and settled near Lexington.

"My father, Elbert Jeter, married Sarah Irvin at Lexington, Ky., January 6, 1820; moved to Indiana in the fall of 1823 and in the spring of 1824 settled in Bloomington, Indiana. In the fall of 1827 he moved to Bedford, Indiana, and in the spring of 1834 moved to Orleans, Indiana, where he lived until his death in October, 1888.

"He was a minister of the Primitive Baptist Church, and preached until age incapacitated him.

"My mother, Sarah Irvin Jeter was the daughter of William Irvin (a soldier in the Revolutionary War, Virginia troops) and Mary Pigman. She was born near Lexington, Ky., September 27, 1797, and died September 11, 1873, at Orleans, Ind.

"So far as I know all the Jeters in America are related, as I know of but one who emigrated to America.

"My father's brother was Horatio Jeter, who lived and died in Bedford, Indiana, where he was married in 1827."

Brookfield, Illinois, December 31, 1929.

I hereby certify that the above history of John Jeter, Sr., and his descendants was copied by me from a family record made by my uncle, William Oliver Jeter, who was a great-grandson of John Jeter, Sr., the emigrant.   (Signed) BERTRAND JETER.

State of Illinois⎫
                 ⎬ ss.
Cook County   ⎭

Subscribed and sworn to before me this 31st day of December, 1929.   (Signed) JESSIE M. JETER, *Notary Public.*

My commission expires December 10, 1930.

....

Below are some extracts from a letter from G. Guy Jeter, of Bridgeport, Conn. We have not been able to place him just where he belongs in the family, but feel sure that some of our readers can do so. He says,

"My father was George Madison Jeter who was the son of William Jeter, a doctor and graduate of the Louisville, Ky., Medical College. My grandfather moved to Kentucky from the vicinity of Richmond, Va., and during his course of study became acquainted with and married Miss Albertson of New Albany, Ind. The Albertsons were Pennsylvania Dutch.

Both paternal grandparents died at an early age, and my father found a home with a family whose name, I believe, was Harris. He had several brothers, but became separated from them. The Harris family left New Albany and went to Union, Mo., remaining there during the Civil War. They were not successful and returned to Illinois, settling near Baldwinsville, Edgar County.

"My father died when I was twelve years old, and when my younger brother, Dr. J. Paul Jeter, dentist of Chester, Pa., was seven year old. My father married J. Nettie Sizemore, becoming acquainted with her when he was operating a stave and tile factory at Nevins, Edgar County, Ill. After a railroad accident he took up the practice of law, and was a member of the Illinois bar, practicing in Paris, Ill. He died in 1908, when he was forty-eight years old.

"The only Jeter that I have ever met was a relative—we agreed that we were cousins. He was Theodore Jeter, a real estate man of Champaign, Ill.

DR. JAY PAUL JETER

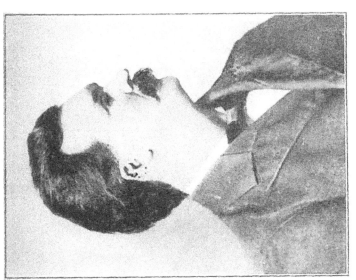

GEORGE MADISON JETER

"My own education was at Paris, where I graduated from high school, University of Illinois B. S. in E. E., post-graduate work at Union College, Schenectady, New York. I have been with General Electric Company since 1910, leaving them this fall (1929) to come to Bridgeport. My last position was Sales Manager, Transformer Department, Pittsfield, Mass. My present work is Manager Power Apparatus Sales for a subsidiary company, General Electric Supply Corporation. During the World War I was stationed at Washington, D. C.

G. GUY JETER.

"My residence address is now 2016 North Ave., Bridgeport, Connecticut."

Dr. J. Paul Jeter, was born July 15, 1893, and is five years younger than his brother, Guy.

He was educated at the public schools of Paris, Ill.; University of Illinois Preparatory School; Mercersburg Academy; and graduated at the University of Pennsylvania in 1918.

He entered the United States Army in the World War in September, 1917; was Private, Corporal, Sergeant, Second Lieutenant, and First Lieutenant of 304th Regiment Engineers. Was Honorably discharged December 31, 1918. Now Captain of Reserves of U. S. Army.

He has lived in Chester, Pa., for the last nine years, where he is a popular dentist.

NOTES OF THE JETER FAMILY MADE FROM KENTUCKY COUNTY RECORDS

JETER—Nicholasville, Jessamine County, Kentucky

Grantors	Grantees	Book	Page	Year
S. Jeter	Elijah J. Young	V.	358	1849
L. F. Jeter	Wm. D. Young, Est.	X.	383	1873
Agnes E. and L. F.	Lucy J. Davis	4	258	1885
Agnes E. and L. F.	Elgin Price	II.	398	1894
Agnes E. and L. F. by Comr.	J. B. Gunn	5	370	1898
Elisha Jeter	Littleton Jeter	D	227	1815
Jacob Ramon	Clement Jeter	N	461	1841
James Uttinger	Leonard F. Jeter	W	796	1872
H. A. Patterson	Leonard F. Jeter	X	337	1873
A. M. Swope	L. F. Jeter	3	328	1884
Ben'j. B. Warfield	L. F. Jeter	3	327	1884

MARRIAGE LICENSE—

Elisha Jeter to Izabellar Long by Rev. John Shackleford. No date given—the ones on either side are Nov. 4, 1817, and Jan. 30, 1806.

MARRIAGE RECORDS—Lexington, Fayette County, Kentucky

	Book	Page
Albert Jeter to Sarah Irvin, Jan. 6, 1820	1	41
Clement Jeter to Amy Bangers, Sept. 15, 18—	1	72
Dorothy Jeter to Willis Carson, Mar. 7, 1821	1	47
Ellen Jeter to Robert Sanders, Nov. 17, 1822	1	54
Harriet Jeter to Geo. W. Ryan, Nov. 2, 1830	1	87
Eliza Jeter to Matthew Alton, Mar. 30, 1834	1	105
Ann Jeter to Jos. S. Gardner, May 11, 1834	1	105
Ben'j Jeter to S. A. Stivers, Mrs. Alcy Stephens, Aug. 14, 1847	2	62
Wm. Jeter to Susan Tyre, Feb. 25, 1851	2	178
John Jeter to Mary Adams	2	248
Elizabeth Jeter to Louis Fredericks, Jan. 19, 1846	2	3
Jane C. Jeter to Stephen Manship, Oct. 26, 1848	2	104
Eliza Mary Jeter to Thos. Sister, Jan. 22, 1851	2	176
Sarah F. Jeter to David P. King, May 23, 1853	2	246

Note:—Sarah and Eliza are given as daughters of Hugh Jeter. Sarah was married by John G. Tompkins.

Hugh Jeter from John L. Candry, Deed Book 22, page 137, June 4, 1844.

John Jeter from Geo. Timberlake, Deed Book 12, page 404, May 3, 1836.

J. T. Gardner to John Jeter, Mgt. Deed, Deed Book 20, page 341, July 8, 1842.

Mtg. Release to Geo. Timberlake from John Jeter, Deed Book 13, page 23, October 1, 1833.

John Jeter to Geo. Timberlake, Deed, Deed Book 13, page 394, June, 1837.

Lyttleton Jeter from Geo. W. Ryan, Deed, Deed Book 10, page 384, February 13, 1835.

Lyttleton Jeter, mtg. to C. F. Brower, Deed Book 35, page 563, April 6, 1860.

Hugh Jeter and James Wood made administrators of estate of Jane Jeter, widow of Littleton Jeter, Jan. 8, 1844. Admr. Bond, Book 3, page 163.

Hugh Jeter admr. of James Jeter, Dec'd. Order Book II, page 163.

THE SALEM, VIRGINIA, JETERS

Horatio Jeter, thought to have been another son of John, Sr., lived and died in Caroline County, Va. His marriage bond—to Elizabeth Rowland of Caroline—bears the same date as that of Littleton Jeter—September 7, 1786—and it is presumed that they were brothers.

His will, made November 29, 1814, and proved February 13, 1815, mentions: wife, Elizabeth; sons, Samuel and Ira; daughters, Nancy Thomson and Harriett Estes; grandson, William Estes. (Will Book 17.)

Ira Jeter, son of Horatio and Elizabeth (Rowland) Jeter of Caroline County, Virginia, was born in Caroline County, March 8, 1796, died in Salem, Roanoke County, Va., January 3, 1876, and is buried in the old Jeter enclosure in East Hill Cemetery of that town.

He married in Botetourt County, Va., July 6, 1820, Sarah White, daughter of Edmund White, who was the original owner of the Fort Lewis estate and who built the brick residence there which was inherited by his son, Alexander White.

Ira Jeter was a pharmacist of Salem for many years. He was also connected with the Salem Tannery. He was a scholar of some note, and contributed material for McCauley's *History of Roanoke County*.

CHILDREN OF IRA AND SARAH (WHITE) JETER WERE:

(1) Samuel W.; married May 26, 1858, Anne E. Ewing, daughter of Rev. John D. and Druscilla Ewing, of Rockbridge County, Va. His marriage bond states that "Sam'l W. Jeter, age 35, occupation, druggist, Salem, Roanoke County, Va., was born in Caroline County, Va. A son of Ira and Sarah Jeter."
(2) Fannie.
(3) Montgomery.
(4) Sarah.
(5) Warren.
(6) James.
(7) Josephine.
(8) Virginia.
(9) Ballard.
(10) Paul.

Montgomery Jeter, born 1829; died 1908; son of Ira and Sarah (White) Jeter, was a cavalryman in the Confederate Army for a few months. He was given an Honorable Discharge on account of a weak heart.

He studied dentistry and practiced his profession in Salem, Va. He was an artist, a cabinet-maker, and a great lover of flowers, seldom appearing in rose season without a bud, from his own garden, worn as a boutonniere. The making of walking canes for his friends was one of his hobbies, and among his many pictures he left several oil paintings of decided merit. His last days were spent in the home of his daughter, Mrs. Florence (Jeter) Kime, in Salem, Va.

Montgomery Jeter married in 1858, Martha Caroline Sagendorf, of Rhineback, Duchess County, New York, who came down to Salem just before the Civil War to be a governess in the family of Alexander White. Their children are:

Warren, Edward, Anne Boleyn, Lulah, Florence, Maurice, and Garland.

Maurice Jeter married Etta Katzenberger of Baltimore, Md., and has children: Thelma, who married J. Leonard Shank; and Lewis.

SAGENDORF—Originally VON SAGENDORF

The Sagendorfs were an old, aristocratic Dutch family who settled in Columbia County, New York, when Peter Stuyvesant was Governor of New Amsterdam. They were large land owners in that state.

Edward Sagendorf, father of Martha Caroline, who married Montgomery Jeter, was the great-grandson of the immigrant, who was a count, and belonged to the nobility of Holland. The history of the family, written in German, with the coat-of-arms, is to be found in the New York Library.

THE JETERS OF AMELIA COUNTY, VIRGINIA

Ambrose Jeter, believed to have been another son of John Jeter, the immigrant, was born in Caroline County, Virginia, before 1735. He was Ensign in the Caroline Militia during the Revolutionary War— commissioned May, 1778.

He married twice—both times in Amelia County, Virginia, where his marriage bonds are to be found. First, in 1760, Jane Stern, daughter of Francis and Ann Elizabeth B. Stern. The marriage bond shows that Ann Stern consented to the marriage of her daughter, and that John Jeter was security.

Francis Stern lived and died in Caroline County. On August 14, 1755, John Jeter was appointed one of the appraisers of the estate of Francis Stern. (Order Book, 1756-1758, page 90. Caroline records.)

Ambrose Jeter married (second) in 1778, Mrs. Mary Farley (widow), by whom he had no children. He died in Amelia County in 1803, and his will, made in 1798, mentions daughters: Tabitha Gills, Mason Crenshaw, and Jane Wood; sons: Allen, Rodophil, and John. (Will Book No. 6, page 355.)

OF THE ABOVE CHILDREN:

(1) Tabitha; married John Gills, March 11, 1786. (His second wife, perhaps.)
(2) Mason; married Anthony Crenshaw, January 3, 1786.
(3) Jane; married William Wood. (See forward.)
(4) Rodophil; married Lucy Gills. (See forward.)
(5) John; married (first) Jane Chaffin; (second) Ann Scott. (See forward.)

Rodophil Jeter, son of Ambrose and Jane (Stern) Jeter, was born in 1765, according to a family tree now in possession of William Jeter, III, of Skipwith, Va., who is his great-great-grandson. He lived in Leigh District of Amelia County, where the Post Office, Rodophil, was named for him. He represented his county in the Legislature, 1818-19-20, and again 1824-25-26-28. He married Lucy Gills, daughter of John Gills of Amelia County, and died in 1843. His will, recorded in Amelia County (Will Book No. 15, page 188) mentions sons: Anderson, John, and William; daughters: Elizabeth, Jane, Harriett, and Lucy Anne; and children of daughter, Rebecca Webster, deceased.

William Jeter, son of Rodophil and Lucy (Gills) Jeter, was born in Mecklenburg County, Virginia, in 1802, and was a tobacconist. He moved to Richmond during the Civil War. His son—

John Rodophil, was born in Mecklenburg County April 18, 1838, and married Roberta Ellis Walker, who was born in Mecklenburg County, June 24, 1839.

CHILDREN:

(1) William.
(2) John Rodophil, Jr., born May 22, 1877, in Henrico County, Virginia; married, April 24, 1907, Sadie Winston Craddock of Amelia County; has been for many years Document Clerk, and Librarian of the State Senate of Virginia.

(3) Wortley; married R. E. Walker, and lives at Skipwith, Va.
(4) Walker; lives in Tennessee.

....

John Jeter, youngest son of Ambrose and Jane (Stern) Jeter, lived and died in Amelia County, Virginia. He was a captain in the War of 1812, as is shown by the following record, furnished by the War Department, at Washington, D. C.:

"Office of Adjutant General.

"The records of this office show that one John Jeter served in the War of 1812 as a Captain of a company designated Captain Jeter's Company of Artillery, Virginia Militia. His service commenced August 1, 1814, and ended February 16, 1815. The record shows that his place of residence was Amelia County, Va."

John Jeter married (first), 1794, Jane Chaffin, daughter of Joshua Chaffin of Amelia County, who was sworn in as Lieutenant under Captain L. Ford, October 26, 1780, and served in the Revolutionary War. He married (second) in 1801, Ann Scott, also of Amelia County.

He died in 1815, and his will recorded in Amelia (Will Book No. 10, page 61) mentions daughter, Emily; sons, John T. and Jarrett A.; wife, Ann; sons, Samuel, James, and George; and daughter, Elizabeth.

The following record of John Jeter and his descendants is taken from the family Bible of his son, Jarrett Allen Jeter:

"John Jeter was born July 17, 1774; died May 15, 1823. Jane Jeter, his wife, was born April 21, 1776.

CHILDREN:

(1) Emily Ellis, born July 16, 1796.
(2) John Tinsley, born November 13, 1798. (See Louisiana Jeters.)
(3) Jarrett Allen, born October 17, 1800.

CHILDREN OF JOHN JETER AND HIS (SECOND) WIFE, ANN JETER:

(4) Samuel Scott, born April 13, 1802; died August 25, 1829.
(5) James Mason, born April 13, 1804. (See forward.)
(6) Elizabeth Evans, born November 7, 1806. (See forward.)
(7) Mary Anna, born June 22, 1809.
(8) George R., born September 10, 1812; married Mary Brazeal.

Ann, wife of John Jeter, was born January 14, 1784; died July 25, 1846.

Jarrett Allen Jeter, son of John and Jane Jeter, married Mary Elizabeth Worsham, who was born in Amelia County, October 9, 1823.

CHILDREN :

(1) Mary Jane, born November 24, 1824.
(2) Daniel Worsham, born January 5, 1831.
(3) Hannah Finney, born September 19, 1833.
(4) Elizabeth Tinsley, born March 9, 1836.
(5) Willia Ann, born January 1, 1839.
(6) Martha Allen, born November 29, 1840.

James Mason Jeter, son of John and Ann Jeter, married (first) in 1826, Susan A. Overton of Amelia County.

CHILDREN :

(1) Marcus Aurelius, born February 16, 1827; died October 12, 1829.
(2) Ann Eliza, born August 31, 1829.
(3) James Richard, born June 5, 1832.
James Mason Jeter married (second) Louisa A. Jones.

CHILDREN :

(4) George Scott, born November 6, 1835.
(5) Henny Jones, born January 20, 1841; died January 26, 1845.
(6) William Mason, born April 9, 1843; married Ida Porter.

CHILDREN :

Ada and Ida (twins), and Carrie.

James Richard Jeter, son of James Mason and Susan (Overton) Jeter, married Hannah Finney Jeter, daughter of Jarrett Allen and Mary (Worsham) Jeter.

CHILDREN :

(1) Linda Mason, born January 29, 1858; died October 12, 1883.
(2) Mary Susan, born February 26, 1860; died June, 1861.
(3) Russell Allen, born January 29, 1865; died September 19, 1866.
(4) Nannie Lee, born October 26, 1862; died October 26, 1881.
(5) Rosa Emmafield, born September 12, 1867; died March, 1885.
(6) Eliza Finney, born October 23, 1869; married Reps Chaffin Jeter,

son of George Scott and Martha (Jeter) Jeter. They live at Jetersville, Va.

Hannah Finney (Jeter) Jeter, wife of James Richard Jeter, died January 5, 1894. He then married her sister, Elizabeth Tinsley Jeter.

James Richard Jeter died February 7, 1906.

Elizabeth Tinsley (Jeter) Jeter died June, 1909.

....

George Scott Jeter, son of James Mason and Louisa (Jones) Jeter, married, June 28, 1860, Martha Allen Jeter, daughter of Jarrett Allen and Mary (Worsham) Jeter.

CHILDREN :

(1) George Scott, Jr., born May 13, 1861; married Esther Martin (died 1911).

CHILDREN :

(a) Norbourne Berkeley, born November 29, 1901.
(b) Mary Pattie, born March 31, 1903.
(c) George Scott, III, born June 17, 1906.
(d) Esther Marion, born May 31, 1909.

(2) Berkeley, born March, 1867; died in infancy.
(3) Lesley, born 1869; died in infancy.
(4) William Norbourne, born April 3, 1863; died 1901.
(5) Pattie A., born January, 1865; died June, 1869.
(6) Reps Chaffin, born October 29, 1871; married Eliza Finney Jeter, daughter of James Richard and Hannah (Jeter) Jeter.

CHILDREN :

(a) Hannah Allen, born September 8, 1897.
(b) James Scott, born March 24, 1900; married, January 14, 1925, Ruth Corban.
(c) Nannie Louise, born August 16, 1903; married, December 14, 1926, Walter W. Anderson.

CHILDREN :

(aa) Walter W., Jr., born August 31, 1927.
(bb) Elmer Ray, born March 12, 1929.

(d) Joyce Keith, born December 26, 1905.
(c) Mary Chaffin, born January 18, 1910.

(7) James Allen, born August 20, 1875; married Elizabeth Pierce.

CHILDREN:

    (a) James Allen, Jr. (twin), born July 1, 1912; died.

    (b) Franklin Scott (twin), born July 1, 1912.

    (c) Norbourne Pierce, born March 6, 1914.

    (d) James Reginal, born August 26, 1915.

    (e) Jarrett Allen, born December, 1918.

    (f) Elizabeth Pattie, born June 29, 1921.

    (g) Charles Jennings, born December, 1923.

    (h) Philip Harvie, born September, 1926.

(8) Warren Hopkins, born September 26, 1878; married Myrtle Turner.

CHILDREN:

    (a) Hazen Boyd.

    (b) Edith.

    (c) Weldon.

    (d) Pattie.

    (e) Ruth.

(9) Mary Louise, born January 23, 1881; married Martin W. Long-fellow.

(10) Charles Old, born June 29, 1883; married Alice Lowry in 1926."

Elizabeth Evans Jeter, daughter of John and Ann (Scott) Jeter, of Amelia County, Va., married, October 5, 1826, Isham Clements Booker.

CHILDREN:

(1) Mary Ann Elizabeth, born September 17, 1827; died July 9, 1852.

(2) Sarah Jane Louise, born December 18, 1829; died January 26, 1911.

(3) William Henry, born July 26, 1832; died July 16, 1903; married (first), November 30, 1871, Elizabeth Rebecca Slater (died June 13, 1877), daughter of Robert Yates and Jane Saunders (Godden) Slater.

CHILD:

    (a) Mary Elizabeth, born August 5, 1873; married, July 9, 1896, Charles Martin Harnish; lives in Richmond, Va.

CHILD:

(aa) Marie, born July 30, 1898.

After the death of his wife, William Henry Booker married her sister, Emma Pleasants Slater.

CHILDREN:

(b) William Lewis, born November 15, 1879; died, unmarried, February 12, 1915.

(c) Robert Henry, born August 14, 1881; married, May 20, 1919, Florence Howard Dyson.

(4) Louisiana Isabella, born April 2, 1835; died March 5, 1855.

(5) Georganna, born February 15, 1837; died March 5, 1863.

(6) John Edmund, born July 5, 1839; died October, 1888.

(7) Virginia Howard, born October 27, 1841; died December 19, 1926.

(8) Indiana Lawson, born August 24, 1844; died July 5, 1864.

(9) Thomas Evans, born November 14, 1845; now living at Hopkinsville, Kentucky.

....

Jean Stern Jeter, youngest daughter of Ambrose and Jean (Stern) Jeter of Amelia County, Va., mentioned in her father's will as his fifth child, was born about 1769 and died after 1831. She married, July 2, 1788, William Wood, Jr. (died 1831) of Amelia County, Va., son of William Wood, Sr.—both officers in the Revolutionary War.

Their daughter, Jean Stern Wood (died 1833); married, October 13, 1824, Ichabod Johnson (born 1801; died 1842) of Cumberland County, Va.

Their son, William Thomas Johnson (born 1825; died 1896) of Cumberland County and Farmville, Va., member of Cumberland Troop, C. S. A.; married, September 10, 1846, Elizabeth Cabell Carrington (born 1825; died 1893), daughter of Tucker Carrington, of Mecklenburg County, Va., and his wife, Mary Watkins.

Their daughter, Julia Jane Johnson, married, December 18, 1895, Joseph DuPuy Eggleston, II, then Superintendent of City Schools of Asheville, N. C.; now President of Hampden-Sydney College, Virginia.

JOHN TINSLEY JETER

SAMUEL JETER

CHILDREN:

(1) Elizabeth Carrington, B. A. of Sweetbriar College, Va.; M. A. of Syracuse University, New York; Honour's A. B., Oxford University, England.

(2) Joseph Du Puy, III, B. S. of Hampden-Sydney College, Va.; now (1929) doing post-graduate work at University of Virginia.

THE LOUISIANA JETERS

John Tinsley Jeter, eldest son of Captain John Jeter of Amelia County, Va., and his first wife, Jane Chaffin, was born in Amelia County, November 13, 1798. He married (first) in Petersburg, Va., October 13, 1823, Elizabeth Lawrence Newman (born April 19, 1802). Their children were all born in Virginia and the family continued to live there until after the death of his wife.

CHILDREN:

(1) Elvira, born December 7, 1825; married Adolphus Motley of Virginia; moved to Tennessee after 1850.

CHILDREN:

   (a) Que (so called); born in Virginia.
   (b) Elvira Elizabeth; born in Tennessee.
   (c) John; born in Tennessee.

(2) John Tinsley, Jr., born May 7, 1827; married, July 15, 1853, Mary Smith Richards of Philadelphia, Pa. They lived and died in Pennsylvania.

CHILDREN:

   (a) John Tinsley, III, born March 26, 1858.
   (b) Harriet Richards, born August 20, 1869; married J. S. Robeson; lives in Pennington, N. J.
   (c) Mary; married Paul Boyer.

(3) Ellen Gray, born July 29, 1831 (?); married in New Orleans, La. Dr. Samuel McLean of Virginia; moved to California in 1849 via Cape Horn, taking six months to make the voyage from New Orleans to San Francisco.

CHILDREN:

(a) Robert Armistead.

(b) Mary.

(c) Elizabeth, born at Point Coupee, La.

(d) John.

A grandson of Dr. Samuel and Ellen (Jeter) McLean is Dr. Herbert McLean Evans of Berkeley, Calif.

(4) Fitz Allen; went to California with his brother-in-law and sister, Dr. and Mrs. Samuel McLean; married there and had two sons.

John Tinsley Jeter, Sr., married (second) in Amelia County, Va., February 20, 1839, Mrs. Ann Watkins (McAshan) Guerrant, widow of William Guerrant. She was born on a plantation in Buckingham County, Va., September 9, 1814, and died July 28, 1878, in the home of her daughter, Mrs. Ann Tinsley (Jeter) Carmouche, at Petit Prairie Bayou St. Landry Parish, La.

John Tinsley Jeter had financial reverses in Amelia County, because of having endorsed too heavily for friends, and left Virginia in 1843, going first to Missouri and later to New Orleans, where his wife owned property. She also had plantations in Louisiana. During the Civil War he started to Bethlehem, Pa., on business and also to see his children by his first marriage, who were living there, but was taken ill of swamp fever on the steamboat and died in Memphis, Tenn., May 13, 1862.

CHILDREN:

(5) Ann Tinsley, born in Virginia July 27, 1843. (See forward.)

(6) William Guerrant; member Delta Rifles of West Baton Rouge in Civil War; was in battles of Corinth, East Baton Rouge and Atlanta; was promoted to Lieutenant and was acting as Captain when killed in Battle of Atlanta, July 28, 1864.

(7) John Warwick, born in New Orleans, La., October 23, 1850. (See forward.)

(8) Bennett; died in infancy.

(12) Ann Watkins McAshan was a descendant of—

Col. Walter Aston, the immigrant, who was born in England in 1606, and came to Virginia about 1628, where he died April 6, 1656, according to the dates on his tombstone, which still stands at Westover. He was the son of Walter Aston of Longden, Stafford County, England, and great-grandson of Sir Walter Aston, knighted in 1560.

Col. Aston represented Shirley Hundred in the House of Burgesses (1629-1630); Shirley Hundred, Mr. Farrar's and Chaplin's (February, 1631-32); Shirley Hundred, Maine and "Carvsey's Care" (September, 1632, and February, 1632-33); and Charles City County (1642-43). He was for years a Justice of the Peace and militia officer for Charles City County, near Shirley Hundred, on King's Creek, of which land 200 acres, known as "Carvsey's Care," were purchased February 7, 1634, from John Carvsey (Causey), the rest of the land was due Aston for the transportation of ten persons to Virginia. More was added October 12, 1641, and the entire grant of 1,040 acres was confirmed to Aston, August 12, 1646.

Col. Aston married (first) Nabon (or Warbon); (second) Hannah Jordan, who survived him. His will was probated in Charles City County, January 25, 1656 or 57.

(11) Mary Aston was the second wife of Richard Cocke, and they were married about 1647. His first wife a widow Brown. Richard Cocke was born in England about 1600, came to Virginia in 1628, and died in 1665. He was County Commandant or Lieutenant of Henrico County, Virginia, and patented 3,000 acres on James River, in Henrico County. He was a member of the House of Burgesses in 1632.

(10) Captain Thomas Cocke was born in 1638, and died in 1696. He was Justice of the Peace, 1678-80; Sheriff of Henrico, 1688; and Member of House of Burgesses. He married Mrs. Margaret (Wood) Jones, widow of Peter Jones, mother of Peter Jones, II, and daughter of General Abraham Wood, who came to Virginia in 1620 on the vessel, "Margaret and John," when ten years of age.

(9) James Cocke was born in 1666, and died 1721-25. He lived at "Curles"; was Clerk of Court; and Burgess in 1699. He married, in 1691, Elizabeth Pleasants, who died in 1751. She was the daughter of John Pleasants, a Quaker of St. Saviors, Norwich, England, who was baptised February 27, 1644-45, and emigrated to Virginia about 1665. He settled at "Curles," on the north side of the James River in Henrico County. He was offered the office of Burgess, but being a Quaker, he could not take the oath. He married Mrs. Jane (Larcome) Tucker, widow of Samuel Tucker, who was Captain of the ship, "Vine Tree." John Pleasants died at "Curles," May 12, 1698.

(8) Elizabeth Pleasants Cocke married Thomas Poythress of Henrico County, Virginia.

(7) Susanna Poythress married William Hall of Virginia, who was born about 1700 and was the son of (6) Robert Hall, a member of the House of Burgesses for Prince George County, Virginia, April 23, 1718. Robert Hall married ———— Pleasants. His father was (7) William Hall of Bermuda, who married Mary Tucker, daughter of George and Frances Tucker of Bermuda. William Tucker and his wife came to Virginia in 1652, and settled at Flower de Hundred.

(5) Dr. Robert Hall, son of William and Susanna (Poythress) Hall, was born in Buckingham County, Va., but removed to Edenton, North Carolina, where he died 1780-1786. He was a surgeon in the 3rd N. C. Infantry Regiment in

the Revolutionary Army, commissioned April 17, 1774. He married Anna Leary, August 4, 1742. (Edenton County, N. C., records.)

(4) Sicily Ann Hall married John Agee in 1772. His grandfather, Mathew Agee, came from France in 1690, because of Huguenot persecution, and settled at Manakin Town, Va., in 1710, where he was still living in 1741. He was a vestryman of King William Parish, and was granted 800 acres of land—two patents—in Henrico County, January 13, 1725. He married in France, and had four children. One son, James Agee, born in 1724; died in 1821; lived near Maysville, in Buckingham County, Va. He married Elizabeth Ford, who was born in 1729, and died in 1821. James Agee was in the Revolutionary Army— 7th Virginia Regiment. His son, John, was also in the Revolutionary Army—7th Virginia Regiment—June 30 to July 31, 1777.

(3) Elizabeth Agee was born March 5, 1790; died in Houston, Texas, November 28, 1874, and is buried in La Grange, Texas. She married, in Virginia, January 8, 1807, Nehemiah McAshan, II, born December 15, 1784; died in Virginia, June 23, 1846; son of Nehemiah McAshan, I, and ——— Chambers.

(2) Ann Watkins McAshan married (first) William Guerrant; (second) John Tinsley Jeter.

....

Annie Tinsley Jeter, daughter of John Tinsley Jeter and his (second) wife, Mrs. Anne Watkins (McAshan) Guerrant, married in New Orleans, Louisiana, April 28, 1864, Captain Emile A. Carmouche, of Point Coupee Parish, Louisiana, who was born January 5, 1836, and was captain of a company of cavalry during the Civil War. He first enlisted with the Delta Rifles, 4th Louisiana Regiment, and was later transterred to the 2nd Louisiana Cavalry. He moved from Point Coupee to St. Landry Parish; served his district as member of Legislature during the reconstruction period following the close of the Civil War; moved to Bossier Parish in 1879; died July 3, 1884.

After his death Mrs. Carmouche continued to live on her farm in Bossier Parish, and there raised and educated her family of five children. She was a woman of strong character, brilliant mind, and unusual business ability. She died in Shreveport, Louisiana, July 18, 1920, leaving a large estate free from encumbrance.

CHILDREN:

(1) Annie E., born February 16, 1865. (See forward.)

(2) Mary Stella, born July 6, 1868. (See forward.)

(3) Bessie, born May 20, 1870. (See forward.)

(4) Emile Aloysius, Jr., born October 30, 1872. (See forward.)

(5) William Jeter, born August 2, 1874. (See forward.)

Annie E. Carmouche, daughter of Emile A. and Annie (Jeter) Carmouche, married Henry Purvis Middleton, who was born April 29, 1861, in Yazoo County, Mississippi. His great-great-uncle, Arthur Middleton, was one of the signers of the Declaration of Independence, and he was also a descendant of Edward Rutledge, another signer of the same document.

CHILDREN:

(1) John Carmouche, born October 9, 1891, at Bluff Plantation, near Shreveport, La.; died, June 9, 1904, at Welcome Plantation in Point Coupee Parish.

(2) Annie Tinsley, born June 2, 1893, at Cane Bend Plantation; married, August 20, 1918, Ernest Brown Nettleton of Bloomington, Illinois, who was educated at Bloomington and Peoria (Ill.) Colleges; was a government engineer, and surveyed the Mississippi River from Cairo to the Delta; now instructor at Carnegie Tech., Pittsburgh, Pennsylvania.

CHILDREN:

(a) Henry Purvis, born, August 2, 1919, New Roads, La.
(b) Elizabeth Anne, born July 26, 1921; died June 18, 1924, at Bloomington, Ill.
(c) Margaret, born September 25, 1922, at Baton Rouge, La.
(d) Mary Eloise, born January 27, 1924, at Bloomington, Ill.
(e) Mary Teresa, born May 31, 1927, at Pittsburgh, Pa.

(3) Loura May, born July 26, 1895, at Jersey Farm, Bossier Parish, La.; died August 20, 1898.

(4) Elizabeth Courtney, born January 25, 1897, at Jersey Farm; married, April 25, 1921, at Welcome Plantation, Thornton Bennett Nettleton, brother of Ernest Brown Nettleton. They live at Baton Rouge, La.

CHILDREN:

(a) Thornton Bennett, Jr., born March 7, 1922.
(b) Margaret Elizabeth, born July 25, 1924.
(c) John Robert, born April 19, 1926.

(5) Margaret Mary, born January 31, 1900, at Jersey Farm; married, June 27, 1923, at Baton Rouge, La., Charles Leslie Osterburger

of Villa, Louisiana, who was instructor of Agricultural Engineering Department of Louisiana State University, and is now head of a department of the Louisiana Power and Light Company in Algiers, La.

CHILDREN:

(a) Charles Leslie, Jr., born October 31, 1926, at Baton Rouge.
(b) Infant, born 1928; died 1929.

Mary Stella Carmouche, daughter of Emile A. and Annie (Jeter) Carmouche; married, September 14, 1887, John Christopher Griggs, born January 23, 1860, son of George Richard Griggs of Devonport, in the County of Devon, England, and his wife, Mary Granfield of London, England. He died May 30, 1906.

CHILDREN:

(1) Emile Carmouche, born and died August 30, 1888.
(2) Thomas William, born June 21, 1889; died August 25, 1906.
(3) John Granfield, born May 17, 1891, at Shreveport, La., married Cora LaCour, daughter of A. J. and Mary (Brown) LaCour of Point Coupee Parish, La.

CHILDREN:

(a) Mary Stella.
(b) John Granfield, Jr.
(c) Emily.
(d) William Jeter.
(e) Frederick.
(f) Cinclair.
(g) August J.
(h) Leo Louis.

(4) George Clifford, born August 30, 1892; married, April 1, 1919, at Caplan, La., Isabelle Mary Deshotels, daughter of Octave Henry and Mary Lilia (Forest) Deshotels of Ville Platte, Louisiana.

CHILDREN:

(a) Henry Octave.
(b) Lilia Ann.

(c) George Clifford, Jr.

(d) Frederick Ivy.

(e) Shirley Rose.

(f) Mary Geraldine.

(5) Mary Stella, born September 7, 1893; now Sister Christina of the Daughters of the Cross.

(6) Joseph Lucas, born June 5, 1896, at New Orleans, La.; married Margaret Ann Conkerton, daughter of John David and Helen (Kreamer) Conkerton of New Orleans. No children.

(7) Virginia Ann, born December 30, 1902, at New Orleans; unmarried.

(8) Henry Purvis, born August 20, 1905, at Shreveport, La.; now studying for the Priesthood in the Order of the Society of Jesus.   ....

Bessie Carmouche, daughter of Emile A. and Annie (Jeter) Carmouche; married, January 15, 1890, George E. Gilmer, who was born October 21, 1863. (See Gilmer family.)

CHILDREN:

(1) Annie Elizabeth, born February 12, 1891; married, December 31, 1914; Oswald E. LaCour of Point Coupee Parish, La.; live near Morganza, La.

CHILDREN:

(a) Oswald Edgar, born March 16, 1917.

(b) Anne Jeter, born January 12, 1919.

(c) George Gilmer, born June 8, 1920.

(d) William Carmouche, born May 6, 1922.

(e) Marie Adele, born May 10, 1924.

(f) Robert H., born June 11, 1925.

(g) Frances Elizabeth, born October 28, 1927.

(2) George Edwin; died in infancy.

(3) George Tinsley, born March 27, 1894; received A. B. degree at Tulane University, New Orleans, La., in 1915; L. L. B. in 1917; now practicing law in Shreveport, La. He married, October 2, 1926, Mrs. Edna Clary Ebey, born in Hickory, Oklahoma, January 30, 1900. Her father was born in Tipperary, Ireland, and her mother, in Virginia. She has one child:

(a) Francis Clary Ebey, born February 6, 1921.

(4) Birdie May; died in infancy.

(5) Peachy Ridgeway, born December 8, 1897; received B. S. degree from Tulane University in 1917, and M. D. in 1921; spent one year in special work at Mayo's, Rochester, Minn.; did interne work at Cleveland, Ohio; returned to Shreveport in 1923 and practiced medicine three years. He then decided to specialize in tuberculosis work, and went to Trudeau Sanitorium, Saranac Lake, New York; completed the course and then studied in Europe. He now has charge of both White and Colored Pines —tubercular institutions of Shreveport, La.

He married, June 6, 1929, Julia Morrow Church, born October 4, 1899, of McKinney, Texas, daughter of Judge John Church, who was born in 1843 at "The Groves," home of the Church family, since the sixteenth century, in Strabane, Londonderry County, Ireland. He graduated at Trinity College, Dublin, and came to McKinney, Texas, in 1873; studied law, and became an able judge and lecturer. He died August 29, 1926.

He married Julia Summerville Coffee, who was born December 8, 1864, at Halcyon Plantation, Brazoria County, Texas, and was the daughter of Aaron Coffee of Bolivar County, Mississippi, and Mary Summerville Smith of Orange County, Virginia, who were married, March 28, 1860, in Galveston, Texas. Mrs. Church owns and operates a large farm in Collins County, Texas.

Julia Morrow (Church) Gilmer is a graduate of Hollins College, Virginia. Since leaving school she has devoted much time to literary work and lecturing; she writes for several magazines, and is a critic of ability.

(6) William Carmouche, born May 14, 1906; now a student of Tulane University, specializing in architecture, for which he has marked talent.

Emile Aloysius Carmouche, Jr., son of Emile A., Sr., and Annie (Jeter) Carmouche, married Nuna Ogden, daughter of John Nash and Celeste (Thompson) Ogden. They live at Crowley, La., where he is a prominent mechanical engineer.

CHILDREN:

(1) Emile A., III, born January 15, 1903; married, August 23, 1924, Thelma Von Eye. He is a lawyer in New Orleans.

CHILD:

(a) Emile A., IV, born September 27, 1927.

(2) Nunamae, born April 5, 1904; married, December 23, 1925, Claud J. Richard; lives at Bayne, La.

CHILDREN:

(a) Ruby Mae, born October 8, 1926.

(b) John Warren, born September 8, 1928.

(3) Henry Purvis, born October 2, 1905; married, August 10, 1929, Margaret Gill; lives at Crowley, La.

(4) William Jeter, Jr., born July 25, 1909.

(5) Robert A., born January 11, 1911.

(6) Ernest Nash, born April 11, 1913.

(7) Ogden, born 1907; died in infancy.

William Jeter Carmouche, son of Emile and Annie (Jeter) Carmouche, graduated from college as valedictorian of his class; studied law at Tulane University; has practiced his profession for many years at Crowley, Louisiana, where he has a large clientele. His work often takes him into other states and even to foreign countries. He has educated many worthy boys in whom he takes a pardonable pride, and it is said that he has more nieces and nephews—if all who call him "Uncle Will" can be considered as such—than any man in Louisiana. Outside of his literary and philanthropic work, his hobby is flowers, of which he has a wonderful collection.

GILMER

The founder of the Gilmer family of America was Dr. George Gilmer, who was born in 1700, near Edinburgh, Scotland; died in Williamsburg, Virginia, January 15, 1757; graduated at University of Edinburgh; went to London, and was associated with Dr. Ridgeway in the practice of medicine. He married (first) the daughter of Dr. Ridgeway, and she died in England while he was in Virginia looking after the interests of the Royal Land Company of London, by whom he had been sent over. He then settled in Williamsburg, continued to superintend the affairs of the Royal Land Company, and practiced medicine.

He married (second) in 1732, Mary Peachy Walker, and they had two sons, Peachy Ridgeway and George, Jr. She died in 1745, and he married (third) Harrison Blair, sister of Hon. John Blair, President of the Virginia Council, and a niece of James Blair, founder and first president of the College of William and Mary. They had two sons, John and William, who died in infancy.

John Gilmer, born April 26, 1747, married Mildred Meriwether, who was born July 25, 1753. Nine children were born to them, the eldest of whom was—

John Thornton Gilmer, born February 20, 1774, in Amherst County, Virginia. He studied medicine and became a noted practitioner. He was perhaps the first to conceive the idea of vaccinating as a preventive for smallpox. Cowpox vaccine had not been discovered at that time, and he was not successful in his method; however, he lived to see his vision realized. He married Martha Gaines Harvey, and seven children were born to them.

Peachy Ridgeway Gilmer, fourth child of Dr. John Thornton and Martha Gaines (Harvey) Gilmer, was born in Wilkes County, Georgia, August 20, 1810. He graduated at the University of Illinois, and practiced law at Quincy, Ill. Later, he moved to Washington, Arkansas, where he practiced his profession until the outbreak of the Mexican War, when he joined the U. S. Army, and was under the command of General Taylor. At the termination of the war, through the advice and persuasion of his uncle, the late George O. Gilmer, a large land and slave owner of Bossier Parish, Louisiana, he gave up his law practice and bought land and slaves and became a farmer. In 1856 he married Elizabeth Dooley, of LaFayette County, Arkansas, whose father was a colonel in the Revolutionary Army and fought in many of the wars against the Indians. He died, from wounds received in the Blackhawk War, many years afterwards. Her mother was a Barton of Arkansas.

Peachy Ridgeway and Elizabeth (Dooley) Gilmer had six children, but only two of them lived to maturity.

CHILDREN:

(1) George Edwin, born October 21, 1863; married Bessie Carmouche. (See Carmouche branch of Louisiana Jeters.)
(2) Mary Peachy, born May 4, 1865; lives at Plain Dealing, La.

John Warwick Jeter (3), son of John Tinsley Jeter and his (second) wife, Mrs. Ann Watkins (McAshan) Guerrant, married, February 23, 1876, Marie Louise Dirmeyer. They moved, in 1879, on steamboat, Marie Louise, to a plantation in Bossier Parish, Louisiana, which he and his sister had inherited. He served as president of Levy Board; member of School Board; represented his county in the Legislature. He died December 18, 1903.

Marie Louise Dirmeyer was born September 9, 1856, in New Orleans, La., and died in Shreveport, La., January 18, 1917. She was the daughter of Dr. George Dirmeyer (died 1880, son of a noted

de Maupassant

musician of Black Forest, Germany, who taught foreign languages in the University of New Orleans) and Rosa Bright, who were married, December 5, 1855. He served on the Board of Health of New Orleans, and was Surgeon at Bass Hospital, Mobile, Alabama, during the Civil War.

Rosa Bright (died December, 1912) was the daughter of Hon. George T. Bright, who married, 1826, in New Orleans, La. Lodoiska de Maupassant (born 1804; died 1882) daughter of Admiral (French) Henri de Maupassant and Massan de Angua. Admiral de Maupassant was descended from an ancient family of Lorraine, France, and his mother was Mme. Rosa Massan (nee Doulan) de Angua, France.

During the insurrection in San Dominique, Admiral de Maupassant was sent there to protect the owners of fruit and coffee plantations. When all was quiet again he took his wife to San Dominique, but he only lived a short time. Soon after his death she left the island, and their daughter Lodoiska, was born off the Isle of Cuba.

George T. Bright (born 1800; died 1877) was a son of George Bright, a native of Jersey. He served with General Anthony Wayne in the French and Indian Wars, and went with the army to Lexington, Ky., where he met and married his wife, a Miss Young, native of Calvert County, Maryland, daughter of George and Helen Young, the latter a cousin to George Bright. The Youngs and Brights were of English descent.

CHILDREN OF JOHN WARWICK AND MARIE LOUISE (DIRMEYER) JETER:

(1) Marie Louise, born December 27, 1876; married, February 17, 1897, John Nixon Birdwell, who was born in Yazoo City, Miss.

CHILDREN:

(a) Warrie Rusell, in World War, did duty overseas, born April 11, 1901; married in 1921, Gladys Baumgardner (born 1901).

CHILDREN:

(aa) Warrie Russell, Jr., born 1922.
(bb) John Roland, born 1924.
(cc) Caroline Louise, born 1927.
(dd) Gladys G., born 1929.

(b) Thomas Malvin, born December 7, 1902, cashier of Oil City Bank; married, June 30, 1924, Erie Kelley, born October, 1906.

CHILDREN:

(aa) Jacquelyn, born 1925.
(bb) Thomas Malvin, born 1929.
(c) Mary Louise, born November 12, 1904; now Sister Mary Fidelis, Daughter of Cross.
(d) Madeline Elizabeth, born March 17, 1906.
(e) John Nixon, born July 4, 1907; married, September 27, 1928, Erie Ra Black, born March 16, 1909.
(f) Maurice Jeter, born December 2, 1908.

(2) John Warrick, Jr., born September 11, 1878; graduated, Soule; married, February 8, 1905, Jessie Elizabeth Herndon, born September 11, 1885.

CHILD:

(a) Beverly Ardis, born August 18, 1907; educated at Foster Hall; married Joseph E. Marshall, born July 2, 1901, in Abbieville, La.

CHILD:

(aa) Jo Ann, born November 26, 1926.

(3) John Tinsley, born July 1, 1880; married, April, 1901, Lillie Belle Gribble, born September 30, 1884, descendant of Gen. Evan Shelby.

CHILDREN:

(a) James Tinsley, Jr., born March 30, 1903; L. L. B. (2); L. S. U. (1). Married at Baton Rouge, La., March 24, 1924, Marie Louise Howell, born February 11, 1902.

CHILD:

(aa) J. T., Jr., born January 17, 1928.
(b) John Robert, born January 28, 1906, educated at Tulane University.

(4) Annie Carmouche, born March 16, 1885; married, December 27, 1906, Andrew Wilson Eason, born at Olive Branch, Miss., January 6, 1879.

CHILD:

(a) Wilson Jeter, born March 27, 1907; specializing in Architecture at Carnegie Tech.

(5) Daisy Elizabeth, born March 3, 1887; married, January 2, 1908, Theodore Doll; born Shreveport, La., July 7, 1883.

CHILDREN:

(a) Howard Francis, born November 27, 1908; graduated from Notre Dame University, B. S. E. E., 1929, at present doing extension work in electricity; General Electric.

(b) Fredericka Adelaide, born March 4, 1914.

(c) Daisy Louise, born August 25, 1916.

(6) Robert McLean, born February 5, 1891; vice-president Continental Bank; married, October 4, 1917, Marion Hearne, born December 11, 1892.

CHILDREN:

(a) Robert McLean, born August 18, 1918.

(b) Horace Hearn, born February 14, 1922.

MARION HEARNE IS DESCENDED FROM:

(9) Thomas Applegate (ca. 1600-1662) of England; was at Weymonth, Mass., as early as 1635; died at Gravesend, Long Island, N. Y.

(8) Thomas Applegate (died 1699) of Middletown, Monmouth County, New Jersey; married Johanna Gibbons. (Richard⁹ Sheriff, 1651-53, a patentee of Middletown, N. J., 1659, one of the twelve Monmouth patentees.)

(7) Benjamin Applegate (ca. 1685; died 1758) Burlington County, New Jersey; married Elizabeth ———.

(6) Benjamine Applegate.

(5) Richard Applegate, private American Revolution; settled near Albany, N. Y.; married ——— Wiggins.

(4) Daniel Applegate (1768-1825), drummer and fifer at eleven, and private at fourteen, in American Revolution; went to Shelby County, Kentucky, 1788; to Henry County, Kentucky, 1806; to Missouri, 1822; married, 1790, Rachel Lindsay.

(3) Judge Lisbon Applegate (1803-75) Chariton County, Missouri, 1837; delegate to Constitutional Convention, 1845; Major C. S. A.; married, 1825, Elizabeth Martin.

(2) William Clarke Applegate married, 1856, Eliza Ann Redding (Qr.), 1834-76.

(9) Edward D'arcy (Dorsey) drowned 1659 (Md. Arch.); from England to Elizabeth River, Virginia, now Portsmouth, with Puritan Colony to Severn River,
Maryland, 1650; married Ann ———, a Quakeress.

(8) Colonel Edward Dorsey (1652-1705) from England to Annapolis, and of
Major's Choice, Anne Arundel County, Maryland; Justice, Burgess, Judge
High Court of Chancery; the first Assemblies met in his house on Prince
George's Street, Annapolis, which is still occupied; married (first) Sarah
Wyatt (Nicholas' married Damaries ——— widow of ———).

(7) Nicholas Dorsey (1689-1717) married, 1709, Frances Hughes (born 1692;
Thomas').

(6) Nicholas Dorsey (1712-80) married Sarah Griffith.

(5) Rachel Dorsey (1737-1805) married, 1758, Anthony Lindsay (1736-1808).

(4) Rachel Lindsay (1769-1816 married, 1790, Daniel Applegate (4 above).

(5) Adam Martin (1755-1835) served in American Revolution, married Mary Mc-
Millon (1762-1850).

(4) Lewis Martin (1779—will proved 1853) married (first) Rachel Wallace (d. ca.
1807).

(3) Elizabeth Martin (1806-90) married Lisbon Applegate (3 above).

....

(9) John Maccubbin (1630-85) from the Lowlands of Scotland (ca. 1659), settled
in Maryland; married (second) Eleanor Carroll (ca. 1640-1711).

(8) Sarah Mccubbin (died 1716) married William Griffith (ca. 1655-1699), of Anne
Arundel County, Maryland.

(7) Orlando Griffith (1688-1757) married, 1717, Katherine Howard.

(6) Sarah Griffith (1718-94) married, 1736, Nicholas Dorsey (6 above).

....

(9) Col. Nicholas Green Berry (ca. 1627-1697), came to Maryland in the "Constant
Friendship," 1674; settled at Greenberry's Point, Ann Arundel County, Md.;
member of the Council of Sir Lionel Copley; acting Governor of the Province
of Maryland, 1693; Chancellor and Keeper of the Great Seal, 1692-94; married
Anne ——— (1648-98).

(8) Katherine Greenberry, 1673-1702, widow of Henry Ridgeley, married (second)
John Howard, Jr. (died 1704; John'), married Susannah Stevens; Mathew[10]
married Sarah Dorsey sister of Col. Edward.

(7) Katherine Howard (1702-83) married Orlando Griffith (7 above).

....

(4) Felix Redding (1782-1863) married Anne Wilson (1787-1865; Captain William').

(3) Isaac Wilson Redding, married Elizabeth Harriman (died 1806).

(2) Eliza Ann Wilson Redding (1834-76) married, 1856, William Clarke Applegate
(1834-83) banker and mathematician.

(1) Luella Applegate (———) married George M. Hearne, September 17, 1891.

....

(7) Adelaide Scanland, born January 6, 1894; married, October 11,
1916, Donald Coty Dickson, born February 28, 1890.

CHILDREN:

(a) Donald Coty, Jr., born November 17, 1917.
(b) Warwick Jeter, born December 13, 1920.
(c) Adelaide Lucile, born January 16, 1923.
(d) Bennet Keth, born January 1, 1927.

....

Donald Coty Dickson is the son of George Bennett Dickson, who was born December 2, 1854, at Greenwood, La.; removed to Pecan Point, La.; educated at Sewanee University, Tenn.; died October, 1889; married, October 22, 1884, at Mansfield, La., Lucile Coty, who was born April 7, 1862, and was educated at Keachie College and Mansfield College (La.).

George Bennett Dickson was the son of Major Bennett Smith Dickson, who was born in Davidson County, Tenn., 1808, and died in 1885. He married, October 18, 1837, Sarah Ann Higginbotham, who was born October 1, 1819, in Green County, Ala., and died October 5, 1873, at Pecan Point, La. He was Major of Tennessee Militia.

Major Bennett Smith Dickson was the son of James Dickson, born in Bedford County, Tenn., in 1766, died 1825; married, 1786, Agnes Nancy Moore. Her father, William Moore, was in the Revolutionary Army, appointed, 1777, for Tryon County, N. C. Commissary Regiment under Major Beatis, and member of the North Carolina General Assembly, 1769-1773.

James Dickson was the son of Joseph Dickson, who was born in 1745, Chester County, Pa., died in North Carolina, 1825; member Committee of Safety of Rowan County, N. C., 1775; Captain Colonial Troops, 1775; Major "Lincoln County Men" at Battle of King's Mountain; Brig. Gen. and State Senator, 1788-1795; founder and one of first trustees of University of North Carolina; member sixth Congress, 1799-1801; married, 1763, Margaret McErwin (born 1741; died 1814) daughter of James McErwin (born in Scotland in 1718; died in Statesville, N. C., in 1776; married in Scotland in 1740, Isabella Miller (born 1720; died 1816), daughter of Sir Michel and Margaret (McNaughton) Miller).

Sarah Ann Higginbotham, wife of Major Bennett Smith Dickson, was the daughter of Green Higginbotham, born in Elbert County, Ala., Major in War of 1812 under General Andrew Jackson; wounded six times; married Sarah Forston and removed to Green County, Ala.; he had two sons—George and Benjamin, who were captains in the Confederate Army.

....

Lucile Coty (1862———), wife of George Bennett Dickson, I (1854-1889), was the daughter of Thomas Davenport Coty, born in Virginia, 1824, died in Shreveport, La., 1908; Justice of Peace in De Soto Parish; "Knight of White Camilla" in reconstruction days; was senior member of firm of Coty & Bowles, which manufactured hats for Confederate soldiers; married, 1857, Mary Jane McDonald, born in Paterson, N. J., November 8, 1837; died in Shreveport, La., April 15, 1912.

Thomas Davenport Coty was the son of James Lucas Coty, born 1754; died 1834; lived in Henrico County, Va., was Fifer Boy in Revolutionary Army; married, ca. 1822, Lucy Donahue.

James Lucas Coty was the son of John Lucas Coty, the immigrant, who married Drusilla Davenport and lived in Halifax County, Va.

Mary Jane McDonald, wife of Thomas Davenport Coty, was the daughter of Mark McDonald, born in Manchester, England; came to Paterson, N. J.; married Hannah Oldham (born 1815; died 1875); was member of firm of Oldham, Alley & McDonald, Brass Manufacturers, Paterson, N. J.

ON BEING AN ANCESTRESS
(*To My Great-great Grandchildren*)

I shall not care for it, I'm sure,
    The being dead, you know, my dears,
And hanging primly on a wall—
    Just looking on for years and years!

Ah, no, I'm sure I shall not like
    To be imprisoned there in paint;
I, who love being up-to-date,
    Shall never like just being-quaint!

Of course I'll do the proper thing,
    And hang serenely in my place
Beside your great-great grandpapa—
    A wifely smile upon my face!

And you will all look up to me—
    Believe, no doubt, I was a saint,
For all my faults, of course, will be
    Quite blotted out by time and—paint!

No doubt your honored parents, dears,
    Will point my portrait out and say:
Your great-great granny would be shocked—
    Things were so different in her day!"

And I'll not say a word, nor smile—
    I'll look demure, show no surprise—
But, dears, if you seek sympathy,
    I think you'll find it in my eyes!

And if you stand and look at me,
    And, wistful, wonder if I knew
The pain, the passion and the stress
    Of life, as they are felt by you,

Come closer, dears, and never tell—
    To you a secret I'll entrust:
Your flaming hearts have caught their fire
    From your great-great grandmother's dust!

—Selected.

JOHNSON

William Johnson of the "Baptist Society" was authorized by the Bedford County Court, April 22, 1782, to celebrate the rite of marriage. On October 27, 1794, "William Johnson, Sr.," of the "Baptist Church" was given a similar license. Whether they were one and the same, we do not know.

William T. Johnson of Moneta, Bedford County, great-grandson of Rev. William Johnson, recalls that he was the first moderator of the Strawberry Association, and the minutes of that organization show that he served three years, 1787-1790. Mr. Johnson also remembers that all of the children of Rev. William went West, except one son, Thomas, who lived and died on the farm near Davis Mill, since owned by the late J. William Hubbard. Thomas married Sarah Dickerson in Bedford County — marriage bond dated October 26, 1895—and from his Bible, now owned by the above grandson, we have taken the following records:

"Thomas Johnson, born October 5, 1770.
Sally Johnson, born May 17, 1778.

CHILDREN:

Francis Johnson, born April 27, 1797.
Patsy Johnson, born January 13, 1800.
Nancy Johnson, born May 27, 1802.
William Johnson, born October 25, 1804.
George Johnson, born November 10, 1806.
Thomas Johnson, born January 31, 1809.
Sallie Johnson, born June 6, 1812.
Robert Johnson, born January 12, 1814.
Joseph Johnson, born December 31, 1816.
Elizabeth Jane Johnson, born March 24, 1819."

The Division of the slaves of Thomas Johnson in 1841 is recorded in Will Book "K," page 395 (Bedford County), so he died before that time. Of his children:

Francis married twice; (first) ———— Holland, and had children: Drury, Thomas J., America (married ———— Hubbard), Susan (married ———— Lipscomb), Jane, Joseph, and Anna;

(second) Nancy Wright, daughter of Matthew and Nancy Wright (see Wright family), and had children: Joseph, Jane, who married Major William F. Graves, and others.

William; married Lucinda Robertson. (See forward.)

George; married Caroline M. Hatcher. (See forward.)

Thomas; married Sarah Burroughs. Children: Sallie, Anna, Fannie, Mattie, Rose, James, and Charles.

Sallie; married Thaddeus Nance.

Robert; married Rebecca Morgan. (See forward.)

Joseph; married Emily Parker, daughter of George and Frances (Oaks) Parker. Children: George T., Alexander, Virginia Frances, and Mamie. (See Parker family.)

Elizabeth Jane; married Rev. Thomas C. Goggin. (See Goggin family.)

....

William Johnson, son of Thomas and Sallie (Dickerson) Johnson, was born in 1804, and died in 1881. He married Lucinda Robertson in 1828. (See Robertson family.)

CHILDREN:

(1) Sarah Virginia; died young.

(2) Otweannah Lelia, born December 3, 1836; died April 13, 1883; married John Mays Wright. (See Wright family.)

(3) Thomas Nicholas; died August, 1856.

(4) William Robert, born December 11, 1840. (See forward.)

(5) John Newton, born February 10, 1843. (See forward.)

(6) George Washington, born June 15, 1845. (See forward.)

(7) Mary Elizabeth (twin), born August 15, 1848. (See forward.)

(8) Martha Frances (twin), born August 15, 1848. (See forward.)

(9) Amanda Alice, born ———; died 1863.

(10) Francis Robertson, born and died in 1855.

William and Lucinda Johnson are buried in the family burying ground on his old home place near Chamblissburg, Bedford County, Va.

....

William Robert Johnson, son of William and Lucinda (Robertson) Johnson, married Matilda Frances Jeter, March 26, 1868. (See Jeter family.)

CHILDREN:

(1) Berta Alice, born May 21, 1869; was educated at Southwest Virginia Institute; now teaching in the city schools of Roanoke.

(2) Nora Earl, born December 11, 1871; was educated at Southwest Virginia Institute; lives in Roanoke with her mother.

(3) James Robert, born April 20, 1875; went to Kansas in 1900; married, August 31, 1902, in McPherson Co., Kan., Nellie Mae Keyte, daughter of George Abraham and Malinda Jane Keyte.

CHILD:

(a) Edna Mae, born November 10, 1903; married Earl Harold Moore, October 24, 1922.

CHILD:

(aa) Bettie Loraine, born July 23, 1923.

James R. Johnson and family live in McPherson County, Kan., where he is a successful farmer.

(4) Annie Laura, born June 1, 1879; educated at Farmville State Normal School, Farmville, Va.; now teaching in Roanoke city schools.

(5) Lelia Ella, born July 1, 1881; married, September 23, 1908, Dr. John F. Thaxton. (See Thaxton branch of White family.)

(6) Thomas Jeter, born February 8, 1885; married in Norfolk, Va., October 11, 1916, Alma Duke Hudgins, born August 28, 1896.

CHILDREN:

(a) Alma Doris, born June 26, 1917.

(b) William Robert, Jr., born November 7, 1920.

Thomas J. Johnson and family live in Norfolk, Va.

(7) Frank Davis, born March 16, 1887; lives in Roanoke.

William Robert Johnson was a member of Company "F," Second Virginia Cavalry, and fought throughout the Civil War. He was neither captured nor wounded, though his horse was shot in a skirmish near Culpeper, while he was holding him by the bridle.

He said of his experiences:

"Company 'F' met and drilled at Davis Mills, Bedford County, several times before going to Lynchburg, May 28, 1861, where the Second Virginia Cavalry was organized.

WILLIAM ROBERT JOHNSON AND WIFE
MATILDA FRANCES JETER

"June 20, the regiment went to Fairfax Court House, where we remained in camp until the first battle of Manassas, which was the first engagement. Later, our regiment was with Jackson in his Valley Campaign, and with Stuart in the Maryland Raid. We also took part in the campaigns of Spottsylvania Court House, The Wilderness, Cold Harbor—in fact, in most of the important battles of the war.

"We were with Lee at Appomattox when he surrendered to Grant. And it was a member of our company—Sergeant Robert W. Parker—who was the last man to give his life for his country in that great struggle, being shot at Appomattox just before the firing ceased. (See Parker family.)

"I was ill of pneumonia while in the army, and was taken to a hospital in Leesburg, November 11, 1862, where I was tenderly nursed by my comrade, William M. Dinwiddie—thus beginning a friendship which has lasted through all these years. When I had been in the hospital nearly a month, my father came and stayed with me two weeks, taking me home with him on December 18th. We traveled twenty-two miles in a closed carriage to Manassas Station, and boarded a train for Lynchburg, where we spent the night, going on to Liberty the next morning. There we were met by "Uncle Austin," the faithful family servant. I remained at home three months, and, after fully recovering returned to the army."

W. Robert Johnson and family lived at his father's old home, near Chamblissburg, until 1912, when fire completely destroyed the residence and out-buildings. The next year they moved to Roanoke and settled in Wasena, a new residence section just being opened up. Here he died August 11, 1925, after a lingering illness, due to infirmities of old age, and was buried in Evergreen Cemetery of that city.

His widow still lives at their home in Wasena (1930), and is being lovingly cared for by her daughters, Berta, Nora, and Laura, and her youngest son, Frank, who live with her, none of whom are married.

John Newton Johnson, born February 10, 1843, son of William and Lucinda (Robertson) Johnson; married, January 22, 1875, Talitha Frances Jamison (born April 13, 1852; died November 30, 1927), daughter of Henry and Sallie (Showalter) Jamison, of Franklin County, Va.

CHILDREN:

(1) Sallye Maude, born January 16, 1876; married Emory Cundiff, October 14, 1903. They live at Altavista, Va., where he is Clerk and Treasurer of the town.

CHILDREN:

    (a) Frances Johnson, born May 7, 1905.
    (b) Emory, Jr., born May 16, 1907.
    (c) Josephine, born July 12, 1910.

(2) Ernest Jamison, born May 6, 1878; married, November 10, 1915, Bessie Evans (born June 6, 1888), daughter of John Roberson and Mary Willie (Moore) Evans. Live in Bluefield, W. Va.

(3) William Henry, born July 23, 1880; married, June 5, 1918, Willie B. Rowan (born January 16, 1892), daughter of M. S. Rowan. Live at War, W. Va.

CHILD:

    (a) Anne R. Johnson, born October 27, 1921.

(4) John Walter, born June 6, 1882; married, May 6, 1916, Irma May Wright (born November 2, 1889), daughter of Joseph Pate and Cornelia A. (Powell) Wright. Live in Bluefield, W. Va.

CHILDREN:

    (a) John Walter, Jr., born September 13, 1917.
    (b) Virginia Powell, born March 6, 1919.
    (c) William Wright, born May 15, 1921.
    (d) Irma Mae, born June 3, 1925.

(5) Cornelius Robert, born September 10, 1884; died December 18, 1888.

(6) Mattie Jane; unmarried; lives with her father in Roanoke, Va.

(7) Samuel Walthall, born April 20, 1889; married, April 16, 1919, Ogilvia Arrington, born May 16, 1891, daughter of Granville Marshall Arrington. They live at the old home place near Chamblissburg, Va.

(8) Pauline Myrtle, born May 27, 1892; married, November 22, 1922, Eslie Rolland Phillips, born September 3, 1874; son of *William Jesse Phillips* (son of Levine W. and Susan E. Phillips (born March 4, 1845)) and his wife, *Margaret Anne Savage* (daughter of *James Kendal Savage* (born June 10, 1846; son of John

and Polly Savage (born August 9, 1808)) and Anne Banfield Harmon (daughter of John Harmon (born April 7, 1908) and *Nancy*, his wife). Live at New Church, Va.

CHILDREN:

(a) Eslie Rolland, Jr., born March 2, 1926.

(b) William Newton, born July 16, 1927.

(9) Grace Evangeline, born August 17, 1895; married, November 12, 1924, Beverly Clifton McManaway, born October 21, 1885; son of Alexander Gilmore and Maria Josephine (Robertson) McManaway. Live in Petersburg, Va. (See Wright family.)

CHILDREN:

(a) Kathryn Jane, born May 27, 1926.

(b) Beverly Newton, born June 22, 1929.

CUNDIFF

Jonathan Cundiff, Ensign in Captain Thomas Buford's Company in the Battle of Point Pleasant, October 10, 1774, married ———— Squires. They had a son—

Isaac Cundiff, who was a soldier in the Revolutionary War, and who married Mary Echols in Bedford County—marriage bond dated October 18, 1787. Their children were—

> Christopher.
> Chesley.
> Jubal.
> Parmelia.

....

Christopher Cundiff, son of Isaac and Mary (Echols) Cundiff, was born February 11, 1792; died December 28, 1879. He married Jane Echols, and their children were:

(1) George M., born May 22, 1826; died January 23, 1901.

(2) Isaac Olin, born June 10, 1830; died July 20, 1924.

(3) John Fletcher, born October 18, 1832; died September 24, 1913.

(4) Marcella; married Alexander Kasey.

....

John Fletcher Cundiff, son of Christopher and Jane (Echols) Cundiff, married Mary Fannie Pate (born December 13, 1844; died February 20, 1916).

CHILDREN:

(1) Emory, born September 13, 1868; married Sallye M. Johnson. (See Johnson family.)

(2) Zulah, born April 16, 1870; died June 14, 1928; married John E. Murrell and had three children: Mary, Frances, who married Bunyan Thaxton, and John D.

(3) Ida, born December 24, 1872; died March 26, 1917.

(4) Annie, born August 17, 1873; died February 20, 1916.

(5) Richard D., born September 3, 1871.

Chesley Cundiff, son of Isaac and Mary (Echols) Cundiff, married Mary A. Moss.

CHILDREN:

(1) Lucy A.; married ———— Newsom.

(2) Mary T.; married ———— Shrewsbury.

(3) Samuel C.

(4) Emma; married C. H. Lloyd.

Affidavit of Mrs. Emma Cundiff Lloyd concerning her ancestry:

I, Emma Cundiff Lloyd, born in Bedford County, Virginia, February 14, 1843, am the daughter of Chesley and Mary A. (Moss) Cundiff. Their children were:

Lucy A. (Cundiff) Newsom, Mary T. (Cundiff) Shrewsbury, Samuel C. Cundiff, and myself.

My father's parents were Isaac Cundiff and his wife, Mary E. Cundiff, and their children were:

Christopher Cundiff, Chesley Cundiff, Jubal Cundiff and Permelia Cundiff.

The parents of my grandfather, Isaac Cundiff, were: Jonathan Cundiff and his wife, who was ———— Squires. Jonathan Cundiff was Ensign in Captain Thomas Buford's Company, which fought in the Battle of Point Pleasant (October 10, 1774) under General Andrew Lewis.   (Signed) EMMA CUNDIFF LLOYD.

Subscribed and sworn before me in Bedford County, Va., this 9th day of August, 1928. A. D.

O. H. WRIGHT.

A Justice of the Peace in and for Bedford County, Virginia."

George W. Johnson, son of William and Lucinda (Robertson) Johnson, married Mary Rebecca Wright, November 2, 1871.

CHILDREN:

(1) Mary Lucinda, born September 10, 1872; married James Randolph Skillman, July 3, 1895; lives in Corinth, Miss.

(2) John William, born February 12, 1874; married Elizabeth Early Michie, April 29, 1897.

CHILDREN:

(a) Mary Elizabeth, born August 27, 1903.

(b) Lucille Johnson, born March 11, 1905; married M. W. Whittaker, November, 1928.

(c) Miriam Olive, born January 24, 1911.

J. William Johnson has been Postal Clerk for the Norfolk and Western Railway for many years, and lives in Lynchburg, Va.

(3) George Leonard, born August 31, 1876; married Mary Elizabeth Fletcher, August 31, 1915; lives in Charleston, W. Va.

CHILDREN:

(a) Elizabeth Anne, born July 30, 1916.

(b) Olive Estelle, born April 23, 1918.

(4) Robert Virgil, born July 10, 1880; unmarried.

(5) Olive Estelle, born May 3, 1884; married Walter Lee Evans, October 20, 1915.

CHILDREN:

(a) Walter Lee, Jr., born April 4, 1921.

(b) Mary Virginia, born June 16, 1924.

Walter L. Evans and family live in Lynchburg, Va.

(6) Homer Fields, born June 29, 1886; married May Stellwell Royall, June 25, 1913; live in Lynchburg, Va.

CHILD:

(a) Homer Fields, born September 4, 1920.

(7) Gilbert, born October 10, 1889; unmarried.

Mary (Wright) Johnson, born November, 1855; died in Lynchburg, Va., October 29, 1917, was the daughter of John Quincy Adams Wright (soldier in the Civil War; born about 1826; died in Lynchburg of typhoid fever on his way home from the army, July 22, 1862) and his wife, Mary Gilbert Williamson (born about 1831; died August 4, 1860, in Paris, Texas).

....

Martha Frances Johnson, daughter of William and Lucinda (Robertson) Johnson; married James R. Stewart, October 20, 1869, in Bedford County, Va., and later moved to Kansas.

CHILDREN:

(1) Charles Walter, born March 4, 1872.

(2) James William, born January 12, 1876; died January 6, 1895.

(3) Mary Jane, born November 20, 1880; married Edward Godfrey Williams, in Kansas, September 6, 1904.

CHILD:

(a) Lelia Belle, born October 7, 1905.

(4) Elizabeth Belle, born February 10, 1883; died March 5, 1905.

(5) Richard Bush, born August 21, 1885.

(6) Alice Lelia, born November 2, 1887.

(7) Samuel Henry, born August 15, 1891; married Ina Lora Williams, October 20, 1914.

CHILDREN:

(a) Florence Pearl, born July 20, 1915.

(b) Ruby Thelma, born July 21, 1918.

(c) Carl Faye, born October 26, 1922.

All of these Stewarts live in Kansas.

....

Mary Elizabeth Johnson, daughter of William and Lucinda (Robertson) Johnson; married George W. Scott, November 12, 1873.

CHILDREN:

(1) George William, born August 17, 1874.

(2) Lucinda Ann, born October 13, 1876.

(3) Minnie Alice, born March 15, 1879.

(4) Walter Eugene, born July 31, 1884.

(5) Pearl Augusta, born November 16, 1889; married Paschal Gibbs, August 18, 1914.

CHILDREN:

(a) Mary Lucille, born January 11, 1916.

(b) Virginia Frances, born February 3, 1920.

(6) Mattie Virginia (twin), born March 18, 1894; died in infancy.

(7) Maude Vernon (twin), born March 18, 1894; died in infancy.

....

George Johnson, son of Thomas and Sarah (Dickerson) Johnson was born November 10, 1806; died February 7, 1896; married

December 22, 1830, Caroline M. Hatcher (born March 13, 1812; died July 19, 1895), daughter of Hardaway and Elizabeth (Nelson) Hatcher of Bedford County, Va. (See Hatcher family.)

CHILDREN:

(1) Matilda F., born December 20, 1831; died July 20, 1833.
(2) Robert Hardaway, born October 1, 1834; died June 20, 1838.
(3) Sarah Frances, born July 28, 1836; died July 24, 1859.
(4) Elizabeth Jane, born April 29, 1840; died August 12, 1876; married Thomas Whitfield Nance.

CHILDREN:

Sarah, Virginia, Maggie, and John.
(5) Lilbourne H., born January 29, 1842; soldier in Civil War, killed in battle near Spotsylvania Court House, May 7, 1864; married Lessie Woodruff, February 13, 1860.

CHILD:

(a) Lee.
(6) Julia Ann, born August 8, 1845; married John P. Wingfield, who was born January 1, 1840; died December 9, 1918.

CHILDREN:

(a) George Dawson; now deceased; married Lucy Logwood McGhee.

CHILDREN:

(aa) Virginia White; married Herbert T. Patterson, Jr.
(bb) Mary Johnson.
(cc) William McGhee.
(dd) Margaret Rice.
(b) Boyd.
(c) William Warren.
(d) Ernest; now deceased; married Coral Burnett.
(e) Mary Lizzie; married Webb Fizer.
(f) Louis Lilbourne; now deceased; married Lizzie May Bush.
(g) Fannie Leslie; married Dr. A. G. Thurman. (See Key family.)

(7) Mary Lucinda, born November 4, 1847; died April 4, 1904; married William Wingfield.

(8) Martha R. C., born March 25, 1850; married George Smith.

CHILDREN:

Zula, Bob, John, Mary, Piercy, Ann, and Lee.

(9) George William, born March 1, 1857; married (first), December 12, 1877, Cordelia Frances Gills, daughter of Asa and Caroline (Poindexter) Gills. (See Poindexter family.)

CHILDREN:

(a) Ada Elizabeth; married, October 27, 1917, A. Raphael Di Cicco; lives in California.

CHILDREN:

(aa) William Raphael, born October 7, 1918.

(bb) Richard Johnson, born May 8, 1923.

(b) Houston, died in infancy.

(c) Mamie E.; married Robert L. James, January 29, 1916.

CHILD:

(aa) Robert Johnson, born April 13, 1918.

George William Johnson married (second) Mrs. Coral (Burnett) Wingfield, December 12, 1928.

Robert Johnson, son of Thomas and Sarah (Dickerson) Johnson; married Rebecca Lazenby.

CHILDREN:

(1) John W.; married Nannie Dickerson Robertson.

(2) Robert A.; married Caroline Pullen.

(3) William T., born May 29, 1855; married, November 14, 1877, Annie Lee Garrett, daughter of Elijah and Margaret (Burgess) Garrett.

CHILDREN:

(a) Olive Rebecca, born September 2, 1878; married September 4, 1901, McLeod Overstreet, son of John H. and Victoria Susan (Morgan) Overstreet.

CHILD:

(aa) Claude Johnson, born September 22, 1905.

(b) Lucy Jane, born March 22, 1882; married, December 24, 1903, James Adkins.

CHILDREN:

(aa) James Burnley, born July 9, 1906.

(bb) William Herbert, born January 19, 1912.

(cc) Marjorie Lee, born December 20, 1915.

(c) Allen Burnley, born November 22, 1884; married, November 8, 1911, Annie Marie Wells.

CHILDREN:

(aa) Eugenia Garrett, born August 31, 1912.

(bb) Rebecca, born May 15, 1924.

(d) Robert Garrett, born November 29, 1895; married, October 25, 1924, Lillian Hancock Nance, daughter of James F. and Ada (Burroughs) Nance. (See Robertson family.)

CHILDREN:

(aa) Robert Garrett, Jr., born April 9, 1926.

(bb) Ada Burroughs, born January 25, 1929.

(4) Samuel D.; married Emma Gills, daughter of Asa and Caroline (Poindexter) Gills.

(5) Jane; married William D. Fields.

(6) Sarah; married William Hancock.

(7) Laura; married Robert Alexander Pollard.

(8) Mildred; married James Robertson.

(9) Ezza; married Edwin Greenwood Garrett.

ROBERTSON

According to family tradition, three brothers—John, Jeffry and Nicholas Robertson—came from England in the ship, "The Blessing." The date of their coming is unknown, but in the records of Prince George County the names "Nicholas Robyson" and "John Robyson and Mary, his wife" appear in 1719.

No record of the marriage of Nicholas Robertson has been found, and the names of only two of his children are known—Nicholas and Elizabeth (Betsy). Betsy married a Bass, and was the mother of twenty-six children. She lived and died in Kentucky.

Nicholas Robertson II, son of Nicholas, the emigrant, was born in Chesterfield County. He married Mary Woolridge of Buckingham County, in 1769.

CHILDREN:

(1) Jeffry, born January 1, 1770. (See forward.)
(2) John; married a Miss Purdy, and died soon after.
(3) Fannie; married John Gilliam of Buckingham County.
(4) Nicholas, born April 12, 1776. (See forward.)

Nicholas Robertson II, moved his family from Chesterfield to Buckingham in 1790, and settled near New Store, where he afterwards died.

....

Jeffry Robertson, son of Nicholas and Mary Woolridge Robertson married Nancy Dickerson of Bedford County, January 9, 1792. (See Dickerson family.)

CHILDREN:

(1) Jannet, born December 28, 1792; married Stephen Goggin (See Goggin family.)
(2) Mills, born November 11, 1796.
(3) John J., born November 21, 1798.
(4) Jeffry G., born July 1, 1803.
(5) Thomas W., born June 6, 1805.
(6) Polly M., born December 5, 1810.

Jeffry Robertson died in Bedford County, October 1856, and was buried on the south side of the county, where he had lived. The inscription on his tombstone reads: "Captain Jeffry Robertson."

His will mentions daughters, Jannet Goggin; Martha Jones; sons: John J.; Jeffry; and Thomas W. (Will Book "Q," page 247.)

....

Nicholas Robertson III, son of Nicholas II and Mary (Woolridge) Robertson, married Sallie Walthall, of Chesterfield County, May 8, 1799.

CHILDREN:

(1) Archer W., born June 1, 1800; married his cousin, Fannie Gilliam, and went to Stokes County, N. C., in 1826, where he died March 17, 1889.
(2) Elizabeth W., born May 15, 1802; died December 21, 1895. (See forward.)
(3) Martha, born March 27, 1804; married Captain John Hatcher; died July 31, 1895.
(4) Mary, born May 30, 1807; married William Washington Reese; died October 4, 1870. (See Reese family.)
(5) Francis W., born September 10, 1809; married (first) Nancy Turner; (second) Mrs. Emma Gibbs; died December 10, 1886.
(6) William Hill, born November 22, 1811; married four times; was the father of sixteen children; died March 13, 1901.
(7) Lucinda, born January 16, 1816; married William Johnson in 1838; died July 14, 1855. (See Johnson family.)
(8) Sallie A. W., born May 14, 1818; married Joseph Parker February 28, 1839; died August 4, 1875. (See Parker family.)
(9) America, born June 24, 1820; married Thomas Holland; died April 24, 1909.

(10) Nicholas IV, born August 26, 1824; married Sallie Law December 12, 1844; died August 24, 1870.

(11) Amanda A., born June 15, 1828; married William Cook; died October 11, 1855.

Nicholas Robertson III lived in Buckingham County until 1806, when he moved his family to Bedford and settled on the south side of the county near a place called Dundee. He was a prosperous farmer and accumulated considerable property, as shown by his inventory, which is recorded in Will Book "N," page 137. (Bedford County records.) He died October 13, 1848.

Sallie Walthall, born April 8, 1871, was the daughter of Frank Walthall and Mary Hill, both of Chesterfield County.

Elizabeth Robertson, daughter of Nicholas III and Sallie (Walthall) Robertson married, August 2, 1818, James Burroughs, son of Joseph Burroughs (Baptist minister) and Mary Pierce, who were married in Maryland and came first to Loudon County, and thence to Bedford.

The Burroughses were originally from France and settled in Maryland.

CHILDREN:

(1) Mary Hill, born September 9, 1819; married John Ayers.

(2) Joseph Nicholas, born April 21, 1821. (See forward.)

(3) Sarah; married Thomas Johnson. (See Johnson family.)

(4) James Benjamin; married Sarah Rucker.

(5) Thomas Robertson; married (first) Julia Bond; (second) Lelia Ballard. (See Bond family.)

(6) Martha; married Charles Noell.

(7) Lucinda; married Ferdinand Price.

(8) William; killed in the Civil War.

(9) Frank; married Fannie Cundiff; died in prison during Civil War.

(10) Ann; married Card Ferguson.

(11) Eliza; married David Witt.

(12) Laura; married Stephen Holland.

(13) Edwin Newton; born July 27, 1844; died September 28, 1922; married (first) Jannie Peters; (second) Roberta Atherson.

(14) Ellen America; married William Goggin. (See Goggin family.)

Elizabeth (Robertson) Burroughs lived to be ninety years old, and at the age of eighty she began to knit counterpanes for her fourteen children, and finished one for each of them. A second eyesight enabled her to knit without glasses, and, at the time of her death, her head was covered with a growth of young hair of a dark brown color.

Jane, the mother of Booker Washington, was a slave of Mrs. Burroughs, and Booker was born and spent his early life at her home in Franklin County, Virginia. He, with his mother and the rest of the family, left their mistress soon after the Civil War, and went to West Virginia to live, where she married a man by the name of Washington. Booker also took the name of his step-father, and was henceforth known as Booker Washington. His home was in Malden, West Virginia, until 1881. when he went to Alabama.

When the estate of James Burroughs was appraised, Booker was valued at $400.00.

The following is taken from the "Inventory and Appraisement of the Estate personal of James Burroughs, dec. 23 Day of November, 1861."

"1 negro man (Monroe)...$ 600.00
1 negro woman (Sophia).. 250.00
1 negro woman (Jane)... 250.00
1 negro man (Lee)... 1000.00
1 negro boy (Green).. 800.00
1 negro girl (Mary Jane)... 800.00
1 negro girl (Sally).. 700.00
1 negro boy (John).. 550.00
1 negro boy (Bowker) (Booker Washington)................ 400.00
1 negro girl (Amanda).. 200.00

In accordance with an order of the County Court of Franklin, made at its November term November 4th, 1861, and directed to the undersigned, we have taken the inventory and made the appraisement of the Estate of James Burroughs dec. which is herewith submitted. November 23, 1861.

B. N. HATCHER,
JAMES WRIGHT,
T. HOLLAND."

The Appraisement, from which the above is taken, is now in possession of the daughter of S. C. Burroughs, a grandson of James Burroughs.

When Booker Washington made his last visit to his old home he asked for this document, but Mr. Burroughs, not being willing to part with it, gave him a copy, instead.

Joseph Nicholas Burroughs, son of James and Elizabeth (Robertson) Burroughs, served in the War of 1812. He married, February 11, 1847, Sarah Morgan (born December 18, 1826; died January 24, 1916), daughter of Christopher and Mary (Anthony) Morgan.

CHILDREN:

(1) Mary, born December 31, 1847; married Thomas W. Morgan (died July 25, 1919), and died August 2, 1919.

CHILDREN:

(a) Lucius; married (first) Janie Moorman; (second) her sister, Willie Moorman.

CHILDREN:

Addison, Mary Burroughs, Kathleen Price, and Janie Moorman.
(b) Thomas Nicholas; married Mary Saunders.

CHILDREN:

(aa) Thomas Robert; (bb) Jesse D. S.; (cc) James Nicholas; (dd) George Garth; (ee) Samuel Clark; and (ff) Mary Mildred.
(c) Beulah; married Cyrus Overstreet.

CHILDREN:

Julia, Elizabeth and Manly.

(d) Lizzie; married R. A. Long.

CHILD:

Bird.

(e) Moses; (f) Flora; (g) Estelle.

(2) Silas C.; married Kate Smith.

CHILD:

(a) Mary, who married Hampton Johnson.

CHILD:

(aa) Kate, who married Clyde Repass, December 25, 1928.

(3) Betty; married Thomas Price.

(4) Thomas.

(5) Amanda; married Jesse Morgan.

(6) Julia; unmarried.

(7) William David; married Marcella Morgan.

(8) Samuel Nicholas; married Emma Hancock.

CHILDREN:

Lillie Hancock, Lucile Mae, and Helen.

(9) Estelle; married William Hubbard.

(10) Ada; born February 5, 1869; married James F. Nance:

CHILDREN:

Lillian Hancock and Julia.

(11) Ida, twin of Ada, died November 27, 1929; married June 15, 1898, Armistead Cary Hatcher, born January 16, 1851; died June 13, 1922; son of Jeremiah G. and Angeline (Wainwright) Hatcher. (See Hatcher family.)

DICKERSON (ALSO SPELLED DICKINSON)

Joseph Dickerson was born April 11, 1742, and came to Bedford County about 1776. He bought his first land from Stephen Goggin, Sr., in 1777. He married Elizabeth Woolridge in Buckingham County, March 6, 1769.

CHILDREN:

(1) Edna, born September 15, 1770; married Archibald Stratton.

(2) William, born January 7, 1772.

(3) Nancy, born October 29, 1773; married Jeffry Robertson. (See Robertson family.)

(4) Sallie, born September 15, 1776; married Joel Shrewsbury.

(5) Pleasant, born April 15, 1785.

Joseph Dickerson died in Bedford County, September 16, 1818. His will mentions wife, Elizabeth; daughters: Edney Stratton, Nancy Robertson, and Sallie Shrewsbury; sons: William and Pleasant.

Executors: son, Pleasant; sons-in-law, Jeffry Robertson, Joel Shrewbury and Archibald Stratton. (Will Book "E," page 37.)

Elizabeth Woolridge was born January 11, 1744, and died November 7, 1818.

In Order Book, 1774-1782, Bedford County records, in the list of those who had furnished supplies for the Revolutionary Army, is the following:

"Joseph Dickerson pr'v'd that he furn'd with 1500 lbs. of Flower, and for which he is allowed 1 2/6 per cwt., and sundry casks for which he is allowed 1, 1s., including sd Flower."

WRIGHT

When Bedford County was formed in 1753 Thomas Wright was already living in its territory, having come from Augusta County about 1748 (Chalkley's Abstracts of Augusta County Records) and settled in the southwestern part of the county, near what is now Stewartsville. His will is among the first recorded in Bedford, and his numerous descendants have been prominent citizens of the county since its formation, many of them still living in the locality in which he lived.

Thomas Wright says in his will that he was a member of the Church of England, but his son John was a charter member of the Beaverdam Baptist Church, and the names of his wife, Elizabeth, and his son, Thomas, appear in the first roll of its members. The membership of that church to the present day has been made up largely of the descendants of the first Thomas Wright, many of them having become ministers of the Gospel.

Will of Thomas Wright (Will Book "A," page 9):

Made December 15, 1762; probated November 22, 1763; mentions wife, Mary; daughters: Elizabeth, Mary Abigale, Sarah, Dorcas, and Catherine; sons: John, and Joseph. It refers to "land on which I did live, part of Randolph's Order."

John Wright, son of Thomas and Mary Wright, married Elizabeth ————.

CHILDREN:

(1) Thomas; married Cynthia Mayse, December 15, 1785. (See forward.)
(2) Sarah; married William Wheeler, December 20, 1785.
(3) Anthony; married (first) Betsy Mayse, December 29, 1789; (second) Kitty, widow of John St. Clair. (See forward.)
(4) Nancy; married James Asbury, November 13, 1792.
(5) Elizabeth; married Thomas Hambleton, May 22, 1783.
(6) Mary (Polly); married Benjamin Watts, December 22, 1786.
(7) Rhoda; married Henry Hurt, December 24, 1798.
(8) John; married Mary Hunter in 1789.
(9) Joseph; married Sallie Edgar, August 17, 1802.
(10) Ruth; married William McGeorge, May 30, 1810.

The will of John Wright, made August 11, 1803; probated September 26, 1803, mentions wife, Elizabeth; children: Tommy, Sarah

Anthony, Nancy Asbury, Betsey, Polly, Rhoda, John, Joseph, and Ruth. (Will Book "C," page 13.)

John Wright proved himself a patriot by furnishing beef to the Revolutionary, for which he was allowed pay at the April Court of Bedford County as follows:

At a Court held April 22, 1782, at the house of David Wright, "John Wright proved that he furnished the said Com: with 550 lbs. Beef for which he is all'd 16/8 per Cwt.—Seven Diets 8d each—Five pecks of Corn 6d each—and Sixteen days pasturage 3d per day." (Order Book, 1774-1782.)

John Wright is listed as a Revolutionary soldier from Bedford County in Virginia Colonial Militia. Edited by Wm. Armstrong Crozier.

....

Thomas Wright, son of John and Elizabeth Wright; married, December 15, 1785, Cynthia Mayse, daughter of James, Sr., and Mary Mayse of Bedford County, Va.

Their son, Joel (born March 25, 1799; died February 25, 1875); married, December 20, 1827, Amanda Jordan (born February 9, 1810; died June 5, 1899), daughter of Leroy and Rhoda (Mayse) Jordan.

CHILDREN (FAMILY BIBLE RECORD):

(1) Elizabeth Rhoda, born May 13, 1829; died May 16, 1876. (See forward.)

(2) Mary Ann, born April 7, 1832. (See forward.)

(3) James A., born March 11, 1834; married Cornelia Adams, October 3, 1860, in Corinth, Miss.

CHILDREN:

(a) Pearl Irene, born September 5, 1861.

(b) George Joel, born January 7, 1864.

(4) John Mays, born September 19, 1836; died March 6, 1901. (See forward.)

....

Elizabeth Rhoda Wright, daughter of Joel and Amanda (Jordan) Wright; married, June 1, 1848, James M. Matthews (born May 13, 1824; died April 7, 1911).

CHILDREN :

(1) Ann Henry, born July 5, 1849. (See forward.)

(2) Lizzie Ella, born and died August 21, 1851.

(3) Caroline Blanche, born September 16, 1853; died January 14, 1871.

(4) Thomas Joel, born January 31, 1856; died June 1, 1917. (See forward.)

(5) Charles M., born December 23, 1858; died December 1, 1910.

(6) John Dunsmore (twin), born July 27, 1865; died July 24, 1866.

(7) James Clifton (twin), born July 27, 1865; died September 9, 1881.

(8) Jennie Lee, born May 29, 1869; died in December, 1869.

Ann Henry, daughter of James M. and Elizabeth (Wright) Matthews; married, October 9, 1866, James Eben Nelms (born July 19, 1839; died July 11, 1911).

CHILDREN :

(1) James Matthews, born May 23, 1868; died December 28, 1923.

(2) William E., born December 19, 1869; married Anna Alexander in October, 1909.

(3) Blanche C., born December 13, 1871; married, May 10, 1910, Rev. Charles T. Kincanon (died 1920).

CHILDREN :

(a) James Nelms, born January 3, 1912.

(b) Ann E., born January 18, 1915.

(4) Virginia S., born June 3, 1873; married A. H. H. Boyd in 1903. He died November 12, 1926.

CHILD :

(a) Virginia Hunter, born February 24, 1906.

(5) Frank C., born September 30, 1875; died June 15, 1908.

(6) Elizabeth A., born March 22, 1878; married, July 12, 1904, Charles G. Bush, son of Eugene and Eliza (Lunsford) Bush.

Thomas Joel Matthews, son of James M. and Elizabeth (Wright) Matthews; married, October 24, 1877, Helen Bell, daughter of Orville P. and Nannie (Gladding) Bell.

CHILDREN:

(1) Clifton, born July 16, 1878.
(2) Orville Thomas, born February 16, 1880; died November 1, 1918.
(3) Elizabeth Douglass, born November, 1881.
(4) Thomas J., Jr., born September, 1885.
(5) Helen Bell, born January, 1887.

BELL

The first recorded ancestor of the Bells of Bedford County, Va., was James Bell, who came from Ireland to America about 1740, and settled in Orange County, Va. He brought up nine children—six of them sons, nearly all of whom fought in the Revolutionary War. One of them, Capt. James Bell, had previously served in the French and Indian Wars and was present at Braddock's defeat.

His son, Thomas Bell, married Ann Mary Wolande and moved to Liberty, Bedford County, Va., in 1798. They had eleven children, among whom the following were brought up in Liberty:

(1) Katherine; married Benjamin Hawkins of Albemarle County, Va.
(2) Juliette; died unmarried.
(3) James; married in West Virginia; moved to Indiana and died there.
(4) William; married Sallie Brown of Bedford County.
(5) Alfred A.; married Mary Isabel Lowry of Bedford County.
(6) Orville; married Nannie Gladding of Rhode Island.
(7) Robert; married Harriet Hopkins of Bedford County.
(8) John; married, lived and died in Tennessee.
(9) Edwin; married Claramore Banks of Lynchburg, Va.

CHILDREN OF ALFRED AND MARY (LOWRY) BELL WERE:

(1) Sarah; married R. D. Buford and had one daughter, Belle.
(2) Mary; married R. B. Claytor and had two children: Evelyn and Alfred B.
(3) Annie; married J. W. Smith and had two daughters: Rosalie and Ethel.
(4) Rose; married O. W. Kelsy of England, and had two children: Gladys and Arthur.
(5) Thomas W.; married, lived and died in Tennessee.

CHILDREN OF ORVILLE AND NANNIE (GLADDING) BELL WERE:

(1) Edmonia, who married L. A. Sale.
(2) Nannie, who married H. W. Moseley.
(3) Charlotte, who married John E. Mitchell.
(4) Roberta, who married M. P. Burks. (See Burks family.)
(5) Josephine, who married (first) E. C. Burks, Jr.; (second) ——— Withers.
(6) Marion, who married Graham Claytor.

(7) Helen, who married Thomas J. Matthews.
(8) Abbie, who married James M. Berry.
(9) Ida, who married T. D. Berry.
(10) Orville Clifton, who married Gretchen Parr.

Mary Ann Wright, daughter of Joel and Amanda (Jordan) Wright, was born April 7, 1832, and died October 9, 1913; She married, December 16, 1852, in Bedford County, Va., Samuel W. Hensley, who died July 4, 1904, in Galesburg, Kansas.

CHILDREN:

(1) James A., born August 1, 1854; married, June 12, 1883, Laura Moss.
(2) Virginia Amanda, born January 15, 1857; married, in Knoxville, Tenn., December 20, 1883, N. B. Ristine, who died at Thoms, Mo., April 12, 1927. CHILDREN:

    (a) Fred Hensley, born January 22, 1885; married in March, 1907, Ora Burkheart Thoms.

CHILDREN:

Charles and Audrey Marie.
    (b) Anne Sue, born February 15, 1889; died March 12, 1901.
    (c) Ruth, born March 2, 1892.
(3) George Dana, born July 7, 1859; died October 15, 1918; married, in Liberty, Va., January 22, 1890, Sallie Otey, daughter of Dr. John A. Otey. CHILDREN:

    (a) Infant; died March 4, 1891.
    (b) Frances Otey, born November 14, 1893; died March 13, 1904.
    (c) Samuel Otey, born January 17, 1895; died October 25, 1897.
(4) William, born October 23, 1866; married in June, 1889, Mollie Cooper of Oseola, Arkansas.

CHILDREN:

Dana Lanier, Edward Raymond, and Fannie Marie.
(5) Lucy, born February 15, 1869; married, January 30, 1889, Ashby Albert Austin.

CHILDREN:

(a) Annie, born January 27, 1890; died January 30, 1890.
(b) Audrey Marie, born May 12, 1896; married, October 6, 1915, Roy Harvey Shaw.

CHILDREN:

(aa) Irwin Austin, born June 3, 1916; died June 6, 1916.
(bb) Phyllis Yvonne, born January 12, 1923.

(6) Ida L., born in Knoxville, Tenn., January 31, 1872; married, July 3, 1895, Harry Sappenfield of Galesburg, Kansas.

CHILDREN:

(a) Walter Ashby, born December 15, 1901; died February 2, 1902.
(b) Samuel W. Hensley, born February 5, 1824; died July 24, 1904.

(7) Albert Wade, born September 25, 1899; married, October 21, 1924, Margaret Chapell.

CHILD:

(a) Dorothy, born October 12, 1925.

John Mays Wright, son of Joel and Amanda (Jordan) Wright, was born near Stewartsville, in Bedford County, Va., September 19, 1836, and died in South Boston, Va., March 6, 1901.

While still a young man he became associated with James M. Matthews, his brother-in-law, in the manufacture of tobacco at Stewartsville, and soon they both moved their families to Liberty, erected a large factory on the northeast corner of Bridge and Jackson Streets, and continued to manufacture the weed until the death of Mr. Matthews.

Mr. Wright then became a partner in the firm of Newsom and Wright, and conducted a warehouse for the sale of tobacco for a number of years, but finally moved his family to South Boston and established a hardware business.

He married, November 10, 1859, Lelia Otweannah Johnson, daughter of William and Lucinda (Robertson) Johnson (see Johnson family), who died soon after the birth of her youngest child. The care of his home and children then fell upon his aged mother, who had always lived with him. She was a gentle, refined, sweet-spirited Christian woman, and her loving ministrations will ever be cherished by her grandchildren.

CHILDREN OF JOHN M. AND LELIA O. (JOHNSON) WRIGHT WERE:

(1) Estelle Amanda, born September 14, 1860, at Liberty, Va.; married, December 20, 1882, Oscar Bayne Barker, born March 15, 1861, son of Rev. Francis Marion and Dematris Anne (Noell) Barker.

Oscar B. Barker began his business career as a clerk in the hardware store of Joshua Thomas, in Liberty, Va. Soon after his marriage he moved to Lynchburg, and has ever since been identified with the interests and development of that city.

He is senior member of the Barker-Jennings Hardware Company; superintendent of the Sunday School of the College Hill Baptist Church; president of the Baptist Hospital Board, and superintendent of the Baptist Hospital, which is located in Lynchburg.

CHILDREN:

(a) John Wright, born May 3, 1884; died July 23, 1884.

(b) Infant daughter, born and died February 7, 1885.

(c) Francis Marion, born May 19, 1886; died November 13, 1913.

(d) Anne Lelia, born February 7, 1888; married, December 30, 1915, McHenry Peters, born May 10, 1881; son of John McHenry Peters of Bedford County (born October 24, 1842; died November 7, 1924) and Louisa Leake Morgan also of Bedford County (born July 20, 1844; died February 15, 1928), who were married, February 14, 1867.

CHILDREN:

(aa) Frances Marion, born May 28, 1917.

(bb) McHenry, Jr., born December 7, 1928.

(e) Oscar Bayne, Jr., born October 14, 1892, in Lynchburg, Va.; married, May 29, 1926, Mary Ogilvie Lefebvre, born July 24, 1898; daughter of William Clayton

Lefebvre of Richmond, Va. (born August 7, 1857; died March 29, 1906), and Martha Harvey Gordon (born March 4, 1861; died July 4, 1899), who were married, January 18, 1888.

CHILD:

(aa) Mary Lefebvre, born July 30, 1927.

(f) Roland Maxwell, born December 9, 1899; unmarried.

(2) John Ashby, born September 29, 1862, in Bedford County; married, October 16, 1894, Flora Redd Drewry, born January 17, 1872, in Henry County, Va.; daughter of Dr. Henry Martyn Drewry (born in Chesterfield County, Va., January 8, 1833; died April 11, 1915, in Martinsville, Va.) and Flora Ruth Redd (born February 14, 1833, in Patrick County, Va.; died October 26, 1914, in Martinsville, Va.). Now in the insurance business in South Boston, Va.

CHILDREN:

(a) Lucie Preston, born January 10, 1896; married, April 26, 1917, Henry Guy Faris, born March 30, 1891; son of William Fitzhugh Faris of Lunenburg County, Va. (born May 4, 1865; died August 26, 1925), and Madeline Love (born April 23, 1870), who were married, March 7, 1888.

CHILDREN:

(aa) Henry Guy, Jr., born November 29, 1918.

(bb) John Wright, born May 4, 1922.

(b) John Ashby, Jr., born September 14, 1897, in Chase City, Va.; married, July 7, 1928, Virginia Shields Sherrill, born March 11, 1908, daughter of Dr. William Marion Sherrill of Statesville, N. C. (born December 25, 1865), and Alice Caroline Moore (born February 6, 1878), who were married, May 3, 1898.

(c) Flora Redd, born in South Boston, Va., May 2, 1901; married, October 16, 1926, Henry Coleman Bethel, born October 16, 1896; son of Charles Thomas Bethel of Rockingham County, N. C. (born July 17, 1855; died July 3, 1914), and Alice Coleman (born September 8, 1871, in Halifax County, Va.).

(d) William Drewry, born March 21, 1903; unmarried.

(e) Lelia Johnson, born April 11, 1905; died July 12, 1906.

(f) Cornelius Tyree, born April 4, 1908; unmarried.

(g) Amelia Davies, born April 18, 1911.

(3) Robert Alexander, born May 2, 1865; died in infancy.

(4) Cora Alice, born April 29, 1866; died in childhood.

(5) William Alexander, born August 15, 1868; died unmarried, December 30, 1891.

(6) Caroline Blanche, born March 17, 1871; died in infancy.

(7) Laura Virginia, born April 29, 1872; married, January 15, 1912, Waiteman Francis Tolley, born February 6, 1871; son of W. Taylor Tolley (born November 1, 1839; died November, 1907) and Jane Elizabeth Sheltman of Rockbridge County, Va.

CHILD:

(a) Frances Virginia, born October 5, 1914, at Kingstree, S. C., where her parents were living at that time, and where her father died in 1924. She and her mother still live there.

(8) Mary Elizabeth, born September 29, 1874; married in Lynchburg, Va., June 8, 1899, John Douglass Moose, born October 6, 1872; son of Major Jacob Eli Moose (born December 8, 1826; died August 30, 1886) and Isabel Jane Steele Eads (born October 4, 1844; died September 25, 1899), who were married, February 6, 1867.

CHILDREN:

(a) John Douglass, Jr., born September 6, 1901; married, July 24, 1929, Christine V. Reinvaldt, born in Detroit, Mich., October 16, 1907; daughter of O. Reinvaldt of Detroit. In business with his father in Lynchburg, Va.

(b) Tyree Wright, born March 11, 1904.

(c) George Francis, born October 29, 1909.

(9) Lelia Johnson, born July 20, 1877; married, June 19, 1907, Floyd Jackson Davis, born in Prince Edward County, Va., June 8, 1882; died in Lynchburg, Va., March 16, 1929; son of John Damin and Mary Frances Davis.

CHILD:

(a) Floyd Jackson, Jr., born May 7, 1912; lives in Lynchburg, Va., with his mother.

(10) Tyree Cornelius, born in Liberty, Va., September 29, 1881; went with his father to South Boston when quite a young man; married, November 6, 1912, Bessie Lewis Lawson, daughter of John James Lawson (born August 27, 1849; died January 3, 1913) and Eliza Jasper Craddock (born December 5, 1858). He is now Treasurer and Purchasing Agent of South Boston, Va.

CHILD:

(a) Tyree Lawson, born May 15, 1917.

BARKER

The will of John Barker was made July 30, 1846, and probated in Bedford County, Va., August 24, 1846. It mentions wife, Polly; sons, Napoleon B. and Francis M.; and Catherine, who married ———— McGregor and went to Alabama. (Will Book "M," page 256.)

NOELL

The will of John C. Noell was made December 11, 1862, and probated in Bedford County, Va., December 22, 1862. It mentions wife, Nancy; children: Alanson L., Palestine W., F. M. Barker and wife, Dematris A. Barker; youngest son, James T. Noell. Gives negro boy to Andrew F. Barker. (Will Book "T," page 148.)

John C. Noell, born in Bedford County, Va., was the son of Thomas Noell, who served in the Revolutionary War. He married Nancy Witt, who was born in Nelson County, Va., and died in September, 1874. (Hardesty's *Encyclopedia*, Sketch of Palestine W. Noell, page 426.)

Anthony Wright, son of John and Elizabeth Wright; married, December 29, 1789, Betsy Mayse, daughter of James, Sr., and Mary Mayse. (See Mayse family.)

CHILDREN:

(1) Rhoda; married William Wright and went to Illinois.
(2) Celia; married Thomas Anthony Wright and went West.

(3) Betsy; married (first) Anthony Wright; (second) Robert Ramsey.

(4) Agnes; married George Wheeler.

(5) Ann; married ———— Crouch.

(6) Martha; married ———— Graham.

(7) Malinda; married Joseph W. Mays. (See Mayse family.)

(8) Solomon; married Phebe Wright.

(9) Joseph; died unmarried.

(10) Mary (Polly); married (first) David Gish; (second) John Brugh. No children by second marriage.

CHILDREN BY FIRST MARRIAGE:

(a) Mary Eliza, born January 4, 1837; married Jacob P. Brugh.

CHILDREN:

(aa) S. Clinton; married (first) Emma Cronise; (second) Willie Kern.

(bb) Leslie H.; married Minnie Firey; lives in Roanoke, Va.

(cc) Ewell J.; married Phebe Ashby of New Orleans.

(dd) Earl Russell; married (first) Pattie Webb; (second) Hettie Graybill; lives in Idaho.

(ee) John Lanier; married Bessie Comer of Winston-Salem, N. C.

(ff) Vista C.; married Floyd Robinson, and lives on part of the old home place near Nace, Botetourt County, Va.

(b) George Russell, born August 10, 1839; married Mary Thrasher of Botetourt County; lived and died near Vinton, Roanoke County, Va.

CHILDREN:

(aa) Ella; died in childhood.

(bb) Thomas Edward; married Belle Williamson; lives in Vinton, Va.

(cc) George William; married (first) Lena Cook; (second) Lillie Fuqua; died in Roanoke, Va.

(dd) Frank Anthony; married Mary Vineyard; lives in Vinton.

(ee) Ola May; married Ellis Bowie; now deceased.

(ff) Joseph Mays; married Annie Kasey; is Farm Demonstrator of Roanoke County.

(gg) Anna; married Marvin Barley; lives in Westbury, Long Island, N. Y. He is now deceased.

(hh) James Emmett; married Mrs. Nannie J. Winfrey; now a lawyer in Roanoke, Va.

(ii) David; went to Oklahoma; married and lives there.

(jj) Elmer; went to Oklahoma; married; lives in Oklahoma.

(kk) Earl; married Ada Biggs; lives in Roanoke.

Joseph Wright, son of Thomas and Mary Wright, married Elizabeth Kemp in Maryland.

CHILDREN:

(1) Barsheba; married Joel Simmons.

(2) Nancy; married ———— Meador.

(3) Judith; married William McCormack, January 4, 1791.

(4) Patsey; married James Mayse, January 3, 1802. (See Mayse family.)

(5) Mary; married Martin Greer.

(6) Agnes; married Samuel Mayse, October 22, 1792.

(7) Thomas; (8) John; (9) Joseph; (10) Matthew; (11) Rite.

No mention has been found of Joseph Wright's having taken a part in the Revolutionary War other than the following record, taken from Order Book, 1774-1782:

At a Court held for Bedford County, April 22, 1782, at the house of David Wright, "Joseph Wright proved that he furnished the said Com: with 475 lbs. Beef for which he is all'd 16/8 per Cwt."

WILL OF JOSEPH WRIGHT

In the name of God, Amen, I, Joseph Wright of the County of Bedford and the State of Virginia, being weak in body but of perfect sound mind and memory, do make and publish this my last will and testament in manner and form following, to-wit:

First, I give and bequeath unto my daughter Barsheba Simmons, wife of Joel Simmons, a tract of land lying in Franklin County on

Staunton River, bounded by said river, Ball's line, and Bruff's Branch, containing one hundred acres, be the same more or less.

Second, I give and bequeath to my grand-children—Jane Meadow, Jubal Meadow, Joseph Meadow, Judith Meadow, and John Meadow—children of my daughter, Nancy Meadow, dec'd, one negro girl, named Juggy to be equally divided between them with her future increase.

Third, I give and bequeath unto my daughter Judith McCormack, wife of William McCormack, one negro girl named Tabb, to be by her possessed during her life, and at her death I give the said negro girl Tabb, and any increase she may have, to the lawful heirs of her body. I also give her one seal skin trunk.

Fourth, I give to my daughter Patsy Mayse, one Iron Bound chest.

Fifth, I give and bequeath to my three oldest sons, Thomas, John and Joseph Wright, and to my five daughters, Mary Greer, Agnes Mayse, Judith McCormack, Patsy Mayse, and Barsheba Simmons, and to the heirs of my daughter, Nancy Meadow, dec'd, one hundred and fifty acres of land in Franklin County whereon my son Joseph Wright now lives, also one hundred and thirty acres adjoining the same, called Ball's place to be equally divided between them.

Sixth, All the balance of my estate, both real and personal of every description after the payment of my just debts and funeral expenses, I give and bequeath to my five sons, Thomas, John, Joseph, Matthew and Rite Wright, and to my five daughters, Mary Greer, Agnes Mayse, Judith McCormack, Patsy Mayse, and Barsheba Simmons, and to the heirs of my daughter Nancy Meadow, dec'd, to be equally divided between them, respectively.

Seventh, and lastly, I do hereby appoint my son Matthew Wright and my son-in-law James Mayse executors of this my last will and testament, hereby revoking all other or former wills heretofore by me made.

In witness whereof I have hereunto set my hand and seal, this 21st day of February, 1815.   JOSEPH WRIGHT [SEAL].

Signed & ack'd in
presence of

 JOHN PATE,
  his
 JAS. x SPRADLIN,
  mark
 JOSHUA NOBLE.

Matthew Wright, born October 19, 1776, youngest son of Joseph and Elizabeth (Kemp) Wright, married Nancy ———.

CHILDREN:

(1) Jane, born September 7, 1800; married Valentine Kemper.

(2) Peter Meador, born May 15, 1802. (See forward.)

(3) Mary, born March 16, 1805; married Wilson Meador.

(4) Joseph, born March 30, 1807; married Eliza Adams.

(5) John A., born February 18, 1809; married Sibyl Craft. Two of their sons were:

> (a) William; married Sarah T. Lloyd.

CHILDREN:

> > (aa) Charles E.; married Leila Moore. One child:
> > (aaa) Mattie.
> > (bb) Lula; unmarried.
> > (cc) Sarah Temperance; died unmarried.
> > (dd) Hugh M.; married Lelia Katherine Gardner.
> > (ee) Frank; unmarried.
> > (ff) Blanche; married John Fuqua. All of these live in Bedford, Va.

> (b) George Delaraine; married Bettie Pannill. (See forward.)

(6) Milly, born December 31, 1810; died unmarried at the home of her niece, Mrs. Edward Brugh.

(7) Nancy, born July 17, 1812; married Frank Johnson. (See Johnson family.)

CHILDREN:

> (a) Jane; married William F. Graves and had a large family of children—among them:
> > Willie, John T., Frank, Nannie, Joseph, Alice, Minnie, Nunie, Florence, Stuart, and Oscar.

> (b) Joseph; married Mrs. Leslie (Woodruff) Johnson.

> (c) Nancy; married John Parker.

(8) Lydia, born February 2, 1814; married John Compton.

(9) Julia, born February 12, 1816; married Isaac Compton.

CHILD:

(a) Nannie, who married (first) William J. Jeter; had one child, which died in infancy; married (second) Edward Brugh and had children:

Pearl, Mary Fannie, Ernest, Frank, Irma, Munford, Nannie and Grover.

(10) Alie, born July 18, 1818; died in youth.

(11) Rite H., born July 30, 1820; married (first) Jane Burford; (second) Minerva Foutz.

George Delaraine Wright, son of John A. and Sibyl (Craft) Wright, was born at Kelso's Mill, Bedford County, Virginia, July 6, 1848, and died in Liberty (now Bedford), Va., August 8, 1890.

He was educated at Washington and Lee University, and became a leading tobacconist of Liberty, being junior member of the firm of Bolling, Wright and Company, Tobacco Manufacturers.

He married, November 4, 1875, Mary Elizabeth (Betty) Pannill, who was born at Glade Hill, Va., November 11, 1850, and died in Cincinnati, Ohio, October 4, 1907. Their children were all born in Liberty, Va., and are as follows:

(1) Harry, born August 25, 1877; business genius; capitalist; philanthropist; world traveler. He has lived in Mexico City for many years and has identified himself with the industrial, fraternal and social life of that city. He is founder and president of the Consolidated Rolling Mills and Foundries Company of Mexico City; trustee of Bank of Montreal, Mexico City; president of American University Club; reorganizer and president of Mexico City Country Club; member American Club; honorary member of Knights of Columbus; a Shriner, an Elk; and a Rotarian.

During the World War he operated a munitions factory at Stamford, Conn.

On September 4, 1906, Harry Wright married Edna Josephine McCauley in Louisville, Kentucky. They have no children.

(2) Della Pannill, born March 27, 1879. Unmarried; lives in Seattle, Washington. Interests: politics, travel, and crippled children. Instructor of surgical dressings for American Red Cross at University of Washington during World War. Has done out-

standing organization work in various charities. Member of Seattle Woman's University Club, Woman's Democratic Club, Seattle Woman's Club, University District Improvement Club, and various charity organizations.

(3) Max, born April 20, 1881; married, December 23, 1904, Annie Fontaine Whiddon of Thomasville, Georgia; lives in Mexico City. He is an expert rollerman and is associated with the Consolidated Rolling Mills and Foundries Company of Mexico City. He is an amateur golf champion, a Mason, an Elk, a Rotarian, and a member of each the American and the Country Clubs of Mexico City.

CHILDREN:

(a) Robert Delaraine, born in Shreveport, Louisiana, March 7, 1906; spent his childhood in Mexico City; was educated at Brown University, Providence, Rhode Island; now foreign representative of the Simmons Bed Company at Barcelona, Spain.

(b) Mackie, born in Mexico City, February 22, 1907; now a student at University of Virginia, where he is an outstanding athlete, and a member of the Delta Tau Delta Fraternity.

(4) Ula Frances, born April 8, 1883; married, August, 1909, Maurice Henry Kayser of El Paso, Texas, who is now legal adviser for the American Smelting and Refining Company at Pachuca, Mexico, where they reside.

CHILDREN:

(a) Elizabeth Davis, born in Mexico City, July 12, 1910; now attending University of Washington. Member Kappa Kappa Gamma Sorority.

(b) Mildred Wright, born in Mexico City, June 20, 1914; now attending John Marshall High School, Seattle, Washington.

(5) George Delaraine, born February 8, 1885; unmarried. Spent his youth in Havana, Cuba, and Latin America; now living in New York City; linguist; writer of short, humorous, negro stories. Exempt from service in World War because of deafness.

(6) Samuel Bolling, born February 14, 1886; married in Mexico City, November 18, 1914, Marion Jennings Conger of Cooperstown, New York. He is vice-president of the Consolidated Rolling Mills and Foundries Company of Mexico City. Was Chairman of Liberty Loan Committee of Mexico City during World War. President of American Board of Education; built present American School; trustee of American Hospital. Member of American Club, University Club, and Country Club. A Shriner, a Rotarian, and a world traveler.

CHILDREN:

(a) Samuel Bolling, Jr., born in Galveston, Texas, July 8, 1915.

(b) Harry, II, born in Mexico City, July 17, 1916.

(c) Evelyn Pannill, born May 6, 1917.

(d) Edward Orrin, born September 19, 1919.

(e) Sydney Conger, born November 18, 1920.

(7) Mildred Sybil, born February 28, 1888; married in Pachuca, Mexico, April 18, 1918, George Hubert Petty of Kansas City, Mo., who died January 4, 1924, in Phoenix, Arizona. She is an interior decorator—graduate of New York School of Interior Decoration; courses in New York and Paris. Resides in Seattle, Washington, where she is a member of the Woman's City Club, University District Improvement Club, and Children's Orthopedic Hospital Board.

(8) Veta Elizabeth, born July 10, 1890; educated at Hollins College; married, August, 1912, at Old Point Comfort, in the chapel of Fortress Monroe, George Lawrence Rihl of Washington, D. C. Resides in Mexico City, where her husband is actively engaged in aviation, being president of the Pacific, American International Aviation Company. She is a well known aviatrix, and is now (January, 1930) on a three months flying tour over South America.

Peter Meador Wright, son of Matthew and Nancy Wright, married, August 24, 1824, Susan James of Bedford County.

CHILDREN:

(1) James Matthew; married Mary Marshall.

CHILDREN:

(a) Susan; married Capt. ———— Albert.
(b) William P.; married ———— Pollard.
(c) Julia Ann; married Rev. Samuel Dooley.
(d) Mary Eliza; married Adam L. Feather ("Coon").
(e) James A.; married Sadie Crenshaw.
(f) Alice Frances; married Stephen Thrasher.
(g) Delia Eoline; married George Blankenship.
(h) Mattie; married Fleming Feather.
(i) Charles; married Kate Kennett.

(2) Mary Jane; married James P. Craft.

CHILDREN:

Abram, Eliza, Mollie, Graves, Elizabeth, Victoria Frances, and Lee.

(3) Nancy Ann, born September 6, 1829; died March 23, 1919; married Charles Harvey McManaway, in 1851.

CHILDREN:

(a) Alexander Gilmer; married Josephine Robertson of Petersburg, Va.; was a Baptist minister.

CHILDREN:

(aa) Clarice Payne; married Thomas Edward Mears.
(bb) Ellen Launice; married Rev. James Gordon Harris.
(cc) Beverly Clifton; married Grace E. Johnson. (See Johnson family.)
(dd) Volney Graham; killed in railroad accident in early life.
(ee) Josephine; married Rev. David Porter Gaines.
(ff) Katrina Ann.

(b) James Meador; married Mary Morgan of Botetourt County, Va.; was a Baptist minister.

CHILDREN:

(aa) Howard Morgan; married Gladys Maxwell.

(bb) Norman Taylor; married Wincia Wilkins.

(cc) Judson McCune; died while in training for World War.

(dd) James Gilmer; married Mary Ruthven.

(ee) Marjory Bates; married Arthur Flynn.

(c) Charles Gustavus; practicing physician; married (first) Rella Harris; (second) Josephine Pharr.

CHILDREN BY FIRST MARRIAGE:

(aa) William Harvey.

(bb) Ivan Morson; married Nervie Ramsey; died while in training in World War.

(cc) Charles Richard; married Eloise Tebeau.

(dd) Minda Lyman; married Arthur Schmidt.

(ee) Rella Mozelle; married Augustus Lowe.

(ff) Hugh Pharr; only child of last marriage.

(d) Ann Harvie; unmarried.

(e) Roberta Lee; married William I. Dooley. (His second wife.)

(f) Mary Eliza; married Thomas S. Wright. (See Wright family.)

(g) John Eugene; Evangelist of Baptist Church; married Virginia Caroline Freeman.

CHILDREN:

(aa) John Eugene, Jr.; married Estelle Payne; was First Lieutenant in the World War.

(bb) Herman Blan; married Roy Jones; was a soldier in World War; won Distinguished Service Medal.

(cc) Caroline Virginia.

(dd) José Antoinette.

(ee) Edward Milton.

(ff) Clayton Albert.

(gg) Gilmer Ware.

(h) Margaret Amanda; unmarried; an invalid since she was sixteen years old, but deeply interested in all affairs of life; mentally alert and actively engaged in research work; a genealogist of experience; and historian of her family.

(4) Peter Meador, II; married Sarah Dearing.

CHILDREN:

(a) Mary Susan; married William I. Dooley. (After her death he married Roberta L. McManaway.)

(b) Samuel Thomas; died in young manhood.

(c) Maria Frances; married (first) Daniel Basham; (second) J. W. Tompkins.

(d) John A.; married Mollie Stratton Brown.

(e) William Chester; married (first) Mary Pendleton.

CHILDREN:

(aa) Carrie, born October 18, 1883.

(bb) Fannie Julia, born March 29, 1886.

(cc) Mary Willie, born March 1, 1889.

Wm. C. Wright married (second) Rosa Ella Meador, May 16, 1894.

CHILDREN:

(aa) Ethel, born May 15, 1895.

(bb) Meador, born September 29, 1896.

(cc) Elsie Starr, born March 1, 1898.

(dd) Hilda, born March 1, 1900.

(ee) Silas Benjamin, born August 15, 1901.

(ff) Emory Frederick, born October 26, 1903.

(gg) Ruby, born October 21, 1905.

(hh) Nancy Starky, born June 6, 1907.

(ii) William Chester, Jr., born June 14, 1910.

(f) Ann Eliza; married John Beard.

(g) Belle; married James Jeter.

(h) Laura; married Marcus D. McCall.

(i) Starr; married Elisha Overstreet.

(5) Eliza Ann; married Joel Lemon of Botetourt County, Va. Lived and died at Nace, Va.

CHILDREN:

(a) Elry Susan; died unmarried.

(b) Rufus Meador; physician; married Kate Brugh.

(c) Louisa Frances; married John Peter Saul; lives in Salem, Va.

(d) Abbie D.; married Willie Watkins.

(e) Joel Bunyan; Baptist minister; married Lelia Parrish.

(f) William Leachman; Baptist minister; Edith Chambers.

(g) Laura Ann; married William Thaxton of Bedford County, Va.

(h) Lee; died in childhood.

(i) Mollie; married Berkeley R. Price.

(j) Walter; died in youth.

(k) Urban.

(l) Allie; married Park Price; lives in Roanoke, Va.

(6) Susan Julia; married William M. Basham. No children.

(7) Stephen Wood; married (first) Narcissus Richardson; (second) Margaret Muse. CHILDREN:

(a) Ida Frances; married John T. Graves.

(b) Dora Ann; married Samuel B. Wood.

(c) Ellis Lyman; married Julia Day.

(8) Joel Wilson; married Eliza Dearing.

CHILDREN:

(a) Libbie Verna; married William Byrd Ferguson.

(b) Thomas Stephen; married Eliza McManaway; lives in Roanoke, Va. CHILDREN:

(aa) Paul Thomas; soldier in World War; minister of Baptist church; married Annie Belle Watkins.

(bb) Mabel Roy.

(cc) Elsie Leroy.

(dd) Norma Christine.

(ee) Guy Silas.

(ff) Mary Kathleen.

(gg) Herman Bruce.

(hh) Ethel, eldest child, died in infancy.

(c) Nancy Frances; married James W. Stephens; lives in Vinton, Va.

CHILDREN:

(aa) Carlie Douglass, born March 19, 1895; married, July 12, 1924, Henry Buff Norfleet, who was born May 30, 1895. They live in Suffolk, Va.

CHILDREN:

(aaa) Carlotta Buff, born July 20, 1927.
(bbb) Ann Elizabeth, born July 20, 1929.
(bb) Clara Barnhardt, born July 6, 1898; married, January 3, 1925; Laurence Livezey Jones who was born November 10, 1898.

CHILD:

(aaa) Ann Douglass, born November 12, 1926.
(d) Fletcher Vermilion; died in childhood.
(e) Abbie Dunsmore; unmarried; now teaching in the public schools of Bedford County.
(f) Pearl Lee; married Rufus D. Foutz; lives near Roanoke, Va.

CHILDREN:

(aa) Roger Williams.
(bb) Louise.
(cc) Blondelle.
(g) Ola Gish; unmarried; teaching in the Blue Ridge Mission School at Buffalo Ridge, Va.
(9) Louisa Frances; thrown from a horse and killed, in young womanhood.
(10) Martin VanBuren; died in infancy.
(11) Elizabeth A.; died in childhood.
(12) Thomas Benton; died in infancy.

LULA EASTMAN JETER
wife of George Pleasant Parker

GEORGE PLEASANT PARKER

PARKER

"September ye 1st, 1673, Will Parker, Arch Deacon of Cornwall and Justice of Peace of ye same County, was second brother of Tho. Parker of Browsholme, Esq'r, who went from Browsh into Cornwall about ye year 1580, whoe he married is not known, but her Christian name was Joanne. . . . Ye said Will had two sons James and Will and his house is called Traugoe in ye parish of Wartegin, in Cornwall about 16 miles of Lauston. . . .

"James, his eldest son, was married to Katteren, eldest daughter of Richard Buller of Shillingham. . . . Will never married. James and Katteren Parker had 21 children.

"Richard, ye 9th, Dr. of Physick, went to Virginny, married a Londoner and had 6 children. Liveth upon St. James River in ye uplands of Virginy and hath been High Sheriff of ye said county.

"George, ye 13th, . . . went to Virginy."

(Taken from an Old English Record, published in the *Virginia Historical Magazine*.)

"The Parkers of Virginia are descended from the Earl of Macclesfield, England, and settled in 1650 in Virginia—one brother, George, in Accomac, and the other brother, Thomas, in Isle of Wight. . . . The English family is one of universal prominence and includes men of title and high rank.

"In America, the name is no less illustrious. Men, high in every profession, in naval and Military life, as well as in business have ever made it a prominent one in affairs of the nation. Bishop Meade, in alluding to an old graveyard, wrote: 'It was honored by the remains of the Washingtons, Lees and Parkers'."

(Taken from *The Encyclopedia* of Virginia History and Biography, by Lyon G. Tyler.)

The following is taken from the *Virginia Historical Magazine*, Vol. 6, pages 412-413:

THE PARKER FAMILY

"Compiled from Records of Accomac and Northampton Counties, Manuscripts and the Family Bible. By R. Ll. S. (Mrs. Edward Shippen).

"The Parker family came early from England to the Colony of Virginia, and are recorded in the records of Northampton County as early as 1654.

"The family seat in England, I believe to be 'Park Hill,' in Staffordshire, descendants of the Earls of Morley and Monteagle . . . same family as the Earls of Macclesfield.

"There appears on the records of Northampton County, Virginia, Vol. IV, page 226, 'Robert Parker and his wife Joan, December 9, 1654.' Vol. VII, page 2, 'Philip Parker, March 28, 1656.'

" 'Capt. George Parker, Gent.,' Vol. IV, page 226, Records of Northampton County, 1656. He was High Sheriff of Accomac County, Va., and a member of the County Courts, both of Northampton and Accomac counties, and was a brother of Robert Parker; and John, Philip and Thomas Parker also appear on the records at the same time; but Thomas is not mentioned again, and it is thought he returned to Isle of Wight County; as my mother's record states that our ancestor, George Parker, came from Isle of Wight County to the Eastern Shore. And a will of Thomas Parker is recorded in Isle of Wight County, dated November 16, 1685, and recorded February 9, 1685, wherein he gives his 'Uplands to his son Thomas,' which land was known afterwards as 'Macclesfield.' The name of 'Macclesfield' was not mentioned in the will as the name of the land, but is now known to be the same land described in his will as my uplands. The same will gives 'my Island land to son John.'

"Captain George Parker, Gent., of the County of Accomac, Eastern Shore, Virginia, bought land in Accomac County called 'Poplar Grove,' and in each will of his descendants, as well as his own, this property has been left by father to eldest son, for many generations, always to son George, except in one instance to 'Thomas,' who in turn leaves the place to his son, Judge George Parker, of Northampton County, who leaves it to his son, Severn Eyre Parker, who sold it to a Mr. Edmund Poulson about 1840.

"Captain George Parker, Gent., who afterwards became major, was commissioner of both Accomac and Northampton counties; a member of the County Court, 1658, and 1663, and a continued justice until his death in 1674. His will is recorded in Vol. 1673 to 1676, page 184, Northampton County Records, September 10, 1674. It mentions wife, Florence; sons: George (to whom he gives his home lands on north side of Onancock Creek which is 'Poplar Grove'), John, Philip and Charles; daughter, Abigail.

"Major George Parker, Gent., eldest son of Captain George Parker, Gent., died in 1724. See Vol. 1715 to 1719, Northampton County Records, page 210. His will was recorded at Accomac County, Va., July 14, 1724. He leaves to his eldest son, George Parker, the half of the home lands, lying on the north side of Onancock Creek, being about 825 acres. To his son Charles he gives all his land lying on Pungoteague Creek, bought of Mr. Justinian Yeo, containing 959 acres. To his son Henry he gives the land lying on 'Back Creek' adjoining that of 'my eldest son, George Parker's land,' also lying on the north side of Onancock Creek, and a part of the original 'home place.' To his son Bennett he gives part of the Wickenough Neck land in Somerset County, Maryland, it being 300 acres. To son Richard he gives the balance of the Wickenough Neck land, being also 300 acres. To his son Philip he gives all the land lying in 'My Neck,' on Onancock Creek, not already given to George and Henry. He had one daughter named Anne Parker. He married Ann Scarborough, the daughter of Charles Scarborough (the son of Edmund Scarborough, Surveyor-General of Virginia) of Accomac County, Va., and Elizabeth Bennett (a daughter of Governor Richard Bennett, of Virginia). See will of Governor Bennett, and also that of his son Richard Bennett, who mention George Parker and Ann Scarborough and their children and also the children of Charles Scarborough and Theoderic Bland."

....

The Parkers, with whom this sketch has to do, are descended from George Parker, who was born in Pittsylvania County, Virginia, in 1769. No record has been found of the names of his parents, but family tradition says that his father came from Maryland, lived for a time in Fauquier County, and came to Pittsylvania between 1765 and 1769, where he died in 1805. It also says that he was the youngest son, and had two brothers in the Colonial Army, who were present at Braddock's Defeat. Family tradition, however, can not always be relied upon, and so all of the early Parkers of the state have been investigated, with the hope of finding some clue to the ancestry of this branch of the family, but, so far, without success.

The Census Report of 1790 gives two William Parkers as heads of families in Pittsylvania County. This, coupled with the fact that

George named his second son William—his oldest was named for his wife's side of the house—leads us to believe that one of these Williams was the father of George.

....

George Parker, born 1769; died April 5, 1859, was the youngest child of his parents. Among his brothers and sisters—how many we do not know—were David and Benjamin, both of whom went to Kentucky, and the family of one of them was poisoned by using arsenic for soda in bread.

George Parker married, May 1, 1797, Frances Oaks, who was born in 1773 and died June 26, 1858.

CHILDREN:

(1) Alexander Oaks, born 1798; married, February 19, 1829, Patsy D. Snow; died January 19, 1840.

(2) Frances, born July 13, 1800; died April 9, 1857; married, 1817, Jabe Snow.

(3) William, born September 25, 1801; died young.

(4) David, born October 10, 1802; died June 17, 1883; married (first) Mary A. Toler; (second) Mary Goggin (born June 12, 1855; died December 25, 1916).

(5) Eli, born November 18, 1804; died December 27, 1878; married (first) Amarilla Snow; (second) Julia Parker.

(6) Ammon Hancock, born March 10, 1807; died May 8, 1880; married (first), December 10, 1835, Frances H. Goggin. (See Goggin family.)

CHILDREN:

(a) Robert William, born August 31, 1838. (See forward.)

(b) George Stephen, born September 23, 1842; member of 58th Virginia Infantry of the Confederate Army; died 1862.

(c) Alexander Clark, born January 14, 1847. (See forward.)

(d) Hester Ann Mary, born August 13, 1849; died November 27, 1907; married William Nicholas Reese, November 22, 1866. (See Reese family.)

He married (second) Elizabeth Parker, June 6, 1878.

(7) Polly, born July 4, 1808; died May 9, 1870; married Richard Snow.

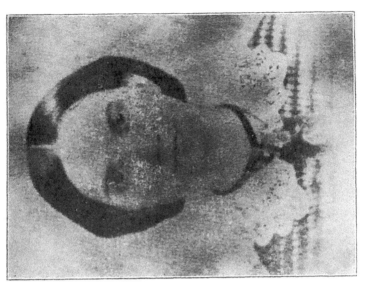

REBECCA WALKER
wife of Robert William Parker

ROBERT WILLIAM PARKER

(8) Bluford, born May 9, 1810; died October 10, 1888; married Polly Williams.

(9) Joseph, born September 7, 1812; died September 16, 1879. (See forward.)

(10) Emily J., born February 3, 1817; died August 5, 1860; married Joseph Johnson in 1842. (See Johnson family.)

....

Robert William Parker, son of Ammon H. and Frances (Goggin) Parker, entered the Confederate Army at the beginning of the Civil War and fought throughout the struggle, giving up his life at Appomattox, April 9, 1865. He was Sergeant of his company.

Andrew Lee, late Lieutenant Company D, 8th Pennsylvania Cavalry, in a letter to Major John W. Daniel of Lynchburg, Va., published in the *Times-Dispatch* of Richmond, Va., about 1904, in telling of the death of Sergeant Parker, said:

"Just before the firing ceased, R. W. Parker of Company F, Second Virginia Cavalry, who was in advance of his regiment, was shot between the lines. He was the last man killed in battle in the Army of Northern Virginia.

"When the firing ceased the officers of both sides met and buried him between the lines. This was one of the saddest and most pathetic scenes witnessed during the war."

Robert William Parker married, December 6, 1860, Rebecca Louise Fitzhugh Walker, daughter of Dr. James Alexander and Nancy (Jopling) Walker. She was born January 6, 1840, and died January 5, 1867. (See Walker family.)

CHILDREN:

(1) Robert Moorman, born November 4, 1861, grew to manhood in the home of his grandfather Walker, going to Liberty and engaging in the hardware business a short time before his marriage. He continued to live in Liberty (now Bedford) until 1898, when he moved his family to Roanoke and accepted a position in the offices of the Norfolk and Western Railway, but his health soon failed and he died November 11, 1902.

He married in Wytheville, Va., May 8, 1888, Sallie Viola Wappett, born January 4, 1868, daughter of Thomas W. and

Nannie (Rider) Wappett. She was a person of rare talents—music, poetry and art were her delight and had she had the necessary training for a career she might easily have made any one of them her life's work. She became ill while on a pleasure trip to California and died July 31, 1923, a few days after reaching her home in Roanoke, Va.

CHILDREN:

(a) Robert Wappett, born 1890; married in Wytheville, Va., June 8, 1918, Hazel Jackson. They now live in Roanoke, Va., where he is engaged in insurance business.

CHILD:

(aa) Ruth Virginia, born April 29, 1919.

(b) Frank Moorman, born April 17, 1892; married Mary Griffith, August 9, 1916. He is a master mechanic and holds a responsible position in Chambersburg, Pennsylvania, where they live.

CHILD:

(aa) Frank Moorman, Jr., born September 20, 1917.

(c) Nannie Eloise, born October 17, 1894; married, December 13, 1913, Horace Blair Gordon, born January 25, 1886, son of Daniel Fletcher Gordon (born in Appomattox County, Va., November 6, 1854) and Mallie Virginia Murrell (born in Campbell County, Va., January 16, 1861), who were married, November 8, 1881. He is a prosperous farmer, and their home is near Goode, in Bedford County, Virginia.

CHILDREN:

(aa) Horace Blair, Jr., born July 5, 1915.
(bb) Nancy Eloise, born September 17, 1916.
(cc) Daniel Parker, born in 1924.

(d) William Alden, born November 7, 1896; married, May 3, 1924, Mary Bernie Ragland, daughter of J. B. and Mary (Miller) Ragland of Roanoke, Va. He is also a master mechanic and holds a position with the Norfolk and Western Railway in Roanoke.

CHILDREN:

(aa) William Alden, Jr., born May 1, 1925.

(bb) Infant; died 1927.

(e) Rice Moorman, born November 24, 1902; attended the public schools of Roanoke, often times working during the day and attending the night school; graduated from High School there in 1922; worked during vacation and defrayed his own expenses for a full course at Emory and Henry, receiving his degree in 1926; continuing his vacation work he has also been enabled to finance his four years at Emory University, where he will receive his degree in June, 1930. He will then enter the ministry of the Methodist Episcopal Church, South.

(2) George Pleasant, born November 17, 1863; was raised by his Parker grand-parents and continued to live with them until the death of his grandmother. He then made his home with his uncle, Alexander C. Parker, until 1887, when he accepted a position with the hardware firm of Jeter and McGhee of Liberty, Va. In 1895, upon the death of Mr. Jeter, he purchased his interest in the business and the firm name was changed to Parker and McGhee. In 1899, this firm was dissolved and in its place a joint stock company was formed, known as the Parker-Ayres Hardware Company, with George P. Parker as senior member and secretary-treasurer of the company. He still holds this position, and is also vice-president of the Overstreet-Smith Lumber Company; a director of the Bedford County Fair Association; a director of the Piedmont Label Company; chairman of the Street Committee of the Town Council. He is an Elk and a Mason—having been treasurer of the local Blue Lodge and the Royal Arch Chapter for more than twenty-five years.

He married, November 11, 1903, Lula Eastman Jeter, daughter of Thomas A., and Laurie Cornelia (Mays) Jeter. (See Jeter family.)

CHILDREN:

(a) Georgette, born August 2, 1907; graduated from Bedford High School in 1925; received degree of B. S. from

College of William and Mary, in Virginia, in February, 1930; member of Phi Sigma.

(b) Laura Jeter, born June 1, 1911; graduated from Bedford High School in 1927; now a student at the College of William and Mary, Williamsburg, Va.

(c) Virginia Hamilton, born July 6, 1913; died September 30, 1919.

(d) Josephine Mays, born June 27, 1914; now a sophomore in the Bedford High School.

(3) Fannie Rebecca, born November 24, 1865; married, January 11, 1887, Robert William Dooley, born November 24, 1862, son of Rev. Thomas William Dooley and Ann Harrison Ownby, who were married, January 28, 1862. Ann Ownby was the daughter of Edward Ownby of Rockbridge County, Va., and Elizabeth Gibbs (born September 20, 1825; died June 29, 1895), daughter of William Gibbs and Susannah Mays, daughter of John and Susannah Mays of Bedford County. (See Mays family.)

CHILDREN:

(a) George Nimmo, born September 17, 1888; married, November 27, 1912, Jessie Elizabeth Reed, born September 29, 1890, daughter of John Henry Reed (born in Rockbridge County, Va., July 2, 1845; died in Bedford County, Va., April 19, 1907) and Margaret Elizabeth Davis (born November 29, 1847), who were married in Staunton, Va., September 5, 1870.

(b) Elizabeth Claire, born March 6, 1890.

(c) Marvin Baker, born August 22, 1892; died November 24, 1894.

(d) Nell Rebecca, born October 22, 1894.

(e) Willie Edith, born September 14, 1896; died January 18, 1898.

(f) Robert Thomas, born September 11, 1899.

(g) Helen Watson, born May 13, 1906.

(h) Faye Virginia, born February 10, 1911.

....

Alexander Clark Parker, son of Ammon H. and Frances (Goggin) Parker, has always lived on the farm on which he was born, having inherited it from his father. His home has ever been a center of old-fashioned southern hospitality, not only for kindred and friends, but strangers have many a time been invited in for a meal or for a night's lodging, when heavy rains had caused the sudden rise of a nearby creek and made travel impossible.

He was a private in the 1st Battalion of the Confederate Army, and Lieutenant in the 60th Virginia Infantry, and served until the close of the war.

He married, January 17, 1877, Elizabeth Ann Teass, born in Campbell County, Va., November 8, 1854, daughter of John F. Teass (born 1811) and Mary M. Crews (born in Amherst County, Va., in 1819; died in Bedford County, October 22, 1860).

CHILDREN:

(1) John Clark, born November 10, 1877; married, March 24, 1910, Emma Lee Teass, born April 15, 1890, daughter of John Thomas and Annie E. (Boswell) Teass, who were married, March 23, 1885. He held responsible positions in West Virginia, with the Lynchburg Trust and Savings Bank in Bedford, and with the Bedford Motor Company. His health began to fail in early manhood and finally, as a last resort, he tried the climate of South Texas, going there with his family in the summer of 1925. He grew steadily worse and only remained a few weeks, coming back to the home of his parents in September. He died November 15, 1925, and was buried in the family burying ground.   CHILDREN:

    (a) Annie Elizabeth, born July 24, 1912; graduated from Roanoke High School in 1929.

    (b) Aileen, born October 25, 1914; now a student in the Roanoke High School.

(2) George Edward, born May 5, 1881; unmarried; lives at home and superintends the farm.

(3) Howard Doane, born July 4, 1882; married, January 27, 1914, Lucy Skinnell, daughter of William Skinnell and Victoria Overstreet. Their home is in Roanoke, Va.

CHILD:

    (a) Howard Doane, Jr., born March 22, 1915.

(4) Mary Antoinette, born February 11, 1885; married George Ira

Ford, son of William H. and Mary M. (Walton) Ford. Live at Lowry, Va., where he was depot agent for the Norfolk and Western Railway for many years.

CHILDREN:

(a) Ruth Elizabeth, born May 27, 1907; married, January 17, 1929, Edward Ayres Holman, born January 14, 1901.
(b) George Ira, Jr., born July 1, 1910.
(c) Iris Parker, born September 11, 1915.

(5) Ruth Frances, born August 14, 1887; married Henry Forest Flowers of Wilson, N. C., born March 11, 1887, son of E. K. and Delphie (Taylor) Flowers. Live in Wilson, N. C.

CHILDREN:

(a) Elizabeth Clark, born December 5, 1921.
(b) Alexander Parker, born November 23, 1925.
(c) Henry Forest, Jr., born May 17, 1928.

(6) Alexander Boyce, born March 24, 1889; enlisted in A. E. F., June 27, 1918, at Sapulpa, Okla.; sent to Camp Travis, Texas; private in Company C, Fifth Engineers; sailed for France, July 30, 1918, on ship H. R. Mallory; landed at Brest, France, August 18, 1918. The principal work of this company was laying out trenches, supervising their construction, and building wire entanglements. They returned from France on the "George Washington," with President Wilson as a fellow passenger; landed in New York, February 25, 1919. He was discharged at Camp Lee, Va., June 1, 1919.

He married in Oklahoma, June, 1926, Mrs. Myrtle Morris of Texas; lived in Oklahoma until 1928; brought his family to Virginia, and is now living in the home of his parents.

CHILD:

(a) Annah Boyce, born July 15, 1927.

(7) Manly Grady, born May 5, 1891; lives at home; is one of the most progressive farmers of Bedford County.
(8) Amanda VanLier, born February 11, 1894; lives at home and is taking care of her parents in their old age.

TEASS

In the *West Virginia Historical Magazine* of October, 1904, is an article entitled, "The Teass Family of Kanawha," in which it is stated that Thomas "Teays" of the Colonial Army, who lived at New London, Bedford County, Va., married Katherine Ley (or Lee) of Germany about 1760 in Bedford County, and that their children were: Katherine, Martha, Mary, Lucy, John, William, and Stephen.

Joseph Parker, son of George and Frances (Oaks) Parker, married Sallie Ann Robertson in Bedford County, February 28, 1839. (See Robertson family.)

CHILDREN:

(1) William Alexander, born March 1, 1840; killed in battle near Stannardsville, Green County, Va., March 1, 1864.
(2) George Nicholas, born October 20, 1841. (See forward.)
(3) Sallie Fannie, born May 3, 1844. (See forward.)
(4) David W., born February 9, 1846. (See forward.)
(5) Mary Rosabell, born April 27, 1848. (See forward.)
(6) Amanda Octavia, born April 18, 1850. (See forward.)
(7) Missouri Rebecca, born November 14, 1852. (See forward.)
(8) Joseph Stanhope, born June 19, 1855. (See forward.)
(9) Bettie Augusta, born August 5, 1857. (See forward.)
(10) Ponta, born April 16, 1860; died January 8, 1862.

Joseph Parker was a minister of the Baptist Church; was ordained in October, 1858. He belonged to old Moodie's Church until 1857, when, upon the organization of Old Fork, he became a charter member of that church. (Old Fork is now Mt. Ivey.)

George Nicholas Parker, son of Joseph and Sallie (Robertson) Parker, was called from school at Mt. Pleasant Academy to enter the Confederate Army. He became a member of Company "D," 2nd Virginia Cavalry; served four years; was captured April 6, 1865, near Richmond, and in prison at Newport News for three months. At Buckland, Prince William County, in 1863, he captured single-handed eighteen Yankees with pistols and turned them over to the guards of the Confederate Army. One of these pistols is still in his possession.

George Nicholas Parker married (first), March 5, 1868, Bettie Margaret Rucker, born December 25, 1844; died December 15, 1891; daughter of Ambrose Clifton Rucker (born June 22, 1817; died

December 23, 1882) and Sarah Jane Board (born March 12, 1819; died May 3, 1895), who were married, December 19, 1843. (See Board family.)

CHILDREN:

(1) William Anthony, born February 20, 1869; married, April 12, 1917, Addie Wirtley Cridlin of Richmond, Va., who was born May 22, 1885, and is a daughter of Rev. Ransdall White Cridlin (a minister of the Baptist Church, born July 18, 1840; died June 22, 1913) and Emma Hasseltine Snellings (born May 12, 1847; died April 15, 1906), who were married in 1871.

CHILD:

(a) Donal Snellings, born September 21, 1921.
William A. Parker served two terms as a member of the State Legislature from Bedford County.

(2) Don Ernest, born August 8, 1870; married, July 12, 1910, Fanny Eva Martin, of Albemarle County, Va., born October 31, 1883; daughter of John Louis Martin (born in Fluvanna County, December 31, 1848; died in Albemarle County, November 8, 1919) and Theodosia Virginia Carter (born in Louisa County, November 14, 1856; died in Albemarle County, August 1, 1924), who were married, February 9, 1881.

CHILDREN:

(a) Mary Theodosia, born February 23, 1912; graduated at Bedford High School in 1928; now a student at the College of William and Mary.
(b) Don Thurston, born August 8, 1915.
(c) Bettie Carolyn, born October 19, 1917.

(The Bedford Co-operative School, a unique institution for girls and young women, was organized by the Parker brothers—William A., Don E., and Joseph N.—in 1900, at the Jeter Institute Building, Bedford, Va.

This school was in successful operation for twelve years, with a total enrollment of about one thousand students. The object of its founders was to furnish a practical means of education at the lowest possible cost, which was done without outside aid or endowment—the tuition charges paid the salaries of the teachers and board was furnished at cost.

The course of study offered was that of an accredited, four years High School, with additional facilities for two years of College work. Also thorough courses in Voice, Instrumental Music and Art.

Mrs. Mary Beaufort, a teacher of long and successful experience was Lady Principal, and among the teachers were Miss Addie Cridlin, who married William A. Parker, and Miss Eva Martin, who married Don E. Parker.)

(3) Ada Florence, born March 30, 1872; married, October 28, 1896, Julius Kemper Dudley of Danville, Va., who was born December 26, 1864, and is the son of James Henry Dudley (born in Franklin County, 1828; died 1905) and Julia Elizabeth Poindexter (born 1832; died 1875), who were married in 1848.

CHILDREN :

(a) Emmett Irvin, born December, 1897; died in infancy.

(b) Guy Rucker, born March 27, 1899; was called by War Department from Wake Forest College, N. C., during World War to enter S. A. T. C. at Richmond. He did not render active service, and finished his education at the University of Virginia. He married. October 13, 1928, Ruth Boyles, and has one child:

(aa) Guy Rucker, Jr., born 1929.

(c) Elizabeth Dorothy, born August 1, 1900; graduated at Randolph-Macon Institute, Danville, Va.; took a two years course in music at Peabody Conservatory of Music in Baltimore, Md., and later attended Columbia University, New York; married, August, 1927, John J. Dratt of Vermont.

(d) Wallace Lee, born May 30, 1904; graduated at Danville High School and took a Commercial Course and Business Management in Richmond, Va.

(e) James Nicholas, born July 14, 1906; graduated at Danville High School; at Randolph-Macon College; entered Medical College of Virginia in 1929.

(f) Carolyn Parker, born September 20, 1909; died July 13, 1910.

(g) Infant, born March 22, 1911; died March 25, 1911.

(4) Mary Reese, born in Franklin County, August 31, 1873; married, November 25, 1897, Gideon Edmund Stone. (See Stone family.)

(5) Sarah Jane, born September 22, 1875; married, June 18, 1902, James Waller Stone. (See Stone family.)

(6) Carrie Lillian, born August 16, 1877; died June 12, 1901; was buried by the side of her mother at Mt. Zion Methodist Church near Penhook, Va.

(7) Ambrose Rucker, born in Pittsylvania County, December 13, 1878; married, January 23, 1907, Mary Louisa Wright of Danville, Va., who was born May 27, 1883, and is the daughter of Capt. John Reuben Wright (born November 12, 1846; died November 8, 1916) and Louisa Jane King of Greensboro, N. C. (born November 22, 1851), who were married, February 28, 1867.

CHILDREN:

(a) Ambrose Rucker, Jr., born November 26, 1907; now a junior at Danville Military Institute.

(b) Reuben Wright, born January 13, 1910; now a senior at Danville Military Institute.

(8) Joseph Nicholas, born December 3, 1880; educated at Bedford Co-operative School; later member of faculty of same.

George Nicholas Parker married (second) Mary Catherine Powell, July 4, 1894. No children. He died in Bedford, January 31, 1930, and was buried in Oakwood Cemetery.

....

Sallie Fannie Parker, daughter of Joseph and Sallie (Robertson) Parker, married Moses Peter Rucker, February 14, 1866. (See Rucker family.)

CHILDREN:

(1) Annie Mary, born January 6, 1867; married William Milton Sutherland, January 4, 1894.

CHILDREN:

(a) Frederick Pelham, born October 6, 1894; married Anna Obrist, June 27, 1920.

CHILD:

(aa) William Pelham, born December 31, 1922.

(b) Willie Maude, born November 30, 1896.

(c) Benjamin Rucker, born May 24, 1898; married Mary Belle Dudley, March, 1923.

CHILD:

(aa) Benjamin Chapman, born January 11, 1924.

(d) James Anthony, born August 12, 1903.

(2) David Hammett, born June 22, 1869; married Lillie Hardy, June 22, 1897.

CHILDREN:

(a) Infant, which died.

(b) Sallie Jane, born February 22, 1900.

(3) Joseph Anthony, born June 28, 1871; married Eliza Vincent Cauthorn, April 30, 1901.

CHILDREN:

(a) Eleanor Jordan, born April 2, 1902; died June 30, 1907.

(b) Joseph Anthony, Jr., born August 21, 1906; graduated at Washington and Lee University; now living in New York City.

(c) George Cauthorn, born November 20, 1908; died November 23, 1914.

(d) William Vincent, born March 29, 1911; now a student at Washington and Lee University.

(e) Ambrose Alexander (twin), born January 24, 1916.

(f) Virginia Browning (twin), born January 24, 1916.

Dr. Joseph A. Rucker was educated at Sunnyside Academy, New London Academy, University of Virginia, and took his M. D. degree at the University of Louisville, Ky. He practiced medicine at Boones Mill, Franklin County, at Thaxton, and came to Bedford in August, 1895. He is now Physician to the Elks National Home, and to Randolph-Macon Academy; Surgeon to the Norfolk and Western Railway; Health Officer of Bedford County since 1914; member of American Medical Society, Virginia Medical Society, and secretary of Bedford Medical Society. He is an Elk and a Mason, a member of the

Sons of Veterans, a deacon and a trustee of the Bedford Baptist Church, and teacher of the Men's Bible Class of that Sunday School.

Eliza (Cauthorn) Rucker, born June 14, 1879, is a daughter of Dr. George Thomas Cauthorn (born in Essex County, Va., January 17, 1833; died in Bedford, August 8, 1903) and Ella Jordan (born April 11, 1854), who were married May 8, 1878. (See Jordan family.)

RUCKER

Peter Rucker (I) died in Orange County, Va., 1743. His son—

John (II) was Captain in the Continental Militia for Orange County in 1740. He assisted in establishing St. Mark's Parish (Church of England) in 1731; was a vestryman, and appears to have been an influential member of the church.

Ambrose (III), son of John, was Captain in the Revolutionary War, from Amherst County. He married Mary Tinsley, and they had fourteen children. Their son—

Ambrose (IV), born 1763; married Elizabeth Lucas; moved to Bedford County and lived near what is now Wheatland.

Anthony (V), born 1793, son of Ambrose and Elizabeth (Lucas) Rucker, married Margaret Hardy, daughter of Joseph Hardy and Margaret McKenzie, of Albemarle County. Anthony Rucker lived and reared his family near Hendrick's Store, in Bedford County, and most of the Ruckers of this county are descended from him.

Moses Peter (VI), born 1837, youngest son of Anthony and Margaret (Hardy) Rucker, married Sallie Fannie Parker, daughter of Joseph and Sallie (Robertson) Parker, February 14, 1866. He was a member of Company "F," Second Virginia Cavalry, C. S. A.

JORDAN

Jonas Jordan (I) appears in the records of Bedford County, Virginia, in 1773, and Absalom, his son, in 1776. Absalom is mentioned as heir-at-law of Jonas. They are first mentioned in Isle of Wight in 1730 and seem to have lived in Amelia, Goochland, and Albemarle counties, before settling in Bedford, as their names are found in the records of all of those counties. No Revolutionary service has been found for either of them except the following:

At a Court held for Bedford County, April 22, 1782, at the house of David Wright, "Jonas Jordan proved that he furnished the said Com: with 835 lbs. Beef for which he is all'd 16/8 per Cwt." (Order Book, 1774-1782.)

Absalom Jordan (II) married Mary Ann ———, and they reared a large family of children. Their son—

Vincent Jordan (III), born 1769; married Elizabeth Mays in 1790. (Leroy, another son, married Rhoda Mays in 1806. Both were daughters of John and Susannah Mays.)

Vincent Jordan lived near Emaus. The old burying ground is near his house, enclosed with a stone wall, and there are tombstones at some of the graves. A brother of Vincent, said to have been an eccentric bachelor, lived at Jordantown, and at his death, left his property to his slaves.

Jubal Jordan (IV), born 1792, son of Vincent and Elizabeth (Mays) Jordan, married in 1817, Priscilla Williamson, daughter of Henry and Ann Rebecca (Mason) Williamson. Four of their sons, Alexander, Tyler, William, and John, served in the Civil War. The first three were Captains, and Tyler was promoted to Major. William was wounded in the war and John was killed.

Alexander Jordan (V), born 1829, son of Jubal and Priscilla (Williamson) Jordan, married in 1851, Lucy Ann Crenshaw, daughter of John and Lucy (Mc-Daniel) Crenshaw.

CHILDREN:

(1) Henry Vincent; married Mary Terry Buford.
(2) Ella; married Dr. George Thomas Cauthorn.

---

(4) William Penn, born October 4, 1873; married Josephine Hardy, April 30, 1908. No children.
(5) Moses Peter, Jr., born June 27, 1876; married Mary Pryor Williams, June 28, 1910.

CHILD:

(a) Nancy Williams, born June 29, 1919.

Dr. M. P. Rucker is also a practicing physician of Bedford.

(6) Sallie Margaret, born December 20, 1881; married Ira Thomas Dickson, November 8, 1905.

CHILDREN:

(a) Byron Rucker, born December 28, 1906.
(b) William Oscar, born February 3, 1908.
(c) Ralph Thomas, born March 5, 1909.
(d) Helen Frances, born January 28, 1912.
(e) Ruth Loraine, born October 27, 1916; died January 18, 1919.

Sallie (Parker) Rucker died in Bedford, February 3, 1925, and was buried in Oakwood Cemetery.

She was a devout member of the Baptist Church and a most loyal and enthusiastic member of Woman's Christian Temperance Union.

David W. Parker, son of Joseph and Sallie (Robertson) Parker, married Mary Ella Moulton, in Bedford County, November 26, 1884.

CHILDREN:

(1) Mary Augusta, born November 8, 1885; married A. P. Albert, May 31, 1924; lives at Coalwood, W. Va.

(2) Joseph Moulton, born August 2, 1887.

(3) Bessie Gertrude, born March 9, 1891.

(4) Grace Winifred, born January 10, 1893.

(5) Wilbur Nicholas, born October 2, 1896.

David W. Parker was a private in Company "D," 2nd Virginia Cavalry, Stewart's Division, C. S. A., which was organized in Franklin County, and started to the army, May 20, 1861. Captain, G. W. B. Hale; First Lieutenant, Wm. A. Parker; Second Lieutenant, M. D. Holland; Third Lieutenant, G. R. Clairborne.

David W. Parker and family live at Moneta, Bedford County, Va., where he has been engaged in farming for a great many years.

Mary Ella (Moulton) Parker, born in Bedford County, near Davis Mills, May 28, 1854; died in 1929; was the daughter of Dr. Benjamin H. Moulton and Mary S. Cundiff.

MOULTON

Dr. Benjamin H. Moulton was born in Sanford, York County, Maine, February 1, 1818; came to Bedford County, Va., after 1840; taught school one or two years near Bunker Hill; entered the University of Virginia and studied medicine. He married (first) in 1848, Mary S. Cundiff, daughter of Jonathan Cundiff and Mrs. ———— Reese (maided name, Boothe), and (second) Mrs. Sarah (Morgan) Wade.

Dr. Moulton was highly esteemed by a wide circle of friends, not only as a physician, but as a citizen. He represented his county in both the Legislature and the State Senate.

He died March 29, 1886, and his wife, Mary (Cundiff) Moulton, died September 25, 1877.

Mary Rosabell Parker, daughter of Joseph and Sallie (Robertson) Parker, married William Dickinson Stone, November 7, 1867.

David Washington Parker

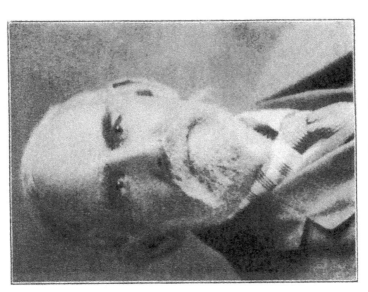

Alexander Clark Parker

CHILDREN:

(1) William Parker, born June 8, 1870; died July 29, 1898.

(2) Bettie Chapman, born April 4, 1872; married Dr. George O. Giles, April 22, 1902. No children.

(3) Sallie Kate, born March 30, 1875; married W. L. T. Hopkins, September 9, 1916. No children.

(4) James Gordon, born November 29, 1877; married (first) Georgia R. Frye, December 30, 1904.

CHILDREN:

(a) William Gordon, born July 30, 1905.

(b) Blair Casper, born October 5, 1908.

Georgia (Frye) Gordon died April 11, 1913. James Gordon Stone married (second) Leta Austin, January 16, 1917.

CHILD:

(a) Mary Esther, born February 18, 1918.

(5) Crispin Clack, born January 23, 1886; married Julia Cooper, December 24, 1921.

CHILDREN:

(a) Mary Elizabeth, born October 27, 1922.

(b) James Crispin, born May 14, 1924.

(6) David Edmund, born August 6, 1883; married Maude Harris, September 12, 1922.

CHILD:

(a) Martha Lee, born July 14, 1924.

(7) Mary Dickinson, born July 26, 1880. Unmarried.

....

Amanda Octavia Parker, daughter of Joseph and Sallie (Robertson) Parker, married Cornelius T. Jamison, April 22, 1875.

CHILDREN:

(1) Joseph Henry, born June 30, 1876; married Ora Maynard, May 22, 1908.

CHILDREN:

(a) Mildred Jane, born May 13, 1910.

(b) Eula May, born October 22, 1911.

(c) Milton Joseph, born April 13, 1913.

(d) William Tazewell, born July 11, 1914.

(e) Gladys Katherine, born September 21, 1916.

(f) Russell Harry, born March 21, 1918.

(g) Royce Parker, born October 4, 1921.

(2) William Cornelius, born January 11, 1878; married Mary Price, June 1, 1904.

CHILDREN:

(a) Christine, born April 9, 1905.

(b) Lucile Price, born February 2, 1913.

(c) Elizabeth Amanda, born July 12, 1914.

(d) William Ferdinand, born March 1, 1919.

(e) Cornelius Tazewell, born August 28, 1921.

(f) Mary Virginia, born May 10, 1924.

(3) Sallie Winifred, born May 26, 1879; married John Pleasant Moore, September 11, 1912.

CHILD:

(a) John Pleasant, Jr., born August 10, 1913.

(4) Katie Fannie, born January 1, 1885; married William Henry Martin, October 9, 1907.

CHILDREN:

(a) Myrtle Winifred, born August 24, 1908.

(b) Cornelius Albert, born December 16, 1909.

(c) Mary Amanda, born June 17, 1911.

William Henry Martin died January 15, 1919.

(5) Stanhope, born May 14, 1889; married Mary Coles, April 24, 1918.

CHILD:

(a) Margaret Louise, born April 22, 1921.

....

Missouri Rebecca, daughter of Joseph and Sallie (Robertson) Parker, married James Sutherland (son of Milton and Angeline (Semones) Sutherland), November 5, 1878.

CHILDREN:

(1) William Joseph, born September 14, 1879; married Aurie Edna Law, June 5, 1921.

CHILDREN:

(a) Frances Rebecca, born October 6, 1922.

(b) James Calvin, born February 29, 1924.

(2) George Washington, born June 23, 1881; married Ruth Eva Phelps, November 7, 1918.

(3) Samuel David, born 1884; died in infancy.

(4) Angeline Winifred, born April 12, 1886; married Clack Stone, April 6, 1910.

(5) Augusta James, born August 19, 1892.

Missouri Rebecca (Parker) Sutherland died September 18, 1894.

....

Joseph Stanhope Parker, son of Joseph and Sallie Ann (Robertson) Parker, married, January 13, 1880, Mary Bell Peters (born February 5, 1856).

CHILDREN:

(1) James Russell, born November 20, 1880; married Lillian Robertson, April 26, 1911; now a practicing physician at Providence Forge, Va.

CHILDREN:

(a) James Russell, Jr., born October 6, 1913.

(b) Joseph Edward, born October 25, 1915.

(c) George Robertson, born November 20, 1916.

(d) Elsie Lillian, born October 26, 1919.

(e) Jean, born December 26, 1922.

(2) Alma May, born March 30, 1882; died July 8, 1883.

(3) George Wesley, born May 19, 1883; a popular dentist of Bedford; married (first) Carlie Huddleston, November 26, 1912; (second) Elizabeth Thaxton, November 7, 1922.

CHILDREN BY SECOND MARRIAGE:

(a) George Thaxton, born May 9, 1925.

(b) Jane Board, born September 13, 1927.

(4) Annie Maude, born April 16, 1885; married Edwin S. Wallace, August 25, 1925.

CHILD:

(a) William Edward, born July 12, 1928.

(5) Joseph Ernest, born January 30, 1887; married Eula Arrington, October 8, 1911.

CHILDREN:

(a) Ruby May, born December 16, 1912.

(b) Earl Lloyd, born January 22, 1914.

(c) Joseph Ernest, Jr., born October 26, 1915.

(d) William Eugene, born October 9, 1916.

(6) Mary Ruth, born April 30, 1889; died May 1, 1890.

(7) Lillian Hope, born August 1, 1891; married John Reid Hicks, November 6, 1917.

CHILD:

(a) John Reid, Jr., born December 13, 1922.

(8) Augusta Bell, born February 5, 1894; married Oscar Crist, November 17, 1914. He was born June 21, 1890.

CHILDREN:

(a) Kathleen French, born November 7, 1915; died July 15, 1918.

(b) Thomas Stanhope, born February 25, 1917.

(c) Virginia Bell, born February 23, 1918; died February 19, 1920.

(d) Jacqueline, born June 27, 1919; died February 8, 1921.

(9) Sallie Lee, born December 9, 1896; died December 21, 1896.

(10) Robert Walthall, born July 8, 1900; married Katherine Blankenship, April 17, 1922.

CHILD:

(a) Mary Virginia, born January 2, 1923.

....

Bettie Augusta Parker, daughter of Joseph and Sallie (Robertson) Parker, married, January 15, 1880, Owen B. Jamison, son of Henry and Sallie (Showalter) Jamison.

CHILDREN:

(1) Frances Marion, born November 15, 1880; married Marshall William Mangus, October 8, 1910.

CHILD:

(a) Julian Edwin, born December 10, 1915.

(2) Parker Cornelius, born March 6, 1882; married Helen Smith Goggin, April 20, 1910.

CHILDREN:

(a) Anita Kathleen.
(b) Cornelius Goggin.
(c) James Clark.

(3) Sallie Missouri, born September 3, 1883; married Dallas Eugene Wigginton, November 15, 1906.

CHILDREN:

(a) Dallas Eugene, Jr., born September 17, 1907.
(b) Parker Jamison, born April 7, 1910.
(c) William Blackwell, born July 20, 1913.
(d) Winifred Jewell, born November 21, 1916.
(e) Virginia Betsey, born July 24, 1919.

(4) Alice Peyton, born May 1, 1886; married John Bascom Thompson, December 6, 1922.

(5) Florence Belle, born March 16, 1888; married Elisha Clark Goggin, October 29, 1914.

CHILDREN:

(a) Augusta Elizabeth, born February 27, 1916.
(b) Elisha Chapman, born July 6, 1918.

(6) Beulah Augusta, born May 29, 1890; married Madison David Hutcherson, June 25, 1919.

CHILDREN:

(a) Ralph Owen, born June 12, 1921.
(b) Lois Katherine, born April 12, 1924.

(7) Owen Orlando, born August 16, 1892; married Cora Lee Dowdy, November 18, 1915.

CHILDREN:

(a) Russell Aubrey, born January 6, 1917.
(b) William Parker, born August 21, 1918.
(c) Cecil Orlando, born May 4, 1920.
(d) Frances Lee, born October 17, 1921.
(e) Elsie Marie, born May 25, 1923.

(8) Lillian Amanda Fleetwood, born May 28, 1894; married Walter Lewis Kayler, February 23, 1918.

CHILDREN:

(a) Walter Owen, born December, 1918.

(b) William, born April, 1920; died young.

(9) Ruth Adelaide, born May 22, 1896; married Lois Chapman Rucker, December 13, 1921.

GOGGIN

Stephen Goggin came to Virginia from Queen's County, Ireland, in 1742, when a mere lad. It is not known with whom he came nor where he lived first, but May 12, 1759, a grant of land was made to him of 204 acres on Flat Creek, in Bedford County, and another of 425 acres, on March 1, 1773, on both sides of Flat Creek.

The name of his first wife is not known, neither is there any record of his children, as such, but it is certain that those Goggins who married in Bedford County in the late 1700's, whose parentage is not given in their marriage bonds, but for whom he was security, were children of Stephen Goggin, Sr., viz.: Stephen, Jr., John, Sarah, and, perhaps, Robert. Richard, who married, Nancy Irvine, in 1791, was probably still another son. John was a lieutenant in the Continental Army, and married Lucy Branch in 1777. The second wife of Stephen Goggin was Susannah Terry of Bedford County—marriage bond dated September 5, 1772.

Stephen Goggin, Jr., son of Stephen, Sr., married in Bedford County, December 21, 1773, Rachel Moorman, daughter of Thomas and Rachel (Clark) Moorman, and died in 1802. He was First Lieutenant in the Revolutionary Army, and his patriotism and that of his father are further attested by the following entry in "Order Book, 1774-1782" of the Bedford County records:

"At a Court held for Bedford County the 22nd day of July, 1782, at the house of David Wright, Stephen Goggin proved that he furnished the sd. Com: with 400 lbs. Beef, for which he is allowed 1 6/8 per cwt.

"Stephen Goggin, Jr., proved that he furnished the sd. Com: with 54 lbs. Bacon, for which he is all'd 7½ per lb."

CHILDREN OF STEPHEN, JR., AND RACHEL (MOORMAN) GOGGIN:

(1) Parmelia; married October 29, 1797, Samuel Clemens; were grandparents of Samuel L. Clemens (Mark Twain).

(2) Mary (Polly); married, November 17, 1801, Alexander Gill.

(3) Nancy; married, December 12, 1798, Obadiah Tate.

(4) William; married November 23, 1810, Pamelia Tate.

(5) Elizabeth; married (first) Samuel Field, June 5, 1827; (second) John B. Witt, December 22, 1830.

(6) Thomas; married Polly Walden, December 23, 1812.

(7) Pleasant Moorman, born February 11, 1777; married, July 31, 1806, Mary Otey Leftwich, daughter of Rev. William Leftwich.

(8) Stephen, III, born April 8, 1789; married, December 29, 1808, Janet Robertson, daughter of Jeffry and Nancy (Dickerson) Robertson. (See Robertson family.)

CHILDREN :

(a) Jeffry R.; married Margaret McGeorge, September 16, 1841.

(b) Thomas Clark. (See forward.)

(c) Frances H.; married Ammon H. Parker. (See Parker family.)

(d) John M.; married, November 14, 1849, Sarah J. Carney.

(e) Mary A.; married David Parker of Pittsylvania County, June 12, 1855. (See Parker family.)

(f) Pleasant M.; married, January 17, 1850, Catherine Stone.

(g) Auville R.; married, February 15, 1855, Emma Catherine Gray.

(h) Ann Elizabeth; married, November 15, 1849, Lawrence McGeorge.

Thomas Clark Goggin, son of Stephen, III, and Janet (Robertson) Goggin, was born January 12, 1815; died April 19, 1895; married, December 4, 1838, Elizabeth Jane Johnson, daughter of Thomas and Sarah (Dickerson) Johnson. (See Johnson family.)

He became a Baptist preacher and was universally beloved and respected. Perhaps no other preacher in Bedford County has been called upon to marry so many couples or to conduct so many funeral services.

CHILDREN OF THOMAS C. AND JANE (JOHNSON) GOGGIN :

(1) Thomas Stephen; unmarried; killed in Civil War.

(2) Sarah Jane, born October 16, 1839; died December 4, 1908; married, March 13, 1866, John B. Gardner, who was born October 21, 1840, and died September 12, 1927.

CHILDREN :

(a) Mary Jane, born April 3, 1869; married J. Wright Bond (See Bond family.)

(b) Berta C.; married James S. McGhee.

(c) Lelia Kate; married Hugh M. Wright.

(d) Willie Frances; married Benjamin B. Fuqua.

(e) Henry F.; died unmarried.

(f) Carrie F.; married William E. Turner.

(3) Martha Frances; married John Lipscomb.

(4) William J.; married (first), September 6, 1871, Ellen A. Burroughs, daughter of James and Elizabeth (Robertson) Burroughs; (second) February 10, 1892, R. Belle Ayres, daughter of Richard P. and Martha Ayres.

(5) James O. L.; married Drucilla Mattox.

MOORMAN

Thomas Moorman and his wife, Elizabeth, came from England in 1670, and settled in Nansemond County, Virginia. The St. Peter's Parish Register gives the baptism of two of their children:

(1) Mary; baptized August, 1686.
(2) Andrew; baptized November, 1689.

Between 1678 and 1688, Thomas Moorman and his family moved to Green Springs, Louisa County, and there another child was born to them—
(3) Charles, born 1690.

....

Charles Moorman, son of Thomas and Elizabeth Moorman, married in 1710, Elizabeth Reynolds, daughter of Christopher Reynolds.

CHILDREN :

(1) Thomas; married Rachel Clark. (See forward.)
(2) Judith; married John Douglass.
(3) Ann; married Thomas Martin. (See Martin family.)
(4) Achilles; married Elizabeth Adams.
(5) Charles, Jr.; married Mary Adams.

The will of Charles Moorman, dated May 9, 1755, was proved in Louisa County, Va., May 24, 1757. (Will Book "I," page 25.) In it he names his three sons: Thomas, Charles and Achilles; his daughter: Judith, the wife of John Douglass, and Ann, the wife of Thomas Martin; and his wife, Elizabeth.

The same children are named by his widow, Elizabeth Moorman, in her will, dated January 9, 1761; and proved in Louisa County, Va., May 11, 1765. (Will Book "I," page 68.)

....

Thomas Moorman, son of Charles and Elizabeth (Reynolds) Moorman, married, January 12, 1730, Rachel Clark, daughter of Christopher and Penelope Clark.

CHILDREN :

(1) Mary, born December 19, 1730; married (first) Benjamin Johnson; (second) John Miller.
(2) Zachariah, born February 2, 1732; married (first) Elizabeth Terrell; (second) Elizabeth Johnson.
(3) Micajah, born January 28, 1735; married Susannah Chiles, May 19, 1754.
(4) Elizabeth, born February 2, 1738.
(5) Thomas, born January 6, 1740.
(6) Mildred, born November 25, 1742; married James Johnson.
(7) Pleasant, born March 19, 1745.
(8) Charles; married (first), Rebecca Leftwich; (second) Nancy Hancock.

(9) Agatha; married William Johnson.

(10) Clark Terrell; married Rachel Harris.

(11) Cilly.

(12) Rachel; married Stephen Goggin, Jr. (See Goggin family.)

....

Thomas Moorman and Rachel Clark were evidently married in Louisa County, and must have lived there a number of years afterwards, since the births of the first seven of their children are recorded in the register of the "Cedar Creek Meeting (Quaker), Hanover County."

The names of their last children are taken from the will of Thomas Moorman.

Thomas Moorman came with his family to Bedford County only a few years before his death, and bought land in that portion of the county which is now Campbell. They were Quakers, and the records of that denomination show that "Thomas and Rachel Moorman removed from the Monthly Meeting, held at Golansville, Caroline County, March 9, 1767, to the Monthly Meeting, held at South River, in Bedford County. (Taken from "Our Quaker Friends," by J. P. Bell of Lynchburg.)

Thomas Moorman's will, made July 22, 1765, and probated in Bedford County, November 25, 1766, mentions wife, Rachel; children: Mary Johnson, Pleasant, Charles, Aggothy Johnson, Clark Terrell, Cilly, Rachel, Andrew, Zachariah; and Micajah. (Will Book "A," page 32.)

After the death of her husband, Rachel (Clark) Moorman married in 1768, William Ballard, of Bedford County. She died in 1792.

_____

CLARK

The following facts about the earliest ancestry of the Clarks have been furnished by various descendants of Christopher Clark. They differ somewhat; but all agree that the Clarks came to America by way of the Barbadoes in the last half of the seventeenth century.

One account says that Christopher Clark was the son of Edward Clark and grandson of Micajah and Sally Ann Moorman Clark, who went to Barbadoes from England in 1669 and came to Virginia the next year.

Another says: In the list of members of Christ Church Parish in Barbadoes, in 1680, appear the following: Christopher Clark having 60 acres of land and 31 negroes; Francis Clark, 15 acres and Edward Clark 1 acre. It is further stated that there were a great many Quakers in Barbadoes at that time, many of whom moved to America.

Christopher Clark married Penelope ———— about 1709. (Some genealogists think she was a Massie, some a Bolling and others a Johnson.)

CHILDREN:

(1) Edward, born 1710, died 1783; married ———— Paulette.

(2) Agnes, born 1712; married, 1728, Benjamin Johnson.

(3) Rachel, born 1714, died 1792; married (first) Thomas Moorman, January 12, 1730, married (second) Wm. Ballard, 1768.

(4) Sarah, born 1716; married (first), 1733, Maj. Charles Lynch; married (second), 1766, Maj. John Ward.

(5) Micajah, born 1718; married, 1736, Judith Adams.

(6) Elizabeth, born 1720; married, 1741, Joseph Anthony.

(7) Bolling, born 1722; married, 1742, Winifred ———.

Abstract of Christopher Clark's will, which was proved May 28, 1754 and recorded in Louisa County, Virginia:

In the name of God, Amen, I, Christopher Clark, being . . . do make this my last will and testament as followeth:

First, I give my loving son Edward one gun and all my wearing clothes, and all things else that he ever was possessed of that were ever mine.

2ndly, I give to my loving daughter Agnes Johnson one negro wench . . . and whatever else she has or ever had in possession that . . . mine.

3rdly, I give my loving daughter Rachell Moorman four hundred acres . . . in Hanover County, near Capt. Dorsey and one negro . . . and all things else that she has had in her possession that ever was mine.

4thly, I give my loving daughter Sarah Lynch one negro boy &c.

5thly, I give my loving son Micajah Clark five hundred acres of . . . in Hanover County, the same whereon I now live, &c.

6thly, I give to my loving son Bowling Clark four hundred acres . . . in Hanover County . . . joining the land of Mr. Thomas Carr . . . ten young negroes . . . my trooping arms, my great Bible and all my law books.

I give my loving daughter Elizabeth Anthony four hundred acres in Goochland County, &c.

I lend to my wife Penelope Clark all the rest of my estate . . . &c.
. . . set my hand and fixed my seal this the fourteenth day of Aug. 1744.

CHRISTOPHER CLARK [SEAL].

Christopher Clark was a wealthy tobacco planter of Hanover—later Louisa County, Va. He was Captain in the Colonial Army and one of the first Justices of Louisa County (1742). He joined the Quaker Society late in life and in 1749 was one of the Overseers of a Friends Meeting near Sugar Loaf Mountain.

REESE

William Washington Reese, born May 10, 1805; died June 3, 1887; married (first), May 5, 1824, Mary Robertson, daughter of Nicholas and Sallie (Walthall) Robertson.

CHILDREN:

(1) John Milton, born May 11, 1829; married Sallie Holt; died about the close of the Civil War.

(2) Missouri Annice, born December 24, 1830; married William C. Shelton; died about 1867.

(3) Sarah Martha, born March 26, 1834; died December 21, 1836.

(4) Robert Whitfield, born April 5, 1836; died December 1, 1841.

(5) Henry Newton, born April 30, 1838; died June 17, 1839.

(6) Laura, born March 27, 1840; married Oliver C. Smith; died January, 1911.

(7) Robert Henry, born August 23, 1843; died January 13, 1847.

(8) Annie Amanda, born September 3, 1844; married Dr. James W. Brown; lives at Sedalia, Mo.

(9) William Nicholas, born July 26, 1846. (See forward.)

(10) Mary Sophia, born September 11, 1848; married William T. Wooding; lives in Danville, Va.

(11) Benjamin Franklin, born November 3, 1852, married Alice Board; died in Kansas City, Mo., December 17, 1921. (See Board family.)

William Washington Reese married (second) Emma P. Creasy in 1879.

CHILD:

(1) Cordie Gertrude, born March 11, 1881; married (first) Frank Barnett; (second) ——— Roundtree. Her children are:

Billy and Russell Roundtree.

The mother of William Washington Reese (who was a Boothe) was twice married; her second husband was Jonathan Cundiff. Her children were: William Washington and Silas Reese; and Christopher Jackson and Mary Cundiff. Mary Cundiff married Dr. Benjamin H. Moulton. (See Moulton family.)

William Nicholas Reese, son of William Washington and Mary (Robertson) Reese, married Hester Mary Parker, November 22, 1866; died July 19, 1917. (See Parker family.)

CHILDREN:

(1) George Robert, born December 17, 1867; married, April 4, 1900, Alma Lipscomb, born August 30, 1877, died February 14, 1923, daughter of *James Joseph Lipscomb* (born September 18, 1833; died November, 1917; son of Jordan W. Lipscomb (born March, 1802; died November 24, 1884) and Mary DeJarnette (died 1836)) and *Sarah Leftwich,* daughter of Granville Leftwich (born December 29, 1829; died April 25, 1905) and Lucy Ann Dallas (born October 8, 1828; died October 9, 1878), *who were married December 6, 1876.*

CHILDREN:

(a) William Werter, born August 24, 1902.

(b) George Clark, born May 12, 1908.

Both children born in Bluefield. W. Va.

(2) Fannie Clark, born September 26, 1869; married, September 14, 1892, Elonzo
Bond (born August 26, 1861; son of William Pleasant Bond and Bettie Ann
Smith). (See Bond family.)

CHILDREN:

(a) William Francis, born at Oakvale, W. Va., July 9, 1893; a veteran of
the World War; married, September 23, 1920, Ethel Thompson,
daughter of William Thompson and Mary Gilmore of Huntington,
W. Va.

(b) Lillian Ora, born June 22, 1897.

(c) Edith Mary, born April 26, 1900; died July 23, 1902.

(d) Elizabeth Rebecca, born June 5, 1903; now a student at Columbia
University, New York.

(3) Mary Washington, born April 25, 1869; married, September 2, 1891, Frank E.
Burroughs (born November 25, 1865; son of Thomas Robertson Burroughs
(born February 8, 1827; died February 19, 1902; son of James Burroughs and
Elizabeth Robertson) and Julia Benson Bond (born February 29, 1836; died
September 9, 1896) who were married, September 25, 1857). (See Bond
family.)

CHILDREN:

(a) Mary Julia, born 1892; married, January 14, 1914, Lewis Waid (born
February 27, 1888; son of Thomas Archer Waid (born February 11,
1860) and Alice Brugh Daken (born February 11, 1863)).

CHILDREN:

(aa) Frank Lewis, born February 4, 1915.

(bb) Archer Dudley, born December 3, 1916.

(cc) Albert Reese, born November 7, 1919.

(dd) Alice Brugh, born October 26, 1921.

(ee) Mary Hester, born January 26, 1923.

(4) Annie Laurie, born March 12, 1872; married, February 17, 1891, Eldridge P.
Watson, son of William D. Watson (born July 4, 1828) and Sarah Jane
Dooley (born July 27, 1831)—both of Bedford County—who were married,
December 18, 1852.

CHILDREN:

(a) Gladys, born November 24, 1891; married Bernard Weekly, January 29,
1918; died January 7, 1919, in Lynchburg, Va.

(b) Frederick W., born January 24, 1894; married Florence Kyle, August
30, 1919.

(c) Hester, born July 18, 1893; married, September 8, 1912, Daniel T. Blue
(born in Hoffman, N. C., April 7, 1891, son of James Blue and
Cornelia Elizabeth Harris).

CHILDREN:

(aa) Elizabeth Reese, born August 6, 1913.

(bb) Lucille Watson, born June 14, 1915.

(cc) Daniel Thomas, Jr., born November 23, 1917.

(dd) Annie Claire, born May 16, 1921.

(ee) James Eldridge, born March 26, 1924.

(5) James Albert, born December 29, 1874; married, June 18, 1907, Mallie Witten of Tazewell County, Va., daughter of Alexander Witten and Albinna Brown. No children.

Dr. James A. Reese is a popular dentist of Lynchburg, Va.

(6) Daisy Lee, born December 5, 1876; married (first), November 21, 1900, Albert Sidney Meador, who died February 17, 1902.

She married (second), June 20, 1910, E. J. Meyer, born June 7, 1862, in Belvidere, N. J.; son of Jacob Meyer (born in Berne, Switzerland, August 28, 1831; died in Belvidere, N. J., 1907; son of Johanns Meyer and Elizabeth Grubs; both born in Berne, Switzerland and died in America and are buried at Catasaqua, Pa.) and Mary Ann Eisenhour (born in Quakertown, Pa., March 13, 1829; died in Bluefield, W. Va., 1914).

CHILDREN :

(a) Bessie Reese, born December 30, 1911.

(b) Frank Emanuel, born October 26, 1913.

(c) Mary Ann, born December 7, 1917.

E. J. Meyer and family live in Bluefield, W. Va.

(7) Emily Parker, born January 29, 1878; married, October 29, 1914, Jesse Cecil Daly. No children.

(8) Sallie Wathall, born August 7, 1881; unmarried; lives in Salem, Va.

(9) William Werter, born November 10, 1883; died August 24. 1002.

(10) Bessie Alexander, born July 8, 1886; married, June 5, 1922, P. S. Zimmerman, born November 23, 1877, at Fincastle, Va., son of Edward Oscar Zimmerman (born March 21, 1842; died April 15, 1908) and Mary Virginia Custer (born August 13, 1848; died May 26, 1912), who were married, September 26, 1865. No children.

(11) Alice Otey, born November 21, 1887; died November 7, 1908.

(12) John Benjamin, born September 3, 1890; married, January 28, 1912, Georgia Nininger, daughter of Milton S. Mininger and Julia Hershberger.

CHILDREN :

(aa) William N., born December 20, 1912.

(bb) Julia Hester, born September 3, 1916.

STONE

The name of Stone in Virginia dates from the coming of George Stone, who was born in London, England, in 1597, and came to Jamestown in 1620. He was a wealthy banker and a stockholder in the Virginia Land Company of London, and was a cousin of Governor William Stone of Maryland. He married Mary Vernon. Their son—

Col. John Stone (2), married Mary Nelson. Their son—

William Stone (3), married Virginia Howard. Their son—

Joshua Stone (4), married Mary Coleman in 1748. He was a soldier in the Revolutionary Army and promoted to captain. (The first marker at the grave of a Revolutionary soldier, placed by the William Pitt Chapter of the D. A. R. of Pittsylvania County, Va., is in the Stone family burying ground, at the grave of Captain Joshua Stone.) Their son—

John Stone (5) (born in Halifax County, Va., November 25, 1754; died in Pittsylvania County in 1824), married Dollie Haskins in 1776. Their son—

Edmund Stone (6) (born 1805; died 1840), married Nancy Chapman Dickinson in 1827. Their son—

James Crispin Stone (7) (born February 8, 1832; died February 27, 1897), a veteran of the War Between the States, was wounded in the hip at Yellow Tavern in the spring of 1864, and was not in active service again. He belonged to Company "E," 6th Virginia Cavalry.

He married, March 8, 1855, Sarah Fannie Edwards, born March 22, 1834; died May 9, 1900; daughter of Gideon Edwards (born February 14, 1801; died March 13, 1870; son of Coleman Edwards and ———— Allen) and Martha A. Gilbert (born January 9, 1812; died April 16, 1863), who were married, January 20, 1828.

CHILDREN :

(1) Martha Chapman, born May 19, 1856; married George Abner Bennett, February 6, 1890; died December 29, 1906.

(2) Gideon Edmund, born September 1, 1859; married Mary Reese Parker, November 25, 1897; died February 26, 1900. (See Parker family.)

CHILD:

(a) Sarah Margaret, born at Penhook, Va., May 9, 1899; graduated at Bedford High School and at the State Normal School, Harrisonburg, Va.; married, February 7, 1923, Rufus Edmund Smith (born in Pittsylvania County, May 1, 1894; son of Edmund Smith (born March 24, 1849; died August 18, 1922) and Ella Anne Hubbard (born November 6, 1855)).

Rufus E. Smith is a veteran of the World War. He enlisted at Chatham, Va., September 18, 1917; was trained at Camp Lee; arrived in France, June 8, 1918; was in battles: Near Heburturne, August 15, 1918; St. Mihiel Offensive, September 12 to 16, 1918; Battle of Argonne-Verdune, September 26-October 12, 1918; Battle of Argonne-Verdune, November 1 to 5, 1918. Left France, May 20, 1918; discharged from Camp Lee, June 12, 1919. Was Private No. 1818299, Company "F," 18th Division, 317th Infantry.

(3) Willie Crispin, born September 1, 1861; died October 4, 1862.

(4) James Waller, born October 27, 1866; married Sarah Jane Parker, June 18, 1902; died November 24, 1905. (See Parker family.)

(a) George Edmund, born at Penhook, Va., May 2, 1903; graduated at Bedford High School in 1920, and is now a senior at Randolph-Macon College and studying medicine at Richmond Medical College, will graduate in 1930.

(b) James William, born May 9, 1906; served three sessions (1922-'23-'24) as page in the Senate at Richmond, Va., educated at Randolph-Macon Academy, Bedford, Va., and at College of William and Mary.

Gideon Edmund and James Waller Stone were born in Pittsylvania County and educated at Hale's Ford Academy, then a widely known private school. Later, they each took a business course at Stuart, Va., and became partners in a mercantile business at Penhook, Va. They were official members of the Liberty Methodist Church; both died in the prime of life and were buried in the "Stone Cemetery," four miles north of Sandy Level, Pittsylvania County, Va. Their widows live together in Bedford, and their children have been raised as one family.

(5) Kate Edwards, born June 14, 1868; died March 14, 1869.

(6) Clack, born August 17, 1872; married Angie Winifred Sutherland, April 6, 1910; died November 28, 1911.

(7) Samuel Coleman, born April 29, 1874; married Angie Hope Preston, October 17, 1900; died April 30, 1921.

WALKER

The first Walker to settle in Virginia was George Walker, Gent., who came in the first supply to Jamestown, in 1607, under Captain Newport, and was a fellow passenger of Captain John Smith. He was left with the infant colony when Newport returned to England in June of the same year. (Smith's *History of Virginia*, Vol. 1, page 153.)

....

"Frances, wife of Alexander Walker, died in 1662." (*Bruton Parish Register*, page 132.)

"Whitehall, December 22, 1677.

"Order of the King in Council on petetion of William Munford, merchant, on behalf of Alexander Walker of Virginia, planter, for restitution of his goods seized by Sir William Berkeley and converted to his own use, petetioner's only offense being the taking of Bacon's unlawful oath, which he was forced by threats; referring same to Lords of Trade and Plantations for their report." (*Colonial Papers*, 2 pages, Archives Virginia State Library.)

Alexander Walker was ordained and licensed to preach in Virginia, September 29, 1699. (*Notes and Queries*, 5th series, Vol. 9, page 22.)

In 1702, the name of Alexander Walker is found in the records of Surry County; later, in Charles City County; and still later, in Prince George County. No will has been found, nor any official proof of the names of his children, but it is generally believed, by those who have studied the history of the family, that Henry, David, and James were sons of Alexander Walker. They were all living in Prince George County in the early part of the eighteenth century and both James and David had sons named Alexander, which in those days of family names, is very good proof.

In the records of Prince George County it is stated that on August 17, 1747, Richard and Alexander Walker, orphans of James Walker, chose Edward Brodnax as their guardian. And again in December of the same year, Henry Walker was appointed guardian of Jane and Mary Walker, orphans of James Walker, deceased.

Henry Walker was one of the first trustees of the City of Petersburg.　................................

David Walker, believed to have been the son of Alexander Walker, married Mary ————— (Munford, perhaps).

CHILDREN:

(1) Alexander, born October 3, 1727.
(2) Robert, born October 10, 1729.
(3) David (twin), born March 6, 1731.
(4) Mary (twin), born March 6, 1731.
(5) Freeman, born September 3, 1734.

David Walker, Sr., was a member of the vestry of Bristol Parish from 1735 to 1743, when Bath Parish was formed from Bristol Parish. He then became a vestryman and churchwarden of Bath Parish. (*Bristol Parish Register.*)

From another source it has been learned that David and Mary Walker had still another son, James, whose name does not appear in the above record.　................................

David Walker, Jr., son of David and Mary Walker, married Peletiah Jones, daughter of William and Mary Jones, of Bristol Parish, in 1756.

CHILDREN:

(1) William Jones, born 1757.
(2) Mary.
(3) Nancy.
(4) Peletiah Jones.
(5) Robert Munford, born August 15, 1772.
(6) Alexander.

David Walker, Jr., entered the Revolutionary War as Lieutenant, and must have risen to the rank of Colonel, since on the back of his will is written "The Will of Colonel David Walker." No official proof of this has been found, however.

A copy of his will, now yellow with age, and worn in the creases, is in the possession of John Key Walker, of Bedford, his great-great-grandson. It reads:

THE WILL OF COLONEL DAVID WALKER

In the name of God Amen: I, David Walker of Dinwiddie County, being of sound mind and memory, thanks to Almighty God for the same, and calling to mind the uncertainty of all terrestrial things, and that it is appointed for man to die once, do ordain this my last will and testament.

It is my desire that my body be decently interred at the discretion of my Executors whom I hereafter appoint.

As to my worldly goods, I dispose of them in manner following:

Imprimis, I give to my son, William Jones Walker, all that I have already possessed him with, and one negro woman named Sue, to him and his heirs forever.

Item, I give to my daughter, Mary Quarles, all that I have already possessed her with, and six head of cows, to her and her heirs forever.

Item, I give to my daughter, Nancy Quarles, all that I have possessed her with, and six head of cows and a young sorrel colt, to her and her heirs forever.

Item, I give to my daughter, Peletiah Jones Walker, one mulatto girl named Lucy and one negro girl named Molly, fifty pounds cash, six head of cows, six head of sheep and bed and furniture, to her and her heirs forever.

Item, I give to my son, Robert M. Walker, all the rest of my land not already disposed of, and one mulatto man named Ned, one negro boy named Daniel, two horses, Darby and Dapple, two work steers and six cows, six sheep and all my stock of hogs, and all the rest of my household and kitchen furniture, to him and his heirs forever.

Item, I give to my grandson, David Walker Quarles, one negro girl named Amy, to him and his heirs forever.

The rest of my stock, the crop and debts on me to be appropriated for the discharge of my debts and legacies, if sufficient (if not) the negroes (Daniel excepted) to be hired till a sufficiency be acquired thereby.

It is my desire that the old negro woman named Beck, be maintained by my children at her discretion. It is also my desire that my three sons above mentioned, viz.: William Jones Walker, Alexander Walker and Robert Munford Walker be my executors, and my desire further is that my estate be not appraised, as witnessed my hand and seal this thirty-first day of December Anno Domini, one thousand seven hundred and ninety-one.

DAVID WALKER [SEAL].

Teste

    THOMAS B. WALKER,
    WILLIAM SMITH,
    ELIZA WALKER.

William Jones Walker, son of David and Peletiah Jones Walker, married (first), about 1798, his cousin, a Miss Jones of Dinwiddie County, and brought her to Bedford. For some reason, she did not like her new home, and after a while, went back to Dinwiddie; but finding that she could not be happy away from her husband, she finally wrote him that she would return with him, if he would come after her. His indignation had not abated, and he replied that he did not send her away, and he would not come after her. She did return, however, and died in Bedford County. She is buried in an unmarked spot in the corner of the family burying ground. This incident so disgusted him with the names of Jones, that he dropped it from his name, and ever after wrote it " William I. Walker."

William I. Walker married (second) in 1816, Betsey Rice, daughter of Benjamin and Catherine Holt Rice, of Bedford County.

There were no children by either marriage.

The following is taken from the Bible of Robert Munford Walker:

Robert Munford Walker, son of David and Peletiah Jones Walker, married (first) Mary Smith, February 18, 1796.

CHILDREN :

(1) William I., born December 8, 1796.
(2) Wilmuth T., born April 11, 1799.
(3) Peletiah J., born August 14, 1800.
(4) James A., born June 15, 1802.
(5) Robert M., born January 6, 1804.
(6) Elizabeth Ann, born October 13, 1805.
(7) Joseph P., born October 2, 1807.

(8) John T., born August 12, 1809.
(9) Mary Adeline, born May 8, 1811.

Mary Smith, born November 30, 1777, was the daughter of Isham and Patience Smith. She died in Bedford County in 1811.

Robert M. Walker married (second) Judith Edgar of Bedford County, June 11, 1812.

CHILDREN:

(10) Peter Ravenscroft, born May 11, 1813.
(11) Katherine Ann, born February 24, 1815.
(12) David Henry, born January 18, 1817.
(13) George M. Anderson, born April 20, 1819.
(14) Samuel Phillips, born February 1, 1824.

Robert M. Walker came from Dinwiddie County to Bedford County about 1798, and settled eight miles southeast of Liberty, where he spent the remainder of his life. He died in 1827. His will is recorded in Will Book "F," page 414.

Judith Edgar, born March 30, 1784, was the daughter of James and Phebe Edgar. She died before her husband.

James Alexander Walker, son of Robert M. and Mary Smith Walker, married (first) Elizabeth Booth, August 1, 1827.

CHILDREN:

(1) Robert; (2) Edward T.; (3) William J.; (4) James E. M.

James A. Walker married (second) Nancy Moorman Jopling, November 13, 1837. (See Jopling family.)

CHILDREN:

(5) Alexander Smith, born January 9, 1839. (See forward.)
(6) Rebecca Louise Fitzhugh, born January 6, 1840; married Robert William Parker. (See Parker family.)
(7) Charles Pleasant, born September 9, 1844. (See forward.)
(8) Lucy Frances, born August 14, 1846. (See forward.)
(9) Jesse Jopling, born January 14, 1850; died March 3, 1912. (See forward.)
(10) Nannie Moorman, born September 16, 1852. (See forward.)

JAMES ALEXANDER WALKER, M. D.

James Alexander Walker studied medicine in Philadelphia and practiced his profession for a great many years in the community in which he was born. He died May 10, 1869.

....

Alexander Smith Walker, son of Dr. James Alexander and Nancy (Jopling) Walker, married, December 20, 1860, Virginia Frances Johnson, daughter of Joseph and Emily (Parker) Johnson. (See Johnson and Parker families.)

CHILDREN:

(1) Emily Moorman; married Thomas Chappelle Wright.

CHILDREN:

Harry Buford, Ernest Thomas, Arthur Walker, Infant (died), and Emily Chappelle.

(2) Alice Virginia; married James Lee Lipscomb.

CHILDREN:

(a) Nerna Marian; died in infancy.
(b) Edna Lee; married William Junius Leftwich, Jr.

CHILDREN:

(aa) William Junius, III.
(bb) Helen Aileen.
(cc) Robert Lee; died in infancy.

(3) Lucy Rebecca; married William A. Rorer.

CHILDREN:

(a) John Alexander; married Mabel Clark.

CHILD:

(aa) John Alexander, Jr.
(b) William Asbury.
(c) Henry.

(4) James Alexander; married Willie Pauline Keesair.

CHILDREN:

James Cline, Alice Virginia, Howard, Alexander, Joseph, and Arthur Walker.

(5) Sallie Waller; married John D. Teass.

CHILDREN:
Helen Asher, Paul Kruger, and Leo.
(6) Joseph Johnson; married Effie Whorley.

CHILDREN:
(a) Lorie May.
(b) Alexander.
(c) Alice Virginia; married Hammett Holland; lives in California.

CHILDREN:
(aa) Nancy Virginia.
(bb) Dorothy June.
(7) Hettie Mary; married William A. Abbott.
(8) Georgie Coleman; married William Henings Teass.

CHILDREN:
(a) Winifred Henings; married L. K. Bryant.

CHILDREN:
(aa) L. K., Jr.
(bb) William Teass.
(b) Horace Argyle.
(c) Alexander Francis.
(d) George Stuart A.
(e) Frances Catherine.
(9) Robert Parker; married Emma Johnson.

CHILDREN:
Virginia Caroline, Robert, Miriam, Margaret Johnson, and Madeline Parker (twins).
(10) Reba Frances; married John R. Abbott.

CHILD:
(a) John Alexander.

Charles Pleasant Walker, son of Dr. James Alexander and Nancy (Jopling) Walker, married Octavia Wells, and died October 26, 1924.

CHILDREN:

(1) Olive Maywood, born June 4, 1868; married, June 4, 1889, William Jeffrey Goggin.

CHILDREN:

(a) Harry Smead, born November 16, 1891.

(b) Mamie Josephine, born September 30, 1893; married, August 15, 1919, Thomas Odell Jacobs.

CHILD:

(aa) Jane Carolyn, born August 15, 1926.

(c) Stanley Bryan, born September 16, 1897.

(d) Samuel Rixey, born January 23, 1901; died October 28, 1913.

(e) William Rucker, born November 12, 1903.

(f) Howard Alexander, born March 5, 1906.

(g) Alvin Kenneth, born November 30, 1908.

(h) Dennis Jeffrey, born January 22, 1910.

(2) Nancy Maude, born March 9, 1870; married, May 19, 1895, James William Compton.

CHILDREN:

(a) Eva Marshall, born March 8, 1897; married, November 23, 1913, Jubal Forest Booth.

(b) Katie Wells, born April 14, 1899.

(c) Ruby Florine, born February 12, 1901; married, November 28, 1924, William Edward Powell.

(d) Ida Lucille, born March 29, 1903.

(e) Helen Hayes, born November 18, 1905; married, September 4, 1926, Howard Guerring Lawder.

(f) Jemmie Octavia, born November 4, 1906.

(g) Leo Dunlop, born July 4, 1908.

(h) Edward Freeman, born May 4, 1911.

(i) Robert Beverly, born February 2, 1916.

(3) Charles Fitzhugh, born December 16, 1871; married, October 30, 1895, Callie Bramblett McGhee.

CHILDREN:

(a) Charles Edward, born September 11, 1896; married, September 20, 1916, Eddie Mack Crowder.

CHILD:

(aa) Jesse Mack, born April 14, 1918.

(b) Nelson Fitzhugh, born January 2, 1901.

(c) Katie Octavia, born August 4, 1902.

(d) Thomas Lee, born March 22, 1904; died November 9, 1906.

(e) Nannie Ruth, born October 28, 1906; married, May 7, 1922, Floyd Ira Crowder.

(f) Marvin Henry, born July 10, 1907.

(g) James Smith, born February 11, 1908; died June 8, 1911.

(h) George Washington, born January 2, 1911.

(i) Mary Edna, born November 28, 1912.

(j) John Wesley, born September 5, 1914.

(k) Elizabeth Rachel, born January 21, 1916.

(l) Samuel Louis, born August 8, 1918.

(4) Ida Braxton, born March 26, 1874; married, July 14, 1914, Gilmo Bunyan Welch. No children.

(5) Flora Lynch, born April 6, 1876; married, February 19, 1896, William Henry Graham.

CHILDREN:

(a) Ada Vogel, born February 6, 1897; died October 10, 1907.

(b) William, born October 27, 1902; died November 1, 1902.

(c) Charles Price, born November 23, 1903; died February 23, 1908.

(d) Thelma Agnes, born August 9, 1905.

(e) Henry Grady, born December 22, 1907.

(f) Ellis Hobson, born September 17, 1910.

(g) Frances Marie, born October 22, 1914.

(h) Viola James, born July 4, 1917.

(i) Wilson Walker, born January 23, 1919.

(6) Mary Agnes, born November 3, 1877; married, February 15, 1908, Thomas Jackson Bryant.

CHILDREN:

(a) Edith Christine, born May 12, 1909.

(b) Herman, born August 10, 1911.

(c) Thomas Jackson, Jr., born October 5, 1913.

(d) Mary Agnes, born March 13, 1921.

(7) Bessie Lee, born July 4, 1886; married, January 30, 1907, Claude Pinkney Burnette.

CHILDREN:

(a) Moorman Walker, born January 11, 1908.

(b) Mike Price, born May 12, 1909.

(c) Warren Lee, born August 6, 1911.

(d) Hallie Elizabeth, born September 15, 1912.

(e) Carleton Claude (twin), born January 10, 1921.

(f) Corbin Padgett (twin), born January 10, 1921.

Lucy Frances Walker, daughter of Dr. James Alexander and Nancy (Jopling) Walker, married, February 26, 1869, Rice McGhee, who was born October 30, 1836, and is the son of Samuel Henry and Margaret (Rice) McGhee.

CHILDREN:

(1) Jessie Rice, born November 30, 1869; married, September 16, 1903, William O. Williams, born September 14, 1863; son of Samuel Thomas (born December 27, 1828) and Susan (Witt) Williams (born August 2, 1835), lives at Badin, N. C.

CHILDREN:

(a) Martha Frances, born February 28.

(b) William VanMeter, born September 12, 1907.

(c) Yetive Elizabeth, born September 7, 1910.

(2) James Alexander, born June 16, 1871; married, June 17, 1923, Mattie Lillian Perrow, born December 20, 1893, daughter of Henry Jackson (born September 25, 1855; died August 19, 1927) and Mattie (Cowling) Perrow (born June 7, 1854; died February 5, 1917).

CHILDREN:

(a) Alexander Perrow, born April 25, 1921.

(b) James Stuart, born March 22, 1926.

(3) Elizabeth Moorman, born March 23, 1873; lives in Farmville, Va.

(4) Mary Lucy, born June 16, 1875; married, December 12, 1906, James Henry Tate, born December 28, 1880, son of William

Clarke Tate (born July 27, 1848; died October 10, 1841) and Rebecca Jane Hatcher (born May 9, 1847; died July 8, 1905), who were married, September 8, 1872; lives in Florida.

CHILDREN:

(a) Virginia, born November 16, 1908; died August 1, 1910.

(b) Henrietta McGhee, born February 8, 1912.

(5) Nancy Ware, born February 8, 1877; died August 7, 1877.

(6) Frances Willie, born April 19, 1878; lives in Farmville, Va.

(7) Genella, born December 11, 1881; married, June 14, 1906, Walter Baine McGhee, son of William Henry and Lucy (White) McGhee. No children.

(8) Edwin, born December 29, 1883; died September 9, 1884.

(10) Stanley Rice, born April 12, 1886; married, October 4, 1919, Katherine Rhodes, daughter of Samuel Thomas and Katherine (Nugent) Rhodes. No children.

(11) Alice Mitchell, born July 5, 1887; lives in Badin, N. C.

(12) Wilbur Irvine, born September 6, 1893; married, December 20, 1916, Ollie Mae Burkholder, daughter of Boyd Burkholder (born February 25, 1873) and Henrietta (Thoms) Burkholder (born December 5, 1871).

CHILDREN:

(a) Rice, born September 28, 1917.

(b) Virginia.

Jesse Jopling Walker, son of Dr. James Alexander and Nancy (Jopling) Walker, married, February 25, 1875, Annie Z. Phelps, daughter of Thomas Jefferson and Malinda Perkins (Key) Phelps. (See Phelps family.)

CHILDREN:

(1) James Thomas, born December 23, 1875; married, July 7, 1898, Elvira Thompson.

CHILD:

(a) James Thomas, Jr., born September 7, 1904; educated at Virginia Military Institute and College of William and Mary.

(2) John Key, born May 13, 1879; married, September 8, 1904, Dewannah Louise Walker, daughter of Capt. N. D. and Janie (Smith) Hawkins. (See Hawkins family.)

CHILDREN:

(a) Dewannah Sydnor, born December 20, 1906; graduated at Bedford High School, 1923; later, student at Randolph-Macon Woman's College, Lynchburg, Va.

(b) Anne Chilton, born August 13, 1916; now a freshman at the Bedford High School.

(c) John Key, Jr., born June 1, 1919.

(3) Jesse Bibb, born August 4, 1881; married, October 27, 1920, Isabel Wharton Cauthorn, born July 22, 1892, daughter of Dr. George T. and Ella (Jordan) Cauthorn. (See Jordan family.)

CHILD:

(a) Jesse Phelps, born April 12, 1922.

(4) Lulinda Phelps, born November 11, 1883.

(5) William Richard, born October 18, 1885; married, January 25, 1915, Iva V. Wright, born December 24, 1892.

CHILDREN:

(a) Lurnene, born January 17, 1916.

(b) William J., born September 2, 1917.

(c) Mildred, born December 23, 1921.

(d) Laura, born August 13, 1926.

(e) Margaret, born February 23, 1928.

(6) Mary Delia, born August 4, 1889; died September 21, 1892.

(7) Frances Moorman, born March 4, 1896.

(8) Elizabeth Nowlin, born July 13, 1899.

....

"AUNT NANNIE"

Perhaps the most widely known and universally beloved member of Bedford branch of Walkers was Nannie Moorman, youngest daughter of Dr. James Alexander and Nancy Moorman (Jopling) Walker. She died unmarried, and, though she was seventy-four years old, she was always active and interested in affairs of the day, mingling constantly with her friends and relatives. In fact her mission in life seems to have been keeping the family in touch with each other by going among them wherever and whenever she was needed, or simply going for her own pleasure.

She was never very robust and always had a remedy at hand for every ill, whether her own or that of another, and was as valuable in a sick room as a trained nurse.

For many years she held positions as housekeeper in the boarding schools of Bedford, going from Randolph-Macon Academy to Belmont Seminary, and from there to the Bedford Co-operative School, and numbered her friends by the hunderds among the students of these institutions.

When she was no longer equal to such activities she spent her time with her nieces and nephews—her brothers and sisters having all passed away—and it was while visiting a niece, Mrs. J. Harry Tate, in Chattanooga, Tenn., that her health began to fail. In 1926, when the Tates decided to move to Florida, she came back to Virginia for a visit, expecting to join them later in their new home. She spent several months seeing her old friends and relatives and then made all preparations to go to Florida, but there was illness in the home of her nephew, George P. Parker, which she made headquarters, at the time set for her departure and she refused to leave, hoping that she might be of some service, but a cold which had troubled her for some time and had weakened her resistance, became worse, pneumonia developed, and she only lived five days, dying November 9, 1926. Preparations recently made by her showed that she must have had some premonition of the end, for her will was found just inside her trunk and the spot she had selected for her grave in the family burying ground had been freshly marked, presumably while she was visiting her old home a few weeks before.

She was a gentle, refined, Christian woman in whom there was no guile. There are none better.

(The following notes were given to me by Nannie Moorman Walker a few weeks before her death. L. E. J. P.) :

William I. Walker married Sallie Hopkins.

Wilmuth T. Walker married ———— Taylor.

Robert M. Walker married America Hudnall.

Elizabeth Ann Walker married ———— Taylor.

Joseph P. went to Missouri and married ————.

John Thomas married Sarah Skinnell.

John Thomas and Sarah Skinnell Walker had two children and she died when the second one, Mary Elizabeth, was an infant. The eldest child died in childhood.

Soon after the death of his wife, Thomas Walker carried his baby daughter to the home of his brother, Dr. James Alexander Walker, and asked his wife to take care of her until he should return for her. In a short time he and two of his neighbors—one of them Alexander McDaniel—went to California. Mr. McDaniel came back after a few years but had been separated from Mr. Walker so long that he could give no account of him, and he was never heard of again. Years after this his great nephew, Dr. Homer Walker, son of Jerome Walker of McPherson, Kansas, who was practicing his profession in Los Angeles had a Mrs. Walker come into his office and tell him that he looked exactly like her son, but not knowing that any of his people had ever gone to California he did not ask any questions. He did write to his father about it, however, and later tried to locate her, but never could do so.

Betty, the baby girl, grew up in the home of her uncle and married Hersey Ayres, whose first wife was a Pullen. She had a large family and died soon after the birth of a son, Pennie Robertson, who was raised by his aunt, Dosia Walker, and her daughter, Nannie.

David Henry Walker married Caroline Shinnell and their children were:

Sarah Frances; died unmarried.
Etherial Thomas; married Rosa Shelton.
Julia; died unmarried.
Mary Jane; went to Colorado and married.
Jerome; married Susan Field and settled in McPherson, Kan.
Proctor; married Mary Cooper.
Caroline; married ———— Overby.
Paul Bowles; went to Colorado.
Aletha Austin; died unmarried.
Cordelia Nelms; married William Mozingo.
Jimmie Pearman; married ———— Reed.

George M. A. Walker married Ann McGhee and they had three children:

Julius Hudnall; married Mary Phelps and had two children: Katherine and Norman.

Susan; died in childhood.

Theodosia Alverda; married Jesse Leftwich Walker and had three children: Grace; George, who died in youth; and Anna, who died in infancy.

Samuel Phillips Walker married his cousin, Theodosia Quarles, daughter of Mary (Walker) Quarles, sister of Robert Munford Walker.

CHILDREN:

Ann Elizabeth; died unmarried.

Roberta David; died unmarried.

Jesse Leftwich; married Alverda Walker.

John Winston; died unmarried.

Alonza Trigg; married Ella Schultz and has one child: Alonza Reginald.

James Wingfield; died unmarried.

Mary Fannie; died in infancy.

Mary, daughter of David and Peletiah Walker of Dinwiddie County, married a Quarles and came to Bedford. Their son, David, married a Leftwich, and his daughter, Theodosia, married Samuel Phillips Walker.

Nancy, another daughter of David and Peletiah (Jones) Walker, married a Quarles, also, and came to Bedford County. She lived and died where Parker Walker now lives. She had a son, John, who married Mary Walker and whose children are:

Walter; married (first) Hetty Franklin; (second) Lettie Coley.

Roger; married ———— Ellis.

Alice; married Lindsay Fisher.

Sallie; married R. Lee Whorley.

Annie; married Robert Lee Robertson—(second) wife.

Frank, son of William I, and Sallie (Hopkins) Walker, married a Carner and had one son, Quincy, who married Blanch Bush and had four daughters: Berta, Sallie, Bettie, and Hettie.

JOPLIN (Spelled Also JOPLING)

The Joplins are of Welsh extraction, and the first of whom we have any definite knowledge settled in the Valley of Virginia.

They have scattered widely—many of them going to the Middle West, while others have made their homes in the Southern States.

Their features are so similar and so characteristic that they are easily recognized by their long, sharp faces, long noses, and, often, blue eyes and auburn hair. Just a few years ago a World War veteran approached a member of the family, who was traveling in Tennessee, and asked, "Is your name Joplin?" He replied, "Yes, but why do you want to know?" The veteran said, "Well, I was in the World War with a young man by the name of Joplin, from Gurley, Alabama, whom you so much resemble that I thought perhaps you were members of the same family. I was standing by his side when he was shot down, and I have tried, ever since I came back, to find some of his people, so that I might tell them that he died an honorable death, in the service of his country." This traveling man knew little of his family, but the story interested him, and he wrote to Gurley, Ala., to see if there were Joplins living there, and found that his father's brother had settled there many years before, and that the young man, killed in France, was his own first cousin, and that his people had never heard any particulars of his death up to this time, and perhaps never would have, but for his unmistakable Joplin features.

Thomas Joplin, the founder of the family in Virginia, was living on Rockfish River, in Albemarle County, in 1749. (Sumner's *History of Southwest Virginia*, page 786.) We find him again in Amherst County as Captain of Minute Men, after that county had been formed from Albemarle (1761).

He died in Amherst in 1789. His will, which was made August 10, 1789, and probated September 7, 1789, mentions: wife, Hannah; children: Josiah, James, Thomas, Martha (married John Griffin), Ann Childress, Jane Davis, Lucy Powell, Rebecca Martin, Hannah Allen; grandson, Jesse Joplin.

Witnesses to his will were Henry Mart·u, Joseph Thomas, Thomas Farrer, and John Joplin. (Will Book No. 3, page 116.)

His eldest son, Ralph, was not mentioned in his will.

....

Josiah Joplin, born 1747, son of Thomas and Hannah Joplin, married, December 1, 1767, in Amherst County, Va., Elizabeth Ware.

We learn from Hardesty's *Encyclopedia*, page 410, that he served as private in the Revolutionary War.

He died in Amherst in 1798. His will, which was made November 16, 1797, and probated April 18, 1798, mentions children: Hannah Bridgewater, James Joplin, William Joplin, Edward Ware Joplin, Holeman(?) Joplin, Thomas Joplin, Bennett Joplin, Elizabeth Bridgewater Joplin, and Sarah Joplin. (Will Book No. 3, page 9.)

....

James Joplin, born October 27, 1769; died October 5, 1852; son of Josiah and Elizabeth (Ware) Joplin, married in Amherst County, October 31, 1793, Nancy Martin, born July 13, 1776.

They lived in Amherst a few years after their marriage, and then moved to Bedford County, about 1806, settling near what is now Peaksville, at the foot of the Peaks of Otter.

For some unknown reason they changed the spelling of their name to "Jopling," and the Bedford branch of the family has ever spelled it thus, while those going elsewhere have stuck to the original "Joplin."

Nancy (Martin) Jopling was a devout Methodist, and upon one occasion, when they were worshipping with the Baptists at Suck Spring Church, the pastor of that church passed the communion plate over her head, making some remark as he did so that offended her husband, and, though he was not a member of any church, he resolved then and there to build a Methodist edifice, in which his wife could worship without embarrassment. He, at once, set about raising funds for this purpose, donating a lot on the corner of his farm, and giving liberally of his own means to the erection of the building. This is the Salem Methodist Church of today.

Miss Maude Hurt of Winthrop College, South Carolina, has the Bible of James Jopling, in which are recorded his birth, that of his wife, the date of their marriage, and the names and dates of births of their children.

CHILDREN:

(1) Elizabeth Ware, born August 25, 1794; died in childhood.
(2) Pleasant M., born December 13, 1796; died in childhood.
(3) Mary Ann B.; born October 15, 1798; married ——— North.
(4) Josiah, born November 22, 1802; married ——— Love; went to Missouri. The town of Joplin, Mo., is named for him.
(5) Louisa Rebecca, born January 4, 1804; married Belfield Porter.
(6) Jesse, born February 5, 1806; married Susan Clark.
(7) James Ware, born November 14, 1807. (See forward.)
(8) Thomas Bennet, born September 25, 1810. (See forward.)
(9) Sally Ware, born February 23, 1812; married Burwell Porter.
(10) Nancy Moorman, born February 16, 1814; married Dr. James Alexander Walker. (See Walker family.)
(11) William Ware, born October 27, 1815; married (first) ——— Thomas; (second) Susan Claytor.
(12) Frances Amanda, born January 26, 1819; married John P. Hurt. (See forward.)
(13) Martha Mildred, born July 13, 1820; married Aaron Wheat.

Mrs. John H. Watts of Bedford, Va., has the Jopling Family Tree made by her mother, Frances (Jopling) Hurt. It is the picture of a tree, drawn in pencil, with the names written on the trunk and branches in ink. It follows:

THE JOPLING FAMILY TREE

James Jopling, son of Josiah Jopling and Elizabeth (Ware) Jopling, married Nancy Martin, daughter of Pleasant Martin and Rebecka (Jopling) Martin.

CHILDREN:

Elizabeth W. Jopling.
Pleasant M. Jopling.
Mary A. B. Jopling.
Josiah Jopling.
Louisa R. Jopling.
Jesse Jopling.
James W. Jopling.
Thomas B. Jopling.
Sallie W. Jopling.
Nancy M. Jopling.
William W. Jopling.
Frances A. Jopling; married J. P. Hurt. Children: C. P. Hurt, M. R. Hurt.
Martha M. Jopling.

The above is a true copy of the family tree of my mother, Mrs. Frances A. (Jopling) Hurt, written by herself, and now in my possession.

(Signed) Mrs. M. R. Watts.

Subscribed and sworn before me at Bedford, Va., this 24th day of March, 1923, A. D.

W. A. Fitzpatrick.

Notary Public in and for Bedford County, Virginia.

After the death of his first wife, James Jopling married Mrs. Booth, who did not live very long, and he married again—his third wife being Sarah Rice, daughter of Benjamin and Catherine (Holt) Rice, of Bedford County.

He died October 5, 1852, and his will is recorded in Will Book "O," page 415, of the records of Bedford County.

....

James W. Jopling, son of James and Nancy (Martin) Jopling, married in December, 1835, Emily Booth (born June, 1816; died August 2, 1869), daughter of Benjamin and Elizabeth (Divers) Booth, of Franklin County, Va.

CHILDREN:

(1) Benjamin; went to Gurley, Alabama, and married.
(2) Thomas; went to Tennessee and married.
(3) Jesse; went to Missouri and married.
(4) William; married Emma Crowley of Louisville, Ky.
(5) Joseph; married Rebecca Boyd, his first cousin, and moved to Santa Anna, California, where he has been County Treasurer for more than forty years, and now, at the age of eighty-nine, is a candidate for re-election.
(6) Ferdinand Martin, born February 2, 1845; married (first) Adelaide Griffin of Hartford, Ky.

CHILDREN:

(a) Francis Warren; married Pearl White.

(b) Pearl; married George W. England, of Baltimore, Md.

(c) Wayne Griffin; married Alice Robertson of Elizabethtown, Ky.

(d) Paul Wilcox; married Sydney Yates of Houston, Texas.

(e) Mary Lou; married Ernest Edmundson, of Crowley, La.

Ferdinand M. Joplin married (second), August 21, 1891, Josephine Saunders, of Rocky Mount, Va.

CHILDREN:

(f) Ann Saunders, born August 16, 1893; lives in Rocky Mount.

(g) Joseph Saunders, born January 26, 1896; married, September 14, 1929, Lucy White Witten, of Albemarle County, Va.

Ferdinand M. Joplin married (third) Mrs. Frances (Slattery) Rue, of Bowling Green, Ky.

CHILD:

(h) John LaRue; went to Houston, Texas, and married.

(7) Elizabeth; married William Martin, of Nashville, Tenn.

(8) Otho Kane; married Elizabeth Stockley, of Memphis, Tenn.; is a wealthy cotton planter, and lives on an island in the Mississippi River.

(9) Charles; drowned in Mississippi River at the age of twelve.

(10) Emma, twin of Charles, died in infancy.

Thomas Bennett Jopling, son of James and Nancy (Martin) Jopling, married Sarah Webb, in Franklin County, Va., September 21, 1845.

CHILDREN:

(1) James Edward; married Betty Goode.

(2) William Bennett; died unmarried.

(3) Thomas Creed; married Annie Wilmer Barnett.

(4) Nancy Rice; married Nelson Hawkins.

(5) John E.; died in infancy.

(6) Morton Irvin; married Ora Newsom.

(7) Jesse S.; died unmarried.

(8) Fannie Willis; married James A. McCauley.

(9) Lemuel Reed; died in infancy.

(10) Ida Woodson; married Achilles Tyree.

(11) Benjamin Wilkes; died unmarried.

(12) Mary Louise; married William T. Evans.

Thomas B. Jopling died at his home near Goode, Va., November 1, 1867. Sarah (Webb) Jopling, born April 18, 1829; died October 12, 1886.

Frances Amanda Jopling, daughter of James and Nancy (Martin) Jopling, married, April 3, 1839, John Pendleton Hurt.

CHILDREN :

(1) Nancy Rice; died in childhood.

(2) Charles Pendleton. (See forward.)

(3) Martha Rebecka; married John H. Watts.

(4) Mary Virginia; died in infancy.

(5) James Jopling; died in childhood.

Frances (Jopling) Hurt died February 23, 1893. John Pendleton Hurt, born February 1, 1810; died January 17, 1892.

....

Charles Pendleton Hurt, born June 7, 1843; died June 23, 1912; son of John Pendleton and Frances (Jopling) Hurt, married Julia Roberta Claytor, who was born April 12, 1848, and died August 14, 1897.

CHILDREN :

(1) Frank Pendleton, born February 26, 1868; married Mrs. Sippie (Crozier) Frye.

(2) Samuel Henry; died in childhood.

(3) James Warren, born June 17, 1873; married in Missouri, Mamie Daisy Pollard. They now live in Missouri.

CHILDREN :

    (a) Charles William.

    (b) Anna Roberta.

    (c) Mamie Daisy.

    (d) Lucile.

(4) Rosa Maude, born October 15, 1876; now a member of the faculty of Winthrop College, S. C.

(5) Elizabeth Rebecca, born September 15, 1879; died November 14, 1890.

(6) Charles Robert, born August 22, 1822; married Grace Trueman Mitchell, September 14, 1914.

CHILDREN :

    (a) Julia Alice.

    (b) Katherine.

    (c) Mary Elizabeth.

(7) John Addison, born June 5, 1887; married, February, 1918, Mamie Burgess; lives in Appalachia, Va.

CHILDREN :

    (a) John Burgess, born December 15, 1918.

    (b) Mary Rebecca, born May 20, 1920.

    (c) Harold Pendleton, born August 3, 1923.

(8) Benjamin Porter, born June 23, 1890; married, October 27, 1917, Lula Virginia Craig; lives on the old home place near Otterville, in Bedford County.

CHILDREN :

    (a) Virginia Frances, born September 27, 1919.

    (b) Winston Porter, born January 3, 1922.

    (c) Maude Mildred, born April 22, 1925.

MARTIN

According to a Martin genealogy compiled by Dr. Samuel Davies of Kentucky, a grandson of Thomas Martin of Albemarle County, the first in America was Abram Martin, a younger son of a wealthy family of Galway, Ireland. He came to America about 1680.

Abram Martin had one son—John, born in Virginia in 1685.

(1) Mary, born 1703; married ———— Clark, and was ancestress of George Rogers Clark.
(2) John.
(3) Eliza, 1708; married ———— Douglass, and was ancestress of Stephen A. Douglass.
(4) Thomas, born 1714; married (first) Ann Moorman, daughter of Charles and Elizabeth Reynolds Moorman; (second) a Miss Glover; and (third) Mary Suddarth.
(5) Abram; was ancestor of the South Carolina branch of the family.

....

Thomas Martin, son of John Martin, married (first) Ann Moorman. (See Moorman family.)

(1) George; married Barbara Woods.
(2) Thomas.
(3) Charles.
(4) John; married Elizabeth Lewis.
(5) Pleasant; married Rebecca Joplin. (See forward.)
(6) Letitia; married Richard Moore.
(7) Mildred; married ———— Oglesby.
(8) Ann; married ———— Blaine.
(9) Mary; married Benjamin Dawson.

Thomas Martin's (second) wife, Miss Glover, had no children; and his (third) wife, Mary Suddarth, had only one son, Abram, who married and lived in Tennessee, where he has numerous descendants.

Thomas Martin lived at "Locust Grove," in Albemarle County, where he was already settled when that county was formed in 1744. He died in 1792, and his will is recorded in Albemarle County.

Clerk's Office Albemarle County, Virginia

1792   Thomas Martin   Will   Book 3, Page 174

In the Name of God Amen. I, Thomas Martin of Albemarle County & Parish of St. Ann's, being in perfect mind and memory &c. Just debts to be paid.

Wife Mary Martin—246 acres in Albemarle County, taking in the Cove Meeting House and adjoining Tandy Key during her life or widowhood. Also slaves, by name, &c., &c. After decease of my wife I give to my son Abraham Martin land & negroes. Land in Kentucky, located by Col. B. Logan.

Son George Martin, land I now live on (Albemarle County) also slaves, by name—and land in Kentucky.

Grandson Martin Moor, land in Kentucky.

Son Thomas Martin, £70 Current Money.

Grand-daughter Milly Moor, feather bed &c.

Rest and residue divided among my following children—Charles Martin; John Martin; Thomas Martin; Pleasant Martin; George Martin; Litty Moor; Milley Oglesby; Nancy M. Blane; Molley Dawson; and Martin Moor.

Lastly I appoint Samuel Murrell, Tandy Key, George Martin, and Pleasant Martin, Executors, to this my last Will.

In witness whereof I have hereunto set my hand and seal this Twenty-fifth day of July, 1792.

THO⁵ MARTIN [SEAL].

Signed, sealed & delivered
In presence of

BENJAMIN NORVELL
THOMAS JOHNSON
     his
WILLIAM M MORAN
     mark

Albemarle December Court, 1792.

Bond and security given by Andrew Hart and Nath¹ Garland. Ordered recorded, John Nicholas, C. A. C.

....

Pleasant Martin, son of Thomas and Ann (Moorman) Martin, married Rebecca Joplin, daughter of Thomas and Hannah Joplin of Amherst County, Va. (Marriage bond dated October 2, 1775. Amherst County records.)

Pleasant Martin and Rebecca, his wife, removed from Amherst County to Bedford County and leased land, in 1812, on the north side of the county from Andrew Donald. (Deed Book "L," page 89.)

In 1816, Pleasant Martin was Commissioner of the Revenue, and James Jopling was one of his securities. (Deed Book "M," page 222.)

....

The marriage bond of James Jopling and Nancy Martin is now in the Archives of the State Library, at Richmond, Va., and has recently been photostated for us. It follows:

MARRIAGE BOND

KNOW ALL MEN BY THESE PRESENTS that we, JAMES JOPLIN and BENJAMIN CHILDRESS are held and firmly bound unto Henry Lee, Esq., Governor of the Commonwealth of Virginia, in the sum of Fifty Pounds current money to be paid to the said Lee, Esq., Governor as aforesaid or to his successors for the use of the said Commonwealth, which payment well and truly to be made we bind ourselves jointly and severally our joint and several heirs firmly by these presents. Sealed with our seal and dated this 21st day of October, 1793.

The condition of the above obligation is such that whereas there is a marriage shortly intended to be solemnized between the above bound JAMES JOPLING, Bachelor, and NANCY MARTIN, Spinster, each of Amherst County and parish of Amht. If therefore to be no lawful cause to obstruct the said marriage, then the above obligation to be void or else to remain in full force and virtue.

JAMES JOPLING [SEAL],
BENJAMIN CHILDRESS [SEAL].

CERTIFICATE

Sir:

You will please to issue for James Jopling to intermarry with my daughter Nancy and this shall be your sufficient warrant. Given under my hand this 21st of October, 1793.

PLEASANT MARTIN [SEAL].

Teste:

BENJ. CHILDRESS,
SAM CHILDRESS.

To Clerk of Amherst.

PHELPS

John Phelps, the first of the name of whom we have any authentic record, was already settled in Brunswick County, Va., when Lunenburg was taken from that county, and was one of the first Justices of the new county. He, with Matthew Talbot and others, was present at the first Court of Lunenburg County, held May 5, 1746.

When the increase in population made it necessary to form still another county from Lunenburg's territory, and Bedford came into being, we find John Phelps again at the head of affairs—"Justice of the Peace, and a Justice of the County Court in Chancery." He and William Callaway were Bedford's first representatives in the House of Burgesses, and from *Hening's Statutes*, Vol. VII, we learn that he was a Colonel in the Colonial Army.

He died in Bedford County in 1772, and his will, recorded in Will Book "A," page 137, mentions wife, Mary; children: Jane, Judith, Sarah, Ann, Mary, Betty, John, and Aggey.

....

John Phelps, Jr., was a lieutenant in the Revolutionary Army. He married (first) Jemima Turner; (second) August 18, 1787, Susannah Younger. He died in 1801. His will, recorded in Bedford (Will Book "B," page 323), mentions: children, Mary Hall, Jemima Forguson, Nancy Forguson, John, Lucy Haynes, Washington, Jeanny, Overton, Robert James, Richard, Thomas, Bethsheba, Glenn, Betsy, Randolph, and William.

....

Thomas Phelps, son of John Phelps, Jr., died in 1851; married, December 1, 1814, Nancy Carter.

CHILDREN:
Richard, Thomas Jefferson, James, Joseph Carter, John Henry Elvira, Bethania, and Ammon.

....

Thomas Jefferson Phelps, son of Thomas and Nancy (Carter) Phelps, born December 28, 1821; died December 15, 1905; married, December 10, 1846, Mrs. Malinda P. (Key) Nelms, widow of William

Nelms. (See Key family.) He was a member of Company "F," Second Virginia Cavalry, C. S. A., and served fifteen months; was honorably discharged because of bad health; then served as collector of taxes in kind for the Army at Liberty, Va. (See Key family.)

CHILDREN:

(1) Thomas Key, born September 21, 1847; died December 27, 1925; married, November 22, 1870, Sarah Elizabeth Moulton, born May 8, 1849; died September 10, 1914, daughter of Dr. Benjamin Hammond and Mary (Cundiff) Moulton. (See Moulton family.) He was one of the cadets of Virginia Military Institute who fought in the Battle of New Market during the Civil War.

CHILDREN:

(a) Mary Malinda, born December 22, 1871; died May 5, 1881.
(b) Thomas Hammond, born August 30, 1873; married in 1904, Annie Lee Blincoe. No children.
(c) Elizabeth Margaret, born January 5, 1875; married in 1900, Dr. Samuel L. Rucker, who is a popular physician and practices on the south side of Bedford County, Va.

CHILDREN:

(aa) Joseph Edward, born October 18, 1901.
(bb) Thomas Francis, born March 8, 1903; married in 1926, Frances Carson.

CHILD:

(aaa) John Blair, born April 28, 1928.
(cc) Elizabeth, born July 4, 1904.
(dd) Frances Elinor, born August 19, 1905.
(ee) Samuel Leonidas, Jr., born October 9, 1906.
(ff) Virginia Moulton, born March 1, 1908.
(gg) James Hammet, born July 19, 1909.
(hh) Mary Kathleen, born October 10, 1910.
(ii) John, born July 2, 1912.
(jj) Margaret Key, born September 28, 1913.
(kk) Ruth, twin of Margaret Key, born September 28, 1913.

(ll) Emily, born 1916; died 1917.

(mm) Richard Anthony, born April 18, 1918.

(d) Ella Docia, born November 22, 1876.

(e) James Key, born August 15, 1878.

(f) Wilbur Moulton, born October 26, 1880; died February 6, 1906.

(g) Harriet May, born May 2, 1882.

(h) Annie Laura, born August 23, 1884.

(i) William Richard, born August 2, 1886; educated at Randolph-Macon College; taught at Randolph-Macon Institute, Danville, Va.; principal of Randolph-Macon Academy, Bedford, Va., since 1921; married, August 9, 1911, Mildred May Davis, born June 24, 1888, daughter of Dr. James Monroe and Rosa (King) Davis of Nottoway County, Va.

CHILDREN:

(aa) Rosa King, born October 30, 1912.

(bb) William Richard, Jr., born September 8, 1917.

(cc) Moulton Davis, born August 20, 1919.

(j) Lucy, born May 13. 1889.

(k) Ruth Eva, born July 19, 1891; married in 1918, Dr. George W. Sutherland. No children.

(2) Mary Elvira, born August 22, 1849; married, December 10, 1874, Robert Mead, who was born February 18, 1846, and died May 15, 1919. He was a member of Company "A," 22nd Virginia Cavalry, and was near Appomattox Court House when Lee surrendered.

CHILDREN:

(a) Mary Malinda, born November 19, 1875; married Herbert E. Burroughs. (See Bond family.)

CHILDREN:

Mary Doris, Thomas, William, Walter Wilson, and Elizabeth.

(b) Thomas Key, born June 6, 1877.

(c) James Oliver, born January 2, 1879; married Julia E. Griggs.

CHILDREN:

Robert Byron, Annie Thelma, and James Edward.

(d) William Richard, born January 1, 1881; married Maud E. Daugherty.

CHILDREN:

Harry Winston, Trumlian, William R., Jr., and Ryland.

(e) Elizabeth Delia, born February 6, 1883.

(f) John Robert, born November 24, 1884.

(g) Annie Cornelia, born March 20, 1887; married Ida E. Torrence.

CHILD:

(aa) Robert Elmo.

(h) Harry Hoffecker, born September 13, 1889; died October 5, 1891.

(i) Ruth Phelps, born September 7, 1894; married John T. Griggs.

CHILDREN:

Ruth Phelps, Frank, Martha, and William Robert.

(3) Annie Z., born November 28, 1850; married Jesse Joplin Walker. (See Walker family.)

(4) William Richard, born April 20, 1854; died October 15, 1882.

KEY

John Key (1) made his first entry of land in Albemarle County, Va., in 1732. His children were Martin, John, and Mary.

Martin Key (2) died in Albemarle County in 1791. His will mentions: wife, Anne; children, Thomas, John, Martin, Tandy, Joshua, William, Henry, Jesse, James, Walter, Elizabeth, and Martha.

Tandy Key (3) died in Fluvanna County, Va., in July, 1838. His will mentions: wife, Mildred; children, Walter, Thomas, Martin, Sally B. Jones, Jesse P., Nancy P. German, Daniel P., Harden; son-in-law, Elijah Brown; and grand-daughter, Mildred Ann Givins.

Thomas Key (4), born August 15, 1779; died April 29, 1818; married in Bedford County, Va., August 29, 1804, Docia Preston, daughter of Stephen and Docia (Smith) Preston.

CHILDREN (BIBLE RECORD) :

(1) Betsy Price, born June 14, 1805.
(2) William Walter, born April 12, 1807; died April 22, 1808.
(3) Nelson, born October 4, 1808; died November 10, 1890.
(4) Malinda Perkins, born July 11, 1811; died February 12, 1894; married (first) in 1836, William Nelms; (second) Thomas Jefferson Phelps. (See Phelps family.)
(5) Jesse Bibb, born May 25, 1813; moved to Cuthbert, Ga.
(6) William Booker, born December 26, 1814.

....

Children of Malinda Perkins Key and her (first) husband, William Nelms:

(1) Elizabeth Cordelia, born July 6, 1837; died December 20, 1914; married (first) James M. Phelps; (second) Thomas W. Nance. No children.
(2) Docia A., born August 5, 1839; died February 28, 1909; married, May 1, 1867, Dr. William Pleasant Thurman, who died March 15, 1910.

CHILDREN :

(a) Jessie Key, born February 20, 1868; married, December 23, 1891, Oscar Wright. One child, which died in infancy.
(b) William Jennings, born August 17, 1867; married, November 27, 1895, Mrs. Sciota Smith.
(c) James Otis, born August 5, 1870; married, Evelyn Hilton.

CHILDREN :
Hilton, Owen, Helen, and Margaret.

(d) John Silas, born March 24, 1872; married Bevie Saunders.

CHILDREN :
William Pleasant, Harry, Otis, John, Vivian, Susie, Marjorie, Lewis, and Anthony.

(e) Delia Nelms, born November 24, 1873; married, June 7, 1899, Robert V. Overstreet.

CHILDREN :
(aa) Robert Thurman, born July 25, 1901; married Lois McCloud.

CHILD :
(aaa) Sydnor Sue.
(bb) William Edwin, born January 2, 1903; married Eula Truxell.

CHILD :
(aaa) William Edwin, Jr.
(cc) Virginia May, born November 29, 1905; married V. B. Smith.

CHILDREN :
(aaa) Stanford B.
(bbb) Alice Nelms.

(dd) Allen G., born April 18, 1907.

(ee) Moulton Phelps, born May 9, 1908.

(ff) Margaret, born June 28, 1909.

(gg) Richard V., Jr., born and died March 15, 1911.

(hh) Infant; died unnamed.

(ii) Rebecca Nelms, born December 12, 1914.

(f) Allen Granberry, born March 29, 1876; died January 31, 1925; married Lessie Wingfield. (See Johnson family.)

CHILDREN :

Allen, Nelson, Warren, Frances, and Wilton.

(g) Mary Susan, born July 27, 1879; married John Hepinstall.

(h) Margaret; died in infancy.

HAWKINS

William Hawkins, the first of the name of whom we have found any authentic record, bought land in Bedford County, Va., in 1781. He removed to Campbell County and died there in 1793. His will mentions: wife, Mary; children, William, Littleberry, Robert, Joseph, Benjamin, James, and Mildred Hicks.

Robert Hawkins died in Bedford County, July 24, 1820. He married, December 30, 1794, Nancy Fourqueran, daughter of John and Mary (Gutry) Fourqueran, who were married in Bedford County, February 26, 1772, her father, Henry Gutry, consenting to the marriage. John Fourqueran is believed to have been the son of Moyse and Susane Fourqueran, French Huguenots of Manakin Town, Va., for the records of that colony give this entry: "Mar. 15, 1736, was born Jean Forqueran, son of Moyse and Susane, his wife. Godfather Pierre Forqueran." (Brock's *Huguenot Emigration*, page 93.)

The Bedford County records show that Peter and John Fourqueran bought land in this county in 1768 and 1772.

CHILDREN OF ROBERT AND NANCY (FOURQUERAN) HAWKINS:

(1) Daughter; died young.

(2) John Fourqueran, born April 24, 1797; died September 26, 1887; married, June 15, 1824, Lucinda Ann Campbell, born November 21, 1806; died March 8, 1880, daughter of Lewis and Susanna (Monroe) Campbell, who were married in Amherst County, Va., October 31, 1803.

CHILDREN :

(a) Sarah Segar, born April 22, 1825; married, September 18, 1854, John G. Apperson.

(b) Robert C., born May 22, 1827; married, December 18, 1850, Mary F. Walthall.

(c) Susan Ann, born May 24, 1829; died November 20, 1911; married, October 22, 1857, N. E. Dinwiddie.

(d) Lucinda Lewis, born June 28, 1832; married, November 17, 1851, Edward W. Dinwiddie.

(e) William James Holcomb, born October 10, 1837; died September 4, 1875; unmarried.

(f) Mary Eliza, born December 27, 1839; died November 27, 1841.

(g) Samuel Morris Hamner, born June 30, 1841; died December 5, 1915; married, November 20, 1860, Elizabeth F. Swinney, born July 29, 1844; died November 9, 1927.

(h) John F., Jr., born September 16, 1843; married, November 22, 1871, Mattie E. Newel.

(i) Nelson S., born May 23, 1847; married (first), December 23, 1868, Nannie R. Jopling; (second) November 8, 1871, Delia H. Haley.

(j) Norment Doniphan, born July 26, 1849. (See forward.)

(k) Edgar T., born November 15, 1851; married (first), May 15, 1878, Lizzie E. Moorman; (second) June 20, 1894, Mrs. Margie E. Singleton.

....

Norment Doniphan Hawkins, son of John F. and Lucinda (Campbell) Hawkins, volunteered at the age of fourteen for service in the Civil War; graduated as First Captain from Virginia Military Institute in 1872, and is now Brigadier-General of the Maryland Division, Confederate Veterans. Lives in Washington, D. C. He married, August 20, 1874, Janie Sydnor Smith, born April 9, 1853. (See Smith family.)

CHILDREN:

(1) Charles Sydnor, born June 4, 1875; died May 24, 1901.

(2) John Hamner, born June 27, 1877; married, September 7, 1904, Rebecca Louise Wright. One child; died in infancy.

(3) Dewannah Louise, born April 12, 1881; married, September 8, 1904, John Key Walker. (See Walker family.)

(4) Mary Forman, born August 1, 1883.

(5) Lula Elizabeth, born August 17, 1885; married, October 4, 1911, Rev. James M. McChesney.

CHILDREN:

(a) James M., Jr., born September 13, 1913.

(b) Janie Katherine, born January 4, 1917.

(c) Lee Doniphan, born November 21, 1918.

(d) Graham Clark, born July 8, 1921.

(e) Charles Sydnor, born September 22, 1923.

(6) Norment Doniphan, Jr., born April 2, 1887; married, September 8, 1909, Ruth J. Burton.

CHILDREN:

(a) Norment Doniphan, III, born August 28, 1910.

(b) Virginia F., born April 9, 1913.

(c) Burton Sydnor, born May 22, 1914.

(d) Norvel Hamner, born May, 1924.
(7) Janie Booker, born October 15, 1889; married, September 6, 1916, Henry Grant Ellis.

(a) Jane Sydnor, born December 14, 1917.
(b) Sarah Grant, born August 17, 1920; died December 8, 1926.
(c) Henry Grant, Jr., born February 16, 1923.
(8) Evelyn Flournoy, born January 17, 1903.

SMITH

The following are records from the family Bible of Robert Smith, which is now in possession of Mrs. J. K. Walker, Bedford, Va.:

Robert Smith, born January 10, 1738; died April 8, 1820; married, March 5, 1760, Sarah Morris, born February 12, 1741.

(1) Robert, born October 30, 1763; died March 26, 1830.
(2) Samuel C., born May 14, 1767; died August 22, 1793.
(3) George, born May 20, 1771.
(4) Ann Sterling, born February 9, 1774.
(5) William, born November 8, 1776.
(6) Francis, born July 10, 1779.
(7) John W., born November 30, 1782.
(8) Thomas, born July, 1785.

Robert Smith, Jr., oldest son of Robert and Sarah (Morris) Smith, married (first) Rebecca Booker, born April 7, 1773, died April 21, 1818, daughter of William and Mary (Flournoy) Booker, who were married in Amelia County, Va., in April, 1755.

(1) Sally Sterling, born September 13, 1790; died October 27, 1832; married Dr. Richard Thornton, of Halifax County, Va.
(2) Mary B., born December 24, 1792; died September, 1832.
(3) Robert, born December 20, 1794; died January 12, 1879; married, June 15, 1822, in Charlotte County, Va., Jane Smith, born 1804, died 1853, daughter of Isaac and Sarah (Hancock) Smith. (Isaac Smith was a Revolutionary soldier.)

(a) Booker Flournoy, born August 5, 1823, died August 23, 1891; married, May 2, 1849, Dewannah Frances Moorman, born August 5, 1830, died

December 25, 1899, daughter of Charles H. and Anne (Chilton) Moorman. (See Chilton family.)

(b) Walter, (c) Sarah, (d) Mary, (e) Vincent, and (f) Helen.

Robert Smith, Jr., married (second), February 25, 1819, Susan A. Watlington.

CHILDREN:

(4) Armistead W., born January 15, 1821.
(5) Rebecca B., born 1825.

Lives of great men all remind us
  We can make our lives sublime,
And, departing, leave behind us
  Footprints on the sands of time.

Footprints, that perhaps another,
  Sailing o'er life's solemn main,
A forlorn and shipwrecked brother,
  Seeing, shall take heart again.

Let us, then be up and doing,
  With a heart for any fate;
Still achieving, still pursuing,
  Learn to labor and to wait."

[FINIS]

INDEX

A

Lucy A., 614.
Marcella, 613.
Mary, 675.
Mary A., 614.
Mary Echols, 613, 614.
Mary S., 664.
Mary T., 614.
Parmelia, 613, 614.
Richard D., 614.

Dabbs, Mrs., 470.
  Mary C., 469.
Daken, Alice Brugh, 676.
Dale, James, 207.
Dallas, Lucy Ann, 675.
Dallice, John, 69, 70.
Dallis, John, 70.
Dalton, James, 409.
Daly, Jesse Cecil, 677.
Dameron, Anna S., 58, 76.
  Chs., 58, 59.
  Chas. D., 58, 76.
  Dunmore, 59.
  Lucy Thomas, 59.
  Mary E., 58.
  Mildred, 58, 76.
  Thomas, 402.
Dandridge, Ann, 336.
  Bartholomew, 349.
  Jane Butler, 336.
  John, 336.
  Mary, 216.
  Nathaniel West, 336.
  Wm., 336.
Daniel, Charles Gillum, 197.
  Elias, 407.
  Fannie McPike, 197.
  John W., 651.
Daniels, G. C., 56.
  Genevieve, 56.
  Sallie Aletha, 197.
Danner, Amelia Stokes, 533.
Darby, Mr., 516.
D'arcy, Edward, 604.
Darr, Mary Lavinia, 284.
Daugherty, Maud E., 706.
  W. L., 522.
Davenport, Betsey, 95.
  Drusilla, 606.
David, Judith, 23.
Davidson, Dorothy, 484.
  James G., 96.
  Jesse Thornhill, 484.
  Joseph Mays, 484.
  Samuel, 484.
Davies, Addison, 349.
  Arthur Landon, 348.

Samuel C., 614.
Zula, 614.
Cunningham, Frank C., 556.
  Marjorie, 556.
Curtler, Frederick Lewis, 269.
Custer, Mary Virginia, 677.
Cutler, Leone John, 521.
  Mary Katherine, 521.

D

Catherine E., 348.
Edith Landon, 348.
H. L., 351, 358.
Henrianne, 348.
Henry L., 347, 348, 350, 356, 357, 358, 361.
Howell, 349.
Lucy Whiting, 361.
N. C., 358.
Nicholas, 347, 348, 355, 356, 362.
Nicholas Clayton, 348, 351, 352, 356, 357, 359, 360, 361.
Sam B., 348, 358, 360, 361.
Samuel, 334, 700.
Tamerlane Whiting, 349.
Wm., 334.
Davis, Miss, 468.
  Mr., 516.
  Abby, 140.
  Absalom, 141.
  Alexander Christopher, 288.
  Alice, 286.
  Amelia May, 309.
  Ann, 139.
  Ann Maria, 284.
  Ann Rachel, 287.
  Annis Elizabeth, 286.
  Annis Lipscomb, 287.
  Arthur, 362.
  August Forsberg, 309.
  Barbara, 231.
  Benj., 288.
  Bettie, 139.
  Betty Elise, 201.
  Betty Nelson. 141.
  Caroline L., 136.
  Catherine, 143.
  Chs., 81, 84, 131, 132, 141, 285.
  Charles D., 135.
  Chs. Edward, 287.
  Chs. Henry, 285, 288.
  Chs. Lewis, 26, 92, 131, 132, 399, 405.
  Charlotte, 285.
  Creed Wills, 286.
  Dabney W., 132.
  Deborah, 288.
  Dolly, 139, 141.

Cora Lee, 669.
Ezekiel, 69.
Dowell, Mr., 172.
Nehemiah, 172.
Downey, Wm., 11.
Doyle, A. M., 310.
Clarence, 169.
R. E., 169.
Dozier, 569.
Drane, James, 333.
Draper, John Claude, 76.
Lyman C., 290.
Dratt, John J., 659.
Drewry, Flora Redd, 632.
Henry Martyn, 632.
Wm. F., 265.
Druery, Jane, 443.
John, 443.
Dudley, Ambrose, 143.
Carolyn Parker, 659.
Elizabeth Dorothy, 659.
Emmett Irvin, 659.
Guy Rucker, 659.
James Henry, 659.
James Nicholas, 659.
Jane, 143.
John, 139, 143, 365.
Julius Kemper, 659.
Mary, 143.

Eads, Isabel Jane, 633.
John, 95.
Jonathan W., 83.
Eager, Alice Rivier, 174.
Auville, 174.
Elizabeth Gish, 174.
George Taylor, 174.
Harriet Ide, 174.
John Howard, 174.
Olive May, 174.
Paul Roman, 174.
Early, Elizabeth, 296, 307, 322.
Jeremiah, 293, 294, 295.
Jerry, 296, 307.
Jubal H., 109.
Ruth, 290, 348.
Sally, 295.
Sarah Anderson, 295.
Easley, Curran Sloan, 543.
Eason, Andrew Wilson, 602.
Wilson Jeter, 603.
Ebey, Edna Clary, 597.
Echols, George, 520.
Jane, 613.
Mary, 613.
Edens, Milly, 167.

Mary Belle, 661.
Nancy, 143, 365.
Peter, 288.
Ursula, 143.
Wallace Lee, 659.
Wm., 143.
Du Duy, Bartholemew, 442.
Dugan, James, 539.
Matilda McDaniel, 539.
Dunbar, David, 135.
Dunning, Eliza, 73.
Joseph, 73.
Virginia, 73.
Dupree, John K., 306.
Marcus K., 306.
Durette, Mary E., 243.
Mary W., 252.
Dutton, Wm., 80.
Duval, Samuel Shepherd, 336.
Dyer, Edna May, 35.
Eugene Vest, 35.
Eva Virginia, 35.
Grace Leonidas, 35.
James Lee, 35.
Roy Bryan, 35.
Wm. Henderson, 35.
Zoula Frances, 35.
Dyerle, Rebecca, 153.
Dyson, Florence Howard, 590.

E

Edgar, James, 684.
Judith, 684.
Phebe, 684.
Sallie, 625.
Edmundson, Ernest, 698.
Richard, 487.
Edwards, Anna C., 395.
Coleman, 678.
Cornelia A., 395.
Eugene, 546.
Gideon, 678.
John N., 272.
Mary Antoinette, 546.
Mary Esther, 103.
Sarah Fannie, 678.
Thos. E., 395.
Effard, Elizabeth, 233.
Eggleston, Elizabeth Carrington, 590.
Mrs. Eugene C., 48.
Eugene Conway, 49, 77.
Joseph Du Puy, 590, 591.
Joseph William, 49.
Lucy Jefferson, 49.
Richard, 50.
Ehite, Lee, 573.
Eidson, Nancy, 212.

H

M

N

O

S

Sadler, Harry Winn, 162.
Safoy, John, 69.
Sagendorf, Edward, 584.
  Martha Caroline, 584.
Sale, Ann A., 124.
  Anna A., 118.
  Channing, 202.
  Charlotte, 118.
  Charlotte A., 124.
  John Wharton, 202.
  L. A., 628.
  Maria L., 117, 124.
  Mary, 277.
  Nelson, 118, 123, 124, 221, 363, 409.
  Richard, 117, 221.
  Richard A., 124.
Sales, Mary Tanner, 563.
Sampson, Florence, 512.
Sanders, Robert, 582.
Sanderson, Coley, 73.
  John, 167, 180.
Sandidge, Wm., 135.
Sanford, Elizabeth, 282.
  James, 281.
  John McD., 282.
  Lelia, 281.
  Lucy, 282.
  Mary Campbell, 282.
  Susan, 572.
Sappenfield, Harry, 630.
  Samuel W. H., 630.
  Walter Ashby, 630.
Sarova, Vestoff, 567.
Sartor, Daniel, 554.
  Julia, 540.
Sasteen, Mr., 210.
Saul, John Peter, 645.
Saunders, Bevie, 707.
Saunders, David, 303, 311.
  George, 218.
  Hillary Abbott, 33.
  Jacob, 95.
  Jas. Hayden, 33.
  John Raeburn, 401.
  Joseph Spottswood, 33.
  Josephine, 698.
  Lelia Edwin, 33.
  Lucinda, 311.
  Martha, 33.
  Mary, 33, 305, 622.
  Nancy Emeline, 474.
  Nelly Rieley, 33.
  Picton L., 276.
  Texana, 286.
  Thomas, 234.
  Virginia, 33.

W. Abbott, 32.
Savage, James Kendal, 612.
  John, 613.
  Margaret Anne, 612.
  Nancy, 184, 185.
  Polly, 613.
Saville, Harry, 408.
  Josephine Deacon, 408.
  Minnie, 408.
Scarbara, James, 207.
Scarborough, Ann, 649.
  Charles, 649.
  Edmund, 649.
Schanbacher, Walter W., 198.
Schenk, Bessie Singleton, 112.
  Earl Nelson, 169.
  Geo. Philip, 169.
  Geo. Winston, 112.
  John Beryl, 112.
  Mary Buford, 112.
  Robt. Beryl, 169.
  Robt. Calvin, 169.
  Wm. Eldridge, 169.
Schmidt, Arthur, 643.
Schnell, August, 160.
  Louise Maier, 160.
Scholl, Peter, 317.
Schooler, Miss, 251.
Schooley, Eli, 224.
Schultz, Ella, 694.
Scott, Ann, 585, 586.
  Ashby, 263, 489.
  Belle M., 58.
  Ben. Jeter, 451.
  Chs. A., 126.
  Clara H., 345, 346.
  Connie Gatewood, 90.
  D. H., 90.
  Daniel, 80.
  Donnie Jeter, 451.
  Elizabeth Brown, 549.
  Francis Bateman, 451.
  Geo., 263.
  George W., 616.
  Geo. Wheeler, 263.
  George William, 616.
  Hampden Warwick, 104.
  Harriet B., 346.
  Helen Tunnell, 273.
  Henry, 159.
  Ida, 250.
  James, 123, 356.
  Jessie M., 451.
  John, 337.
  John Pleasant, 263, 489.
  Jos., 237.

Thomson, A. Wallace, 554.
Alexander S., 177, 179, 200.
Ann H., 552.
Betty Kabler, 179.
Catherine, 180.
Charlotte F., 114, 123, 180.
Christine Henry, 179.
Cornelius Lupton, 179.
Demaris Ann, 177.
Edith Hatcher, 178.
Emily Frances, 178.
Emily Morris, 177.
Emma Lou, 179.
Frances Olivia, 179.
Harry Penn, 178.
Helen, 242.
Helen Temple, 178.
Henry, 178.
Herbert Bruce, 179.
Isabelle, 222.
Isabella, 180.
Isabella M., 180.
James Ralph, 178.
Jesse, 221.
Jesse L., 64, 114, 123, 177, 180.
John, 194.
Lelia, 177.
Lewis Edward, 178.
Lillian Olivia, 178.
Louise Evelyn, 178.
Margaret Louis, 179.
Margaret R., 200.
Marian Jessie, 178.
Mary, 346.
Mary Lewis, 235.
Mary Louise, 177.
Nelson, 241.
Nancy, 583.
Nancy Henderson, 552.
Nathaniel Brown, 222.
Nathaniel W., 64, 72, 179, 180.
Olivia Alexander, 177.
Rhoda M., 64, 114, 123.
Sallie W., 177.
Sarah, 180.
Sophia Davis, 180.
Spotswood Edward, 178, 200, 201.
Virginia Elizabeth, 179.
Virginia Spotswood, 178.
Waddy, 235.
Wallace, 552.
Wm., 346.
William Alexander, Jr., 178.
Thornell, Agnes, 345, 346.
John, 345, 346.
Thornhill, Elizabeth, 484.
Thornton, Elizabeth, 252.

Frances, 259.
Reuben, 259.
Rich., 237, 710.
Sarah, 259.
Thorp, Betsey, 295.
Francis, 269, 295, 321.
Kitty, 295.
Mary, 269.
Polly, 282.
Sophia, 295.
Theodosia, 295.
Thorpe, Mary, 267, 325, 468.
Sarah Triplett, 468.
Thomas, 468.
Thrasher, Mary, 635.
Stephen, 642.
Thurber, C. H., 122.
Jack, 122.
Thurman, A. G., 617.
Allen, 708.
Allen Granberry, 708.
Anthony, 707.
Delia Nelms, 707.
Frances, 708.
Harry, 707.
Helen, 707.
Hilton, 707.
James Otis, 707.
Jessie Key, 707.
John, 707.
John Silas, 707.
Lewis, 707.
Margaret, 707, 708.
Marjorie, 707.
Mary Susan, 708.
Nelson, 708.
Otis, 707.
Owen, 707.
Susie, 707.
Vivian, 707.
Warren, 708.
Wm. Jennings, 707.
Wm. Pleasant, 707.
Wilton, 708.
Thweatt, Fannie York, 451.
Joseph, 451.
Robt. Wharton, 451.
Tilford, Mr., 210.
Tiller, Thomas, 230.
Tilley, Elizabeth, 294, 310.
Timberlake, Geo., 582.
Wm., 328.
Tinsley, Absalom, 123.
Ann Burks, 139.
Betsy Burks, 46, 89, 92.
Charlotte Ann, 270, 271, 282
Eliza, 409.
Eliza Eldridge, 384.

W

John, 303.
John H., 115, 125, 696, 699.
Katherine Sallings, 93, 386.
Lewis Poindexter, 135.
Lucy, 522.
Lucy Dudley, 136, 405.
Ludwell, 92, 135, 405.
M. R., 697.
Mary Ellen, 135.
Mary Eliza, 239, 241, 261.
Mary Elizabeth, 125.
Nancy, 136.
Nancy Brown, 92, 135.
Nancy Sallings, 92, 405.
Nannie, 136.
Overton Ludwell, 136.
Parmelia Jane, 563.
Rebecca, 115, 125.
Richard, 135.
Susan Frances, 135.
Thos., 93.
Walter Douglas, 93.
Wm. Beverly, 92, 135, 386.
William Miller. 136.
Waugh, Mr., 207.
Wayman, Sinclair, 94.
Wayne, Anthony, 601.
Weakley, Anna E., 274.
　Leonard A., 274.
　Victorine Hammett, 274.
Weaver, Cornelia Frances, 199.
　John, 230.
　John L., 199.
　Lula Kipps, 199.
Webb, Pattie, 635.
　Sarah, 698.
　Theo., 304.
Webster, M. A., 336.
　Rebecca, 585.
Weekly, Bernard, 676.
Weir, Adolphus Gus, 345, 346.
Weisiger, Bolling, 269.
Welch, Geo., 261.
　Gilmo Bunyan, 688.
　Hannah White, 261.
　John, 207.
　Levi, 261.
Wells, Annie Marie, 619.
　Lillie, 386.
　Margaret, 319, 326.
　Mary Katherine, 51.
　Octavia, 686.
　Samuel, 279.
Welsh, Mary, 210.
　Nicholas, 210.
West, Laura Virginia, 287.
　Thos., 335.
Westbrook, John Minniece, 514.

Lizzie Alice, 514.
Polk, 514.
Sidney Ivey, 514.
Thaddeus Phillips, 514.
Thaddeus W., 514.
William Henry, 514.
Wharton, Alice, 223.
Ann Aiken, 221.
Catherine Amanda, 221.
Charles W., 223.
Charles William, 223, 467.
Charlott, 469.
Charlotte Eliza, 221, 223.
Dabney Miller, 221.
Edmund, 221.
Estelle Steptoe, 467.
Frances I., 222, 225.
Isabella Brown, 180.
Jesse, 221.
John, 219, 220, 221.
John A., 124, 180, 221, 222.
John Edmund, 222.
Lyman B., 220, 222, 223.
Maria Louisa, 221.
Marie Louise, 223.
Martha, 221.
Mary Jane, 222.
Mary Johnson, 221.
Rhoda Morris, 177, 221.
Sallie, 217.
Sally Logwood, 221.
Sally Temple, 221.
Sarah Virginia, 179, 222.
Sophia Hill, 221.
Thomas Jefferson, 221.
William Adolphus, 221.
Whealton, Virginia, 49.
Wheat, Miss, 48.
Mr., 219.
Aaron, 696.
Bessie, 127.
Curtis, 127.
Edith B., 220.
Eliza, 72.
Eliza H., 125.
Floy, 127.
Harry, 127.
Hazarel, 72.
Hugh, 127.
Jack O., 220.
John W., 75.
Joseph F., 125.
Levi, 209.
Lucy D., 72.
Lydia, 218.
Otho W., 126.
Sallie, 121.
Sallie Ethel, 125.

ADDENDUM

How To Use The Addendum

Listed on the following pages are the corrections, deletions and additions which have been recorded. The number of the page involved is found in the center of these pages. Following the page number is the line or lines in the original text, on the page indicated. It is suggested that the researcher, after locating the subject in the index, turn to the Addendum to ascertain if any changes have been indicated for that page.

....

PAGE 14

Line 28 A—Boline, Barnabas (wife, Elizabeth).
Line 29 A—Boyd, James (wife, Elizabeth).

PAGE 15

Line 11 A—Garvin, Hugh (wife, Susanna).
Line 20 A—Goodman, Ansel (wife, Edith).
Line 22 A—Graham, James (wife, Deborah).
Line 37 A—Hutts, Jacob (wife, Lena; 2nd., Christiana).
Line 8 B—Kelley, Michael (wife, Mary).
Line 12 B—Lahorn, Henry (wife, Sarah).
Line 14 B—Leister, William (wife, Mary).

PAGE 16

Line 3 A—Piles, Henry (wife, Susanna).
Line 16 A—Robinson, Stephen (wife, Mary Ann).
Line 17 A—Rose, Thomas (wife, Jean).
Line 18 A—Ruff, Benjamin (wife, Sarah).
Line 21 A—Runyon, John (wife, Susannah).
Line 23 A—Smith, James (wife, Susannah).
Line 26 A—Snow, Henry (wife, Elizabeth).
Line 30 A—Suter, Charles (wife, Elizabeth).
Line 21 B—Watts, Aaron (wife, Rebeckah).
Line 35 B—Bond, Wright—Sgt.

PAGE 17

Line 9 A—Childress, Henry
Line 14 A—Conner, William
Line 9 B—Holly, John (wife, Judith).
Line 25 B—Leftwich, William, Captain, Rev.

PAGE 18

Line 33 A—Ross, William (wife, Mary).
Add:
Line 45 A—Johnson, Benjamin, Pension Claim R5674.
Line 46 A—Snow, Thomas.
Line 47 A—Snow, Vincent.

PAGE 24

Line 18—Daniel White . . . bond secured but marriage did not take place. Daniel was son of John White who died in Charlotte Co. in 1788.
Line 19—Jeremiah White was son of James White and Lucy Terry of Bedford Co. He married Lucinda Buford.

PAGE 26

Line 17—John A., born 1788.
Line 20—Nancy R., born 1790.
Line 26—Rebecca H., born 1794.
Line 28—Elizabeth, born 1796.
Line 30—William Allen, born 1798.
Line 33—Samuel D., born 1799.
Line 35—Polly, born Mar. 13, 1801, married Jan. 30, 1817, died Aug. 9, 1876 in Tennessee.

PAGE 39

Line 9—John William, died Oct. 21, 1939.

PAGE 40

Line 2—Louis Embree, died June 24, 1932.

PAGE 46

Line 24—Richard Emmett, born March 10, 1877.

PAGE 47

Line 12—Marion Louise, born 1899.

PAGE 51

Line 23—Mary Walter Barnett, born 1860, died Jan., 1941.

PAGE 59

Line 37—Rebecca Joyner married John Victor Garnoc, 1945.

PAGE 69

Line 14—(Correction) Rhoda Arthur, not Pheola.
Line 33—(Correction) John Lafoy and Mary White, widow of Jacob White, 10 Jan., 1805.
Line 36—Jeremiah White, son of James.

PAGE 70

Line 31—Lucinda H. White, widow of Jeremiah White, daughter of William Buford.

PAGE 71

Line 31—Theodosia A. White, widow of James White, Jr.

PAGE 74

Line 29—Leonidas Rosser White.

PAGE 75

Line 27—Mary Walter White (Widow of Leonidas R. White).

PAGE 111

Line 1—Susie Doswell Epes.
Line 20—Margaret Burks Kasey died Dec. 23, 1937.

PAGE 112

Line 5—Margaret, born Dec. 9, 1897.

PAGE 114

Line 25—Jesse Spinner died at his home "Wyoming".
Line 32—Now living at "Wyoming".

PAGE 121

Line 21—Frances Burks married R. Edward Dennis.

PAGE 147

Line 6—Mary Ward, daughter of Seth Ward, and granddaughter of Captain John Ward, who
         came to Virginia in 1619 and was living in Indian Thickett in 1623. Member of House
         of Burgesses. Son Seth married Katherine Smith.

PAGE 154

Line 12—Angeline Wainwright, daughter of Mack and Mary C. Wainwright.

PAGE 155

Line 16—Mary Frances married Dr. A. A. Walker.

PAGE 156

Line 32—(Addition) One child, Diana.

PAGE 158

Line 34—Ada Burroughs married Sept. 2, 1933, Ollie Clarence Hancock. One daughter, Cary
          Hatcher born Nov. 24, 1936.
Line 35—Angeline Wainwright married Sept. 29, 1934, Carter Cowles, Jr. One child, Carter,
          III born May 31, 1936.
Line 36—Sallie Anthony, married June 20, 1942, Raymond Talley.

PAGE 173

Add:
Line 18—Susanna Moseley Board, married Clifton Coppedge Peters.

PAGE 175

Line 12—. . . One child, Emelyn Browning.

PAGE 178

Line 33—Henry died June 3, 1940.

PAGE 184

Line 10—Married in Pittsylvania County.

PAGE 204

Line 5—August 1, 1635.
Line 27—. . . son of Richard, the immigrant, and a daughter of John Vause.
Line 33—Richard Parrott, Sr. mar. 1st. Elizabeth Thompson, 2nd. Sarah Dale, widow of Nicholas
          Dale. Their son Richard, Jr. was the first male child born of English parents on
          the Rappahannock River (Christ Church Register).
        —Margaret Parrott, sister of Anthony Haywood of Boston. She had been previously
          married to _____ Dedman.

PAGE 205

Line 1—Richard Parrott, Sr. rec'd payment for his services as a Burgess, in October, 1676,
          in the levy of Middlesex Co. for 1677. (Virginia Colonial Register, p. 81, also p.
          82).
Line 16—Judith (delete "Phillippe") daughter of Count Claude Phillippe, Minister de Richebourg.
          Family tradition says she was an Early, and no proof of the Phillippe de Richebourg
          marriage has been found after years of research. L.E.J.P.
Line 20—Delete "Phillippe".
Line 25
 & 26—Delete "perhaps his brother-in-law".

PAGE 206

Line 10—Delete "Phillippe".
Line 16—Ann Watts died in 1797.
Line 37B—Add John Fields.

PAGE 207

Line 4 A—William McAllister.
Line 21 A—John McLaughtin.
Line 30   —The same members of the family afterwards mentioned remembering hearing that
          he died at the block house which is just a very short distance from where he
          was buried.

PAGE 208

Line 2—Elizabeth married James Field Oct. 10, 1814.
Line 19—. . . John and Judith (Early), delete ("Phillippe").
Line 38—William Bramlett, Jr.'s will (W.B. "A", page 351) made 1779, mentions wife Ann,
          son James and "all my children", but does not name them. Deeds made by them,
          to lands they inherited, show them to have been James, William, Milly, (wife of
          John Hancock, married 1787), Reuben, Matilda, (wife of Jesse Watson, married 1801),
          Elizabeth and Elknah (son). There may have been others.

          Reuben, Matilda and Elknah sold to James C. Steptoe in 1805, for $ 1,000.00, the
          place on "the headwaters of Little Otter, adjoining the town of Liberty, whereon
          William Bramblett, dec'd, had resided". The residence is now the rear of the home
          of Mrs. Ella Cauthorn in Bedford (D.B. "K", p. 1210).

          Order Book 1774-1782, Sept. 22, 1777—William Bramblett, a Baptist Preacher, came
          into Court and took the Oath of Allegiance to this state.

          Same book—Ann Bramblett prd. that she furnished yd. sd. Com. F. Provisions for
          Men and Forage for Horses for which she was al*d* 2 3/4.

PAGE 209

Line 5—William, born 1766.
Line 11—Lucinda married 1st. Jeremiah White, 2nd. Jasper Clayton.

PAGE 210

Line 1—Delete "Phillippe".

PAGE 211

Line 24—Delete "Phillippe".

PAGE 215

Line 3—Column "C", add Philipe.

PAGE 216

Line 24—. . . and bought up a large . . .

PAGE 217

Line 10—married Dec. 20, 1815.
Line 25—married July 19, 1794

PAGE 218

Line 12—She had two children.
Line 19—. . . and William H. White who married Lucy D. Wheat in 1858; killed in Civil
        War.
Line 31—Elizabeth Johnson, daughter of Lilburn and Frances Jordan Johnson—Quakers.
Line 35—Polly (Mary Gwatkin).

PAGE 222

Line 21—Frances married . . . , 2nd, Bryan.

PAGE 223

Line 7—Charles William, Jr. died 1940.

PAGE 228

Line 1—. . . married 1st. Elizabeth Buford, 2nd. Mrs. Mary C. Wainwright.

PAGE 235

Line 4—. . . Anne Poindexter, 1790?
Line 5—Sarah Garth, mar. 1798.
Line 6—Martha, married 1828.

PAGE 263

Line 3—Allen married May 29, 1814, Martha Thornton.
Line 8—Pollina Mettert married Thomas Hunter Jones.

PAGE 264

Line 8—Mertie M. died 1947.

PAGE 265

Line 2—Emmett L., Jr. married Bettie Carolyn Parker (see p. 658).

PAGE 282

Line 18—Delete "Bixler".
Line 19—Delete "Bixler".
Line 21—Delete "Bixler".

PAGE 284

Line 5—. . . (4) Evan, sons of John Davis . . .

PAGE 295

Line 22—. . . and his wife Sarah (delete name in parenthesis).

PAGE 311

Line 30—James M. Harris, Esq. "Crow".

PAGE 312

Line 1—Fannie Otey Horsley died June, 1934.
Line 6—John Callaway Brown, Jr. died Dec. 22, 1941.

PAGE 332

Line 5—Martha Kennon, sister of Mary, married Robert Munford (see Walker Family).
—Richard Kennon was a Burgess for Henrico County in 1685.

PAGE 344

Line 16—Tradition says that the officiating clergyman upon this occasion was Rev. William
Mays, first rector of Old St. John's Church, Hampton, Va. (see Mays Family).

PAGE 363

Line 25—Jasper Clayton and Mrs. Lucinda H. White, widow of Jeremiah White.

PAGE 448

Line 24—Oliver Jeter died in 1807 in Lincoln Co., Ga.
Line 31—. . . who married John Hardy (correction).

PAGE 453

Line 31—James Jeter, born Sept. 11, 1769.
Line 32—He married Martha Jennings, born Oct. 9, 1772.

PAGE 457

Line 17—John Overstreet, Oct. 4, 1797.
Line 34—Caleb died Aug. 4, 1819.

PAGE 460

Line 31—Henry married Chelsea Dent.
Line 32—Allison married Mar. 26, 1827.
Line 35—Margaret P. married Blair D. Bowling, Apr. 29, 1833.

PAGE 462

Line 5—Chelsea Dent, daughter of Peter Dent.
Line 18—Chelsea (Dent) Jeter.

PAGE 467

Line 27
   & 28—Ellis Brown Bibb died 1940.
Line 33—Charles William Wharton died 1940.
Line 35—Robert Quarles Lowry died 1934.

PAGE 469

Line 6—Andrew Fuller, physician, left one son, Dudley.
Line 7—Margaret married Capt. John Sharp; died in Mo.
Line 8—Edith Jane married John H. Diggs; died in Montgomery Co., Mo.
Line 9—Betsey mar. Joshua Sharp; lived and died in Mo.
Line 10—Sarah mar. Charles G. Buchanan; lived and died in Mo.

PAGE 470

Line 14—Sovereign Jeter, born ca. 1780.
Line 15—Matilda Vaughan, born ca. 1785; d. 1833.

PAGE 471

Line 20—Obedience married John Mitchell.

PAGE 475

Line 22—Mamie Turner . . . ; mar. Dec. 5, 1933, E. G. Fitzgerald.

PAGE 476

Line 19—George W. Snow, son of Jabez & Frances (Parker) Snow (see Parker Family).

PAGE 484

Line 10—. . . a Methodist and a Democrat.
Line 15—Joseph Mays Davidson's children; Mildred Randolph, born June 21, 1930; Joseph
          Mays, Jr., born May 1, 1936.
Line 24—Jesse Thornhill, Jr. married Maxwell Dudley; child Gene Maxwell.
Line 26—Dorothy married June 24, 1939, Stuart T. Saunders, son of W. Hammett and Lucy
          Smith Saunders; children Stuart Thomas, Jr., born Mar. 19, 1941; Laura Jeter, born
          Apr. 15, 1944.
Line 34—Jesse Thornhill Davidson died Feb., 1947.

PAGE 485

Line 16—William Mays, tradition says, performed the marriage ceremony of John Rolfe and

PAGE 485 (Cont'd)

Pocahontas. He was 1st. rector of Old St. John's Church, Hampton, Va.
Line 22—John Maise had sons Daniel and Henry, and perhaps others. His wife was _____
Newcomb.

PAGE 486

Line 6—Henry Mayes had sons Thomas, William and Mattox.
Line 33—Elijah married Patsey Pryor Jan. 6, 1801.
       —Richard married Peggy Pryor July 26, 1806.
       —John married Nancy McConohea June 21, 1817.
       —Susannah married John William Gibbs Feb. 27, 1802.

PAGE 487

Line 2—Samuel C. married Annis Linton in Davidson County, Tenn.
Line 5—Martha (Patsey) married William P. Carter Jan. 23, 1836.
Line 8—Agnes . . . married Nov. 7, 1842.
Line 10—Parmelia married John Deyerly Oct. 14, 1846.
Line 11—William S., correction, William L., married Feb. 10, 1843, Susan R. Claytor, dau.
       of Dr. John Claytor.
Line 33—Betsy (Mayse) Wright, born July 12, 1812.
Line 37—Joseph W. Mays died Mar. 5, 1900.

PAGE 491

Line 36—Charlotte C. Morgan died Jan. 31, 1948.

PAGE 493

Line 6—Tilghman Buford Jeter died Mar. 31, 1932.

PAGE 501

Line 31—Ann (Nannie) Pannill (Ficklen) Jeter died in Lynchburg, Va. Oct. 13, 1936.

PAGE 507

Line 1—Vivian Vaughan died July 21, 1954.
Line 6—Virginia Elaine mar. June, 1944, Jack Kines.
Line 16—Thomas Edwin died Jan. 20, 1936.
Line 28—Clark mar. Aug. 27, 1946, John Morrow.

PAGE 556

Line 22—Thomas Bothwell died 1931.

PAGE 562

Line 24—; married Ann Moseley.

PAGE 568

Line 35
& 36—. . . Elizabeth Satterwhite. Will of John Satterwhite, dated 1772, proved in Essex
Co., 1779, mentions his daughter Elizabeth and her husband Elijah Jeater (Essex
Co. Records, W.B. 13, p. 258).

PAGE 577

Line 8—(Correction)—William Oscar.

PAGE 578

Line 12—Bertrand; died, 1935.
Line 14—Fred; married Lorene Morgan.

PAGE 585

Line 9—. . . he died 1798. She married (2) Jacob Lockett in 1804. Mason (Jeter) Crenshaw
had 4 sons; Nathaniel A., William T., Allen J. and Anthony W. Her husband was
the son of Elkanah Crenshaw of Amelia Co.

PAGE 599

Line 17—William Jeter Carmouche died Oct., 1930.

PAGE 603

Line 11—Fredericka Adelaide mar. Aug. 5, 1933, Baron Marcellus Donald A.R. von Redlich,
an Austrian nobleman, now consul to the U.S.A. from Monaco.

PAGE 608

Line 8—Wife of Rev. William Johnson was Patty. They sold land on Goose Creek in 1794
and went to Tennessee, where he died in 1814.

PAGE 609

Line 13—Elizabeth Jane died Sept. 9, 1874.

PAGE 610

Line 2—Berta Alice died Feb. 21, 1939.

PAGE 611

Line 29—Matilda Frances Jeter Johnson died Nov. 11, 1942, aged 99 years & 21 days.
Line 32—John Newton Johnson died Sept. 27, 1930.

PAGE 613

Line 16—. . . married Mary Squires.

PAGE 615

Line 25—Mary Rebecca Wright was the daughter of John Q. A. and Mary Gilbert Williamson. John Q. A. was the son of John and Sally (Hardy) Wright (See page 626). Mary Gilbert Williamson was the granddaughter of John and Susannah Mayse Gibbs. Susannah was dau. of John and Susannah Mayse (p. 486).

PAGE 616

Line 18—Mary Elizabeth Johnson died 1930.

PAGE 620

Line 11—Nancy Dickerson, born Oct. 29, 1773, died June 30, 1846.
Line 13—Jannet died Aug. 6, 1875.

PAGE 621

Line 10—(Correction)—Sallie Walthall born April 8, 1771.

PAGE 625

Line 21—John Wright, son of Thomas and Mary Wright, married Elizabeth Pate, dau. of Anthony and Sarah Pate. Elizabeth died after 1817.

Note: There were two other John Wrights in Bedford County at the same time, and marriages of four of their children are incorrectly given in "Our Kin". L.E.J.P.
Line 24—Thomas, born about 1760-62, died about 1849; went blind.
Line 26—Sarah went to Jackson Co., Tenn.
Line 30—Elizabeth married William Corley June 1, 1798 (see D. B. "L", p. 379). (. . . married Thomas Hambleton is an error).
Line 31—Mary (Polly) married Ballinger Mays Dec. 21, 1811., (. . . married Benjamin Watts, incorrect).
Line 33—John (. . . married Mary Hunter, incorrect).
Line 34—Joseph (. . . married Sallie Edgar, incorrect). He married Agnes Brown and was living in Breckenbridge Co., Ky. in 1806 & 1811 (see D. B. "M" pp. 452 & 628).

Marriage bond, June 26, 1805—Joseph Wright and Aggy Brown, John Brown, surety. National Hist. Mag. (D. A. R.) vol. LXIII, # 1, p. 63. Joseph Wright b. June 1, 1785, Bedford Co., Va., d. Apr. 19, 1842; mar. Agnes Brown, b. June 10, 1788, Bedford Co., Va., d. Jan 19, 1842; moved to Ralls Co., Mo., 1819. Ch., Peyton, Carson, John A., William C., Scott, Agnes, Rhoda and Elizabeth.

Agnes, dau. Capt. John Brown, cousin to Gen. Winfield Scott.

PAGE 626

Line 16—Children (D. B. "R", p. 315, Bedford Co. Records) James, Joel, Jubal, John, Betsy Meador, Polly Mayse and Nancy Wright.

John married Nov. 13, 1820, Sally B. Hardy, dau. of Robert and Mary Hardy, and had children Robert W., John Q. A., James A. and Mary S.

PAGE 626 (Cont'd)

John Q. A. was father of Mrs. Geo. W. Johnson (see p. 614).

Nancy Wright mar. Henry Chapman July 13, 1824.

PAGE 627

Line 2—Ann Henry died 1946.

Line 14—James Eben Nelms, son of Eben and Sinor (Mitchell) Nelms. Eben Nelms was the son of Serg't. Charles N. Nelms (1752-1838) soldier of the Revolution. Enlisted in Northumberland Co. Allowed pension in Bedford Co., 1832, for 2 years actual service in Virginia line.

PAGE 634

Line 24—Anthony Wright, son of John and Elizabeth Pate Wright, d. 1850; married 1st., Dec. 29, 1789, Betsy Mayse (d. after 1841) . . . 2nd., Mrs. Kitty St. Clair, Sept. 24, 1846. Children, 1st. marriage, Rhoda, born 1812; Celia, married Nov. 8, 1817.

PAGE 635

Line 1
& 2—Betsy; married (first) Archibald Wright, d. 1827; (second), Robert C. Ramsey, Sept. 23, 1847

Line 3—Agnes, married Aug. 6, 1839.

PAGE 636

Line 14—. . . ca. 1765, Joseph Wright married Elizabeth Kemp.

Line 17—Nancy; married John Meador Sept. 2, 1793.

Line 21—Mary; married Martin Greer Feb. 25, 1788.

Line 22—Agnes; . . . went to Davidson Co., Tenn.

PAGE 638

Line 1
& 2—Matthew Wright d. 1841 . . . married Nancy Holland.

Line 8—John Asher Wright died Aug. 10, 1886. Sibyl Craft Wright, b. Mar. 7, 1811, died Aug. 2, 1875. Three sons; William, b. in Botetourt Co., married Sarah T. Lloyd; James Edward, b. Mar., 1838, died Aug. 18, 1879, had married Sallie H. Anderson; and George (see line 20).

Line 33—Lydia and John Compton, married in 1834, had children Rev. James W., Mary E. and John Nelson.

PAGE 639

Line 13—George Delaraine Wright was educated at Virginia Military Institute.

PAGE 644

Line 4—Delete "II" after Peter Meador.

PAGE 645

Line 23—(8) Joel Wilson; married Eliza Dearing.

Children

(a) Libbie Verna; married William Byrd Ferguson.

Children

(aa) Clyde; married (first) Bessie Settle; (second) Helen? of Missouri.
Earnest; married Shirley? from England.
Lorene; married Orval Putnam.
Margaret.
(bb) Katie; died in infancy.
(cc) Tolbert Morgan; married Hennie Dearing.
Marvin; married Della Stacy; Four children.
Hazel; married Ralph Johnson; Two children.
Maxine; married Alvin Kitts; Two children died in infancy.
Hillary; married Jean Overstreet; One child.
(dd) Hester Clair; married (first) Elmer Baker.
Mildred; married Bruce Edwards; Two children.
Inez; married James R. Rogers; Four Children.
Margaret; died in infancy.
Ailene; married (first) Edward McCuine; (second) George Fallon.
Dorothy; married Oran Marshall.
Hester Clair; married (second) William H. Stephens; No children.
(ee) Edmund Twilley; married Addie Dickinson.
Christine: married John Francis Huddleston; One child.
Edmund T., Jr.; married Frances Austin; Two children.
Jeanne; married Perry Creasy; One child.
(ff) Laura; married Glen Pinkerton White.
Murry; married Mildred Mills.
Clarissa Ethel; died in infancy.
(gg) Corynne; married Finis Boulware.
Woodrow; married Jalie Davis; One child.
Verna; married G. H. Shryock; One child.
(hh) Marie; died in childhood.

PAGE 647

Line 18—Earldom created in 1710.
—Motto of Parker arms, "Dare to be just (wise)".

PAGE 648

Line 10—In October, 1653, Mr. George Parker (son of Robert Parker, a native of Hampshire, England) living in Northampton County, sued Mr. John Elsey, etc. (Va. Hist. & Biog. Mag., Vol. 29, p. 346).

PAGE 650

Line 9—The mother of Frances Oaks Parker was Frances Toler, dau. of William Toler, whose will recorded in Pittsylvania Co. in 1799, mentions his daughter Frances Dixon.

PAGE 650 (Cont'd)

Then the grandfather of Frances Oaks Parker was William Toler, and her stepfather was William Dixon, who mentions her first among his children, and names her husband George Parker as one of his executors.

Unquestionably she named her second son for these Williams rather than for the father of her husband, whose name has not been preserved. He may have been Alexander.

The mother of Frances Oaks (also named Frances) married for her second husband, William Dixon, and had seven children. She had another Oaks daughter, Lavinia, who married John Howell in 1795.

Line 12
& 13—Patsy D. Snow, born Apr. 1, 1806.
Line 18—. . . Mary Goggin mar. June 12, 1855. She died Dec. 25, 1916 (see Goggin Family).
—William David, son of David and Mary (Goggin) Parker, was b. June 7, 1858; died Nov. 7, 1930; mar. Dec. 20, 1876, Susan Joanna Graves, b. May 29, 1858; died Oct. 10, 1929. Their son Leslie Oliver, b. 1877, mar. 1897, Elizabeth Ann Howard, b. 1878.
Line 21—(Correction) Barilla Snow.
Line 35—Elizabeth Parker, dau. of Caleb.
Line 36
& 37—Richard Snow, b. Nov. 29, 1804. ? Richard and Mary Parker Snow had children Hester Ann (1828-1844), Anselm T. (1831-   ), Emily C. (1834-1836), David Richard (1836-   ) and Catherine (d. 1836).

PAGE 652

Line 29—Nancy Eloise mar. Oct., 1936, Joseph Riddick.

PAGE 653

Line 3—Add: (cc) Mary Ellen, born 1931.
Line 14—Methodist Episcopal Church, South. Baltimore Conference, Oct., 1931. He married Sept. 8, 1931, Marie Rickey. Children, David Lambert, Stephen Moorman (b. May 30, 1939) and Nelson.
Line 15—George Pleasant died Jan. 26, 1939.

PAGE 654

Line 5—. . . Class of 1932.
Line 8—Josephine Mays mar. Nov. 8, 1941, John Carson Woodford. Child, Georgette Parker Woodford, born Sept. 23, 1944.

PAGE 655

Line 9—Elizabeth Ann Teass d. June 16, 1941. (Correction) Born 1851.
—Alexander Clark Parker died Jan. 15, 1931.
Line 31—George Edward died unmarried.

PAGE 656

Line 7—. . . child, Betty Ann born Feb. 2, 1931.
Line 9—Iris Parker mar., 1939, Ralph Dorer.

PAGE 656 (Cont'd)

Line 17—Alexander Boyce died Jan., 1947.
Line 32—Manly Grady m. Mabel Cochran.

PAGE 658

Line 27—Bettie Carolyn mar. Nov. 17, 1945, Emmet Leslie Talbot (see p. 265); child Emily
        Parker, b. 1946.

PAGE 662

Line 4—Eliza (Cauthorn) Rucker d. May, 1941.
Line 38—Absalom Jordan (II) married Mary Ann Williamson. Daughter, Rosanna, married William
        Dickerson in 1890. William, son of Joseph (see Dickerson Family).

PAGE 663

Line 2—Delete "another son" . . . married Rhoda Mays, Dec. 22, 1806. Leroy Jordan, son
        of Ezekiel and Jane Jordan (mar. bond).

PAGE 664

Line 15—David W. Parker died 1932.
Line 25—. . . Mrs. Mary Smith Booth Reese (maiden name Boothe) mar. 1st., William Reese,
        mar. bond in Franklin Co.

PAGE 670

Line 7—Stephen Goggin. . . His name appeared first in Bedford Co. in 1754 in a suit against
        Ray. Order Book 1754-61, Suit of Ray vs Goggin, 1754. License to Stephen Goggin
        to keep an ordinary, Sept. 27, 1756.
       —Stephen Goggin died 1790.
Line 20—Stephen Goggin, Jr. died 1801 (correction).
Line 21—Rachel Moorman Goggin died in 1835.
Line 39—Children of Pleasant Moorman and Mary Otey Leftwich Goggin; (a) William Leftwich
        Goggin, b. 1807, d. 1870; (b) Sarah Paulina Goggin, mar. John R. Steptoe.

PAGE 671

Line 1—Stephen, III d. Jan 29, 1872.
Line 7—Frances H. Goggin, born Dec. 8, 1812, died Aug. 14, 1877. Frances H. Goggin,
        1st. cousin to John Marshall Clemens. Son Robert William Parker, 2nd. cousin to
        Samuel Langhorn Clemens (Mark Twain).

PAGE 673

Line 19—"Cilly" a son. Name was Achilles.
Line 22—William Ballard's 1st. wife was Mary Byron, dau. of Henry Byron of Yorkshire,
        England. William Ballard was born in England and married before coming to Virginia.

PAGE 675

Line 18—(Correction) William Washington Reese married Emma P. Creasy Dec., 1877.
Line 22—Delete "Billy and Russell Roundtree".

PAGE 676

Line 11—Elizabeth Rebecca mar. W. C. Robertson.

PAGE 677

Line 32—Milton S. Nininger.

PAGE 681

Line 3—David Walker married Mary Munford, daughter of Colonel Robert and Martha (Kennon) Munford. Robert Munford was son of James and _____ (Wyatt) Munford and grandson of Thomas Munford, who was in Nansemond Co., Va. in 1664. (This not yet proved). Martha Kennon was daughter of Col. Richard and Elizabeth (Worsham) Kennon.

Both Robert Munford (1720 & 1722) and Richard Kennon (1685) were members of the House of Burgesses. (see p. 332).
Line 19—Peletiah Jones Walker married Rev. William Early (born 1766) in 1793.

PAGE 691

Line 5—Dewannah Sydnor married April 8, 1933, James Washington Hayes.
Line 8—Anne Chilton mar. Bernard Cunningham Dec., 1938. Child, Irene Sydnor, b. Mar. 22, 1940.

PAGE 694

Line 7—Theodosia Quarles, granddaughter of Mary (Walker) Quarles.
Line 19—Mary . . . married James Quarles. James Quarles mar. 2nd., Elizabeth Rives and went to Tennessee in 1804.
Line 23—Nancy . . . married John Quarles.

PAGE 695

Line 26—Hannah married 1st., _____ Wood; 2nd., Samuel Bridgewater, Apr. 24, 1789.
         —Henrico Co. records give Hannah Freeman as wife of Thomas Jopling, Sr., and daughter of George Freeman.

PAGE 696

Line 21—Mary Ann B. married John R. North.
Line 24— . . . married Belfield J. Porter.
Line 25—. . . married Susan J. Clark.
Line 28—Sally Ware . . . mar. July 9, 1832.
Line 29—Nancy Moorman died 1873.

PAGE 697

Line 23—. . . he married again Jan. 11, 1836. . .

Line 28—James W. Jopling . . . mar. Dec. 2, 1835.

Line 35—William A., b. 1842, married Emma Cromley Nov. 4, 1882, d. Mar. 26, 1902. Children, William A., Jr. and Mary K.

PAGE 700

Line 3—Thomas Martin, Sr. came to Albemarle Co. from New Kent Co. in 1750 (see D.B. # 1, p. 248, Albemarle records).

Line 4—Abram Martin was a colonial officer. Abram's son John married Letitia _____. He died, 1756; was a member of Virginia Assembly.

Line 10—John, b. 1710, d. 1783, mar. Ann Farish of King William co., Va.

Line 24—According to Pension Claim S2729, Pleasant Martin was born Dec. 21, 1756 in Albermarle Co., Va. He lived 35 years in Albemarle Co., 20 years in Amherst Co., about 15 years in Bedford Co., and then went to Wilson Co., Tenn. in 1827, where he died Oct. 16, 1836 (Pension Bureau).

—Pleasant Martin was born 1756.

PAGE 701

Line 26—Pleasant Martin was 1st Lt. in Revolutionary Army.

Children of Pleasant and Rebecca (Joplin) Martin.

1. Nancy, married James Joplin.
2. Ralph, married Signas Price.
3. Martha (Patsy), married John Hawkins, went to Tenn.
4. George, married (1) Sarah Walker, (2nd.) Mrs. Elizabeth Woodward Bowers.
5. Mildred, married John Palmer.
6. Thomas, married Mary Boyd.
7. James, married Elizabeth Owsley.
8. Pleasant, married Rebecca Preston.
9. Elizabeth, married William Powell.

PAGE 705

Line 18—William Richard, Jr. d. 1934.

PAGE 709

Line 16—Norment Doniphan Hawkins died Jan. 10, 1931.

PAGE 710

Line 8—Evelyn Flournoy, born Jan. 17, 1893.

BIBLIOGRAPHY

WILLIAM AND MARY QUARTERLY.
VIRGINIA HISTORICAL MAGAZINE.
Wallace's HISTORICAL MAGAZINE.
Tyler's QUARTERLY HISTORICAL AND GENEALOGICAL MAGAZINE.
STATUTES AT LARGE—*Hening.*
OLD CHURCHES AND FAMILIES OF VIRGINIA—*Meade.*
HISTORY OF KENTUCKY—*Collins.*
COLONIAL FAMILIES OF THE UNITED STATES—*Mackenzie.*
ABSTRACTS OF AUGUSTA COUNTY—*Chalkley.*
ST. MARK'S PARISH, VIRGINIA—*Slaughter.*
VIRGINIA MILITIA IN THE REVOLUTION—*McAllister.*
REVOLUTIONARY SOLDIERS—*Eckenrode.*
REGISTER OF CONTINENTAL OFFICERS—*Heitman.*
VIRGINIA BIOGRAPHY—*Tyler.*
HISTORIC FAMILIES OF KENTUCKY—*Green.*
GENEALOGICAL NOTES OF CULPEPER COUNTY, VA.—*Green.*
Hardesty's ENCYCLOPEDIA.
SCOTTISH CLANS AND THEIR TARTANS—*Johnston.*
PATRONYMICA BRITANNICA—*Lower.*
LANDED GENTRY—*Burke.*
Burke's HERALDRY.
CAMPBELL CHRONICLES AND FAMILY SKETCHES—*Early.*
LIFE OF BOONE—*Draper.*
LIFE OF BOONE—*Thwaite.*
POCAHONTAS AND HER DESCENDANTS—*Robertson.*
THE PENN FAMILY OF VIRGINIA—*Clemens.*
CABELLS AND THEIR KIN—*Brown.*
VIRGINIA COUSINS—*Goode.*
WILLIAMSBURG WILLS—*Crozier.*
HISTORY OF HALIFAX COUNTY, VIRGINIA—*Carrington.*
HISTORY OF CAROLINE COUNTY, VIRGINIA—*Wingfield.*
HISTORY OF ALBEMARLE COUNTY, VIRGINIA—*Wood.*
HISTORY OF SOUTHWEST VIRGINIA—*Sumner.*
BRISTOL PARISH REGISTER—*Slaughter.*
LIFE OF J. B. JETER—*Hatcher.*
THE BUFORD FAMILY IN AMERICA—*Minter.*
HUGUENOT EMIGRATION TO VIRGINIA—*Brock.*
THE DOUGLAS REGISTER.
Records of the following counties of Virginia:
ALBEMARLE, AMELIA, AMHERST, AUGUSTA, BEDFORD, BOTETOURT, BUCKINGHAM
CAMPBELL, CAROLINE, CHARLOTTE, CHESTERFIELD, CULPEPER, CUMBERLAND, ESSEX
FAUQUIER, HALIFAX, KING WILLIAM, KING AND QUEEN, LUNENBURG, MECKLENBURG
MONTGOMERY, NOTTOWAY, ORANGE, PITTSYLVANIA, POWHATAN, PRINCE GEORGE
ROCKBRIDGE, SPOTSYLVANIA, AND YORK.